Praise for Italy Guide!

"Douglas E. Morris knows Italy from the inside; and what is more, he knows Italians. Choose one of his books to be your guide, and you will not be disappointed."
— Martin Stiglio, Director, Italian Cultural Institute

"Using *Italy Guide* is like having your own personal tour guide. Don't leave without it!"
— Mary Ann Puglisi, President, eduVacations

"Raised in Italy, Morris has the perspective of an insider, but the sensibility of an American traveler. An unbeatable combination."
— Alice Leccese Powers, editor, *Italy in Mind* and *Tuscany in Mind*

"As someone who has lived and travelled widely in Italy, I can vouch for Mr. Morris' sophisticated insights and expertise. Whether you are a first-time visitor or an experienced traveler, *Italy Guide* will inspire you to create the vacation of your dreams."
— Michele Micalizzi McCarthy, Senior Editor, *Primo Magazine*

"A reliable, fun and delicious volume, packed with insights and suggestions that will ensure your trip to Italy is unforgettable."
— Marsha Weiner, *Slow Food USA*

"Mr Morris has written a guide that can be used by budget and luxury travelers alike. This is the only book you'll need."
— Andy Herbach, author, *Eating & Drinking in Italy*

"*Italy Guide* is a gem of a book... Ignore the glut of travel books filling store shelves, this is the only one you'll need."
— Paul Rosetti, Editor, *The Italian Tribune*

About the Author

Having spent more than eight years living in Italy and exploring the country, Douglas E. Morris has put his extensive travel experiences down on paper with *Italy Guide*. Morris's other Open Road guides include *Rome Guide* and *Tuscany & Umbria Guide*, and *Become a Travel Writer* available from fabjob.com. Doug is also preparing to move back to Italy in 2005, further ensuring that his guides to Italy give you the most accurate, up-to-date, and comprehensive information about restaurants, nightlife, hotels and sights in Italy.

Doug in Roma

Open Road *is* Travel!

Open Road Publishing has guide books to exciting, fun destinations on four continents. As veteran travelers, our goal is to bring you the best travel guides available anywhere!

No small task, but here's what we offer:

• All Open Road travel guides are written by authors with a distinct, opinionated point of view – not some sterile committee or team of writers. Our authors are experts in the areas covered and are polished writers.

• Our guides are geared to people who want to make their own travel choices. We'll show you how to discover the real destination – not just see some place from a tour bus window.

• We're strong on the basics, but we also provide terrific choices for those looking to get off the beaten path and experience the country or city – not just see it or pass through it.

• We give you the best, but we also tell you about the worst and what to avoid. Nobody should waste their time and money on their hard-earned vacation because of bad or inadequate travel advice.

• Our guides assume nothing. We tell you everything you need to know to have the trip of a lifetime – presented in a fun, literate, no-nonsense style.

• And, above all, we welcome your input, ideas, and suggestions to help us put out the best travel guides possible.

❧

Italy
Guide

Open Road *is* Travel!

Douglas E. Morris

Open Road Publishing

Open Road Publishing

We offer travel guides to American and foreign locales. Our books tell it like it is, often with an opinionated edge, and our experienced authors always give you all the information you need to have the trip of a lifetime.

Open Road Publishing
P.O. Box 284, Cold Spring Harbor, NY 11724
E-mail: Jopenroad@aol.com

Acknowledgments

Many people assisted considerably in the development of this book, but I wish to extend special gratitude to my departed parents, Don and Denise, for being the world travelers and citizens of the world that they were. Without them I would never have lived in Italy and developed the experience to write this book. I also wish to thank Heddi Goodrich for her unique insight into Naples. My brother Dan was a valuable resource. Alain deCocke's editorial assistance, in both English and Italian, was much appreciated. I am also indebted to Anamaria Porcaro, Theresa Luis and the MMI class of '76 for their thoughtful insights about how to travel in Italy as women. And most of all this book is better for the invaluable suggestions and feedback offered by our many readers including: Jack and Joan Sawinski, Pamela A. Motta, Donna and Mike Lareau, Steve and Sheila Cech, Hugh L. Curtin, Senator Paul Simon, and many others.

Please forgive me if I did not include you here. And please keep your e-mails coming to *Roma79@aol.com*.

Contents

14. Florence & Tuscany   230

15. Umbria   354

Maps

Maps *continued*

෨

Sidebars

Sidebars *continued*

ItalyGuide

INTRODUCTION

If you're looking for a wide variety of entertainment, stunning architecture, passionate people, soul refreshing relaxation, beautiful beaches, unparalleled artwork, dazzling museums, ruins from ancient civilizations, world-class accommodations, superb restaurants, first-rate ski resorts, championship golf courses, wonderful water sports and continuous recreation, then Italy is the place for you! And the food – by far the best and most varied in the world. Created with the freshest ingredients and always with a distinctly local flair, not only is the cooking healthy and nutritious, but the variety of flavors and tastes will tantalize and satisfy like no other cuisine. Not to mention great wines like Chianti, Ruffino, Frascati and many more. Add onto all of that the Italian passion for living, and in Italy you have an ideal vacation destination.

With this Open Road guide, your days and nights in Italy will be filled with all the exciting possibilities the land of *La Dolce Vita* has to offer. I've given you a multiplicity of options for shopping, eating, traveling and much more so that you can tailor the perfect vacation for your particular needs.

It's easy to see why so many Americans choose to visit the boot-shaped peninsula that juts into the Mediterranean. From the big tourist cities of Rome, Florence, and Venice to historic hill towns like Perugia, Ravello and Lucca, small mountain villages like Nocelle, Gubbio or Todi, and the abundant breathtaking coastal resorts, Italy is romantic, beautiful, fun and exciting. If you are looking for an adventure like no other, read on!

Chapter 2

OVERVIEW

Italy is generally divided into three main parts: northern central, and southern Italy.

Northern Italy

Northern Italy is dominated by the lowland formed by the **Po River** and its tributaries. The **Alps** form the northern and western boundaries, and the **Apennines** are the southern boundary. The main ports on northern Italy's eastern side, that which is accessible to the **Adriatic Sea**, is Venezia and Trieste. On the western side there is access to the **Ligurian Sea**, mainly from the port of Genoa. The north of Italy has the largest portion of the nation's population and is the leading agricultural and industrial area. Good climate and soil composition in the north are favorable for farming; and easy access to the rest of Europe has made northern Italy more economically viable and industrially successful than the rest of Italy.

There are a variety of interesting travel locations in the north. Besides **Venice**, with its fairy tale architecture surrounded by the canals that are the city's roads, you can also find the beautiful city of **Bolzano** deep in the Alps of Sud Tirol. Here you can explore hiking trails in the summer, or ski down mountain slopes in the winter, while savoring the unique mixture of Italian and Austrian cultures. Sud Tirol is the beauty of Tuscany with the Alps as a backdrop instead of rolling hills.

If life by the sea is your thing, try the **Italian Riviera**. Filled with all sorts of fun water sports, stunning beaches, and quaint little towns, the seaside resort areas along the Ligurian coast are the ideal place to relax or to sample *La Dolce Vita*. If rustic is more your taste, try the **Cinque Terre**, five little

villages cut into the cliffs along the Ligurian coast of the Mediterranean that are breathtakingly beautiful.

Central Italy

Central Italy includes and extends north of Rome through the Tuscany region. **Florence** and **Rome** are the main tourist cities in Central Italy and contain the most amazing art, architecture, museums and churches in Italy, and some would say the world.

One small overlooked town that shouldn't be missed while in Tuscany is **Lucca**. One of only two completely walled medieval cities left in Europe, the ramparts and battlements that surround the city have been converted into the most romantic tree-lined walkway you will find anywhere.

Not to be missed but a little more difficult to get to are the colorful medieval hill towns of **Umbria**. Though strategically located between Rome and Florence, the province of Umbria is on the periphery of the well worn tourist path. Since many of Umbria's cities are not on main rail lines, Italy's chief form of inter-city transportation, getting to many locations in Umbria can be time consuming. But once you are here, Umbria is a beautiful slice of mother nature's paradise. Covered with lush green forests, manicured fields and wonderful medieval hill towns like **Perugia**, **Gubbio**, **Assisi**, **Orvieto** and

Todi, Umbria is an ideal destination. And since it has yet to be overrun by the thundering herd of mass tourism you will have the scenery and history all to yourself.

Southern Italy & Sicily

Southern Italy is generally considered to be everything south of Rome. In terms of significant tourist locations, the **Bay of Naples** and the **Amalfi Coast** are the places to visit.

Naples is a vast port city that boasts one of the best museums in Italy. It is a vibrant metropolis, as are all ports, and can be a little dicey at times if you're out late at night in the wrong place; but if you look beyond its reputation as being less than meets the eye, and look into its heart, Naples is a fun city to visit. In its old section it has the ambiance of a large medieval city with its tiny streets and shops of skilled artisans practicing crafts you would never have thought still existed. You can find violin makers, doll makers, cabinet makers and similar craftsmen hidden down the side streets and on the second stories of Naples' *centro storico*.

Naples is the perfect stopping-over point on your way to the quaint islands of **Capri**, **Ischia** or **Procida** in the bay of the city; and is the perfect transit stop for visits to **Pompeii** and **Herculaneum**, those ancient cities smothered but preserved by the lava and ash of the local volcano. These two ancient Roman cities have to be visited if you are a student of history. If sunning and funning is more your speed, the towns along the **Amalfi Coast** are a summer vacation paradise. Beautifully set on the hills overlooking the sea, these little towns offer stunning vistas and all types of summer recreation.

If you want to venture a little further afield, and are an experience traveler, **Sicily** is a historian's dream. As the island was one of ancient Greece's main colonies, here you'll find the most complete Greek ruins outside of Greece, some of which are located just below the town of **Agrigento**. You can also find ancient medieval hill towns like **Erice**, located 80 km west of Palermo, complete with walls, fortress and even an ancient temple dedicated to Venus. Sicily is also a summer sportsman's paradise, and as a result many resorts have sprung up to accommodate this need.

Experience History

Home to the ancient world's most powerful empire, Italy is alive in history. Daily life revolves around ruins thousands of years old. Modern buildings incorporate ancient structures into their walls. Medieval streets snake through almost all cities including Rome, Florence, and especially Venice. In Italy you can see the tapestry of history woven directly in front of you. Museums abound with ancient artifacts, beautiful paintings, and stunning sculpture. You can easily spend an entire trip roaming through museums – or for that matter inside the beautiful churches where you'll see some of the most exquisite paintings and sculptures anywhere on earth!

Movies to Set the Scene

As you're planning your trip, you might want to rent a few movies to get you in the mood for your travels (save the novels for the airplane trips and beach visits!). Some modern classics include:

- **Amarcord**, Fellini's great film about youth and coming of age
- **Christ Stopped at Eboli**, about a sophisticated left-wing doctor sent to a small hill town during the Fascist era
- **Cinema Paradiso**, about growing up in southern Italy
- **The Garden of the Finzi-Cantinis**, tale of what happens to a wealthy Jewish family before and during World War II
- **Il Postino**, a romantic movie about a postman, a poet, and the island of Procida
- **Life is Beautiful**, a celebration of living, Italian-style, even in the worst of times

A Feast for the Eyes

Even though you could spend an entire trip inside museums or churches, if you decided to do so you would miss out on what makes Italy such a wonderful vacation: its ancient beauty, charm, and ambiance. Being in Italy is like walking through a fairy tale. The old winding streets, twisting around the quaint refurbished buildings, leading to a tiny piazza centered with a sparkling fountain seems like something out of a dream. And you'll find a similar scene in virtually every city you visit in Italy.

If cities are not your cup of tea, you can't surpass the natural beauty of Italy's **Alpine** region, the crystal clear **Northern Lakes**, the pristine southern coastline, or the little villages perched on hills scattered across the land, especially in Tuscany and Umbria. A feast for the eyes awaits you in Italy.

Food & Wine

Eye candy is not all you'll get. Italy has, arguably (pipe down, you Francophiles!), the best food you'll find anywhere in the world. In most cases it's simple food, but with bountiful taste. Take, for example, a Roman favorite: *abbacchio arrosto*. This is a succulent lamb dish slowly cooked over an open flame until the meat is tender and inviting. It is usually accompanied by *patate arrosto*, roast potatoes cooked with rosemary, olive oil, and salt that makes my mouth water just thinking about them.

Since Italy is surrounded on almost all sides by water you can also sample any flavor of seafood imaginable. Usually caught the same day, especially in the small towns along the coast, the seafood in Italy will have you coming back for more.

And don't forget the pasta. You'll find all shapes and sizes covered with sauces of every description and variety. Regions are known for certain pasta dishes and when there you have to sample them all. The area around Bologna is known for the production of the best ham in the world, *Prosciutto di Parma*. To make this ham so succulent, the pigs are fed from the scraps of the magnificent cheese they make in the same region, *Parmigiano Reggiano*. Both of these foods feature prominently in *spaghetti alla bolognese* making it a favorite in the region and throughout Italy.

To wash down all these savory dishes you need look no further than the local wine list. Italian wines may not have a reputation as being as full-bodied and robust as French or California wines, but they have an intimate, down to earth, rustic flavor. Order from the wine list or get a carafe of the house wine, which is usually delicious and more often than not comes from local vineyards.

Sports

If you've noticed your waistband stretching a little from all the wonderful food and wine you've been enjoying, have no fear – Italy has plenty of activities for you to shave off some of those unwanted pounds. A land of sea and mountains, you can find some of the best skiing in the world in the **Alps** as well as wonderfully clear water and beaches all along the **Mediterranean Sea** and the **Adriatic Sea**.

You can go water-skiing, snorkeling, skin diving, sailing or just lie on the beach and sunbathe. Many vacation beaches are topless today, an unheard of activity a decade ago, so you'll be treated to an added adventure either participating or appreciating the presentation.

There are also many top-level golf courses all over Italy, plenty of tennis courts in most major cities, horseback riding in the country, fishing in lakes and sailing in the seas. Italy has it all.

Open Road's Italy

Besides offering the many sights to see, museums and churches to visit, and places to go, I've also listed the best sights to see while visiting a certain destination. In conjunction I've detailed for you the best hotels from each star category, as well as the restaurants where you'll find the best atmosphere and most satisfying cuisine. And to help you plan the perfect vacation and find everything the instant you arrive, this book offers you the **most complete set of city maps** you'll find in virtually any travel guide to Italy.

🙠

Chapter 3

SUGGESTED ITINERARIES

If you only have a short period of time in **Rome** and you want to fill it up with the best sights, restaurants, hotels, cafés at which to lounge, and pubs from which you can crawl back to your bed, all you have to do is follow the itineraries listed below. The hotels, sights, and restaurants mentioned are all described in more detail later in the book.

The places listed in these itineraries are among my favorites in Rome, but there were plenty of close calls! So follow my advice if you wish, or plow through the rest of the information included here and find the perfect itinerary tailor made for your needs.

The Perfect Three Days
Day One

This is going to be a somewhat slow day since you'll have just arrived and will be slightly jet-lagged.

• Arrive at Rome's Leonardo da Vinci airport in the morning.
• Take a cab to your hotel shower and unpack.
• To start off your Roman adventure head to the **Spanish Steps**.
• Get your picture taken while you lean over and grab a drink from the fountain in front of the steps.
• Walk to the top of the steps for the magnificent view over the city
• It should be about lunch time now, so walk back down the steps, cross the street, and take a left into the third street at the edge of the piazza, **Via della Croce**. Follow this to the end, find an outside seat at the superb local restaurant **Otello alla Concordia**, Via Della Croce 81. *Tel. 06/679-1178.*

Try any of their exquisite Roman pasta specialties – *arrabbiata, amatriciana*, or *vongole verace*.
- After lunch it should be about nap time. But remember to only take a 2-3 hour nap, wake up right away, take a shower and get out again – otherwise you'll sleep until 10:00pm and be wide awake because jet-lag will have set in.
- Now it's time to explore the streets around the **Piazza di Spagna**, **Via della Croce**, **Via del Corso**, **Via dei Condotti** and admire all the different shops.
- After shopping/exploring, take a small walk (or short cab ride) to **Piazza Navona**.
- Stop at **Le Tre Scalini** and sample some of the world famous Italian *gelato* (ice cream). If you sit at the tables outside the cost will double or triple.
- If some liquid refreshment is more your style, exit the Piazza Navona on the other side, cross the **Via Vittorio Emanuele**, visit the **Campo dei Fiori** (where they have a superb market in the mornings which we'll get to in a few days) and stop in at the **Drunken Ship** for some Guinness, Harp, or Kilkenny. Enjoy the English speaking bartenders, and have a few ales for me.
- From here you are within striking distance of **Trastevere**, the place for Roman nightlife, on the other side the river. Cross the pedestrian bridge **Ponte Sisto** and make your way to **Piazza Santa Maria** in Trastevere.
- If it's too early for dinner (7:30pm or 8:00pm is the beginning time) stop at one of the outdoor cafés and replenish your fluids.
- For dinner stop at **La Canonica** just outside of the piazza. Here you should also try one of the typical Roman pasta specialties, *arrabbiata, amatriciana*, or *vongole verace*; as well as some *sogliola alla griglia* (grilled sole) for seconds.
- After dinner, if you're not too tired, let's go to the **Trevi Fountain**. It is beautiful lit up at night. To do so walk down the long road leading to the Piazza, **Via della Lungaretta**, to the large main road **Viale Trastevere**. From here catch a cab to Piazza Colonna, near the fountain. The side streets leading up to the fountain are usually packed and the cab wouldn't be able to move through the crowds anyway. Go across the big road, Via del Corso and take Via di Sabini to the fountain.

Day Two
- Today is museum day. Start off at the best in the city, the **Vatican Museum** and the **Sistine Chapel**. This should take you all morning.
- After your museum visit, instead of a long sit-down meal, on your way to St. Peter's stop at one of the many cafés and order a light snack. This will be a truly authentic way to eat a quick meal in Rome. My suggestion is getting a *Medallione*, a grilled ham and cheese concoction that is tasty and filling.

You don't order at the counter, you first pay for your order with the cashier (order your drink at the same time), then bring the receipt up to the counter and tell the bartender what you'll have. A good tip to leave is about Euro 50 cents.

- After your meal, let's explore **St. Peter's**. Guys will need slacks and cannot wear tank tops for this adventure, and women cannot wear short skirts, shorts or tank top-like shirts either. While here, make a point of walking to the top, or taking the elevator, to get a great view over St. Peter's square.
- Once done here, which should be late afternoon, let's take a brief walk to the **Castel St. Angelo** and explore the ancient armaments museum and fortifications of the fortress that protected the Vatican in the past.
- Now it's time to go home for a 2-3 hour nap, if you need it.
- Dinner tonight is at the nearby **La Buca di Ripetta**, on Via di Ripetta, where you should try either the *Lasagna al Forno, Saltimbocca alla Romana,* or the *Ossobuco di Vitello.*
- After dinner, if you missed the **Trevi Fountain** last night.
- If not, you must return to the **Piazza Navona** to soak up the ambiance there at night with its fountains lit up. Either bring your own bottle of wine and sit at one of the benches or grab a table at one of the cafés and enjoy a beautiful Roman evening.

Day Three

- Time to explore some serious ruins. First stop the Forum on **Via dei Foro Imperiali** Up ahead you'll see the **Colosseum**, our next destination.
- Wander around the forum in the morning. After which head to the Colosseum.
- Lunch will be a wonderful meal at the at fantastic little wine bar **Cavour 313**, located at Via Cavour 313. It is only open from 12:30pm - 2:30pm for lunch so make sure you get there on time.
- After lunch let's walk back down the Via dei Foro Imperiali towards the Piazza Venezia to get to the **Campidoglio**. Remember to find *La Buca della Verita*. The museums on the Campidoglio should take most of the afternoon.
- When completed, make your way to the **Pantheon** (or back to the hotel if you're tired) and sit at one of the outside cafés and savor the sight of one of Rome's oldest buildings in a quaint medieval square. If it is super hot, sit by the pillars at the entrance of the Pantheon since it is always wonderfully cool there.
- Now it's back to the hotel to freshen up for your meal this evening at **La Carbonara** in **Campo dei Fiori**. Remember you were in this piazza on Day One at the Drunken Ship? They make the best *spaghetti alla vongole verace* I've ever had.

• You can stay in Campo dei Fiori for the whole evening and take in the sights and sounds of one of Rome's most popular nighttime piazzas. Most evenings they have live bands playing. You've already been to Navona, Santa Maria in Trastevere, and Trevi, the other three great piazzas where you can get a true taste of Roman nightlife.

The Perfect Four Days

Follow the above itinerary and add Day Four immediately below.

Day Four
• Time to go to church (you don't have to pray if you that's not your thing). To get to these places of worship you're going to need to take the metro and buses or rely on Roman taxis. Our first stop is the cathedral of Rome, which isn't St. Peter's, it is **San Giovanni in Laterano**.
• From here walk back towards the Colloseum on Via San Giovanni in Laterano or grab a quick cab to the **Church of San Clemente**.
• After this small church walk up to **San Pietro in Vincoli** to see some of Michelangelo's beautiful statues.
• From here **Santa Maria Sopra Minerva** is only a hop skip and a jump up the Via Cavour.
• By now you must be exhausted, and hungry, and planning ways to make the travel writer who wrote this itinerary pay. Let me assuage your frustrations by offering the chance for a repast at **Enotecantina** on Via del Croce 76. This is near the Spanish Steps so hop in a cab and direct it there. Your feet will thank me for having you take a cab.
• After lunch, when the stores re-open, let's do some antique and art shopping on the nearby streets of **Via del Babuino** and the **Via Margutta**, Rome's best for antiques.
• You were in this area on day 1. It is Rome's best shopping area. Once again explore the streets around the **Piazza di Spagna**, **Via della Croce**, **Via del Corso**, **Via dei Condotti** and admire all the different shops
• If you sustain yourself until dinner time, we will be going to try the hidden **Al Piccolo Arancio** at Vicolo Scandberg 112 near the Trevi Fountin.
• For an after-dinner snack let's visit the best ice cream parlor in Rome, **San Crispino**, on Via della Panetteria 42. Now its time to wander to the Trevi Fountain and savor the sight one more time.

The Perfect Seven Days

Follow the above itinerary for the first four days, then add Days Five through Seven immediately below.

Day Five
• Now the fun begins. We're going to a terrific town – **Frascati**. If we are lucky

and it's September, we may stumble into their wine festival (and definitely stumble out).

- To get to Frascati, go to the train station, buy a ticket, go to track 27, board the small local train (takes 35 minutes and costs Euro [E] 4), and enjoy the scenery along the way.
- Enjoy the views, exploring the winding medieval streets and the relative peace and quiet compared to Rome. Don't forget to search out some of the little wine stores. My favorite is **Cantina Via Campania**.
- For dinner, let's give the wild and raucous **Pergatolo** at Via del Castello 20 a try. If you're into something more sedate, **Zaraza** at Viale Regina Margherita 21 should be your choice.
- Once dinner is done, make your way back to Rome.
- After arriving at the train station, let's go to a nearby Irish pub, **The Fiddler's Elbow** on Via dell'Olmata, that serves up fine ales, an authentic atmosphere, English conversation, and a fun evening to end an adventurous day.

Day Six
- Let's start off the day at the nearby **Mercato de Stampe**, at Piazza Fontanella, which is open from 9:00am–6:00pm Monday through Saturday. Here you can find maps, stamps, books, almost anything on the intellectual side.
- When done here, take a cab or stroll the short distance to the Church of Bones. Yes you heard me correctly. This is **Santa Maria della Concezione** at the foot of the Via Veneto. Here you will find the crypt layered with the bones of the Capuccin monks. Definitely a once in a lifetime sight.
- Next we'll stop in the **Palazzo Barberini**, located on the Via Quattro Fontane that leads up the hill from the Piazza. This palazzo is the home of the **National Portrait Gallery**.
- After soaking up the art, walk back to the Via Veneto , the street that embodies the good life – *la dolce vita*. Halfway up you'll pass by the **American Embassy** on the right hand side.
- Near the top, just off of the Via Veneto, you will find **Giovanni** at Via Marche 64, a great place to eat.
- After your meal, go through the massive gate at the top of the Via Veneto, cross the street and enter the beautiful park, **Villa Borghese**. Take a leisurely stroll through the gardens to the **Galleria Borghese.** This place has beautiful paintings and sculptures galore. Wander ing the park, and savoring the art should take most of the afternoon.
- Dinner tonight is at **Dal Bolognese** in the Piazza del Popolo. Try their *fritto misto*, a fried mix of veggies, cheese, and meat.
- End the evening by going to the top of the **Spanish Steps** for a view over the city at night.

Day Seven
• Assuming today is a Sunday, you must visit the **Porta Portese** market that lines the Tevere every Sunday. Starting at the **Ponte Sublico**, you'll find all sorts of interesting antiques and junk here. A must visit if you're in Rome on a Sunday.
• After the market, it's time to return to the restaurant you have already visited which you liked best. I always do this wherever I travel. It ensures that one of my last meals is going be great, and it makes me feel somewhat like I belong.
• Return to your hotel and pack, and afterwards go for a stroll back the area you liked best. Just like eating at a favorite restaurant, revisiting a favorite place makes you feel connected, and it helps you say good bye.
• End your stroll at the top of the **Spanish Steps** again. Tonight we're going to the terrace restaurant in the **Villa Hassler** for one of the most scenic and romantic you can find in Rome. Try their specialty, *abbacchio al forno*.

Chapter 4

LAND & PEOPLE

Land

From the top of the boot to the toe, Italy is a little more than 675 miles (1,090 kilometers) long. The widest part, in the north, measures about only 355 miles (570 kilometers) from east to west. The rest of the peninsula varies in width from 100 to 150 miles (160 to 240 kilometers) making it an easily traveled country, at least side to side. In total the peninsula of Italy fills an area of about 116,000 square miles (300,400 square kilometers).

A mountainous country, Italy is dominated by two large mountain systems – the **Alps** in the north and the **Apennines** which run down the center of the peninsula. The Alps, which are the highest mountains in Europe, extend in a great curve from the northwestern coast of Italy to the point where they merge with Austria and Slovenia in the east. Just west of the port city of Genoa, the **Maritime Alps** are the beginning of the chain. Despite mighty peaks and steep-sided valleys, the Alps are pierced by modern engineering marvels of mountain passes that have allowed commerce between Italy and its northern neighbors to flow freely. These highway and railroad tunnels provide year-round access through the mountains encouraging trade, tourism and transit.

The Apennine mountain system is an eastern continuation of the Maritime Alps. It forms a long curve that makes up the backbone of the Italian peninsula. The Apennines extend across Italy in the north, follow the east coast across the central region, then turn toward the west coast, and, interrupted by the narrow Strait of Messina, continue into Sicily.

There are numerous smaller mountains in Italy, many of volcanic ancestry, most of which are thankfully extinct. But that does not mean mother nature

remains dormant in Italy. Because of the volcanic nature of the peninsula, which is caused by the earth plates shifting, Italy is prone to earthquakes. In the summer of 1997 an earthquake hit Umbria and destroyed not only towns and villages but some of Giotto's precious frescoes in the cathedral in Assisi. The region was still active for months and aftershocks were felt in Rome in November of that year. I can personally attest to that since the aftershocks woke me up at 3 o'clock one November morning.

People

The Italian people are now considered to be one of the most homogeneous, in language and religion, of all the European populations. About 95 percent of the Italian people speak Italian, which for more than seven centuries the standard form of the language has been the one spoken in Tuscany. However, there are many dialects, some of which are difficult even for Italians to understand. Three of these principal dialects, those of Venice, Sicily and Sardinia, sound like a foreign language, even to most Italians.

But all this is just about where they live and how they speak. What are the Italians like?

Shakespeare was enamored with Italians and things Italian, as is evidenced by having many of his plays set in Italy. And when he wrote "All the world's a stage," he definitely had Italy in mind. Filled with stunningly beautiful architecture and ancient ruins, Italy's physical landscape is a perfect backdrop for the performance that is Italian life. In Italy everyone is an actor, dramatically emphasizing a point with their hands, facial expressions leaving no doubt about what is being discussed and voices rising or falling based on what the scene requires.

Performances in the Piazza

Italians are some of the most animated people in the world and watching them is more than half the fun of going to Italy. These people relish living and are unafraid to express themselves with gusto. There is a tense, dramatic, exciting directness about Italians which is refreshing to foreigners accustomed to Anglo-Saxon self-control. In Italy most travelers find, without even realizing it was missing, that combination of sensuality, love and sincerity that is so lacking in their own lives.

In every piazza, on every street, there is some act being played. Whether it's two neighbors quarreling, vendors extolling the virtues of their wares, a group of older ladies chatting across the street as they lean out their windows, lovers whose whispering hands caress each other as they walk, or a man noticing his reflection in the mirror, there is something about the daily street scenes all over Italy that make this country seem more alive, more animated than the rest or the world. Italians really know how to enjoy the production of living; and they love to watch these everyday scenes unfold.

Seats are strategically placed in cafés to catch all that occurs. And it is easy, even for the uninitiated, to see what is transpiring a distance away because Italians are so expressive. On the faces of Italians it is easy to read joy, sorrow, hope, anger, lust, desire, relief, boredom, despair, adoration and disappointment as easily as if they were spoken aloud. When Italians visit Northern Europe, England, or America they seem lost. Because everyone is so expressionless in other countries, Italians seldom know what is going.

Fashion, Art & Warfare?

Virtually all Italians share a love for fashion. The Italians are some of the best dressed people in the world, and they love to prance around like peacocks displaying their finery. 'Style over substance' is an adage that well describes Italians; but they live it with such flair that it can be forgiven. Along with the clothes they wear, the intrinsic beauty of the Italian people is unparalleled. All manner of coloration, including the stereotypical sensual brown eyed and brown haired beauties abound.

Besides fashion, Italians love art. If you ask an Italian to take your photograph expect to be posed and re-posed for at least five minutes. All Italians imagine themselves to be Federico Fellini, the famous film producer. They want to get the light just right, the shading perfect and the framing ideal. They'll pose you until you're almost blue in the face, but you'll get a great picture.

They also love architecture. What happened in the United States where beautiful buildings were destroyed all over the country to erect parking lots would never happen in Italy. You also be hard pressed to find garish strip malls or ugly suburban sprawl. For example, the McDonalds' in Italy do not stand out the way they do in America with neon golden arches glowing the location for all to see. The store signs have been blended to the architecture of the building in which they are located. A balance has been found between commercialism and aesthetic appeal that has been forgotten in America.

Their love for style over substance is why Italians have always excelled in activities where appearance is paramount, such as architecture, decorating, landscaping, fireworks, opera, industrial design, graphic design, fashion and cinema. It could be conjectured that because of this pursuit of such 'effeminate' pastimes, warfare has never been Italy's forte.

During the Renaissance, battles were mere window dressing. Well paid condottieri headed beautifully appointed companies of men, resplendent in their finest silks, carrying colorful flags bearing the emblem of the families who were paying them. Martial music was played, songs were sung, and bloodcurdling cries were bellowed. But there was not much war being made. There were limited casualties, and when blood was shed it was usually by accident. "Armies" would pursue each other back and forth for weeks in a pageantry of color and celebration until a settlement was decided by negotiation, not bloodshed. This may seem to be a ludicrous form of warfare, but it is a brilliant expression of life, and certainly an appreciation for living.

Religion & Family

The best way to describe Italians is that they are fun. They will "live while they have life to live, and love while they have love to give," as my father used to say. But they are also traditional in their religion. As the center of Roman Catholicism, Italy is a shining example of Christian piety, even though many of the saints they worship are only decorated pagan gods dating back to the pre-Christian era. The Pope is revered as if he truly is sitting at the right hand of the Lord. Virtually every holiday in Italy has some religious undertones and the people perform the associated rites and rituals with enthusiasm.

Christmas is a prime example of this. In Italy it is not as garish and commercial an activity as it is in North America. Religion takes precedence over mass consumption. Having a lavish dinner with family and friends is more important than going into debt to show people you love them through product purchases. Most decorations are of religious figures, not the commercial icons like Santa Claus and Rudolph.

Religion may guide the people and present a foundation for living, but the family is paramount. In a society where legal authority is weak, the law is resented and resisted (estimates place the number of people that actually pay income tax at around 20%) and the safety and welfare of each person is mainly due to the strength of the family. Family gatherings, especially over meals are common. Knowing your third cousins is not rare. And many family members live and die all in the same small neighborhoods where they were born, even in the large cities of Florence, Venice, Naples and Rome. Family traditions are maintained, strengthened and passed on. The young interact, learn from, and respect their elders. The family is the core of Italian society, strong and durable; and from it grows a healthy sense of community. We have much to learn from Italians.

Useful Phrases

If you want to take a few virtual language lessons before you go, visit the "Foreign Language for Travelers" website at *www.travlang.com/languages*. It's helpful and fun.

Pronunciation

Even though Italian is basically pronounced the way you see it, there are few pronunciation idiosyncrasies you should be aware of before attempting to speak the language.

In Italian you pronounce every letter. Vowels are pronounced differently in Italian than in English. In general **e** is pronounced 'ay,' **i** is 'ee,' **a** is 'ah,' **o** is always 'oh,' and **u** is 'oo.' Which would make our vowel list, a-e-i-o-u pronounced ah-ay-ee-oh-oo. Also, an 'e' at the end of a word is always pronounced. And 'e' and 'i' when used with consonants are soft.

Also, and this is important, the second to last syllable is stressed. This is different from English where the first syllable is usually stressed. For example, we pronounce 'rodeo' with the stress on the 'RO' part. The Italians would put the stress on the 'E' part. We would say **RO**deo. They would say rod**E**o. And they would pronounced the **e** as 'ay.'

Other than that, Italian is pretty simple. What you see is how it is pronounced. Sure there are exceptions to that rule, but in general simplicity is the rule. Listed below should not be a considered a comprehensive pronunciation guide for each letter, but it should serve you well.

a - as in father

au - as the 'ow' in cow

b - same as in English

c, cca, ca, cco, co, cchi and **cu** - as the hard 'k' in keep

cci, ci and **ce** - as the 'ch' in cheap

(**c** is the toughest letter with many variations, including: **ca** - ka, **ce** - chay, **ci** - chee, **chi** - key, **che** - kay)

d - same as in English

e - as the 'ay' in day

f - same as in English

g, ga, go, gh and **gu** - as the hard 'g' in gate

ge and **gi** - as the soft 'g' in jar

gl - as the 'll' in million

gn - as the 'ni' in onion

h - silent. OK so not everything is as it appears.

i - as the 'ee' in keep

j - in rare appearances is soft like a 'y' in you.

k/l/m/n - same as in English

o - as the 'o' in float

p/q - same as in English

r - same as in English except for a rolling of the letter. Think of cat purring.

s - majority of cases is as the hard 's' in sit. Between two vowels is soft 's' as in hose.

sc, sca, sco, scu - as the hard sound 'sc' in scout

sce and **sci** - as the soft sound 'sh' in sheep

t - same as in English

u - preceded by a consonant is pronounced as a 'w'

u - all other occurrences pronounced 'oo' (as in an exclamation over fireworks, oooh)

v - preceded by a consonant is pronounced as a 'w. All other times as in English.

z - like the 'ts' sound in cats

Italian is really easy when you grasp the simple pronunciation rules. Yes these rules are different from those in English, but that helps make the Italian language sound so lyrical.

General
• Excuse me, but ....
    Mi scusi, ma .... (This is a good introduction to virtually any and all inquiries listed below. It is a polite way of introducing your questions.)
• Thank you
    Grazie
• Please
    Per favore
• If you are in trouble, yell "Help"
    Aiuto (eye-yoo-toh)

If you are looking for something, a restaurant, a hotel, a museum, simply ask "where is ...:"
• Where is the restaurant(name of restaurant)
    Dov'é il ristorante_____?
• Where is the hotel (name of hotel)
    Dov'é l'hotel _____?
• Where is the museum (name of museum)
    Dov'é il museo _____?
    Note: *(Dov'é* is pronounced "Dove [as in the past tense of dive] -ay")

Travel-Trains
• Where is track number ...
    Dov'é binnario ...

1	*uno*	11	*undici*
2	*due*	12	*dodici*
3	*tre*	13	*tredici*
4	*quatro*	14	*quatordici*
5	*cinque*	15	*quindici*
6	*sei*	16	*sédici*
7	*sette*	17	*diciassette*
8	*otto*	18	*diciotto*
9	*nove*	19	*dicianove*
10	*dieci*	20	*venti*

• Is this the train for Florence (Roma)?
    E questo il treno per Firenze (Roma)?
• When does the train leave?
    Quando partirà il treno?

• When is the next train for Naples/Milan?
Quando é il prossimo treno per Napoli/Milano?

Travel-Cars
• Where is the next gas station?
Dov'é la prossima stazione di benzina?
• I would like some oil for my car.
Voglio un po di olio per la mia automobile.
• Can you change my oil?
Puo fare un cambio dell'olio per me?
• I need a new oil filter.
Voglio un nuovo filtro dell'olio.

Travel-Public Transport
• Where is the (name of station) metro station?
Dov'é la stazione del Metró _____?
• Where can I buy a Metro ticket?
Dove posso prendere un biglietto per il Metro?
• How much is the ticket?
Quanto costa il biglietto?
• Where is the bus stop for bus number ___.
Dov'é la fermata per il bus numero ___?
• Excuse me, but I want to get off.
Mi scusi, ma voglio scendere.
• Where can I catch a taxi?
Dov'é posso prendere un taxi?

Purchasing
The following you can usually get at a pharmacy (*Farmacia*).
• Where can I get...?
Dov'é posso prendere ...?
• toothpaste
dentifricio
• a razor
un rasoio
• some deodorant
un po di deodorante
• a comb
un pettine
• rubbers
dei profilattici
• a toothbrush
un spazzolino da denti

- some aspirin
  un po di aspirina

    The following you can usually get at a *Tabacchaio*:
- stamps
  francobolli
- a newspaper
  un giornale
- a pen
  una penna
- envelopes
  buste per lettere
- some postcards
  delle cartoline

    The following you can usually get at an *Alimentari:*
- some mustard
  un po di senape
- some mayonnaise
  un po di maionese
- tomatoes
  pomodoro
- olive oil
  olio d'oliva
- I would like ... *Vorrei ...*
- 1/4 of a pound of this salami
  un etto di questo salami
- 1/2 of a pound of Milanese salami
  due etti di salame milanese
- 3/4 of a pound of this cheese
  tre etti di questo formaggio
- a small piece of mozzarella
  un po di mozzarrella
- a portion of that cheese
  una porzione di quel' formaggio
- a slice of ham
  una fetta (or una trancia) di prosciutto
- one roll
  un panino
- two/three/four rolls
  due/tre/quattro panini
- How much for the toothpaste, razor, etc?
  Quanto costa per il dentifrico, il rasoio, etc.

- How much for this?
  Quanto costa per questo?
- Excuse me, but where I can find a ...?
  Mi scusi, ma dov'é un ... ?
- pharmacy
  Farmacia
- tobacconist
  Tabaccaio
- food store
  Alimentari
- bakery
  Panificio

Communications
- Where is the post office?
  Dov'é l'ufficio postale?
- Where is a post box?
  Dov'é una buca delle lettere
- Where is a public telephone?
  Dov'é una cabina telefonica?
- May I use this telephone?
  Posso usare questo telefono?

Hotel
- How much is a double for one night/two nights?
  Quanto costa una doppia per una notte/due notti?
- How much is a single for one night/two nights?
  Quanto costa una singola per una notte/due notte?
- Where is the Exit/Entrance?
  Dov'é l'uscita/l'ingresso?
- What time is breakfast?
  A che ora é la prima colazione?
- Can I get another....for the room?
  Posso prendere un altro ... per la camera?
- blanket
  coperta
- pillow
  cuscino
- bed
  letto

Miscellaneous
- Where is the bathroom?

Dov'é il bagno?
- What time is it?

Che ore sono?
- Sorry, I don't speak Italian.

Mi scusi, ma non parlo italiano.
- Where can I get a ticket for ...?

Dove posso prendere un biglietto per ...?
- a soccer game

una partita di calcio
- a basketball game

una partita di pallacanestro
- the theater

il teatro

the opera

l'opera
- You are truly beautiful.

Tu sei veramente bella (spoken to a woman informally)

lei é veramente bella (spoken to woman formally)

Tu sei veramente bello (spoken to a man)

lei é veramente bello (spoken to man formally)
- Can I buy you a drink?

Posso comprarti una bevanda?
- Do you speak any English?

Parli un po d'Inglese?
- Do you want to go for a walk with me?

Voi andare a una passeggiata con me?
- Is there anyplace to go dancing nearby?

C'é un posto per ballare vicino?

Chapter 5

A SHORT HISTORY

A short Italian history is a contradiction in terms. Italy has been home to the Etruscans, Romans, Greeks, 'Barbarian' hordes, Holy Roman Emperors, the Papacy (although not the whole time – the seat of the Catholic Church was moved to Avignon, France from 1305 until 1377), painters, sculptors, the Renaissance, the Medici family, Crusaders, Muslim invaders, French marauders, Spanish conquistadors, Anarchists, Fascists, American soldiers, Communists, Red Brigades, and much more. So much has occurred in that narrow strip of land which has affected the direction of the entire Western world, that it is difficult to succinctly describe its history in a brief outline.

What follows is an attempt at a brief outline of the major events on the Italian peninsula.

Etruscans

Long before Romulus and Remus were being raised by a she-wolf to become the founders of Rome, Italy was the home of a people with an already advanced civilization – the **Etruscans**. This powerful and prosperous society almost vanished from recorded history because not only were they conquered by Rome but were also devastated by marauding **Gauls**. During these conquests once from the south, the other from the north, it is assumed that most of their written history was destroyed, and little remains of it today. The **Eugubine Tablets**, the Rosetta Stone for Central Italy, are the best link we have to understanding the Etruscan language. These tablets have corresponding Umbrian language text, which evolved from the Etruscan, and a corresponding rudimentary form of Latin.

Because of the lack of preserved examples of their language, and the fact that the inscriptions on their monuments has been only partially deciphered, archaeologists have gained most of their knowledge of the Etruscans from studying the remains of their city walls, houses, monuments, and tombs.

From their research, archaeologists have been able to ascertain that the Etruscans were a seafaring people from Asia Minor, and that as early as 1000 BCE (Before the Common Era) they had settled in Italy in the region that is today **Tuscany** and **Lazio**. An area basically from Rome's Tiber River north almost to Florence's Arno River. Their influence eventually embraced a large part of western Italy, including Rome.

As a seafaring people, the Etruscans controlled the commerce of the Tyrrhenian Sea on their western border. After losing control of Rome, they strengthened their naval power through an alliance with Carthage against Greece. In 474 BCE, their fleet was destroyed by the Greeks of Syracuse. This left them vulnerable not only to Rome, but the Gauls from the north. The Gauls overran the country from the north, and the Etruscans' strong southern fortress of **Veii** fell to Rome after a ten-year siege (396 BCE). But as was the Roman way, the Etruscans were absorbed into their society, and eventually Rome adopted many of their advanced arts, their customs, and their institutions.

The Etruscan Kings of Early Rome

When Greece was reaching the height of its prosperity, Rome was just beginning its ascent to power. Rome didn't have any plan for its climb to world domination; it just seemed to evolve. There were plenty of setbacks along the way, but everything seemed to fall into place at the right time; and the end result was that at its apex, Rome ruled most of the known world.

The early Romans kept no written records and their history is so mixed with fables and myths that historians have difficulty distinguishing truth from fiction. The old legends say that **Romulus** founded the city in 753 BCE when the settlements on the seven hills were united. But this date is probably later than the actual founding of the city. As is the case with many emerging societies, the founders are mythical figures, as was Romulus, but there is some evidence that the kings who followed him in the ancient stories actually existed.

Shortly before 600 BCE, Rome was conquered by several Etruscan princes. The Etruscans were benevolent conquerors, an attitude that Rome would itself adopt, and set about improving the native lifestyles to match their own.

The Etruscans built Rome into the center of all Latium, their southern province. Impressive public works were constructed, like the huge sewer **Cloaca Maxima**, which is still in use today. Trade also expanded and prospered, and by the end of the 6th century BCE Rome had become the largest and richest city in Italy.

The Native Romans Revolt

But in spite of all this progress and development, the old Latin aristocracy wanted their power back from the Etruscans. **Junius Brutus** led a successful revolt around 509 BCE, which expelled the Etruscans from the city. That was when the people of Rome made themselves a **republic**.

Rome's successful thwarting of the Etruscans helped the young republic gain the confidence it needed to begin its long history of almost constant conquest. At the time Rome was only a tiny city-state, much like the city-states that were flourishing at the same time in Greece, with a population of roughly 150,000. But in a few centuries this small republic would eventually rule the known world.

Roman Conquest of Italy

The Latin League started to develop a dislike for the growing power and arrogance of their ally and attempted to break away from its control; but Rome won the two year war that followed (340-338 BCE) and firmly established their dominance. The truce that was made between Rome and the Latin League was broken a few years later (326 BCE) by the **Samnites**, and a wild-fought struggle ensued, with a variety of interruptions, until the decisive battle of **Sentinum** (295 BCE), which made Rome supreme over all central and northern Italy.

Southern Italy, still occupied by a disunited group of Greek city-states, still remained independent. Alarmed at the spread of Roman power, the Greek cities appealed to **Pyrrhus**, king of Epirus in Greece, who heeded their warning and inflicted two telling defeats on the Roman army. He then crossed to Sicily to aid the Greek cities there in eliminating Carthaginian rule. Unfortunately this was a classic example of spreading your forces too thin and trying to fight a war on two fronts. Encouraged by the arrival of a Carthaginian fleet to combat the Greeks, Rome renewed its struggle for the Greek city-states in southern Italy, and in 275 BCE defeated Pyrrhus in the battle of **Beneventum** and a new phrase was born: a Pyrrhic victory – where you win the war but at excessive cost. Eventually, one by one the Greek cities were taken, and just like that Rome was ruler of all Italy.

Keeping the Conquered Lands Happy

Rome gradually wove the lands conquered into the fabric of a single nation, contented and unified. Rome could have exploited the conquered cities of Italy for its own interests, but instead made them partners in the future success of the entire empire.

Rome also set about establishing colonies of its citizens all over Italy. Almost one sixth of all Italy was annexed and distributed among these colonizing Roman citizens. By encouraging this colonization, a common interest in the welfare of Rome spread throughout the Italian peninsula. The Roman republic eventually gave way to the Roman empire, which brought about two centuries of peace and prosperity known as the **Roman Peace** (*Pax Romana*).

But all was not well at home. The rich amused themselves by giving splendid feasts. The poor had their circuses where free bread and wine was distributed. Slave labor had degraded the once sturdy peasantry to the status of serfs or beggars, and the middle class, who once had been the backbone of the nation, had almost disappeared. A welfare mentality overcame the population. And Roman governors of the provinces once again began to concentrate on siphoning off as much money as possible during their short term of office, instead of keeping abreast of the economic and political climate.

The Fall of the Roman Empire

Political decay, economic troubles, and decadent living were sapping the strength and discipline of the Roman Empire. At this time, German 'barbarians,' who were a violent people living on the fringes of the empire and led by warrior chiefs, began to attack the edges of the empire in the 4th century CE (Common Era). These **Goths, Vandals, Lombards, Franks, Angles, Saxons,** and other tribes defeated unprepared Roman garrison after garrison, and sacking and pillaging the decadent and crumbling empire. In 330 CE, when the Roman emperor **Constantine** moved the capital to **Constantinople** (today's Istanbul in Turkey), the Western Roman Empire began a gradual decline. Order made way for chaos and rival governors fought over fragments of Italian territory to increase their power.

With the fall of the Western Roman Empire in CE 476, this was the beginning of the period called the **Dark Ages**. They were so called because Roman civilization and law collapse along with its artistic and engineering achievements. Order was lost, well developed distribution trade routes evaporated, people went back to the way life was like prior to Roman rule and in most cases it was a step backward in time. Coordinated agriculture disappeared, the roads fell into ruin, irrigation system were not maintained, public health measures were ignored and the resulting poor hygiene set the stage for the coming of the Black Plague.

What the 'barbarians' did bring with them, however, was an aspect of their freedom and independence that helped shape the future of Western civilization. This was their belief that the individual was important, more so than the state. In contrast, the Romans believed in the rule of the state over the people – in despotism, or the concept of a benevolent dictator. The 'barbarians' gave us a rudimentary form of personal rights, including more respect for women, government by the people for the people, and a system of law which represented the needs and wishes of the people being governed.

In essence, these 'barbarians' lived under the beginnings of democracy in Europe.

After the Roman Empire

Even **Charlemagne**, who had conquered the Lombard rulers and had himself crowned emperor of the **Holy Roman Empire** in 800 CE, could not stop the disintegration of everything the Roman Empire had built. To maintain a semblance of order, the Holy Roman Empire became a union between the Papacy and Charlemagne in which management of the empire was shared.

But Charlemagne's Holy Roman Empire fell apart after his death, only to be refounded by the Saxon **Otto I** in 962 CE, bringing Italy into a close alliance with Germany. From that time until the 1800s, the Holy Roman Empire took on many shapes, sizes, and rulers. It included at different times France, Germany, Luxembourg, the north of Italy (because the Muslims, and then the Normans had taken control of Italy south of Naples), Austria, Switzerland, and more. It had rulers from the Saxon Line, Franconian Line, Hohenstaufen Line, Luxembourg Line, and the Hapsburg Line. It may have been constantly in flux but it did last over 1,000 years in some shape or form.

While the Holy Roman Empire expanded and contracted, it eventually contracted itself outside of Italy, leaving Italy an amalgamation of warring city-states. Florence, Venice, Milan, and the Papacy became the strongest of these contending powers and they came to dominate the countryside while feudalism declined. They drew their riches from the produce of their fertile river valleys and from profits generated in commerce between the Orient and Europe. This trade flowed in through Venice, Pisa, Genoa and Naples and passed through to other European cities on its way across the Alps.

The Italian Renaissance

Under the patronage of the Papacy and of the increasingly prosperous princes of the city-states, such as the **Medici** of Florence, the scholars, writers, sculptors and painters created the masterpieces of literature, art, and science that made the **Italian Renaissance** one of the most influential movements in history. In this period many splendid churches, palaces, and public buildings were built that still inspire awe in Italians and visitors alike. But at the same time as this resurgence in artistic expression, almost completely lost after the fall of the Roman Empire the dominant city states in Italy – Florence, Pisa, Siena, Venice, Perugia, Milan, the Papal States and more – were filled with social strife and political unrest.

Pawn of Strong Nations

While Italy was being torn by struggles between the local rulers and the Papacy, and among themselves, strong nations were developing elsewhere in

Europe. As a result of this, Italy became an area of conquest for the other powers struggling for European supremacy. French and Spanish rivalry over Italy began in 1494. **Charles VIII of France** valiantly fought his way through the peninsula to Naples, but by 1544 **Charles I of Spain** had defeated the French three times and had become ruler of Sicily, Naples, and Milan.

For centuries the city-states of Italy remained mere pawns in other nations' massive chess games of power. Italian city-states passed from one to another of Europe's rulers through war, marriage, death, or treaty. The **Papacy** was, however, usually strong enough to protect its temporal power over the areas in central Italy known as the **States of the Church**, or the **Papal States**.

Movement for Political Unity

Eventually hatred of foreign rule mounted, and with it grew the **Risorgimento**, or movement for political unity. Such secret societies as the Carbonari (charcoal burners, the name given from their use of charcoal burners' huts for meeting places), plotted against the Austrians, but the **Carbonari Revolts** were crushed in 1821 and again in 1831 by Austrian troops.

Then the idealistic republican leader, **Giuseppe Mazzini**, organized his revolutionary society, **Young Italy**, and called upon **Charles Albert**, king of Sardinia-Piedmont and a member of the ancient House of Savoy, to head a movement to liberate Italy. By early 1848, revolts had broken out in many regions, and constitutions had been granted to Naples, Piedmont, and Tuscany. But when Mazzini drove out the pope and set up a short lived republic in Rome the French came to the pope's aid, and Austria quelled the revolt in the north. Despite this outside interference, the ball was rolling, and when Charles Albert abdicated his rule in Sardinia-Piedmont to his son **Victor Emmanuel II**, the stage was set for a run at independence.

Under the able leadership of the shrewd diplomat **Count Camillo di Cavour**, Victor Emmanuel's minister, Sardinia-Piedmont grew strong in resources and in alliances. Cavour was also aware that no matter how real Italian patriotic fervor was, the country would never be unified without help from abroad, so he cleverly forged an alliance with **Napoleon III** of France. Then in the spring of 1859 Austria was goaded into declaring war against Sardinia-Piedmont and France, and was defeated by the combined French and Italian forces. Italy claimed the lands of Lombardy for a united Italy, but France kept as its bounty the kingdom of Venezia.

To consolidate their power, Cavour and Victor Emmanuel lobbied the peoples of Tuscany, Modena, Parma, and Emilia who eventually voted to cast out their princes and join Sardinia-Piedmont as parts of a unified Italy. Napoleon III consented to such an arrangement, but only if Savoy and Nice voted to join France. (Politics is too complicated. I'll stick to travel writing).

Garibaldi to the Rescue

The second step toward a united Italy came the next year, when the famous soldier of fortune **Giuseppe Garibaldi** and his thousand red-shirted volunteers stormed the island of Sicily and the rest of the Kingdom of Naples on the mainland. The people everywhere hailed him as a liberator, and the hated Bourbon king was driven out.

In February 1861 **Victor Emmanuel II** was proclaimed king of Italy, and he began working closely with Garibaldi. Now only the Papal States and Venezia remained outside of the new Italian nation. Venezia joined in 1866 after Prussia defeated Austria in alliance with Italy. The Papal States and **San Marino** were now the only entities on the peninsula outside the Italian kingdom. Not yet as small and isolated as it is today, San Marino was then about the size the current region of Lazio making it a valuable prize for a unified Italy.

Vatican Captured – Kingdom of Italy United

Since French troops still guarded the pope's sovereignty, Victor Emmanuel, being the apt pupil of Cavour (who had died in 1861), did not want to attack the French and perhaps undo all that had been accomplished. Then, miraculously in 1870, the **Franco-Prussian War** forced France to withdraw its soldiers from Rome, at which time Italian forces immediately marched in.

Pope Pius IX, in his infinite lack of wisdom and understanding, excommunicated the invaders and withdrew behind the walls of the Vatican. There he and his successors remained 'voluntary prisoners' until the **Concordat of 1929**, or **Lateran Treaty**, between Italy and the Holy See, which recognized the temporal power of the pope as sovereign ruler over Vatican City (all 108.7 acres of it, or about 1/6 of a square mile!). The rest of the Papal States was absorbed into the new unified Italy, as was San Marino, except for the small, fortified town on top of a butte-like hill that remains independent today.

Modern Italy

Staggering under a load of debt and heavy taxation, giant steps needed to still be taken for Italy to survive. Leaders of the various regions, always trying to gain an edge, were in constant disagreement – even in active conflict. At the same time citizens, used to the ultimate control of despotic rule, found it difficult to adopt the ways of parliamentary government. As a result, riots and other forms of civil disorder were the rule in the latter half of the 19th century.

Despite all of these problems, in the typical Italian mode of functioning despite complete political chaos, an army and navy were developed; railroads, ports, and schools were constructed; and a merchant marine was developed. At the same time, industrial manufacturing started to flourish as it was all over the world.

But then, in 1900, **King Umberto I** (son of Victor Emmanuel II) was assassinated by anarchists – in what was to turn out to be a string of assassinations during that time period all over Europe – and his son, **Victor Emmanuel III**, rose to the throne. Although having joined with Germany and Austria in the **Triple Alliance** in 1882, by the early 1900s Italy began to befriend France and England. With Austria's invasion of Serbia in 1914 after the assassination of Archduke Ferdinand of Austria, Italy declared its neutrality despite being Austria's ally. In April 1915, Italy signed a secret treaty with the **Allies** (Russia, France, and England), and the next month it stated that it had withdrawn from the Triple Alliance. On May 23, 1915, the king of Italy declared war on Austria.

When World War I ended in 1918, the old Austro-Hungarian Empire was broken up. Italy was granted territory formerly under Austrian rule, including "unredeemed Italy" of the Trentino in the north and the peninsula of Istria at the head of the Adriatic.

Mussolini & Fascism

The massive worldwide depression after World War I brought strikes and riots, which were fomented by anarchists, socialists, and Communists. The government of Victor Emmanuel III seemed powerless to stop bands of former servicemen lawlessly roaming the country. In these bands, **Benito Mussolini** saw his opportunity to gain power. With his gift of oratory he soon molded this rabble into enthusiastic, organized groups in many communities all over Italy, armed them, and set them to preserving the order which had been had destroyed. These bands formed the nucleus of his black-shirted **Fascist** party, whose emblem was the *fasces*, the bundle of sticks that had symbolized the authority of the Roman Empire.

On Oct. 28, 1922, the **Blackshirts**, meeting in Naples, were strong enough, well enough prepared, and willing to march on Rome and seize the government. The king, fearing civil war and his own life, refused to proclaim martial law, forced the premier to resign, and asked Mussolini to form a shared government. Within a few years Mussolini, *Il Duce* (The Leader), had reorganized the government so that the people had no voice at all. Mussolini first abolished all parties except his own Fascist party, and took from the Chamber of Deputies the power to consider any laws not proposed by him. The king remained as a figurehead because he was revered by the people and had the support of many wealthy and important families. In 1939 when Mussolini replaced the Chamber of Deputies with the Chamber of Fasces and Corporations, composed of all his henchmen, no semblance of popular rule remained.

Intimidation or violence crushed all opposition. Suspected critics of the regime were sentenced to prison by special courts or were terrorized, tortured, or murdered by Blackshirt thugs. News was censored and public meetings could not be held without the government's permission. The new Fascist state was based on the doctrine that the welfare of the state is all-important and that the individual exists only for the state, owes everything to it, and has no right of protection against it. It was a return to the despotism of the later Roman Empire.

A Return to the Roman Empire?

Mussolini, like other Italian leaders before him, longed to create a new Roman empire and to bring back Italy's lost glory. So, in 1935, with his large army and recently expanded navy, he attacked and conquered the weak, backward, and poorly defended African country of Ethiopia.

In October 1936, at Mussolini's invitation, the **Rome-Berlin Axis** was formed between Italy and Nazi Germany to oppose the power of France and England. At this time Mussolini was considered the stronger ally of the two. In April 1939, Italy invaded Albania, and which that time Italy and Germany became formal military allies.

But when Germany's program of aggression plunged it into war with England and France on September 3, 1939, Italy at first adopted the position of a non-belligerent. But on June 10, 1940, Italian forces attacked southeastern France in an invasion coordinated with German forces in the north.

Defeat in World War II

Italy lacked the military power, resources, and national will to fight a large-scale modern war. Within six months, Italian armies met defeat in Greece and North Africa. In fact a running joke during World War II was that Italian tanks had only one gear: reverse. Italy then humbly accepted the military assistance of Germany. This soon grew into complete economic and military dependence, and Italy was forced to let Germany occupy it, control its home affairs, and Mussolini became a German puppet.

The end of the war found Italy with the majority of its industry and agriculture shattered. During its occupation, the Germans had almost stripped Italy's industry bare by commandeering supplies. Italian factories, roads, docks, and entire villages were ruined by the Allied bombing raids and during the invasion. To make things worse, as the Germans retreated they had wrecked whatever industries and transportation remained.

Even with the Allies contributing substantial quantities of food, clothing, and other supplies, the people were cold, hungry, and jobless. After the war, the United Nations Relief and Rehabilitation Administration gave more aid to Italy than to any other country. Reconstruction lagged, however, because of internal political turmoil, a situation that has become something of a theme in postwar Italian politics.

Postwar Political Change

On June 2, 1946, the Italian people voted to found a republic. They then elected deputies to a Constituent Assembly to draft a new constitution. On February 10, 1947, the peace treaty between Italy and the Allies was ready to be signed. The treaty stripped Italy of its African 'empire' of Libya, Italian Somaliland, and Eritrea. The pact also ceded the Dodecanese Islands to Greece, placed Trieste under UN protection, made minor boundary changes with France, and gave about 3,000 square miles to Yugoslavia, including most of the Istrian peninsula.

Italy had to pay $360 million in reparations, and was also forced to restore independence to Ethiopia and Albania. One lone gain was that **South Tyrol**, which Austria had been forced to cede after World War I, remained with Italy, and eventually, in 1954, **Trieste** was given to Italy through a pact with Yugoslavia.

On January 1, 1948, Italy's newly formed constitution became effective. It banned the Fascist party – though today there are a number of political parties in Italy that go by another name but informally call themselves *Fascisti* – and the monarchy. Freedom of religion was guaranteed, though Catholicism remained the state religion.

But a constitution alone cannot recreate a country. Italian leaders had the double task of creating a stable parliamentary system of government while at the same time restoring the economy. (They still haven't solved the first problem.) The main economic hindrance was the poverty-stricken, agriculturally dependent south contributing little to the improving industrial economy of the north. As a result there were many riots and moments of intense civil unrest.

Land Reform

One of the reasons that the south of Italy was so poor was because much the lands there, as well as in Sicily and Sardinia, were among the last aristocratic strongholds of large-scale landowners. The estates of these landowners covered many thousands of acres and employed only small numbers of laborers, mostly at harvest time. These landless peasants, who had no work during much of the year, lived in nearby villages and small towns and barely made ends meet all year. These people either stayed peaceful and subservient, contributed to civil unrest, or emigrated to find better employment and living conditions elsewhere.

In the early 1950s, the Italian parliament passed special land reform laws that divided large private estates into small farms and distributed them to the peasants. The new owners were given substantial government support for their first years on the land, and the previous owners received cash compensation. Thousands of new small farms were created in this way during the

1950s, and farm production, as a result of the land reform and other measures, rose quickly.

The Italian government not only invested large sums of money in land reform but at the same time also started to develop the infrastructure in the south to help the farmers. New roads were built to help carry produce to market, and new irrigation systems, needed during the long, dry summers, were constructed. Warehouses and cold storage facilities for farm products were provided, and the government also helped to introduce new crops.

Chaos Mixed With Stability

Even with the south's new-found prosperity, Italy's economic development was mainly due to spectacular gains in industrial production in the north. But then during the mid-1960s, Italy began to suffer from severe inflation. A government austerity program to combat this trend produced a decline in profits and a lag in investments. To add insult to injury, devastating floods – the worst in 700 years which were caused by severe soil erosion – hit the country in 1966, ravaging one third of the land and causing losses of more than $1.5 billion. To make matters even worse, some of the priceless art treasures of Florence were irreparably damaged when the flood waters poured through that city.

In 1971 Italy had its largest economic recession since the country's post-World War II recovery. Strikes affected nearly every sector of the economy as Italian workers demanded social reforms. The problems of inflation, unemployment, lack of housing, and unfavorable balance of payments continued in the 1970s.

When Italy was about to pull out of its economic problems, political terrorism escalated, culminating in March 1978, when **Aldo Moro**, leader of the Christian Democratic party and former premier, was abducted in Rome by the **Red Brigades**, an extreme left-wing terrorist group. During the two months that Moro was held, Rome was like an armed camp, with military roadblocks everywhere. I was living there at that time and the memory of sub-machine guns being pointed at me still lingers. Eventually Moro was found murdered and left in the trunk of his car.

In 1980, in Italy's worst natural disaster in more than 70 years, an earthquake killed more than 3,000 persons in the Naples area. As if things could only get worse, in May 1981 a Turkish political dissident tried to kill Pope John Paul II in St. Peter's Square. Also in 1981, a corruption scandal involving hundreds of public servants who were allegedly members of a secret society erupted and brought down the government.

Economic conditions in the early 1980s were affected by growing recession and rising inflation. The Vatican Bank and the Banco Ambrosiano of Milan, Italy's biggest private banking group, were involved in a major banking scandal that forced the liquidation of Banco Ambrosiano in 1982. Two more natural disasters, an earthquake and a landslide, caused widespread damage in the regions of Perugia and Ancona in late 1982.

In 1989, another bank became involved in a scandal when it was revealed that an American branch of the Banca Nazionale del Lavoro had loaned billions of dollars to Iraq. Then severe drought occurred throughout Italy in the winter of 1989 and in Venice some canals were unusable because water levels had dropped so low. And still, into the late 1990s, the Italian government is under intense investigation for rampant corruption which includes officials taking bribes from, or actively colluding with members of the Mafia.

Despite all of this, the Italian economy continues to improve, to the point where it is one of the more successful in Europe. Throughout all of this chaos, Italy perseveres. It's almost as if without a reasonable amount of disorder, Italy could not survive.

What's New?

Italy has raced into the 21st century along with the rest of Europe by adopting a new currency, the **Euro**, which will join the economies of a number of countries and help the Europeans counterbalance the economic power of America and the almighty dollar. The jury is still out on the impact this will have.

To get to the point where they could be included in this economic gambit, Italy had to pass some rather unpopular laws. The most controversial were those associated with food production. Italy is home to some of the world's most diverse food products, all made with time-honored tradition, but sometimes these traditions did not meet hygienic standards required by the European Union. Despite the outcry over having to change the way their beloved food is made, since these standards were imposed food poisonings have decreased all over Italy and the quality and taste of the food products have stayed the same.

Immigration is another issue Italy shares with its European brethren. The economies of Third World countries are not keeping pace with those in the First World. As a result all of Europe is experiencing unparalleled immigration pressure from Africa, the Middle East, Asia, and Eastern Europe. Italy is being especially overrun with refugees from the Balkans, who initially came to avoid the recent war there, but are now escaping their stagnant economies as well.

What to do with these people is a big concern for Italians. Housing is getting scarce, social services are becoming overwhelmed, and society and culture are changing. All of which has enhanced the pleasant chaos that is life in Italy.

Chapter 6

PLANNING YOUR TRIP

Climate & Weather

The climate in Italy is as varied as the country itself, but it never seems to get too harsh. Most of the country has a Mediterranean type of climate, meaning cool, slightly rainy winters and warm, dry summers.

The summers are mild in the north, but winters there tend to be colder because these regions are in or near the Alps. The Alps do play a role in protecting the rest of Italy from cold northern winds. Because Italy is a peninsula and thus surrounded by water, the entire country never seems to get too hot except for the south and Sicily.

Winter is the rainy season, when stream beds that remain empty during much of the year fill to overflowing. Rome has the mildest climate all year round, although the *scirocco* – a hot and humid red sand tinged wind blowing from North Africa – can produce stifling weather in August every other year or so. The climate in Tuscany and Umbria is very similar to Rome's, although winters are colder in Florence. But overall winters are very moderate with snow being extremely rare; still, it is wise to dress warmly.

When to Go

Basically, anytime is good time to travel to Italy. The climate doesn't vary greatly making Italy a pleasant trip any time of year. Then again I'm biased – I spent close to ten wonderful years in Italy and I think it's fantastic all year round. The busiest tourist season is from May to October, leaving the off-season of spring and autumn as the choice times to have Italy all to yourself.

A visit in April or November can be best in terms of cost, both for airfare and lodging, and there will be less tourists about. December is also fun because there are so many festivals during the Christmas season.

Most people come during the summer, making many of the most popular tourist cities such as Rome, Florence and Venice over crowded. Then in August the entire country literally shuts down, since most Italians abandon the cities to vacation at the beach or in the mountains. Personally I find August a wonderful time to visit too, since the cities become sparse with people. Granted many restaurants, shops and businesses are closed during this time, but the country is still as scenic and beautiful.

The early summer months, though packed with people in the cities, are great months to come and visit the hiking trails of the Alps and Appenines. Remember to bring clothing for colder weather even though it is summer.

What to Pack

One suitcase and a carry-on should suffice for your average ten day trip. Maybe the best advice for shoppers is to pack light and buy clothes while you're there, since there are countless clothing stores from which you can buy yourself any needed item. Also if you pack light it will be easier to transport your belongings. A suitcase with wheels is important, but since there are endless numbers of stairs even the wheels won't relieve the burden of lifting your bag every once and awhile. And even if there are no stairs, because of the uneven state of Italian pavements, and in some cases non-existent sidewalks, pulling a wheel suitcase can be cumbersome. I prefer a wheeled carry-on, but if you're the rugged type, a back pack is the best choice.

You can always find a local *Tintoria* (dry cleaner) if your hotel does not supply such a service. If you want to clean your own clothes, it's best to look for a Lavanderia – coin operated laundromat – instead. Remember also to pack all your personal cosmetic items that you've grown accustomed to, since, more than likely, they're not available in Italian stores. The Italian culture just hasn't seemed to grasp the necessity of having 400 types of toothpaste, or 200 types of tampons. If you take medication remember to get the drug's generic name because name brands on medications are different all over the world.

Important items to remember, especially if you're traveling in the winter time, is an umbrella, a raincoat, and water-proof shoes. You never know when the rain will fall in the winter. You should also bring a small pack, or knapsack to carry with you on day trips. A money belt is also advised, because of pick pockets though I've never had any problems. The same can be said for handbags and purses to thwart the potential risk of purse snatchers.

But most importantly, bring a good pair of comfortable walking shoes or hiking boots. A light travel iron is not a bad idea if you cannot abide wrinkles; but a more sensible option is to pack wrinkle free clothes. And in the summer, if you want to get into most of the churches, remember to pack long pants or something to cover your legs. Tank tops and halter top type shirts are also not considered appropriate attire.

Public Holidays

Offices and shops in Italy are closed on the dates below. So prepare for the eventuality of having virtually everything closed and stock up on picnic snacks, soda, whatever, because in most cities and towns there is no such thing as a 24 hour a day 7-11. The Italians take their free time seriously. To them the concept of having something open 24 hours a day is, well, a little crazy. Florence's feast day is June 24th; St. John the Baptist is the patron saint.

- **January 1**, New Year's Day
- **January 6**, Epiphany
- **April 25**, Liberation Day (1945)
- **Easter Monday**
- **May 1**, Labor Day
- **August 15**, *Ferragosto* and Assumption of the Blessed Virgin (climax of Italian family holiday season. Hardly anything stays open in the big cities through the month of August)
- **November 1**, All Saints Day
- **December 8**, Immaculate Conception
- **December 25/26**, Christmas

Listed below are some dates that may be considered public holidays in different areas of Italy, so prepare for them as well:
- **Ascension**
- **Corpus Christi**
- **June 2**, Proclamation of Republic (celebrated on the following Saturday)
- **November 4**, National Unity Day (celebrated on following Saturday)

Making Airline Reservations

Since airfares can vary so widely it is advised to contact a reputable travel agent and stay abreast of all promotional fares advertised in the newspapers. Once you're ticketed getting there is a breeze. Just hop on the plane and 6-8 hours later you're there. Italy's two main international airports are Rome's **Fiumicino** (also known as **Leonardo da Vinci**) and Milan's **Malpensa**, which handle all incoming flights from North America and Australia. There are other, smaller regional airports in Bologna, Florence, Pisa and Venice that accept flights from all over Europe as well as the United Kingdom, but not from North America or Australia. For more information see the *Getting to Italy* section.

Fares are highest during the peak summer months (June through mid-September) and lowest from November through March (except during peak

Christmas travel time). You can get the best fares by booking far in advance. This will also assure you a good seat. Getting a non-stop flight to Italy at the last minute is simply an impossibility during the high season. If you are concerned about having to change your schedule at the last minute, and do not want to book far in advance, look into some special **travel insurance** that will cover the cost of your ticket under such circumstances. Check with your travel agent about details and pricing since these, like ticket prices, change almost on a daily basis.

Passport Regulations

A visa is not required for US or Canadian citizens, or members of the European Union, who are holding a valid passport, unless that person expects to stay in Italy longer than 90 days and/or study or seek employment. While in Italy, you can apply for a longer stay at any police station for an extension of an additional 90 days. You will be asked to prove that you're not seeking such an extension for study or employment, and that you have adequate means of support. Usually permission is granted almost immediately.

When staying at a hotel, you will need to produce your passport when you register; and most likely the desk clerk will need to keep your passport overnight to transcribe the relevant details for their records. Your passport will most likely be returned that same day. If not, make sure you request it since it is an Italian law that identification papers be carried at all times. Usually a native driver's license will suffice but I always carry my passport. If you are concerned about pickpockets, keep your passport in the front pocket of your pants. I keep mine in a small zip lock bag so it won't get moist with perspiration.

To find out all the information you need to know about applying for a US Passport go to the State Department website at *http://travel.state.gov/ passport_services.html.*

If you have failed to renew your passport and you need one right away try **Instant Passport**, *Tel. 800/284-2564, www.instantpassport.com.* They promise to give you 24-hour turnaround from the time they receive your passport pictures and requisite forms. They charge $100 plus overnight shipping on top of all fees associated with passport issuance.

Another company, **American Passport Express**, *Tel. 800/841-6778, www.americanpassport.com,* offers three types of service – expedited (24 hours), express (three to four business days) and regular. Prices range from $245 to $135.

For **Canadian travelers**, the Canadian Passport Office *(www.dfait-maeci.gc.ca/passport/menu.asp)* also offers an excellent web site to help walk you through the steps to apply for the passport.

For **British travelers**, the UK's Passport Agency *(www.ukpa.gov.uk)* offers a similar level of exemplary service on their web site.

Vaccinations

No vaccinations are required to enter Italy, or for that matter, to re-enter the U.S., Canada, or any other European country. But some people are starting to think it may be wise, especially for Hepatitis A. One of those people is Donna Shipley, B.S.N, R.N. and President of Smart Travel, an international health service organization. She says, "Even though the perception is that Italy is safe and clean, it is still not like North America. In other words it is better to be safe than sorry. Prevention makes sense."

For information about vaccinations contact:
• **Smart Travel**, *Tel. 800/730-3170*

Travel Insurance

This is the most frequently forgotten precaution in travel. Just like other insurance, this is for 'just in case' scenarios. The beauty of travel insurance is that it covers a wide variety of occurrences, such as trip cancellation or interruption, trip delay/missed connection, itinerary change, accident medical expense, sickness medical expense, baggage and baggage delay, and medical evacuation/repatriation. And to get all that for a week long trip will only cost you $25. You'll spend more than that on the cab ride from the airport when you arrive.

For travel insurance look in your local yellow pages or contact the well-known international organization below:
• **Travelex**, *Tel. 800/228-9792*

Customs

Duty free entry is allowed for personal effects that will not be sold, given away, or traded while in Italy: clothing, bicycle, moped no bigger than 50cc, books, camping and household equipment, fishing tackle, one pair of skis, two tennis racquets, portable computer, record player with 10 records, tape recorder or Dictaphone, baby carriage, two still cameras with 10 rolls of film for each, one movie camera with 10 rolls of film (I suppose they mean 10 cassette tapes now), binoculars, personal jewelry, portable radio set (may be subject to small license fee), 400 cigarettes, and a quantity of cigars or pipe tobacco not to exceed 500 grams (1.1 lbs), two bottles of wine and one bottle of liquor, 4.4 lbs of coffee, 6.6 lbs of sugar, and 2.2 lbs of cocoa.

This is Italy's official list, but they are very flexible with personal items. As well they should be, since technology is changing so rapidly that items not listed last year could be a personal item for most people this year (i.e. Sony Watchmans, portable video games, etc.).

Flying to Italy

Book well in advance. As the airline industry continues to contract, fewer and fewer flights are scheduled to Italy. That being as it may, sometimes if you wait until close to the last minute, you can get some good deals on airfare. However, there is a risk that you might not get flights at all. The choice is yours.

The main airports that carriers from North America fly into are Rome, Milan or Venice. See each of those specific sections for information about getting from the airport into town. Below is a list of some other major carriers that have flights to Italy:

- **Alitalia**, *Tel. 800/223-5730 in US, www.alitalia.it/eng/index.html. Toll free in Italy 800/1478/65642.* Address in Rome – Via Bissolati 13. Flights from the United States, Canada, and the United Kingdom.
- **Air Canada**, *Tel. 800/776-3000; www.aircanada.com. Toll free in Italy 800/ 862-216.* Rome address – Via C. Veneziani 58. Flights from Canada to London or Paris, then connections on another carrier to Rome or Milan.
- **American Airlines**, *Tel. 800/433-7300; www.americanair.com. Rome Tel. 06/4274-1240,* Via Sicilia 50. *Italy E-mail: abtvlaa@tin.it.* Direct flights from Chicago to Milan.
- **British Airways**, *Tel. 800/247-9297; www.british-airways.com. Toll free in Italy 1478/12266.* Rome address – Via Bissolati 54. Connections through London's Heathrow to Rome, Milan, Bologna, Venice, and Palermo.
- **Delta**, *Tel. 800/221-1212; www.delta-air.com. Toll free in Italy 800/864-114.* Rome address – Via Po 10. Direct flights from New York to Rome or Milan.
- **Northwest**, *Tel. 800/2245-2525; www.nwa.com. KLM in Rome 06/652-9286.* Flights to Amsterdam connecting to KLM and onto Rome or Milan.
- **TWA**, *Tel. 800/221-2000; www.twa.com. Toll free in Italy 800/841-843.* Rome address – Via Barberini 59. Direct flights from New York's JFK to Rome or Milan.
- **United**, *Tel. 800/538-2929; www.ual.com. Rome Tel. 06/4890-4140,* Via Bissolati 54. Direct flights from Washington Dulles to Milan.
- **US Airways**, *Tel. 800/622-1015; www.ual.com. Toll free in Italy 800/870-945.* Direct flights from Philadelphia to Rome.

Discount Travel Agents

The best way to find a travel agency for your travel to Italy is by looking in your local yellow pages; but if you want to get the same flights for less, the three organizations below offer the lowest fares available. I have had the best service and best prices from *www.lowestfare.com*, but the others are good also.

- **Fly Cheap**, *Tel. 800/FLY-CHEAP*
- **Fare Deals, Ltd.**, *Tel. 800/347-7006*

• **Lowestfare.com**, *Tel. 888/777-2222*
• **Airdeals.com**, *Tel. 888/999-2174*

In conjunction, listed below are some online travel booking services that offer great fares. Online travel searching can be cumbersome, since there is a registration process and each has a different approach to the reservation and booking process. In essence, what you learn from these services is what your travel agent goes through when they work with reservation systems like Apollo, Worldspan and System One. Also, if you shop here to find out what prices and availability are and then book your flights the regular way, from the airline or a live travel agent, these online service do not like that. Some will even terminate your registration if you shop too frequently without buying.

With that said, here are some websites:
• **Internet Travel Network**, *www.itn.net*
• **Preview Travel**, *www.previewtravel.com*
• **Expedia**, *www.expedia.com*
• **Travelocity**, *www.travelocity.com*

Courier Flights

Acting as an air courier – whereby you accompany shipments sent by air in your cargo space in return for discounted airfare – can be one of the least expensive ways to fly. It can also be a little restrictive and inconvenient. But if you want to travel to Italy, at almost half the regular fare, being a courier is for you.

The hassles are (1) in most cases you have to get to the courier company's offices before your flight adding to your travel time, (2) most flights only originate from one city and that may not be the one where you are, (3) since you usually check in later than all other flyers you may not get your choice of seating, (4) you can only use a carry-on since your cargo space is being allocated for the shipment you are accompanying, (5) your length of stay is usually only 7-10 days – no longer, and (6) courier flights don't do companion tickets, which means you fly alone.

But contrary to the common impression, as a courier you usually do not even see the goods being transported and you don't need to check them through customs. Also you are not legally responsible for the shipment's contents – that's the courier company's responsibility – according to industry sources and US Customs. All this aside, if you are interested in saving a large chunk of change, give these services a try:
• **Halbart Express**, *Tel. 718/656-8189 or 718 656-8279*
• **Discount Travel International**, *Tel. 212/362-8113 or 212/362-3636*
• **Airhitch**, *Tel. 212/864-2000; www.airhitch.org*. Air hitching is the least expensive but they are also the most restrictive. You really need to be very flexible, i.e. can travel at the drop of a hat.

Accommodations
What to Expect at Hotels

Don't be surprised by hotel taxes, additional charges, and requests for payment for extras, such as air conditioning that make your bill larger than expected. Sometimes these taxes/service charges are included in room rates but you should check upon arrival or when you make your reservation. Remember to save receipts from hotels and car rentals, as 15% to 20% of the value-added taxes (VAT) on these services may be refunded if you are a non-resident. For more information, call **I.T.S. Fabry**, *Tel. 803/720-8646* or see Chapter 9, *Shopping*, Tax-Free Shopping section.

The Italian Tourist Board categorizes all of the hotels in Italy with a star rating. A five star deluxe hotel (*****) is the best, a one star hotel (*) is the least desirable and usually the least expensive too. The term *Pensione* is in the process of being phased out, and these smaller, bed-and-breakfast type inns are being replaced with a designation of one-star (*), two-star (**), or three star (***) hotel.

Making Reservations

I recommend faxing or emailing the hotel(s) of your choice inquiring about availability for the dates you are interested in, as well as the rate for those dates. Faxing or emailing is preferable to calling since you can quickly and easily communicate your information, reducing any long distance telephone charges.

Also, since most Italians who run hotels speak English, it is possible to write your fax or e-mail in English; but if you want to practice your Italian, they usually appreciate any effort at communicating in their own language. Personally, I write my requests in both English and Italian so that there is no confusion as to the information imparted.

When writing the dates you are interested in, make sure you spell out the month, since here in America we transpose the month and day in numeric dates. For example, in the US January 10, 2005 would appear numerically as 1/10/05. In Europe, it would appear as 10/01/05. See where the confusion could come in?

Expect a reply to your communication within a few days. If you do not get a reply, send another message. Sometimes faxes or emails get lost on the night shift. To book your room you will need to send the hotel a credit card number with expiration date in a reply communication. This will ensure that you show up. So if you have to cancel your trip for whatever reason, make sure you contact the hotel and cancel your room – otherwise you will be charged.

Hotel Prices

The prices that are listed sometimes include a range, for example E50-75. The first number in the range indicates what the price is during the off-season, the second price is the going rate during high season. If there is no range, then the hotel doesn't change its rate for the off-season.

The high season is generally April through September, with Christmas and New Year's week thrown in. Other high seasons will include local festivals, like the **Palio** in Siena or **Calcio in Costume** in Florence. Also, the high season for the ski areas will be winter, not summer, so it is important to inquire up front about what the actual rates will be.

Hotel Rating System

The star rating system that the Italian Tourist Board officially uses has little to do with the prices of the hotels, but more to do with the amenities you will find. The prices for each category will vary according to the locale, so if it's a big city, a four star will be super-expensive; if it's a small town, it will be priced like a three or two star in a big city.

In the ambiguous way of the Italians, nothing is ever as it seems, which means that even the amenities will be different for each star category depending on whether you are in a big city or a smaller town. Hence the need for travel guides. But basically the list below is what the ratings mean by star category:

*****Five star, deluxe hotel**: Professional service, great restaurant, perfectly immaculate large rooms and bathrooms with air conditioning, satellite TV, mini-bar, room service, laundry service, and every convenience you could imagine to make you feel like a king or queen. Bathrooms in every room.

****Four star hotel**: professional service, most probably they have a restaurant, clean rooms not so large, air conditioning, TV (usually via satellite), mini-bar, room service, laundry service and maybe a few more North American-like amenities. Bathrooms in every room.

***Three star hotel**: a little less professional service, most probably do not have room service, should have air conditioning, TV and mini bar, but the rooms are mostly small as are their bathrooms. Some rooms in small town hotels may not have bathrooms.

Two star hotel: Usually a family run place, some not so immaculate and well taken care of as higher rated hotels. Mostly you'll only find a telephone in the room, and in big cities you'll be lucky to get air conditioning. About 50% of the rooms have either a shower/bath or water closet and sometimes not both together. Hardly any amenities, just a place to lay your head. The exception to this is in small towns, where some two stars are as well appointed as some of the best three stars.

*One star hotel**: Here you usually get a small room with a bed, sometimes you have to share the rooms with other travelers. The bathroom is usually in the hall. No air conditioning, no telephone in the room, just a room with bed. These are what used to be the low-end *pensiones*. Definitely for budget travelers.

Diplomatic & Consular Offices In Italy

These are the places you'll need to contact if you lose your passport or have some unfortunate brush with the law. Remember that the employees of these offices are merely your government's representatives in a foreign country, not God. They cannot fix your problems in the blink of an eye, but they will do their best on your behalf. For a list of the consular offices in each city, refer to that section.

Agriturismo

If you have ever wanted to work on a farm, Italy has a well organized system where you can do just that. Initially the idea behind **Agriturismo** started as a way for urban Italians to re-connect with their old towns and villages, and through that to the earth again; but every year it has grown in popularity. Traditionally you would rent rooms in family farmhouses, but some accommodations have evolved into more hotel type, bed-and-breakfast like situations with separate buildings on the farms for agriturists. Since there is such a large demand for agriturism, two separate competing bodies have published directories to assist people trying to reconnect with mother nature.

Both of the books sold by these groups are also available at selected bookstores, like the Feltrinelli Bookstores listed in this guide:
- **Agriturist**, Via Vittorio Emanuele 89, 00186 Roma, *Tel. 06/658-342*. Open Monday-Friday 10:00am-noon and Tuesday, Wednesday, Thursday 3:30-5:30pm. Closed Saturday and Sunday.
- **Turismo Verde** (Green Tourism), Via Mariano Fortuny 20, 00196 Roma, *Tel. 06/361-1051*.

Mountain Refuges

There are a number of mountain refuges (*rifugi*) available for rent in the Alps and Apennines, many of which are run by the **Club Alpino Italiano (CAI)**. If you are a member, you can get maps and information about hiking, and all necessary information about the *rifugi*. The CAI has offices all over Italy, but there is limited centralization of resources and information, and most offices are run by volunteers and/or avid hikers. Contact the CAI offices listed below, or the local tourist office in the city nearby where you want to go hiking, for any available information.

The *rifugi* are generally dormitory style and meals are available at a cost of around E12 per person. There are private *rifugi* which charge rates comparable to about one or two star hotel accommodations. All rifugi are

usually only open from July to September and are booked well in advance.
• **CAI–Milano**, Via Silvio Pellico 6, *Tel. 02/8646-3516.*
• **CAI–Roma**, 305 Corso Vittorio Emanuelle II, 4th floor, *Tel. 06/686-1011, Fax 06/6880-3424, www.frascati.enea.it/cai*

Renting Villas & Apartments
One of the best ways to spend a vacation in Italy is in a rented villa in the country or in an apartment in the center of town. It makes you feel as if you actually are living in Italy and not just passing through. Staying in "your own place" gives your trip that little extra sense of belonging.

The best way to find a place of your own in Italy is to contact one of the agencies listed below that specialize in the rental of villas and apartments in Italy:
• **At Home Abroad Inc**, 405 East 56 Street, Suite 6H, New York, NY 10022-2466, *Tel. 212/421-9165. Fax 212/752-1591, Web: www.athomeabroadinc.com*
• **B&B's in Italy**, *Web: www.bbitalia.com*
• **Hideaways International**, *Tel. 800/843-4433, Web: www.hideaways.com*
• **Holiday Homes**, *Web: www.holidayhomes.com*
• **Homebase Abroad**, 29 Mary's Lane, Scituate, MA 02066, *Tel. 781545-5112, Fax 781/545-1808, Web: www.homebase-abroad.com*
• **Individual Travellers Company**, *Web: www.indiv-travellers.com*
• **Italian Villa Rentals**, 900 County Line Road, Bryn Mawr, PA 19010-2502, *Tel: 610/520-0806 or 800/261-4460, Fax 610/520-0807 Email: info@doorwaysltd.com, Web: www.villavacations.com*
• **Italian Farm Holiday**, *Web: www.italyfarmhouse.it*
• **InterHome**, *Web: www.interhome.com*
• **International Vacation Homes**, 9920 S. La Cienega Blvd., Suite 900, Inglewood, CA 90301, *Tel. 800/282-1594, 310/568-8510, Fax 310/568-8289, Web: www.ivacation.com*
• **Invitation to Tuscany**, *Web: www.invitationtotuscany.com*
• **Overseas Connection**, *Web: www.villasoftheworld.com*
• **Tuscan Villa UK**, *Web: www.tuscany-villas.co.uk*
• **Villa Net**, *Tel. 800/964-1891, Email: info@rentavilla.com, Web: www.rentavilla.com*
• **Villas and Apartments Abroad**, 370 Lexington Ave Suite 1401, New York 10017, *Tel. 212/897-5045, Fax 212/897-5039, Email: villas@vaanyc.com, Web: www.vaanyc.com*
• **Villas International**, *Web: www.villasintl.com*
• **Windows on Tuscany**, *Email: info@windowsontuscany.com, Web: www.windowsontuscany.com*
• **Worldwide Villas**, *Email: villas@villasintl.com, Web: www.4vacationers.com*

Youth Hostels

Youth Hostels (ostelli per la gioventú) provide reasonably priced accommodations, specifically for younger travelers. A membership card is needed that is associated with the youth hostel's organization, i.e. a student ID card. Advanced booking is a must during the high season since these low priced accommodations fill up fast. Hundreds of youth hostels are located all over Italy. Contact the Tourist Information office when you arrive in the city to locate them.

Getting Around Italy

Italy is connected by an extensive highway system **(Autostrada)**, a superb train system, a series of regional airports, and naturally, since Italy is virtually surrounded by water and has a number of islands, a complete maritime service involving ferries and hydrofoils. The mode of transportation you select will depend on how long you're staying in Italy and where you are going.

In general the best way to get around Italy is by train. No traffic, no parking hassles, no dealing with fuel, just sit back and watch the scenery pass by. That being said, if you are going to rural, off-the-beaten path locations, you'll need a car, but in overall, you can get almost anywhere imaginable quickly and easily by train.

By Air

You can fly between many Italian destinations quite easily. If you are on business, using air travel makes sense to fly from Milan to Rome, but not if you are a tourist. You could enjoy a relaxing three hour train ride in the morning to Florence, spend a day shopping and sightseeing, then get on another three hour train ride to Rome and get there in time for dinner. And the entire cost would only be around $100, a lot less than if you had flown.

But if you insist on flying, here is a list of towns that have airports that receive service from the larger venues in Rome and Milan: Alghero, Ancona, Bari, Bologna, Brindisi, Cagliari, Catania, Firenze, Genoa, Lamezia Terme, Lampedusa, Napoli, Olbia, Pantelleria, Pescara, Pisa, Reggio Calabria, Torino, Trapani, Trieste, Venice, Verona.

By Bicycle

A great way to get around Italy is with an organized bicycle tour group. Two such organizations are **Ciclismo Classico**, and **BCT Tours**. They offer magnificent tours all over Italy, from Sardinia to Venice and beyond. Their guides are extremely knowledgeable and professional and speak impeccable English. And you stay at fine hotels, eat fantastic food, meet wonderful people, and constantly interact with the locals – all while seeing Italy up close and personal on a bicycle.

To get more information, contact **Ciclismo Classico**, 13 Marathon Street, Arlington MA 02174, *Tel. 800/866-7314 or 781/646-3377, Fax 617/641-1512, E-mail:info@ciclismoclassico.com, Web: www.ciclismoclassico.com.* **BCT Tours**, 2506 N. Clark St #150, Chicago, IL 60614, *Tel. 800/736-BIKE, Fax 773/404-1833, E-mail: adventure@cbttours. Web: www.bcttours.com.*

Home Exchange

A less expensive way to have "a home of your own" in Italy is to join a **home swapping club**. These clubs have reputable members all over the world. All you'd need to do is coordinate travel plans with a family in a location you'd like to stay in Italy, and exchange houses. This type of accommodation will save you a lot of money.

The best one that we know is **Home Link**, PO Box, Key West FL 33041, *Tel. 305/294-3720, Tel. 800/638-3841, Fax 305/294-1448.*

By Bus

Most long distance travel is done by train, but the regional bus systems can be beneficial for inter-city trips to smaller towns not serviced by rail lines. If you're not a rental car person, and you simply have to get to that beautiful little medieval hill town you saw from the train window, the only way you're going to get there is by regional bus.

Conveniently, most bus stations are next door to or near the train station in most towns and cities. The Italian transportation system is something to be admired since they make it so convenient, and comfortable too. Hopefully one day Americans will wake up and learn that having a multiplicity of transportation options is better than being completely dependent on the automobile. In Italy, most long range buses are equipped with bathrooms and some have televisions on them. The regional inter-town buses are a little less comfortable but still palatial compared to the same type of bus in Central America.

By Car

The world's first automobile expressways were built in northern Italy during the 1920s. Today, Italy and Germany have the most extensive networks of fast, limited-access highways in Europe. Motorists can drive without encountering traffic lights or crossroads – stopping only for border crossings, rest, or fuel – from Belgium, Holland, France, or Germany across the Alps all the way to Sicily. Unlike in America, where our highways were designed for short trips with access every other mile or less, in Europe the highways are for long distance travel.

Two highway tunnels through the Alps, under the Great St. Bernard Pass and through Mont Blanc, enable motor vehicles to travel between Italy and the rest of Europe via car regardless of weather. The expressways, called *Autostrada*, are superhighways and toll roads. They connect all major Italian cities and have contributed to the tremendous increase in tourist travel.

Driving is a good way to see Italy's smaller towns, villages, seascapes, landscapes, and monuments. The Italian drivers may be a little *pazzo* (crazy), but if you drive confidently and carefully you should be fine. If you remain aware and keep your eyes on the car in front of you, you should be fine. Still, be alert on Italy's roadways, because Italian drivers are like nothing you have ever experienced.

Driver's Licenses

US, British, and Canadian automobile driving licenses are valid in Italy. If you want to rent a motorcycle, you will need a motorcycle license from your country of origin. To rent a scooter up to 150 cc, all you need is a pulse.

Car Rental

In all major cities there are a variety of car rental locations, and even such American stalwarts as Avis and Hertz (see each city's individual section for specifics). All you need to do to rent a car is contact the agency in question.

Driving through the back roads of Italy can offer you some of the best access to secluded little hill towns, clear mountain lakes, snow capped mountains and more; but it can also be one of the most expensive items on your trip, not only because of the exorbitant cost of the rental itself, but also because of the price of gasoline, which can run up to $6 or more per gallon. Naturally, there are ways to keep the cost down, one of which is to make the best use of your car.

Don't rent a car for your entire trip, allowing it to sit in a garage when you are in a big city and you are getting around on foot or by bus, metro, or taxi. Use a rental car to travel through the isolated hills and valleys in between the big cities and drop off the car once you arrive at your destination. Compared to the cost of the rental, drop-off charges are minimal. And of course, make sure you have unlimited mileage, otherwise the cost will creep up by the kilometer.

But always be aware of the wild Italian drivers. Unless you are from Boston and are used to aggressive driving tactics, driving a car to get around Italy should be avoided. So think twice about renting a car. Italian drivers are like nothing you've ever seen.

Another caveat against car rental is that it will isolate you from many experiences while traveling. Going by train allows you to become a part of the daily lives of the locals. You experience life from their perspective. Behind the glass and steel of an automobile you tend to be isolated from pure cultural experiences.

Since 1945 in America we have not really known anything other than getting around by automobile, but in Europe, and especially in Italy, there are a multiplicity of other transportation options, whether it is inter or intra-city. The inter-urban Italian train system is one of the best in the world, and where trains don't go, frequent bus service exists. So think twice about car rental because there are many other transportation options to choose from in Italy, unlike here in America.

If you do choose to rent a car, Hertz and Avis have offices all over Italy. To book a car in advance, contact their toll free numbers in the U.S. or websites in Italy: **Hertz**, *Tel. 800/654-3001, Web: www.hertz.it;* **Avis**, *Tel. 800/331-1084, Web: www.avisautonoleggio.it.*

Road Maps

If you're going to be our of Rome you are going to want adequate maps, and the only place to get really good maps is from the **Touring Club Italiano**. Your rental company should supply you something that will enable you to get the car out of their parking lot, but after that you are on your own. The place that has the best road maps of Italy is the **Touring Club Italiano**, Via Marsala 8, Roma, *Tel. 06/499-899, www.touringclub.it/.* Their website is in Italian. You can also get maps from the **Italian Government Tourist Office**, *www.italiantourism.com*, or any high-level travel book store.

By Hiking

If you are an avid hiker, and enjoy seeing a country from the perspective of the back roads or trails, contact this excellent organization, **BCT** (British Coastal Trails) **Scenic Walking**, which offers some great walking tours of Italy, England and the rest of the European continent. **BCT Scenic Tours**, 703 Palomar Airport Road, Suite 200, Carlsbad CA 92009, *Tel. 800/473-1210 or 760/431-7306, Web: www.bctwalk.com.*

By Train

Taking the train is by far the most expedient, most relaxing, and definitely the best way to travel throughout Italy. Trains go almost every place you'd like to visit, they are comfortable, run on time, and free you from having to drive. The railroad system is more extensive in north and central Italy, but main lines run along both coasts, and other routes cross the peninsula in several places.

The Italian railroad system is owned by the government and provides convenient and extensive transportation throughout the country. A great web site that contains everything you need to know about rail travel in Italy is for the Italian Rail Company (**Ferrovie dello Stato** – FS) at *www.fs-on-line.com.*

Eurostar Style

A feather in the cap of the European rail system is the **Eurostar trains**. These are very comfortable, luxurious and fast. Travel between Rome and Florence (and Venice and Florence) has been reduced to less than two hours each way. The seats on these trains are large and accommodating in both first and second class. In first class they serve you a snack with free beverage service, and offer you headphones that you can keep. A truly wonderful way to travel. So if you are going by train and want to enjoy luxury on the rails, try the Eurostar. Price is rather expensive at E55 (about $55) each way, but well worth it.

Types of Train Tickets

There are two main levels of seating on most every train in Italy: **first class** and **second class**. The difference in price is usually only a few dollars, but the difference in convenience is astounding. An example of the price difference between first class and second when traveling between Rome and Florence is $35 for first class, $22 for second class. First class ticket holders can make reservations in advance and the trains are air-conditioned.

Buying a Ticket

When buying your train ticket, if the line at the ticket office in the train station (Bigletteria) is so long that you feel the next ice age will arrive prior to you being able to buy a ticket, there are options.

First, there are usually automated ticket machines sprinkled around most well traveled stations. Usually they take credit cards only. Some take bills. Instructions can be selected to be presented in English.

Second, also in most well traveled stations there are travel agencies (Angezia di Viaggio) that sell train tickets. Without charging a commission.

Boarding the Right Train

When taking a train in Italy the ultimate destination that is listed on the train schedule and the departure listing by the track may not be the same city or town to which you are going. To get to Pisa, for example, sometimes you have to board a train whose ultimate destination is Livorno. To make sure you're boarding the proper train, first ask the information desk in the train station when your train is leaving and which track it is leaving from, then try one of two things (or both):

1. Consult one of the large glass-enclosed schedules (see graphic on page 81) located in the information offices and usually at the head of the tracks. Normally they have a wildly gesturing crowd hovering around them, so you may have to squeeze your way through for a view. Match your intended departure time with the time printed on the sheet. Then check directly to the right of the time to see the list of all the destinations for the train. If the name of your destination is listed, you've found your train. Next write down the ultimate destination of the train so you can check the main board at the station that lists **partenze** (trains leaving) to see which **binario** (track) you should board.

2. If that still doesn't soothe your concerns, ask someone waiting at the track or inside the train if it is going to your destination. Ask at least two people, since I've had someone erroneously tell me a train doesn't go where I asked. It seems that these people, some of whom have been riding the same train to and from work for forty years haven't bothered to pay attention to where the train actually stops.

Whatever the case, to ask someone politely in Italian whether the train is going to your destination say **"Scusa, ma questo treno va a Lucca?"** ("Excuse me, but does this train go to Lucca?") Obviously substitute the underlined city name for the destination to which you wish to go. This question is asked countless times by many people, including Italians.

Finally, if you're standing on the platform waiting for the train to come and you suddenly see all the Italians moving away en masse, that usually means that the public address announcer just declared a track change. Ask one of the departing Italians "Has the track for the train to Lucca changed?" **(é cambiato il binario per il treno per Lucca?)** If the answer is yes (si), either get the number and go there or simply follow them, and as you pass the board that lists the trains leaving, you'll see the change already officially noted.

Train Layouts

If you want to be in the right place on the boarding track (binario) to board the train, which will give you a better chance of finding a good seat, this is what you need to do. Generally there is a sign at your track, or in larger stations at the head of all the tracks, that graphically depicts the make-up of trains

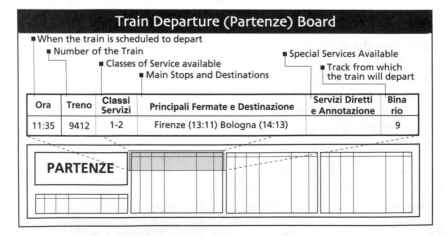

Train Departure (Partenze) Board

- When the train is scheduled to depart
  - Number of the Train
    - Classes of Service available
      - Main Stops and Destinations
- Special Services Available
  - Track from which the train will depart

Ora	Treno	Classi Servizi	Principali Fermate e Destinazione	Servizi Diretti e Annotazione	Binario
11:35	9412	1-2	Firenze (13:11) Bologna (14:13)		9

PARTENZE

stopping at that track or in that station. Locate the time of your departure on the board, make sure it's the proper destination, and you will see a graphic representation of your train and where all the cars will be at the track once it arrives.

Each track in Italian train stations is segmented into lettered sections (A, B, C, D, etc.). The sign board depicting your train will indicate which lettered section 1st and 2nd classa and the club car will be located. Now look over your head to find the proper lettered section where you need to stand.

Once located you can position yourself perfectly to board the train without having to run along the track when it arrives, or board at the wrong spot, then have to muscle your way through the train.

Ticket Discounts
The Italian Railway System offers a variety of discounts on its tickets. Check out their web site for more details (*www.fs-on-line.com*). These tickets are can be purchased directly through the web site.

Types of Trains
• **Eurostar**: Top notch services and speed. Air-conditioned, comfortable seats, snacks served at your seat and headphones available for use.
• **IC-Intercity**: Both first and second class seating is available with most first class compartments air-conditioned. Dining cars are also available.
• **EC-Eurocity**: These are the trains that are used in international rail service.
• **EXPR-Expresso**: Ordinary express trains usually carry first and second class passengers. No supplemental fare and reservations are necessary, but I recommend you make them. Food and drink service is available. These are the trains to take. Hardly any stops at all. Kind of like the MetroLiner Service on Amtrak between Washington DC and New York.
• **DIR-Diretto**: Semi-express trains that make plenty of stops. They often have second class seating only. During off-peak hours they are not crowded, but at peak hours they're sardine-city.
• **Locale**: These trains stop everywhere on their route and take forever, but to get to rural locations these are the only options.

Remember to Validate Your Ticket
Whatever train you are taking, whatever type of ticket you have, remember to validate your ticket at the yellow boxes at the station by each track before you board the train. This is true for all tickets except Eurorail passes. If you do not validate your ticket, you can get fined. To validate your ticket, simply push one end into the yellow box and it will automatically date and time stamp it.

&

Chapter 7

BASIC INFORMATION

Banking

Banks in Italy are generally open Monday through Friday, 8:30am to 1:30pm and from 2:45pm to 4:00pm, and are closed all day Saturday and Sunday and on national holidays. In some cities the afternoon open hour may not even exist, and in some cities, like Rome, banks may open on Saturday mornings. Once again, bank hours, like business hours, vary region-to-region and even city-to-city within the region. Check outside of banks for their posted hours of operation. Even if the bank is closed, most travelers' checks can be exchanged for Italian currency at hotels as well as shops and at the many foreign exchange offices in railway stations and at airports.

Shop around for the best exchange rate. Each bank offers a different rate and exchange fee, as do the **Casa di Cambio**, smaller exchange establishments. Sometimes the rate charged to exchange your money is a set fee, which is best when you change a large amount of money. Other places charge a percentage of the total which is generally more beneficial for smaller amounts.

Lost or Stolen Travelers Checks & Credit Cards

The toll free numbers listed below should be called if your credit cards or traveler's checks are stolen:
- **American Express**, *Tel. 800/872-000 (travelers checks)*
- **American Express**, *Tel. 800/874-333 (credit cards)*
- **Diner's Club**, *Tel. 800/864-064*
- **Mastercard**, *Tel. 800/870-866*

• **Thomas Cook/Mastercard**, *Tel. 800/872-050 (traveler's checks)*
• **VISA**, *Tel. 800/874-155 (traveler's checks)*
• **VISA**, *Tel. 800/877-232 (credit cards)*

Business Hours

Store hours vary all over Italy, but as a rule they are open from Monday through Friday, 9:00am to 1:00pm, then re-open at 3:30 or 4:00pm to 7:30/8:00pm, and Saturdays from 9:00am to 1:00pm. In large towns, mainly to cater to tourists, stores are open on Saturday afternoons and Sundays as well. Most stores everywhere else in Italy are closed on Sundays, and everywhere they are closed on national holidays. Don't expect to find any 24-hour convenience stores just around the corner in Italy. If you want some soda in your room after a long day of touring you need to plan ahead.

Food stores (*alimentari*) keep their own hours entirely but generally follow the regular business hours listed above. *Alimentari* also close at least one other day of the week besides Sunday. Usually this day is Thursday (*Giovedì*), but it varies region to region, and even city to city within the region. There is a sign outside each *alimentari* that you can check to see which day they are closed (*chiuso*).

Basically, you must plan on most stores being closed from 1:00pm to 4:00pm, since this is the Italian siesta time. During that time, the only places open are restaurants, and most of those close at 3pm.

Currency – The Euro

On January 1, 2002, the official currency for all participating members of the European Community, to which Italy belongs, became the **Euro**. (In this book the Euro is represented by this symbol: E.) It took about two months to become seamlessly adopted in each participating country, and now the lira is no longer in circulation.

The Euro will have far reaching economic and political effects, but the impact is also grammatical. In most European languages, the name of the old currency was a feminine word, such as the now extinct Italian lira, which ends in an 'a.' But the word 'Euro' is masculine since it ends in an 'o.' Another grammatical conundrum is the plural. In Italian a masculine plural is usually represented by an 'i.' But with the Euro all of Europe has adopted the English way by adding an 's' - i.e. 'Euros.' This is truly a big step for Europe. Everyone, not least of which the United States, is waiting to see the Euro's long-term impact.

The Euro comes in coin denominations of 50, 20, 10, 5, 2 and 1 cent, and bill denominations of 500, 200, 100, 50, 20, 10, 5, 2, and 1 Euro.

Dollar-Euro Exchange Rates

The exchange rate between the Euro and the dollar fluctuates all the time. At printing, the rate was approximately $1.20=E1. Please check your local paper for up-to-date exchange rates.

Electricity

The standard electric current in Italy is 220v, but check with your hotel first before you plug in! If you want to use your blow dryer, electric razor, radio, or plug in your laptop you are going to need a hardware adapter to switch your appliance from a two prong to a three prong insert. Also check before you leave to see if your appliance automatically changes the voltage from 110v to 220v. If it doesn't, you will need to purchase a converter.

If you can't find these devices at your hardware store or local Radio Shack, you can order them from the **Magellan**, *www.magellan.com,* which also have other cool travel products.

Express Couriers

• **DHL**, Toll free in Italy *800/345-345, Fax 06/7932-0051,* Via Lucrezia Romana 87a; *E-mail: dhl@dhl.com, Web www.dhl.it*
• **UPS**, Toll free in Italy *800/822-054, Fax 06/5226-8200*, Via della Magliana 329.

Gypsies

You may have the misfortune of being confronted with a pack of gypsies whose only interest is to relieve you of your wallet and other valuables. These situations are rare but they do happen. Gypsies are not violent, and usually you will only encounter women and children, but they tend to swarm all around you, poke pieces of cardboard in your midsection and generally distract you to the point where they are able to pilfer your pockets, fanny packs, back packs, or knapsacks. So if you are swarmed by gypsies, do not be polite, push back if you need to, make a scene, yell, scream, start running, do anything you can to get out of their midst. Gypsies will not harm you, but if you do not act quickly you will lose your valuables.

Staying out of trouble with the law is paramount, because in Italy you are guilty until proven innocent, unlike in the States where it's the other way around. And most importantly, if arrested you are not simply placed in a holding cell. The Italian officials take you directly to a maximum security prison and lock you up. And that's where you'll stay for as long as it takes your traveling partners to figure out where you are, bribe your case to the top of the local judge's pile, and have your case heard. That whole process can sometimes take months.

So if you like your drinks strong and your nights long, remember to keep your temper in check. And don't even think about smuggling any banned substance into the country, or God forbid, buying something illicit when you're in Italy. If you are approached to buy some hashish or something else, say politely, *No Grazie* (no thank you) and walk away.

Health Concerns

A wonderful "just in case..." option is Personal Physicians Worldwide. This organization can provide you with a list of physicians and hospitals at your destination. If you have a medical condition that may need treatment, or you just want to be safe, they can help. Your personal medical history will be confidentially reviewed by the Medical Director, Dr. David Abramson. He will then contact screened and qualified physicians at your destination to see if they will agree to be available and to care for you if the need arises, while you are in their location.

• **Personal Physicians Worldwide**, *Tel. 888/657-8114, Fax 301/718-7725; E-mail Myra Altschuler, Director, at myra@personalphysicians.com, or Dr. David Abramson, Medical Director at doctors@personalphysicians.com; Web: www.personalphysicians.com.*

Italian Government Tourist Offices

These offices are designed to promote tourism to Italy. However, the receive so many requests for information, they have an incredible back log. Check out their website for information: *www.italiantourism.com.* If you are looking for more information, either contact them through the website or at the following locations: 500 N. Michigan Ave, Chicago, IL 60611, *Tel. 312/644-0990;* 630 Fifth Ave, Suite 1565, New York, NY 10111, *Tel. 212/245-4822, Fax 212/586-9249;* 360 Post Street, Suite 801, San Francisco CA 94109, *Tel. 415/392-6206;* in Canada: Store 56, Plaza 3, 3 Place Ville Marie, Montreal, Quebec, *Tel. 514/866 7667.*

Newspapers & Magazines

At most newsstands in Italy you can find the world renowned *International Herald Tribune*, which is published by The New York Times and printed in Bologna. You will also be able to find a condensed version of *USA Today.* Besides these two, you can also find newspapers from all over the world at almost any newsstand.

Pets

If you're bringing your precious pooch (your dog will have to be on a leash and wear a muzzle in public in Italy) or kitty into Italy with you, you must have a veterinarian's certificate stating that your pet has been vaccinated against rabies between 20 days and 11 months before entry into Italy, and that your pet is in overall good health. The certificate must contain the breed, age, sex, and color of your pet and your name and address. This certificate will be valid only for 30 days. The specific forms that the vet needs to fill out are available at all Italian diplomatic and consular offices.

Parrots, parakeets, rabbits, and hares are also subject to health certification by a vet, and will also be examined further upon entry into Italy. Also Customs officials may require a health examination of your pet if you have just come from a tropical region or that they suspect the pet to be ill. All this means that they can do whatever they want whenever they want, so it might be wise to leave your pet at home.

Postal Service

Stamps can be purchased at any post office or *tabacchi*. If you send a letter airmail with insufficient postage it will not be returned to sender, but will be sent surface mail, which could take months. So make sure you have the correct postage. Air mail prices for post cards is E1.3 to the US and Canada. Air mail letters cost E1.5.

Post boxes are red. International post boxes are blue. Both have silver slots on the front near the top. If you put your correspondence in a red post box, remember to put it in the right hand slot, which reads *Per tutte le altre desinazione* (for all other destinations other — other than the city where you are).

The main post office in each city is generally open from 8:30am to 6:00 or 7:00pm Monday through Friday and Saturday they close at noon. Smaller post offices are only open from 8:30am to 2:00pm Monday through Friday.

Restaurant Hours

Restaurants in Italy keep rather rigid hours, which are usually 12:30 or 1:00pm for lunch until 3:00 or 3:30pm. The dinner hours start at either 7:30 or 8:00pm and usually run until 10:00pm. Some late night restaurants, stay open until the early morning hours.

Safety & Avoiding Trouble

Italian cities are definitely much safer than any equivalent American city. You can walk almost anywhere without fear of harm, but that doesn't mean you shouldn't play it safe. Listed below are some simple rules to follow to ensure that nothing bad occurs:
• At night, make sure the streets you are strolling along have plenty of other people. Like I said, most cities are safe, but it doesn't hurt to be cautious.

• Always have your knapsack or purse flung over the shoulder that is not directly next to the road. Why? There have been cases of Italians on motor bikes snatching purses off old ladies and in some cases dragging them a few blocks.
• Better yet, have your companion walk on the street side, while you walk on the inside of the sidewalk with the knapsack or purse.
• Better still is to buy one of those tummy wallets that goes under your shirt so no one can even be tempted to purse-snatch you.
• Always follow basic common sense. If you feel threatened, scared, or alone, retrace your steps back to a place where there are other people.

Taxis

Taxi service is widely available in all major cities in Italy, and a little less so in smaller cities such as Pisa or Lucca, and almost non-existent in remote towns and villages. Rates are comparable to those charged in your large American cities, which means expensive. Generally taxis locate themselves in special stands located at railway stations and main parts of the city, but many can be waved down as they cruise the streets for fares. At these taxi stands there are usually telephones that you can call directly from your hotel, but remember, in Italy, if called, the meter starts at the point of origin, so you'll be paying the cabby to come pick you up. The same goes for radio taxis if called to come pick you up.

Fares will vary from city to city, but basically when you get in the cab there will be a fixed starting charge of approximately E 1-2, and a cost per kilometer of approximately E 0.50 to E 1. If you are stuck in traffic, every minute another E 0.50 cents or so will be added to the fare. Some extra charges may come into play, like the **nighttime supplement** (between 10:00pm and 6:00am), a **Sunday and public holiday supplement**, as well as a **per item luggage charge**. You will also be charged for every piece of luggage. All of these vary from city to city.

On long trips, like from airports, it is advised to agree upon a price before heading out. Ask at the information booth inside each airport what the expected charge should be.

Telephones & Fax
Calling Italy

Even when making local calls the area code must be used. In conjunction, before it was necessary to discard the leading zero of the area code (for example Rome's area code is 06), but now you need to use the leading zero in all area codes.

To dial Rome from the United States, first dial the international prefix, **011**, then the country code, **39**, then the city code for Rome, **06**, then the number you wish to reach.

Long Distance Calling From Italy

To call the U.S. from Italy, dial **001**, then the area code and number. Listed below are some of the major telecommunications carriers for North America and their access numbers:

AT&T – *Tel. 172-1011* (a toll free number in Italy) to gain access to an AT&T operator (or English language prompts) for efficient service. You can bill your AT&T calling card, local phone company card, or call direct.

Canada Direct – *Tel. 172-1001* (a toll free number in Italy) and you will be connected to the Canadian telephone network with access to a bilingual operator. You can bill your *Calling Card, Call Me*™ service, your *Hello!* Phone Pass or call collect.

MCI – *Tel. 172-1022* (a toll free number in Italy) for MCI's World Phone and to use your MCI credit card or call collect. All done through English speaking MCI operators.

Sprint – *Tel. 172-1877* (a toll free number in Italy) for access to an English speaking Sprint operator who can charge your phone card or make your call collect.

Modem or Fax Usage In Italy

To connect you modem or fax to the wall you will need an adapter. These too can be bought from a hardware store or from the **Franzus Company** (see above under Electricity). Many hotels in Italy are starting to use the American standard phone plug, so this may not be a concern. When making your reservations, inquire about the type of plugs in use to insure you can communicate with home without a problem.

Pay Phones

The days of the *gettone* phones are long past. Most pay phones in Italy only use **domestic phone cards** (which you can buy in denominations of E2.5, E5 or E7.5) but some use a combination of cards and coins. You can buy phone cards at most *tabacchi* (the stores with the **T** out in front of them), newsstand, post office and some bars.

Phone Cards

An inexpensive option for international calling is to buy an **international phone card** (*carta telefonica internationale*) which are sold at most *tabacchi* and newsstands. You can get cards for E10, which have 300 minutes available on them. This translates to about 3 cents a minute, a steal for international calling. These cards can be used in your hotel room or at public phone booths simply by following the directions on the back. This usually entails calling a toll free number, receiving instructions in a variety of languages, including English, punching in the number of your specific card (usually found on the back after rubbing off a covering), then keying in the number you wish to call. Your connection is crisp and clear. Discerning travelers who do not want to spend an arm and a leg to call home, generally pick up a phone card.

Generally, you can use international phone cards at pay phones. Sometimes, you cannot. And sometimes you need a domestic phone card to get the pay phone to work so you can use the international phone card. This is Italy. Nothing is set in stone. Everything is chaotic.

Time

Most of the year, Italy is **six hours ahead of Eastern Standard Time** in North America, so if it's noon in New York it's 6:00pm in Rome. Daylight savings time goes into effect each year in Italy usually from the end of March to the end of September.

Tipping

Hotels

A service charge of 15-18% is usually added to your hotel bill, but it is customary to leave a little something for the maid. Whatever you deem sufficient, but anything over E 1-2 per service rendered can be extravagant.

Restaurants

A service charge of around 15% is usually automatically added to all restaurant bills. But if you felt the service was good, it is customary to leave a little something extra. There is no set percentage, and a good rule of thumb is to leave whatever change is returned, as long as it is not above between 5-10%. The same applies in cafés and bars. For example, around E 0.50 is normal if you're standing at the counter drinking a soda, cappuccino, etc. Leaving change in this manner is a good way to rid myself of burdensome coins.

Tipping at the Right Time

Most people tip at the end of a stay in a hotel indicating an appreciation for the services rendered. But if you want to ensure that the services rendered are exemplary, tip in the beginning of your stay. Giving on the spot tips for services rendered usually guarantees the best possible service. Slip a Euro or two to the person who checks you in; leave a Euro on the bed for the maid with a note saying "Grazie" will almost always ensure service above and beyond the call of duty.

Weights & Measures

Italy uses the metric system, where everything is a factor of ten. The table below gives you a list of weights and measures with approximate values.

Weights

Italy	14 grams	Etto	Kilo
US	1/2 oz	1/4 lb	2 lb 2oz

Liquid Measure

Italy	Litro
US	1.065 quart

Distance Measure

Italy	Centimeter	Meter	Kilometer
US	2/5 inch	39 inches	3/5 mile

Websites of Interest

Before you head off to Italy, I've listed some websites below that you may find interesting or useful. Some of them are featured elsewhere in this book.

Airfare
- *www.bestfares.com*
- *www.lowestfare.com*
- *www.cheaptickets.com*
- *www.airdeals.com*
- *www.lastminutetravel.com*

Currency
- *www.oanda.com/converter/travel* – to create a pocket currency conversion chart to bring with you, visit this website

General Information
- *www.italiantourism.com* – website for the Italian government tourist office; filled with lots of great information
- *www.itwg.com* – an all-inclusive website featuring loads of useful information about Italy
- *www.travel.it/welcome.html* – another all encompassing website produced by yet another Italian government agency
- *www.enjoyrome.com* – offers walking tours of Rome
- *www.mondoweb.it/livinginrome* – the complete guide to living in Rome for foreigners

Hotels
- *www.venere.it* – you can get hotel reservations for thousands of hotels all over Italy at this site, including many that are in this book

Language
- *www.travlang.com/languages* – if you want to take a few virtual language lessons before you go, visit the *Foreign Language for Travelers* website
- *www.arcodidruso.com* – Italian language and culture for foreigners

Medical
- *www.personalphysicians.com* – provides you with a list of physicians and hospitals at your destination; if you have a medical condition that may need treatment, or you just want to be safe, they can help

Passport
- *www.instantpassport.com* – this website promises to give you 24-hour turnaround from the time they receive your passport pictures and requisite forms; they charge $100 plus overnight shipping on top of all fees associated with passport issuance.
- *www.americanpassport.com* – this site offers three types of service: expedited (24 hours), express (three to four business days) and regular; prices range from $245 to $135.
- *www.travel.state.gov* – download passport application forms, international travel advisories, and listings of embassies and consulates worldwide

'Where Rome'

This is the title of a good tourist magazine usually found in hotel rooms. In it you can locate all sorts of up-to-date information about events in Rome, new restaurants, cafes, bars, shops etc. If you do not have one at your hotel, you can contact the publishers, *Tel. 06/578-1615*, and pick up a copy or they can tell you where to get one. A great resource for events and current goings-on while in Rome.

Women Travelers

As stated in the Safety section above, Italy is a safe country, but generally women traveling alone will find themselves the recipients of unwanted attention from men. In most cases the attention you receive will be limited to whistles, stares, comments (in Italian which you will probably not understand), catcalls and the like. This may happen whether you are in groups or alone. But usually if you are with a male companion this type of unwanted attention doesn't occur.

If you choose to be alone, whether it's going for a walk, seeing a sight, or stopping for a coffee, don't expect to be alone for long. Since foreign women have a reputation for being easy, ignoring unwanted suitors won't work because they think they can charm their way into your heart and elsewhere. My suggestion is to politely tell them you are waiting for your boyfriend (*aspetto mio fidanzato*) or husband (*marito*). If that doesn't work, raise your voice, look them in the eye angrily and tell them to *lasciami stare* (lash-ah me star-ay), which means leave you alone.

If these ploys do not work, simply walk away. If the man continues to badger you, find a local policeman for assistance, but always remain in a populated area. In the vast majority of cases there is truly nothing to fear. Most Italians just want to get lucky and when rebuffed they will go find easier prey. In conjunction, most of the attention falls into the nuisance category, but like I said in the Safety section, please use common sense. Avoid unpopulated areas, avoid walking alone on dark streets, avoid hitchhiking alone and things like that. Just be smart. Italy is much safer than America and is not even remotely as violent, but it's better to be safe than sorry.

In general too, the further south you go, the more you will be hassled. Something about the warm climate must heat the male's blood or stimulate their libido. Also in port cities women traveling alone will be pegged as targets for petty theft. So be extra careful in those types of cities.

And all over the country, when you ride public transportation you may very well be confronted with wandering hands, especially when the bus or train is crowded. To avoid this, keep your back to the wall. If someone does start to fondle your posterior or elsewhere, make a loud fuss – otherwise it will continue unabated.

Yellow Pages

There is an excellent **English Yellow Pages (EYP)** in Italy. It is the annual telephone directory of English-speaking professionals, organizations, services and commercial activities in Rome, Florence, Milan, Naples, Genoa and Bologna. The EYP is a well-known resource and reference source among the international community in Italy, from which you can easily find numbers for airlines and embassies, English-speaking doctors and dentists, international schools and organizations, hotels, moving companies, real estate agents, accountants, attorneys, consultants, plumbers, electricians, mechanics and much more. Listings are complete with address including zip code, phone and fax numbers, e-mail and web sites.

You can find copies at embassies, international organizations, schools & universities, social and professional associations, English-language churches, foreign press offices, local events within the expat community and various businesses that deal directly with an international clientele. Also copies of it are on sale at most international bookstores. This is a great resource for any resident or visitor to Italy. Their website is *www.intoitaly.it*.

Chapter 8

SPORTS & RECREATION

Italians are active sports enthusiasts. Besides soccer they participate in skiing, golf, tennis, scuba diving, mountain climbing, hiking, fishing, hunting, and more. Any sport you can play at home you can also enjoy in Italy!

Golf

In the summer you can also enjoy some excellent golf courses. Located all over Italy, except for the poor south, there are plenty of accessible courses around the main tourist areas of Rome, Milan and Florence (see regional chapters for more information). You can also find courses around the many seaside resort areas that dot Italy's coastline.

Since Constatino Rocca choked in the Ryder Cup in 1994 for the whole world to see, and when he made that miraculous putt after chili dipping his chip in the British Open in 1995 on the final hole (he eventually lost to John Daly), Italian golf has started to get recognition. Maybe not the kind of recognition it wants but, nonetheless, the *cognoscenti* have begun to discover some gems of courses all over Italy. It's only natural that a country filled with such natural beauty would provide superb golf.

Hunting & Fishing

If you are looking for the more rustic pursuits like sport fishing and hunting, Italy has lakes, streams and rivers filled with trout. In the **Alpine and Apennine regions** you can actually bag a wild boar *(cinghiale)*, which is on the menu at many northern Italian restaurants. Hunting is popular all over Italy but the seasons vary according to region. Contact the **Italian Government**

Travel Office in New York, *Tel. 212/245-4822,* to find information about the hunting and fishing seasons and how to get licenses for each activity.

Skiing

From December through April, ski resorts all over Italy are swarming with people willing to sacrifice life and limb to get the adrenaline flow that only plummeting down a sheer cliff covered with snow can offer them. Most winter sports areas are found in the north of Italy in the Alps; one of the most famous is **Courmayeur,** but there are also some near Rome in the Central Apennines, **Cortina d'Ampezzo** being the most notable.

These same mountain ranges are used as hiking locations during the summer. If you like breathtaking views without the risk of tearing a medial collateral ligament, try hiking the trails of the **Italian Alps** in the summer.

Spectator Sports

If watching from the sidelines is more up your alley, Italy goes **soccer** crazy every Sunday from September to May. Virtually every city and every town has a team that plays professionally. The Italian league is separated into four divisions, or *Serie*. The first division is Serie A, which plays the best soccer in the world, and the lowest fully professional division is Serie C1. Some cities have several teams, such as Rome, which has two Serie A teams (Lazio and Roma) and several nearby Serie C2 and C1 teams. The Serie A and B games are the most fun to go to since the fans are so passionate. Tickets can be hard to come by since the games are so popular, but contact your hotel's concierge and s/he may be able to scrape some up for you.

If you don't want to go to the game you may still choose to go to the stadium, not only to revel in the atmosphere, but also to get some great gifts from the vendors who sell team paraphernalia outside. Certain types of product piracy is legal in Italy, and putting the names and logos of sports teams on unofficial products is one of them. The quality of the shirts, hats, and scarves is just as good and about one fourth the price of the official products.

Another popular spectator sport is **auto** and **motorcycle racing**. At Monza, just outside of Milan, the **Italian Grand Prix** is held every September; and at Imola, near Bologna, you can find the **San Marino Grand Prix** every May. Equally as popular is **cycling**, which culminates in the **Tour d'Italia** in May.

And surprisingly enough, **basketball** and **baseball** both have professional leagues, and most major cities now have teams. Professional baseball has been around for only about twenty five years, and is still at the level of the CBA (Continental Basketball Association), a minor league in the US, but is starting to catch on in popularity. Ask your concierge about upcoming games.

Tennis

In virtually every city in Italy there are courts that can be rented if you are interested. Italians are passionate tennis fans and if you are in Rome during the summer, the entire city is caught up in the Italian Open tennis tournament. Where available we list places where you can rent tennis courts. But since the Italians seem to build more courts each year, ask your concierge for advice. There are bound to be some whereever you are.

Water Sports

You'll find scuba diving, sailing, snorkeling, and para-sailing along Italy's various coasts. Since the country is surrounded on three sides by water, Italians are fanatical about their water sports and activities, which has started to include topless bathing, an unheard of activity 10 years ago. At some beaches frequented by northern Europeans, there are days when not a suit is in sight.

Chapter 9

SHOPPING

As mentioned in Chapter 7, store hours are usually Monday through Friday 9:00am to 1:00pm, 3:30/4:00pm to 7:30/8:00pm, and Saturday 9:00am to 1:00pm. In major cities like Rome, shops will also open in the afternoons on Saturday, but everywhere in Italy they will be closed on Sunday. This may vary in Milan and/or Turin, where sometimes the lunch break is shorter so shops can close earlier.

The big Italian chain stores are **La Rinascente, Coin, UPIM,** and **STANDA**. In Coin, UPIM, and STANDA, you will also find supermarkets filled with all manner of Italian delectables. At the end of this chapter I'll make some suggestions about what you could buy at a local Italian *Supermercato* or *Alimentari* (smaller food store) to bring home with you so you can make a fine Italian meal with authentic ingredients!

Besides food and clothing, Italy has a wide variety of handicrafts. Any one of Italy's crafts would be a perfect memento of your stay. Works in alabaster and marble can be readily found in and around Florence, Milan, and Venice. Wood carvings are the specialty of many of the cities in the south, such as Palermo and Messina. Beautiful glasswork is at its best in and around Venice and Pisa. Embroidery and lace work can be found all over Italy, and rugs from Sardinia rival those of most other European countries. Sardinia is also known for its straw bags, hats, and mats, as is Florence.

Exquisite gold and silver jewelry is a specialty of Florence, where, on the Ponte Vecchio, you'll find shop after shop of jewelry stores. In other parts of Tuscany you can find hand-wrought iron work as well as beautiful tiles.

And finally, the main fashion centers in Italy are, of course, Milan, Florence and Rome, with Florence specializing in shoes and gloves, and Milan and Rome everything else. Each regional chapter will describe for you specific places to visit to find the most exquisite and authentic regional handicrafts.

Tax-Free Shopping

Italian law entitles all non-European Union residents to a **VAT (IVA) tax refund** with a minimum purchase exceeding E150. Ask for an invoice (*fattura* in Italian) or a **Tax-Free Check** when completing a purchase. Upon departure from Italy, purchased goods must be shown to a customs agent at the airport or border station and a customs stamp must be obtained no later than three months after the date of purchase. The stamped invoice must be returned to the store or the VAT Refund Companies Office in Italy no later than four months after the date of purchase.

Direct refunds at the airport or the border are offered albeit at a lower rate. There are also a number of tax free services, such as **Cashback**, **Global Refund Italia**, **Tax-Free for Tourists**, etc. and each have a different window at the airport. Be aware of this when you make your purchases so that your time spent in lines at the airport getting refunds is lessened. You will usually see the tax back signs in most upscale stores.

Tax Rebate on Purchases

If you acquire products at the same merchant in excess of E150 (about $150), you can claim an **IVA** (purchase tax) **rebate**. You must ask the vendor for the proper receipt (*la ricevuta per l'IVA per favore*), have the receipt stamped at Italian customs, then mail no later than 90 days after the date of the receipt back to the vendor. The vendor will then send you the IVA rebate. You can also do this at the airport, but will receive less money in return. If you spend a fair chunk of money in Italy on clothing or other items, this is a good way to get some money back. Also be aware that there is more than one tax free service available.

Clothing Sizes

The chart below is a comparison guide between US and Italian sizes. Many sizes are not standardized, so you will need to try everything on anyway. Generally if you are above 6'2" and weigh over 200 pounds you may have trouble finding clothing in Italy because the Italians just are not big people. The following conversions should help you out in your shopping quest:

WOMEN'S CLOTHING SIZES

US	2	4	6	8	10	12	14	16
Italy	36	38	40	42	44	46	48	50

Continued

18	20	24
52	54	56

WOMEN'S SHOE SIZES

US	5 1/2	6 1/2	7	7 1/2	8	8 1/2	9	10
Italy	35	36	37	38	38 1/2	39	40	41

WOMEN'S HOSIERY SIZES

US	Petite	Small	Medium	Large
Italy	I	II	III	IV

MEN'S SUITES, OVERCOATS, SWEATERS, & PAJAMAS

US	34	36	38	40	42	44	46	48
Italy	44	46	48	50	52	54	56	58

MEN'S SHIRTS

US	14	14 1/2	15	15 1/2	16	16 1/2	17	17 1/2
Italy	36	37	38	39	40	41	42	43

MEN'S SHOES

US	6	6 1/2	7	7 1/2	8	8 1/2	9	9 1/2
Italy	30	40	40 1/2	41	41 11/2	42	42 1/2	43

Continued

10	10 1/2	11-11 1/2
43 1/2	44-44 1/2	45

MEN'S HATS

US	6 7/8	7	7 1/8	7 1/4	7 3/8	7 1/2	7 5/8	7 3/4
Italy	55	56	57	58	59	60	61	62

CHILDREN'S SIZES

US	1	2	3	4	5	6	7	8
Italy	35	40	45	50	55	60	65	70

Continued

9	10	11	12	13	14
75	80	85	90	95	100

CHILDREN'S SHOES

US	4	5	6	7	8	9	10	10 1/2
Italy	21	21	22	23	24	25	26	27

Continued
11	12	13
28	29	30

Key Shopping & Bargaining Phrases

Italian	**English**
Quanto costa?	How much is this?
E Troppo	That's too much
No Grazie	No thank you
Voglio pagare meno	I want to pay less
C'é l'hai questo piú grande?	Do have this in a bigger size?
..... pui piccolo	..... in a smaller size
..... in nero	..... in black
..... in bianco	..... in white
..... in rosso	..... in red
..... in verde	..... in green

When to Bargain

In all stores, even the smallest shops, bargaining is not accepted, just like here in North America. But you can bargain at any street vending location, even if they have placed a sign indicating the price. Don't be afraid to bargain, or you'll end up spending more than you (ahem) 'bargained' for.

Most Italian vendors see foreigners as easy marks to make a few more lire because they know it is not in our culture to bargain, while in theirs it is a way of life.

The best way to bargain, if the street vendor doesn't speak English, is by writing your request on a piece of paper. This keeps it subdued in case you're embarrassed about haggling over money. Basically while in Italy try to let go of that cultural bias. Anyway, you and the vendor will probably pass the paper back and forth a few times changing the numbers before a price is finally agreed upon. And of course, the Italian vendor will be waving his arms about, jabbering away, most probably describing how you're trying to rip him off, all in an effort to get you to pay a higher price. Remember, this is all done in fun – so enjoy it.

What You Can Bring Back Through Customs

See Chapter 6, *Planning Your Trip,* for more details, but in short you can bring back to the US $400 worth of goods duty free. On the next $1,000 worth of purchases you will be assessed a flat 10% fee. These products must be with you when you go through customs.

You can mail products duty free, providing the total value of each package sent is not more than $50 *and* no one person is receiving more than one package a day. Also, each package sent must be stamped "Unsolicited Gift" and the amount paid and the contents of the package must be displayed. They'll be able to tell you all this again at the post office.

What you cannot bring back to North America are any fruits, vegetables, and in most cases meats and cheeses, even if they're for your consumption alone, and even if they are vacuum sealed. Customs has to do this to prevent any potential parasites from entering our country and destroying our crops. Unfortunately, this means all those great salamis and cheeses you bought at those quaint outdoor food markets and had on one of your picnics will not be let back into North America.

But there are some things you can buy. Hard cheeses, like *Parmigiano Reggiano* and *Pecorino*, will be let through because they have been cured long enough. But soft cheeses and salamis will not be let in.

Chapter 10

CULTURE & ARTS

From Etruscans to the Renaissance

Italy is perhaps best known for its great contributions to painting and sculpture; and many art lovers have described the country as one vast museum. Italy gave birth to such world renowned artists as Giotto, Donatello, Raphael, Michelangelo, Leonardo da Vinci, and Botticelli, who are revered the world over.

The oldest works of art in Italy are those of the **Etruscans**, and they date back to the 9th century BCE. This mysterious society's main cities and art centers were in the middle of the peninsula, between Rome and Florence, mainly in the province now know as Tuscany (the region was named after them ... Etruscans ... Tuscany). In Tarquinia, Volterra, Cerveteri, and Veio, the Etruscans have left behind magnificent temples, sculptures, and bronzes as well as other fascinating testimonies to their presence. The best museum collections of Etruscan art can be found in Rome's **Etruscan Museum**, Florence's **Archaeological Museum**, the **Bologna Municipal Museum**, and the **Municipal Museum of Volterra**.

Italy is also known for being a repository of ancient Greek art. During the time of the Etruscans, the Greeks established colonies in the south of modern-day Italy as well as Sicily. Magnificent ruins of temples exist today in some of these ancient Greek colonies: **Syracuse, Agrigento**, and **Taormina** in Sicily; and **Peastum** and **Coma** in Campania. There are good collections of Hellenic art in the **National Museum of Naples**, and in the museums in Palermo, Syracuse, Reggio Calabria, Paestum, and Taranto.

After the Greeks and Etruscans, the Roman Empire left its lasting impression all over Italy. There are still roads, bridges, aqueducts, arches, and theaters built by the Romans still in use today, some of which are over 2,000 years old. The most extensive excavations of ancient Roman ruins have been made at the **Forum** in Rome, at **Ostia** near Rome by the beach, and at **Pompeii** and **Herculaneum** - the cities that the volcanic **Mount Vesuvius** buried. For a first-hand, up-front feel of what life was like in the Roman Empire, don't miss these sites.

After the fall of the Roman Empire, the Byzantine Empire ruled many parts of the southern and eastern regions of Italy. This period left behind many churches, with their glorious mosaics, like those of the 6th century in Ravenna near the east coast; as well as the morbid but powerful **catacombs** outside of Rome.

Then after the Dark Ages, when the Roman Empire's progress reverted back to tribalism, the Renaissance came. This artistic period, meaning "rebirth," began in Italy in the 14th century and lasted for two hundred years. The Renaissance left us an extensive array of churches, palaces, paintings, statues, and beautiful city squares in almost every city of Italy. The main cities of Florence, Rome, Venice, Milan, and Naples have most of the treasures and beauty of this period, but smaller towns like Ferrara and Rimini also have their share. The best museums for viewing Renaissance art are the **Uffizi Gallery** and **Pitti Palace** in Florence, as well as the **Vatican** and **Borghese Galleries** (in the Borghese Gardens just outside the walls) in Rome.

After the Renaissance, **baroque art** became fashionable. And Rome, more than any other Italian city, contains a dazzling array of churches, paintings, and statues recalling the splendor of such famous artists as Bernini, Borromini, and Caravaggio of the late 16th and 17th centuries.

Renaissance Painting

In Italy (with France and Germany soon following suit) during the 14th and 15th centuries, the Renaissance was a period of exploration, invention, and discovery. Mariners from all over Europe set sail in search of new lands. Scientists like **Leonardo da Vinci** studied the mysteries of the world and the heavens. Artists found the human body to be a marvel of mechanics and beauty (but had to secretly study it, as Michelangelo did, lest the Church condemn them for heresy). This was undoubtedly one of Italy's most exciting periods in the history of artistic and scientific advancement.

Many consider the birthplace of Renaissance art to be Florence. It seemed to start with a young painter named **Masaccio**, who began introducing many bold new ideas into his work. He made his paintings vibrantly interesting by drawing each person completely different from another, as well as making each person as realistic as possible. In conjunction with his ability to express the human form, Masaccio used combinations of colors to give the impression of space and dimension in his landscapes. Now every art student studies how brown makes objects appear closer, and blue makes them appear as if they in the distance.

Paolo Uccello, another Florentine, worked at the same time as Masaccio. A mathematician as well as an artist, he expanded on the mechanical and scientific issues of painting rather than on the human and psychological ones. One of his paintings, *The Battle of San Romano*, circa 1457, celebrated the victory of Florence over Siena some 25 years earlier, and is a brilliant study in **perspective**. His depiction of objects, men, and horses all help to accentuate the sense of real perspective he was trying to achieve. One technique he used, which is now part of any good art school's curriculum, is **foreshortening**. In the left foreground of *The Battle of San Romano* is a fallen soldier with his feet facing the front of the picture. To give this figure a proper perspective, Uccello had to shorten the perceived length of the body, an extremely difficult task, and one not usually seen in other artists' previous works. In conjunction, Uccello drew roads, fields, etc., going back into the painting towards the horizon, to give the impression of distance. Now these are all well used and rather pedestrian artistic techniques, but back then they revolutionized the art world.

But most definitely three of the most influential Renaissance artists were **Raphael**, **Leonardo da Vinci**, and **Michelangelo**. Raphael was mainly known for his paintings of the Madonna and Child, from which our conceptual image of the Mother of Jesus is largely based. All of his paintings reflect a harmony that leaves the viewer with a warm and positive feeling of content-ment.

Leonardo da Vinci is most well known for his *Mona Lisa*, painted in Tuscany in 1505-06 and now hanging in the Louvre, but he was also a versatile architect and scientist as well. Leonardo studied botany, geology, zoology, hydraulics, military engineering, anatomy, perspective, optics, and physiology. You name it, he did it – the original Renaissance Man!

Another versatile artist of the Italian Renaissance, and definitely its most popular then and now – he was always being commissioned to paint or sculpt all the wealthy people's portraits – was Michelangelo Buonarroti. Although he considered himself chiefly a sculptor – he trained as a young boy to become a stone carver – he left us equally great works as a painter and architect. As a painter he created the huge **Sistine Chapel** frescoes in the Vatican, encompassing more than 10,000 square feet in area. As an architect he helped complete the designs for **St. Peter's**, where his world renowned statue, *La Pieta*, currently resides.

Renaissance Sculpture

Besides painting and architecture, Michelangelo was also the pre-eminent sculptor of the Renaissance. By the age of 26 he had carved *La Pieta*, his amazing version of Virgin Mary supporting the dead Christ on her knees; and was in the process of carving the huge and heroic marble *David*. He also created the memorable **Medici tombs** in the Chapel of San Lorenzo, Florence. Even though Michelangelo was commissioned to create many works by the Popes themselves, he had learned his amazing knowledge of the human anatomy by dissecting cadavers in his home town of Florence as a young man, a crime punishable by death and/or excommunication at the time.

During the Renaissance there were many other sculptors of note, but Michelangelo was truly the best. One of the others was **Lorenzo Ghiberti**, who died a few years before Michelangelo was born. For 29 years he labored to produce ten bronze panels, depicting Biblical episodes, for the doors of the Baptistery of Florence. Michelangelo was said to have been inspired to become a great artist because of these beautiful bronze doors.

Music

Italy also has a great tradition in music. Even today, Italian folk music has made a resurgence, mainly because of the theme song for the *Godfather* movie series. Can't you just hear it playing in your head right now?

Besides folk music and Gregorian chants, Italy is known for its opera. If you are an opera fan you cannot miss taking a tour of the world famous **La Scala** in Milan. Getting a ticket to a performance is another matter. But have no fear, if your appetite cannot be sated without the shrill explosion of an *aria* there are other famous opera houses in Italy: **The Opera** in Rome, **The San Carlos** in Naples, **La Fenice** in Venice, **The Reggio** in Turin, **The Communale** in Bologna, **The Petruzzelli** in Bari, **The Communale** in Genoa, and **Massimo Bellini** in Catania (see addresses and phone numbers below).

These are also many opera festivals all over Italy virtually year-round.

Italian Opera

Italian opera began in the 16th century. Over time such composers as Gioacchino Rossini, Gaetano Donizetti, and Vincenzo Bellini created **bel canto** opera – opera that prizes beautiful singing above all else. The best singers were indulged with *arias* that gave them ample opportunity for a prominent display of their vocal resources of range and agility.

Rossini, who reigned as Italy's foremost composer of the early 19th century, was a master of both melody and stage effects. Success came easily, and while still in his teens he composed the first of a string of 32 operas that he completed by the age of 30. Many of these are comic operas, a genre in which Rossini excelled, and his masterpieces in this form are still performed and admired today. Among them is one you probably recognize, *The Barber of Seville* (1816).

Rossini's immediate successor as Italy's leading operatic composer was **Donizetti**, who composed more than 70 works in the genre. A less refined composer than Rossini, Donizetti left his finest work in comic operas, including *Don Pasquale* (1843) and *Lucia di Lammermoor* (1835).

Although he lived for a shorter time than either Rossini or Donizetti and enjoyed a far briefer career, **Bellini** wrote music that many believe surpassed theirs in refinement. Among the finest of his ten operas are *La Sonnambula* (The Sleepwalker, 1831), *Norma* (1831), and *I Puritani* (The Puritans, 1835), all of which blend acute dramatic perceptions with florid virtuosity.

From these roots came Italy's greatest opera composers of all times, **Puccini** and **Verdi**. Giacomo Puccini lived from 1858-1924 and composed twelve operas in all. Considered by many to be a close second to Verdi in skill of composition, Puccini's music remains alive in the popular mind because of enduring works like *Madame Butterfly* and *La Boheme*. Even though Puccini was the fifth generation of musicians in his family, he was mainly influenced to pursue his career after hearing Verdi's *Aida*.

Giuseppe Verdi lived from 1813-1901, and is best known for his operas *Rigoletto* (1851), *Il Trovatore* and *La Traviata* (both 1853), and what could be the grandest opera of them all, *Aida* (1871). Verdi composed his thirtieth and last opera *Falstaff* at the age of 79. Since he mainly composed out of Milan and many of his operas opened at La Scala opera house in that city, today a **Verdi museum** has been established there to honor his work.

Opera, Music, Drama, & Ballet Festivals

As the birthplace of opera, Italy offers visitors a variety of choices during the operatic seasons, which are almost year-round. In the summer months there are wonderful open-air operas presented at the **Terme di Caracalla** (Baths of Caracalla) in the center of Rome near the main train station from July to August, at the **Arena** in Verona from July to August, and at the **Arena Sferisterio** in Macerata in July. In general the opera season lasts from December to June.

Two of the most spectacular festivals for Italian performing arts are the **Maggio Musicale Fiorentino** with opera, concerts, ballet, and drama performances in Florence from May to June, and the **Festival of Two Worlds** with opera, concerts, ballet, drama performances and art exhibits in Spoleto from mid-June to mid-July.

If you wish to obtain tickets to opera performances, concerts, ballet, and other performances you can either write directly to the theater in question or ask your travel agent to obtain the ticket for you. When you are in Italy, your hotel should be able to assist you in obtaining tickets for performances in their city.

Regional & National Folk Festivals

Despite the encroachment of the modern world, the traditional festivals and their accompanying costumes and folk music have survived surprisingly well all over Italy. In many cases they have been successfully woven into the pattern of modern life so as to seem quite normal. Despite all possible modern influences these festivals (both secular and religious) have preserved their distinctive character.

Two of the most famous, the secular festivals of the **Palio** in Siena and **Calcio in Costume** in Florence give foreigners a glimpse into the past customs and way of life of medieval Italians. Both of these festivals pit different sections of their respective cities against each other to see who can earn bragging rights for the year. In Siena, a heated horse race takes place in a crowded city square. In Florence the Piazza della Signorina is turned into a veritable battleground when a game that is a cross between boxing, soccer, rugby, and martial arts is played. And what is most impressive of all in these festivals, besides the competition, is the fact that all participants dress in colorful period garb making each city appear to come alive with the past.

Since Italy is the home of the Catholic church, religious festivals also play a large part in Italian life. Particularly interesting are the processions on the occasion of **Corpus Christi**, **Assumption**, and **Holy Week**. In Italy, holiday times such as Easter and Christmas have not lost their religious intent as they have in most other places, and commercialism takes a back seat to the Almighty. This also means that tradition has not made way for consumerism, allowing us to experience a rich display of costumes, statues, parades, masses and more that evoke a simpler, more peaceful time.

Before you come, make sure you do your research and find out if there any festivals being held during the times you are visiting. In each section of this book you will find a listing of festivals available for each destination.

Crafts

Hundreds of thousands of skillful Italian artisans are the heirs to a 2,000-year tradition of craftsmanship. Their products – fashioned of leather, gold, silver, glass, and silk – are widely sought by tourists who flock to Florence, Rome, Milan, and Venice. Cameos made from seashells, an ancient Italian art form, are as popular today as they were in the days of the Roman Empire. The work of Italian artists and artisans is also exported for sale in the great department stores of France, Germany, the United Kingdom, and the United States.

Italian clothing designers are world famous, especially for precise tailoring, unusual knits, and the imaginative use of fur and leather.

The best place to see Italian artisans at work is in the glass blowing factories of Venice. There you'll be amazed at how easily they can manipulate molten balls into some of the most delicate, colorful, and beautiful pieces you've ever seen. Each chapter in this book highlights specific traditional crafts by region.

Literature

Perhaps Italy's most famous author/poet is **Dante Aligheri**, who wrote the *Divine Comedy*, in which he describes his own dream-journey through Hell *(l'Inferno)* Purgatory *(Purgatorio)*, and Paradise *(Paradiso)*. At the time it was extremely controversial, since it is a poem about free will and how man can damn or save his soul as he chooses, which was contrary to church teachings. Even today it sparks controversy since it seems apparent that Dante's description of Purgatory is actually describing the life we all lead on earth, and shows his belief in reincarnation.

Two other notable Italian writers (you should remember these for quality cocktail party conversation) are **Petrarch**, famous for his sonnets to Laura, a beautiful girl from Avignon who died quite young, and is known as the "First of the Romantics;" and **Boccaccio**, the Robin Williams of his time, except he wrote, not performed, his famous *Decameron*, a charming and sometimes ribald series of short stories told by ten young people in a span of ten days. He was sort of like the Chaucer of Italy.

Among contemporary Italian writers, **Umberto Eco** stands out on his own. You may know two of his books that have been translated into English: *The Name of the Rose* and the more recent *Foucault's Pendulum*. If you are looking for complex, insightful, intriguing, and intellectual reading, Eco's your man. Last but not least, one Italian writer whom children all over the world should know is **Carlo Collodi**, who wrote *Pinnochio*.

Shakespeare's Italy

The Immortal Bard chose Italy as the setting for a number of his best-known masterpieces: **Othello** takes place in part in Venice, and features both honorable and conniving Venetians; **Two Gentlemen from Verona** and **Romeo & Juliet** take place in Verona (the latter was pretty much lifted from Luigi da Porto's identical story, and today you can visit Juliet's House in Verona); **The Merchant of Venice** takes place in Venice; **The Taming of the Shrew** concerns the doings of rich Paduans, Pisans, and Veronans; about half of **A Winter's Tale** takes part in Sicily; all of **Much Ado About Nothing** takes place in Sicily; and **All's Well That Ends Well** has one part set in Florence.

Ancient Rome and the ageless themes of power, love, and intrigue also held great allure for Shakespeare: pick up **Julius Caesar, Titus Andronicus, Troilius & Cressida**, or **Coriolanus** for some light reading about the tragic nature of the men and women who made the Roman Empire the world's first superpower!

చ

Chapter 11

FOOD & DRINK

Food

Most Italian food is cooked with the freshest ingredients, making their dishes not only healthy but tasty and satisfying. There are many restaurants in Italy of international renown, but you shouldn't limit yourself only to the upper echelon. In most cases you can find as good a meal at a fraction of the cost at any trattoria. Also, many of the upper echelon restaurants you read about are only in business because they cater to the tourist trade. Their food is acceptable, but doesn't warrant the prices charged. I list the best restaurants in every city, where you can get a wonderful meal every time. As you will notice in each regional chapter, I feature some top-of-the-line restaurants as well as many local places, but each are well off the regular tourist path, and each offers a magnificently Italian experience for your enjoyment.

The traditional Italian meal consists of an antipasto (appetizer) and/or soup, and/or pasta and is called primo, a main course called secondo (usually meat or fish), with separately ordered side dishes of contorni (vegetables) or insalata (salad) which come either verdi (green) or mista (mixed), then dolci (dessert), which can be cheese, fruit, or gelato (ice cream). After which you then order your coffee and/or after dinner drink.

Note: Pasta is never served as an accompanying side dish with a secondo. In Italy, it is always served as a separate course. It is time to forget everything you thought you knew about "Italian" food that was learned at some run-of-the-mill restaurant chain.

Many North Americans think that there is one type of Italian food, and that's usually spaghetti and meatballs. As a result they don't know what they are missing. Region by region Italy's food has adapted itself to the culture of the people and land. In Florence you have some of the best steaks in the world, in the south the tomato-based pastas and pizzas are exquisite; in Genoa you can't miss the pesto sauce (usually garlic, pine nuts, parmiggiano and basil); and don't forget the seafood all along the coast.

When you are in Italy and you tell someone where you are going, the first thing they will do is exclaim the wonders of whatever food comes from that region – cheese, meats, fish, wines. Italians know the cuisine of the different regions and sigh with longing at the bounties one can find in each.

Restaurant Listings in This Book

Here's a sample listing of what you will find in this book in each of our *Where to Eat* sections. The number preceding the name of the restaurant tells you where to find it on the accompanying city or town map.

"**3. LA LEPANTO**, *Via Carlo Alberto 135, Tel. 079/979-116. Closed Mondays in the winter. All credit cards accepted. Dinner for two E70.*

A fine place with a quaint terrace located in the heart of the old city, but the preparation of dishes is haphazard. Sometimes it's great, other times so-so. Maybe it's because they try to do too much. The menu is extensive and seems to have everything that surf and turf could offer. I've always been pleased with the *i polpi tiepido con le patate* (roasted octopus in an oil and garlic sauce with roasted potatoes) and the *spaghetti con gamberi e melanzane* (with shrimp and eggplant). For antipasto, try the exquisite *antipasto misto di pesce spada affumicato* (smoked swordfish) or the *insalata mista* (mixed salad) with fresh vegetables from the region."

The restaurant listings indicate which credit cards are accepted by using the following phrases:
• **Credit cards accepted** = generally American Express, Visa, and/or Mastercard
• **All credit cards accepted** = everything imaginable is accepted
• **No credit cards accepted** = only cash or travelers checks

Each restaurant listing will give a ballpark price for a dinner for two in Euros. For example: "Dinner for two E40." This price represents the cost for two people who choose to eat a full meal of an antipasto, pasta dish and an entrée. In most cases you can get by with one course, which will make the actual price you will pay less than indicated. With the exchange rate at roughly $1.20 = Euro (E)1, for this example the dollar price would be about $48 for the meal.

Wine

Italy is also famous for its wines. The experts say the reds are not robust enough, and the whites are too light, but I'm not an expert. Personally I think Italian wines are great, one and all. Most importantly, to get a good bottle of wine, you don't have to spend a fortune. You can find some excellent wines straight out of vats in small wine stores in every city in Italy.

At any restaurant, all you'll need to order is the house wine to have a satisfying and excellent wine. (*Vino della casa*: House Wine; *Rosso*: Red; *Bianco*: White). But if you're a connoisseur, or simply want to try a wine for which a certain Italian region is known, in the sidebar above you'll find a selected list of wines and their regions (if you like red wine, try the Chianti, and if it's white you prefer, try Verdicchio or Frascati).

Order Like a Native: Reading an Italian Menu

Here are a few choice words to assist you when you're ordering from a menu while in Italy. Usually, the waiter should be able to assist you, but if not, this will make your dining more pleasurable. You wouldn't want to order octopus, rabbit or horse by surprise, would you?

And if you do not find this list adequate, I can recommend a superb pocket-sized booklet published by Open Road Publishing, *Eating and Drinking in Italy*, by food experts Andy Herbach and Michael Dillon. You will find these ever so useful guides in any bookstore, online or at their website: *www.eatndrink.com.*

ENGLISH	ITALIAN	ENGLISH	ITALIAN
Menu	*Lista (for wine)*	Teaspoon	*Cucchiaino*
	Carta (for food)		
Breakfast	*Prima Colazione*	Knife	*Cotello*
Lunch	*Pranzo*	Fork	*Forchetta*
Dinner	*Cena*	Plate	*Piatto*
		Glass	*Bicchiere*
Cover	*Coperto*	Cup	*Tazza*
Spoon	*Cucchiaio*	Napkin	*Tovagliolo*

Antipasto

Soup	*Zuppa*	Broth	*Brodo*
Fish Soup	*Zuppa di Pesce*	Vegetable soup	*Minestrone*
Broth with beaten egg	*Stracciatella*		

Pasta

Ravioli with meat stuffing	*Agnolotti*	Egg noodles	*Fettucine*

Large rolls of pasta	*Cannelloni*	Potato-filled, ravioli-like pasta	*Gnocchi*
Thin angel hair pasta	*Capellini*	Thin pasta	*Vermicelli*
Little hat pasta	*Capelletti*	Macaroni-like pasta	*Penne*

Eggs — *Uova*

soft-boiled	*al guscio*	hard boiled	*sode*
fried	*al piatto*	omelet	*frittata*

Fish — *Pesce*

Seafood	*Frutti di mare*	Eel	*Anguilla*
Lobster	*Aragosta*	herring	*Aringa*
Squid	*Calamari*	Carp	*Carpa*
Mullet	*Cefalo*	Grouper	*Cernia*
Mussels	*Cozze*	Perch	*Pesce Persico*
Salmon	*Salmone*	Clams	*Vongole*
Octopus	*Polipo*	Bass	*Spigola*
Oysters	*Ostriche*	Mixed fried fish	*Fritto Misto* *Mare*

Meat — *Carne*

Spring Lamb	*Abbacchio*	Lamb	*Agnello*
Rabbit	*Coniglio*	Chicken	*Pollo*
Small Pig	*Porchetta*	Veal	*Vitello*
Steak	*Bistecca*	Breast	*Petto*
Pork	*Maiale*	Liver	*Fegato*
Cutlet	*Costoletta*	Deer	*Cervo*
Wild Pig	*Cinghiale*	Pheasant	*Fagiono*
Duck	*Anitra*	Turkey	*Tacchino*

Methods of Cooking

Roast	*Arrosto*	Boiled	*Bollito*
On the Fire	*Ai Ferri*	Spit-roasted	*Al Girarrosto*
Grilled	*Alla Griglia*		
Rare	*Al Sangue*	Grilled	*Alla Griglia*
Well Done	*Ben Cotto*	Medium Rare	*Mezzo Cotto*

Miscellaneous

French fries	*Patate Fritte*	Cheese	*Formaggio*
Butter Sauce	*al burro*	Tomato and Meat Sauce	*Salsa Bolognese*

Tomato Sauce	*salsa di pomodoro*	Garlic	*Aglio*
Oil	*Olio*	Pepper	*Pepe*
Salt	*Sale*	Fruit	*Frutta*
Orange	*Arancia*	Cherries	*Ciliegie*
Strawberry	*Fragola*	Lemon	*Limone*
Apple	*Mela*	Melon	*Melone*
Beer	*Birra*	Mineral Water	*Aqcua Minerale*
Orange Soda	*Aranciata*	7 Up-like	*Gassosa*
Lemon Soda	*Limonata*	Juice (of)	*Succo (di)*
Wine	*Vino*		
Red	*Roso*	White	*Bianco*
House wine	*Vino della Casa*	Dry	*Secco*
Slightly Sweet	*Amabile*	Sweet	*Dolce*
Local Wine	*Vino del Paese*	Liter	*Litro*
Half Liter	*Mezzo Litro*	Quarter Liter	*Un Quarto*
A Glass	*Un Bicchiere*		

A feature on most menus are **piatti del giorno** (daily specials) and **prezzo fisso** (fixed price offerings.) The latter can be a good buy if you like the choices and is usually a better deal than ordering a la carte. If you have trouble reading the menu, ask your waiter for assistance. Usually they will speak enough English to help. And in many restaurants there are menus in different languages to help you choose the food you want.

Deciphering a Restaurant Bill

In all restaurants in Italy there is a universal cover charge, **pane e coperto** (literally "bread and cover"), which is different restaurant to restaurant, and in some cases can be quite expensive. **Pane e coperto** is tacked on to your bill above and beyond any tip you decide to leave. Therefore if your bill has an extra E5 or so, that is the pane e coperto, which covers the cost of the basket of bread at your table and gives you the right to sit there.

There should also be a statement about whether service is included, **servizio incluso**, or not, **servizio non incluso**. If service is included it is usually 15% of the bill. If you felt the service was good, it is customary to leave between around 5% more for the waiter.

Chapter 12

BEST PLACES TO STAY

Rome

EDEN, *Via Ludovisi, 49, Tel. 06/474-3551, Fax 06/482-1584. E-mail: Reservations@hotel-eden.it. Web: www.hotel-eden.it/index_e.html. 100 rooms all with private bath. Single E280-495; Double E450-825, Suites E700. Continental breakfast is E14 extra, buffet breakfast is E20.* *****

Located west of Via Veneto in the exclusive Ludovisi section but still in the middle of everything, the Eden is but steps from the famous Via Voneto and Spanish Steps, and the Trevi Fountain is just down the street. The Eden is ideally situated for sightseeing. With a long tradition of excellent service, year after year it maintains its top-ranked exclusivity, attracting all the cognoscenti (those in the know) to its exquisite accommodations. Declared one of the *Leading Hotels of the World*, it has an ultra-sophisticated level of service and comes with amenities virtually unmatched the world over.

Some of the amenities here include the terrace restaurant, which has a spectacular view over the city. Guests and locals alike flock to this restaurant, not just because of the view but because of the excellence of Chef Enrico Derflingher. The former personal chef to the Prince and Princess of Wales, Chef Derflingher prepares food fit for royalty. And after a sumptuous meal you can work it off in their fully appointed gym with everything from cardiovascular equipment to free weights. If you want to stay in the lap of luxury while in Rome, the Eden is the paradise you've been looking for.

LE GRAND HOTEL, *Via Vittorio Emanuele Orlando, Tel. 06/4709, Fax 06/ 474-7307. Web: www.romeguide.it/legrandhotel/legrandhotel.html. Single E195-310; Double E275-450; Suites E950. Extra bed costs E75. Breakfast E20.*
*****
Opulence knows no bounds in this extra fine hotel. Located between the Piazza della Repubblica and Piazza San Bernardo, near the American speaking church in Rome, Santa Susanna, this top-class luxury hotel has everything you'd ever need, and the prices to match. The rooms and suites are palatial, some with 16 to 17 foot ceilings, and the bathrooms have every imaginable amenity. The elegance and professional service here are refined including the hairdresser, beauty salons, and sauna. When staying here you will definitely feel like a prince or princess.

Afternoon tea is served downstairs everyday at 5:00pm. They also have a very relaxing but expensive American-style bar. The Grand Hotel has recently undergone an incredible face lift and has returned to its status as a premier hotel, not just in Rome, but the entire world.

VILLA HASSLER, *Piazza Trinita Dei Monti 6, Tel. 06/678-2651, Fax 06/ 678-9991. E-mail: hasslerroma@mclink.it. Web: www.hotelhasslerroma.com. All credit cards accepted. 80 rooms all with bath. Single E370-460; Double E500-660. Continental breakfast E23 extra. Buffet breakfast E35 extra.*
*****
The Villa Hassler may not be as opulent as the Eden, but it is just as refined and equally as elegant. In many travelers' opinions this is the best hotel in Rome, not just because of it's excellent location at the top of the Spanish Steps, but mainly because of the ultra-professional service and amazingly comfortable accommodations. Oil sheiks, movie stars, the nouveau riche, the landed gentry all have made the Hassler home, at one time or another, for over a century. They have a relaxing courtyard and an excellent (but expensive) roof garden restaurant with a superb view of the city.

These same views are shared with a number of the rooms on the upper floors facing the Spanish Steps, so remember to request one of these. Every imaginable amenity awaits you at the Hassler, and in a city filled with great restaurants, they have one of the best. So you don't even have to leave your hotel to have a first class meal. Even if you don't stay here, come to the restaurant, sample the food, and enjoy the superb view.

One of the best, most famous, and ideally located hotels in Rome. If you have the means, I recommend it highly.

BAROCCO, *Piazza Barberini 9 (entrance on Via della Purificazione 4), Tel. 06/ 487-2001/2/3, 487-2005, Fax 06/485-994. E-mail: hotelbarocco@holelbarocco.it. Web: www.hotelbarocco.com. 37 rooms all with bath. Single E150-200; Double E240-290. Breakfast included. All credit cards accepted. ****

A four star of the highest quality, but also one that is the smallest size. This allows for incredibly attentive service which helps to add to your stay. Here you can have an intimate and elegant four-star experience and you won't get lost in the shuffle as you would at a larger hotel. The entrance hall is a tastefully introduction to its elegance with its beautiful photos of Roman scenes.

The rooms are all as refined, even though each room is different from the other. Some of the best have two levels, others have small terraces, and all offer a unique, comfortable and accommodating living experience while in Rome. All rooms come with an electronic safe, TV, A/C and everything else befitting a four star.

Every decoration and piece of furniture is supremely elegant. The bathrooms are a little small but come with hair dryer and courtesy toiletry kit. In the summer, breakfast is served on the roof terrace. A great location for an evening's relaxation. Centrally located with the Trevi Fountain, Spanish Steps, Via Veneto all around the corner. A great place to spend an entire vacation, or simply the last night of a long one. I love this quaint, intimate little place.

LOCARNO, *Via della Penna 22, Tel. 06/361-0841, Fax 06/321-5249. E-mail: info@hotellocarno.com. Web: www.hotellocarno.com/. All credit cards accepted. 38 rooms all with bath. Single E207; Double E155-230; Suite E245 and up. Breakfast E12.* ***

Though only a three star I simply adore this hotel. The professional service, the ideal location, and the quality of the rooms, all point to a higher star rating. But let it be our little secret that though only a three star, this place offers exemplary accommodations. Situated between the Piazza del Popolo and the Tiber River, in a nice neighborhood of stores, galleries, and restaurant this hotel is wonderfully situated and amazingly comfortable. It has a very relaxing American-style bar, spacious common areas, a small side-garden patio, and a roof terrace where breakfast is served in good weather. In regular weather the downstair solarium/green house is where you will be served.

The rooms are large and tastefully decorated with all possible amenities. Situated on a side street, the Locarno offers a refined respite from the hectic pace of Rome. The best three star Rome has to offer. One that gives the big boys a run for their money.

Florence

HOTEL TORRE DI BELLOSGUARDO, *Via Roti Michelozzi 2, Tel. 055/ 229-8145, Fax 055/229-008. E-mail: torredibellosguardo@dada.it. Web: www.torrebellosguardo.com/. 16 room all with bath. Single E195; Double E265; Suites E275-325. All credit cards accepted.* ****

If you have the means, this is definitely the most memorable place to stay while in Florence. With stunning views over all of Florence, a swimming pool with a bar at which to relax, olive gardens in which to take an evening stroll, the Bellosguardo is like no other hotel in Florence. Housed in a huge old castle that has been separated into only 16 luxury rooms, it goes without saying that the size of accommodations are quite impressive. The interior common areas with their vaulted stone ceilings and arches, as well as staircases leading off into hidden passages, all make you feel as if you've stepped back in time.

The hotel is a short distance outside of the old city walls in the middle of pristine farmland. You will find pure romance, complete peace, and soothing tranquillity all with stunning views of the city of Florence. In fact the hotel is so well thought of that they are booked solid year round, so you have to reserve well in advance. I can't say enough about the Bellosguardo, it is simply something you have to experience. Also, and most importantly, if you aren't already in love, you'll find it or rekindle it in this wonderfully majestic hideaway.

LOGGIATO DEI SERVITI, *Piazza SS. Annunziata 3, Tel. 055/289-593/4, Fax 055/289-595. E-mail: info@loggiatodeiservitihotel.it. Web: www.loggiatodeiservitihotel.it/. All credit cards accepted. 29 rooms all with private bath. Single E139; Double E201; Suite E268-382. Breakfast included. E40 for an extra bed. ****

Located in a 16th century *loggia* facing the quiet, quaint and colorful Piazza della SS Annunziata, this hotel is filled with charm, character and is a three star of the highest quality. The interior common areas consist of polished terra-cotta floors, gray stone columns and high white ceilings.

The rooms are pleasant and comfortable and are filled with elegant antique furnishings. All are designed to make you feel like you just walked into the 17th century, and it works. But they do have the modern amenities necessary to keep us weary travelers happy, especially the air conditioning in August.

The best room possible would definitely be #30. From here you have unobstructed views of the Duomo, the spire of the Palazzo Vecchio, and Fort Belvedere beyond the Arno. Out the side windows of this unique room, you can look down into the Accademia and the skylight under which the David stands! A special treat for any traveler.

Some rooms face what many believe is one of the most beautiful piazzas in Italy (no cars allowed), while many of the rest face onto a lush interior garden. They are finished renovation on five additional rooms on the third floor, which will be top of the line accommodations. This place only gets better and better. All the bathrooms come with every modern comfort. The service, the accommodations, everything is at the top of the three star category. So, if you want to have a wonderful stay and also to feel as if you've stepped back in time, book a room here. They also have facilities for weddings and business functions.

Venice

HOTEL CIPRIANI, *Fondamenta San Giovanni 10, La Guidecca, Venezia. Tel. 041/520-7744. Fax 041/520-3930. American Express, Diners Club, Mastercard and Visa accepted. 98 rooms all with bath. Single E250-500; Double E380-700. ****.*

This exquisite hotel occupies three beautiful acres at the east end of La Isola del Guidecca and comes with a swimming pool, saunas, Jacuzzis, a private harbor for yachts, a private launch to ferry guests back and forth from the center, an American-style bar with every drink imaginable, two superb restaurants, and professional staff waiting on you hand and foot. There are sixty rooms overlooking the lagoon, while many of the others look out over the pool. Each room is stunningly appointed with only the best furnishings and every conceivable comfort.

This hotel is probably as close to heaven on earth as you'll find in Venice. The ambiance is exquisite, the service sublime, and the accommodations impeccable. Staying here makes a visit to Venice almost a fantasy.

HOTEL DANIELI, *Riva degli Schiavoni 4196, Venezia. Tel. 041/522-6480, Fax 041/520-0208. American Express, Diners Club, Mastercard and Visa accepted. 235 rooms all with bath. Single E150-300; Double E250-450. Suites E600-1,400. *****

A completely different style of atmopshere than the Cipriani, but still ultra-luxurious. First opened in 1882 with only 16 rooms, the Danieli has expanded to encompass many surrounding buildings. After encompassing all the fine architectural features of each, the Danieli has developed a beguiling, romantic and enticing atmosphere.

The magnificent lobby, which is built around a Gothic courtyard with its intertwining staircases and columns, is truly awe-inspiring. It makes you feel as if you're suddenly thrust back in time into an ancient medieval castle. One of the largest and best hotels in Venice as well as the most romantic, each room comes perfectly appointed with only the best furnishings and all imaginable modern conveniences. And one of the best places for a meal in all of Venice is the rooftop dining room, with its exquisite view of the Lagoon looking towards the Cipriani.

Courmayeur

GALLIA GRAN BAITA, *Strada Larzy, 11013 Courmayeur. Tel. 0165/844-040, Fax 0165/844-805 (US & Canada Tel. 402/398-3200, Fax 402/398-5484; Australia Toll Free 800/810-862; England, Tel. 071/413-8886, Fax 071/413-8883). 50 rooms and 3 junior suites all with bath. Single E75-140; Double E100-250; Suite E350. Breakfast E12 extra. Credit cards accepted. ****

Even though it was only established in 1994, the Gran Baita has been created with tradition, style, character and ambiance in mind. The entrance hall comes complete with antique furnishings from the 1600s where you are served tea in the afternoons. The rooms are large, comfortable, and accommodating and come richly decorated in coordinated green or yellow color schemes that complement the furnishings well. The marble bathrooms are amazingly appointed and come complete with every imaginable modern convenience.

They have a heated pool for your use, a free shuttle bus to pick you up and drop you off wherever and whenever you choose, a sun room, a workout room, a spa/beauty room that offers everything from being wrapped in seaweed to getting a wax treatment, and they also have baby-sitting services. A great place to stay while in Courmayeur.

Positano – Amalfi Coast

HOTEL LE SIRENUSE, *Via Cristoforo Colombo 30, 84071 Positano. Tel. 089/875-066, Fax 089/811-798. 60 rooms all with bath. Single E200-250. Double E250-320. Credit cards accepted. Breakfast included. Full board E200-280. ******

Definitely the place to stay in Positano – everything about this hotel is beautiful. Nothing overly fancy, nothing too ostentatious, just simply radiant. The rooms are furnished with antiques but nothing too frilly. The bathrooms are complete with every conceivable comfort. The breakfast buffet is so ample as to dissuade most from lunch. There is a stunningly beautiful pool at your disposal, a sauna, and a small boat to ferry you along the coast. The service is extremely attentive.

Their restaurant is one of the best, if not the best, in the city. Expensive, yes, but when the food is combined with the great views from the terrace, the price is irrelevant. All the food they make here is great, but I believe the chef concocts the best *spaghetti alla vongole* (with spicy clam sauce) in Positano.

Capri – Southern Italy

LA SCALINATELLA, *Via Tragara 10, 80073 Capri. Tel. 081/837-0633, Fax 081/837-8291. 30 rooms, 2 suites, all with bath. Single E150-220; Double 170-320. All credit cards accepted. Closed November to March. *****

Located on the sea, this small intimate hotel offers you serene ambiance and excellent service, and is the place to stay when on Capri. This four star is run by the same family that operates the Quisisana, except that here you receive much more personal attention since there are only 30 rooms compared to 150. Many prefer the Quisisana, which is considered one of the leading hotels in the world, but for my choice I prefer its sister, La Scalinatella, because of its intimate, romantic charm.

Besides the ample rooms, all with excellent views and decorated with quality furnishings, the hotel has a pool where you can relax or receive your meals. The restaurant, with its stunningly panoramic views, offers warm and welcoming dining experience. This is definitely the most romantic place to stay in Capri.

Umbria – Perugia
RESIDENZA DELL'OSCANA, *06134 Locanda Cenerente, Perugia. Tel. 075/690-125, Fax 075/690-666. Web: www.umbria.org/hotel/oscano. 100 rooms. All credit cards accepted. Breakfast included. Castle: Only 11 rooms in the castle E210-290. Villa Ada: Double E110. La Macina: Weekly rates E300 to E625. Buffet breakfast included and is served in the dining room of the Castle.*

Stunning. Incredibly beautiful. Amazing. Like something out of a fairy tale. Simply unbelievable. By far the best place to stay in all of Umbria. If you have a car, and you have the means, this is definitely the place to stay in Umbria. Near Perugia but set deep in the surrounding verdant forested hills, this amazing medieval castle offers an atmosphere of unparalleled charm and ambiance.

There are three locations to choose from: the Castle (a medieval structure complete with towers and turrets that is simply but elegantly decorated and equipped with every comfort); the Villa Ada (a 19th century residence adjoining the castle that is more modern but no less accommodating); and La Macina (a country house down the hill from the other two structures, which comes with complete apartments and an adjacent pool). All three offer the setting for an ideal vacation, but the castle is the place to stay because of its unique, one of a kind, medieval ambiance and charm. A perfect place to spend a honeymoon or simply have the vacation of a lifetime.

Besides the excellent accommodations, you will also find the finest quality cuisine served nightly in the grand hall in the castle. World class chefs cater to your every need as they creatively concoct regional and international dishes from fresh locally grown produce and game. This is a residence and not a hotel, so it does not carry a star rating, but it would easily receive four stars if it decides to allow itself to be regulated by the tourist industry.

Umbria – Orvieto
LA BADIA, *1a Cat., 05019 Orvieto. Tel 0763/301-959 or 305-455, Fax 0763/305-396. All credit cards accepted. Single E140; Double E320. ✶✶✶✶*

An unbelievably beautiful 12th century abbey at the foot of Orvieto is now an incredibly beautiful hotel and restaurant. Located only an hour from Rome, you will find one of the most unique and memorable experiences in the entire world. This historic abbey became a holiday resort for Cardinals in the 15th century, and today, through painstakingly detailed renovations, you can stay or dine in incomparable ambiance and charm.

The rooms are immense, the accommodations exemplary, the service impeccable, and the atmosphere like something out of the Middle Ages. For a fairy tale vacation stay here, and make sure that you eat at least once at their soon to be world renowned restaurant that offers refined local dishes — many ingredients culled from owner Count Fiumi's farms and vineyards — in an incredibly historic and romantic atmosphere.

Milan

PRINCIPE DI SAVOIA, *Piazza della Repubblica 17 (near the Giardini Publici). Tel. 02/62-301, Fax 02/659-5838. All credit cards accepted. 285 rooms all with bath. Single E300-360; Double E360-520. All credit cards accepted. Breakfast E15.* *****

This is one of the most elegant and prestigious hotel in of all Italy. Expensive, ritzy, filled with every amenity imaginable, the service is impeccable and caters to your every need. Situated in a neoclassic palazzo that evokes a feeling of refined elegance, this hotel has an historic tradition of accommodating the most dicerning travelers. When in Milan this is a great place to stay, if you have the means.

Recently absorbed into the ITT Sheraton chain, an amazing transformation has been made, while the overall tone and ambiance of elegance remains. While the Principe has always been elegant, Sheraton's influence has dusted off its hidden charm, and polished the ambiance so the true beauty of this hotel can shine through. The rooms are enormous and delicately furnished with beautiful antiques. The bathrooms are awash in marble and every modern convenience. If you have the means, at over 500 square meters, the Presidential suite is the largest in all of Europe.

The hotel comes complete with the Caffé Doney for breakfast, the Galleria restaurant for lunch and dinner, a fitness center with a lap pool and sauna, and a beauty center. You are also afforded courtesy limousine service to the center. When you stay here, you reside in the lap of luxury.

Chapter 13

ROME

Rome is a magical city, filled with ancient ruins, winding Medieval streets, superb restaurants, great nightlife, relaxing cafes, authentic wine bars, unique shopping, and everything else needed to make your vacation enjoyable. At the same time, Rome is a city of 3 million people, and as such is somewhat crowded and rather fast paced. Many first time travelers to Rome tend to feel overwhelmed, at least in comparison to other popular Italian cities such as Florence or Venice. Both of these cities are much smaller and more easily walkable.

Even if you feel a little discombobulated by Rome's pace, you will still love coming here. Rome is a great place to visit, and a fantastic city to in which to live for. I spent seven years here and loved it. Where else can you see ancient Roman ruins such as the Colosseum, interspersed with the Renaissance glory of the Sistine Chapel and the Pieta? And eat at fantastic restaurants every night?

Rome was not always the largest and most powerful city in the region. Prior to the Roman Empire, another culture, the **Etruscans**, dominated the area around Rome. Cerveteri and Tarquinia, north of Rome, were two of the richest Etruscan cities. Now they are home to magnificent *Necropoli*, cities of the dead. The Etruscans took great care in laying their dead to rest in cemeteries set up like actual towns; and those found in Tarquinia and Cerveteri are two of the finest. **Cerveteri** is the closest, so this may be the best alternative for a quick day trip.

Besides Rome, the other locations, towns, and cities featured in this chapter include **Vatican City, Tivoli Gardens, Frascati,** and **Ostia Antica**.

Websites for Rome
Rome has much to offer and the proliferation of websites reflects that. However, here are a few you may want to take a look at, to help you get a feel for this wonderful city. *www.ciaorome.com, www.allaroundrome.com, www.romecity.it,* and *www.comune.roma.it.*

The Eternal City
For a millennium and a half, Rome was the cultural center of Europe. At the time of the Empire, it controlled territory extending from Scotland to North Africa, and from the Atlantic Ocean to the Persian Gulf. During and after the Renaissance (14th century CE), Rome was also a center of artistic expression. Hundreds of churches were built by the Vatican, and many artists were sponsored to fill them with beautiful works. **Michelangelo** spent much time here, working on the Sistine Chapel, helping to design St. Peter's, carving the Pieta, as well as other projects.

Because of this extensive history, dating all the way back to before the time of Christ, Rome has a wide variety of sights to see, which is why many people describe Rome as a living museum. You'll see ancient Roman ruins nestled side by side with buildings built three to four centuries ago, and sometimes these ruins have been incorporated into the design of a 'new' building built at the end of the 19th century.

If You Haven't Done This, You Haven't Been to Rome
Rome has so many options that it's easy to neglect seeing a certain sight, or going to a specific restaurant, or visiting a particular spot late in the evening to enjoy the ambiance and charm. If you do not have the time to sift through the rest of this chapter - which is filled with the most authentic and enjoyable places to stay, eat, and see while in Rome - I have conveniently listed the best of those options below.

Even if you are not religious, make the effort to see **St. Peter's** and the **Vatican Museums**. This will take the better part of a day if you do a proper tour. No church is more magnificent and no museum is more complete.

That night, make sure you get to the **Trastevere** district and sample the atmosphere of **La Canonica**, a converted chapel and now a restaurant that also has many tables spilling out along the street. Reserve a spot inside since this may be your last chance to have a meal in a quaint converted chapel. Try their *spaghetti alla carbonara* (with a light cream sauce, covered with ham, peas, and grated parmesan cheese) for *primo* and for your main course sample the light fish dish, *sogliola alla griglia* (grilled Sole). Then sojourn to **Ombre Rosse**, in Piazza Sant'Egidio around the corner, grab a drink, and savor the evening.

It is also imperative that you visit **Piazza Navona** and grab an ice cream at one of the cafés. A good place to sit and eat your *gelato* is near Bernini's magnificent **Fontana Dei Quattro Fiumi** (Fountain of Four Rivers). The four figures supporting the large obelisk (a Bernini trademark) represent the Danube, the Ganges, the Nile, and the Plata rivers. Notice the figure representing the Nile. It is shielding its eyes from the facade of the church it is facing, **Santa Agnese in Agone**, which was designed by Bernini's rival at the time, Borromini. An ancient artistic quarrel comes to life everyday in Piazza Navona.

From there, only a few blocks away is the piazza **Campo dei Fiori** where you'll find one of Rome's best fruit and vegetable markets every day until 1:00pm, except Sundays. Make sure you get here to shop or just to enjoy the atmosphere of a boisterous Roman *mercato*.

There is a restaurant in the square where you should enjoy at least one meal, **La Carbonara**. Even though the name would lead you to believe that the best dish to get is the *spaghetti alla carbonara*, my favorite here is the *spaghetti alla vongole verace* (with a spicy oil, garlic, and clam sauce).

Other dishes you need to sample while in Rome are *penne all'arrabbiata* (literally means angry pasta and is a tubular pasta made with a spicy garlic, oil, and tomato-based sauce), *tortellini alla panna* (meat or cheese filled pasta in a thick cream sauce), and any *abbacchio* (lamb) or *maiale alla griglia* (grilled pork).

In the evening, don't miss the **Trevi Fountain** all lit up and surrounded by locals and tourists strumming on guitars and drinking wine. It's definitely a party atmosphere. Come here with friends or arrive and meet new ones. For one of your evening meals, there's a place nearby called **Al Piccolo Arancio** on Vicolo Scandberg.

Located on a small side street near the Trevi fountain, you can either sit at one of the tables outside, or in their colorful local atmosphere inside. They serve excellent pastas, great meat dishes, and all come with wonderful service. To finish the meal, order a *sambucca con mosce* (this is a sweet liquor with three flies with three coffee beans floating in it). Remember to bite into the beans as you have the sweet liquor in your mouth. The combination of tastes is exquisite.

There is obviously much more to do in Rome than this, but if you only have a little time, make sure you get to the places mentioned above. Then you can say you really have seen Rome.

Arrivals & Departures
By Air
Rome Fiumicino (Leonardo da Vinci) Airport
Most travelers will arrive at Rome's **Fiumicino** (**Leonardo da Vinci**) **Airport**, which handles most incoming flights from North America, Australia, and the United Kingdom. If you are arriving from other points in Europe you

may arrive at Rome's **Ciampino** airport. The website for Rome's airports is: *www.adr.it.*

Rome's Fiumicino has a dedicated **train** to whisk you directly to the central train station (**Termini**). If your hotel is in the center of town, this is by far the best, and least expensive, way to make it to your destination.

When the train arrives at Stazione Termini (Rome's main train station), you catch a taxi to your hotel from the taxi stand in front of the station. You can also hop on the Metro, which is underneath the train station, or take one of the many city buses located outside the front of Stazione Termini.

Direct Link. A train service is available from the airport directly to Stazione Termini (Rome's Central Railway Station). The trip costs Euro (E) 8.5 one way and takes 30 minutes. There are trains every half hour. They start operating from the airport to Termini at 7:38am and end at 10:08pm. Returning to the airport the trains also run every half hour, from track 25-29, but start at 6:52am and ends at 9:22pm. Note: You can pick up a schedule for the train when you buy your tickets. This will help you plan for your departure.

Metropolitan Link. There is train service from the Airport to Stazione Tiburtina stopping at the following stations: Ponte Galleria, Muratella, Magliana, Trastevere, Ostiense, and Tuscolana. Departures are every 20 minutes from 6:00am to 10:00pm. Trip takes about 45 minutes. Trains are air-conditioned.

Night Arrivals and Departures. There is a night bus running between Fiumicino and Tiburtina station, which stops at Termini. From Fiumicino the bus leaves at 1:15am, 2:15am, 3:30am and 5:00am. From Tiburtina station to the airport the bus runs at 12:30am, 1:15am, 2:30am and 3:45am. The trip takes about half and hour.

Car Rental. If you are renting a car, you can get explicit driving directions from your rental company. See the *Renting a Car* section below for more complete information. If they neglect to give you directions, make sure you get on the large road – SS 201 – leading away from the airport to the GRA *(Grande Raccordo Anulare)*, which is Rome's beltway and is commonly known as the Anulare, going north. Get off at SS 1 (Via Aurelia) and follow this road all the way into town.

Airport Shuttles. In the past few years a number of shuttle services have sprouted up to ferry tourists back and forth between Rome's airports and downtown. These are great options if you arrive into either Roman airport, need a ride to Rome and don't want to pay an arm and leg to a taxi. Listed below are two of the best:

• **Airport Shuttle** – *Tel. 06/4201-4507, Web: www.airportshuttle.it, Email: airportshuttle@airportshuttle.it*. Office hours 6:30am-10:30pm, 7 days a week. No credit cards. Cash only. E30 for one or two passengers. For service between 8pm and 8am it's 30% more. Pick-up service at Ciampino or Fiumicino add an additional E12. Fluent English spoken.

• **Airport Connection Services** – *Tel. 06/338-3221. Web: www.airportconnection.it.* Available 7:00am to 7:00pm. Major credit cards accepted. Must be booked at least a day in advance; closed Christmas and New Year's Day. For E25 per person (shared with others) will take you from the airport to your hotel and vice versa. They also offer a private Mercedes for E40 to perform the same service.

Rome Ciampino Airport

If you arrive at Rome's **Ciampino** (which is really only used for flights from European counties), there are dedicated airport buses that leave for the Anagnina Metro Station every half an hour. If you rent a car, simply take Via Appia all the way into town. For the scenic view get on the Via Appia Antica a kilometer or so after passing the GRA aka the Annulare.

Bus Link – Buses leave from the airport starting at 6:00am and end at 10:30pm and will take you to the Anagnina Metro stop, where you can catch the subway to Termini station. The only other option is taking a taxi or the Airport Connection Service.

Airport Shuttles. See information above.

By Car

To get into Rome you will have to either get on or pass by the Anulare, Rome's beltway. If arriving from the north you will be using Via Cassia (which can get congested), Via Flaminia, Via Salaria or the fastest route, the A1 *(Autostrada del Sole)*, which will dump you onto the Annulare (GRA).

If arriving from the south, the fastest route is the A2, also referred to as the *Autostrada del Sole*. A more scenic route is along the Via Appia.

Sample trip lengths on the main roads:
• **Florence**: 3 1/2 hours
• **Venice**: 6 1/2 hours
• **Naples**: 3 hours

By Train

When arriving by train, you will be let off at Rome's main train station, **Stazione Termini**. From here you can catch a **taxi** at the row of cabs outside the front entrance, catch the **Metro**, or hop on one of the **buses** in the main square (Piazza Cinquecento) just in front of the station.

Termini is a zoo. Packed with people from all over the world, queuing up to buy tickets, trying to cut in line to get information, and in some cases looking for unprotected belongings. So don't leave your bags unattended here or in any train station in Italy. The **Tourist Information** office is located near the train tracks, *Tel. 06/487-1270.* You can get a good map here and make a hotel reservation. The **Railway Information** office faces the front entrance along with the taxis and buses. If you're planning a trip, you should come here to find out when your train will be leaving. All attendants speak enough English to get by. There is a **baggage storage area** at Termini which is open from 5:15am to 12:20am. For E2.5 you can store an item there for 12 hours. There are also lockers available for E2 for 6 hours.

Sample trip lengths and costs for direct *(diretto)* trains:
• **Florence**: 2 1/2 hours, E23
• **Venice**: 5 hours, E33
• **Naples**: 2 hours, E16

Getting Around Town
By Car
Unless you are from Boston and are acclimated to aggressive driving tactics, driving a car to get around Rome is nuts. Especially considering that the public transportation system is so good.

So think twice about renting a car while in Rome, unless you are taking excursions to the outskirts that are not accessible by train. Remember also, that if you rent a car you'll need to buy gas, which besides being expensive can sometimes be inconvenient. Many stations in Italy are unmanned self-service and the pumps only take crisp Euro bills. Some have converted to taking credit cards, but not many.

Renting a Car

Cars can be rented at Fiumicino or Ciampino airports, booked in advance by a travel agent, or rented at many offices in the city, especially at the Stazione Termini. Try the following places:
• **Avis**, Information *Tel. 06/41998*. Their office at Termini Station is open Monday-Saturday 7:00am-8:00pm, and Sundays from 8:00am-11:00pm *(Tel. 06/413-0812)*. Their office at Fiumicino is open every day from 7:30am-11:00pm *(Tel. 06/7934-0195)*.
• **Hertz**, Customer Service *06/5429-4500*. Main Office is on the Via Veneto #156, *Tel. 06/821-6881 or 06/321-6834*. The office number at Fiumicino is *06/6501-1448*; at Ciampino it's *06/7934-0095*. *Web: www.hertz.com*.
• **National/Maggiore**, Car reservations in Italy, *Tel. 1478/67067*. Van Reservations in Italy, *Tel. 1478/48844*. *Web: www.maggior .it*. At Fiumicino airport, *Tel . 06/65-010-678*.

The fees usually include the costs for towing, minor repairs, and basic insurance, but you should ask just to make sure. Also most firms require a deposit equal to the daily cost of the rental, which is usually between E70 and E100. The minimum age for rental usually is 21 and you must have had a drivers license for at least a year. Rules and regulations will vary according to company, since the concept of standard industry practices hasn't hit Italy yet.

Parking Your Car in Rome

If you are just passing through, you are going to have to deal with the Byzantine Roman parking system. There are spaces on the street indicated by blue lines where you can park for E1 per hour. This is usually only from 8am – 8pm. The tickets can be purchased at the vending machines along the sidewalks (which use coin only) or at *tabacchi* stores or newsstands. Ask for a *biglietto per parcheggio* (parking ticket). There are also some large public and private parking garages situated all around the city, where you can leave your car overnight if the hotel you are staying at does not have a garage. These public lots are located at: ParkSi in Villa Borghese, Parking Ludovisi on Via Ludovisi 60, and Parking Termini in front of the main train station.

Towed Car?

If your car happens to have been towed, it means you parked in an illegal spot. To find out where your car has been taken call **Vigili Urbani**, *Tel. 06/67691*. Give them the registration number, make of car and place where it was removed. They will tell you where your car has been placed, but you can only pick up your car after you have paid your fine at Via della Consolazione 4. Take your receipt with you when you retrieve your car. On Sundays the office to pay your fine is closed, but the tow trucks are still working – so don't park illegally on Sundays.

By Moped

If you are looking for a new experience, try renting a moped. A moped gives you freedom, and the ability to go from one corner of Rome to another, quickly. Riding a moped makes you feel in tune with the flow of the city. With no plan, no structure, no itinerary, no boundaries, you can go from the tourist areas to a part of Rome tourists rarely see. You can find monuments and markets in Rome you would never have seen if not on a moped. It makes you feel a part of the city, and this familiarity gives you the confidence to widen your explorations.

Now that I've almost convinced you to rent one, I'll counsel you to think hard about not renting one. Traffic in Rome is like nothing you have ever experienced, and as such makes riding a moped rather dicey. Only if you feel extremely confident about your motorcycle driving abilities should you even contemplate renting a moped.

A sizable deposit (around E100+) is generally required for each moped. The deposit will increase based on the size of moped you want to rent. Your deposit can be cash in any currency, travelers checks, or on a credit card. This is standard procedure for all rental companies. Daily rates are between E25 and E40. Renting for a more extended period can be a better bargain. Rates should be prominently posted.

Moped Caution & Rates

If you cannot ride a bicycle, please do not rent a moped. The concept is the same, one vehicle just goes a little faster. Also, start off renting a 50 cc (**cinquanta**), not a 125 cc (**cento venti cinque**). With more than twice the engine capacity, the 125 cc is a big difference, and in the traffic of Rome it's best to start slow. But if you insist on riding two to a moped, then a 125 cc is necessary. It's the law too. (Not that any Italians abide by it). Also you need to be at least sixteen years old to rent a moped, but you don't need a motorcycle license. Just hop on, and ride away ... but don't let Mom and Dad know about it.

Renting a Moped

• **Bici e Baci**, Via del Viminale 5, *Tel. 06/482-8443. Web: www.romeguide.it/ bicibaci/ bicibaci.html.* Open 8:00am-7:00pm. All credit cards accepted. Extensive selection of bicycles, scooter, and cars. They also organize guided bike tours or scooter tours in English.

• **Scooters for Rent**, Via Quattro Novembre 96, *Tel. 488-5685.* Open 8:30am-8:00pm, seven days a week. A centrally located moped rental, just off the Piazza Venezia.

• **I Bike Rome di Cortessi Ferruccio**, Viale Galappatoio, near Via Veneto. *Tel. 06/322-5240.* Open Monday-Saturday 9:00am-1:00pm and 4:00pm-8:00pm, and Sundays 9:00am-8:00pm. They rent from the same underground parking garage (connecting the Piazza di Spagna Metro Stop and the Via Veneto) as does Hertz. Maybe that's why you get a 50% discount with a Hertz card.

• **Happy Rent**, Via Farini 3, *Tel/Fax 06/481-8185. Web: www.happyrent.com.* They also have other rental locations by the Colosseum and the Spanish Steps, they rent bicycles, scooters, and cars.

By Bicycle

Bicycles make getting from one spot in Rome to another quicker and easier, but if you haven't been on one in awhile, trying to re-learn on the streets of Rome is not a good idea. And don't even think about having children younger than 14 try and ride around Rome unattended. Not only could they get lost very easily, but the traffic laws are so different they may not be able to adapt very well.

Renting a Bicycle

Please refer to the scooter rental place above that I listed as they also rent bicycles. The cost for an entire day varies from place to place, and year to year, but the latest price is around E15 per day and E5 per hour, except at the one below, which is only E13 a day and E4 per hour.

- **Bici Pincio**, Viale di Villa Medici & Viale della Pineta, *Tel. 06/678-4374*. A location in the Borghese Gardens and one near the Piazza del Popolo, this company has this side of Rome to themselves and only rents bicycles.

By Taxi

Taxis are the best, but also the most expensive, way to get around Rome. They are everywhere so flagging one down is not a problem. And **cab stands** are dispersed all over the city too.

Since taxis are expensive I wouldn't rely on them as your main form of transportation. Use them as a last resort, such as when you start to get tired from walking. Also have a map handy when a cabby is taking you somewhere. Since they are on a meter, they sometimes decide to take you on a little longer journey than necessary.

Rome also has several radio taxi cooperatives: **La Capitale** *(Tel. 4994)*, **Roma Sud** *(Tel. 6645)*, **Roma** *(Tel. 3570)*, **Cosmos** *(Tel. 88177)* and **RadioTaxi Tevere** *(Tel. 4157)*. Be warned that when you call for a taxi the cab's meter starts running when it is summoned, not when it arrives to pick you up, so by the time a cab arrives at your location there will already be a substantial amount on the meter.

The going rate as of publication was E2 for the first 2/3 of a kilometer or the first minute (which usually comes first during the rush hours), then it's Euro 30 cents every 1/3 of a kilometer or minute. At night you'll also pay a surcharge of E2.5, and Sundays you'll pay E1 extra. If you bring luggage aboard, you'll be charged E1 extra for each bag. In conjunction, if you go from Rome to Fiumicino you will charged E7 extra, Fiumicino to Rome E6, and between Ciampino and Rome you will be charged E5 extra.

By Bus

At each bus stop, called **fermata**, there are signs that list all the buses that stop there. These signs also give the streets that the buses will follow along their route so you can check your map to see if this is the bus for you. Also, on the side of the bus are listed highlights of the route for your convenience. Nighttime routes (since many of them stop at midnight) are indicated by black spaces on newer signs, and are placed at the bottom of the older signs. In conjunction the times listed on the signs indicate when the bus will pass the *fermata* so you can plan accordingly.

Riding the bus during rush hour is like becoming a sardine, complete with the odor, so try to avoid the rush hours of 8:00am to 9:00am, 12:30pm to 1:30pm, 3:30 to 4:30pm, and 7:30pm to 8:30pm. Yes, they have an added rush hour in the middle of the day because of their siesta time in the afternoon.

The bus fare costs E0.77 cents and lasts for 75 minutes, during which time you can transfer to any other bus, but you can only ride the Metro once. Despite the convenience and extent of the Roman bus system, I recommend taking the Metro as it is easier, quicker, less crowded, and more understandable.

Never board the Metro or a bus without a ticket. Tickets can be bought at any ATAC booth or kiosk and at tobacco shops (*tabacchi*), newsstands (*giornalaio*) and vending machines in the Metro stations. To enter the Metro system you need to stamp your ticket; but you need to remember to do it once on board a bus. There are yellow stamp machines at both the front and back of buses.

If you do not have a ticket or have one and do not stamp it with the date and time, and an inspector catches you, you face an instantaneous E25 fine. For more information (though only in Italian), call **ATAC**, *Tel. 06/4695-4444;* or **ACOTRAL**, *Tel. 06/5912-5551.*

ATAC Bus Tours

If you like the local scene, take the no-frills Giro di Roma tour on the **silver bus #110** offered by **ATAC**, the intra-city bus company, *Tel. 06/4695-2252.* This three hour circuit of the city leaves from the information booth in the middle of the **Piazza Cinquecento** in front of the train station daily at 10:30am, 2:00pm, 3:00pm, 5:00pm and 6:00pm, and takes you to over 80 sites of historic and artistic significance, and stops at the most important sights like the Colosseum, Piazza Venezia, St. Peter's, and more.

Cost is only E7.5 and you can pay by credit card. To book a seat on these luxury buses with tour guides and an illustrated guide book call the number above 9:00am and 7:00pm. Or stop by one of the ATAC ticket booths in from of Termini Station.

Bus Passes

If you are staying in Rome for a while or will be using the buses frequently, you can buy one of the following bus tickets at most newsstands, *tabacchi*, or ATAC booths by the station, and in the Metro. These tickets are:
• **Daily Ticket** (B.I.G.): E3 (Valid for unlimited Metro, Bus, Trolley and Train with the Commune di Roma which includes going to Ostia but not Fiumicino Airport or Tivoli)
• **Weekly Ticket** (C.I.S.): E12 (Valid for everything under the B.I.G.)

By Metro

The Roman *Metropolitana* (**Metro**) has two lines (Linea A and Linea B) that intersect in the basement of Termini station. You'll find these and all other stations marked with a prominent white "M" inside a red square up on a sign. The Metro can get quite crowded around **Stazione Termini** and during rush hours.

Also, always be on the lookout for pickpockets. There are signs (in Italian) in the Metro and on buses warning people about them, so be prepared. The best way to do that is to put your wallet in your front pants pocket, or buy one of those fanny packs, wear it in front of you, and lock the pouch, so that no unwanted hands cannot get inside.

For women, to make sure you are not the recipient of unwanted gropes on your derriere, keep your back to the wall if possible. And if you feel hands on you, be sure to push them away and say "Basta" (enough) or "Non toccare" (do not touch) loud enough for others to hear. The Italians are good about coming to the aid of a damsel in distress. This is not generally a problem, but I felt a warning should be given anyway.

The Metro runs from 5:30am to 11:30pm.

Metro Lost & Found

If you misplace something on the metro or the bus, you can report the item missing at the office at the main station, *Servizio Movimento delle Ferrovie dello Stato (Tel. 06/4669, ext. 7682)*. However, it is more than likely that you won't get it back, especially if it is an expensive item. However, a report should be filed for insurance purposes when you get home. Otherwise you may not be able to claim the loss.

Take the Metro to the Beach!

If you're interested in going to the beach or visiting the ruins at Ostia Antica, take the Linea B Metro to the Magliana stop and transfer to a train that

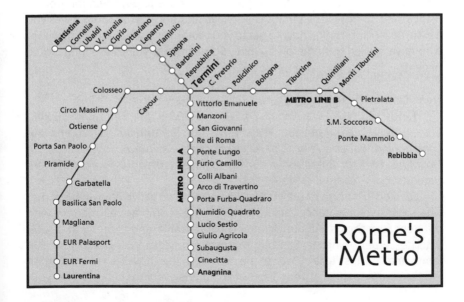

will take you from there. Follow signs to Spiaggia (Beach) or Ostia. Your metro ticket is valid for the train as well.

Using the Metro

It is best to have a ticket in hand when you head down to the Metro since the machines that dispense tickets are, in true Italian fashion, usually out of service. So, get a ticket at a tabacchi or newsstand before coming to the Metro. These cost E0.77. Before entering the Metro, you will need to stamp these tickets in the yellow stamp machines at the turnstiles. On buses, you would be able to ride anywhere for 75 minutes from the moment of the stamp, but on the Metro, it is only valid for one trip.

Where To Stay

Hotels in Italy are strictly controlled by a government rating system that categorizes them from "no star" hotels to "five star deluxe" hotels. Each and every hotel must prominently display their official ranking. See Chapter 6, *Planning Your Trip*, for more details on accommodations and ratings.

No Hotel Reservations?

If you get to Rome without a reservation, there is a free hotel finding service located at the end of **track #10** at the train station that will get you a room. They do not charge a fee, but you usually have to pay them for the first night's stay up front. The service calls ahead and books your room, gives you a map, and will show you how to get to your hotel. It's a great service for those who have arrived in Rome on a whim. Sometimes the lines are long, so be patient.

Near Termini Station

1. **BRITANNIA**, *Via Napoli 64, Tel. 06/488-3153, Fax 06/488-2343. Email: info@hotelbritannia.it. Web: www.hotelbritannia.it. 32 rooms. Air conditioning. Parking Available. All credit cards accepted. Single E135-210; Double E160-240. Breakfast included. Children up to 10 years old share parent's room for free. (Map A)* ***

Located just north of the Via Nazionale, this is an efficiently run hotel that offers guests every conceivable attention. The rooms are all modern with different furnishings. All are clean and comfortable and come with a safe, satellite TV and mini-bar. The bathrooms are modern with hair dryers, sun lamps and courtesy toiletry kits. In the mornings, they have Italian and English language newspapers at your disposal and in the evenings chocolate on your

Hotels By Map

Map A – see pages 120-121

1. Brittania
2. Columbia
3. Grand Hotel
4. Mecentate Palace
6. Venezia
7. Ambasciatori Palace
8. Barocco
9. Bernini Bristol
10. Eden
11. Excelsior
12. Flora
13. Golden
14. Merano
15. Savoy
16. Fontana
17. Trevi
18. Julia
19. De Petris
20. Carriage
21. Hassler
22. Homs
23. Internazionale
24. Manfredi
25. Scalinata di Spagna
26. Lydia Venier
27. Erdarelli
28. Gregoriana
29. Margutta
30. Parlamento

Map B – see pages 140-141

29. Margutta
31. Locarno
32. Valadier
33. Campo dei Fiori
34. Genio
35. Portoghesi
36. Arenula
37. Del Sole
38. Markus
39. Sole Al Pantheon
40. Santa Chiara
41. Trastevere

Map C – see pages 156-157

5. Richmond

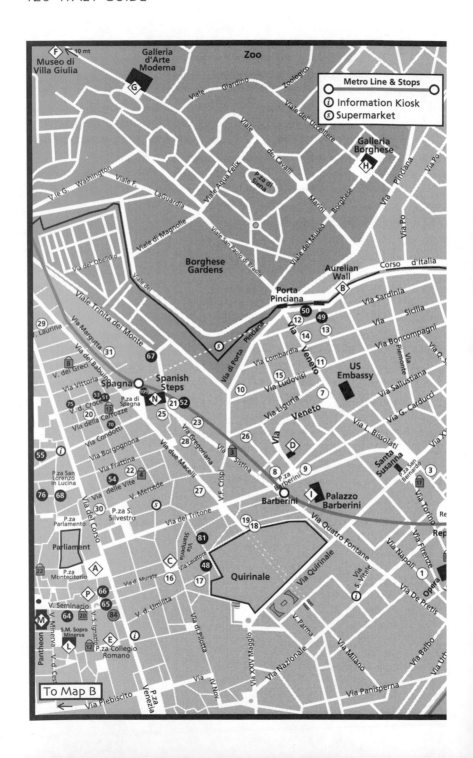

Roma
Map A

0   100   200

Meters

Sights ◇
A. Column of Marcus Aurelius
B. Aurelian Wall
C. Trevi Fountain
D. Church of Bones
E. Museo Doria Pamphili
F. Museo di Villa Giulia
G. Galleria d'Arte Moderna
H. Galleria Boghese
I. Palazzo Barberini
J. Baths of Diocletian
K. SM Maggiore
L. SM Sopra Minerva
M. Pantheon
N. Spanish Steps
O. Borghese Gardens
P. Temple of Hadrian

Via Cavlari
Via Collina
Via Plave
Via Flavia
Settembre
Via Cernaia
Via Montebello
Via Gaeta
Via Volturno
Castro Pretorio
Via Palestro
Via Steffidarni
P.za Indipendenza
J
Baths of Diocletian
(Nat'l Museum)
Servian Wall
Via Vicenza
Via Marghera
P.za d. pubblica
Piazza Cinquecento
pubblica
Via Viminale
Via D'Azeglio
Via Manin
V. Giobetti
Termini Station
Via Vicenza
V. Farini
Via Cavour
S. Maria Maggiore
86
K
S
Via C. Alberto
Via Napoleone
Via Giovanni
Via Prin. ne Ame
Via F. Turati
To Map C

Hotels ○
1. Brittania
2. Columbia
3. Grand Hotel
4. Mecentate Palace
6. Venezia
7. Ambasciatori Palace
8. Barocco
9. Bernini Bristol
10. Eden
11. Excelsior
12. Flora
13. Golden
14. Merano
15. Savoy
16. Fontana
17. Trevi
18. Julia
19. De Petris
20. Carriage
21. Hassler
22. Homs
23. Internazionale
24. Manfredi
25. Scalinata di Spagna
26. Modigliani
27. Erdarelli
28. Gregoriana
29. Margutta
30. Parlamento

Eateries ●
48. Al Piccolo Arancio
49. Giovanni
50. Girarrosto Toscano
51. Re degli Amici
52. Hassler
53. Otello alla Concordia
54. Le Grotte
55. Arancio d'Oro
64. La Sacrestia
65. Da Sabatino (do not go here)
66. La Caffetteria
67. Al Cafe du Jardin
68. Teichner
69. Babbington's
70. Cafe Greco
72. Bar Herbier Nature
75. Enotecantica
76. Vini e Buffet
81. San Crispino

Nightlife ●
84. Trinity College
86. Fiddler's Elbow

Shopping 🛍
3. Flea Market
4. Anglo-American Bookstore
6. Economy Book Center
8. The Lion Bookshop
12. Moriando & Gariglio
13. Puyricard
17. Terrecotte Persiane
20. Chimera
22. Il Papiro

pillow. The service is supremely courteous and professional. Situated near a Metro stop for easy access to all parts of the city.

2. COLUMBIA, *Via del Viminale 15, Tel. 06/474-4289, Fax 06/474-0209. Email: info@hotelcolumbia.com. Web: www.hotelcolumbia.com. 45 rooms. Single E190; Double E200. (Map A) ****

Owned by the ever accommodating Patrizia Diletti, who is also the proprietor of the excellent hotel Venezia. This hotel has all of the positive features of the Venezia, plus a small roof garden. What makes this hotel and the Venezia stand out is the attentive and friendly service, as well as the clean and comfortable rooms. The lobby here is nothing to write home about, but the rooms have all gone through a year and half renovation making the Columbia is a wonderful place to stay. Located by the Opera and the Via Nazionale, you are also close to the train station, and have easy access to the Metro and buses to get you anywhere you want to be when in Rome. An excellent choice for a stay in Rome.

3. ST. REGIS GRAND HOTEL, *Via Vittorio Emanuele Orlando, Tel. 06/47091, Fax 06/474-7307. Web: www.starwood.com. 150 rooms. Single E195-310; Double E275-450; Suites E950. Extra bed costs E75. Breakfast E20. (Map A) ******

Located between the Piazza della Repubblica and Piazza San Bernardo, this top-class luxury hotel has everything you'd ever need, and the prices to match. There is a hairdresser service, beauty salons, and saunas. The rooms and suites are palatial, some with 16 to 17 foot ceilings. You'll feel like royalty when they serve you afternoon tea downstairs at 5:00pm. If tea is not your style, there's a very relaxing but expensive American-style bar. A wonderful place to stay if you are part of the jet-setting world elite.

Selected as one of my *Best Places to Stay* – see Chapter 12.

My Favorite Hotels in Rome

These are my ten favorites hotels in the Eternal City, from least to most expensive. See each listing for full info:

14. MERANO**
30. PARLAMENTO**
31. LOCARNO***
5. RICHMOND***
25. SCALINATA DI SPAGNA***
6. VENEZIA***
8. BAROCCO****
4. MECENATE PALACE****
10. EDEN*****
21. HASSLER*****

4. MECENATE PALACE, *Via Carlo Alberto 3, Tel. 06/4470-2024, Fax 06/446-1354. Email: info@mecenatepalace.com. Web: www.mecenatepalace.com. All credit cards accepted. 62 rooms. Single E260-320; Double E370. Breakfast included. (Map A) *****

Attentive service, elegant accommodations, first class dining, and a spectacular view of Rome all add up to a wonderful stay. This hotel is a study in cozy elegance and is new, having only opened in 1995. Conveniently located near the train station, it boasts its own roof garden with a wonderful view of St. Peter's in the distance and Piazza Santa Maria Maggiore nearby. Fast becoming famous for its exceptional service and beautifully appointed, welcoming rooms, the Mecentate is one of Rome's most sophisticated hotels. They also have a great restaurant: Terrazza dei Papi.

5. RICHMOND, *Largo Corrado Ricci 36, Tel. 06/6994-1256, Fax 06/6994-4145. Email: romint@flashnet.it. Web: www.hotelrichmondroma.com. 13 rooms. Single E130-170; Double E200. Breakfast included. (Map C) ****

This colorful little hotel is simply fantastic. The rooms are large and incredibly accommodating, and all expected three star amenities are included. The main feature is the terrace, which has a stupendous view over the Forum, Victor Emanuel Monument and Colosseum and is the ideal place to relax in the evenings. Somewhat distant from the main tourist area of the Pantheon, Navona and the Spanish Steps, but this helps to make your stay tranquil. I recommend this hotel highly for your stay in Rome.

6. VENEZIA, *Via Varese 18, Tel. 06/445-7101, Fax 06/495-7687. Email: info@hotelvenezia.com. Web: www.hotelvenezia.com. Credit cards accepted. 61 rooms. Single E180-190; Double E200. Generous buffet breakfast included. (Map A) ****

This is definitely the best hotel near the Stazione Termini. For a three star the prices are quite good and the service is excellent. If you are traveling alone ask for one of the single rooms on the fifth floor so you can relax and enjoy the wonderful Roman evenings on the individual balconies. The hotel caters to travelers, business customers, and visiting academics since the University is just around the corner. You'll love the 16th century altar that serves as buffet table for breakfast and bar at night; as well as the huge 16th century table in the conference room. The ever charming and hospitable owner and operator, Patrizia Diletti, will bend over backwards to make your stay pleasant This is a wonderful hotel with some of the most attentive, friendly and multi-lingual service I have encountered in the Eternal City.

Via Veneto Area

7. AMBASCIATORI PALACE, *Via Vittorio Veneto 62, Tel. 06/47-493, Fax 06/474-3601. Email: reservationgrp@ambasciatoripalace.com. Web: www.hotelambasciatori.com. 140 rooms and 8 suites. All credit cards* accepted. *Single E300-360; Double E360-500; Suite E570-830. Buffet break-fast included. (Map A)* *****

This hotel deserves its luxury rating since it has impeccable service, palatial rooms, and a top class restaurant La Terrazza to complement its fine ambiance. Your every need can be taken care of here: massage, evening companion, theater reservations, travel arrangements, etc. If you're looking for deluxe treatment at a deluxe price, look no further. A simply marvelous hotel on one of Rome's most fashionable streets.

8. BAROCCO, *Piazza Barberini 9 (entrance on Via della Purificazione 4), Tel. 06/487-2001/2/3, 487-2005, Fax 06/485-994. Email: hotelbarocco@holelbarocco.it. Web: www.hotelbarocco.com. 37 rooms. Single E170-220; Double E250-330. Breakfast included. All credit cards accepted. (Map A)* ****

If you're looking for an intimate and elegant four-star experience and don't want to get lost in the crowd at a larger hotel, this is the place for you. Each room is different from the other, some with two levels, others with small terraces; and all come with an electronic safe, TV, A/C and everything else befitting a four star. The bathrooms come with hair dryer and courtesy toiletry kit. In the summer, breakfast is served on the roof terrace. I love this hotel.

Selected as one of my *Best Places to Stay* – see Chapter 12.

9. BERNINI BRISTOL, *Piazza Barberini 23, Tel. 06/488-3051, Fax 06/482-4266. Web: www.berninibristol.com. 124 rooms. Single E300-360; Double E460; Suite E680-1,400. American breakfast buffet E26. (Map A)* *****

The hotel is located in the Piazza Barberini at the foot of the Via Veneto facing Bernini's Triton Fountain. Established in 1870, this hotel still retains the charm and atmosphere of that era. The entrance salon is beautifully appointed with antique furniture and lamps as well as a crystal chandelier. All rooms are elegantly furnished (each in its own style), well lit, and quite large. The bathrooms are large and come with a phone and courtesy toiletry kit. They offer every possible convenience and comfort here and are definitely waiting on that fifth star. The suites on the top floor all have wonderful terraces with splendid views. The Olimpo restaurant where you are served an abundant breakfast has a panoramic view over the rooftops of Rome. Perfectly located for shopping and sightseeing. A good choice if you have the means.

10. EDEN, *Via Ludovisi, 49, Tel. 06/474-3551, Fax 06/482-1584. Email: reservations@hotel-eden.it. Web: www.hotel-eden.it. 100 rooms. Single E440-460; Double E650-750, Suites E1,800-3,400. Continental breakfast is E14 extra, buffet breakfast is E20. (Map A)* *****

The best just got more expensive, but if you can afford it, this place is well worth it. Located in the exclusive Ludovisi section, the Eden is a long-established top-ranked, exclusive hotel. One of the *Leading Hotels of The World*, it has a sophisticated level of service and virtually unmatched ameni-ties. Located just off the Via Veneto here you are in the center of it all, but it is supremely quiet too. The terrace restaurant has a spectacular view of the city and the Villa Borghese. Also available is a complete gym with everything from cardiovascular equipment to free weights. The Eden is a paradise in Rome. Selected as one of my *Best Places to Stay* – see Chapter 12.

11. WESTIN EXCELSIOR, *Via Vittorio Veneto 125, Tel. 06/47081, Fax 06/482-6205. Web: www.starwood.com. 244 doubles, 38 singles, and 45 suites. Double E350-730, Suite E1,600-6,500. An extra bed costs E50. Continental breakfast is E15 extra and American breakfast is E25. (Map A)* *****

Named to Condé Nast Traveler's 2002 Gold List, this hotel is a monument to turn-of-the-century style. Located on the east side of the Via Veneto right across the street from the American Embassy. All rooms and common areas are done up with ornate moldings and elegant decorations. A truly palatial experience. They have a world-renowned restaurant, La Cuppola, as well as a piano bar at night. A wonderfully elite hotel, now owned by the Westin chain. Though thoroughly modernized, it retains superb ambiance and charm.

12. GRAND HOTEL FLORA, *Via Vittorio Veneto 191, Tel. 06/489-929, Fax 06/482-0359. Web: www.marriotthotels.com. 21 suites and 155 rooms. All credit cards accepted. Single E200-280; Double E350-450. Breakfast included. (Map A)* ****

Located immediately at the top of the Via Veneto by the old Roman walls, this old-fashioned hotel has first class traditional service. The public rooms are elaborately decorated with antiques, oriental rugs, and soothingly light color schemes reminiscent of the turn of the century. The rooms are immense and some have wonderful views over the walls into the lush greenery of Villa Borghese. The bathrooms have been recently renovated and come with all modern creature comforts. This hotel offers everything you could want: location, service, and great rooms. Now owned by Marriott.

13. RESIDENCE GOLDEN, *Via Marche 84, Tel. 06/482-1659, Web: www.venere.com/it/roma/golden. 12 of the 13 rooms have private baths. All credit cards accepted. Single E60-95; Double E90-150. (Map A)* **

An upscale pensione with air-conditioning, TV, phone, and mini-bar in every room. And the prices in the high season reflect their high level two-star accommodations. The hotel is located on the first floor of an old house, on a quiet street off of the Via Veneto. All the amenities of a three star, in a great location at the prices of an upscale two star. Clean, comfortable and well situated.

14. MERANO, *Via Vittorio Veneto 155, Tel. 06/482-1796, Fax 06/482-1810. Web: www.guestinitaly.com/hotels/rome/r002.htm. All credit cards accepted. 30 rooms 28 with bath. Single without bath E50-60; Single E60-70; Double without bath E70-90; Double E90-120. (Map A)* **

Ideally located on the Via Veneto at rock bottom prices. The only reason the prices are so low is that you have to ride an elevator up to the third floor of a building to get to the hotel. The entranceway is dark but the rooms are warm and cozy. Everything is spic and span in the bathrooms, and you don't have to worry about remembering to buy your drinks for the evening, since they sell beer, soda, and water. If you want to enjoy Rome inexpensively, this is one of the best places from which to do it.

15. SAVOY, *Via Ludovisi 15, Tel. 06/421-551, Fax 06/474-68122. Web: www.savoy.it. 135 rooms. All credit cards accepted. Single E200-320; Double E250-400; Suite E450-650. Breakfast extra. (Map A)* ****

Located in the upscale Ludovisi section west of Via Veneto, this is a comfortable and well run hotel that has recently jacked up their prices astronomically. They have an excellent restaurant, offering both a la carte and a superb buffet and a lively but still relaxing bar downstairs. The service is impeccable as it should be and the decor is elaborately expensive. The rooms, even the ones that face the Via Veneto are quiet and comfortable. The location is perfect, especially if you're a spy since the hotel is almost directly across the street from the American Embassy.

All in the Family

A husband and wife team of hoteliers, Patrizia Diletti and Andrea Gnecco own four great 3-star hotels in Rome: **Internazionale**, **Richmond**, **Venezia** and **Columbia**. The service in each is ultra professional and the rooms comfortable and accommodating. I recommend all highly. If you contact any of these, and they are full, try one of the other three and you will not be disappointed. In conjunction, the mother of Patrizia, Rosmarie Truninger Diletti, has started her own bed and breakfast, the **Villa Delros**, *Tel/Fax 06/33678402 or 06/33679837, Email: info@hotelvenezia.com*). Located some distance outside of Rome, if you do not want to face the chaos of the Eternal City, this is an option for you to try.

Trevi Fountain Area

16. FONTANA, *Piazza di Trevi 96, Tel. 06/678-6113, 06/679-1056. Web: www.hotelfontana-trevi.com. 24 rooms. Single E190-225; Double E270. A/ C costs E15 extra. All credit cards accepted. Breakfast included. (Map A)* ***

The location of this hotel is great, but is not secluded or tranquil because it is in the same square as one of Rome's most famous monuments, the Trevi Fountain. You can hear the cascading waters and ever-present crowds far into the night. If you're a heavy sleeper this hotel's location is perfect, but if not try elsewhere. The rooms are sparse but comfortable and since this is a converted monastery, some rooms have been made by joining two monk's cells together.

There is also a pleasant roof garden from which you can sip a drink and gaze over the rooftops of Rome.

17. TREVI, *Vicolo del Babuccio 20/21, Tel. 06/6994-1406, Fax 06/6994-1407. Web: www.gruppotrevi.it. 29 rooms. Single E190-225; Double E270. All credit cards accepted. Breakfast included. (Map A)* ***

Located on a quiet side street near the Trevi Fountain, this ideal little three-star is in a wonderful location. Each room comes with every conceivable modern convenience. They have a roof garden, which is a great place to relax in the evenings and is where the buffet breakfast is served in good weather. Though only a three-star, the prices here are rather dear, but the location and accommodations warrant them. Very professional service. An elite, upscale hotel.

18. JULIA, *Via Rasella 29, Tel. 06/488-1637, Fax 06/481-7044. Email: info@hoteljulia.it. Web: www.hoteljulia.it. 33 rooms. Single E50-120; Double E90-170. All credit cards accepted. Breakfast included. (Map A)* ***

In the heart of Rome, on a small, tranquil side street near the Trevi Fountain, the Julia is a hotel of great comfort and style. And it is relatively inexpensive. It's main selling point is being in an ideal location. The rooms are clean and comfortable, and come with every three star comfort. A good choice in Rome.

19. DE PETRIS, *Via Rasella 142, Tel. 06/481-9626. Fax 06/482-0733. Email: hoteldepe@tiscalinet.it. Web: www.hoteldepetris.com. 53 rooms. Single E130-180; Double E130-230. All credit cards accepted. Breakfast E15. (Map A)* ***

Just across the street from the Julia, this is also in an ideal and tranquil location. Very accommodating and comfortable with all necessary three star amenities. Each room is different from the other in terms of furnishings and layout. The bathrooms are well-appointed. The breakfast is extensive and is served in a quaint room. A good choice in the heart of Rome.

Piazza di Spagna Area

20. CARRIAGE, *Via delle Carrozze 36, Tel. 06/600-8279, Fax 06/678-8279. Email: hotelcarriage@alfanet.it. Web: www.hotelcarriage.net. All credit cards accepted. 30 rooms. Single E130-190; Double E170-230; Suite E360. Breakfast included. (Map A)* ***

Located near the Piazza di Spagna on a pedestrian side street, this elegant little hotel is luxuriously furnished with a variety of antiques and has a courteous and professional staff. They have a lovely roof garden terrace from which you can have your breakfast or an evening drink. The rooms are comfortable and come with every four star convenience. The bathrooms are immaculately clean and have hair dryers and courtesy toiletry kit. A character-filled, comfortable and convenient place to stay.

21. HASSLER ROMA, *Piazza Trinita Dei Monti 6, Tel. 06/699-340, Fax 06/678-2651. Email: info@hotelhasslerroma.com. Web: www.hotelhasslerroma.com. All credit cards accepted. 80 rooms. Single E430-460; Double E520-790. Suites E1,800-3,200. Continental breakfast E23 extra. Buffet breakfast E35 extra. (Map A)* *****

In many travelers' opinions this is the best hotel in Rome. Oil sheiks, movie stars, travel publishers, nouveau riche, and landed gentry all have made the Hassler their home away from home for over a century. Located at the top of the Spanish Steps, with its own garage, a relaxing courtyard restaurant in the summer, and an excellent (but expensive) roof garden restaurant with a great view of the city. Remember to request one of the nicer rooms facing the church belfry and the Spanish Steps because the view is stupendous. One of the best, most famous, and ideally located hotels in Rome. If you have the means, I recommend it highly.

Selected as one of my *Best Places to Stay* – see Chapter 12.

22. HOMS, *Via Delle Vite 71, Tel. 0/679-2976, Fax 06/678-0482. Web: www.hotelhoms.it. All credit cards accepted. 50 rooms. Single E150; Double E230. Breakfast included. (Map A)* ***

This hotel is in between the Trevi Fountain and the Spanish Steps, and has a quaint, pleasant ambiance and decor. The rooms are all comfortably appointed and come with every three star amenity. Since Via Delle Vite is not well traveled here you will be able escape Rome's traffic noise. There is also a wonderful terrace with great views of the rooftops of Rome. Nothing spectacular except good prices.

23. INTERNAZIONALE, *Via Sistina 79, Tel. 06/6994-1823, Fax 06/678-4764. Email: info@hotelinternazionale.com. Web: hotelinternazionale.com. All credit cards accepted. 42 rooms. Single E150-180; Double E220-240; Extra bed E55. Buffet breakfast included. (Map A)* ***

Written up in both *Travel & Leisure* and *Forbes,* this little Roman hideaway offers old-world charm, modern comfort and super rates for its ideal location. Located just a stone's throw away from the top of the Spanish Steps, the building was erected in first century BCE, and the lobby contains artifacts from that period, which have been unearthed within the walls of the hotel during recent renovations. The rooms are accommodating and comfortable and the staff professional and very attentive. The rooms are all different from one another with a wide variety of unique decorations and furnishings, supplied by Andrea Gnecco, owner and architect. This family-owned gem is a superb hotel in an ideal location, one of my favorite choices when in Rome. But remember to request a room on a higher floor, or on the inside to avoid traffic noise at night.

24. MANFREDI, *Via Margutta 61, Tel. 06/320-7676, Fax 06/320-7736. Web: www.romeby.com/manfredi. Credit cards accepted. 18 rooms. Single*

E160-210; Double E180-300. American style breakfast buffet included. (Map A) ***

This cozy, accommodating hotel is located near the Spanish Steps and has all the charm, service, and amenities of a three star. They even have VCRs in some rooms as well as movies to rent at the front desk for your convenience. The street they're located on is cute, extremely quiet, and home to some of Rome's best antique stores and art galleries. If you only stay here for the American style buffet breakfast of ham, eggs, cheese, fruit etc., it is worth it. A good place to stay in a great location.

25. SCALINATA DI SPAGNA, *Piazza Trinita Dei Monte 17, Tel. 06/679-3006 and 06/679-0896, Fax 06/684-0598. Meail: info@hotelscalinata.com. Web: www.hotelscalinata.com. All credit cards accepted. 16 rooms all with baths. Single E150-310; Double E160-360. Breakfast included. (Map A)* ***

Just across the piazza from the Hassler at the top of the Spanish Steps, this used to be a moderately priced, quaint little pensione, but once it received its three star rating the prices here have skyrocketed. Nothing much else has changed, but it is still well worth the price because of the view from their large roof terrace, which is open in the summer months for breakfast. The rooms are basic, but accommodating and comfortable in three star style. This place has plenty of character and ambiance and you will simply adore the roof terrace. Highly recommended.

26. MODIGLIANI, *Via della Purificazione 42, Tel. 06/4281-5226, Email: info@hotelmodigliani.com, Web: www.hotelmodigliani.com. 28 rooms. Single E120-160; Double E160-200. All credit cards accepted. (Map A)* ***

Named after Amadeo Modigliani, an Italian painter and sculptor from the turn of the 20th century, who achieved some elevated renown. This hotel is as artistic and welcoming as many of Modigliani's works. The owners, Giulia and Marco di Tillo offer you every conceivable comfort in their lovely boutique hotel. If you need more space, they also have apartment rentals and larger rooms that can be shared with up to four people. An excellent choice while in Rome. A veritable artist's hotel. Also, The di Tillo's have published an excellent book that guides you through some wonderful walks around Rome.

27. ERDARELLI, *Via Due Macelli 28, Tel. 06/679-1265, Fax 06/679-0705. Web: www.hotelerdarelli.com. 28 rooms. All credit cards accepted. Single E100; Double E150. (Map A)* **

Just down from the Piazza di Spagna in a building that looks like it has seen better days on the outside but which is clean and accommodating on the inside. The singles are minuscule and the doubles functional but the real selling point for this budget two-star is its ideal location. You can get A/C for an extra E10 and in August this is a necessity. Nothing grand but clean and comfortable at a good price for Rome.

28. GREGORIANA, *Via Gregoriana 18, Tel. 06/679-4269. Fax 06/678-4258. 20 rooms. Single E150; Double E230. No credit cards accepted. (Map A)* *******

Situated in a building that used to be a convent, on a small side street just off the top of the Spanish Steps, the Gregoriana is a small hotel that is tranquil and comfortable with all three star amenities. The rooms are decorated in Deco style and come with A/C and TV and a few have a small terrace. The bathrooms are small but clean and functional. Breakfast is served in the room except in warm weather when they open their little roof terrace. An intimate and comfortable place to stay while in Rome. But they do not accept credit cards so be prepared to have cash available.

29. MARGUTTA, *Via Laurina 34, Tel. 06/322-3674, Fax 06/320-0395. All credit cards accepted. 24 rooms. Single E70-95; Double E80-120. Breakfast included. (Map A&B)* ******

This place a rare gem of price/quality considerations. The hotel has been totally renovated and is as modern as can be. There's a relaxing lounge area and the rooms are spacious and airy. Rooms 50 and 52 share a terrace and are very nice, and #59 is another great place to stay too. The bathrooms are micro, especially those with showers. The location is fantastic, right between the Piazza del Popolo and the Spanish Steps. But there's no A/C, a problem in the summer.

30. PARLAMENTO, *Via delle Convertite 5, Tel. 06/6992-1000, Fax 06/679-2082. Email: hotelparlamento@libero.it. Web: www.hotelparlamento.it. All credit cards accepted. 22 rooms, 19 with bath. Single without bath E65. Single E70-120. Double E90-160. Breakfast included. (Map A)* ******

A homey atmosphere with simply furnished rooms. There is small roof terrace, where in the summer you are served your breakfast. In a completely renovated building, the common rooms are decorated with panoramic Roman scenes. The rooms are all decorated differently, some have antique style furniture, and all have TVs and sound-proof windows. The bathrooms are new and immaculate; some even have a phone. Most of the staff speaks English and are more than willing to help you find what you're looking for. There is a small elevator available, though you will still need to carry your bags up a few flights of stairs to get to it. A great price/quality option. One of the best two stars in Rome.

31. LOCARNO, *Via della Penna 22, Tel. 06/361-0841, Fax 06/321-5249. Email: info@hotellocarno.com. Web: www.hotellocarno.com. All credit cards accepted. 38 rooms. Single E130; Double E200-210; Suite E310-510. Breakfast included. (Map B)* *******

I simply adore this hotel. Situated between the Piazza del Popolo and the Tiber River, in a nice neighborhood of stores and galleries, this hotel is wonderfully accommodating and amazingly comfortable. It has a very relaxing American-style bar, spacious common areas, a small side-garden patio, and a roof terrace where breakfast is served in good weather. The rooms are tastefully decorated with all possible amenities, and the service is superb and utterly professional. Definitely one of the best three stars Rome has to offer.

32. VALADIER, *Via della Fontanella 15, Tel. 06/361-0592, 361-0559, 361-2344, Fax 06/320-1558. Email: info@hotelvaladier.com. Web: www.hotelvaladier.com. 48 rooms. Single E110-270; Double E130-360. Suite E210-780. All credit cards accepted. (Map B)* ****

The first word that comes to mind concerning this place is opulent. There is black marble everywhere and the effect is doubled by the placement of the many mirrors and shining brass fixtures. The wood paneling here sparkles, it's so well shined. The rooms are no less ostentatious with lights, mirrors – some on the ceilings for you exotically amorous types – and the ever-present marble. The bathrooms are a little small but accommodating and have every amenity. If you want to feel like an oil sheik who has money to burn, spend your stay in Rome here. Ideally located between the Piazza del Popolo and the Spanish Steps, you are in walking distance to many sights and shops.

Centro Storico – Piazza Navona, Pantheon, Campo dei Fiori Area

33. CAMPO DEI FIORI, *Via del Biscione 6, Tel. 06/687-4886, Fax 06/687-6003. All credit cards accepted. Four singles with shower each E120; Nine doubles with shower each E165, 14 doubles without shower each E140. Breakfast E10. (Map B)* **

Another hotel with a great roof terrace in Rome. Located on six floors in a sliver of a building without an elevator. This can make this hotel an exercise routine in and of itself. Also there's no air conditioning, which could be a problem in August. Only a few blocks away from the Trastevere area and its nightlife, here you are also in the perfect location to visit the best outdoor market in the city, the Campo dei Fiori. Breakfast is served in a basement dining area, but you are free to bring it to the roof with you. Ask for one of the inside rooms since the windows do not have double paned glass to cut the noise from the street.

34. GENIO, *Via Zanardelli 28, Tel 06/683-2191, 06/683-3781, Fax 06/6830-7246. Email: genio@leonardihotels.com. Web: www.leonardihotels.com. Credit cards accepted. 60 rooms. Single E170-190; Double E230-250 An extra bed costs E35. Breakfast included. (Map B)* ****

Located near the Piazza Navona, here you get a great location in the Old City of Rome. The rooms are well-appointed with tasteful paintings, Persian rugs, and cream colored wall coverings. The lobby/common areas seem a little rough around the edges but the roof garden terrace has a spectacular view. An ideal place to be served your breakfast in the morning. Nothing spectacular, but if you choose the Genio, you have chosen well.

35. PORTOGHESI, *Via dei Portoghesi 1, Tel. 06/686-4231, Fax 06/687-6976. Email: info@hotelportoghesiroma.com. Web: www.hotelportoghesiroma.com/.*

*Credit cards accepted. 27 rooms. Single E150-175; Double E195. Suite E210-310. Breakfast included. (Map B) ****

Nestled beside the church of Sant'Antonio, on a narrow medieval street, this small hotel's central location is ideal. It may be not be near a Metro line but the restaurants, shops, food stores, small streets, and sights all around it make this place ideally suited for a wonderful vacation in Rome. There are a smattering of antiques all over the hotel to give the place a feeling of old world charm that matches its unique location. The rooms are small but comfortable and there is a relaxing roof garden to enjoy. A great bed and breakfast type place to stay. Highly recommended.

36. ARENULA, *Via Santa Maria de' Calderari, 47, Tel. 06/687-9454, Fax 06/689-6188. Email: info@hotelarenula.com. Web: www.hotelarenula.com. 50 rooms. Single E100; Double E130. All credit cards accepted. Breakfast included. (Map B) ***

On the inside of an old building from the last century, in the Jewish Ghetto and situated on a small street, this is a great two star. Here you have everything that a modern hotel would have with amazing charm and ambiance. They have A/C and TV in the rooms and have recently given each room their own bath. The hotel is bucking for three star status but right now they are a great price/quality place to stay while in Rome.

37. DEL SOLE, *Via del Biscione 76, Tel. 06/6880-6873 or 687-9446, Fax 06/689-3787. Email: info@solealbiscione.it. Web: www.solealbiscione.it. 58 rooms only 24 with bath. Single without E70; Single E90. Double without E100; Double E110-150. No breakfast. No credit cards accepted. (Map B) ***

A wonderful two star in a great location with two relaxing roof garden areas. Supposedly the oldest hotel in Rome, it seems its age as you enter, but the rooms are clean and comfortable. Ten rooms have TV and only 24 with private bath. A good place to stay for those on a budget, and the staff is very accommodating. Keep a look out for Cleopatra, the resident cat.

38. MARCUS, *Via del Clementino 94, Tel. 06/6830-0320, Fax 06/6830-0312. Web: www.hotelmarcus.com. 18 rooms. Single E100; Double E150. All credit cards accepted. (Map B) ***

This small two-star is in an ideal location deep in the heart of the *centro storico* by the Pantheon. The atmosphere here is pleasant and accommodating and filled with the character of a 17th century building. The entryway thatleads to the second floor lobby is beautiful. The rooms are very spacious and come with A/C and double windows to keep out noise. The bathrooms are minuscule and only have showers. If they had a lobby on the ground floor, and added a few more amenities, this would be a three-star; but for now it is a wonderful two-star.

39. SOLE AL PANTHEON, *Piazza dell Rotunda 63, Tel. 06/788-0441, Fax 06/6994-0689. Email: info@hotelsolealpantheon.com. Web: www.hotelsolealpantheon.com.*

All credit cards accepted. 62 rooms. Single E210; Double E260; Apartment E320. Breakfast E15. (Map B) ****

This is a place that used to be a small, well-appointed *pensione* and is now a fantastic four-star hotel. The clean white walls and delicate furnishings attest to its status as one of Rome's best small hotels. Most of the furniture is of the neo-classic mold leaning towards modern. Some of the rooms have a view over the *Piazza della Rotunda* and the Pantheon, which is a beautiful people watching scene, and come with soundproof windows so it's relatively quiet at night. The building has been around since 1513 so you'll be staying in history while here. The service is exquisite and everything conforms to the highest standards, making this a well-located fine little four-star hotel. For those with the means, a great place to stay.

40. SANTA CHIARA, *Via Santa Chiara 21, 00186 Roma. Tel. 06/687-2979, Fax 06/687-3144. Email: stchiara@tin.it. Web: www.albergosantachiara.com. All credit cards accepted. 96 rooms. Single E120-210; Double E180-240; Suite E370-420. Breakfast included. (Map B)* ***

A three star that should be a four star, and their prices reflect that. This is a supremely elegant hotel in the heart of Rome near the Pantheon. Once you enter the lobby you feel as if you've been whisked away to a palace. Everything is marble, buffed to a high polish, and the ceilings reach to the sky. The rooms are all tastefully decorated and the ones on the top floors get great breezes, if you don't want to use your air conditioning, and some have small balconies. There is also a tranquil inside terrace area, the service is impeccable and the breakfast buffet huge. This place is great.

Trastevere

41. TRASTEVERE, *Via Luciano Manara 24/25, Tel. 06/58-14-713, Fax 06/58-81-016. Email: info@hoteltrastevere.com. Web: www.hoteltrastevere.com. 30 rooms. All credit cards accepted. Single E100; Double E140. (Map B)* **

Located in the heart of Trastevere, one of the city's oldest and most distinctive neighborhoods, here you will be surrounded by locals and far from the thundering herd of tourists. The Roma Trastevere train station is only 700 meters away, which means you should get the local train from the airport and not the one that goes directly to Termini. The rooms are all spacious and accommodating, though simply furnished. If you want to stay in local atmosphere of Trastevere, this is the best option.

Bed & Breakfasts in Rome

The city of Rome has formalized - into the Bed & Breakfast Association of Rome - an already existing cadre of top notch apartments and villas which have been housing travelers for years. To find out more information about these places, visit the association's website at *www.bbitalia.com (Email: info@bbitalia.com, Tel/Fax 06/687-7348).*

Stay in a Convent – For Less
Some of the best and least known places to stay, which can reduce the cost of a stay in Rome, are convents. While you may think that convents would only take women pilgrims as guests, most also welcome single men, married couples, and families with children. Couples 'traveling in sin' are usually not welcome, but some well placed pieces of jewelry can usually fool the best nun. All these convents are immaculate (no pun intended) since the nuns take pride in their work.

• **Suore Teatine**, Salita Monte del Gallo 25, 00165 Roma. *Tel. 06/637-4084 or 06/637-4653, Fax 06/3937-9050.* E35 per person with full board. E30 with half board. E25 with only breakfast. Not all rooms have private bath. Curfew is 11:00pm.

• **Franciscan Sisters of the Atonement**, Via Monte del Gallo 105, 00165 Roma. *Tel. 06/630-782, Fax 06/638-6149.*E35 per person with full board. E30 with half board. E25 with only breakfast. All rooms have private bath. Curfew is 11:00pm. English spoken. Parking available. Great spacious pine-shaded garden.

• **Suore Dorotee**, Via del Gianicolo 4a, 00165 Roma. *Tel. 06/6880-3349, Fax 06/6880-3311.* E40 full board. E35 half board. Some rooms have private baths. Curfew is 11:00pm. Recommended by the Vatican Tourist Information Bureau.

• **Pensione Suore Francescane**, Via Nicolo V 35, 00165 Roma. *Tel. 06/3936-6531.* E27 per person with breakfast. No private baths. No curfew. Small but lovely roof garden with views of St. Peter's. English spoken. Great location.

• **Domus Aurelia-Suore Orsoline**, Via Aurelia 218, 00165 Roma. *Tel. 06/636-784, Fax 06/3937-6480.* E50 for a double. E37 for a single. E60 for room with three beds. All rooms with private bath. Breakfast extra. 11:30pm curfew.

• **Suore Pallotini**, Viale della Mura Aurelie 7b, 00165 Roma. *Tel. 06/635-697, Fax 06/635-699.* E27 for single with breakfast. E50 for double without private bath. E65 for double with private bath. 10:00pm curfew for first night. Any night after that they give you a key.

• **Fraterna Domus**, Via di Monte Brianzo 62, 00186 Roma. *Tel. 06/6880-2727, Fax 06/683-2691.* E35 per person with full board. E30 with half board. E27 with breakfast only. Single rooms add E9 extra. All rooms with private bath. Curfew is 11:00pm.

• **Le Suore Di Lourdes**, Via Sistina 113, 00187 Roma. *Tel. 06/474-5324, Fax 06/488-1144.* E25 per person without bath. E27 per person with bath and breakfast. Curfew is 10:30pm.

Where To Eat

Before I guide you to the wonderful restaurants Rome has awaiting you, below I've prepared an augmented, Rome-specific version of Chapter 11, *Food & Wine*. The list of restaurants by map is on the next page.

Roman Cuisine

"Italian Food" is definitely a misnomer, because each region of Italy has its special dishes, and in most cases so do each province and locality. As a rule, Roman cooking is not elegantly refined and is considered a rustic cuisine. The food is basic, unpretentious , and enjoyable. Gone are the days of the Roman Empire's lavish banquets.

Authentic Roman dishes today are often based on simple ingredients, such as tomatoes, garlic, hot pepper, and parmesan cheese, and the results are magnificent. If you are bold try some of the favorite dishes, like brains, tripe, oxtail, and pig's snout. If not treat yourself to the omnipresent pasta and grilled meats.

Besides these staples, Romans enjoy a harvest of seafood from the shores just 15 miles from their city; and as a result prepare excellent grilled seafood dishes, the famous *spaghetti alla vongole verace* (spicy clam sauce), as well as other pastas brimming with many fruits from the sea. The Roman countryside provides exquisite fresh greens and vegetables, which arrive daily at the city's open air markets. Also in never-ending supply are the local cheeses like *pecorino*, made from sheep's milk, and plump *mozzarella* balls, generally made from the milk of water buffaloes.

The Jewish ghetto has made a lasting impression on Roman cuisine. The most memorable dish to come from there is the *carciofo alla giudia*, a small artichoke flattened and fried. What I'm trying to say is that it is very difficult not to eat well in any one of Rome's 5,000-plus restaurants. But what I have supplied you with here are some of the best in and around your hotel choices.

In case you didn't know, lunch hour is usually from 12:30pm to 3:00pm, and dinner anywhere from 7:30pm to 10:00pm, but is usually served at 8:30pm. So enjoy your meal and remember to take your time. Meals are supposed to be savored, not rushed through.

Traditional Roman Fare

You don't have to eat all the traditional courses [**antipasto** (appetizer); then soup and/or pasta which is called **primo**; next a main course, **secondo** (usually meat or fish) with separately ordered side dishes of *contorni* (vegetables) or *insalata* (salad) which come either *verdi* (green) or *mista* (mixed); then **dolci** (dessert), which can be cheese, fruit, or *gelato* (ice-cream). After which you then order your coffee and/or after-dinner drink], but in some restaurants it is considered bad form not to. That may be the case, but most Italians accept the difference in our culture, even if they don't understand it.

So don't feel embarrassed if all you order is a pasta dish or an entrée with a salad or appetizer.

However, if you want to order the way the Italians do, expect to spend a lot of time over dinner. A long drawn out meal is the traditional way to spend an evening.

Antipasto – Appetizer
• **Bruschetta** – Garlic bread brushed with olive oil
• **Antipasto Misto** – Mixed appetizer plate. Differs from restaurant to restaurant
• **Pomodoro, Mozzarella ed olio** – Tomato and mozzarella slices covered in olive oil with a hint of basil

Primo Piatto – First Course
Pasta
• **Spaghetti alla carbonara** – Spaghetti tossed with bacon, garlic, peppers, grated cheese, and a raw beaten egg
• **Bucatini all'amatriciana** –Thin tubes of pasta with red pepper, bacon, and pecorino cheese
• **Penne all'arrabbiata** – Literally means angry pasta. It is short ribbed pasta tubes with a hot and spicy tomato base, garlic and parsley sauce (this is my favorite, but if your stomach can't handle spicy food, steer clear of this delicacy)
• **Fettucine al burro** – Fettucine with butter and parmesan
• **Spaghetti alla puttanesca** – Literally means whore's spaghetti! So named because the ingredients, peppers, tomato, black olives and garlic are so basic that prostitutes could quickly create a meal between tricks.

Zuppa – Soup
• **Stracciatella** – a light egg–drop soup
• **Pasta e ceci** – a filling pasta and chick pea soup
• **Zuppa di telline** – soup made from tiny clams

Secondo Piatto – Entrée
Carne – Meat
• **Abbacchio** – Milk-fed baby lamb. Can be grilled (*alla griglia*), sautéed in a sauce of rosemary, garlic, onions, tomatoes, and white wine (*alla cacciatore*), or roasted (*al forno*)
• **Saltimbocca alla Romana** – Veal fillets that are covered in sage and prosciutto and cooked in butter and white wine
• **Pollo alla Romana** – Chicken stewed with yellow and red bell peppers
• **Lombata di vitello** – Grilled veal chop

- **Porchetta** – Tender suckling pork roasted with herbs
- **Maile arrosto can patate** – Roasted pork with exquisite roast potatoes

Pesce – Fish
- **Sogliola alla griglia** – Thin sole lightly grilled
- **Ciriole** – Small tender eels dredged from the Tiber

Contorno – Vegetable
- **Carciofi alla giuda** – Jewish-style artichokes, pressed flat and fried. Usually served with an anchovy garlic sauce.
- **Patate arrosto** – Roasted potatoes that usually come with a grilled meats but can be ordered separately.
- **Insalata Mista** – Mixed salad. You have to prepare your own olive oil and vinegar dressing. American's thirst for countless types of salad dressings hasn't hit Italy yet.

Dolci
Desserts can be gelato, cake, pudding, fresh fruit, and in many cases is accompanied by an after dinner drink. One of the most popular is sambuca, a liquorice flavored, syrupy concoction. However, my favorite is Limoncello, which sometimes is made prohibition-style, by each restaurant in their own stills.

Buy Some Wine to Take Home!

The most complete and best located store to buy your duty free wine quota (three liters per person) is **Buccone**, Via di Ripetta 19-20, *Tel/Fax 06/361-2154*, near the Piazza del Popolo. The walls of these two storefronts are lined from floor to ceiling with bottles from every different region in Italy, as well as other countries. Extensive does not do this place justice. The prices here are comparable with duty free at the airport and you get a much better selection. The prices for Sambuca and Limoncello are better at the airport, but get your wine here.

Reviews Explained
The reviews below are arranged first according to establishment – first **ristorante/trattorie/pizzerie**, then **spuntini veloci** (Italian fast food), then **enoteche** (wine bars), and finally **gelateria** (ice cream shops) and **pasticcerie** (pastry shops). Within the first section the eating establishments are separated into specific areas in Rome. Each entry mentions a price that reflects dinner for two, if two people order two dishes apiece (i.e., a pasta and a meat for one

List of Restaurants by Map

Map A – see pages 120-121
47. Sora Lella
48. Al Piccolo Arancio
49. Giovanni
50. Girarrosto Toscano
51. Re degli Amici
52. Hassler
53. Otello alla Concordia
54. Le Grotte
55. Arancio d'Oro
64. La Sacrestia
65. Da Sabatino *(do not go here)*
66. La Caffetteria
67. Al Cafe du Jardin
68. Teichner
69. Babbington's Tea Rooms
70. Cafe Greco
72. Bar Herbier Nature
75. Enotecantica
76. Vini e Buffet
80. San Crispino

Map B – see pages 140-141
42. La Canonica
43. Camparone
44. Gino in Trastevere
45. Sabatini I
46. La Tana de Noantri
47. Sora Lella
55. Arancio d'Oro
56. Da Alfredo All'Angoletto
58. Dal Bolognese
59. Buca di Ripetta
60. La Carbonara
61. Hostaria Giulio
62. Orso "80"
63. Vecchia Roma
64. La Sacrestia
68. Teichner
71. Antica Caffe del'Isola
73. Anacleto Bleve
74. Buccone

76. Vini e Buffet
77. Cul de Sac
78. Vineria Reggio
79. Cul de Sac
81. Cremeria Monteforte
82. Tre Scalini

Map C – see pages 156-157
63. Vecchia Roma
77. Cavour 313

person and an antipasto and a fish dish for the other, etc.) exclusive of wine. Obviously, if you only choose to eat one dish per sitting, which we Americans are apt to do, the actual price for your meal will be significantly less than what is indicated in this guide.

RISTORANTE, TRATTORIE & PIZZERIE

Ristorante, **trattorie** and **pizzerie** are all traditional Italian eateries. The ristorante are more formal, trattorie are more rustic and pizzerie usually serve only pizza's and other baked goods. But all the places listed here will offer you an excellent meal, quality service and an authentically Roman dining experience. If you want to take a peek at other places to eat, **www.ristorantidiroma.com** lists some good restaurants in Rome.

Trastevere

Trastevere literally means "across the river," and until recently it was one of the poorest sections of Rome, but now it has become gentrified, though these changes have not altered Trastevere's charm. You'll find interesting shops and boutiques, and plenty of excellent restaurants among the small narrow streets and *piazzetta* (small squares). The maze of streets is a fun place to wander.

This area offers some of the best dining and casual nightlife in town. Here you can sit in a piazza cafe, sipping Sambuca or wine and watch the life of Rome pass before your eyes.

42. LA CANONICA, *Vicolo dei Piede 13, just off of the Piazza Santa Maria in Trastevere. Closed Mondays. Major credit cards accepted. Tel. 06/580-3845. Dinner for two E40. (Map B)*

In the capital of the Catholic world, what better way to dine than in a deconsecrated chapel transformed into one of Rome's most entrancing restaurants? Located near Rome's only exclusive English language movie theater, Il Pasquino, La Canonica's Baroque facade is delicately covered with vines and flowers. In the summer months tables are set outside. For me, the best place to sit is inside where it is always cool and you can soak in the atmosphere of a renovated chapel that now has meats, kegs, and bottles hanging from the ceiling.

The menu is dominated by seafood and pasta. My recommendations: *spaghetti alla vongole verace* (spicy clam sauce of garlic, basil, oil, and hot peppers) or the *spaghetti alla carbonara* (a light cream sauce, covered with ham, peas, and grated parmesan cheese). For the main course, try the light fish dish of *sogliola alla griglia* (grilled sole). The *grigliato misto di pesce* (mixed grilled fish) is also good.

43. COMPARONE, *Piazza in Piscinula 47. Tel 06/581-6249. Web: www.ilpastarellaro.it/comparone. Closed Mondays. Credit cards accepted. Dinner for two E38. (Map B)*

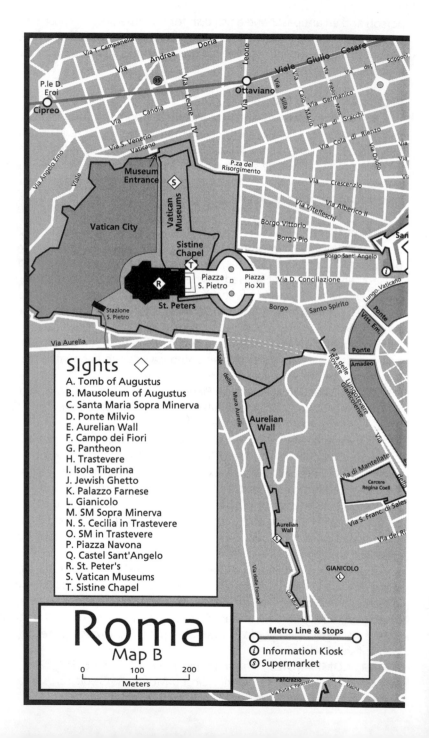

Sights ◇

A. Tomb of Augustus
B. Mausoleum of Augustus
C. Santa Maria Sopra Minerva
D. Ponte Milvio
E. Aurelian Wall
F. Campo dei Fiori
G. Pantheon
H. Trastevere
I. Isola Tiberina
J. Jewish Ghetto
K. Palazzo Farnese
L. Gianicolo
M. SM Sopra Minerva
N. S. Cecilia in Trastevere
O. SM in Trastevere
P. Piazza Navona
Q. Castel Sant'Angelo
R. St. Peter's
S. Vatican Museums
T. Sistine Chapel

Roma
Map B

0   100   200

Meters

Metro Line & Stops

ⓘ Information Kiosk
Ⓢ Supermarket

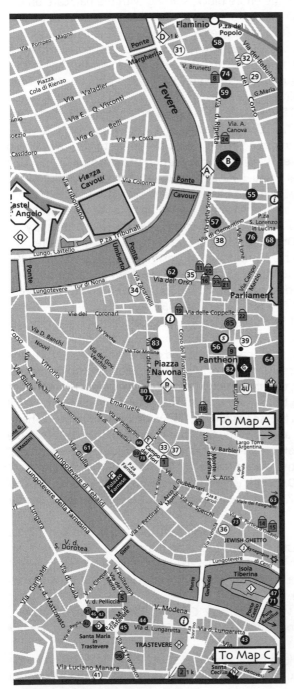

Hotels ○

29. Margutta
31. Locarno
32. Valadier
33. Campo dei Fiori
34. Genio
35. Portoghesi
36. Arenula
37. Del Sole
38. Markus
39. Sole Al Pantheon
40. Santa Chiara
41. Trastevere

Eateries ●

42. La Canonica
43. Camparone
44. Gino in Trastevere
45. Sabatini I
46. La Tana de Noantri
47. Sora Lella
55. Arancio d'Oro
56. Da Alfredo all'Angoletto
57. Alfredo alla Scrofa
58. Dal Bolognese
59. Buca di Ripetta
60. La Carbonara
61. Hostaria Guilio
62. Orso "80"
63. Vecchia Roma
64. La Sacrestia
68. Teichner
71. Antico Caffe del'Isola
73. Anacleto Bleve
74. Buccone
76. Vini e Buffet
77. L'Insalata Ricca
79. Vineria Reggio
80. Cul de Sac
82. Cremeria Monteforte
83. Tre Scalini

Nightlife ●

85. Black Duke
87. John Bull Pub
89. Drunken Ship
91. Ombre Rosse
92. Birreria Artu
95. Alexander Platz
96. Big Mama

Shopping 🛍

1. Campo dei Fiori Market
2. Porta Portese Market
5. Corner Bookshop
7. English Bookshop
9. Antica Salumieria
10. Volpetti
11. Antica Norcineria
14. Dolceroma
15. Il Forno del Ghetto
16. L'Antico Forno
18. L'Impronta
19. L'Antico Forno
21. Fefe Aldo
22. Il Papiro
23. Scatole
24. Gusto

This restaurant owns the entire block, starting with the bar/café on the left, the restaurant in the middle, and the pizzeria/birreria on the right. The outside seating at the restaurant is the best place to enjoy a true Trastevere evening. Their food includes an excellent rendition of *ossobuco alla Romana* which they prepare with *fungi* (mushrooms). Mainly known for their grilled meats and some of their pastas. Located off the beaten path near the Tiber River and the Isola Tiberina.

44. GINO IN TRASTEVERE, *Via Della Lungaretta 85, 00153 Roma. Tel. 06/580-3403. 06/580-6226. Closed Wednesdays. Dinner for two E40.*

The food here is exceptional. Since it's popular it tends to get crowded, so get there early (7ish) or late (10ish) otherwise you may be in for a wait. They have an extensive fish and meat menu: try the *sogliola alla griglia* (grilled sole), or the *saltimbocca alla Romana* (veal shanks in sauce and spices) for seconds. Your primo piatto has to be one of their great Roman pasta dishes like *arrabiatta* (tomato-based with garlic and peppers), or *vongole verace* (clams in a spicy oil, garlic, and basil sauce). Or if the desire for pizza hits you, it's great here.

45. SABATINI I, *Piazza Santa Maria in Trastevere 13, Tel. 06/581-8307 (outside seating) or 06/581-2026 (inside seating with an entrance on side). Closed Wednesdays, and two weeks in August. No credit cards accepted. Very expensive. At least E50 for dinner. (Map B)*

Besides the excellent fish dishes here, you can soak up the Trastevere life-style, especially in summer when outside seating is available. At night the floodlights keep the church at the opposite end of the piazza aglow. Try the *spaghetti alle cozze* (mussels), *zuppa di pesce*, the *spiedino misto di pesce al forno* (mixed grilled fish), and the grilled sole (*sogliola alla griglia*). If you want to see the fish grilled go to the very back of the restaurant and there they'll be roasting over an open fire, scales and all. (The waiter will de-bone, de-head and de-tail either at your table or by the fire). The inside is cozy and comfortable and they have singers walking through the tables serenading the customers, which is nice if you like that sort of thing.

46. LA TANA DE NOANTRI, *Via della Paglia 1-2-3, 00158 Roma. Tel. 06/ 580-6404 or 06/589-6575. Credit cards accepted. Closed Tuesdays. Dinner for two E38. (Map B)*

Located past Piazza Santa Maria and past the tables laid out for La Canonica, this superb restaurant has rather boring seating inside, but oh so wonderful places outside in the Piazza di San Egidio at night. Here you can sit under awnings and savor succulently seasoned Roman specialties. An excellent choice in Trastevere.

47. SORA LELLA, *Via di Ponte IV Capi 16, Tel. 06/686-1601. Web: www.ristorantidiroma.com. Closed Sundays. Credit cards accepted. Dinner for two E60. (Map B)*

A wonderful local place magically situated on the Isola Tibertina in the middle of the Tiber River. Here you'll find great atmosphere and wonderful food. Family-run for generations, they prepare real *cucina romana* (Roman cooking). There are only two rooms that can seat maybe 45 people so if you come in the evenings, call first for reservations. Try their *gnocchi alla amatriciana* (dumplings in a red pepper, bacon and pecorino cheese sauce) or the *spaghetti al tonno* (with a tuna sauce). For seconds their *abbacchio* (lamb) is some of the best in Rome. It may seem expensive but the food and exclusive atmosphere justifies the cost.

During the day, the Isola Tibertina is a great place to come and relax, either at the cafe next to Sora Lella, or especially down some stairs and in a quiet slice of Rome, on the banks of Tiber.

Rome's Best Eateries

You'll find plenty of good eateries in Rome, but for a truly great meal every time, here is my list of favorites (in no particular order).

42. LA CANONICA
47. SORA LELLA
48. AL PICCOLO ARANCIO
54. LE GROTTE
59. LA BUCA DI RIPETTA
60. LA CARBONARA
75. ENOTECANTICA
76. VINI E BUFFET
77. CAVOUR 313
79. CUL DE SAC

Trevi Fountain Area

The **Trevi Fountain** is the place where you toss a coin at Neptune's feet for a guarantee that you will one day return to Rome. It is an impressive 18th century baroque statue that dominates the square it is in. All around Trevi are shoe stores and small *pizzerie* and is one of the most popular spots in Rome.

48. AL PICCOLO ARANCIO, *Vicolo Scandberg 112, Tel. 06/678-6139. Web: www.ristorantidiroma.com. Closed Mondays. Credit cards accepted. Dinner for two E45. (Map A)*

Located on a side street near the Trevi fountain you would walk right past if you did not know this place existed. Great food served either at the few tables outside, or in the boisterous inside rooms. Excellent pastas, great meat dishes, wonderful service. An ideal choice when in Rome.

Via Veneto Area

The **Via Veneto** was backdrop for the 1959 film *La Dolce Vita*. It used to be the chic gathering place for international movie stars but now it's simply an expensive place to stay, shop, and eat. Yet is still retains a lot of character. The area is filled with shopping opportunities, upscale apartments, offices, and the American Embassy.

49. **GIOVANNI**, *Via Marche 64, Tel. 06/482-1834. Closed Saturdays and the entire month of August. Credit cards accepted. Dinner for two E75. (Map A)*

Close to the hustle and bustle of the Via Veneto is this good restaurant with an Adriatic flair. The owners are from Ancona and they serve fresh fish brought in from there. The soups in their restaurant are also very good, so if you've had your fill of pasta, come here and try the seafood and soups. I really like the *calamaretti ai ferri* (small shrimp cooked over an open flame). The house white from the Verdicchio region is quite good.

50. **GIRARROSTO TOSCANO**, *Via Campania 29, Tel. 06/482-1899. Closed Wednesdays. No credit cards accepted. Dinner for two E60. (Map A)*

Located in the cellar of a huge building facing onto the Aurelian Wall, this is a first-class restaurant that accepts orders until 1am. The food is mainly veal and beef grilled on a spit over an open wood fired oven. Prior to the meal you can indulge in melon, *prosciutto di Parma* and *ovoline* (small mozzarella cheeses). The servings are large and so are the prices. Beside the food you'll enjoy the rustic atmosphere, with hams hanging in the entrance way along with a table filled with fresh produce. In the dining area bottles of wine line the walls above the tables, and the wood paneling adds to the peasant appeal at princely prices.

Dine With a View Over Rome

Listed below are some cafes and restaurants where you can grab a bite to eat, take a load off, and savor a tantalizing view over the rooftops of Rome. Don't forget your camera.

52. HASSLER HOTEL RESTAURANT,
9. OLIMPO RESTAURANT OF THE BERNINI BRISTOL HOTEL
10. EDEN HOTEL ROOF

These two are not located on our maps:
CAFFE DEL VITTORIANO, Piazza Venezia, *Tel. 06/699-1718*
CAFFE CAPITOLINO, Piazzale Caffarelli 4, *Tel. 06/678-8821*

Piazza di Spagna Area

Around the **Piazza di Spagna** is where it all happens in Rome. You have the best shops, great restaurants, wonderful cafes, and beautiful buildings. Stately *palazzos* lining the streets look like an ideal place to live, but today much of the housing has been replaced by offices, shops, boutiques, or restaurants. Only the lucky few can afford an apartment in this location.

This area is home to the **Spanish Steps**, which gets its name from the Piazza it is in. In turn this piazza gets its name from the Spanish Embassy to the Holy See that used to sit on the sit, and s now down the road.

The area also used to be called *il ghetto degli Inglesi*, the English ghetto, since it was adopted by British travelers in the 18th and 19th centuries. This Anglo presence is still here in the form of **Babbington's Tea Rooms**, as well as the **Keats/Shelley Memorial.** At the beginning of Spring, the Spanish Steps are laden with banks of flowers that make the whole area look like a garden. Even though you are not supposed to sit and relax on the steps anymore (a law passed 1996), you'll find many doing it. So sit a spell and watch the world walk by.

51. RE DEGLI AMICI, *Via della Croce 33b. Tel. 06/679-5380 or 678-2555. Credit cards accepted. Closed Mondays and the last three weeks in June. (Map A)*

This *trattoria* close to the Spanish Steps has been serving traditional Roman food for years. If you don't want a full meal their antipasto bar will more than suffice, and after 7:30pm, you can get one of their excellent pizzas. My favorite is the one named after the restaurant, made with sausage, mozzarella, oregano and tomatoes. The pasta dishes here are also something that shouldn't be missed. Try any of the Roman specialties: *carbonara, amatriciana,* or *arrabiata.*

52. HASSLER, *Piazza Trinita dei Monti 6, Tel. 06/678-2651. Web: www.hotelhasslerroma.com. Credit cards accepted. Open 7 days a week. Dinner for two E60. (Map A)*

If you have the money to spend, the view down the Spanish Steps and over the rooftops of Rome from the glassed-in and air-conditioned terrace is worth every penny. The food used to only be passable, but now the Italian and Continental menu has begun to sparkle. The multilingual waiters will tell you that the *abbacchio al forno* is excellent, and I'd agree. There are many fine dishes on the menu, so you can order anything, but remember it's expensive.

53. OTELLO ALLA CONCORDIA, *Via Della Croce 81. Tel. 06/679-1178. No credit cards accepted. Closed Sundays. Dinner for two E40. (Map A)*

This is a family-run, small trattoria set off of Via della Croce. You enter through a tiny entrance then a small shady garden to get to the restaurant. The prices are perfect and the food is simple, basic, and good. I loved the *abbacchio arrosto can patate* (roast lamb with grilled potatoes). They open at 7:30pm. Make sure you get here early (or make reservations) or else you'll have a wait. The help is surly, but in a congenial Roman way. They have now made the garden eating area enclosed in removable glass, so people can eat out here all year round.

54. LE GROTTE, *Via delle Vite 37. Tel. 06/679-5336. . Credit cards accepted. Dinner for two E35. (Map A)*

This place has superb atmosphere and exquisite food. While dining here you really do feel as if you are in a series of caves (grotte). They are known for their excellent antipasto bar and great pizza. The food is down-to-earth peasant style in the true Roman fashion, and mixes well with the rustic ambiance. I've had the *spaghetti alla vongole verace* (spicy clam sauce) and the *pollo arrosto* (spit roasted chicken) and loved them both.

55. ARANCIO D'ORO, *Via Monte d'Oro 17, Tel. 06/686-5026. Web: www.ristorantidiroma.com. Credit cards accepted. Closed Mondays. Dinner for two E45. (Map C)*

Refine, elegant and not frequented by tourists. This is gem of a restaurant hidden down a small side street, with a small sign and curtains hindering the view inside so people who do not know of it walk right on by. Tuesdays and Thursday are fresh fish days. Excellent food, great service, wonderful atmosphere. Come here for a true local meal when in Rome.

56. DA ALFREDO ALL'ANGOLETO, *Piazza Rondanini 51, Tel. 06/686-8019, 06/686-1203. Credit cards accepted. Closed Mondays and August 11-15. Dinner for two E50. (Map C)*

A vibrant and noisy trattoria specializing in fish. Try to resist the lure of the innumerable, mouth-watering *antipasti* or you won't have room for the superbly fresh fish, the enormous Mediterranean prawns, or the still live lobsters in the display case awaiting your cooking instructions. Mushrooms are another Alfredo specialty from late summer to late autumn. There is outside seating on the small piazza as well as air-conditioned inside seating. The decor is simple, with wine bottles lining the shelves set above the tables. Come here for great food and wonderful atmosphere.

57. ALFREDO ALLA SCROFA, *Via della Scrofa 104, Tel. 06/654-0163. Web: www.ristorantealfredo1907.com. Closed Tuesdays. Credit cards accepted. Dinner for two E55. (Map C)*

There are photographs of the very rich and famous literally papering the walls. The restaurant has been in business for over half a century and was even frequented by Douglas Fairbanks and Mary Pickford which should give you an idea of what the prices are like now: high. All the pasta dishes are superb, especially *fettucine al triplo burro* (a rich artery clogging concoction made with triple butter sauce). The wine list is excellent and so are their house variations. If you like music with your meal, there is a strolling guitarist inside, if you are into that sort of thing.

58. DAL BOLOGNESE, *Piazza del Popolo 1-2, Tel. 06/361-1426.. Closed Mondays and Sunday evenings, and August 9-25. Credit cards accepted. Dinner for two E47. (Map C)*

The cooking is Bolognese in style, which some claim is the best in Italy. They have a menu in English to help you search through their great dishes. The *fritto misto alla bolognese*, which includes fried cheeses, meats and vegetables, is great. The *misto di paste* (mixed pasta and sauces) was filling enough for two. By ordering this dish you get to sample a variety of dishes while only ordering one. They have outside seating, perfect for people watching, but the intimacy of their inside rooms decorated with a fine collection of modern paintings is also appealing.

59. LA BUCA DI RIPETTA, *Via di Ripetta 36, Tel. 06/321-9391. Closed Mondays and the whole month of August. No credit cards accepted. Dinner for two E35. (Map C)*

This is a very small, friendly local trattoria that serves straightforward extra tasty Roman cooking. Try the *lasagna al forno, saltimbocca alla romana,* or the *ossobuco di vitello.* The restaurant is only one tiny room, its high walls covered with cooking and farming paraphernalia like enormous bellows, great copper pans, etc. Reservations are needed. When in Rome, you simply must dine here. Remember to make reservations. Immensely popular for its food, reasonable prices, and festive atmosphere.

Centro Storico
Piazza Navona, Pantheon and Campo dei Fiori Area

The **centro storico** (historic center) is the old medieval heart of Rome. This is where you will find many of Rome's main sights, as well some of the best nightlife, restaurants and cafes. **Piazza Navona** is the perfect place to explore Rome's tapestry of history. The square itself is like a living architectural gallery, with its baroque churches and buildings lining the square and the immense statues standing majestic in the square itself.

On a hot day, the fountains here are a visitor's oasis, allowing for needed foot soaking refreshment. You'll also find great ice cream, wonderful cafes, good restaurants as well as fire-eaters, painters, jugglers, caricaturists, tourists, rampaging Italian children, and much more.

And from mid-December to mid-January, the square becomes a giant Christmas market with booths and stalls selling stuffed animals, toys, handicrafts, and candy that looks like coal. Since it is the central focus of the holiday season there are also some great toy stores in the piazza which I loved to visit as a kid.

Another focal point of the area is the **Pantheon**, built almost two thousand years ago by Consul Marcus Agrippa as a pantheistic temple, hence its name. The city's population was centered in this area during the Middle Ages, and except for the disappearance of a large fish market, the area has remained virtually unchanged.

The area is completed by the **Campo dei Fiori** (literally translated this means "field of flowers") which has a produce and flower market every morning except Sundays. The entire centro storico is authentically picturesque, with a maze of interconnecting narrow streets, *piazzette* (small squares), and centuries-old buildings. All of which evokes a feeling of what Rome was once like long ago.

60. LA CARBONARA, *Campo dei Fiori 23, Tel. 06/686-4783. Credit cards accepted. Closed Tuesdays. Dinner for two E45. (Map B)*

Located in the best piazza for atmosphere, and the food's great as well. As could be expected, *rigatoni alla carbonara* is the house specialty so give that a try here. It is prepared to perfection in a rich peppery sauce of egg, cheese, and bacon. They also make the best *spaghetti alla vongole verace* (spicy clam sauce) I've ever had anywhere. I also love the *abbacchio alla griglia* (roast baby lamb) and the roasted potatoes. A word of warning. Periodically minstrels will play tunes for patrons. Some people find this to be too touristy. So if you do not like music played for you when you eat, do not come here.

61. GUILIO, *Via della Barchetta 19, Tel. 06/6880-6466. Credit cards accepted. Dinner for two E37. (Map B)*

They have a beautiful arched interior with brown tiled floors that emits all the character of Rome. The dishes are great Roman fare, such as the *penne all'arrabbiata* or the *spaghetti alla vongole*. Besides the pasta, which they make in house, they have fresh fish and grilled meats. This place off the beaten track and seems to have lost its lustre with the locals, but the food and atmosphere is still excellent.

62. ORSO "80," *Via dell'Orso 33, Tel. 06/333-8709. Credit cards accepted. Closed Mondays. Dinner for two E43. (Map C)*

The place to come for some classic pasta dishes, good fresh fish, and juicy meats. They also bake their breads on-site in their red-brick pizza oven. Basically this is a restaurant with a little bit of everything for everybody. Pasta, pizza, fish, grilled meats, home-made breads, extensive antipasto, etc. I really like the Roman favorite *spaghetti alla carbonara* as well as the *abbacchio alla griglia* (grilled baby lamb). Ever popular, remember to make reservations.

63. VECCHIA ROMA, *Piazza di Campitelli 18, Tel. 06/656-4604. No credit cards accepted. Closed Wednesdays. Dinner for two E43. (Map B)*

The setting of the piazza with its Baroque church and three beautiful palazzos makes your meal worthwhile, even if the buildings are covered in grime. This menu changes constantly, but the basics are the wide variety of antipasto (which could be a meal in itself), as well as *agnello* (lamb) and *capretto* (goat) or their grilled artichokes. You have to try the artichoke, since this is the Jewish ghetto and the dish is a local favorite. One of Rome's best locations. The ambiance is delightful, the service great, and the food *fantastico*.

64. LA SACRESTIA, *Via del Seminario 89, Tel. 06/679-7581. Closed Wednesdays. No credit cards accepted. Dinner for two E43. (Map C)*

Close to the Pantheon, this restaurant has over 200 places for seating, and offers good food at reasonable prices. The decorations leave much to be desired, especially the garish ceiling and fruit-clustered grotto. Come for their pizzas, served both during the day and at night, an unusual offering for an Italian restaurant. They also serve good cuts of grilled meat, and the pasta is typically Roman.

65. DA SABATINO, *Piazza S. Ignazio 169, Tel. 06/679-7821. (Map A)*
Do not eat here!! Not only have I been rudely received here, but fellow travelers I have conferred with have confirmed that this place despises tourists. I have never, ever experienced such rude, belligerent, antagonistic behavior in my life. And it is not a theme they are trying to present. This is not a game. They honestly do not care for tourists. Sadly, this place is located in one of the most beautiful piazzas in Rome. But do not be swayed by the attractive setting. The waiters' behavior will make your meal and the time you spend here ugly.

CAFES

Rome is filled with cafés. They are the heart and soul of the city, the place where locals gather. If you want to grab drink or a snack at some of the most authentic and picturesque, try any of those listed here. Regular café hours vary, but most are open early (6am) for breakfast, and close late (around 10pm).

66. LA CAFETTERIA, *Piazza di Pietra 65, Tel. 06/679-8147. Closed in August and Sundays in July. Hours 7am-9pm. Meal for two E25. (Map C)*
Near the Pantheon and Piazza della Colonna, this upscale and traditional little cafe serves up scrumptious breakfast, lunch and dinner. You can find some of the best quick and healthy food in the city here, at a good price. Always a little crowded, but if you want good eats in a relaxing ambiance in the old historic center this is the place to come. No outside seating.

67. CIAMPINI AL CAFÉ DU JARDIN, *Viale Trinita dei Monti, Tel. 06/678-5678. Closed Wednesdays and all of March. Hours 8am-7pm. Summer hours 8am-1am Meal for two E20. (Map A)*
In a fantastic location near the Villa Borghese, Villa Medici and the top of the Spanish Steps this frenzied and always full local place is perfect for hungry tourists and locals alike. A combination cafeteria, ice cream parlor and restaurant, here you'll find many choices, both hot and cold, and you can get some excellent ice cream for dessert.

68. TEICHNER, *Piazza San Lorenzo in Lucina 17, Tel 06/687-1683. Closed Sundays. Open 8am–midnight.*
A classic cafe in a calm and relaxing piazza amid the chaos of Rome, generally overlooked by tourists. My favorite place to grab a cup of coffee or gelato in Rome. You can get all sorts of snacks to nibble on as well as foodstuffs to bring home with you from the small store inside. Just off the main shopping street, Via del Corso, this is a perfect cafe at which to stop for a break. If the tables are all full, there are also two other cafes to choose from in this, the most relaxing piazza in Rome.

69. BABBINGTON'S TEA ROOMS, *23 Piazza di Spagna, Tel. 06/678-6027. Web: www.babbingtons.com. Credit cards accepted. Closed Thursdays.*
A great place to grab a spot of tea. In the mornings they serve breakfasts of scones, and other British favorites. This ancient café, with its heavy

furniture, musty decor, and creaky floors has been serving customers for several centuries. The service is out of the 18th century, but the prices are from the 21st. A required stop on the literary tour of Rome.

70. CAFÉ GRECO, *Via Condotti 86, Tel. 06/679-1700. Closed Sundays. Open 8am to midnight.*

This places has been here since 1740 and has been a stop on the grand tour of Rome since then. A unique and elegant café where you can get all sorts of drinks, snacks and pastries. Expensive, but worth at least one stop just to be a part of the history. Another required stop on the literary tour of Rome.

71. ANTICO CAFFE DEL'ISOLA, *Via Ponte IV Capi 18, Tel. 06/6880-1774.*

Situated on the Isola Tibertina, right next to the great restaurant Sora Lella, this cafe is a great place to come on a warm, sunny day, and sit on their terrace, far from the maddening crowds of Rome. Not really anything special except for its supreme location. This cafe and the island it is on, are an oasis of calm.

72. BAR HERBIER NATURE, *Via s. Claudio 87, Tel. 06/678-5897.*

Located in the central courtyard of a building that is on the hectic Via del Corso. If you want a respite from that frenzy, stop in here for a coffee or a snack, sit at one of their tables in the courtyard and relax. Nothing scenic or spectacular about this place, but entering here is like walking into a world of calm and serenity. From the Via del Corso, enter directly to the right of the Spizzico cafe.

ENOTECHE

Wine bars (*enoteche*) have existed in Italy since the beginning of grape cultivation, but in the past have usually been dark places populated by older men playing cards at rickety tables, slurping hearty local vintages from chipped mismatched glasses. Most of those places have been replaced with newer, upscale, more ambient establishments such as those listed below. Usually open mid-day until the wee hours of the morning, with a break in the afternoon, *enoteche* are an upscale place for Italians to go for lunch, an early meal, a light dinner or just for a quiet evening out. In general they only offer excellent light food such as salads, sandwiches, crepes, quiches, and salami and cheese plates.

73. ANACLETO BLEVE, *Via S. Maria del Pianto 9a, Tel. 06/686-5970. Meal for two E25. (Map B)*

Located at the entrance to the Jewish quarter, just off the Via Arenula this place has one of the best selections of wines in all of Rome. Lunch is served in the side room and is an exquisite buffet, with hot plates prepared quickly, as well as typical local artesian cheeses and salamis, all accompanied by their superb vintages served by the glass. Wonderfully courteous service. A superb option when near the Campo dei Fiori. It's hard to find especially since their sign is upside down and backwards.

74. BUCCONE, *Via di Ripetta 19, Tel. 06/361-2154. Lunch served everyday, dinner only Thursday-Saturday. Meal for two E25. (Map C)*

A great enoteca in Rome, not only because of the offerings by the glass but also the bottled selection you can choose from. Mentioned in a sidebar in this book as the best place to buy wine to bring home, Buccone also stands on its own as a place to come in and grab a tasty, light and healthy snack and a glass of wine at either their counter serving area or side room. An excellent choice for wine lovers, in a fun local area near the main shopping street of Via Del Corso.

75. ENOTECANTICA, *Via del Croce 76, Tel. 06/679-0896. Web: www.enoteantica.com. Closed Sundays. Meal for two E28. All credit cards accepted. (Map A)*

Opened in 1860, until a few years ago this was an old-fashioned wine store selling local vintages directly from large vats. Now it's a fern-filled wine bar with wooden stools with ceramic seats. Light meals and snacks of all sorts are served here, and wine by the glass. A great place to stop in a perfect location.

76. VINI E BUFFET, *Piazza della Torretta 60, Tel 06/687-1445. Open 12:30pm-2:30pm and 7:30pm to midnight. Closed Sundays. Meal for two E25. (Map C)*

Set on a tiny side street, near the Parliament building, just off the Via del Corso, this little wine shop and café is a breath of fresh air. A fantastic place to grab a light lunch (sandwiches, crepes, salads, etc.) and some great wine. The rustic and charming setting is authentically Roman and offers a unique dining experience. By far my favorite enoteca in Rome – so much so that we include a map next to this review so you'll have no problem getting here!

77. L'INSALATA RICCA, *Piazza Pasquino 72, Tel. 06/6830-7881. Web: www.linsalataricca.it. Open Open 12:30pm-2:30pm and 7:30pm-12:30am. Closed Sundays. Meal for two E25. (Map B)*

If you ever get tired of pasta, the staple of the Roman diet, you can come

here for a salad of gargantuan proportions. They also serve other dishes if you still want to "carb-out;" but the mainstay of this place, and the others in this excellent Italian group of restaurants, is fresh and wholesome salads. Ricca has outside seating and an interior that is simply decorated. There are 12 more of these superb eateries all over Rome, so if you stumble onto one of them, and desire some greens, stop in.

78. CAVOUR 313, *Via Cavour 313, Tel. 06/678-5496. Open 12:30pm-2:30pm and 7:30pm-12:30am. Closed Sundays. Meal for two E25. (Map C)*
Wow. What a great wine bar. Rustic and down-to-earth atmosphere. Superb light and healthy local food, prepared fresh. If you happen by the Colosseum or Forum, you simply must stop here for lunch, an afternoon snack or a light dinner. An excellent menu of local salamis, cheeses, sandwiches, salads and much more, all accompanied by a varied and extensive wine list. My second favorite place to Vini e Buffet above.

79. VINERIA REGGIO, *Campo dei Fiori 15, Tel. 06/6880-3268. Open 12:30pm – 2:30pm and 7:30pm – 2:00am. Closed Sundays. Meal for two E25. (Map B)*
An ideal location, this wine bar has great seating outside in one of Rome's best piazza's. An adequate menu and wine list, what really makes this place is their location in the Campo dei Fiori.

80. CUL DE SAC, *Piazza di Pasquino 73, Tel. 06/6880-1094. Open 12:30pm-3:30pm and 7:00pm-12:30am. Closed Mondays for lunch. Meal for two E25. (Map B&C)*
This intimate wine bar with outdoor tables set up in nice weather has over 1,400 Italian and foreign vintages for you to sample. This place has been around since the 1970s and serves up hot and cold light meals as well as dessert and ice cream. Quick informal service and a stunning ambiance, especially inside among the bottles lining the walls and at the marble topped tables.

GELATERIE

Gelato, or what we call ice cream, is a combination of whole milk, eggs, sugar, and natural flavoring – or fresh fruit and sugar in the fruit flavors. It is softer, more intensely flavored and colored creation than what we know as ice cream here in North America. The best fruit *gelato* is made from crushed fresh ripe seasonal produce. The best milk-based *gelato* is flavored with all-natural ingredients and has a silky consistency. They will all melt faster than the ice cream we are used to does, so be prepared for that on a hot summer day.

Besides *gelato* there are also three different types of frozen concoctions savored by the Italians:

Semifreddo, which means "half cold," and refers to any of a variety of chilled or partially frozen desserts including whipped ice cream. It vaguely resembles a mousse, which is what the chocolate flavor is called.

Sorbetto is basically a fruit sorbet and has become popular in many Italian restaurants as a separator between the fish and meat courses to act as a palate cleanser. It also makes a wonderful dessert.

Granita is frozen flavored ice water. It usually, but not always, comes in lemon, orange or coffee flavors.

Some gelato shops for you to try include:

81. SAN CRISPINO, *Via della Panetteria 42, Tel. 06/679-3924. Open Noon to 12:30am Mondays, Wednesdays, Thursdays and Sundays; and Noon to 1:30am Fridays and Saturdays. Closed Tuesdays.*

Easily the best *gelateria* in Rome. Here you can find any flavor imaginable and all are made from scratch. All ingredients are natural, without preservative so you cannot choose by color, since the *nocciola* (hazelnut) looks like vanilla, the *pistacchio* looks like chocolate, and the *Stracciatella* (chocolate chip) looks like mud.

82. CREMERIA MONTEFORTE, *Via della Rotonda 22, Tel. 06/686-7720. Closed Mondays.*

The ice cream in this minuscule little local *gelateria* is some of the best in the entire city. Since there's not much room, grab a cone or a cup here and wander out and sit by the Pantheon. All natural ingredients.

83. TRE SCALINI, *Piazza Navona 28, Tel. 06/6880-1996.Web: www.paginegialle.it/trescalini. Closed Wednesdays.*

A staple in Rome for many years, here you can grab a cone and eat in the piazza, or sit at a table outside and watch the world go by. Very upscale and very pricey, but this is place is world renowned as a great *gelateria* in Rome.

Seeing the Sights

For the Jubilee year, Rome introduced nine tourist information kiosks run by multilingual staff from 9:00am-6:00pm every day. At the locations below, you can get excellent maps of Rome, wonderful color brochures of the local museums and tons of information about virtually anything to do in Rome.

Rome has realized the importance of these kiosks has kept them open past the Jubilee, dispensing similar information though not as extensive. They will also act as ticket booths for theatrical performances, museums, special events and sporting events.

You should make a point of stopping at one of these kiosks when you first arrive in Rome. The information they dispense is invaluable, and their free maps the best available. On the maps in this book, the location of each kiosk is noted. Look for these kiosks at:

• **Termini Train Station**, *Tel. 06/4890-6300.* Open 8:00am-9:00pm daily
• **Termini**, Piazza Cinquecento, *Tel. 06/4782-5194*
• **Castel S. Angelo**, Piazza Pia, *Tel. 06/6880-9707*
• **Imperial Forums**, Piazza Tempio della Pace, *Tel. 06/6992-4307*
• **Piazza di Spagna**, Largo Goldoni, *Tel. 06/6813-6061*

• **Piazza Navona**, Piazza Cinque Lune, *Tel. 06/6880-9240*
• **Via Nazionale**, Palazzo delle Esposizioni, *Tel. 06/4782-4525*
• **Trastevere**, Piazza Sonnino, *Tel. 06/5833-3457*
• **San Giovanni**, Piazza S. Giovanni in Laterano, *Tel. 06/7720-3535*

The chief difficulty most visitors have is that there is so much to see in this huge historic city. With even a month's worth of concentrated touring, you'd only scratch the surface. If your time is limited, consider a sightseeing tour or series of tours by bus. This way you can be sure to see at least the greatest sights in Rome and its environs. See information on Tour Guides at the end of this chapter.

The Vatican Museums alone can take you an entire day to work through, so don't believe that you can do all of these places justice in a few short days. Also, when you visit Piazza Navona, Piazza di Spagna, and Trevi Fountain, you will get a different experience depending on the time of day you go. At night each of these places livens up with Italians of all ages strolling, chatting, sipping wine, strumming guitars, while during the day they may only be swarmed by tourists. Take your time – don't do too much, and don't rush through. Take your time, be Italian and savor the experience. Below is a sidebar for the must-see sights' these ten could easily last you a week.

Ten Must-See Sights in Rome

Sistine Chapel – Michelangelo's magnificent frescoed ceiling and walls.

Vatican Museums – Greek & Roman artifacts, as well as the best collection of paintings and sculptures anywhere in the world.

St. Peter's – The world's largest cathedral, exquisitely decorated.

Castel Sant'Angelo – The fortress that used to protect the Vatican now houses a wonderful armaments museum.

Imperial and Roman Forums – The center of ancient Roman life.

Capitoline Museum on the Campidoglio – The second best museum in Rome, with many fine sculptures and paintings.

Piazza Navona – A lively piazza filled with wonderful fountains, churches, and palazzi as well as good cafés and restaurants.

Piazza di Spagna – Walk to the top and get a great view of the city. Sit by the fountain during siesta and enjoy Rome as it passes you by.

Trevi Fountain – One of the most beautiful fountains in Italy. At night when lit up, it is a magnificent sight.

Saint Paul's Outside the Walls – Location of many buried Saints, some fine sculptures and mosaics. Walls ringed with portraits of all the popes.

List of Sights by Map

Sight	Map	Sight	Map
Altar/Mausoleum of Augustus	B	Pantheon	A & B
Arch of Constantine	C	Piazza del Popolo	B
Aurelian Wall	A,B,C	Piazza di Spagna	A
Basilica of Maxentius Constantine	D	Piazza Navona	B
Baths of Caracalla	C	Ponte Frabricio	B
Baths of Diocletian	A	Ponte Milvio	B
Borghese Gardens	A & C	Pyramid	C
Campidoglio	C	Roman Forum & Palatine Hill	D
Campo dei Fiori	B	S Cecilia in Trastevere	B
Capitoline Museum	C	S Clemente	C
Castel St. Angelo	B	S Giovanni in Laterano	C
Circus Maximus	C	S Maria Sopra Minerva	C & B
Colosseum	C	S Pietro in Vincoli	C
Column of M. Aurelius	A	SM in Trastevere	B
Forum of Augustus	C	SM Maggiore	A & C
Forum of Caesar	C	St. Paul's Outside the Walls	C
Galleria Borghese	A	St. Peter's	B
Galleria Borghese	A	Temple of Hadrian	A
Gianicolo	B	Trajan's Forum & Market	C
Imperial Forums	C	Trastevere	B
Isola Tiberina	B	Trevi Fountain	A
Jewish Ghetto	B	Vatican City	B
Museo della Civilta Romana	C	Vatican Museums	B
Museo di Villa Giulia	A	Via Veneto	A
National Museum	A	Via Appia Antica/Catacombs	C
Palazzo Barberini	A	Vittorio Emanuelle Memorial	C
Palazzo Farnese	B		

Rome maps can be found on the following pages:
Map A: pages 120-121
Map B: pages 140-141
Map C: pages 156-157
Map D: pages 163

≈

A map of Rome (which you can get at any newsstand or the information kiosks listed above), some walking shoes, and a spirit of adventure are all you need to explore the innumerable piazzas, churches, galleries, parks, and fountains of this unique city. If you want the most up to date information about what is happening in Rome, whether a museum exhibit, performing arts festival, or simply what is going on in the local American community, pick up

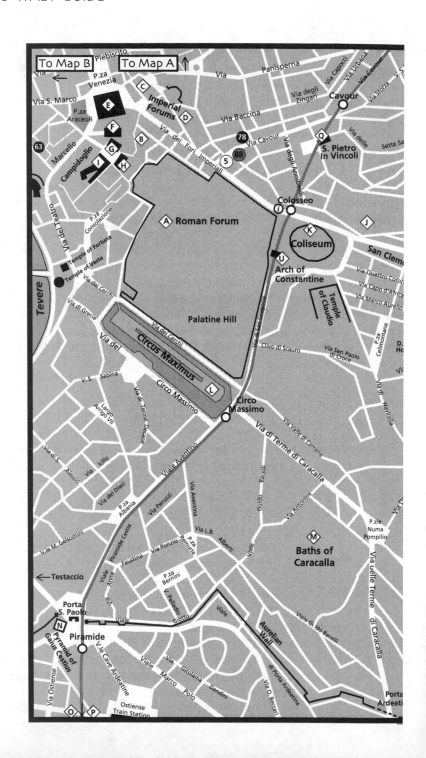

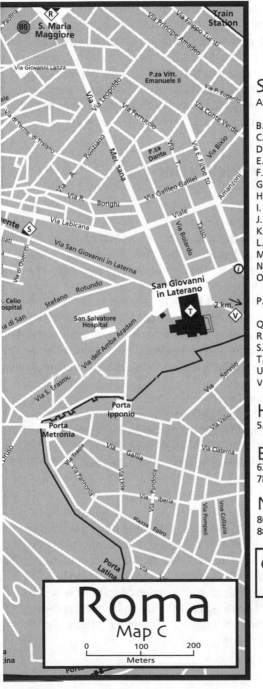

Sights ◇

A. Roman Forum
   (see separate map)
B. Caesar's Forum
C. Trajan's Forum/Column/Market
D. Augustus' Forum
E. Vitt. Emanuele II Monument
F. S.M. d'Araceoli
G. Capitoline Museum
H. Senatorial Palace
I. Conservatorio
J. Nero's Golden House
K. Coliseum
L. Circus Maximus
M. Baths of Caracalla
N. Pyramid
O. St Paul's Outside the Walls
   Metro - San Paolo
P. Museo della Civilta Romana
   Metro - EUR Palasport or Fermi
Q. S. Pietro in Vincoli
R. Santa Maria Maggiore
S. San Clemente
T. San Giovanni (St. John's)
U. Arch of Constantine
V. Appia Antica/Catacombs

Hotels ○

5. Richmond

Eateries ●

63. Vecchia Roma
78. Cavour 313

Nightlife ◐

86. Fiddler's Elbow
88. Shamrock

Metro Line & Stops
○━━━━━━━━○
ⓘ Information Kiosks

Roma
Map C

0   100   200
Meters

a copy of *Wanted in Rome* (Euro 75 cents) at any newsstand. This is the resource for the ex-pat community to know exactly what's going on in Rome.

If you saunter through the narrow streets of old Rome, behind the **Piazza Navona**, for example, or along the **Via Giulia** or near the **Pantheon**, you'll get many unexpected and revealing glimpses of flower hung balconies, inner courtyards, and fountains. Here, perhaps more than in the impressive ruins of antiquity, you will get the feeling of this city where civilizations have been built on the ruins of the previous ones for centuries. Rome is an ancient city whose vitality seems to be renewed perpetually by each new generation.

Ancient Rome

The Imperial Forums
Via IV Novembre 94. Admission E2.5. *Tel. 06/679-0048.* Open 9:00am-8:00pm and in the summers on Saturday until midnight. Metro-Colosseo.

The Imperial Forums were built in the last days of the Republic, when the Roman Forum became inadequate to accommodate the ever-increasing population, and the emperors needed space to celebrate their own magnificence. These forums were used as meeting places for Romans to exchange views, as lively street markets, or as places where official announcements could be proclaimed to the populace. The first was built by Julius Caesar, and those that followed were created by Augustus, Vespasian, Domitian, Trajan, Nerva, and Hadrian.

After the fall of the Roman Empire, these places of great import fell into disrepair; by the time of the Middle Ages and the Renaissance all that was left are the ruins we see today. Gradually, over the centuries, these monumental ruins became covered with soil. Modern excavation began in 1924 by Mussolini's regime as a way of heralding the glory of Italy and thus Mussolini himself.

Trajan's Forum
Located well below current street level, this is the most grandiose of the Forums of the imperial age and reflects the emperor's eclectic taste in art and architecture. Here you can see one of the finest monuments in these Imperial Forums, Trajan's Column, built to honor the Victories of Trajan in 113 CE. It is over 30 meters high and is covered with a series of spiral reliefs depicting the military exploits of the Emperor against the Dacins in the 1st century CE. At the summit of this large column is a statue of St. Peter that was placed there by Pope Sixtus V in the 17th century.

Trajan's Market

This is a large and imposing set of buildings attached to Trajan's Forum, where people gathered and goods were sold. In the vast semi-circle is where the merchants displayed their wares.

Forum of Caesar

Located near the Roman Forum, on the other side of the Via dei Fori Imperiali (the road itself was built in 1932 on the site of a far more ancient road to more adequately display the monuments of ancient Rome), this was the earliest of the Imperial Forums. It was begun in 54 BCE to commemorate the Battle of Pharsalus, and finished in 44 BCE. Trajan redesigned many parts of this Forum to meet his needs in 113 CE and to celebrate some of his victories

For example, Trajan added the Basilica Argentaria (Silver Basilica), which was a meeting place for bankers and money changers. Originally a bronze statue of Julius Caesar stood in the center of this Forum. This statue is now located in the Campidoglio.

Forum of Augustus

Built around the time of Christ's birth, this Forum commemorates the deaths of Brutus and Cassius (the traitors who allied against Caesar) at the Battle of Philippi in 42 BCE. Here you'll find some remains of the Temple of Mars, the god of war, including a high podium and some trabeated (horizontally decorated) columns. To the side of the temple you'll find the remains of two triumphal arches and two porticos.

THE COLOSSEUM

Piazza del Colosseo. Admission E6. Hours in the summer 9:00am-7:00pm. In the winter 9:00am-5:00pm. Buses 11, 27, 81, 85, 87. Metro-Colosseo.

The **Colosseum** (*Flavian Amphitheater*) remains the most recognized monument surviving from ancient Rome. Its construction began in 72 CE by Vespasian on the site of the Stagnum Neronis, an artificial lake built by Emperor Nero near his house on the adjacent Oppian Hill. The Colosseum was eventually dedicated by Titus in 80 CE. It is recorded that at the building's opening ceremony, which lasted three months, over 500 exotic beasts and many hundreds of gladiators were slain in the arena. These types of bloody spectacles lasted until 405 CE, when they were abolished. The building was severely damaged by an earthquake in the fifth century CE and saw little use afterwards as a theater. Since then it has been used as a fortress and as a quarry for construction material for Vatican buildings.

What we see today is nothing compared to what the building used to look like. In its prime it was covered with marble, and each portico was filled with a marble statue of some important Roman.

The Colosseum used to be fully elliptical and could hold over 50,000 people. Each of the three tiers is supported by a different set of columns: Doric for the base, Ionic for the middle and Corinthian for the top. Inside, the first tier of seats was reserved for the tribunes and other dignitaries such as knights (Which is where the Medieval Age got the term for their chivalric representatives. In fact the plumed helmets, courteous manner, and colorful banners of Medieval knights were all based on ancient Roman officers, their garb, and emblems). The second tier in the Colosseum was for citizens, and the third tier for the lower classes and slaves. The Emperor, Senators, Government Officials and Vestal Virgins sat on marble thrones on a raised platform that went around the entire arena.

Inside the arena, below where the floor once was, we can see vestiges of the subterranean passages that were used to transport the wild beasts. Human-powered elevators were employed to get the animals up to the Colosseum floor. At times the arena was flooded to allow for the performance of mock naval battles. Unremarkable architecturally, the Colosseum is still an engineering remnant from the past which deserves admiration. A great site for kids and adults to explore.

NERO'S GOLDEN HOUSE
Viale della Domus Aurea. *Tel. 06/399-67700.* Buses 11, 27, 81, 85, 87. Metro-Colosseo. Hours: 9am to 8pm summer; 9am to 5pm winter; closed on Tuesdays. Admission E6.

After 15 years of excavations, the **Domus Aurea** is once again open to public viewing. Known as Nero's Golden House, Nero built the Domus Aurea after the great fire of 64 CE destroyed his first abode, not to mention a great deal of Rome. Nero appropriated a huge amount of land in much of central Rome and had the finest craftsmen of the day work on the structure. Nero only lived in the palace a few short years, after which most of it was abandoned (as a result of the general dislike for Nero) and much of the grounds given back to the people of Rome.

You can view eight rooms today, all underground, and admire the vaulted ceilings, extant pieces of frescoes and stone reliefs, beautiful floor mosaics, and pieces of broken sculpture here and there. It's a magnificent building, and well worth the sight if you are in the neighborhood of the Colosseum and have the time. Be sure and get the audio guide, since you will be accompanied by someone who is only there to show you from room to room . You have to call in advance and make a reservation, since only small groups are allowed in at a time.

ARCH OF CONSTANTINE
Piazza Colosseo. Buses 11, 27, 81, 85, 87. Metro-Colosseo.
Located near the Colosseum, this monument was built in 312 CE to

commemorate the Emperor's victory over Maxentius at the Ponte Milvio (the oldest standing bridge in Rome) and is comprised of three archways. This is the largest and best preserved triumphal arch in Rome. The attic is not continuous but is broken into three parts corresponding to the placement of the arches. Even though this is the Arch of Constantine, the attic panels are from a monument to Marcus Aurelius. On one side of the attic the bas-reliefs represent Marcus Aurelius in his battle with the Dacians, and on the opposite side there are episodes of deeds by Marcus Aurelius and Constantine. On the lower areas there are bas-reliefs from earlier arches of Trajan and Hadrian.

THE ROMAN FORUM, PALATINE HILL & NEARBY SIGHTS

Largo Romolo e Remo 1 Tel. 06/699-0110. Admission €6. Open 9:00am-8:00pm and in the summers on Saturday until midnight. Buses 11, 27, 85, 97, 181, 186, 718, and 719. Metro-Colosseo.

The best way to get an overall view of the **Roman Forum** is to descend from the Piazza del Campidoglio by way of the Via del Campidoglio, which is to the right of the Senatorial Palace. You get a clear view of the Forums in the front, with the Colosseum in the background, and the Palatine Hill on the right. The entrance to the forum is some distance down the *Via dei Fori Imperiali*. You can also enter from the Via di San Gregorio near the Colosseum.

The Roman Forum lies between the Palatine and Quirinale hills and was first a burial ground for the early settlers of both hills. Later the area became the center for the religious, commercial and political activities of the early settlers. The surrounding area was greatly expanded in the Imperial era when Roman emperors began building self-contained *Fora* in their own honor. The entire area has been decimated by war, used as a quarry for other buildings in Rome, and has been haphazardly excavated, but is still a wonder to behold. A great site for kids to explore.

In the Roman Forum you'll find the following sights and more:

Arch of Septimus Severus

Built in 203 CE to celebrate the tenth anniversary of the Emperor Septimus Severus' reign. This triumphal arch is constructed with two lower archways flanking a larger central one and is the one of the finest and most imposing structures remaining from ancient Rome. Over the side arches are bas-reliefs depicting scenes from victorious battles fought by the Emperor over the Parthians and the Mesopotamians.

Rostra

Located next to the Arch of Septimus Severus, this building was decorated with the ramrods, or rostra, of ships captured by the Romans at Antium in 338 BCE. It was the meeting place for Roman orators. All that remains now is the semi-circular flight of entry stairs. In front of it is the **Column of Phocas**, erected in honor of the Eastern Emperor of the Roman Empire, Nicephorus Phocas, in 608 CE. The column was the last monument to be erected in the Forum.

Temple of Saturn

Built in 497 BCE, it was restored with eight ionic columns in the 42 BC that were bounty from the Syrian wars. In the temple's basement was the Treasury of State. Only the threshold of the door which opens towards the Forum remains.

Basilica Giulia

Started in 54 BCE by Julius Caesar on the site of the destroyed Baslica Sempronmia and completed by Augustus, it was destroyed by fire and restored in 12 BCE, and restored a final time in 416 CE. The Basilica consisted of a huge 2 storied hall with five aisles. It once housed the Roman law courts.

Basilica Emilia

Located to the right of the entrance to the Forum, this is the only remaining Republican Basiclia and was built in 179 BCE. It was restored on several occasions by Gens Aemilia and now bares his name. Because of the ravages of fire, destruction by "barbarian hordes" and neglect, little remains today. The facade consisted of a two story portico and 16 arches. It was one of the largest buildings in Rome and was used by money-changers and other business people.

The Curia

Founded by Tullus Hostilius and initially erected between 80 BCE and 44 BCE, it was completed in 29 BCE by Augustus and restored several times. It was the house of the Senate, the government of Rome in the Republican period, and the puppet government during the empire. It was once covered with exquisite marble but is today a combination of stucco and brick. The structure was rebuilt after a fire in 283 CE, and converted into a church in the seventh century CE. The interior is still a large plain hall, with marble steps that were used as the senator's seats. Take the time to go inside and sit where the Roman Senators sat ages ago. In this room is where many of the major decisions associated with governing Rome were debated.

Temple of Anthony & Faustina

Built by Antonius Pius in honor of his wife Faustina in 141 CE, after his death the temple was dedicated to the emperor as well. The temple was later converted to a church in the 11th century, **San Lorenzo in Miranda**. All that remains of the original Roman temple are the ten monolithic columns that are 17 meters high, and an elegant frieze. The baroque facade is from the 1600s.

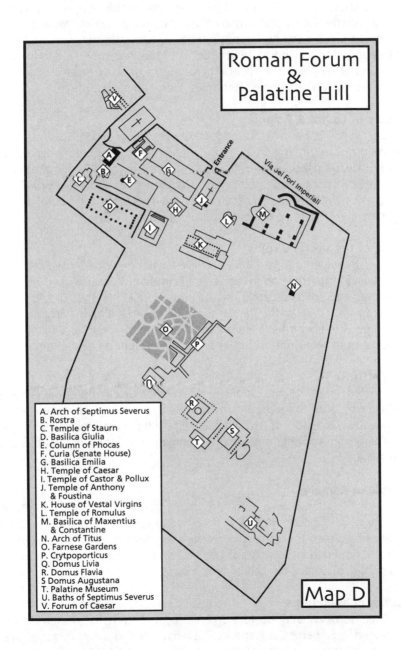

Roman Forum & Palatine Hill

A. Arch of Septimus Severus
B. Rostra
C. Temple of Staurn
D. Basilica Giulia
E. Column of Phocas
F. Curia (Senate House)
G. Basilica Emilia
H. Temple of Caesar
I. Temple of Castor & Pollux
J. Temple of Anthony
   & Foustina
K. House of Vestal Virgins
L. Temple of Romulus
M. Basilica of Maxentius
   & Constantine
N. Arch of Titus
O. Farnese Gardens
P. Crytpoporticus
Q. Domus Livia
R. Domus Flavia
S Domus Augustana
T. Palatine Museum
U. Baths of Septimus Severus
V. Forum of Caesar

Map D

Temple of Caesar
Also known as the Temple of the Divine Julius, this temple was built by Augustus on the site where the body of Julius Caesar was cremated and where Marcus Antonius made his famous funeral oration after the assassination. It was inaugurated on August 18 29 BCE. The little that now remains includes the round altar where the funeral pyre was most likely erected. Septimus Severus restored the Temple after it has been damaged by fire.

Temple of Castor & Pollux
Built in 484 BCE and dedicated to the cult of Castor and Pollux, the temple has been restored many times, most notably by Hadrian and Tiberius. The facade once faced the square of the forum and there were 19 original columns (only three remain). Inside, the Senate would meet periodically to deal with concerns of weights and measures. At the foot of the podium, money changers, bankers and barbers would set up shop.

House of the Vestal Virgins
This is where the vestal virgins lived who dedicated themselves to maintaining the sacred fires in the nearby **Temple of Vesta**. Why you needed to be a virgin to do has escaped into the mists of time. A portico of two stories adorned with statues of the Vestals surrounded a round open court that was decorated with flower beds and three cisterns. In the court you can still see the remains of some of the statues and the pedestals on which they sat.

Arch of Titus
Erected in 81 CE by Domitian to commemorate the conquering of Jerusalem by Titus. The arch contains bas-reliefs of the Emperor and of soldiers carrying away the spoils of Jerusalem. It is one of the most imposing structures remaining from ancient Rome, and a pilgrimage site for every Jewish tourist to the city.

Temple of Romulus
Once considered as a commemorative building for Romulus, son of Maxentius, who died in 309 CE at a very young age. It is now know as the Temple of Jupiter Stator. The brick construction dates back to the Maxentius-Constantine period and consists of a domed, round, central location, preceded by a semi-circular face flanked by two rectangular sections.

Basilica of Maxentius
Built between 306 CE and 312 CE by the Emperor Maxentius and completed by Emperor Constantine. The last remaining column was removed in 1613 and placed in front of the Santa Maria Maggiore to commemorate Christianity's dominance over paganism. This is the location where the giant

statue of Constantine once stood, the head and foot of which are now on display at the Capitoline Museum.

The Palatine Hill

Of the Seven Hills of Rome, this one's ancient structures have not been paved over with modern progress and new constructs. This hill was the residence of the Roman emperors during the Golden Age and Imperial Period. In addition, it was here, in 754 BCE, that Romulus is said to have founded the city of Rome. However, actual records and not just myth have indicated that settlement was actually established in the 9th century BCE.

Aristocratic families also resided here, leaving behind wonderful architectural relics most of which have been excavated today, making the Palatine Hill one of the must-see places when you tour the Forum. It is also a wonderful respite from the hectic pace of Rome, filled with lush greenery and plenty of shade; it's a great place to have a picnic or go on a relaxing walk through history.

Entering the Palatine, you pass through the **Farnese Gardens**. Originally called the Domus Tiberiana, these gardens were laid out in the sixteenth century and were fill of orange trees and gurgling fountains. They were created for Cardinal Allessandro Farnese who used them for lavish parties. Underneath the gardens is the **Cryptoporticus**, a subterranean tunnel built by Nero for hot-weather walks and as a secret route from the Palatine and his palace (Nero's Golden House) across the valley on the Oppian Hill.

Further up the hill is the **Domus Livia** named after Augustus' wife. The wall paintings here date from the late Republic period. Nearby is the **Domus Flavia** with the foundations of what appear to be a maze. Next to that is the **Domus Augustana**, the emperor's private residence. The oval building may have been a garden or a theater for the emperor's private entertainment.

In between the Domus Flavia and Domus Augustana is the **Palatine Museum**. A nondescript gray building which houses human remains and artifacts from the earliest communities in Rome, which existed around the ninth century BCE. In the upstairs rooms are busts and other works from the fourth century CE.

Finally, at the farthest corner of the Palatine lie the remains of the small palace and **Baths of Septimus Severus**. These are some of the best-preserved buildings on the hill, quite possibly because it was the most difficult point to reach, deterring the scavengers from looting its structure for building materials. This simple explanation is the main reason for state of decay exhibited in the Forum, Colosseum and other Roman era sights. Quite simply, these older buildings were used as a quarry, mainly by the Papacy for the construction of new churches. Also, the common person would grab whatever was available as well to help in the construction of their domicile.

BATHS OF CARACALLA

Via Terme di Caracalla, *Tel. 06/575-8626.* Admission E4. Hours Monday–Saturday 9:00am until one hour before dark. Mondays and Holidays 9:00am–1:00pm. Buses 90, 90b, 118. Metro-Circo Massimo.

Built in 217 CE by the Emperor Caracalla, these baths were second in size only to the Baths of Diocletian. They were used until the sixth century at which time they were destroyed by Gothic invaders. Today it takes quite an imagination to reconstruct the building mentally. The baths were once rich with marble and statues and decorated with stucco and mosaic work. All that is left are the weathered remains of the massive brick structure which offers an insight into the scale of the baths, but doesn't offer a glimpse of their beauty. Today, on summer evenings, opera performances are held among the ruins of the **Calidarium**, the circular vapor bath area.

BATHS OF DIOCLETIAN

Viale E de Nicola. Open 9:00am-2:00pm, Holidays only until 1:00pm. Buses 57, 64, 65, 75, 170, 492, and 910. Metro-Repubblica.

These were the most extensive baths of their times in which more than 3,000 bathers could be accommodated together. They were built by Maximilian and Diocletian from 196–306 CE. Today the **National Museum** (a great museum in Rome) is located within their walls, as is the **Church of Santa Maria Degli Angeli**.

CAMPIDOGLIO

Piazza del Campidoglio 1. Open 9:00am-7:00pm. Closed Mondays. E5. Buses 94, 95, 713, 716. Metro-Colosseo.

The Capitoline Hill is one of the seven hills of Rome. It forms the northwest boundary of the Forum and today is home to the **Capitoline Museum**, **Senatorial Palace**, the **Palace of the Conservatori**, the **Church of Santa Maria D'Aracoeli** (formerly the Temple of Juno Moneta), and the bronze **statue of Marcus Aurelius**. The Palazzo di Senatori (Senatorial Palace) was finished in the beginning of the 14th century; the statue was placed there in 1528, and the piazza along with the other two buildings were completed in 1570. These last three structures as well as the stairs leading up to them were based on a design developed by Michelangelo, who died in 1564 not seeing his plan completed.

The **Capitoline Museums** were founded by the Popes Clement XII and Benedict XIV and house some exquisite works (see Capitoline Museum in the *Museums* section below).

To ascend the hill, take either the steep stairway that leads to the church, the winding ramp of the Via delle Tre Pile, or from between the two of these by way of the monumental stairs, Cordonate, which were designed by

Michelangelo. At the entrance to these stairs you'll find two imposing Egyptian lions and at the top you'll find the statues of Castor and Pollux.

The church of Santa Maria D'Aracoeli was originally a pagan temple then was converted for use as a Christian church. In the 12th century it was given its present form with a colonnade of mismatched ancient columns, stolen from a nearby Roman ruin, and a wide nave. The enormous set of stairs in front are one of the church's main features.

You must visit the museums on this hill, since they are second in magnificence only to the Vatican Museums, and certain exhibits are even better. Also, having your picture taken in front of the large pieces of Constantine's statue is a wonderful memento.

CIRCUS MAXIMUS

Via del Circo Massimo. Buses 15, 90, 90b, 94. Metro-Circo Massimo.

This is where the predecessors of Barnum and Bailey got their start. Known then as Barnumus and Baileum, they were famous throughout the Roman world, especially for that trick with a bucket and shreds of paper. Or was that the Globetrotteri?

Seriously, this circus (or circuit, i.e. race-track) is located on the flat lands to the south of the Palatine Hill. It was erected in 309 CE by the Emperor Maxentius in honor of his deified son Romulus, whose temple is on the Palatine. Then in Imperial times it was expanded, destroyed, enlarged and used as a quarry until little is left of the original marble.

However, today its shape is clearly visible underneath the contoured grass and earth, and some of the original seats remain at the turning circle of the southwestern end. The slight hump running through the center marks the location of the *spina*, around which the chariots, and at times runners, would race. In its prime the Circo Massimo could hold between 150,000-200,000 spectators, more than most modern stadiums.

CATACOMBS

Saint Callistus (Via Appia Antica 110, *Tel. 06/513-6725.* Closed Wednesday.); San Sebastian (Via Appia Antica 132, *Tel. 06/788-7035.* Closed Thursday.); Santa Domitilla (Via di Sette Chiese 282, *Tel. 06/511-0342.* Closed Tuesday.)

Entrance for each E5. Hours for each 8:30am-12:00pm and 2:30pm-5:00pm. Buses 118 and 218.

Located next door to one another on and around the Via Appia Antica south of the city, these tombs were originally an ancient Roman necropolis. They were then used by the early Christians as a meeting place as well as one of worship, and were finally a haven for them from prosecution. Here you can visit the **crypts of the Popes**, the crypt of Saint Cecilia, the crypt of Pope Eusebius, as well as frescoes dating back to the 3rd century CE. All three are an eerie reminder of the time before Christianity dominated the Western world. A time when Christians were actually the ones being persecuted instead of doing the persecuting. A great site for kids to explore.

ALTAR & MAUSOLEUM OF AUGUSTUS

Piazza Augosto Imperatore. Altar open 9:00am-2:00pm. You need to call to gain access to the mausoleum, *Tel. 06/6710-3819.* Closed Sundays. Buses 81, 90, 119, 926. Metro-Spagna.

The excellently preserved altar was built from 13-9 BCE to celebrate the peace established by Emperor Augustus following his victories in Gaul and Spain. It consists of a simple raised altar enclosed by a four-walled screen with openings at the front and back. Reconstructed and housed in a temporary structure in 1938 by Mussolini to glorify Italy's past, the carved friezes of flowers on the lower walls were created by Greek masons imported to Rome. The upper section displays mythical scenes in the history of Rome as well as scenes form the consecration ceremonies of the altar itself.

The altar originally stood in the Campo Marzio. Fragments came to light in 1568 during reconstruction on the Palazzo Fiano. Additional pieces were excavated in the mid-19th and early 20th centuries. Finally in 1938 a professional excavation and reassembly was undertaken. Currently a more permanent structure is on the verge of being completed to house the altar, which will also contain a small museum.

The mausoleum of Augustus is the circular structure nearby that is overrun with grass and shrubs. It used to be a series of intricate passageways where niches of urns filled with funeral ashes were located, and once was topped with a large statue of Augustus. It has been used as a fort, a bull ring, a theater and a concert hall. In 1938 when the altar of Augustus was dedicated, the medieval buildings surrounding the mausoleum were razed and the present bland piazza was built, creating a modern backdrop to this ancient historic site.

PYRAMID OF GAIUS CESTIUS

Piazzale Ostiense. Buses 13, 23, 57, 95, 716. Metro-Piramide.

Built in 12 BCE as a tomb for the Praetor Gaius Cestius, this structure is a prime example of the influence that Egypt and its religion had on ancient Rome. During the time of early Rome, a cult of Egyptology was one of the largest of the pagan religions. Built of brick and rock and covered with limestone, this is one of the more striking structures left from that time period and as such is a great photo op, one that my family has been coming back to since the '50s.

If you're out here at night, or in the evenings, the **Testaccio** section nearby is the place to be for nightlife. Rome's best discos are located here, as are number of restaurants.

PONTE MILVIO

Via Flaminia/Piazza Cardinale Consalvi. Take the 225 bus to Piazza Mancini and walk to Piazza Cardinale Consalvi, or take the 201 bus from Piazza Mancini.

Located north of the Aurelian and Servian walls, the Ponte Milvio was the first Roman bridge over the Tiber and was built in 109 CE. This bridge was the location of many military campaigns throughout Italian history, including one battle that helped establish Christianity as the world's dominant religion. Here in 312 CE Emperor Constantine defeated forces led by Maxentius. Constantine made a pact that if he won the battle, he would convert to Christianity. If he had not won this battle, pagan worship would more than likely be much more prominent than it is today.

The current bridge has been destroyed and rebuilt countless times but retains its original form. It was last destroyed in 1849 when Garibaldi's troops blew it up to prevent the advance of the French army. In 1985 it was closed to vehicular traffic for restoration and remains a pedestrian bridge today. The is a daily market on the side farthest from the city center which is worth visiting if you are in the area.

AURELIAN WALL

Built from 272-279 CE, this wall is a testament to the faded glory of the Roman Empire. Built to protect Rome from an incursion of Germanic tribes, one of the best places to witness its protective shield is at the top of the Via Veneto at the **Porta Pinciana**. The walls enclosed not only the old city of Rome but also what used to be farmland.

Today the walls extend to the Baths of Caracalla in the south, Piazza del Popolo in the north, Trastevere and Saint Peter's in the west, and the University and Stazione Termini in the East. They have a total length of about 12 miles, and consist of concrete rubble encased in brick almost 12 feet thick and 25 feet high. In some places the wall's height is 50 feet. In some places there is a parapet running across the top. Also there are 380 square towers interspersed along its length. These towers are a distance of two arrow shots apart, which was one hundred ancient Roman feet or just under 30 meters, or about 100 modern American feet.

There were 18 main roads over which gates were built. Many have been rebuilt to accommodate different defense strategies throughout the ages; most recently they were adapted for the onslaught of automobile traffic. The ones that are the best preserved with most of their Roman features are the **Porta San Sebastiano** (take bus 188 from San Giovanni in Laterano), **Porta Asinara** (next to Porta San Giovanni) and the **Porta Toscolana** (behind the train station).

COLUMN OF MARCUS AURELIUS

Piazza Colonna. Buses 56, 60, 62, 85. Metro-Barberini.

Carved between 180 and 196 CE, this column is a continuous spiral of bas reliefs celebrating Marcus Aurelius' military victories. It used to be surrounded by buildings from its own era, but only the ruins of the Temple of Hadrian located in the wall of the *Borsa* remain (see description below). Statues of Marcus Aurelius and his wife once adorned the top of the column, but they were replaced by a statue of St. Paul in the 16th century. Today this piazza has been made into another of Rome's car-free zones, since the citizens of this city, as well as other cities in Europe, are realizing that automobiles drastically eliminate community livability.

TEMPLE OF HADRIAN

Piazza di Pietra. Buses 56, 60, 62, 85. Metro-Barberini.

Located near Piazza Colonna and the Via del Corso, this is a fantastic example of architectural pastiche, where structures from different eras are blended together into one building. In this case, one wall of the modern Roman Stock Exchange (*Borsa*) has eleven Corinthian columns from the temple dedicated by Antonius Pius to his father Hadrian in 145 CE.

This is a great place for photos of how Rome's ancient past is woven together with the present. While here please note the path that runs in front of this sight. It leads to the Trevi Fountain and the Pantheon, and is marked with exhibit signs describing what the significance of this sight is. By building this pathway and erecting these signs, Rome has decided to forgo simply being a museum in spirit and has started to formally make itself into one.

Piazzas, Neighborhoods, Monuments & More

BORGHESE GARDENS

Buses 95, 490, 495, 910. Metro-Spagna.

The most picturesque park in Rome, complete with bike and jogging paths (you can rent bikes in the park), a lake where you can rent boats, a wonderful museum – **Galleria Borghese** – lush vegetation, expansive grass fields, the Roman **zoological park**, a large riding ring, and more.

This is the perfect place to come and relax in the middle of a hard day of touring. Sundays fill the park with families, couples and groups of people biking, jogging, walking their dogs, playing soccer, strolling or simply relaxing in Rome's largest green space. Small food stands are interspersed in the park offering refreshments and snacks.

The gardens are a great sanctuary just outside the ancient walls of Rome. If you want an afternoon's respite from the sights of the city, or you're tired of spending time in your hotel room during the siesta hours, escape to these luscious and spacious gardens.

To get to the gardens either exit the old walls of Rome through the gates at the Piazza del Popolo or at the top of the Via Veneto. From the Piazza del Popolo exit, the gardens will be on your right through the iron gates just across the busy Piazzale Flaminio. Once you enter you will be on the Viale Washington. Anywhere to the left of you, after a few hundred meters, will be prime park land. From the Via Veneto gate of the Aurelian wall, cross the major thoroughfare in front of you and you're in the Borghese. From here stroll to your right and you will instantly find a pleasant area to picnic or take a small nap for the afternoon. Make sure you keep an eye out for those heated Italian couples if you have kids in tow.

Galleria Borghese

One of Rome's finest museums is in the Borghese Gardens, the **Galleria Borghese**. For those of you who entered the Gardens from Piazza del Popolo, it will be a long hike up the Viale Washington to the lake, and around it to the Viale Dell'Uccelleria (the zoo will be on your left) which leads directly to the Galleria Borghese.

From the Via Veneto it is not quite as long. From where you first entered the gardens, there is a road, Viale Del Museo Borghese, on your right. Take this all the way to the Galleria.

The Galleria Borghese was built by Dutch architect Hans van Santes during the 1820's. It houses a large number of rare masterpieces from many disciplines and countries. There are classical works of Greeks and Romans, along with 16th and 17th century paintings by such notables as Raphael, Titian, Caravaggio, and Antonella da Messina. Sculptures are also featured with works by Lorenzo Bernini, Pietro Bernini, and Houndon. A must see when in Rome.

For more details, see the Galleria Borghese description below under *Museums*.

CAMPO DEI FIORI

Campo dei Fiori. Buses 46, 62, 64, 65, 70.

This is a typically Roman piazza that hosts a lively flower and food market every morning, except Sundays, until 1:00pm. You'll hear the cries of the vendors blending with the bargaining of the customers. Though there are now some vendors specifically catering to the tacky souvenir needs of tourists, most stands are for the locals, and the majority of the visitors are the same. A perfect place to see and smell the vibrant local beauty and bounty of Rome.

The campo used to be a square where heretics were burned at the stake and criminals were hanged. The monument in the middle is in memory of Giordano Bruno, a famous philosopher who was burned here in 1600.

This is a great place to come at night, because it is home to a great restaurant, **La Carbonara**, that serves the best *spaghetti alla vongole verace* I've ever had, and a great American-style bar, **The Drunken Ship**. It is also an active local shopping area. So if you're looking for intriguing and original items, or rare antiques, wander through the back streets around this piazza, Piazza Navona and the Pantheon.

GIANICOLO
Piazza Garibaldi. Bus 41.

Offering one of the best panoramas of Rome, the **Gianicolo Hill** is located between Trastevere and the Vatican, across the river from the old city of Rome. At the terrace of the Piazza Garibaldi, you'll find the equestrian statue of Giuseppe Garibaldi, as well as a panoramic photo, with accompanying titles for all the domes and buildings of note, of the scene laid out in front of you This is a perfect photo opportunity. The walk may be a little tiring but the view is calming and serene.

ISOLA TIBERINA
Buses 44, 75, 170, 710, 718, 719.

Halfway across the river on the way towards Trastevere, this island used to be a dumping ground for dead and sick slaves. At that time, the 3rd century BCE, there was also a cult of healing (aesculapius) located here. Currently half the island is taken up by a hospital showing that traditions do live on. The church on the island, **San Bartolomeo** was built in the 12th century, and was substantially altered in the seventeenth. A fun place to relax with wide walkways around the island and along the river. The perfect place for a relaxing picnic. The remains of the Pons Aemilius, the oldest bridge in Rome, can be seen south of the Isola Tiberina. The bridge was washed away in 1598 and never rebuilt.

JEWISH GHETTO
Buses 780, 774, 717.

Long before any Pope reigned in Rome, another religion thrived here: Judaism. The ancient Jewish quarter is a peaceful, tiny riverside neighborhood with narrow curving street and ocher apartment buildings. It looks much like any other section of Rome until closer inspection reveals Kosher food signs, men in skullcaps and spray painted stars of David. Technically the Ghetto ceased to exist in 1846 when its walls were torn down, but the neighborhood that retains its name remains home to Europe's oldest and proudest Jewish community.

The history of the Jews in Rome dates back to 161 BCE when Judas Maccabaeus sent ambassadors to Rome to seek protection against the Syrians. Over time many traders followed these emissaries and a Jewish community sprouted. After Rome colonized and eventually conquered the Land of Israel culminating in 70 CE with the fall of Jerusalem and the destruction of its Temple (an event etched in stone on the Arch of Titus), over a short time as many 40,000 Jews settled in Rome. They contributed in all aspects of Roman society and they and their religion were accepted as different but equal. But that was before Christianity became the religion of the state, at which point discrimination against the Jews became widespread.

In the 13th century, for instance, the Catholic Church ordered Jews to wear a distinctive sign on their clothing: a yellow circle for men and two blue stripes for women. Anti-Semitism continued to grow to the point where in 1556, Pope Paul IV confined all Jews to this small poor section of the city and closed it in with high walls. This was not the first virtual imprisonment of its kind, because the Venetians did the same thing to its Jewish population four decades earlier. In Venice the Jews were forced to live on the site of an old cannon foundry, or *getto*. The name stuck and has since evolved to mean any section of a city that is composed of one type of activity (e.g., an Office Ghetto), or is inhabited by one group of people.

Today there are over 16,000 Jews living in Rome and the Ghetto is still the meeting place. To find out more about this neighborhood stop in the **Jewish Museum** in the **Sinagoga** (Lungotevere de Cenci, *Tel. 06/684-0061, Fax 06/6840-0684;* open 9:00am-6:30pm Tuesday-Friday, until 8:00pm on Sundays and also from 9:00pm-midnight on Saturdays in the summer. English tours E7.). Inside you will find a plan of the original ghetto, as well as artifacts from the 17th century Jewish community.

Besides learning about the history of the ghetto, you can find some of Rome's truly great restaurants here along with many ancient Roman buildings, arches, and columns completely incorporated into modern day buildings. It seems as if a number of structures have been better preserved in this area. Maybe it is because the locals did not have the resources to tear them down and replace them. Whatever the situation, visit the Ghetto and feel history come alive.

PANTHEON
Piazza della Rotonda. *Tel. 06/6830-0230.* Open Monday-Saturday 9:00am-6:30pm, Sundays 9:00am-1:00pm. At 10:00am on Sundays is a mass. Tel. 06/6830-0230. Buses 70, 81, 87, 90.

Located in a vibrant piazza, the **Pantheon** is one of the most famous and best preserved monuments of ancient Rome. Besides the architectural beauty, the entrance area to the Pantheon is by far the coolest place in Rome during the heat wave of August. So if you want to relax in cool comfort in the middle of a hot day, park yourself just in front of the entrance under the portico.

First constructed by Agrippa in 27 BCE, it was restored after a fire in 80 CE and returned to its original rotunda shape by the Emperor Hadrian. In 609

CE, it was dedicated as a Christian Church and called Santa Maria Rotunda. In the Middle Ages it served as a fortress. In 1620 the building's bronze ceiling was removed and melted into the cannons for Castel Sant'Angelo and used for Bernini's Baldacchino (Grand Canopy) in Saint Peter's.

The building is made up of red and gray Egyptian granite. Each of the sixteen columns is 12.5 meters high and is composed of a single block.

You enter the building by way of the cool and comfortable portal area and the original bronze door. As you enter it is impossible not to feel the perfect symmetry of space and harmony of its architectural lines. This feeling is somewhat lessened by the fact that the Roman authorities have placed a ticket booth inside along with a small souvenir stand, each of which detracts from the perfection of the structure. Nonetheless you will still be awed by the marvelous dome (diameter 43 meters) with the hole in the middle through which rain cascades during moments of inclement weather.

There are three niches in the building, two of which contain tombs: **Victor Emmanuel II** (died 1878), one of Italy's few war heroes, **Umberto I** (died 1900) and **Queen Margherita** (died 1926), and in another niche the tomb of renowned artist **Raphael Sanzio** (died 1520).

PIAZZA DEL POPOLO
Buses 90, 119. Metro-Flaminio.

This impressive piazza is the base of the ascent to the **Pincio**, a relaxing area of Rome where you can get some great views of the city. It was consolidated as a piazza in 1538 during the Renaissance, and today has been made another car-free zone in the city of Rome. Citizens of this city, as well as other cities in Europe, are realizing that automobiles may enhance individual transportation possibilities, but they drastically eliminate livability. In 1589, the **Egyptian Obelisk** which is 24 meters high and came from Egypt during the time of Ramses II in the 8th century BCE, was moved from the Circus Maximus and erected in the middle of the square. The present layout was designed by G. Valadier at the beginning of the 19th century and is decorated on its sides

Eerie Roman Trivia

There is a movie theater immediately next to Santa Maria dei Miracoli (near Piazza del Popolo) that played the first-run release of *The Exorcist* when it came out in the 1970's. During the first showing of the film, the cross on the top of the church was inexplicably dislodged from its perch, and as it fell miraculously avoided the rooftops, and shattered directly in front of the movie theater. No one was hurt but all of Italy was shocked. This is a true story.

∂

with two semi-cycles of flowers and statues. During this re-design the obelisk was placed in a new fountain with the present sculpted lions.

There are two symmetrical baroque churches at the south end of the piazza flanking the intersection of the Via del Corso. These two churches, **Santa Maria dei Miracoli** (1678) — also called Santa Maria del Popolo — and **Santa Maria in Monesanto** (1675) both have picturesque cupolas that were begun by C. Rainaldi and finished by Bernini and Carlo Fontana respectively.

PIAZZA NAVONA

Buses 70, 81, 87, 90.

The piazza is on the site of a stadium built by Domitian in 86 CE that he used for mock naval battles, other gladiatorial contests, as well as horse races. The stadium's north entrance has been excavated and you can see the stone arch of the entrance outside of the Piazza Navona toward the Tiber on the south side of the Piazza di Tor Sanguigna. Located some 20 feet below the current street level, this is a glance back in time at how much sediment has built up in Rome over the past 2,000 years.

After the Roman era the piazza was lined with small squatters' homes which followed the tiers of the stadium, but because of its wide open space it soon became a prime spot for large buildings. Today the style of the piazza is richly Baroque, featuring works by two great masters, **Bernini** and **Borromini**.

Located in the middle of the square is Bernini's fantastic **Fontana Dei Quattro Fiumi** (Fountain of Four Rivers), sculpted from 1647-51. The four figures supporting the large obelisk (a Bernini trademark) represent the four major rivers known at the time: the Danube, the Ganges, the Nile, and the Plata Rivers. The idea behind the representation of the statues is that the Catholic church reigns triumphant over the world.

Besides the statue's obvious beauty and meaning, Bernini has hidden a subtle treasure in this piece. Notice the figure representing the Nile shielding its eyes. Some historians interpret the position of the figure's hand blocking its view of the facade of the church it is facing, **Santa Agnese in Agone**, as a statement of revulsion. This church was designed by Bernini's rival at the time, Borromini, and Bernini, as the story is told, playfully showed his disdain for his rival's design through the sculpted disgust in his statue. Others claim the revulsion comes from the fact that the church, built as a family chapel for Pope Innocent X's Palazzo Doria Pamphili, is located on the site of an old neighborhood brothel. Maybe both are true?

To the south of the piazza is the **Statue of Il Moro** (actually a replica) created by Bernini from 1652-1654. To the north is a basin with a 19th century **Statue of Neptune** struggling with a sea monster.

To savor the artistic and architectural beauty, as well as the vibrant nightlife of the piazza, choose a table at one of the local bars or cafés and sample some excellent Roman *gelato* (ice cream), grab a coffee, or have a meal and watch the people go by. Navona has been one of Rome's many gathering spots for people of all ages since the early 18th century. You'll find local art vendors, caricaturists, hippies selling string bracelets, and much more. This is the place to come for ice cream in Rome, and Tre Scalini is the most famous *gelateria*. The piazza is also home to a fun Christmas fair that lasts from mid-December to mid-January. Filled with booths and performers, it is much like an old fashioned carnival that kids of all age love. Another feature of Navona that kids will love is that it contains two of Rome's best toy stores. This is a piazza you cannot miss if you come to Rome.

PIAZZA DI SPAGNA & THE SPANISH STEPS

Buses 52, 53, 56, 58, 60, 61, 62, 71, 81. Metro-Spagna.

This is one of the most beautiful spots in Rome. It is named after the old Spanish Embassy to the Holy See that used to stand on the site. The current Spanish Embassy is just down the road. The 137 steps are officially called the Scalinata della Trinita dei Monti, and are named for the church at the top. But most people just call them the **Spanish Steps**.

The fountain in the middle of the piazza is known as the **Barcaccia** and was designed in 1628 by Pietro Bernini in commemoration of the big flood of 1598. To the right is the column of the **Immaculate Conception** erected in 1865 by Pius IX. The Spanish Steps were built in the 17th century. Besides being the location of fine works of art and architecture, it is also a favorite gathering spot for Italians of all ages.

TRASTEVERE

Buses 44, 75, 170, 710, 718, 719.

This is the perfect place to immerse yourself in Roman life. **Trastevere** literally means "across the river" and this separation has allowed the area to remain virtually untouched by the advances of time. Until recently it was one of the poorest sections of Rome, but now it is starting to become gentrified. Yet these changes have not altered Trastevere's charm. You'll find interesting shops and boutiques, and plenty of excellent restaurants among the small narrow streets and *piazzette* (small squares). The maze of streets is a fun place to wander and wonder where you're going to end up.

During the month of July the *Trasteverini* express their feeling of separation from the rest of Rome with their summertime festival called **Noiantri**, meaning "we the others," in which they mix wine-induced revelry with religious celebration in a party of true bacchanalian proportions. *Trasteverini* cling to their roots of selling clothing and furnishings to make ends meet by continuing to hold the **Porta Portese** flea market on Sundays. The market and event are true Trastevere even though the area has been gentrified for decades.

This area offers some of the best dining and casual nightlife in town. Here you can sit in a piazza bar sipping Sambuca or wine and watch the life of Rome pass before your eyes. To accommodate this type of activity many stores have begun to stay open later. Trastevere is a great place to enjoy for a day or even more, because it is the way Rome used to be.

TREVI FOUNTAIN
Piazza di Trevi. Buses 52, 53, 56, 58, 60, 61, 62, 71, 81. Metro-Barberini.

This is the largest and most impressive of the famous fountains in Rome and is truly spectacular when it is lit up at night. Commissioned by Clement XII, it was built by Nicola Salvi in 1762 from a design he borrowed from Bernini and takes up an entire wall of the Palazzo Poli built in 1730. In the central niche you see Neptune on his chariot drawn by marine horses preceded by two tritons. In the left niche you see the statue representing Abundance, and to the right Health. The four statues up top depict the seasons and the crest is of the family of Clement XII, Corsini.

There is an ancient custom, legend, or myth, that says that all those who throw a coin into the fountain are destined to return to Rome. So turn your back to the fountain and throw a coin over your left shoulder with your right hand into the fountain and fate will carry you back. That is if you can get close enough. In the summer, and especially at night, this place is packed wall to wall with people. Also, please don't try and recreate Anita Ekberg's scene in the film *La Dolce Vita* when she waded through the fountain to taunt Marcello Mastroiani. It is completely illegal to walk in the fountain, and the authorities enforce this regulation severely. If they didn't, the local kids would all swim in and collect the coins thrown by tourists.

VATICAN CITY
Piazza San Pietro. Buses 19, 62, 64, or 492. Metro-Ottaviano. The city is generally inaccessible except for official business, but you can look into gardens from the cupola of St. Peter's.

The Vatican (officially referred to as **The Holy See**) is a completely autonomous country within the Italian Republic and has its own radio station, railway, newspaper, stamps, money, and diplomatic representatives in major capitals. Though it doesn't have an army, the **Swiss Guards** volunteer to protect it.

La Citta Vaticano sits on the right bank of the Tiber river, in the foothills of the Monte Mario and Gianicolo section of Rome. In ancient Rome this was the site of the Gardens of Nero and the main circus where thousands of Christians were martyred. Saint Peter met his fate here around 67 CE. Today it is the world center for the Catholic Church, rich in priceless art, antiques, and spiritual guidance. (See Vatican Museums.)

VIA APPIA ANTICA
Buses 118 and 218.
The most celebrated of all ancient Roman roads was begun by Appius Claudius Caecus in 312 BCE. The road has been preserved in its original character as have the original monuments. At first it was the chief line of communication between Rome and Southern Italy, Greece, and the eastern possessions of the Roman Empire. Now it is a well traveled picturesque road to the country and the famous Roman/Christian **catacombs**.

VIA VENETO
Buses 52, 53, 56, 58. Metro-Barberini.
Definitely the most famous and fashionable street in Rome. It used to be the center of all artistic activities as well as the meeting place for the jet set, but it doesn't quite have the same allure it used to. Nonetheless, it's still a great place to wander since it is flanked by wonderful hotels, stores, and cafés.
At the bottom of the street is the **Piazza Barberini**, where you'll find the graceful **Fontana delle Api** (Fountain of the Bees) as well as the more famous **Fontana del Tritone**, both designed and sculpted by Bernini. Both sculptures were created to celebrate the Barberini family and their new palace just up the Via delle Quattro Fontane. Up the Via Veneto a little ways from the Piazza Barberini is the grandiose **Palazzo Margherita**, built by G. Koch in 1890 and is now the home of the American Embassy. You'll recognize it by the armed guards and the American flag flying out front.

VITTORIO EMANUELE II MONUMENT
Piazza Vittorio Emanuele. Buses 70, 81, 87, 90.
A monument to the first king of Italy who died in 1878. Work started in 1885 but was not finished until 1910. It is an inflated version of the Temple of Fortune on the hillside at Praenestina. To natives it is affectionately called "The Wedding Cake," since its shape and white marble make it look eerily like a larger version of one. The monument is also home to the tomb of the unknown soldier.

Churches

SANTA CECILIA IN TRASTEVERE
Via Anicia. Hours 10:00am–noon and 4:00pm–6:00pm. Buses 181, 280, 44, 75, 717, 170, 23, 65.
Normally visitors don't go to Trastevere to visit churches. Instead they are attracted by the more secular delights of this part of Rome. But if you're

interested in beautiful churches, **Santa Cecilia** is one to visit in Trastevere; the other is Santa Maria.

Santa Cecilia's was founded in the fifth century and had a make-over in the ninth century as well as the 16th. A baroque door leads to a picturesque court, beyond which is a baroque facade, with a mosaic frieze above the portico, and a beautiful bell tower erected in the 12th century. There are several important works of art to be found in the church, not the least of which is the expressive statue of Santa Cecilia by Stefano Maderno. It represents the body of the saint in the exact position it was found when the tomb was opened in 1559.

Another place of interest to visit on the church grounds is the Roman house where Santa Cecilia suffered her martyrdom. There are two rooms preserved, one of them has the bath where she died. It still has the pipes and large bronze cauldron for heating water. Which is how she was martyred, with hot water and steam. A great church to visit, not just for the art, but also for the history.

SAN CLEMENTE

Via di San Giovanni Laterano. Admission E2 (to the lower church). Hours to visit the basement 9:00am–1:00pm. Not on Sundays. Catch bus 65. Metro-San Giovanni.

Located between the Colosseum and St. John Lateran is this hidden gem of a church, **San Clemente**. One of the better preserved medieval churches in Rome, it was originally built in the fifth century. The Normans destroyed it in 1084 but it was reconstructed in 1108 by Pachal II. Today when you enter you are in what is called the **Upper Church**, a simple and basic basilica divided by two rows of columns. Above the altar are some intricately inlaid 12th century mosaics.

The thrill of this church is that you can descend a set of stairs to the **Lower Church**, which was discovered in 1857, and immediately you have left the Middle Ages and are now in subterranean passages that housed an early Christian place of worship, from the days when Christians had to practice their religion below ground for fear of persecution.

Even further below that are the remains of a temple dedicated to Mithraic, a religion that practised in the 4th century CE known for their barbaric blood rites. Brought to Rome from Asia Minor in 67 BCE by soldiers of Rome's Legions, this pagan religion became entrenched in the military because of its bonds of violence, fidelity, loyalty and secrecy. Before the Roman Legions adopted it, Mithraic was the religion of Alexander the Great's army.

This is a must see church while in Rome. They also have a bucolic little porticoed garden, where you can relax, with a spritzing fountain in the center.

SAN GIOVANNI IN LATERANO

Piazza San Giovanni in Laterano 4, *Tel. 06/7720-7991.* Hours Bapistery: 6:00am–12:30pm and 4:00–7:00pm; Cloisters 9:00am-5:00pm. Buses 16, 85, 87, and 650. Metro-San Giovanni.

Another of the great basilicas of Rome. Most people don't realize that this church is the cathedral of Rome as well as the whole Catholic world, and not St. Peter's. Established on land donated by Constantine in 312 CE, that first building has long been replaced by many reconstructions, fires, sackings and earthquakes over the centuries. Today, the simple and monumental facade of the church, created by Allessandro Galiliei in 1735, is topped by fourteen colossal statues of Christ, the Apostles, and saints. It rises on the site of the ancient palace of Plautinus Lateranus (hence the name), one of the noble families of Rome many eons ago.

To get inside, you must pass through the bronze door that used to be attached to the old Roman Senate house. The interior of the church, laid out in the form of a Latin cross, has five naves filled with historical and artistic objects. In total it is 150 meters long, while the **central nave** is 87 meters long. This central nave is flanked by 12 spires from which appear 12 statues of the Apostles from the 18th century. The wooden ceiling and the marble flooring are from the 15th century.

The most beautiful artistic aspect of the church is the vast transept, which is richly decorated with marbles and frescoes portraying the *Leggenda Aurea* of Constantine. One piece of historical interest is the wooden table, on which it is said that Saint Peter served mass, which you'll find in the **Papal Altar**.

SAN PIETRO (SAINT PETER'S)

Piazza San Pietro. Hours 8:00am–6:00pm, but only until 5:00pm in the winter. *Tel. 06/6988-4466.* Buses 19, 62, 64, or 492. Metro-Ottaviano.

Located in the monumental square **Piazza San Pietro**, Saint Peter's is a masterpiece created by **Bernini** between 1655 and 1667, and is the largest church in the world. The square itself is oval and 240 meters at its largest diameter. It is composed of 284 massive marble columns, and 88 pilasters forming three galleries 15 meters wide. Surrounding the square, above the oval structure are 140 statues of saints.

In the center of the square is an obelisk 25.5 meters high with four bronze lions at its base, all of which were brought from Heliopolis during the reign of Caligula (circa 40 CE) and which originally stood in the circus of Nero. All of them were placed here in 1586. Below the monument you can see the points of the compass and the names of the winds.

Around this obelisk during the Christmas season a life-sized crèche is erected, and since 1980 has become a site that many Italians come to admire during that season. If in Italy during this time, come out and pay a visit, especially at night, when it is all lit up.

Also of interest are two porphyry's (disks) in the ground in St. Peter's Square, located on either side of the obelisk. If you stand on either disk and look at the columns (which run four deep) surrounding the square, it appears as if there is only one column instead of four! People line up to stand on the disks and witness the brilliance of the architects of the structure.

To reach Saint Peter's you must pass the obelisk and walk up a gradual incline. The church rises on the site where Saint Peter is buried. The early Christians erected a small oratory on the site of the tomb, but that was destroyed in 326 when Constantine the Great erected the first Basilica on this site. Over the centuries the church began to expand and became incongruously and lavishly decorated, so that by 1452 Pope Nicholas V decided to make it more uniform. He commissioned Bernardo Rossellino to design a new structure. When the Pope died three years late this work was interrupted, but in 1506 Pope Julius II, with the assistance of **Bramante**, continued the work on a grander scale.

Bramante died in 1514 before his work could be finished. His successor was **Raphael**, and when he died four years later, **Baldassare Peruzzi** and **Antonio de Sangallo the Younger** took over the responsibility jointly. Work was interrupted by the sack of Rome in 1527, then again in 1536 when Peruzzi died. When Sangallo died in 1546, the project was taken over and modified by the 72-year old **Michelangelo**. Before he died eight years later, he had modified Bramante's plan for the dome and we are blessed with his pointed Florentine version today. His design is obviously modeled after Brunelleschi's brilliant dome on the Duomo in Florence.

After Michelangelo died, the plans he made for St. Peter's were more or less adhered to by his successors Vignola, Pizzo Ligorio, Giacomo dell Porta, Domenico Fontana, and finally Carlo Maderno, who designed the facade according to his plan. On November 1, 1626, Urbano VIII dedicated the Basilica as we know it today.

The Facade
Rounding off, the **facade** is 115 meters long and 45 meters high, and is

Proper Attire at Museums & Churches
When you're visiting most museums and monuments in Italy, follow these necessary rules: **Women** should wear either long pants or a long skirt or dress, and a top with sleeves. **Men** should wear long pants and no tank tops. Both men and women will be denied entry to St. Peter's, and to many other sights as well, if wearing shorts or short skirts and/ or a revealing top! Don't expect Italy to adapt to you. You are in another country. Adapt to Italy.

☙

approached by a gradually sloping grand staircase. At the sides of this staircase are the statues of **Saint Peter** (by De Fabis) and **Saint Paul** (by Adamo Tadolini). On the balustrade, held up by eight Corinthian columns and four pilasters, are the colossal statues of the Savior and St. John the Baptist surrounded by the Apostles, excluding Saint Peter.

There are nine balconies, and from the central one the Pope gives his Christmas and Easter benedictions. There are five doors from which to enter the church, but today only the large central one is used.

The Interior

The church is more than 15,000 square meters in area, 211 meters long and 46 meters high. There are 229 marble columns: 533 of travertine, 16 of bronze, 90 of stucco, and 44 altars. On the floor of the central nave you'll find lines drawn identifying where other churches in the world would fit if placed in Saint Peter's. Kids love to explore this aspect of the basilica.

Also on the floor, near the front entrance, is a red disk indicating the spot where **Charlemagne** was crowned Holy Roman Emperor by Leo III on Christmas Day in 800 CE. To the right of this, in the first chapel, is the world famous *Pieta* created by Michelangelo when he was only 24, in the year 1498. In the niches of the pilasters that support the arches are statues of the founders of many religious orders. In the last one on the right you'll find the seated bronze statue of Saint Peter. The statue's foot has been rubbed by so many people for good luck that its toes has all but disappeared.

Just past the statue is the grand **cupola** created by Michelangelo. One of the most amazing architectural wonders of all times, it is held up by four colossal spires which lead to a number of open chapels. Under the cupola, above the high altar rises the famous **Baldacchino** (or Grand Canopy) made by Bernini. It is constructed of bronze taken mainly from the roof of the

Free English-Language Tours of St. Peter's

One of the best ways to see St. Peter's, and one of the least known is on a FREE **English-language tour** of the basilica by trained volunteer guides. Available seven days a week, Monday-Saturday at 3:00pm and Sundays at 2:30pm, the tour lasts an hour and a half and offers an in-depth historical and religious perspective of this magnificent church. The tours start at the information desk to the right as you enter the portico of St. Peter's. For more information: *Tel. 06/6972.*

To coordinate your day, go to the Vatican museums in the morning, have a light lunch, get here for the tour about half an hour early, and enjoy a stimulating and fact-filled afternoon.

‿ঌ

Pantheon. In front of the altar is the **Chapel of Confessions** made by Maderno, around which are 95 perpetually lit lamps illuminating the **Tomb of Saint Peters**. In front of the shrine is the kneeling **Statue of Pius VI** made by Canova in 1822.

Throughout the rest of the Basilica you'll find a variety of superb statues and monuments (including the magnificent *Pieta* by Michelangelo), many tombs of Popes, and a wealth of chapels, not the least of which is the **Gregorian Chapel** designed by Michelangelo and executed by Giacomo della Porta. It is rich in marbles, stuccos, and mosaics, all put together in the creative Venetian style by Madonna del Soccorso in the 12th century.

If you grow tired of the many beautiful works of art and wish to get a bird's eye view of everything, you can ascend into Michelangelo's Cupola either by stairs (537 of them) or by elevator. If you come to Saint Peter's, you should do this. Kids of all age love it.

SANTA MARIA DELLA CONCEZIONE aka "CHURCH OF BONES"

Right at the bottom of the Via Veneto you will find the famous 'Church of Bones.' In the **Cappucin crypt** of the church there is a macabre arrangement of the bones of over 4,000 skeletons of ancient friars who were exhumed and decoratively placed on the walls. The reason this display exists is that a law was passed many centuries ago which decreed that no graveyards or burial grounds could exist inside the walls of Rome. Rather than part with the remains of their brothers by re-burying them in a cemetery outside the walls, the Cappucin brothers exhumed the fraternal remains and decorated the crypt with them. I guarantee that you'll never see a sight like this anywhere else.

SANTA MARIA MAGGIORE

Piazza di Santa Maria Maggiore. *Tel. 06/483-195.* Hours 8:00am– 7:00pm. Buses 4, 9, 16, 27, 714, 715. Metro-Termini.

Like St. Paul's Outside the Walls, St. Peter's, and St. John Lateran, this is one of the four patriarchal basilicas of Rome. Its name derives from the fact that it is the largest church (*maggiore*) in Rome dedicated to the Madonna (*maria*). The facade, originally built in the 12th century, was redone in the 18th century to include the two canon's houses flanking the church. It is a simple two story facade and as such is nothing magnificent to look at, and as result, if you are not going out of your way to come here, many people simply amble on by.

But the interior, in all its 86 meters of splendor, is interesting and inspiring mainly because of the 5th-century mosaics, definitely the best in Rome, its frescoes, and multi-colored marble. On the right wall of the **Papal Altar** is the funeral monument to Sixtus V and on the left wall the monument to Pius V, both created by Fontana with excellent bas-reliefs. Opposite this chapel is the **Borghese Chapel**, so called since the sepulchral vaults of the wealthy

Borghese family lie beneath it. Here you'll view the beautiful bas-relief monumental tombs to Paul V and Clement VIII on its left and right walls. Towards the west end of the church is the **Sforza Chapel** with its intricately designed vault. Pius VI's eerie crypt is below and in front of the main altar.

SANTA MARIA SOPRA MINERVA
Piazza della Minerva (behind the Pantheon). Hours 7:00am–7:00pm. Buses 70, 81, 87, 90.

Built on the pagan ruins of a temple to Minerva (hence the name) this must-see church was begun in 1280 by the Dominican Order which also commissioned the beautiful Santa Maria Novella in Florence. With their wide Gothic vaulted nave and aisles, the two churches are much alike in design. The facade was created during the Renaissance by Meo del Caprino in 1453.

In this expansive church, you can find many tombs of famous personages of the 15th through the 16th centuries as well as beautiful paintings, sculptures, frescoes and bas relief work. Saint Catherine of Siena, who died in Rome in 1380, rests at the high altar. To the left of the altar is the statue of *Christ Carrying the Cross* created by Michelangelo in 1521. The bronze drapes were added later for modesty. If you compare this work to the one to the right of the altar, *John the Baptist* by Obici, you can easily see why Michelangelo is considered such a master. His statue looks like it could come to life, while the one by Obici simply appears carved out of stone.

Behind the altar are the tombs of Pope Clement VII and Leo X which were created by the Florentine sculptor Baccio Bandanelli. In the Sacristy is a chapel covered with frescoes by Antoniazzo Romano, brought here in 1637 from the house where Catherine of Siena died.

In front of the church is a wonderful sculpture of an elephant with an obelisk on his bac, which was designed by Bernini and carved by Ercole Ferrata called *Il Pulcino*.

SANTA MARIA IN TRASTEVERE
Piazza Santa Maria in Trastevere 1. Hours 7:00am–7:00pm. Mass at 9:00am, 10:30am, noon, and 6:00pm. Buses 181, 280, 44, 75, 717, 170, 23, 65.

A small church in Trastevere, in a piazza of the same name that is frequented by many locals and tourists alike, making the church one of the most visited. Around this church are some of the best restaurants and cafés in all of Rome, a popular English language theater, a handsome 17th century fountain where hippies hang out, and the Palace of San Calisto.

This was one of Rome's earliest churches and the first to be dedicated to the Virgin Mary. It was built in the 4th century and remodeled between 1130-1143. It is best known for its prized mosaics, especially the 12th and 13th century representation of the Madonna which adorns the facade of the church. The Romanesque bell-tower was built in the 12th century. The interior is of three naves separated by columns purloined from ancient Roman temples.

On the vault you'll find exquisite mosaics depicting the Cross, emblems of the Evangelists, and Christ and the Madonna enthroned among the Saints (created by Domenichino in 1140). Lower down, the mosaics of Pietro Cavallini done in 1291 portray, in six panels, the life of the Virgin.

SAN PAOLO FUORI LE MURA

Via Ostiense. Church open 7:00am–6:00pm. Cloisters Open 9:00am–1:00pm and 3:00pm–6:00pm. Metro-San Paolo.

Located a short distance beyond the Porta Paolo, **St. Paul's Outside the Walls** (San Paolo Fuori le Mura) is the fourth of the patriarchal basilicas in Rome. It is second only in size to St. Peter's and sits above the tomb of St. Paul. It was built by Constantine in 314 CE and then enlarged by Valentinian in 386 CE and later by Theodosius. It was finally completed by Honorius, his son.

In 1823, the church was almost completely destroyed by a terrible fire and many of its great works of art were lost. Immediately afterward, its renovation began and today it seems as magnificent as ever. (So much so that every time my family returns to Rome, whoever is left lines up just inside to the left of the entrance to the *quadroportici* with its 150 granite columns and get our picture taken with the palm trees in the background. We've been doing this since the 1950's and in that time the palms have grown from stubby bushes into gigantic trees.) With the beautiful garden surrounded by the great rows of columns, the palms growing in the center, the gigantic statue of St. Paul, and the facade with mosaics of four prophets (Isaiah, Jeremaih, Ezekial, and Daniel), just getting inside this church is a visual treat.

The interior is 120 meters long and has four rows of columns and five naves. The columns in the central nave are Corinthian that can be identified by their splendidly ornate capitals. The walls contain Medallion Portraits of the Popes from Saint Peter to Pius XI. On the High Altar still sits the ancient Gothic tabernacle of Arnolfo di Cambio (13th century) that was saved from the fire in 1823. Saint Paul rests beneath the altar in the confessional. The mosaic in the apse, with its dominating figure of Christ, was created by artists from the Republic of San Marino in 1220.

To the left of the apse is the **Chapel of St. Stephen**, with the large statue of the saint created by R. Rainaldi, and the **Chapel of the Crucifix** created by Carlo Maderno. This chapel contains the crucifix which is said to have spoken to Saint Bridget in 1370. Also here is St. Ignatius de Loyola, who took the formal vows that established the Jesuits as a religious order. To the right of the apse is the **Chapel of San Lorenzo** and the **Chapel of Saint Benedict** with its 12 columns. One other place of note in the church are the cloisters that contain fragments of ancient inscriptions and sarcophagi from the early Christian era.

The Masters in Rome

Listed here are where you can find some of the works of the Masters of Italian art:

Michelangelo — Sistine Chapel, Statue of Moses (San Pietro in Vincoli), Pieta (St. Peter's), Dome of St. Peter's, Christ Carrying the Cross (SM Sopra Minerva), Campidoglio square and steps.

Bernini — The Ecstasy of Santa Teresa (SM della Vittoria, Via XX Settembre 17), Ecstasy of Beata Ludovica Albertoni (S. Francesco a Ripa, P.za S. Fracesco d'Assisi), the Baldacchino (St. Peter's), the Throne (St. Peter's), the Tomb of Pope Alexander VII (St. Peter's) the square and colonade of St. Peter's, Fountain of the Four Rivers (Piazza Navona), San Andrea al Quirinale, Elephant Obelisk (outside of SM Sopra Minerva), Ponte San Angelo.

Caravaggio — Painting of Saints Peter and Paul (SM del Popolo), Madonna dei Pellegrini (SanAgostino, Via della Scrofa 80), The Life of St. Matthew (three paintings in S. Luigi dei Fracesi), and a number of works, including Young Girl with Basket of Fruit, and The Sick Bacchus (which is a self-portrait) in the Borghese Gallery.

Raphael — Numerous works, including Lady of the Unicorn and Deposition in the Borghese Gallery, Chigi Chapel (SM del Popolo), La Fornarina (Palazzo Barberini), Cherub holding a Festoon (Academy of San Luca), Double Portrait (Doria Pamphili Gallery), The Prophet Isaiah (Sant'Agostino), the Loggia di Psiche (Villa Farnesina), and a number of works, including the School of Athens, in the Vatican Museums.

SAN PIETRO IN VINCOLI

Piazza di San Pietro in Vincoli. Hours 7:00am–12:30pm and 3:30pm–6:00pm. Metro-Cavour.

Located only a few blocks from the Colosseum, this church was founded in 442 by the Empress Eudoxia as a shrine dedicated to preserving the chains with which Herod bound St. Peter in Jerusalem. These chains are in a crypt under the main altar.

But the reason to come to this church is the tomb of Julius II. Not really the tomb itself, because the great patron of the arts Julius is actually interred in St. Peter's, but come for the unforgettable seated figure of *Moses*. Created by the master himself, Michelangelo, this statue captures the powerful personification of justice and law of the Old Testament.

In fact, Moses appears as if he is ready to leap to his feet and pass judgment on you as you stand there admiring him. You can almost see the cloth covering his legs, or the long beard covering his face move in the breeze.

Flanking Moses are equally exquisite statues of *Leah* and *Rachel* also done by Michelangelo. Everything else was carved by his pupils. Because of this one work, this church is definitely worth your time.

Museums

CASTEL SANT'ANGELO
Lungotevere Castello 50, *Tel. 06/687-5036.* Admission E5. Open 9:00am–7:00pm. Closed the second and fourth Tuesdays of the month. Last entrance time is 1 hour before closing. Buses 23, 34, 64, 280, 982. Metro Lepanto.

Also known as the **Mausoleum of Hadrian** since it was built for Hadrian and his successors, for eighty years it was used as a funeral monument where the ashes of Roman emperors were stored. As the papacy began to establish itself near the tomb of St. Peter's during the Middle Ages, the structure was converted into a fortress for the Popes. During that period the bulky battlements and other military fortifications were added. A covered walkway leads from Saint Peter's to the Castel Sant'Angelo and, because of the volatile political situation in Italy for many centuries, this walkway was used more than once to protect the Pope. Since then it has been used as a residence for popes and princes, as a prison, and as a military barracks.

On the summit of the building is the statue of an angel (hence the name of the castle), and rumor has it that in 590 CE, Gregory the Great saw a vision with an avenging angel sheathing its sword at the summit of the castle. He took this to mean the plague that had ravaged Rome was over. To commemorate this event he placed an angel on top of the building. Today the castle houses a museum with a wonderful collection of armaments from the Stone Age to the present day. There are also some nondescript art exhibits and luxuriously preserved Papal apartments. A must-see when in Rome. A great site for kids and adults to explore.

GALLERIA BORGHESE
Villa Borghese, Piazza dell'Uccelliera 5. *Tel. 06/632-8101.* Admission E6. Hours 9:00am–9:00pm, until midnight on Saturdays, only until 8:00pm on Sundays. Closed Mondays. Entrance is only available in two-hour increments starting at 9am. Closed Mondays. Buses 95, 490, 495, 910. Metro-Spagna.

Located in the most picturesque public park in Rome, and housed in a beautiful villa constructed in the 17th century, the ground floor contains the sculpture collection, which would be considered without peer if not for the fact that it is located in Rome where there are a number of other superb collections. The sculptures are just the appetizer because the main draw of this museum is the beauty of the gallery of paintings on the first floor.

But before you abandon the sculptures, take note of the reclining *Pauline Borghese*, created by Antonio Canova in 1805. She was the sister of Napoleon, and was married off to one of the wealthiest families in the world at the time to ensure peace and prosperity. She looks quite enticing posing half naked on a lounge chair. Another work not to miss is *David and the Slingshot* by Bernini in 1619. It is a self-portrait of the sculptor. Other works by Bernini are spotlighted and intermixed with ancient Roman statuary.

On the first floor there are many great paintings, especially the *Madonna and Child* by Bellini, *Young Lady with a Unicorn* by Raphael, *Madonna with Saints* by Lotto, and some wonderful works by Caravaggio. If you are in Rome, you have to visit this museum. Advanced booking is suggested from **www.ticketeria.it**, otherwise you may not gain access since there are a limited number of spaces available. There is a gift shop and snack bar in the basement area where you pick up your reserved tickets. You will also have to relinquish your handbags, camera, umbrellas, etc., for safekeeping at the basement baggage area.

GALLERIA COMUNALE D'ARTE MODERNA

Via Reggio Emilia 54, *Tel. 06/884-4930*. Admission E3. Open everyday from 10:00am-9:00pm. Holidays and Sundays 9:00am-2:00pm. Email: GalleriaModerna@comune.roma.it. Metro B – Policlinico.

Situated in the old Peroni brewery, whose renovated open spaces make for a perfect backdrop for this superb gallery of modern art. A working museum with laboratories as well as exhibit space, multimedia rooms, bookshops and also displays of the recent history of the building when it used to cater to the more 'spiritual' interests of the citizens of Rome. If you want a change of pace, or simply a taste of something different, stop by this brand new, just opened gallery of modern art in Rome. Nearby, in another section of the Peroni Brewery, is a Coin department store, so you can satisfy some consumer needs while here too.

GALLERIA DORIA-PAMPHILI

Piazza del Collegio Romano, 2. *Tel. 06/679-7323; www.doriapamphilj.it.* Open 10am-5pm, closed Thursday, E8 museum, E4 private apartments (these are only open 10:30am to noon).

A private home just off the Via del Corso is also home to a fantastic museum, recently reopened to the general public. Here you can tour their incredible art collection and a number of private apartments dolled up with exquisite furnishings. Audio tour in English narrated by the owner is available and recommended. Works by Caravaggio, Titian, Velasquez, Lippi, and other incredible artists. The family came into prominence when their relative became Pope Innocent X in the 1600s. This place is unusual because not too many private homes have been opened up to the public for viewing.

MUSEO CAPITOLINA

Piazza del Campidoglio 1. *Tel. 06/6710-2071.* Admission E5. Hours 9:00am-7:00pm. Closed Mondays. Buses 44, 46, 56, 57, 90, 90, 94, 186, 710, 713, 718, 719. Entrance E5.

The **Capitoline Museum** is actually two museums, the **Capitoline** and the **Palazzo dei Conservatori**. The Capitoline Museum is the perfect place to come to see what ancient Romans looked like. Unlike Greek sculpture, which glorified the subject, Roman sculpture captured every realistic characteristic and flaw. There are rooms full of portrait busts dating back to the republic and imperial Rome, where you have many individuals of significance immortalized here, whether they were short, fat, thin, ugly. Here they remain, warts and all. Because of these very real depictions of actual Romans, and many other more famous sculptures, this museum ranks only second in importance to the Vatican collections.

Besides the busts, you'll find a variety of celebrated pieces from antiquity including *Dying Gaul*, *Cupid and Psyche*, the *Faun*, and the nude and voluptuous *Capitoline Venice*. Then in the **Room of the Doves** you'll find two wonderful mosaics that were taken from Hadrian's Villa many centuries ago. One mosaic is of the doves drinking from a basin, and the other is of the masks of comedy and tragedy. Besides these items in the interior, the exterior itself was designed by none other than the master himself, Michelangelo.

The **Palace of the Conservatori** is actually three museums in one, the **Museum of the Conservatori**, the **New Museum**, and the **Pinocoteca Capitolina**. It too was also constructed by a design from Michelangelo. What draws me to them, as well as most people young at heart, are the largest stone head, hand and foot you're ever likely to see. A great place to take a few pictures. These pieces are fragments from a huge seated statue of Constantine.

You could wander here among the many ancient Roman and Greek sculptures and paintings but remember to see the famous *Boy with a Thorn*, a graceful Greek sculpture of a boy pulling a thorn out of his foot, the *She-Wolf of the Capitol*, an Etruscan work of Romulus and Remus being suckled by the mythical wolf of Rome, the death mask bust of Michelangelo, the marble *Medusa* head by Bernini, the celebrated painting *St. Sebastian* by Guido Reni that shows the saint with arrows shot into his body, and the famous Caravaggio work, *St. John the Baptist*.

MUSEO DELLA CIVILTA ROMANA

Piazza G Agnelli 10, *Tel. 06/592-6041.* Open 9:00am – 7:00pm. Holidays only until 1:30pm. Closed Mondays. Metro-EUR Palasport (Marconi) or Fermi.

If you've always wanted to see a scale model of ancient Rome, you have to visit this museum. In it you'll find a perfect replica of Rome during the height of empire in the 4th century BCE. This piece is an exquisitely detailed plastic model that brings ancient Rome to life. It really helps to bring some sense to the ruins that now litter the center of Rome. Even if you are not a museum person, this exhibit is well worth seeing. Ideal for kids of all ages.

The rest of the museum contains little original material, and is made up of plaster casts of Roman artifacts. The museum is located in the section of Rome called **EUR** (Esposizione Universale di Roma), which was built as an exposition site for an event that was to take place in 1941. It is a perfect example of grandiose fascist architecture and its attempt to intimidate through size. Built with Mussolini's guidance halfway between Rome and its old port of Ostia, it was an attempt to reclaim some of Rome's glory and add to its grandeur. EUR has none of the human feel of the rest of Rome, since it is in essence an urban office park with a connected residential ghetto eerily similar to American suburbs, but with a little more style.

Rome the Museum

For years Rome has been considered a museum in and of itself, but finally the city fathers have made it official. Rome has built a pathway between many of the major sights in the *centro storico* area (including Trevi Fountain and the Pantheon) with a signdescribing the history and significance of each sight – in Italian, English, and Braille.

MUSEO STORICO NAZIONALE DELL'ARTE SANITARIA
Lungotevere in Sassia, *Tel. 06/68351.* Open Mon., Wed. & Fri. 9:30am-1:30pm.

Located in the interior of a hospital founded by Pope Innocent III in 1198, the museum holds pieces, surgical instruments, apothecary cases, wax models, apothecary pots, a laboratory and an extensive library that are precious records of the history of medicine and how it has been practiced over the ages. If you think doctors are a bunch of quacks today, wait until you see what they worked with and believed years ago.

MUSEO DELLE TERME aka MUSEO NAZIONALE
Baths of Diocletian, Viale delle Terme. Admission E1. Hours 9:00am-2:00pm. Holidays until 1:00pm. Closed Mondays. Buses 57, 64, 65, 75, 170, 492, 910. Metro-Repubblica.

If you like ancient sculpture you'll enjoy this collection of classical Greek and Roman works, as well as some early Christian sarcophagi and other bas-relief work. Located in the **Baths of Diocletian**, which are something to see in and of themselves, this museum is easily accessible since it is located near the train station and right across from the Repubblica Metro stop. Since there are so many fine works here, you should spend a good half day perusing the items, but remember to start with the best, which are located in the *Hall of Masterpieces*. Here you'll find the *Pugilist*, a bronze work of a seated boxer, and the *Discobolus*, a partial sculpture of a discus thrower celebrated for its amazing muscle development.

At the turn of the century this collection was graced with the Ludovisi assembled, collected by Cardinal Ludovico Ludovisi and a number of Roman princes. The most inspiring of these many fine works of art is the celebrated *Dying Gaul and His Wife*, a colossal sculpture from Pergamon created in the third century BCE. The collection also contains the famous Ludovisi throne, created in the 5th century BCE and which is adorned with fine Greek bas-reliefs.

Another must-see in the museum is the *Great Cloister,* a perfectly square space surrounded by an arcade of one hundred Doric columns. It is one of the most beautiful architectural spaces in Rome, which is saying something. Rumor has it that it was designed and built by Michelangelo in 1565, which may be the case, but since he was so busy many experts believe that it is actually the work of one of his more famous, and possibly intimate pupils, Jacopo del Duca. Another great museum to see in Rome.

MUSEO TIPOLOGICO NAZIONALE DEL PRESEPIO

Via Tor de' Conti 31a, *Tel. 06/679-6146.* Open 5:00-8:00pm (weekdays) and 10:00am-1:00pm & 5:00-8:00pm holidays. Admission E3.

This museum exhibits crèches and individual statuettes for creches (over 3,000) from all over the world, made from all kinds of materials. Each of these nativity scenes and figurines help illuminate for us the way in which Christmas is celebrated worldwide. If you are an aficionado of crèches, as is my mother, you simply must make a point of visiting this great little museum.

MUSEO DI VILLA GIULIA

Piazza di Villa Giulia 9. *Tel. 06/332-6571.* Admission E5. Hours 9:00am–6:30pm Tues-Fri, Sundays until 8:00pm and Saturdays in the summer open also from 9:00pm-midnight. Closed Mondays. Buses 19b or 30b. Metro-Flaminio.

Located in the Palazzo di Villa Giulia, built in 1533 by Julius III, and situated amid the Borghese Gardens, this incredible archaeological museum contains 34 rooms of ancient sculptures, sarcophagi, bas-reliefs, and more, mainly focusing on the Etruscan civilization.

Items of interest include the statues created in the 5th century BCE of a *Centaur*, and *Man on a Marine Monster;* Etruscan clay sculptures of *Apollo, Hercules with a Deer*, and *Goddess with Child*; objects from the Necropoli at Cerveteri including a terra-cotta work of *Amazons with Horses* created in the 6th century BCE and a sarcophagus of a "married couple," a masterpiece of Etruscan sculpture from the 6th century BCE.

PICCOLO MUSEO DELLE ANIME DEL PURGATORIO

Lungotevere Prati 12, inside the Chiesa del Sacro Cuore del Suffragio. Open every day 7:30-11:30am and 4:30-7:30pm.

This has got to be the weirdest museum in Rome. It is the museum for the souls in purgatory and used to be called the Christian Afterlife Museum. There are supposedly records of souls in purgatory expressing their displeasure of where they are by impacting the physical world, such as a burnt handprint that appears on a missal, which suddenly appeared there during mass one day.

PALAZZO ALTEMPS

Museo Nazionale Romano, Piazza Sant'Appolinare 44, *Tel. 06/683-3759.* Open 9:00am-9:00pm Tues-Thurs and until midnight every other day except Monday when it is closed. Admission E5.

A must-see museum while in Rome. Located just outside the Piazza Navona, this little museum has an elegant collection of sculptures and paintings, but best of all it is a respite from the frenetic pace of Rome, and is an architectural curiosity in and of itself. Besides the excellent pieces inside, the building itself offers a glimpse into what life was like many years ago in Rome. The inner courtyard is mesmerizing and the private chapel an oasis of calm. Though it does not have as many pieces as the Vatican or the Campidoglio, you will able to savor each piece without having to fight the crowds at those other places.

PALAZZO BARBERINI

Via delle Quattro Fontane, 13. *Tel. 06/482-4184.* Admission E5. Hours 9:00am–9:00pm Tuesday-Friday, until midnight on Saturdays, until 8:00pm on Sundays. Closed Mondays. Buses 95, 490, 495, 910. Metro-Barberini.

Located just off the Piazza Barberini on the Via Quattro Fontane, this baroque palace was started by Carlo Maderno in 1623 with the help of Borromini and was finished in 1633 by Bernini. When the entrance was rearranged to the south from the northeast in 1864, the baroque iron gates were designed, built and installed by Francesco Azzuri.

One wing of the palace is the site of the **Galleria Nazionale d'Arte Antica**. Besides the wonderful architecture which is impossible to miss, the gallery has many wonderful paintings such as *Marriage of St. Catherine* by Sodoma, *Portrait of a Lady* by Piero di Cossimo, and *Rape of the Sabines* by Sodoma. A wonderful little museum, and a great place to visit in the evenings since it stays open so late.

VATICAN MUSEUMS

Viale Vaticano. *Tel. 06/6988-4466.* Admission E6.5. From November to the first half of March and the second half of June through August open 8:45am to 12:45pm. From the second half of March to the first half of June and September and October open 8:45am to 3:45pm. Closed most Sundays and all major religious holidays like Christmas and Easter. The last Sunday of every month in January, February, April, May, July, Aug., September, October, November and December are open and the entrance is free. Buses 19, 23, 32, 45, 51, 81, 492, 907, and 991. Metro-Ottaviano.

The Vatican Museums keep rather short hours, so make a point of getting here early since the lines are very long. There are a number of self-guided tape cassette tours available that take you through different sections of the Vatican Museums. Touring the museums is almost like an amusement park ride, except the sights you see are amazing works of art. These are the best way to get an insight into the many splendid works you are witnessing.

Pinacoteca Vaticana

A wonderful collection of masterpieces from many periods, covering many styles all the way from primitive to modern paintings. Here you can find paintings by Giotto (who was the great innovator of Italian painting, since prior to his work Italian paintings had been Byzantine in style), many works by Raphael, the famous *Brussels Tapestries* with episodes from the Acts of the Apostles created by Pieter van Aelsten in 1516 from sketches by Raphael, and countless paintings of the Madonna, Virgin, Mother and Child, etc.

Pius Clementine Museum

Known mainly as a sculpture museum, it was founded by Pius VI and Clement XIV. You can also find mosaic work and sarcophagi from the 2nd, 3rd and 4th centuries. One mosaic in particular is worth noting, the *Battle between the Greeks and the Centaurs*, created in the first century CE. The bronze statue of Hercules and the **Hall of the Muses** that contain statues of the Muses and the patrons of the arts are also worth noting. Here you can also find many busts of illustrious Romans including Caracalla, Trajan, Octavian and more.

In the **Octagonal Court** are some of the most important and the beautiful statues in the history of Western art, especially the *Cabinet of the Laocoon*. This statue portrays the revenge of the gods on a Trojan priest, Laocoon, who had invoked the wrath of the gods by warning his countrymen not to admit the Trojan horse. In revenge the gods sent two enormous serpents out of the sea to destroy Laocoon and his two sons.

Chiaramonti Museum

Founded by Pope Pius VII, whose family name was Chiaramonti, this museum includes a collection of over 5,000 Pagan and Christian works. Here you can find Roman Sarcophagi, *Silenus Nursing the Infant Bacchus*, busts of Caesar, the Statue of Demosthenes, the famous *Statue of the Nile* with the 16 boys representing the 16 cubits of the annual rise of the Nile, as well as a magnificent Roman chariot recreated in marble by the sculptor Franzone in 1788.

Etruscan Museum

If you can't make it to any of the Necropoli around Rome, at least come here and see the relics of a civilization that preceded Ancient Rome. Founded in 1837 by Gregory XVI, it contains objects excavated in the Southern part of Etruria from 1828-1836, as well as pieces from later excavations around Rome. Here you'll find an Etruscan tomb from Cerveteri, as well as bronzes, gold objects, glass work, candelabra, necklaces, rings, funeral urns, amphora and much more.

Egyptian Museum

If you can't make it to Cairo to see their splendid exhibit of material excavated from a variety of Egyptian tombs, stop in here. Created by Gregory XVI in 1839, this museum contains a valuable documentary of the art and civilization of ancient Egypt.

There are sarcophagi, reproductions of portraits of famous Egyptian personalities, works by Roman artists who were inspired by Egyptian art, a collection of wooden mummy cases and funeral steles, mummies of animals, a collection of papyri with hieroglyphics, and much more.

Library of the Vatican

Founded through the efforts and collections of many Popes, this museum contains many documents and incunabula. Today the library contains over 500,000 volumes, 60,000 ancient manuscripts, and 7,000 incunabuli. My favorite are the precious manuscripts, especially the *Codex Vaticanus B* or the 4th century Bible in Greek.

Appartamento Borgia

Named after Pope Alexander VI, whose family name was Borgia, since he designed and lived in these lavish surroundings. (What about that vow of poverty?) From the furnishings to the paintings to the frescoes of Isis and Osiris on the ceiling, this little "museum" is worth a look.

Sistine Chapel

This is the private chapel of the popes famous for some of the most wonderful masterpieces ever created, many by **Michelangelo** himself. He started painting the ceiling of the chapel in 1508 and it took him four years to finish it. On the ceiling you'll find scenes from the Bible, among them the *Creation*, where God comes near Adam, who is lying down, and with a simple touch of his hand imparts the magic spark of life. You can also see the *Separation of Light and Darkness*, the *Creation of the Sun and Moon*,

Creation of Trees and Plants, Creation of Adam, Creation of Eve, The Fall and the Expulsion from Paradise, the *Sacrifice of Noah and his Family* and the *Deluge.*

On the wall behind the altar is the great fresco of the *Last Judgment* by Michelangelo. It occupies the entire area (20 meters by 10 meters) and was commissioned by Clement VII. Michelangelo was past 60 when he started the project in 1535. He completed it seven years later in 1542. Michelangelo painted people he didn't like into situations with evil connotation in this fresco. The figure of Midas, with asses' ears, is the likeness of the Master of Ceremonies of Paul III, who first suggested that other painters cover Michelangelo's nude figures.

This covering was eventually done by order of Pius IV, who had Daniele da Volterra drape the most prominent figures with painted cloth. These changes were left in when the entire chapel underwent its marvelous transformation a few years back, bringing out the vibrant colors of the original frescoes that had been covered by centuries of dirt and soot.

Rooms of Raphael

Initially these rooms were decorated with the works of many artists of the 15th century, but because Pope Julius II loved the work of Raphael so much, he had the other paintings destroyed, and commissioned Raphael to paint the entire room himself. He did so spending the rest of his life in the task. Not nearly as stupendous as the Sistine Chapel work by Michelangelo, but it still is one of the world's masterpieces.

Chapel of Nicholas V

Decorated with frescoes from 1448-1451 by Giovanni da Fiesole. The works represent scenes from the life of Saint Stephan in the upper portion and Saint Lawrence in the lower.

The Loggia of Raphael

Divided into 13 arcades with 48 scenes from the Old and New Testaments, these were executed from the designs of Raphael by his students, Giulo Romano, Perin del Vaga, and F. Penni. The most outstanding to see are the *Creation of the World, Creation of Eve, The Deluge, Jacob's Dream, Moses Receiving the Tablets of Law, King David,* and the *Birth of Jesus.*

Grotte Vaticano

The Vatican caves seem to be a well-kept secret even though they've been around for some time. I think that's because you need special permission to enter them, and if you haven't made plans prior to your arrival it is quite difficult to gain access at short notice. To gain permission you need to contact the **North American College** in Rome (Via dell'Umita 30, *Tel. 06/672-256 or*

678-9184). The entrance to the Grotte is to the left of the basilica of St. Peter's where the Swiss Guards are posted. The Grotte were dug out of the stratum between the floor of the actual cathedral and the previous Basilica of Constantine. This layer was first excavated during the Renaissance. After passing fragments of inscriptions and mosaic compositions, tombstones, and sarcophagi, you descend a steep staircase to get to the Lower Grottos, also called the **Grotte Vecchie** (the Old Grottos).

Here you'll find pagan and Christian Necropoli dating from the 2nd and 3rd century. The Grotte are divided into three naves separated by massive pilasters that support the floor of St. Peter's above. Along the walls are numerous tombs of popes and altars adorned with mosaics and sculptures. At the altar is the entrance to the **Grotte Nuove** (New Grottos), with their frescoed walls, marble statues, and bas-reliefs.

Literary Rome

For centuries Rome has been luring artists from all over the world to be inspired by its charms. Here you can explore the city with the realization that Virgil, Robert and Elizabeth Browning, Hans Christian Anderson, Henry James, Lord Byron, Mark Twain, Goethe and more all traced the same steps you are taking.

If you are interested in following almost exactly in these famous writers' footsteps, read on, for we are going to trace for you the paths taken, the places stayed and the restaurants/cafés frequented by literati of times gone by.

The perfect place to start is the **Piazza di Spagna**. In the 18th and 19th century this piazza was literally (no pun intended) the end of the line for many traveling coaches entering the city. Near the western end of the piazza, the **Via delle Carrozze** (Carriage Road) reminds us that this is where these great coaches tied up at the end of their long journeys. More often than not, travelers would make their homes in and around this area.

At Piazza di Spagna #23, you'll find **Babbington's Tea Rooms** (see above, *Where to Eat*) where Byron, Keats, Shelley, and Tobias Smollett all shared at one time or another some afternoon tea. Across the piazza, at #26, is the **Keats/Shelley Memorial** where Keats spent the three months before his death in 1821 at the age of 25. The memorial contains some of Keats' manuscripts, letters and memorabilia, as well as relics from Shelley and other British writers. Keats and Shelley still reside in Rome, in the **Protestant Cemetery** near the metro stop Piramide. Located at Via Ciao Cestio 6, it is open all day, but visitors must ring the bell for admittance. Next, at #66 in the piazza, the grand poet George Gordon (Lord) Byron took lodging in 1817 and performed work on *Child Harolde's Pilgrimage*.

From here, you can explore the **Via Condotti**, Rome's center for high level consumerism. **Caffe Greco**, at #86, is where, in its double row of interconnecting rooms, you could have found Goethe, Hans Christian Anderson or Mark Twain sipping an aperitif and other drinks that were a little stronger than can be found at Babbington's. In 1861, one of the upper rooms was also the lodging for Hans Christian Anderson of *Ugly Duckling* fame. A little further along, at #11 Via Condotti, poet Alfred Lord Tennyson and writer William Thackeray made their home when they visited Rome.

Just off the Via Condotti, at Via Bocca di Leone #14, is the **Hotel d'Inghlitera** where Mark Twain scratched many pages for *Innocents Abroad* in 1867 and where Henry James initially stayed during his forays into the Eternal City. Later on, James would reside at the **Hotel Plaza** at Via del Corso 126 where he began his work *From a Roman Notebook,* which described his exploration of the city, its culture, history, and expatriate social activities.

Further down the Corso, at #20, is where the German poet Goethe made his home from 1786 to 1788. Here he penned his immortal travel diary *Italian Journey.* Goethe's old house now contains a small museum of photographs, prints, journals, books, and other material relating to the poet's travels in Italy.

At Bocca di Leone, #43, you'll see where Robert and Elizabeth Browning lived in 1853. This is where Robert got the inspiration for his epic poem *The Ring and the Book,* a tragic tale of the murder of the Comparini family and their daughter Pompilia (who had lived on the Via Bocca di Leone in 1698), by Pompilia's husband, Count Franchescini.

Another famous writer who resided in Rome was the magnificent Charles Dickens, who wrote part of his *Pictures From Italy* at Via del Babuino #9. If you get a chance, try and read this book, since it brings the Rome of that time to life as vividly as he brought London to life in his many other books.

Nightlife & Entertainment

Rome is filled with many discos and pubs where you can spend your evening and nights having wild and raucous times. If that's what you want to do, I've compiled a list of the best places to go. But if you want to do like most of the Romans do for evening and nightly entertainment, seat yourself at a bar/café or restaurant, savor your meal or a few drinks and revel in the beauty that is Rome. Lingering in the evening air while recalling the day's events or planning tomorrow's is a great way to relax, slow down, and adapt to the Italian culture.

There are a few ideal places in Rome where you can do that. The best is in **Trastevere** at one of the little open air cafés where you can either stay all night sipping a few glasses of wine, or visit after you've had your dinner in one of the restaurants around the piazza (see Trastevere, *Where to Eat*). This is definitely *the* best place to go for a night out in Rome.

Another is **Campo dei Fiori**, which also has many cafés and restaurants where you can sit while you watch the life of Rome amble past. Three other great nightspots are the **Piazza Navona**, around the **Pantheon**, and around the **Trevi Fountain** though these last three are more well known. Hence more tourists. However, if this relaxed, slow-paced lifestyle is not for you, by all means try one of the following. I found them all perfect for letting off some steam.

However, if you are looking for late night dancing, **Testaccio** is the place for you (see separate Rome-Testaccio map). Though fun, this is a little off the beaten path, so I would recommend taking a cab there and back.

Map references for the nightlife entries are as follows: numbers 84 and 86 are on map A (pages 120-121); numbers 85,86,89-92, 95, and 96 are on map B (pages 140-141); and numbers 86 and 88 are on map C (pages 156-157). Numbers 90, 93, and 94 are on the smaller Testaccio map on page 200.

Pubs, Bars & Discos

84. TRINITY COLLEGE, *Via del Collegio Romano 6, Tel. 06/678-64-72. Email: trinity-pub@flashnet.it. Web: www.trinity-rome.com. Open 7:30am to 3:00pm and 8:00pm to 2:00am. Credit cards accepted. (Map A)*

An upscale place to have a good meal and a few pints, and a watering hole in which to drink the night away. The menu comes complete with pub fare such as sandwiches, Shepherd's Pie, salads, hamburgers, hot dogs, french fries and more. They also have an extensive and excellent Roman menu. The atmosphere and ambiance are impeccably upper crust. A great place to relax over one of the many complimentary newspapers in a variety of languages. Another plus to this place is that in the summer, the air conditioning is cranked, so it's the perfect spot to escape the heat of Rome. An upscale crowd hangs out here.

85. BLACK DUKE, *Via della Maddelena 29, Tel. 06/6830-0381. Open for lunch in the summers. Open until 2:00am all year long, every day. (Map C)*

Located near the Pantheon there is outside seating bordered by large shrubs that separate you from the street. You can also sit inside in the large downstairs dining and bar area that seats 120 people. The air circulation is not that great so non-smokers beware...even in the small area designated for your use, breathing can be quite difficult. Here you can savor a full menu of authentic pub grub in the traditional dark and dinghy (yet clean and comfortable) English/Irish pub setting of dark wood decor and furnishings. More of an upscale crowd.

86. FIDDLERS ELBOW, *Via dell'Olmata 43, Tel. 487-2110. Open 7 days a week 5:00pm -1:15am. (Maps A&D)*

Rome's oldest authentic pub, which has knock-offs in Florence and Venice, this place has a slightly run-down feel but that gives it a truly Irish flavor. Located near the Piazza Santa Maria Maggiore, you'll get a taste of home here but no real food. Only snacks like potato chips, peanuts and salami sticks are served. A little off the beaten path, unless you are staying near the Train Station.

87. JOHN BULL PUB, *Corso Vittorio Emanuele II 107a, Tel. 06/687-1537. Open 12:00pm to 2:00am. (Map B)*

The English John Bull company's version of what the Irish Guinness is promoting all over the world: authentic pub experience in which to sell their beer. There is wood, brass, glass, and mirrors, and English knickknacks everywhere. Totally British, including the friendly service. Ideally located near Piazza Navona, Pantheon and Campo dei Fiori on Via Vittorio Emanuele, this is a fun place to come for a few drinks or their extensive antipasto spread at happy hour. Besides that you can muster up some sandwiches, salads, or other basic pub food.

88. SHAMROCK, *Via del Colosseo 1/c, Tel. 06/679-1729. Web: www.shamrockpub.com. Open noon to 2:00am. (Map D)*

The place to play darts in Rome. A truly authentic Irish pub, located near the Colosseum. If you are looking for great pub food, cold beer, a fun crowd, stop in here. Highly recommended.

89. DRUNKEN SHIP, *Campo dei Fiori 20/21, Tel. 06/683-00-535. Web: www.drunkenship.com. Open 1:00pm-2:00am. Some days (the schedule changes ... this is Italy, remember), they don't open until 6:00pm. Happy Hour 6:00-9:00pm. (Map B)*

The best American bar in the best location in Rome. The decor is dark wood and the whole place has a slight tilt to it befitting, I suppose, a drunken ship. American owner Regan Smith has created a wild and raucous American style bar in one of Rome's oldest piazzas. Loud music, rowdy crowd, great drinks, draft beer and bilingual and beautiful waitresses. The crowd is mainly Italian with a sprinkling of foreign students and travelers. This is the place to come for a pint or two in the early evenings as well as the best place to party the night away. They have specials every night to keep you coming back for more.

90. RADIO LONDRA, *Via di Monte Testaccio, 65B. Tel. 06/575-0044. Open Monday-Friday 10:00pm to 3:00am, and Saturdays until 4:00am. All credit cards accepted. (Testaccio Map)*

This place is a bunker dug into the Testaccio hill with military style furnishings and decorations. You have segments of all parts of society here, making for a wild time. If the goings-on inside this inferno get too hot, you can always sojourn to one of the tables on the terrace. A great place to meet other single people, not necessarily tourists. The interior is complete with an 18th century vaulted ceiling. They offer live music Tuesday through Friday. Food specialties are house pizza and grilled steaks. Located in the trendy Testaccio section of town, where you will find most of Rome's dance clubs and hot night spots.

91. OMBRE ROSSE, *Piazza Sant'Egidio 12, Tel. 06/588-4155. Hours 7am-2am. (Map B)*

Wonderful service from morning 'til the wee hours. Strange for a late night place to open so early, but they are, and their breakfasts are excellent. There are all kinds of wines, as well as beer on tap in this oasis of calm in the frenzy of late night Trastevere. Inside or out, here you'll be able to grab a quick bite to eat and a superb glass of wine. One of my favorites.

92. BIRRERIA ARTU, *Largo MD Fumasoni Biondi 5, Tel. 06/588-0398. Closed Mondays. Open 6:00pm-2:00am. (Map B)*

As you enter there'll be a comfortable room with a few tables, a fireplace leading to a cozy bar area, which leads to a back room where the hip locals hang out. This place has a great feel, an extensive snack menu, an adequate wine list, and friendly wait staff. It's one of my favorite places to come for a late night after dinner drink when I'm in Trastevere.

93. ALIBI, *Via di Monte Testaccio 40/44, Tel. 06/574-3448. Web: www.alibionline.it. (Testaccio Map). Free admission Wed, Thur, and Sun. Fri & Sat E8-13. Open after 11pm.*

This started out as a gay dance club in Rome, but has turned into something for everyone. Spread over three floors, the terrace is the place to be in the summer. Located in the Testaccio section of Rome, an area that contains the highest concentration of establishments catering to the night owl party crowd. Come to Testaccio starting at around 10pm and the place is hopping. It's best to take a cab here and back, as it is not easily accessible by public transport.

94. BUSH, *Via Galvani 46, Tel. 06/5728-8691. Web: www.bush.it. (Testaccio Map)*

Ever crowded with late night revelers that offers a great variety of house music in the heart of the nightlife district of

Testaccio. Come to Testaccio for this place, but if it does not meet your fancy, there are plenty of other options to choose from.

95. ALEXANDER PLATZ, *Via Ostia 9, Tel. 06/3974-2171. Membership entry E6.*

Of all the jazz clubs in Rome, this is without a doubt the best. For 16 years it has hosted top quality acts, gaining for itself national and international renown. The walls are covered with photos of the musicians who have played there. Dinner is served. Concerts every evening starting at 10:30pm.

96. BIG MAMA, *Via San Francesco a Ripa 18, Tel. 06/581-2551. Web: www.bigmama.it. Membership entry E5.*

This club, deep in the heart of Trastevere is dedicated to Blues-Rock-Ethnic music earning it the title "House of Blues" in Rome. In keeping with the music, the ambiance is laid back and informal. Food served from 9pm. Concerts every evening at 10:30pm.

Opera

If you are in Rome from December to June, the traditional opera season, have the proper attire (suits for men, dresses for women), and a taste for something out of the ordinary, try the spectacle of the opera:

• **Teatro dell'Opera**, Piazza D. Gigli 1, 00184 Roma. *Tel. 06/481-601, Fax 06/488-1253.*

Movies in English

• **Pasquino**, Piazza San Egideo 10, *Tel. 06/580-3622.* Three screens. Daily films in English.

• **Quirinetta**, Via M. Minghetti 4, *Tel. 06/679-0012.* Original Language films daily.

Sports & Recreation

There are many different sporting activities to participate in and around Rome, since the city is only 15 miles from the beach and 65 miles from great skiing country. Below is a list of possible activities:

Bicycling

Reckless Roman drivers can make biking on the city streets dangerous if you're not careful, and especially if you're a young North American used to the defensive drivers in the States and Canada. But if you are interested in riding a bicycle you can rent them at many different locations (see *Getting Around Town*) and take them for a trip through the **Borghese Gardens** (see *Seeing the Sights*, above) or along the city streets. I find it easy and manageable but I ride a bike a lot back home. So if you don't ride a bicycle normally I would advise against trying to do so here in Rome. This is not the Bahamas.

Boating
Rowboats can be rented at the **Giardino del Lago** in the Villa Borghese. You can also rent dinghies at **Lido di Ostia** (see *Excursions & Day Trips* below). If you are in Italy near the end of April, you may want to try the annual Tiber Descent starting near Perugia and ending up in Rome. Canoeists travel about 15km a day and lasts for six days. You can join for any or all of the days. For more information visit the descent's website *www.discesadeltevere.org* or contact the organizer Andrea Ricci at *andrearicci@libero.it*.

In July and August you can take a river trip through central Rome. The trips are organized by the **Amici del Tevere**. Check the journal *This Week in Rome* for details, a local periodical available in most hotels and at the American Express office.

Bowling
There are two good bowling alleys *(bocciodromi)* in Rome, but unless you have your own car, both of these places are far outside of the old walls of the city and thus rather difficult to get to except by taxi:
- **Bowling Brunswick**, Lungotevere Aqua Acetosa, *Tel. 396-6696*
- **Bowling Roma**, Viale Regina Margherita 181, *Tel. 861-184*

Golf
- **Golf Club Castel Gandolpho**, Via Santo Spirito 13, 00040 Castel Gandolpho. *Tel. 06/931-2301, Fax 06/931-2244.* This is an 18 hole par 72 course near the Pope's summer residence that is 5,855 meters long. It's open all year except on Mondays. They have a driving range, carts, pro shop, swimming pool, and a restaurant/bar.
- **Olgiata**, Largo Olgiata 15, Roma 00123, *Tel. 06/378-9141. Fax 06/378-9968.* Located 19 km from the center of Rome, in a housing development similar to many golf courses in the U.S. At Olgiata there is an 18 hole par 72 course that is 6,396 meters long and a 9 hole par 34 course that is 2,968 meters long. The course is open all year except on Mondays. They have a driving range, pro shop, swimming pool and a bar/restaurant.

Swimming
You can gain entry to private pools at hotels for a fee. Below is a list of those available:
- **Hotel Parco dei Principi**, Via G. Frescobaldi 5, *Tel. 06/854-421.* Open 10am-6pm M-F. E25.
- **Shangri La**, Viale Algeria 141, *Tel. 06/591-6441.* Open 9am - 6:30pm M-Sat. E6 half day; E10 full day. Sun E10 half day; E15 full day.
- **Cavalieri Hiton**, Via Cadlolo 101, *Tel. 06/35-101.* Open 9am - 7pm M-F E40, Sat and Sun E50. Under 12 half price.

• **Villa Pamphili**, Via della Nocetta 107, *Tel. 06/6615-8555*. Open 9am - 9pm. E12. Under 12 half price.

The best nearby beach is at **Lido di Ostia**, less than an hour west-northwest of Rome. The beaches are large, and they have plenty of *cabanas* to rent where you can change your clothes. And you can get there by Metro then public train, all for the price of a subway ticket. There are also some excellent seafood restaurants where you can leisurely eat, sip wine, and enjoy the beautiful Italian summers. A wonderful respite from the city.

Shopping

The very best of Italian design and craftsmanship are conveniently located all over Rome, making this city one of the finest shopping experiences in the world. You can find the finest items made from the very best material, though cut-price bargains are hard to find. Leather and silk goods predominate, but Rome is also an important location for jewelry, antiques and general top of the line *pret-a-porter* (ready to wear) fashion.

The main shopping area is near the Spanish Steps and is a network of streets featuring the **Via della Croce** in the north to **Via Frattina** in the south, and **Via del Corso** in the west to **Piazza di Spagna** in the east. This area includes the famous **Via Condotti**.

Romans, like most Italians, prefer to shop in boutiques, and the Via Condotti area has these quaint little shops selling everything from shirts to gloves. This specialization originated from the village craft shops of old, and generally ensures top quality and personal service.

In Italy, **department stores** are the exception rather than the rule, but in this shopping area there are some that warrant a look, like **La Rinascente**, **STANDA**, **UPIM**, and **Coin**. Both STANDA and UPIM are designed for the Italian on a budget, while Rinascente and Coin are a little more upscale.

In any store, to get instant respect, you may have to dress the part here in Italy. It's not like in the malls back home where it doesn't matter how you dress; here in Rome the wealthier you look the better assistance you'll get. Unfortunately as tourists we usually leave our best attire back home, but try the best you can. Shorts and tank tops usually will get you no respect at all, particularly if you're shopping on the Via Condotti and Via Borgognona. This holds true, and I can vouch for this personally, if you're shopping on some of the parallel streets like Via Frattina, some of the little cross-streets, and even in Piazza di Spagna or Via del Babuino.

Antiques

Today, the typical Roman antique can be either a precious Roman artifact or pieces in the baroque and neoclassical style. There are also many French and English antiques masquerading as Italian. One thing that they all have in common is that they are extremely expensive.

Some good antique shops in Rome can be found in the **Via del Babuino** and the **Via Margutta**. Other shops can be found on the **Via dei Coronari**, and the **Via Giulia**. And don't forget to check out the **Porta Portese** Sunday market (open 6:30am-2:30pm). You'll find some interesting antiques there, but not too many.

However, the best area to visit to find antiques is the area of the old city of Rome, the *centro storico* from **Piazza Navona** and **Campo dei Fiori** to the tip of the peninsula that points towards St. Peter's. This is an area filled with artisan's stores, creative little shops, and is a great area to get a feel for what real Roman life is like, far away from the thundering herd of tourists. So take some time to explore this area. You will not be disappointed.

Fantastico Shopping Streets!

Top of the Line Shopping – Via Condotti, Via Borgognona, Via Bocca di Leone, Via del Corso

Mid-Range Fashion – Via Nazionale, Via Cola di Rienzo, Via del Tritone, Via Giubbonari

Antiques – Via del Babuino, Via Giulia, Via dei Coronari, around Piazza Navona

Leather Goods and Apparel – Via due Macelli, Via Francesco Crispi

Straw and Wicker Products – Via dei Deiari, Via del Teatro Valle

Outdoor Markets

Besides these places listed below, Rome also has many colorful street markets offering a vast selection of top quality fruit, flowers, vegetables, prosciutto, salami, cheeses, meat and fish, as well as cheap and inexpensive clothes. Be aware that bargaining is an accepted practice in most markets. Also you can try asking for a *sconto* (discount). Reasons for meriting a *sconto* may be numerous – buying two articles at once is a good example – but if you are bold you will ask for a *sconto* for no good reason at all, and will usually get one. This practice applies even to shopping in stores. Try it in hotels too.

Map references for shops are as follows: numbers 3, 4, 6, 8, 12, 13, 17, 20, 22 are on map A (pages 120-121); and numbers1, 2, 5, 7, 9-11, 14-16, 18, 19, 21-24 are on map B (pages 140-141).

1. CAMPO DEI FIORI, *Piazza Campo dei Fiori. Closed afternoons and Mondays.*

Rome's oldest and definitely best market held in the cobblestone square in the center of Rome's old medieval city. You can buy flowers (the name Campo dei Fiori means fields of flowers), fruits and vegetables, all delicately presented under makeshift awnings or giant umbrellas. Also available are hardware products, clothing and more. Surrounding the square are some *Alimentari* and *Panneterie* where you can pick up cold cuts, cheeses, and bread for picnics.

2. PORTA PORTESE, *Ponte Sublico. Open 6:30am–2:30pm, Sundays only.*

This flea market stretches along the Tiber from Ponte Sublico (where the Porta Portese is) in the north to the Ponte Testaccio in the south. That's roughly south of the center of Trastevere along the river. It is not even on most maps, but tell a cab driver where you're going and he'll know, since it is truly a Roman institution where anything and everything under the sun is sold: from live rabbits to stolen antiques to trendy clothes to kitchen items and all sorts of odds and ends. The clothes and accessories are inexpensive but are not of the highest quality, as befits most flea markets. Not many tourists venture here, but it's safe (though beware of pickpockets), and if you like flea markets, it is a whole lot of fun. A great place to come and get Italian soccer jerseys, hats and scarves. And it goes without saying that you have to bargain.

3. FLEA MARKET, *Via Fr. Crispi, Tel. 06/3600-5345, Admission E2. Open First Saturday (5:00-8:00pm) and Sunday (10:30am-7:30pm) of every month. Saturdays.*

Though technically not an outside market, this is a fantastic flea market that should be visited if you are in Rome on the First Saturday and Sunday of every month. Located in an underground parking garage near the Via Veneto and the Spanish Steps, you can find all sorts of interesting knick-knacks and antiques here.

English-Language Bookstores

If you have finished the book you have been reading, want a spare one for the trip home, or simply have the need to browse in a store surrounded by the English language (sometimes a necessary respite after being inundated with another language), here are some bookstores to try:

4. ANGLO-AMERICAN BOOKSTORE, *Via delle Vite 102. Tel. 06/679-5222. Web: www.aab.it. Credit cards accepted.*

5. THE CORNER BOOKSHOP, *Via del Moro 48, Tel. 06/583-6942. Email: almostcorner@libero.it. Credit cards accepted.*

6. ECONOMY BOOK CENTER, *Via Torino 136, Tel. 06/474-6877. Email: books@booksitaly.com, Web: www.booksitaly.com. Credit cards accepted.*

7. THE ENGLISH BOOKSHOP, *Via di Ripetta 248, Tel. 06/320-3301. Email: theenglishbookshop@katamail.com. Credit cards accepted.*

8. THE LION BOOKSHOP, *Via dei Gresci 36, Tel. 06/3265-4007. Email: thelionbookshop@hotmail.com. Credit cards accepted.*

AUTHENTIC ITALIAN FOOD STORES

When in Italy, you simply have to visit a small Italian food store. Whether they are **alimentari**, where you can find some authentic food products and unique gift items, or **pasticcerie** or **ciocolatterie** where you can find home-made pastries and chocolate to snack on, you will receive a unique and authentic shopping experience in any of the Italian food stores listed below. And, you will get some tasty edibles as well.

Alimentari
9. ANTICA SALUMIERIA, *Piazza della Rotonda 4, Tel. 06/687-5989. Closed Thursday afternoons and Saturday afternoons in the summer.*

Located in the same piazza as the Pantheon, the entry display is tantalizingly filled with smoked fish, mushrooms, truffles and an assortment of many different typically Italian food products. Here you can also find all sorts of cheese, salamis, olive oils, and packaged goods.

10. VOLPETTI, *Via della Scrofa 31/32, Tel. 06/686-1940. Closed Sundays and Tuesday afternoons.*

One of the most famous and best *gastronomie* in the center of town. They have an ample supply of cheeses and salamis, as well as local and foreign delicacies. There is also an excellent *rosticceria* inside with an inviting buffet of quick dishes such as *pasta al forno* (baked pasta), *gnocchi* (on Thursdays), *pollo arrosto* (juicy roasted chicken ... you have to try this), and a variety of *verdure* (green veggies) and *contorni* (vegetable side dishes). A great place to come for a quick bite, to load up on gift food items, or to get something great to eat to bring back to your room.

11. ANTICA NORCINERIA, *Via della Scrofa 100, Tel. 06/6880-1074.*

Almost directly across the street from Volpetti this place has a good selection of salamis, and they also carry bread. Another typical Italian food store.

Cioccolaterie
12. MORIANDO & GARIGLIO, *Via del Pie di Marmo, Tel. 06/699-0856. Closed Sundays, August, and Saturdays in July.*

A gem of a chocolate store in terms of ambiance, presentation, flavor and price. This place began in Rome in 1886 bringing with it a grand tradition of chocolate making from the Alps. Still a family business they use nothing but the best chocolates and mix their ingredients in traditional ways. In all there are 80 varieties of chocolate covered sweets to choose from. My favorite chocolate store in Rome.

13. PUYRICARD, *Via delle Carrozze 26, Tel. 06/6929-1932. Closed Sundays.*

A transplanted French chocolate maker has made its home on one of Rome's best shopping streets near the Spanish Steps. With 92 varieties to choose from, and many awards for excellence to their name, you can find something here to satisfy even the most discerning palate. You can also get items gift wrapped to bring home with you. Everything here is rather pricey, but well worth it.

Pasticcerie

14. DOLCEROMA, *Via dei Portico d'Ottavia 20b, Tel. 06/689-2196. Closed Sunday afternoons and Mondays.*

Here you will find exquisite Austrian and American style pastries made by Stefano Ceccarelli and which are famous city wide. All sorts of pastries abound in this wonderful little shop including strudels and tarts all covered in rich abundance of chocolate, marzipan, fruit preserves and anything else that is delectable and attractive. You can also find cherry, lemon and pecan pies and chocolate chip cookies.

15. IL FORNO DEL GHETTO, *Via del Portico d'Ottavia 2, Tel. 06/687-8637. Closed Saturdays.*

In this small store located in the heart of the Jewish quarter in Rome, you can sample the creations of three generations of pastry makers. Traditional Italian and Jewish-Roman pies and pastries abound, filled with fruit, covered in chocolate and begging to be eaten. My favorite is the tasty cheese cake. In the mornings you can sample their home-made breakfast creations.

16. L'ANTICO FORNO, *Via della Scrofa 33, Tel. 06/686-5405. Closed Sundays.*

Right next door to Volpetti, the great alimentari mentioned earlier, here you can get all sorts of tasty pastries, breads, and pizza by the slice. Everything is made in-house in the their extensive back room, so it is all fresh and oh-so-tasty.

Unique Little Shops

Rome is filled with all sorts of great little shops and exotic clothing boutiques, all stuffed with many different types of products that shopping at the mall will seem boring in comparison.

17. TERECOTTE PERSIANE, *Via Napoli 92, Tel. 06/488-3886, Open 10:00am-1:30pm and 3:30pm-8:00pm.*

Come here for an eclectic mix of terra cotta figures, tiles, masks, planters and post boxes. Located in a small courtyard just down from the American church in Rome, Santa Susanna's, the place is filled with everything terra-cotta you can imagine. The prices are rather high, so do not be afraid to bargain.

18. L'IMPRONTA, *Via del Teatro Valle 53, Tel. 06/686-7821.*

For the most amazing, intricate and colorful prints of the piazzas, monuments, and buildings of Rome, in all shapes and sizes, framed or unframed, visit this wonderful little shop. Tucked away on a tiny side street between the Pantheon and Piazza Navona.

19. AI MONESTARI, *Corso Rinascimento 72, Tel 06/6880-2783. Closed Thursday afternoons. In the summer closed Saturday afternoons.*

Located just outside the Piazza Navona, this tiny shop is filled with soaps, jams, patés, olive oils, wines, all made by men of the cloth. Hence the name of the place – *Ai Monestari* means 'of the monastery.' These monk-made products are all made with the best ingredients, have ever so quaint packaging and make perfect keepsakes or gifts.

20. CHIMERA, *Via del Seminario 121, Tel. 06/679-2126; open Mon. 3:15pm-7:30pm, Tuesday-Thursday 10:30am-7:00pm; Friday 10:30am-5:30pm; Mondays and Saturdays 1:00-7:00pm; closed Sundays.*

This consignment shop/antique store specializes in elegant objects such as paintings, drawings, porcelain, silver, jewelry, art, coins, and much more. A short walk from the Pantheon, located in the basement of a 16th century palazzo, this is where Rome's well-heeled pawn their family heirlooms so they can continue living the life of luxury. An antique shop of the utmost tradition and discretion.

21. FEFE ALDO, *Via della Stelletta 20b, Tel. 06/6880-3585. Open 8:00am – 8:00pm.*

A small store near the Pantheon that is an outlet for handmade stationery crafts, journals, address books, and artisan book binding products. Here you can find all of the same stuff that is in the far more upscale and expensive Il Papiro (see below). Not really a place to peruse, the store's a mess, since it is really a small warehouse, but if you take the time to look through what they have you will find some real gems at great prices.

22. IL PAPIRO, *Via del Pantheon 50, Tel 06/679-5597, Email info@ilpapirofirenze.it, Web: www.ilpapirofirenze.it.*

This is one of three stores of the same name surrounding the Pantheon. Here you can get all sorts of unique stationery gift items like journals, pens, blotters, cards, wrapping paper and more. They started in Florence but have now firmly established themselves all over Italy. A great store, but look at Fefe Aldo and Scatole (see below) for similar items at a lower price.

23. SCATOLE, *Via della Stelletta 27, Tel. 06/6880-2053. Open 9am-7pm.*

Just down the street from Fefe Aldo, this place is a cute little shop that makes decorative boxes in all shapes and sizes. It is a little cluttered since the shop is really a small artisan factory. However, come here and price boxes before you go to either Il Papiro. If you like what you see here, you'll save a lot of money.

24. GUSTO, *Piazza Augusto Imperatore 9, Tel. 06/322-6273.*

This is by far the most extensive and complete kitchenware store I have seen in Rome. Also one of the most expensive. But if you want that certain little something for the kitchen, this is the place to come. It is also an enoteca and restaurant.

Excursions & Day Trips

I've planned some fun excursions for you: **Tivoli Gardens**, **Frascati**, **Ostia Antica** and **Cerveteri**. And if you've got the time, you can also visit the ancient ruins of **Pompeii** and **Herculaneum**, or the **Isle of Capri** (listed in the *Naples, Southern Italy and Sicily* chapter).

Exploring Beyond Rome

Whether you wish to explore outside of Rome for a day, a weekend or longer, **Flegant Etruria** is a travel organization to consider. They help find the best accommodations, offer sightseeing tours, and make your travel easier and worry-free. So if you want to explore the best of the little hill towns around Rome and want someone else to make all the arrangements for you, contact Mary Jane Cryan at Elegant Etruria.

Elegant Etruria, Palazzo Pieri Piatti, Vetralla (VT) 01019 Italia, *Tel.* 0761/485008, *Fax* 0761/485002, *Email: macryan@tin.it*, *Web: www.dbws.com/Etruria/Home.htm*.

TIVOLI GARDENS

Tivoli is situated on the Aniene, a tributary of the Tiber, overlooking Rome from its place on the Sabine Hills. This town is where the wealthy ancient Romans built their magnificent summer villas. The three main attractions are **Villa Adriana** (Hadrian's Villa), **Villa d'Este**, and **Villa Gregoriana**.

The **Villa Adriana's** main attraction is its huge grounds. There are plenty of secluded spots to relax or enjoy a picnic on the grass. The building itself was begun in 125 CE and completed 10 years later, and was at the time the largest and most impressive villa in the Roman Empire. From his travels **Hadrian**, an accomplished architect, found ideas that he recreated in his palace. The idea for the **Poikile**, the massive colonnade through which you enter the villa, came from Athens. And the **Serapeum** and **Canal of Canopus** were based on the Temple of Serapis near Alexandria, Egypt.

Another villa is the **Villa D'Este's**, the main draw of which are its many wonderful fountains. The villa itself was built on the site of a Benedictine convent in the mid-16th century. The **Owl Fountain** and **Organ Fountain** are especially beautiful, as is the secluded pathway of the **Terrace of the Hundred Fountains**. If you make it out to Tivoli, these gardens and their fountains cannot be missed, especially at night during the months of May through September when they are floodlit. They are simply spectacular then.

The **Villa Gregoriana** is known for the **Grande Cascata** (the Great Fall), which is a result of Gregory XVI diverting the river to avoid flooding. The park around the cascade has smaller ones as well as grottoes. This is the least interesting of the three villas.

The addresses and hours of the three villas are:
- **Villa Adriana**, Bivio Villa Adriana, 3.5 miles southwest of Tivoli. Open Tuesday–Sunday, 9:30am–1 hour before sunset. Closed Mondays. Small fee required.
- **Villa d'Este**, Viale delle Centro Fontane. Open Tuesday–Sunday, 9:30am to 1.5 hours before sunset. May–September also open 9:00pm–11:30pm with the garden floodlit. Closed Mondays. Small fee required. Sundays free.
- **Villa Gregoriana**, Largo Sant'Angelo. Open Tuesday–Sunday 9:30am to 1 hour before sunset. Closed Mondays. Small fee required. Sundays free.

Arrivals & Departures

Tivoli is about 23 miles east of Rome. Take the Via Tiburtina (SS5). The Villa Adriana lies to the right about 3.5 miles before the town. By train from Stazione Termini, the trip takes about 40 minutes.

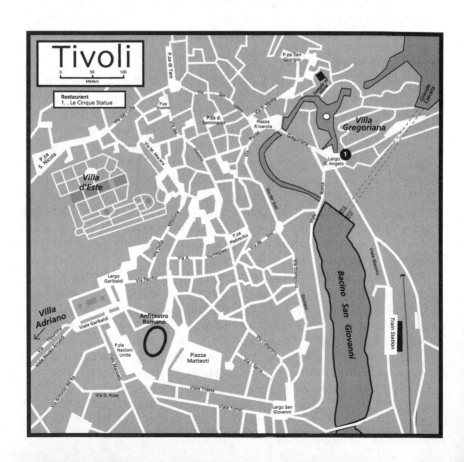

Where To Eat

Tivoli simply abounds with restaurants, many offering a magnificent panoramic view of Rome. Try this one if you can:

1. LE CINQUE STATUE, *Largo S Angelo 1, Tel. 0774/20366. Closed Fridays. All credit cards accepted. Dinner for two E55.*

In front of the entrance to Villa Gregoriana this place has outside seating where you can enjoy the local cuisine. They make many of their pastas in house and smother them in tantalizing sauces. They also specialize in meats, like *maialino* (baby pork) and *abbacchio* (lamb) *arrosto* as well as their *verdure fritte* (fried vegetables).

FRASCATI

Rome can be a bit overwhelming both for a first-time visitor and a veteran traveler to the city. So if you are someone who would rather see Rome but not stay in Rome, consider **Frascati**. This quaint, charming, quiet, little hill town is the perfect place to get away from it all while still having access to everything. The town is only 35 minutes away by train (the fare is E5) and the trains run every 45 minutes or so until 10:00pm.

In Frascati, you'll be able enjoy many good restaurants, sample the fine local wines from quaint little wine stores located all over the city. They serve you glasses or carafes from huge vats. You'll also be able to savor the ambiance of an ancient medieval town, with its cobblestone streets and twisting alleys. Here you'll be able to gaze out your windows and see lush valleys below. And if you come in October, you'll be able to experience a wine festival of bacchanalian proportions. So if you are used to the calm serenity of country life, but still want to experience the beauty that Rome has to offer, Frascati may be your answer.

Since this is still primarily an excursion, I've listed more restaurants and wine bars than hotels – though I hope some of you will opt to stay here and enjoy Frascati's many charms.

Arrivals & Departures

Frascati is roughly 14 miles southeast of Rome. Take the Via Tuscolana (SS215) up to the hill town (25 minute drive). By train from Stazione Termini, board a local train that leaves every forty minutes or so from Track 27. The ride lasts a little over 35 minutes. Cost E5.

Where to Stay

1. BELLAVISTA, *Piazza Roma 2, Tel. 06/942-1068, Fax 06/942-1068. Web: www.hbellavista.it. 18 rooms. Single E70-75. Double E95-100. Breakfast included. All credit cards accepted.* ***

A simple, comfortable hotel with all three star comforts, and all at great prices. A three-star with similar amenities in Rome would cost 2 and half times as much, or more. Here you have room service, TV in your room, and a hotel bar, as well as a nice view of the valley. The building is quite quaint and old, but restored perfectly for your comfort. The high ceilings in the rooms make them feel much larger.

2. **FLORA**, *Via Vittorio Veneto 8, Tel. 06/941-5110, Fax 06/942-0198. Email: info@hotel-flora.it. Web: www.hotel-flora.it. 37 rooms. Single E120-140; Double E150-190. Suite E210-270. Breakfast included. All credit cards accepted.* ***

An old hotel, decorated with style, located in a central position in Frascati. Similar amenities to the Bellavista, but not as good a view. Located a little ways outside of town, this hotel is set in a wonderfully tranquil environment. A good place to stay.

3. **PINNOCCHIO**, *Piazza del Mercata 20, Tel. 06/941-7883, Fax 06/941-7884. Single E60; Double E80. Seven rooms all with bath, mini-bar, and TV. No credit cards accepted.* **

Large comfortable rooms with gigantic bathrooms, located upstairs from a restaurant of the same name. The office is in the restaurant so you'll need to enter there to get your key. Located on the central market square.

Where to Eat & Drink

Some of the wine bars are so small that they don't even have names. Also many of the places do not have telephones. One of the owners explained to me, *"Why should we have telephones when we can walk over and talk in person?"* That makes sense, since Frascati is such a small intimate little town.

Don't be put off by this casual hill town attitude, since the ones without names or phones are some of the best places to visit. Enjoy.

Wine Bars

4. **CANTINA VIA SEPULCRO DI LUCURO**, *Via Sepulcro di Lucuro 6. No Telephone.*

Located just off the main road (Via Catone), this place has a small area for seating outside separated from the rest of the world by large planters. The inside is quite cool, like a wine cellar. Just inside the door is an antique wine press that they still use during the pressing season. Inside or out you'll get some of the best wines Frascati has to offer.

5. **CANTINA VIA CAMPANIA**, *Via Campania 17. No Telephone.*

Just down the road from the wine bar listed above, this place has one and a half of its four inside walls covered with wine vats, and the rest of the space taken up with strange looking tools used in the wine trade, as well as large empty bottles that you only wish you could take home with you ... full. The owner is quite friendly and if it's not too crowded will sit down and chat. Great wine. Wonderful atmosphere.

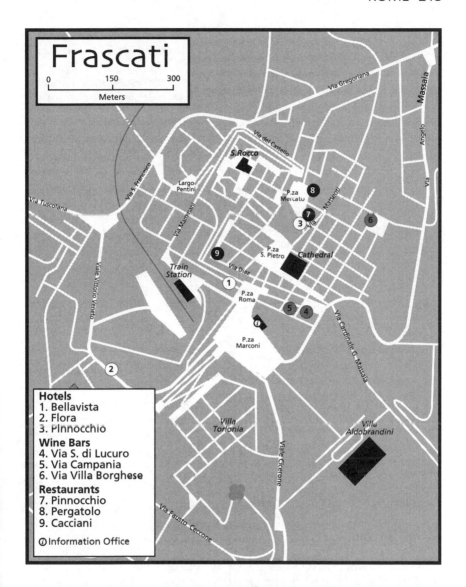

Frascati

0   150   300

Meters

Hotels
1. Bellavista
2. Flora
3. Pinnocchio

Wine Bars
4. Via S. di Lucuro
5. Via Campania
6. Via Villa Borghese

Restaurants
7. Pinnocchio
8. Pergatolo
9. Cacciani

ⓘ Information Office

6. CANTINA VIA VILLA BORGHESE, *Via Villa Borghese 20. No Telephone.*

Small wine store filled with large 1,000,000 liter barrels called *botte*, and 500,000 liter barrels called *mezza botte*. Each cask is numbered and initialed with the vineyard it came from. Not very scenic atmosphere and no tables to sit at, but they will sell you a bottle of their finest for only E1. That's about a dollar for an excellent bottle of Frascati wine.

Restaurants

7. **PINNOCCHIO,** *Piazza del Mercato 20, Tel. 06/941-6694 or 942-0330. Dinner for two E28.*

A large statue of Pinnocchio advertises this superb restaurant in Frascati's quaintest and most vibrant square (it's actually a triangle). There is outside seating with large planters separating you from the pace of this market-dominated piazza. Inside you'll find tiled floors and wood paneling giving the place a nice rustic flair. They serve great *canneloni ai quattro formaggi* (with four cheeses), as well as great Roman staples such as *amatriciana, carbonara, and vongole.*

8. **PERGATOLO,** *Via del Castello 20, Tel. 06/942-04-64. E7-Cold plate with wine and bread; E10-First course of pasta, pizza, or meat, second course of the cold plate with wine and bread.*

Wild and fun atmosphere, a little on the touristy side with singers serenading the diners. You can either enjoy or ignore it in this large and spacious restaurant that has a deli counter displaying all the available meats, cheeses, breads, salamis, etc., that you'll be served. There are roaring fires behind the counter where your meats are all prepared. If you've come to Frascati for the day or the week, this is one place you have to try, just for the fun of it.

9. **CACCIANI,** *Via Alberto Diaz 13, Tel. 06/942-0378. Closed Mondays. Holidays January 7-15 and 10 days after Ferragosto. All credit cards accepted. Dinner for two E55.*

One of the most famous restaurants in this region. It has a beautiful terrace that offers a tranquil and serene atmosphere. For starters, try the *crostini con verdure* (baked pastry appetizer filled with vegetables). Then try the home-made *fettuccine alla Romana* (made with tomatoes, chicken and spices) or *spaghetti con le vongole verace* (with clams in a hot oil and garlic sauce). For the entrée try the *fritto misto di carne* (mixed fried meats) the *saltimbocca*, or any of their grilled fish.

Seeing the Sights

If you've driven to Frascati, you were able to savor the lovely scenic route along the old **Appia Antica** past the Catacombs and ruined tombs. The town is perched halfway up a hill, and on a clear day you will have splendid views of all of Rome and its scenic countryside.

Besides the great views, the wine, and the chance for some relaxation, Frascati has a wealth of villas and spacious parks that were formerly residences of princes and popes. One of these residences, **Villa Aldobrandini** which sits just above the town, and has a magnificent garden in which you can find solitude. To enter the villa's grounds you need to first get a free pass from the **Aziendo di Soggiorno e Turismo**, in Frascati's Piazza Marconi. The hours are Monday–Friday 9:00am–1:00pm.

Besides the beauty of its old villas, Frascati's draw is the fine **white wine** that bears its name. To enjoy this succulent nectar, there are old, dark wine stores, with heavy wooden tables and chairs located all over town. At one of these you can sit and enjoy this unspoiled and inexpensive wine, the way the natives have been doing for centuries.

Frascati is the perfect place to wander through, getting lost in the alleys, side streets, steps leading nowhere, and winding roads. If you follow the sporadically placed yellow signs that say *Ferrario Pedonale*, you'll be guided through all the major sights and sounds of this hill town. These signs are prominently displayed so that the revelers who come for the wine festival can find their way around even after having a glass or two of the local vintage.

If you are fortunate enough to be in Frascati during the month of October, the town celebrates a **wine festival** of pagan proportions that lasts several days and nights. Come out to witness and partake in the debauchery, but please do not drive back to Rome afterwards – take the train or spend the night.

CERVETERI

Cerveteri used to be the Etruscan capital of Caere, and today Cerveteri is popular for the towns of the dead the Etruscans built, called **Necropoli**. These are large circular mounds of tombs laid out in a pattern of a street, like houses in a city.

Today these round roofs are densely covered with grasses and wild flowers. Inside they have been furnished with replicas of household furnishings carved from stone. Most of the original artifacts are in the **Villa Giulia Museum** or **Vatican Museums** in Rome, but the burial sites themselves are eerily significant. The site is open Tuesday to Sunday 9:00am–4:00pm. Admission E4.

After viewing the necropolis you can settle down among the mounds and have a picnic lunch, and imagine what life would be like during that time. After sightseeing you can return to the town by taxi, or by car if you have one, and take in the limited sights the little town has to offer. From the crowded main piazza you can climb steps to a **museum** with a lovely medieval courtyard. But the main sights out here are the Necropoli.

Arrivals & Departures

Cerveteri is about 28 miles west northwest of Rome. A 45 minute drive up the Via Aurelia (SS1), which will give you a more scenic view, or the Autostrada A12, which connects to the 'beltway' around Rome by route 201. By train from Stazione Termini it takes 1 hour and 10 minutes; from Roma Tiburtina it takes 50 minute to get to Cerveteri-Ladispoli. Once in the town, to reach the **Necropolis** you can grab a local taxi, or take the two kilometer walk along a little road. There are signs on the road to guide you where you're going.

Where to Eat
  DA FIORE, *near Procoio di Ceri, Tel. 06/9920-4250. Closed Wednesdays. Dinner for two E30. No credit cards accepted.*

A simple little local *trattoria* in the open country not far from the ruins and only four kilometers from the Via Aurelia. They make great pastas like *penne al funghi* (with mushrooms) *al ragu* (with tomato and meat sauce) or *con salsiccia* (with sausage). They also have grilled meats and their famous *bruschetta* (garlic bread as an appetizer) and pizza – all cooked in a wood burning oven.

OSTIA ANTICA

If you can't get down to Pompeii or Herculaneum, come here. Founded in the fourth century BCE, **Ostia Antica** feels about as far away from Rome as you can get, but is actually only 15 miles southwest of the city, a mere 45 minutes by subway and train. As with excursions to Pompeii or Herculaneum, you get the sensation that the clock has been turned back nearly 2,000 years. And what most people do not know is that Ostia contains the largest sampling of mosaic floors anywhere in Italy. Some of which are as intricate as tapestries.

This city was once the bustling seaport of Ancient Rome, but today it is calm and serene respite from the hectic pace of modern Rome. The mosaic tile floors document the great variety of goods and services available in Ostia, documenting how busy the port was at one time. Commodities included furs, wood, grain, beans, melons, oil, fish, wine, mirrors, flowers, ivory, gold, and silk. Among the services offered were caulkers, grain measurers, maintenance men, warehousing, shipwrights, barge men, carpenters, masons, mule drivers, stevedores and divers for sunken cargoes.

As at Pompeii, the houses are the most interesting part of the city. There were large villas and average sized abodes but the majority of Ostian residences were apartment buildings. There were also many public amenities including a theater, baths, and a fire department. The theater is small but is still put to use today for modern renditions of Greek and Roman plays.

Ostia was abandoned starting in the 5th century CE. By that time no new burials were being made in its cemetery and the road to Rome was overgrown with bushes and trees. What led to Ostia's decline was that its two harbors were silting up and were thus of no use to Rome anymore. This silting is documented today by the beach at Ostia (Ostia Lido) being three miles beyond the ancient seawall of the town.

Without an identity or commercial base of its own – as Pisa had, Florence's old port city, which no longer is on the Mediterranean – archeological records indicate that citizens began leaving the decaying town of Ostia in droves. When Saint Augustine was passing through the city in the 4th century CE, it was already in full decline. By that time the Emperor Constantine had revoked its municipal status and assigned it to be governed by the village of Portus, which had grown up around a 'new,' harbor built by Trajan.

If you are interested in seeing an ancient Roman city being unearthed from its tomb and you do not have the time to get to Pompeii, Ostia Antica is an option which will not disappoint. Also, Ostia Antica is a wonderful respite from the hectic pace of Rome and is great place for kids to wander around.

Arrivals & Departures
By Train
Ostia Antica is about 15 miles southwest of Rome. By car, take the Via del Mare (SS8) for about 25 minutes. By metro and train, take Linea B to the Piramide station, and catch the train to Ostia Antica. It takes about 15 minutes from Stazione Termini. Your Metro ticket is valid for both Metro and train so it will only cost you E1. Once at Piramide follow the signs for "Lido."

On the way back, check the signboard at the Ostia station for the return train. You can either catch a train that goes to the Magliana Metro station or Piramide.

By Boat
You can also get to Ostia Antica on the Tiber river. Boats set off from the Ponte Marconi on Fri, Sat and Sun (and Tues, Wed and Thurs through reservations) at 9;15am, arriving at Ostia Antica at 1:30pm, returning at 3:45pm. Tickets cost E10 one way and E11 return. Web: *www.battellidiroma.it*

Seeing the Sights
Ostia Antica gives an excellent notion of what life in the metropolis was like at the height of the Empire. This city presents to the modern world a picture of Roman life only a shade less vivid than that of Pompeii. The plan of the city is regular but not too regimented. It is scenic, monumental and functional. Its backbone is the major east-west street, the *Decumanus Maximus*, nearly a mile long, which was once colonnaded, and runs from the **Porta Romana** straight to the **Forum**.

You enter the excavations in Ostia at the aforementioned **Porta Romana**. The Decumanus Maximus, takes you past the well-preserved old **theater** and the **Piazzale dei Corporazione** (Corporation Square), a tree-lined boulevard once filled with over seventy commercial offices of wine importers, ship owners, oil merchants, or rope makers. All of these shops are worth a visit, but the well-preserved laundry and wine shop are best because these offices are tastefully decorated with more exquisite mosaic tiled floors representing their trades. A must see stop around this area is the site museum which has many of the excavated statues.

Farther down the Decumanus Maximus you arrive at the **Capitolium**, a temple dedicated to Jupiter and Minerva, located at the end of the **Forum**. The

insulae (apartment blocks) are of particular interest since they are often four or five stories high. This is where the regular people and smaller merchants lived. Only the most wealthy of the merchants were able to build themselves separate villas. The *insulae* were well lighted, had running water, and a means for sanitation (i.e., garbage removal and toilets) on each floor.

Two private home of interest that should be visited are the **House of the Cupid and Psyche**, which is west of the Capitolium, and the **House of the Dioscuri**, which is at the southwest end of town.

My favorite way to tour this site as well as most other archeological sites is to go off of the beaten path. Leave the already excavated section and wander through the areas, which have not yet been dug up. This helps to give you an idea as to the amount of labor involved in actually excavating sections, and usually makes for great places to relax. And who knows maybe you'll turn up and ancient artifact or two.

The site is open daily 9:00am–6:00pm in summer, 9:00am–4:00pm in winter. Admission E5. The museum is open one hour less.

RURAL RETREATS AROUND ROME

I've provided a three day plan if you want to escape Rome. Peace and tranquility are but a drive away in the hills surrounding the Eternal City. Some of these excursions are mentioned in greater detailed earlier in this chapter.

Day One

The perfect place to start is **Tivoli**, an ancient vacation spot famous for its large villas, lush gardens and picturesque waterfalls. The best way to get out to Tivoli from Rome is to make your way to the Raccordo Annulare, the beltway around the city. Follow this east until you get to the Via Tiburtina exit. This will take you all the way out. If it is easy for you to get directly on the Via Tiburtina downtown do so instead.

Drive first to **Villa d'Este**. Originally built as a Benedictine convent, it was transformed into a sumptuous villa by Cardinal Ippolito II of Este. Here you will be transfixed with the stunning beauty of the lush gardens and beautiful fountains.

After wandering the paths that cut through the vegetation, get back in the car for the short jaunt up to the **Villa Gregoriana**, in the town of Tivoli itself. Walking along the dirt path in the Villa's grounds you pass the Grotta delle Sibille and then are able to witness the panorama of the Grande Cascata with its wonderful waterfall.

After bathing in the beauty of these two villas it's time for some repast before you venture into the third, Hadrian's Villa.

For lunch stop in **Adriano** (Via di Villa Adriano 194, *Tel. 0774/529-174*) located just outside of Hadrian's Villa. Sample some of their *crostini di verdure* (fried dough with vegetables inside), or *raviolini primavera con ricotta e spinaci* (ravioli with spring vegetables, spinach and fresh ricotta).

After lunch venture onto the grounds of Hadrian's Villa. The building itself was begun in 125 CE and completed 10 years later, and was at the time the largest and most impressive villa in the Roman Empire. From his travels Hadrian, an accomplished architect, found ideas that he recreated in his palace.

Once you have satisfied all your architectural voyeurism, it's onto **Frascati** where we will spend the night.

To get to Frascati, take route 636 under the A24 highway, past the Via Prenestina and the Via Casalina. Once there we will check into our quaint old hotel, the **Bellavista** *(Piazza Roma 2, Tel. 06/942-1068)*. Evening is the perfect time to spend at an outside café or wine bar in Frascati, savoring the quiet ambiance of this Roman hill town as well as the full bodied white of the region. If you want to be in the center of everything for dinner try **Pizzeria Pinnocchio** *(Piazza del Mercato 20, Tel. 06/941-6694)*. If you want a quiet meal overlooking the fields of Frascati, try **Zaraza** (Viale Regina Margherita 21, *Tel. 06/942-2053)*.

Day Two

The next day take a leisurely stroll through the thriving gardens of the **Villa Aldobrandini**. Afterwards simply wander the streets of this lovely medieval town, watching the tapestry of daily life unfold around you.

For lunch, let's go to **Pagnanelli** (Piazza A Gramsci 4, *Tel. 06/936-0004)* in **Castel Gandolpho**, only a few minutes drive away. Take route 216 through the town of Marino. There's not much to see here except for the wonderful **Palazzo Pontificio**, the summer residence of the Pope, located in the **Piazza del Plebiscito**. From the piazza and the restaurant you have wonderful views of the lake below. The scene is truly enchanting. After lunch take the car for a spin down to the lake and around the beautiful blue waters.

The afternoon and early evening will be spent getting to **Velletri** and **Anagni** then finally onto **Fiuggi** for the night and their curative baths the next morning. Don't hesitate to stop along the way and take some amazing photos of the picturesque Italian countryside.

To get to **Velletri** from Castel Gandolpho you can either take the less scenic Route 7, or the more pleasant route 217. You can get on Route 7 straight from Castel Gandolfo, but to catch the 217 you need to drive down to the lake and go south around it until the junction for 217. In Velletri we can admire the fourth century **Cattedrale di San Clemente** and walk slowly through the historical center of the town, taking in the small details of everyday life.

Next on our tour is **Anagni**, which we arrive at by taking Route 600 north out of town, which hooks up with Route 6 at Collefore and will take us to

Anagni. This is a wonderful medieval town with steep, narrow streets winding around beautiful palazzi. The town's cathedral rises solitary on the highest point in town. Beside this eleventh century monument with its simple facade is the powerful twelfth century bell tower. If you're hungry stop for a small snack at one of the cafés in town, but don't eat too much; in Fiuggi we're going to have a great meal.

To get to **Fiuggi**, only a short drive away, we catch the Route 155r. Fiuggi is famous for its curative waters at the **Fonte di Bonifacio** or the **Fonte Anticolana**. The waters and the tranquility are always an excuse to linger here for a day. We will spend the night at the **Grand Hotel Palazzo Delle Fonte** (Via dei Villini 7, Tel. 0775/5081) a spectacular four star hotel, founded in 1913 with tennis courts, indoor and outdoor swimming pools, luscious gardens and more. If you don't want something so upscale, try **Hotel Fiuggi Terme** (Via Prenestina 9, Tel. 0775/551-212), another four star that runs about half the price since it has about half the amenities.

Fiuggi is a city split in two: Fiuggi Fonte where the curative waters are, and Fiuggi Citta with its quaint winding streets. We will be eating dinner in the old city at **La Torre dal 1961** (Piazza Trento e Trieste 18, Tel. 0775/55382) so you may want to drive to the restaurant. Eating here at Antonio and Maria Ciminelli's wonderful restaurant is a culinary delight. Everything they serve is exquisite. I especially like the filet of trout (*filetto di trota*) lightly cooked in extra virgin olive oil.

Day Three

Today will be leisurely, spent being 'cured' by the waters, savoring the peace and quiet of the hills, and sampling the fine food and atmosphere of Fiuggi. For lunch try **Villa Hernicus** (Corso Nuova Italia 30, Tel. 0775/55254) near the waters. Their *spaghetti con vongole e peperoncini verdi* (with clams and green peppers) is wonderful.

After you've had enough peace and quiet to last a life time ... it's back to Rome. We can get back by taking the Via Prenestina all the way.

Practical Information for Rome
ATM Machines

Called **Bancomat** machines, ATM's are everywhere in Italy, making it convenient for you to withdraw money directly from your checking account. One drawback is that you can withdraw around E300 each day. But the advantages of using an ATM over traditional travelers checks are easy to discern.

The ATM gives you excellent, up-to-date exchange rates that are better than most exchange offices. Also, the transaction fee, a fixed rate of around $2.00, is usually lower than the fees charged by currency exchange places.

Another advantage is that you are not constrained by bank or business hours. You can access your money anytime.

Despite the advantages of ATMs I would strongly suggest bringing some travelers checks with you. Why? If there is a bank strike (and that could happen at any time in Italy), the ATMs won't be filled up with cash and you'd be left without money. And also have a credit card handy just in case as well.

Babysitters

A list of reliable, English-speaking baby-sitters can be obtained through the **American Women's Association of Rome** (AWAR), *Tel. 06/482-5268.* In addition the American Embassy also has babysitter listings.

Banking & Changing Money

Banks in Rome are generally open Monday through Friday, 8:30am to 1:30pm and from 2:45pm to 4:00pm, and are closed all day Saturday and Sunday and on national holidays.

Shop around for the best exchange rate. Each bank offers a different rate and exchange fee, as do the **Casa di Cambio**, smaller exchange establishments. Sometimes the rate charged to exchange your money is a set fee, a situation that is best when you change a large amount of money. Other places charge a percentage of the total which is generally more beneficial for smaller amounts.

One such exchange place that is open until 9:00pm on weekdays and until 2:00pm on Saturdays, is in the **Stazione Termini**. Some other places to change your money are:
- **American Express**, Piazza di Spagna 38, *Tel. 06/67-64-1.* Open weekdays 9:00am to 5:30pm, and Saturdays from 9:00am to 12:30pm.
- **Banco Nazionale del Lavoro**, Via Veneto 11, *Tel. 06/475-0421.* Open 8:30am to 6:00pm Monday through Saturday.

Boat Service on the Tiber

With ample fanfare and inevitable glitches, Roman officials on May 3rd, 2003 inaugurated boat service along the Tiber, which has not been navigated for more than a century. Cleaners have been down by the river scouring the marble, pulling up weeds, whacking down trees, and shooing away vagrants, so tourists and residents alike can you use the new boat service and avoid Rome's traffic while getting a view of Rome that most people have not seen for over one hundred years.

Five river boats now ply the Tiber from Tiber Island to the Olympic Stadium – a distance of eight kilometers – all for only E1 per person. Landing areas are near these bridges: Garibaldi, Sisto, S. Angelo, Cavour, Risorgimento, Duca d'Aosta. The regular service sets off daily from Ponte Garibaldi at 8:50am.

Cruises with commentaries set off daily at: 10.00, 11.30, 15.30, 17.00. Tickets cost E10. Dinner cruises leave Ponte S. Angelo at 10pm. Tickets cost E43 per person. For information and bookings: *Tel. 066789361*, or visit *www.battellidiroma.it.*

Business Hours

Though hours vary, as a rule store in Rome are open from Monday - Friday, 9:00am-1:00pm, then re-open at 3:30 or 4:00pm to 7:30/8:00pm, and Saturdays from 9:00am to 1:00pm. Recently stores are now open on Saturday afternoons and Sundays as well.

Basically, you must plan on most stores being closed from 1:00pm to 4:00pm, since this is the Italian siesta time. During that time, the only places open are restaurants, and most of those close at 2:30pm or 3:00pm. 24/7 is not a concept here in Rome ... yet.

Church Ceremonies in English

• **All Saints' Church** (Anglican), Via del Babuino 153b, *Tel.06/3600-2171. Email: allsaintsEroma@hotmail.com.* Sunday Mass 8:30am and 10:30am (sung)
• **Church of Jesus Christ of Latter Day Saints**, Piazza Camaro 20, *Tel. 06/ 827-2708.*
• **Methodist Church**, Via del Banco di Santo Spirito 3, *Tel. 06/686-8314. Email: iasb.trad@tiscalinet.it.* 10:30 Sunday Service.
• **Rome Baptist Church**, Piazza San Lorenzo in Lucina 35, *Tel. 06/687-6652. Email: rombaptist@compuserve.com.* 10am Sunday worship.
• **St. Andrews** (Scottish Presbyterian), Via XX Settembre 7, *Tel. 06/482-7627.* Sunday Service at 11:00am
• **St. Patrick's** (English-speaking Catholic), Via Boncompagni 31, *Tel. 06/420-3121.* Sunday mass at 10:00am.
• **St. Paul's within the Walls** (American Episcopal), Via Napoli 58, *Tel. 06/ 488-3339. Email: stpaul@mclink.it.* Sunday Mass 8:30am and 10:30pm (sung)
• **San Silvestro** (English-speaking Catholic), Piazza San Silvestro 1, *Tel. 06/ 679-7775.* Sunday Mass at 10:00am and 6:00pm.
• **Santa Susanna** (American Catholic), Piazza San Bernardo, *Tel. 06/488-2748, Web: www.santasusanna.com.* Sunday Mass at 9:00am, and 10:30am. Saturdays and weekdays at 6:00pm. 11am services at Marymount International school out the Via Cassia.
• **Synagogue**, (no services in English) Via Lungotevere dei Cenci, *Tel. 06/684-0061*

Computers in Rome

Plan ahead. If you decide to bring your laptop, remember to carry an adapter so you can plug it into the wall to recharge your batteries. You can get them at most Circuit City or Radio Shack stores in North America.

Credit Card Lost?
If you lose your credit card, these numbers in Italy will come in handy:
- **American Express**, *Tel. 800/872-000* (travelers checks), *Tel. 800/874-333* (credit cards)
- **Bank Americard**, Toll free in Italy *167/821-001*
- **Citibank**, *Tel. 06/854-561*
- **Diner's Club**, *Tel. 800/864-064*
- **Mastercard**, *Tel. 800/870-866*
- **Thomas Cook/Mastercard**, *Tel. 800/872 050* (traveler's checks)
- **VISA**, *Tel. 800/874-155* (traveler's checks), *Tel. 800/877-232* (credit cards)

Doctors & Dentists (English-speaking)
In case of need, the **American Embassy** (Via Vittorio Veneto 119, *Tel. 06/46741)* will gladly supply you with a recommended list of English-speaking doctors and dentists. A hospital where English is spoken is **Salvator Mundi**, Viale della Mura Gianicolensi 67, *Tel. 06/588-961, Website: www.smih.pcn.net, Email: dg.smih@pcn.net.* I had my tonsils out there and am doing fine today. Another place is the **Rome American Hospital**, Via VE Longoni 69, *Tel. 06/22551, Web: www.rah.it.* They have a physician on call 24 hours a day.

An organization that can hook you up with physicians all over the world is **Personal Physician Worldwide**. See Chapter 7 for contact information. A recommended heart specialist is **Aleardo William Madden**, MD, a Fellow in the American Heart Association. For an appointment, call *06/7049-1747* (Via Baldo degli Ubaldi 272.)

A well-recommended dental clinic is **Bazzucchi Dental Center**, Via I Vivanti 201, *Tel 06/520-0202, Email: Bazzucchi@mail.wing.it, Web: www.bazzucchi.it.*

Embassies & Consulates
- **Australia**, Via Alessandria 205, *Tel. 06/852-721*
- **Canadian Embassy**, Via GB de Rossi 27, *Tel. 06/445-981*
- **Great Britain**, Via XX Settembre 80a, *Tel. 06/482-5441, Web: www.grbr.it*
- **Ireland**, Piazza di Campitelli 3, *Tel. 06/697-912*
- **New Zealand**, Via Zara 28, *Tel. 06/441-7171, Email: nzemb.roma@flashnet.it*
- **South Africa**, Via Tanaro 1, *Tel. 06/852-541, Email: sae@flashnet.it*
- **United States**, Via Veneto 199, *Tel. 06/46741*

Emergencies
The following numbers should be used in case of emergency: **113**- Police;

112 – Caribinieri (military police), **118** – Ambulance (Red Cross), and **115** – Fire. There are police and caribinieri offices in Termini station by the tracks. Other **Caribinieri** stations include: Via Mentana 6 and Piazza Venezia. Other **Polizia** stations include: Via Farini 40, Via S Vitale 15, or Piazza del Collegio Romano.

Festivals in Rome
- **January 1**, Candle-lit processional in the Catacombs of Priscilla to mark the martyrdom of the early Christians.
- **January 5**, Last day of the Epiphany Fair in the Piazza Navona. A carnival celebrates the ending.
- **January 21**, *Festa di Sant'Agnese*. Two lambs are blessed then shorn. Held at Sant'Agnese Fuori le Mura.
- **March 9**, *Festa di Santa Francesca Romana*. Cars are blessed at the Piazzale del Colosseo near the church of Santa Francesca Romana.
- **March 19**, *Festa di San Giuseppe*. The statue of the saint is decorated with lamps and placed in the Trionfale Quarter, north of the Vatican. There are food stalls, sporting events and concerts.
- **April**, *Festa della Primavera* (festival of Spring). The Spanish Steps are festooned with rows upon rows of azaleas.
- **Good Friday**, The Pope leads a candlelit procession at 9:00pm in the Colosseum.
- **Easter Sunday**, Pope gives his annual blessing from his balcony at noon.
- **April 21**, Anniversary of the founding of Rome held in Piazza del Campidoglio with flag waving ceremonies and other pageantry.
- **May 1**, *Festa del Lavoro*. Public Holiday
- **First 10 days of May**, international horse show held in the Villa Borghese at Piazza di Siena.
- **May 6**, Swearing in of the new guards at the Vatican in St. Peter's square. Anniversary of the sacking of Rome in 1527.
- **Mid-May**, Antiques fair along Via dei Coronari
- **First Sunday in June**, *Festa della Repubblica* involving a military parade centered on the Via dei Fori Imperiali. It's like something you'd see in Moscow during the Cold War.
- **June 23-24**, *Festa di San Giovanni*. Held in the Piazza di Porta San Giovanni. Traditional food sold: roast baby pig and snails.
- **June 29**, *Festa di San Pietro*. Festival to Saint Peter. Very important religious ceremony for Romans.
- **July**, *Tevere Expo* involving booths and stalls displaying arts and crafts, with food and wine lined up along the Tiber. At night there are fireworks displays and folk music festivals.

• **July 4**, A picnic organized by the American community outside Rome. Need to contact the American Embassy *(06/46741)* to make reservations for the buses to take you out there.

• **Last 2 weeks in July**, *Festa de Noiantri* involving procession, other festivities, feasting and abundance of wine all in Trastevere.

• **July & August**, Open air opera performances in the Baths of Caracalla.

• **August 15**, *Ferragosto*. Midsummer holiday. Everything closes down.

• **Early September**, *Sagra dell'Uva*. A harvest festival with reduced price grapes and music provided by performers in period costumes held in the Roman Forum.

• **Last week of September**, Crafts show held in Via dell'Orso near Piazza Navona.

• **Early November**, Santa Susanna Church Bazaar. Organized by the church for the Catholic American community to raise money for the church. Great home-made pies and cookies as well as used books and clothes. Auction of more expensive items held also.

• **December 8**, Festa della Madonna Immacolata in Piazza di Spagna. Floral wreaths inlaid around the column of the Madonna and one is laid at the top by firefighters.

• **Mid-December**, Start of the Epiphany Fair in the Piazza Navona. All throughout the piazza a fair filled with food stands, candy stands, toy shops opens to the public. Lasts a week. A must see.

• **December 20-January 10**, Many churches display elaborate nativity scenes.

• **December 24**, Midnight Mass at many churches. I recommend the one at Santa Maria Maggiore.

• **December 25**, Pope gives his blessing at noon from his Balcony at St. Peter's. The entire square is packed with people.

• **December 31**, New Year's Eve. Much revelry. At the strike of midnight people start throwing old furniture out their windows into the streets, so be off the streets by that time, or else your headache from the evening's festivities will be much worse.

Health Clubs

• **Roman Sports Center**, Via del Galoppatoio 33, *Tel. 06/320-1667.* Open 9:00am-10:00pm.

• **Le Club**, Via Igea 15, *Tel. 06/307-1024.* Open Monday-Friday 7:30am–7:00pm, Saturday 4:00pm-6:00pm.

Internet Access

• **Easy Internet Cafe**, Via Barberini 2, *Tel. 06/42-903-388. Web: www.easyinternetcafe.it.* Only 0.80 Euro per hour. The BEST place to access the internet in Rome. Tons of computers, professional space, and a Subway shop inside to satisfy your munchies while surfing.

- **Freedom Traveller**, Via Gaeta 25, *Tel. 06/478-23-862. Email: info@freedom-traveller.it. Web: www.freedom-traveller.it.* Access for E2.5 for 30 minutes or less. Student discount for an hour E4.
- **Splashnet**, Via Varese 33, *Tel. 06/4938-2073.* Open in the summers from 9:00am to 1:00pm and Winter from 9:00am to 10:00pm. E2.5 per half hour on line time.
- **The Netgate**, Piazza Firenze 25, *Tel 06/689-3445, Email: roma.pantheon@thenetgate.it; Borgo S. Spirito 17, Tel. 06/6813-4082, Email: roma.vaticano@thenetgate.it; Termini Station, Tel. 06/8740-6008, Email: roma.terminie@thenetgate.it. Website: www.thenetgate.it.* Rates start at E2 per hour.

Language Study

If you want to travel in Italy and actively pursue learning the language at the same time there are many different schools all over the country. But the best way to do this would be to have everything arranged for you by organizations that specifically connect students with schools in Italy. Two of the best to contact, with quite similar names, are:
- **Language Studies Abroad**, *Tel. 800/424-5522.*
- **Language Study Abroad**, *Tel. 818/242-5263.*

Laundry Service

- **Uondo Blu**, Principe Amadeo 70, *Tel. 06/474-4647.* Coin operated laundry open seven days a week from 8:00am to 10:00pm. Wash E3. Dry E3. Convenient to the train station.
- **Aqua & Sapone**, Via Montebello 66, *Tel. 06/488-3209.* Self-service wash and dry E3 each. Open every day from 8:00am to 10:00pm. Convenient to the train station.

Papal Audiences

General audiences with the Pope are usually held once a week (Wednesday at 11:00am) in Vatican City. To participate in a general audience, get information through the **North American College** (Via dell'Umita 30, *Tel. 06/679-0658, Fax 06/679-1448),* the American seminary in Rome. Catholics are requested to have a letter of introduction from their parish priest. Ticket pickup is the Tuesday before the Wednesday audience.

For attendance at a Papal audience women should dress modestly, with arms and head covered, and dark or subdued colors are requested. Men are asked to wear a tie and a jacket.

At noon every Sunday, the Pope addresses the crowds gathered beneath his window in St. Peter's square. During the latter part of the summer, because of the heat in Rome, and now more so for tradition, the Pope moves to his summer residence at **Castel Gandolpho** in the Alban Hills about sixteen miles southeast of Rome. Audiences are also regularly held there.

Pharmacies

Farmacia are open from 9:00am to 1:00pm and reopen from 3:30pm to 7:30pm. At nights and on Sundays and holidays, one pharmacy in each district remains open on a rotating schedule. For information, dial 192 then 1 through 5 depending on the zone (see phone book for zones) for the location of the pharmacy nearest you (in Italian). Also a list of open pharmacies for holidays and Sundays is published in the Rome daily, *Il Messagero*.

Police

- **Pubblica Sicurezza**, *Tel. 06/4686* (for theft, lost and found, petty crimes)
- **City Police** (Vigili Urbani), *Tel. 06/67691* (for towed cars)
- **Carabinieri**, *Tel. 112* (for emergencies, violent crimes, etc.)
- **Highway Police** (Polizia Stradale), *Tel. 06/557-7905* (for parking tickets, etc.)

Postal Services Rome

You can buy stamps at local tobacconists (they are marked with a "T" outside) as well as post offices. Mailboxes are colored red, except for the international ones, which are blue. Post offices are open from 8:25am to 1:50pm on weekdays, and 8:25am to 11:50am Saturday. Some, like the one on Via Firenze, near the Economy bookstore are open until 5:00pm, Monday through Saturday. The two exceptions to this rule are: the **Main Post Office** (Piazza San Silvestro), which is open Monday through Friday from 9:00am to 6:00pm, and Saturday from 8:30am to 12:50pm; and the branch at **Stazione Termini** (*Via Terme Diocleziane 30*, near the McDonalds on the Piazza della Repubblica), which is open 8:30am-6:00pm Monday – Friday and Saturdays 8:30am – 2:00pm.

Postal Services Vatican

If you want to have your postcards mailed by the Vatican, with their official stamp, go to the **Vatican Post Office** (Via di Porta Angelica 23, close to Piaza Risorgimento) which is open 8:30am-6:00pm Monday – Friday and Saturdays 8:30am–11:50am.

Public Restrooms

These are scarcer than flying pigs, even though many were built for the year 2000 celebrations. When in need, there are always McDonalds, which have sprouted up all over Rome after they bought out the Italian burger chain *Burghy*. If no McDonalds is around, try a well-heeled restaurant or hotel. Ask for the *servizio, toilette,* or *bagno*.

Supermarkets

You can usually find all the food you need at an *alimentari*, but if you want a wider selection, there are four supermarkets in the center of Rome, three of which are marked on Map A with an "S" in a circle. One, **GS**, is in the Metro tunnel system between the Piazza di Spagna and the Via Veneto. Another, **SMA**, is in the Piazza Santa Maria Maggiore near the train station. A **Despar** supermarket is at Via del Pozzetto 119-124 near the Via del Tritone and Via del Corso. Finally, there is a supermarket near the Pantheon at Via Giustiniani 18-20, noted on Map B.

Support Groups

- **Alcoholic Anonymous**, *Tel. 06/474-2913*
- **Narcotics Anonymous**, *Tel. 06/860-4788*
- **Overeaters Anonymous**, *Tel. 06/884-5105*

Tour Companies

Some of the companies that offer you a variety of tourist services and tours are listed below:
- **Appian Line**, Piazza dell'Esquilino 6, *Tel. 06/487-861*
- **Carrani**, Via Vittorio E. Orlando 95, *Tel. 06/474-2501*
- **Green Line**, Via Farini 5, *Tel. 06/483-787*
- **Vastours**, Via Pienmonte 34, *Tel. 06/481-4309.*
- **Stop 'n' Go Bus Tours**, *Tel. 06/321-7054*, is one of the best and stops at a number of different sights in Rome and also offers half day trips to Tivoli and Ostia Antica and a full day trip to Cerveteri and Tarquinia.

If you want a personalized tour of Rome, by licensed tour guides, contact one of the following organization:
- **Centro Guide Roma**, Via S. Maria delle Fornaci 8, *Tel. 06/639-0409, Fax 06/630-601*
- **Centro Assistenza Servizi Turistici**, Via Cavour 184, *Tel. 06/482-5698,*
- **Italian Language and Culture for Foreigners**, Via Tunisi 4, *Tel. 06/3975-0984; www.arcodidruso.com; Email: cultura@arcodisdruso.com,*
- **Walking Tours of Rome**, Via Varese 39, *Tel. 06/44-51-843, Fax 06/44-50-734; www.enjoyrome.com.*

Tourist Information & Maps

Besides the tourist kiosks mentioned in the *Seeing the Sights* section, you can buy maps and guide books at most newsstands and bookstores. This may be necessary even the tourist kiosks tend to run out of information fast. Also, the maps given out at the tourist offices and kiosks may not be as extensive as is needed when in Rome, especially if you want to use the bus system. There are maps which you can buy at newsstands which not only list the bus routes but also have an index of streets which will help you locate places of interest in Rome. The cost for these maps is anywhere from E3.5-5. A bargain as well as a great keepsake of your trip to Rome.

Wanted in Rome
An excellent periodical that features classified ads about accommodations, jobs, and more. Also included are the latest performing arts activities in Rome. A great resource for tourists and ex-pats alike. Cost is E75 cents and you can find it at most English language bookstores. Office located at Via dei Delfini 17, *Tel. 06/679-0190, Email: wantedinrome@compuserve.com, Web: www.wantedinrome.com.*

Chapter 14

FLORENCE & TUSCANY

A visit to Italy is not complete without a trip to **Firenze** (**Florence**), one of the most awe-inspiring cities in all of Europe. The Renaissance achieved the bloom of artistic expression here, and it was in Florence that countless master artists, writers, inventors, political theorists and artisans lived and learned their craft, then excelled at filling the world with the glow of their brilliance. Michelangelo and Leonardo da Vinci may be the best known outside of Italy, but I'll wager you've also heard of Dante, Petrarch, Brunelleschi, Machiavelli, Giotto, Raphael as well as many other learned and talented Florentines.

Strolling through the cobblestone streets of Florence is like being in a history book come to life. The sights, smells, and sounds of this wonderful city must be experienced first-hand to appreciate and fully understand the magical atmosphere. So read on, and I'll guide you through the amazing city of Florence. And later in this chapter, find separate sections for some of the best cities in **Tuscany** — including **Cortona**, **Siena**, **Pisa**, **Lucca**, **San Gimignano**, and **Montepulciano** — as well as a bonus excursion to the incredible city of **Bologna** in Emiglia Romagna.

Alive with History – Beautiful Firenze!

Florence has humble beginnings as a marketplace for the ancient Etruscan town of **Fiesole**, which is located on a hill about three miles (five kilometers) to the northeast. Farmers displayed their fruits and vegetables on the clearing along the **Arno**, and the Fiesole people came down to buy. About 187 BCE, the Romans built a road through the marketplace, and later a military garrison was established here.

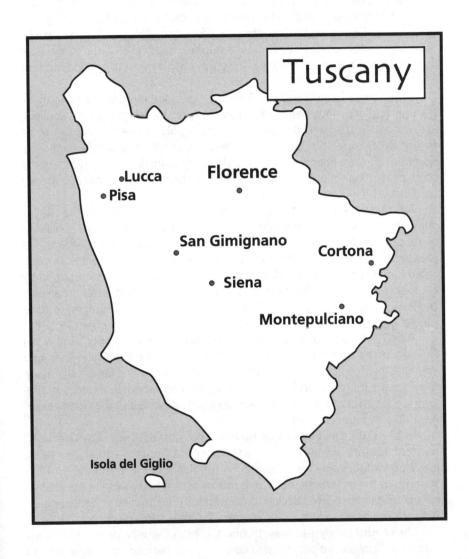

As the Roman roads extended through central and northern Italy, Florence grew and prospered, and it became a trade center for goods brought down from the north. Because of its significance invaders sought its spoils; and in 401 CE a horde of Ostrogoths besieged the city; then in 542 the Goths made an unsuccessful attack. Soon after, the Lombard conquest swept over Florence, and the city became the capital of a Lombard dukedom. In time, the Holy Roman Empire led by Charlemagne drove the Lombards out and in 799 ordered new fortifications built. Charlemagne's death in 814 ended the Holy Roman Empire's hold on Florence, at which time it became an independent city-state.

With its newfound freedom, Florence expanded rapidly. The Florentines became energetic merchants and bankers, expert workmen, brave soldiers, and shrewd statesmen. By the 1100s their guilds were among the most powerful in Europe, and Florentine textiles were sold throughout the continent. Florentine bankers financed enterprises in many countries, and in 1252 the city coined its first gold pieces, called **florins**, which became the accepted currency for all of Europe.

Although Florence was largely self-governing, for a long time the city fell under the auspices of German princes. The last to hold it was Countess Matilda of Tuscany. At her death in 1115, the countess bequeathed Florence to the papacy. In the early 1200s, the papal power was supported by a political group called the **Guelfa**, while the claims of the German emperor were backed by another group, the **Ghibellines**. This conflict lasted almost a hundred years and was formally initiated in 1215 when the rival factions each tried to seize control of the city.

Aided by several popes, the Guelfa held power in the city until 1260 when their army was almost wiped out at a battle near Siena. The Ghibellines held the reins for six years, until in 1266, Charles of Anjou, the champion of Pope Clement IV, marched down from France and smashed the forces of the German emperor at the battle of Benevento. At which point the Guelfa exiles were able to return to Florence.

In 1293, the **Ordinances of Justice** were passed. These laws excluded from public office anyone who was a member of a Florentine guild. As a result many powerful people were barred from holding public positions, and the strength of the merchant-nobles was reduced for a time. Despite these laws, control of the city, passed back into the hands of the guilded citizens, and the Florence remained a democratic republic for about 150 years.

The **Medici** family gradually, through its extensive economic power, took control of Florence, helping to get citizens sympathetic to their cause elected into city government. Giovanni de' Medici was the first of this family to gain real wealth and influence. His son Cosimo was the de facto ruler of Florence for many years. It was Cosimo who helped to re-initiate an appreciation for classical Greek and Roman teachings, a harbinger of the Renaissance. Under

Cosimo's grandson **Lorenzo the Magnificent**, Florence ascended to its greatest heights as a cultural center.

An Incredible Statue, a Fabulous Inn!

If this is your first visit to la bella Italia, you must visit Florence. The small Renaissance streets, the countless art galleries, the friendly people, and the fine food all make this city a joy to visit. But not in high season. Florence in the summer is a zoo of tourists (not quite as bad as Venice, but close) all crammed together or queued for blocks to see the main sights. Florence definitely should be visited in the off-season, not only to save on your hotel bills (hotels drop their rates dramatically in the off-season) but also to make your entire stay more enjoyable and relaxing.

It is one thing to savor the excellence of Michelangelo's **David** virtually alone, and almost believe that you saw it move, but quite another to have to fight your way through a crowd just to get close enough to try and see that majestic statue without an obstructing head in the way. But no matter when you visit, if you're looking for some peace and tranquility, try the unmatched **Torre Di Bellosguardo**, one of my favorite hotels anywhere.

A medieval castle perched prominently above the city, here you'll find some of the best views of Florence. It is a supremely romantic spot filled with gardens, olive trees where horses graze, an open lawn in front, and a pool with a bar all overlooking this magnificent city. There are only 16 rooms here, so if you want to experience the best accommodations Florence has to offer you must plan far enough in advance.

Before and after Lorenzo died in 1492, the city's excesses brought on a reform movement headed by **Girolamo Savonarola**, a Dominican friar. The Medici family was expelled in 1494 and Savonarola ruled Florence as a fundamentalist theological dictator until 1498, when a popular reaction to his rule erupted and he was put to death.

In 1512 "la famiglia Medici" was restored to the city. After years of consolidating power, in 1537 the city became part of the Grand Duchy of Tuscany. Upon the death of the last Medici in 1737, Tuscany passed to the Hapsburgs of Austria. Ultimately, in 1861 the city was formally annexed to the newly created Kingdom of Italy, of which Florence was the capital from 1865 to 1870.

In World War II, Florence was a battleground, as was most of the country of Italy. Italy entered the war on the German side in 1940, and soon after German troops occupied Florence. When the Allies advanced in 1944, the

Germans destroyed all the bridges except the Ponte Vecchio, and demolished many medieval dwellings to hinder the progress of the advancing Allies. Later the Allied Military Government restored the less seriously damaged structures, helping to maintain the charm that Florence retains today. Irony of ironies is that as the United States was helping to restore of the buildings in Florence, as well as throughout all of Europe, America was initiating domestic programs which razed their own vibrant city neighborhoods to replace them with desolate "ghettoes" of office buildings, empty parking structures, and wastelands of highways slicing through the heart of every American city.

But enough editorializing ... in 1966 Florence's had its own problems when the Arno River overflowed its banks, rising as high as 20 feet (6 meters) in some places. As a result of this watery onslaught, hundreds of artistic masterpieces were lost. Many of the damaged works have since been restored, but thousands of irreplaceable treasures were lost.

Rebirth of Art & Science in Florence

Florence was the cradle of the Italian **Renaissance**, a rebirth of classical knowledge that precipitated a new creativity in art and literature. **Dante's** magnificent poetry made the Tuscan dialect the official language of Italy. **Francesco Petrarch** composed his lovely sonnets here, and **Giovanni Boccaccio's** *Decameron* was penned here as well. **Machiavelli**, another Florentine, set down his brilliant, though cynical observations on politics based on the intrigue intrinsic to Florentine politics.

Giotto was the first of many immortal Florentine painters and sculptors. **Michelangelo** worked on the city's fortifications as well as his paintings and statues. **Ghiberti** labored almost a lifetime on the doors for the Florentine Baptistery. His rival **Brunelleschi** created the immense dome atop the Duomo. Many other great artists studied or worked in Florence, among them **Leonardo da Vinci**, **Donatello**, and **Raphael**.

Four Day Itinerary In & Around Florence
DAY ONE
Morning

To begin, let's walk to the **Accademia** and see Michelangelo's *David*. Make sure that you have made reservations already by going to *www.firenze.net* and booking specific entry times. Take in all the other works by the master which are located here.

Lunch

Walk back to the **Piazza San Lorenzo** where there is a daily market. Go to **Nerbone's** in the **Mercato Centrale** for lunch. Try one of their amazing

Panini (boiled beef or pork) served on a Panino bread roll. Order a beverage and sit at one of the tables directly in front of the quaint little place. After your meal, wander through the market. Check out all the different cuts of meat the Italians use in their recipes. Upstairs is the vegetable and fruit market. A good place to buy some healthy snacks for later.

Afternoon

After you're done shopping head to the nearby **Piazza Duomo**. Admire the bronze doors on the baptistery, and the impressive expanse of the church. Take the time to go all the way up top of the dome.

If needed, take a little siesta. If not, head to the **Piazza della Signoria** and admire the statues in the Loggia. Also go into the **Palazzo della Signoria** and admire the staircase that leads to their museum. This was the residence of the Medici until the Palazzo Pitti was made available. If you're interested go upstairs and pay the fee to see the inside.

Just outside of the Piazza dell Signoria is the **Uffizi Gallery**, which you'll be going to tomorrow. Remember to have made your reservations well in advance using *www.firenze.net.* Now make your way to the **Ponte Vecchio** over the river **Arno**. Shop for jewelry in the many little stores if you want. Follow the bridge over to the other side of the Arno.

From here we're going to the **Pitti Palace** and the **Boboli Gardens**. Each museum has beautiful artwork in the building, and the gardens offer peace and tranquility as well as many wonderful statues. If you bought some snacks at the **Mercato Centrale** you may want to take the time to have a brief picnic in the gardens. When you leave, check out the store **Firenze Papier Mache** in the piazza across from the palace.

Evening

Return to your room to freshen up and get ready for dinner. Tonight we're going to a wonderful local place called **La Bussola**, Via Porta Rossa 58, *Tel. 055/293-376.* You can either sit at the counter and have a simple meal of pizza or sit in the back and soak up all the ambiance and romance of Florence. Try their spaghetti alla Bolognese (with a meat and tomato sauce) or their tortellini alla panna (cheese or meat stuffed tortellini in a cream sauce).

After dinner wander over to the Piazza Santa Maria Novella and stop at the **Fiddler's Elbow** for a pint. This place has an authentic Irish Pub atmosphere, great Italian people and fun times. If dancing is your desire, try the **Space Electronic** nearby at Via Palazzuolo 37, *Tel. 055/292-082.*

DAY TWO
Morning

Get to the **Uffizi Gallery** a half an hour before your reservations indicate you should and pick up your tickets. You'll probably spend all morning here.

Lunch

For lunch try a quaint basement restaurant between the **Duomo** and the train station and near Piazza Santa Maria Novella, **Buca Lapi**, Via del Trebbio 1, *Tel. 055/213-768*. There are old travel posters plastered all over the walls and ceiling, and the tables surround the cooking area so you can view quite a display while you wait for your food. Depending on the season, it may be closed for lunch. Try their cinghiale con patate fritte (roasted wild boar with fried potatoes) or their pollo al cacciatore con spinacio (chicken 'hunter style' which is made with tomatoes, spices and brandy and comes with spinach)

Afternoon

Remember the church in the piazza where the **Fiddler's Elbow** was last night? We're going there now (**Chiesa di Santa Maria Novella**) to check out the overall ambiance and to admire the frescoes painted by Michelangelo when he was beginning his career as an artist. While we're in this area of town, check out the store **Il Tricolore**, Via della Scala 25, just off the piazza. This is the official outlet for the police and military in Florence where you can buy a variety of items like pins, hats, shirts, badges, that you can take home as gifts. Some items they won't sell to you, like guns, knives, and uniforms.

Next we're walking slightly across town to get to the place where Michelangelo is buried, **Chiesa di Santa Croce**. Inside the church you will also find many other graves of prominent Florentines including Dante Aligheri. There is a leather shop attached to the church where you can find some of the best hand-made leather goods anywhere. It is also a treat to watch them work the leather. A great place to visit and/or shop.

Late Afternoon

From here, we're going up to the **Piazzale Michelangelo** to watch the sun set. This is really a hike. If you do not want to walk, the cab ride will be quite dear, but the view is worth it. Remember to take your camera and high speed film to catch all the light possible. You'll get some of the best shots of Florence from up here. If you want to splurge on a fantastic meal, try **La Loggia**, Piazzale Michelangelo 1, once you get up here. It's very expensive but well worth it. Or, on the way back down the hill into town, stop at **Il Rifrullo**, Via San Niccolo 55, to get a pint of beer or glass of wine. At night this is an isolated and relaxing place to come and savor the Florentine evenings.

From here take the long walk across the river to the train station to establish your itinerary for tomorrow. You may have to wait a little while in the information office, but it's worth it so you won't have to do it in the morning.

Evening

For dinner tonight we're going to the **Tredici Gobbi** (which means "13 hunchbacks") located on Via Porcellana. Situated down a small side street near the Arno, here you can enjoy a combination of Italian and Hungarian cuisine. For an after-diner drink wander over to the nearby **Excelsior Hotel** and go up to their roof deck. Enjoy a sambuca con tre mosce, literally translated it means "sambuca (a liquorice drink) with three flies," but in actuality the flies are coffee beans. When you bite into the beans as you sip the Sambuca the combination of tastes is phenomenal. Here you have a view over all of Florence as it lines the Arno.

DAY THREE

Since you've now seen virtually everything that a traveler is supposed to see in Florence, let's take a day trip outside of the city to **Pisa** and **Lucca**. We'll first go to Pisa to admire the leaning tower, and its cute little market near the Arno. Next we'll go to Lucca to walk around the romantic walls and see a virtually perfectly preserved old medieval town.

Pisa

Once you arrive in Pisa, stop in the tourist office just outside the station to the left and pick up a map of the city. Then if you're tired take the No. I bus directly to the **Piazza dei Miracoli** which has the church, baptistery and leaning tower. Admire them all and take plenty of pictures. If you decide to walk (it only takes about 15 minutes to get to the Piazza dei Miracoli) you must pass by the colorful market of **Piazza Vettovaglie** near the river and just off of the **Borgo Stretto**, the street with the famous covered sidewalk. It's well worth the visit.

For lunch we'll stop at the **Dei Cavalieri**, Via San Frediano 16, *Tel. 050/ 49-008*. It's off the beaten tourist path and that's one reason why the food is so great. Try the spaghetti con funghi porcini (with mushrooms), or vongole verace (clams in a garlic and oil sauce).

Lucca

Now it's back to the train station and onto Lucca. Once you arrive simply walk out of the station towards the old walls of the city. Follow the path leading to the walls where you will find an entrance into the walls themselves. Follow the stairs inside up to the top. Now you're on the old battlements and ramparts. Walk around them to your left about 400 meters until you get to the **Piazza Verdi/Vecchia Porto San Donato** where the tourist office is located. You'll know you're there by the size of the piazza inside the walls and the fact that this is where tour buses park. Descend and pick up a map of the city from the tourist office, you'll need it.

Now it's time to go to the **Torre del Guinigio**. This tower has trees and bushes growing on its top. Go up here to get great views of the city and the surrounding area. Use the map to explore the old Roman amphitheater,

Puccini's museum, the cathedral, and more. And of course, take some more walks along the romantic tree-lined battlements.

For dinner, we'll be going to **Da Leo Fratelli Buralli**, Via Tegrini, *Tel. 0583/492-236.* This is the best, most authentic restaurant in Lucca. It caters to the locals, the food is stupendous and the atmosphere festive. Try the fettucine all rucola e gamberi (pasta with a cheese and shrimp sauce), the pollo arrosto con patate (exquisite roasted chicken and potatoes flavored with rosemary and olive oil), or the pollo fritto e zucchini (chicken and zucchini fried in olive oil).

DAY FOUR
Siena

Located about an hour and a half from Florence, Siena is a great day trip. Here you have the famous **Campo**, a tower that rises above the city for great photos, quaint medieval streets and plenty of ambiance to spare. The cathedral seems out of place since it is so large in a relatively small square. If the Florentines hadn't conquered the city when they did, the locals would have made the tower almost twice as large. Did you know that in its hey-day Siena was larger than either London or Paris?

Once you arrive at the station take bus number 1 or 8 to get dropped off near the tourist office, or catch a cab.

Despite its past prominence, you can wander around Siena quite easily. If you want a great meal at a wonderful local place, try **Marlborghetto**, Via di Porta Giustizia 6, *Tel. 0577/289-258.*

Arrivals & Departures
By Air
THE FLORENCE AIRPORT

Florence's **Aeroporto Amerigo Vespucci,** *www.airport.florence.it,* has an information desk in the arrival terminal open from 7:30am to 11:30pm everyday. It provides tourist information, *Tel. 055/315874,* and information on flight arrivals and departures, *Tel. 055/3061300,* as well as information on lost baggage, *Tel. 055/30061302.* The information desk can also be reached by fax at *055/315874* or *Email: infoaeroporto@safnet.it.* Automated flight information is available also: domestic flights *Tel. 055/306-1700,* international flights *Tel. 055/306-1702.*

Taxi Service

The bus service is the best and least expensive way to get to Florence from the airport, but if you want to go by taxi, there is a taxi stand outside the main exit from the airport. *Tel. 055/4242, 4798, 4390, 4499.*

Bus Service

The SITA station (Via Caterina da Siena 17- Florence, *Tel. 055/214-721*, Toll-free in Italy *800/373-760, 800/424-500)* is located next to the train station in Florence. Buses leave frequently between the bus station and the airport, typically once or twice an hour for most of the day.

Car Rental
• **Avis**, *Tel. 055/315-588* (open 8:00am-11:30pm)
• **Hertz**, *Tel. 055/307-370* (open 8:30am-10:30pm; Saturday-Sunday 9:30am-10:30pm)
• **Maggiore/National**, *Tel. 055/311-256* (open 8:30am-10:50pm)

THE PISA AIRPORT

Pisa's **Aeroporto Galileo Galilei,** *www.pisa-airport.com* (in Italian), has an information office open every day from 8:00am until 10:00pm, *Tel. 050/ 500-707.*They dispense tourist information, flight information, and can store your bags for you.

Taxi Service

At the airport the taxi stand is right outside the exit of the airport. To call a radio taxi: *Tel. 050/541600.*

The train station in Pisa is about five minutes from the airport; the taxi stand is located directly in front of the station, *Tel. 050/41252.* In town, there's a taxi stand in the Piazza Duomo, *Tel. 050/561-878.*

Train Schedule

You can take a train from the Pisa Airport directly into Florence in a little over an hour and a half. Trains leave frequently for other destinations throughout Tuscany and the rest of Italy, for the most part once an hour or more every day for most of the day.

Car Rental
• **Avis**, *Tel. 050/42028, 42028*
• **Hertz**, *Tel. 050/43220, 49156*
• **Thrifty**, *Tel. 050/45490, 45356*

By Bus

There are many different bus companies in Italy, each serving a different set of cities and sometimes the same ones. Buses should be used only if the train does not go to your destination since traffic is becoming more and more of a problem in Italy.

The most convenient bus company in Florence is located directly next to the train station in **Piazza Adua**, called **Autolinee Lazzi**, *Tel. 055/215-154*

. They have over 50 arrivals and departures a day to and from a variety of different locations like Pisa, Lucca, Prato, and Pistoia. Two other bus companies are: **Autolinee Sita**, *Tel. 055/214721 or 284661*, and **Autolinee CAP**, *Tel. 055/218603*.

If You Miss These Places, You Haven't Been to Florence

After spending all your time and money to come to this Renaissance paradise, there are a few sights that if you don't see you can't really say you've been to Florence. The first of which, the **Duomo** with its campanile and baptistery, is hard to miss. The next, the **Ponte Vecchio**, is a gem of medieval and Renaissance architecture and is filled with gold and jewelry shops. And if you miss Michelangelo's **David** in the Accademia you shouldn't show your face back in your hometown. That work of art is as close to sculpted perfection as any artist will ever achieve.

Last but not least is the art collection in the **Uffizi Gallery**. To actually do this museum justice you may need to spend close to one day wandering through its many rooms. And don't forget to shop at the **San Lorenzo Market** or browse through the local **Mercato Centrale**.

There are countless other wonderful sights to see and places to go in Florence. Walking the streets is like walking through a fairy tale. But if you haven't seen the items above, you haven't been to Florence.

By Car

If arriving in Florence from the south, for speed you will be on the **A1**. If you were looking for a more scenic adventure, you would be on the **Via Cassia** which you can take all the way from Rome. If arriving from the north in a hurry, you would also take the **A1**, but if in no rush you would probably take the **SS 65**.

If you need to rent a car while in Florence, please refer to the *Getting Around Town* section of this chapter, below. Sample trip lengths on the main roads:
• **Rome**: 3 1/2 hours
• **Venice**: 4 hours

By Train

The station, **Stazione Santa Maria Novella**, is located near the center of town and is easily accessible on foot to and from most hotels. The **tourist information office** in the station, *Tel. 055/278-785*, is open daily from 7:00am to 10:00pm and is your first stop if you don't have a reservation at a hotel. The **railway office**, at the opposite end of the station from the tourist information office, is where you plan your train trip from Florence.

There are **taxis** located just outside the entrance near the tourist information office as well as **buses** that can take you all over the city.

Sample trip lengths and costs for direct (diretto) trains:
• **Rome**: 2 1/2 hours, E40
• **Venice**: 3 1/2 hours, E20

Getting Around Town
By Bus
Florence is so small that you will more than likely never need to use the buses. But if you do, first get information from the booth at the **Piazza della Stazione** across the piazza from the station itself. Here they can give you all the information you need to get anywhere you want to go. A ticket costs E1 and is reusable within an hour.

The information number for the local bus company, **ATAF-Autobus Urbani** , is Tel. 055/5650-222.

By Car
Renting a car is relatively simple, as things go in Italy, but it is somewhat expensive. You can rent a car from a variety of agencies all over Florence. All prices will vary by agency so please call them for an up-to-date quote.
• **Avis**, Borgo Ognissanti 128r, Tel 055/21-36-29 or 239-8826
• **Budget**, Borgo Ognissanti 134r, Tel. 055/29-30-21 or 28-71-61
• **Hertz**, Via Maso Finiguerra 33, Tel. 055/239-8205, Fax 055/230-2011

Most companies require a deposit that amounts to the cost of the rental, as well as a 19% VAT added to the final cost, which can be reimbursed once you're home (see Chapter 6, Basic Information). A basic rental of a Fiat Panda costs E80 per day, but the biggest expense is gasoline. In Italy it costs more than twice as much per gallon as it does in the States. If you're adventurous enough to think of renting a car, remember that the rates become more advantageous if you rent for more than a week.

By Moped
Only if you feel extremely confident about your motorcycle driving abilities should you even contemplate renting a moped.

Rentals for a moped (50cc) are about E30 per day, and for a 125cc (which you'll need to transport two people) about E60 per day. From some companies you can rent even bigger bikes, but I would strongly advise against it. You can also rent the cycles for an hour or any multiples thereof.
• **Happy Rent**, Via Borgo Ognissanti 153r, Tel. 055/239-9696. Web: www.happyrent.com. A great place to rent mopeds, motorcycle and

cars, including the tiny and adorable Smart Cars. My favorite in Florence. You will be happy renting from Happy Rent.
• **Noleggio della Fortezza** (two locations), Corner of Via Strozzi and Via del Pratello, Open 9:00am to 8:00pm, the 15th of March to 31st of October; and Via Faenza 107-109r. *Tel. 055/283-448.*

By Bicycle
• **Florence By Bike**, Via San Zanobi 120/122, *Tel./Fax 055/488-992, Email: info@florencebybike.it, Web: www.florencebybike.it.* Open from 9:00am-7:30pm every day. Credit cards accepted. A great place to rent bikes. Very helpful staff. They also have guided city tours and countryside tours. They also offer moped rentals.

By Taxi
Florence is a city made for walking, but if you get tired, taxis are good but expensive way to get around. They are everywhere so flagging one down is not a problem.

The going rate as of publication was E2.5 for the first 2/3 of a kilometer or the first minute (which usually comes first during the rush hours), then its Euro 50 cents every 1/3 of a kilometer or minute. At night you'll also pay a surcharge of E1.5, and Sundays you'll pay E0.50 extra. If you bring bags aboard, say for example after you've been shopping, you'll be charged E0.50 extra for each bag.

There are strategically placed cab stands all over the city. But if you cannot locate one, here are some radio taxi numbers:
• **Radio Taxi**, *Tel. 055/4242 or 4798 or 4390*
• **Taxi Merci**, *Tel. 055/296230 or 210321 or 371334*
• **Moto Taxi**, *Tel. 055/4386 or 355741 or 359767*

Where To Stay
Centro Storico
The **centro storico** is the heart of Florence. Anywhere you stay, shop, eat, or drink will be relatively expensive, since this is the prime tourist area of Florence. Here you will find the **Duomo** dominated by Brunelleschi's huge dome; the **Baptistery** next door with its beautiful bronze doors; the **Piazza della Signoria** with its copy of Michelangelo's *David,* and under all the cobblestones you are walking on are Bronze age relics proving that Florence is centuries older than anyone ever thought.

There is also the unforgettable collection of art in the **Uffizi Gallery**; the **Ponte Vecchio**, built in 1345 and once home to butchers, blacksmiths, greengrocers, tanners and leather workers but now filled with gold shops; the **Piazza della Repubblica** that once was the site of a Roman Forum; the **Jewish ghetto**, which was until the end of the 19th century an open air

Florence Website

You can book museum tickets, find special events, locate quaint little stores, book hotels, and help plan all aspects of your trip with *www.firenze.net.*

market; the **Mercato Nuovo** or Straw Market with its many fine examples of Tuscan craftsmanship; and the Fifth Avenue of Florence, the **Via Tornabuoni**.

1. ALDINI, *Via Calzaiuoli 13, Tel 055/214-752, Fax 055/216-410. Web: http://aldini.hotelinfirenze.com/. Credit cards accepted. 15 rooms all with private bath, telephone, and air conditioning. Single E60-90; Double E95-140. Breakfast Included.* ******

This centrally located two-star charges what it does because some of the rooms have views of the Duomo. There are no TVs in the rooms and truly limited ambiance with few amenities. What used to be a bargain is now just trying to suck tourists dry. Avoid at all cost despite the location. If they add more amenities or drop their price back down to a reasonable level I'll recommend this place again. Until then read on.

2. BEACCI-TORNABUONI, *Via Tornabuoni 3, Tel. 055/212-645, Fax 055/283-594. Email: info@bthotel.it. Web: www.bthotel.it. All credit cards accepted. 28 rooms. Single E130-160; Double E190-250. Extra bed E30. Buffet breakfast included.* *******

Located on the top three floors of a 14th century palazzo on the world famous and elegant shopping street, Via Tornabuoni, this is a classic hotel. There is a wonderful rooftop garden terrace that will make you fall in love with Florence every evening you spend up there. This place is coordinated like an old castle, with nooks and crannies everywhere, and plenty of common space besides the terrace to sit and write your postcards home. You'll be surrounded by antiques and will feel as if you've stepped into an Agatha Christie novel. The breakfast is an abundant buffet which can be served to you in your room at no extra charge. The rooms are all furnished differently but with the finest taste and character. An excellent place to stay.

3. BERNINI PALACE, *P.za di San Firenze 29, Tel. 055/288-621, Fax 055/268-272. Web: www.hotelbernini.com. All credit cards accepted. 86 rooms. Single E250-400; Double E300-500. Breakfast included. Parking E25.* ********

Centrally located just behind the Palazzo Vecchio, the Bernini is an elegant and refined hotel. The breakfast room is once where the Italian Parliament met when Florence was the capital of the country. An auspicious location for an equally impressive buffet. The rooms are spacious, the windows are soundproof, and the hotel come complete with all necessary four-star amenities. The

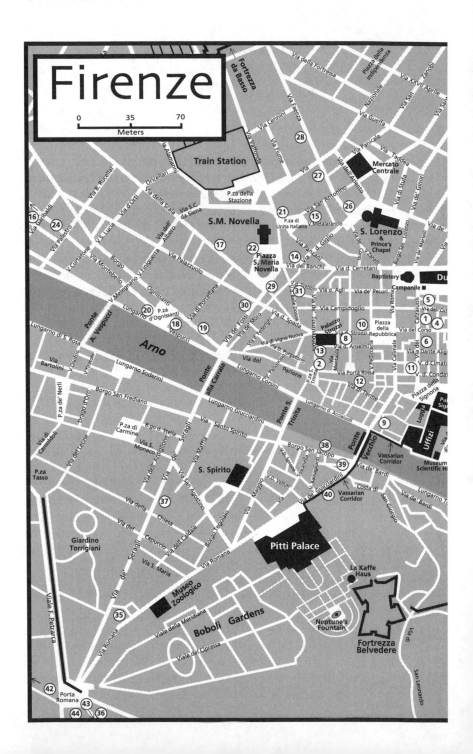

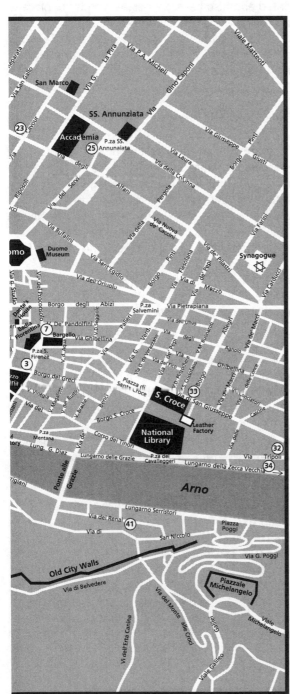

Hotels ○

Centro Storico
1. Aldini
2. Tornabuoni-Beacci
3. Bernini Palace
4. Brunelleschi
5. Calzaiuoli
6. Firenze
7. Grand Hotel Cavour
8. Helvetia & Bristol
9. Hermitage
10. Pendini
11. Pierre
12. Porta Rossa
13. La Residenza

Centro
14. Astoria
15. City
16. Crocini
17. Elite
18. Excelsior
19. Goldoni
20. Grand Hotel
21. Grand Hotel Bagioni
22. Grand Hotel Minerva
23. Il Guelfo Bianco
24. Kraft
25. Loggiato dei Serviti
26. Lorena
27. Nuova Italia
28. Porta Faenza
29. Roma
30. Unicorno
31. De La Ville

Santa Croce
32. Claridge
33. Dante
34. Ville Sull'Arno

Oltrarno
35. Annalena
36. Classic
37. Istituto Gould
38. Lungarno
39. Pitti Palace
40. La Scaletta
41. Silla
42. Torre di Bellosguardo
43. Villa Carlotta
44. Villa Cora

bathrooms are well appointed and also have phones. A wonderful place to stay in Florence. Professional, high end, attentive service.

4. BRUNELLESCHI, *P.za Sant'Elisabetta 3, Tel. 055/290-311. Fax 055/ 219-653. Email: info@hotelbrunelleschi.it. Web: www.hotelbrunelleschi.it. All credit cards accepted. 96 rooms. Single E250; Double E360. Breakfast included. Parking E25.* ****

Filled with an antique ambiance, accentuated by the 6th century Byzantine tower and the 12th century medieval church which have been absorbed into the hotel, this place is characterized by a rustic elegance and Tuscan refinement. The furnishings are a mixture of modern and antique, the structure is bathed in history accentuated by a small museum with a few Roman artifacts. The rooms are large and filled with every imaginable comfort, as are the bathrooms with their double sinks, courtesy toiletry kit and hairdryers. The breakfast buffet is abundant. From the terrace you have a wonderful view of the Duomo. Located in a tiny piazza in the heart of Florence, near all the sights, and in the middle of the best shopping in the city, this four-star is a great choice.

5. CALZAIUOLI, *Via Calzaiuoli 6, Tel 055/212-456, Fax 055/268-310. Web: www.calzaiuoli.it. All credit cards accepted. 45 rooms all with private bath, TV, Telephone, mini-bar, and air conditioning. Breakfast included. Single E140-210; Double E160-260. Extra bed E35.* ***

Located in a recently renovated old palazzo and perfectly situated in the quiet pedestrian zone between the Duomo and Palazzo Vecchio. The rooms are spacious enough, as are the bathrooms, and have a nice floral and ribbon print motif. The rooms on the Via Calzaiuoli are perfect for people watching, but can be a little noisy on the weekend evenings. Other rooms have views of the Duomo. You can't beat the location or the service.

6. FIRENZE, *Piazza dei Donati 4 (off of Via del Corso), Tel. 055/268-301, Fax 055/212-370. No credit cards accepted. 60 rooms, 35 with private bath. Single without bath E30-40; Single E40-50; Double without bath E50-60; Double E60-80. Breakfast included.* *

This is two different hotels. One is new, the other's left in a time warp from the 1950s. My recommendation is based on the new section, so call in advance to get your reservations. Even though this place doesn't have air conditioning, it should be higher than a one star. The lobby is all three-star, as are the rooms in the new wing with their phones and TVs. Room 503 caught my fancy since it has a great view of the Duomo from the bed: when you wake up in the morning there's the most romantically picturesque scene right in front of you. Besides the beauty and comfort of the new wing, the lobby and breakfast area is of a much higher standard than any other one star I've been in. It's beautiful and quite inexpensive.

7. GRAND HOTEL CAVOUR, *Via del Proconsolo 3, Tel. 055/282-461. Fax 055/218-955. Email: info@hotelcavour.com. Web: www.hotelcavour.com. Credit cards accepted. 89 rooms. Single E100-160; Double E150-190. Breakfast included. Parking E20.* ***

Near the Bargello and the Uffizi, this old hotel has traditional and regal common areas filled with authentic antiques. The rooms are large and very comfortable and the bathrooms come with all necessary amenities. The rooms on the top floor are the best because of the wonderful views. Make a point of requesting them. The terrace on the top floor, accessible by all guests, though less than quaint in and of itself, has panoramic views over the city. A wonderful three-star in a prime location.

8. HELVETIA & BRISTOL, *Via del Pescioni 2, Tel. 055/287-814. Fax 055/288-353. Web: www.florence-hotels.ws/hotels/helvetia-and-bristol.html. Credit cards accepted. 52 rooms. Single E300-350; Double E400-550. Breakfast E20. Parking E23.* *****

Located in the heart of the centro storico right by the Palazzo Strozzi, this is a refined and super elegant five star hotel. The common areas are anything but common, the bar is situated in a magnificent garden in the summer, and the restaurant is of the highest level. The rooms, each different from the other, are all furnished tastefully and the bathrooms are awash in marble. This hotel is stupendous, the staff is superb and the services offered sublime, including professional babysitting. A top of the line hotel in Florence.

9. HERMITAGE, *Vicolo Marzio 1 (Piazza del Pesce), Tel. 055/287-216, Fax 055/212-208. Email: florence@hermitagehotel.com. Web: www.hermitagehotel.com. Credit cards accepted. 16 rooms all with private bath and jacuzzi. All rooms E250. Breakfast included.* ***

Only steps from the Ponte Vecchio this wonderful little hotel is on the top three floors of palazzo and is reached by a private elevator. It has the most beautiful roof terrace, complete with greenery and flowers and a great view over Florence. They serve breakfast up there in good weather and it is a great place to relax in the evenings. The rooms are not that large but the ambiance and the location make up for it, as does the spacious terrace and common areas. A great three-star that has been updated with jacuzzi style baths in every room so you can luxuriate here at the end of the day.

10. PENDINI, *Via Strozzi 2, Tel. 055/211-170, Fax 055/-281-807. Email -pendini@florenceitaly.net. Web: www.florenceitaly.net/hotel.html. All credit cards accepted. 42 rooms. Only 25 with air conditioning. Single E90-120; Double E120-160. Breakfast included. Extra bed costs E30.* ***

Ideally situated in the heart of Florence by the Piazza della Repubblica in a quaint old palazzo. The breakfast room is located in an archway between two buildings. They have twelve rooms that overlook the piazza and all are well appointed and quite large, perfect for family stays. Most bedrooms have brass or wooden beds, pretty floral wallpaper, and soft pastel carpeting. The staff is more than accommodating, and they speak perfect English. An ideal central location for your stay in Florence.

11. PIERRE, *Viale de' Lamberti 5, Tel. 055/216-218, Fax 055/239-6573. Web: www.florenceby.com/pierre. All credit cards accepted. 39 rooms. Single E240; Double E330. Breakfast included. Parking E22.* ****

The courtesy, hospitality and professionalism of the staff helps to make a stay here wonderful. The entry hall is adjacent to a spacious bar where many guests congregate in the evenings before and after dinner. The rooms, all rather large by Italian standards, have fine furnishings and colorful carpets to complement the various amenities of this excellent four-star hotel. It's located right by the Piazza della Signoria, deep in the heart of Florence's best shopping district. The continental breakfast comes complete with local Tuscan cheeses and salamis and an assortment of breakfast cereal. A good choice for a relaxing stay in Florence.

12. PORTA ROSSA, *Via Porta Rossa 19, Tel. 055/287-551, Fax 055/282-179. Credit cards accepted. 80 rooms. Single E150; Double E220.* ***

Don't even think of staying here. Yes it's quaint, yes the rooms are large, yes the prices are relatively inexpensive, but it is rather run-down and the staff is surly. If your tour group has booked you here, make the best of it. The rooms are comfortably appointed with Liberty style antiques, and you are in the middle of everything in Florence, so the stay won't be all bad. But if you have a choice, avoid this hotel like the plague.

13. LA RESIDENZA, *Via de' Tournabuoni 8, Tel. 055/218-684, Fax 055/284-197. Web: www.florenceby.com/residenza. All credit cards accepted. 24 rooms. Single E80-140; Double without bathroom E80-140. Double E130-220. Breakfast included. Parking E15.* ***

A small but accommodating hotel in a central location with a clientele that

The Best Hotels in Florence

These are my favorite places to stay in Florence:

6. FIRENZE*
37. ISTITUTO GOULD*
16. CROCINI**
40. LA SCALETTA**
9. HERMITAGE***
36. CLASSIC***
25. LOGGIATO DEI SERVITI***
42. TORRE DI BELLOSGUARDO****
21. GRAND HOTEL BAGLIONI****
20. GRAND HOTEL*****
44. VILLA CORA*****

&

is very international, many who come to have access to the world famous shopping street on which the hotel is located. The roof garden is a great place to relax in the evenings. The bar and restaurant are also located in the roof, and it is also where breakfast is served in the mornings. The rooms, many of which have some grand terraces, are simple yet comfortable, but the bathrooms are quite small.

Centro

This section of town is north of the Duomo and west of the Via Tornabuoni, and is home to many reasonably priced hotels, restaurants, and stores. Here you'll find the **Mercato of San Lorenzo**, a huge daily outdoor clothing market, and the **Mercato Generale**, Florence's main food market. Also located in Centro is the train station from which you'll be embarking on the terrific excursions I've planned for you in the next chapter.

14. ASTORIA, *Via del Giglio 9, Tel. 055/239-8095, Fax 055/214-632. Email: reception@astoria.boscolo.com. Web: www.florenceby.com/boscoloastoria. All credit cards accepted. 103 rooms. Single E170-280; Double E220-340. Breakfast E15. Parking E20.* ****

Within walking distance of the train station, down a quaint side street, this is an elegant hotel. The communal area – bar, piano salon, and the in-house restaurant, Palazzo Gaddi - are all pleasantly refined. In the summer the hotel restaurant's garden is a wonderful place for a meal. The hotel encompasses a number of different buildings, including the 16th century structure after which the restaurant is named and where the conference facilities are located. The rooms are all soundproofed against Florence's buzzing traffic and come complete with all necessary four-star amenities; and the bathrooms are more than adequate. A well situated four-star, which will make your stay in Firenze a pleasant one.

15. CITY, *Via Sant'Antonino 18, Tel. 055/211-543, Fax 055/295-451. Email: info@hotelcity.net. Web: www.hotelcityflorence.com. All credit cards accepted. 18 rooms. Single E80-160; Double E100-205. Breakfast included. Parking E15.* ***

Located within walking distance of the train station and right by the superb San Lorenzo Market, this is a wonderful three-star deep in the heart of Florence. Filled with spacious rooms, soundproofed from Florence's city noise, each filled with wonderful furnishings and well equipped bathrooms. The common areas are nicely decorated in cathedral-like vaulted rooms. This is a wonderfully intimate three-star. More of a bed and breakfast than a hotel, since there are only 18 rooms.

16. CROCINI, *Corso Italia 28, Tel. 055/212-905, Fax 055/239-8345. Email: hotel.crocini@firenze.net. Web: www.hotelcrocini.com. Closed December 18-26. All credit cards accepted. 1 suite, 20 rooms (17 with private* *bath, 2 with shared bath, 1 with private bath outside of room). Single E100; Double E120. Breakfast E8. Parking E10.* **

Situated in a tranquil residential area outside of the central tourist area, near the Teatro Communale and the big park Le Cascine, this is a professionally run little two-star that I recommend highly. A stay here not only does not drain your bank account, but it also liberates your soul. A member of the Family Hotels consortium, this hotel is located in a wonderful palazzo and the rooms are well, if simply appointed. A good choice for travelers to Florence who want high quality accommodations but do not want to spend too much for it.

17. ELITE, *Via della Scala 12, Tel. and Fax 055/215-395. 10 rooms all with bath or shower. Single E90. Double E120. Breakfast E7. All credit cards accepted.* **

A quaint little hotel located on a great street in a perfect area for sightseeing, shopping, or dining. You'll love the wooden staircase that takes you from the lobby and breakfast salon to your quiet and spacious rooms. The prices are good for the location even though there are only a few amenities other than comfort and cleanliness, not to mention accommodating service. More of an inexpensive bed and breakfast than a hotel.

18. WESTIN EXCELSIOR, *Piazza Ognissanti 3, Tel. 055/264-201, Fax 055/210-278. Toll free number in America 1-800-221-2340. Web: www.westin.com. All credit cards accepted. 200 rooms. Single E415-460; Double E520-580. Continental breakfast E15. American breakfast E22.* *****

Directly across from its sister, The Grand Hotel, everything here is of the highest standard, especially the roof garden/restaurant. Great rooms and perfect service. A superb five-star, luxury hotel. They have everything and more that you could want during your stay. If you can afford it, this is one of the best luxury hotels in Florence.

19. GOLDONI, *Borgo Ognissanti 8, Tel. 055/284-080, Fax 055/282-576. Email: info@hotelgoldoni.com. Web: www.hotelgoldoni.com. Credit cards accepted. 20 rooms. Single E110-160; Double E130-200. Breakfast included. Parking E10.* ***

In a somewhat removed location near the Arno river, this small three-star hotel is situated on the second floor of an 18th century palazzo. Most of the rooms face onto a quiet courtyard garden, and all are of different size but are comfortably furnished. The bathrooms are basic but come with all three-star amenities. The breakfast buffet is abundant. A quiet, comfortable place to stay, slightly off the beaten path.

20. GRAND HOTEL, *Piazza Ognissanti 1, Tel. 055/288-781, Fax 055/217-400. Toll free number in America 1-800-221-2340. Web: www.westin.com. All credit cards accepted. 106 rooms. Single E395; Double E615; Continental breakfast E15. American breakfast E22.* *****

Aptly named, this hotel is definitely grand. Located in a pale yellow and gray palazzo built in 1571, everything has been superbly restored to offer modern comforts while retaining the old world charm. The reception area is classically elegant. Each bedroom has beautiful neo-classic furniture and elegant decorations and frescoes; the bathrooms are a luscious oasis. Your breakfast is served on a small balcony overlooking an internal garden. An excellent choice for the high end traveler.

21. GRAND HOTEL BAGLIONI, *P.za dell'Unita Italiana 6, Tel. 055/23-580, Fax 055/235-8895. Email: info@hotelbaglioni.it. Web: www.hotelbaglioni.it. All credit cards accepted. 195 rooms. Single E200-280; Double E280-380. Breakfast included. Parking E25.* ****

Within walking distance of the train station, set in a piazza off the main road near the San Lorenzo market, this is a hotel of grand tradition situated in an austere palazzo from the 18th century. There is an elegant and spacious entry hall; and roof garden restaurant with panoramic views over the rooftops of Florence with a dramatic presentation of the Duomo. The breakfast buffet is served up here in good weather. The rooms are large and well appointed in four-star style, the best of which face the piazza; the bathrooms are simply elegant. A top quality hotel in Florence.

22. GRAND HOTEL MINERVA, *P.za Santa Maria Novella 16, Tel. 055/284-555, Fax 055/268-281. Email: info@grandhotelminerva.com. Web: www.grandhotelminerva.it. All credit cards accepted. 99 rooms. Single E200-280; Double E320-400. Breakfast included. Parking E22.* ****

Located in one of the best piazzas in the city, within walking distance of the train station, the Minerva is a comfortable and modern hotel. The entry hall with its garden is elegantly accommodating, off of which you will find the restaurant and breakfast room. All rooms are equipped with the necessary four-star amenities and more, including video players. The bathrooms are lavish and some have hydro-massage and sauna. Available to guests for free is a pool and fitness center. And guests also receive free bicycle rentals. This is a great place to stay in a prime location.

23. IL GUELFO BIANCO, *Via Cavour 29, Tel. 055/288-330, Fax 055/295-203. Email: info@ilguelfobianco.it. Web: www.ilguelfobianco.it. Credit cards accepted. 29 rooms. Single E145; Double E190-240. Continental breakfast included.* ***

Not in my favorite area of Florence, even though it is close to everything important; but there is something about this hotel that catches my heart. Maybe it's Room 24, with the only terrace located on the inside courtyard. A perfect place to unwind after a day of sightseeing. Or maybe number 27 and 28, two large doubles that are basically suites with living and sleeping space. If you stay here, call well in advance to book either of these rooms. Every room has all necessary modern comforts, and the bathrooms are modern, large and brilliantly white. There are many places to sit and relax, such as two different courtyards downstairs, and little balconies and terraces strewn everywhere.

24. KRAFT, *Via Solfernino 2, Tel 055/284-273, Fax 055/239-8267. Email: info@krafthotel.it. Web: www.krafthotel.it. All credit cards accepted. 80 rooms. Single E220-290; Double E350-470. Breakfast included. Parking E20.* ****

This refined hotel is out of the city center in a tranquil area, but close enough for walking access. The roof garden, where breakfast is served, offers exquisite panoramic views along the Arno. The piano bar and restaurant also have views over the rooftops of Florence, making it a wonderful place to end the day. The rooms are spacious and furnished with style and come with every imaginable four-star amenity. A wonderful choice for those who want elegance outside of the main tourist area. There is also a terrace with an elongated lap pool for summer cooling and sightseeing of a different sort.

25. LOGGIATO DEI SERVITI, *Piazza SS. Annunziata 3, Tel. 055/289-593/4, Fax 055/289-595. Email: info@loggiatodeiservitihotel.it. Web: www.loggiatodeiservitihotel.it. All credit cards accepted. 29 rooms. Single E150; Double E215; Suite E270-390. Breakfast included. E40 for an extra bed.* ***

Located in a 16th century *loggia* that faces the beautiful Piazza della SS Annunziata, this hotel is filled with ambiance. The interior common areas consist of polished terra-cotta floors, gray stone columns and high white ceilings. The rooms are pleasant and comfortable and are filled with elegant antique furnishings. All are designed to make you feel like you just walked into the 17th century, and it works.

They also have the modern amenities necessary to keep us weary travelers happy, especially the air conditioning in August. Some rooms face what many believe is one of the most beautiful piazzas in Italy (no cars allowed), while the rest face onto a lush interior garden. The bathrooms come with every modern comfort. The service, the accommodations, everything is at the top of the three-star category. So, if you want to have a wonderful stay and also to feel as if you've stepped back in time, book a room here.

Selected as one of my *Best Places to Stay* – see Chapter 10.

26. LORENA, *Via Faenza 1, Tel. 055/282-785, Fax 055/288-300. Email: info@hotellorena.com. Web: www.hotellorena.com. 16 rooms, 10 with bath. Single without bath E45-60; Single E60-75; Double without bath E65-80; Double E60-115. All credit cards accepted. Continental Breakfast E4. Hotel closes its doors from 2:00am to 6:00pm.* **

A pleasantly run hotel located just off of the large San Lorenzo market. Perfectly located for shopping and sightseeing. The rooms are nondescript but comfortable and the prices are good. Not many amenities except for location, comfort and cleanliness. They have added A/C and TV in each room as a prelude to moving to three-star status. There is still some work to go, but for now they are on the high end of two-stars both in quality and price.

27. NUOVA ITALIA, *Via Faenza 26, Tel. 055/287-508, Fax 055/210-941. Web: http://nuovaitalia.hotelinfirenze.com. Credit cards accepted. 21 rooms. Single E80. Double E115. Extra person E25. Breakfast included.* **

This family-run hotel is ideally located near most of the sights and night spots, and the prices are very good. You'll just love the old Mama as she caters to you during your meals in the breakfast area, which looks just like a country *trattoria*. Not many real amenities, just a pleasant place to lay your head with friendly and accommodating service. Some rooms have A/C so request those in late summer. Each room is plainly but comfortable furnished.

28. PORTA FAENZA, *Via Faenza 77, Tel 055/214-287, Fax 055/210-101. Email: info@hotelportafaenza.it. Web: www.hotelportafaenza.it/home.html. All credit cards accepted. 25 rooms. Single E120-180, Double E140 210. Breakfast included. Parking E12.* ***

Situated in a beautiful and completely refurbished old palazzo from the 1700s, this hotel is located near the train station, a bit removed from the centro storico. The Lelli family, including Canadian wife Rose, operates this cute little hotel. A recent series of renovations have made visible some older architectural details which lends an air of history. The rooms are spaciously spartan and filled with modern but comfortable furnishings and come with all necessary three-star amenities. Not in my favorite location in Florence, but overall a good three-star.

29. ROMA, *Piazza Santa Maria Novella 8, Tel. 055/210-366, Fax 055/ 215-306. Email: hotel.roma.fi@dada.it. Web: www.firenzealbergo.it/ hotelroma/. Credit cards accepted. 60 rooms. Single E115-190; Double E170-280.* ****

A discrete hotel with expansive common areas, and large, clean and comfortable rooms with all necessary four-star amenities. The hotel is on one of Florence's best piazza's, the beautiful Piazza Santa Maria Novella. The common areas are elegantly appointed with marble, columns, and frescoes with an omnipresent pastel blue shade; and are a perfect place to unwind. A wonderfully accommodating hotel without unnecessary frills. If you are looking for a spacious room, at a good price, look no further. Another major plus is their massive breakfast of rolls, croissants, cheese, ham, salami, cereal, juice, coffee, tea, and fruit. A great way to start your day.

30. UNICORNO, *Via dei Fossi 27, Tel. 055/287-313, Fax 055/268-332. Web: www.florenceby.com/unicorno. 27 rooms,. Single E95-160; Double E140-180. All credit cards accepted. Breakfast included. Parking E15.* ***

Near Piazza Santa Maria Novella, this hotel is situated in a palazzo from the 1400s. Completed renovated and complete with all modern amenities, this is a wonderfully located and comfortably accommodating three-star. The rooms and bathrooms come with all necessary three-star features and the staff goes out of its way to make you comfortable. The breakfast buffet is large and filling. Though not spectacular, I would definitely recommend this hotel for a stay in Florence.

31. DE LA VILLE, P.za Antinori 1, Tel. 055/238-1805/6, Fax 055/238-1809. Email: delaville@firenze.net. Web: www.hoteldelaville.it. All credit cards accepted. 69 rooms. Single E210-260; Double E270-430. Breakfast included. Parking E22. ****

An elegant hotel within walking distance of the station, in an optimal location between the Duomo, the Ponte Vecchio and the Piazza Santa Maria Novella. The rooms are very comfortable, soundproof, each uniquely furnished, and have all necessary three-star amenities including satellite TV. The bathrooms are well appointed, and come complete with all amenities including a phone. The common areas are charming, especially the terrace, which is great place to relax at the end of the day. Breakfast is superb and the staff is professional and courteous.

Santa Croce

This is the area of Florence in which Michelangelo played as a child. Located to the east of the Centro Storico, Santa Croce is more of an authentic, residential, working class neighborhood and seems far from the maddening tourist crowds, even though it's just around the corner from them. The church that gives this area its name, Santa Croce, contains the graves of Michelangelo, Galileo, and other Italian greats.

32. CLARIDGE, Piazza Piace 3, Tel 055/234-6736, Fax 055/234-1199. Web: www.florence-hotels.ws/hotels/claridge-hotel.htm. All credit cards accepted. 32 rooms. Single E90-110; Double E120-190. Breakfast included. Parking E15. ***

A comfortable and functional three-star hotel that has an ample entrance hall and a covered cortile in the center of this elegant villa. The rooms are simply decorated but come with all necessary three-star comforts. What sets this hotel apart is its location. Outside of the main tourist center, here you can get away from it all while being only a short walk from everything. The highest floor has wonderful views of Santa Croce. A wonderful three-star for those who want to be in Florence but not surrounded by tourists.

33. DANTE, Via San Cristofano 2, Tel. 055/241-772, Fax 055/234-5819. Web: http://dante.hotelinfirenze.com. All credit cards accepted. 14 rooms. Single E90-110; Double E120-190. Breakfast E10. Parking E12. ***

A small hotel, only 14 rooms, near the picturesque piazza of Santa Croce. The main draw of this bed and breakfast style hotel are the ten rooms with kitchenette. These are very useful for families, as are the spacious and comfortable rooms and bathrooms. The common areas are tiny but overall this is a rather pleasant place to stay in Florence, near enough to everything, but just outside the main tourist center to make your stay here authentically local.

34. **VILLE SULL'ARNO**, *Lungarno C. Colombo 3, Tel. 055/67-09-71, Fax 055/678-244. Email: info@villesullarno.it. Web: www.hotelvillesullarno.com. 47 rooms. Single E150; Double E210-230. Breakfast included. All credit cards accepted.* ****

Located away from the center of things, about ten minutes by car. They have a good-sized swimming pool and a lovely garden where breakfast is served in the summer. The rooms are large and comfortable with all the amenities of a four-star, including A/C and cable TV. The ones on the river are wonderfully tranquil as are the others because in this location you are definitely away from the hustle and bustle of Florence. A good choice for those that do not like the pace of city life. Also, they have some rather large rooms, great for families.

Country Living Near Florence

Surrounded by 25 acres of olive groves vineyards, **La Fornella** is a former monastery turned into a beautiful bed & breakfast villa located only 18 kilometers southeast of Florence. Stay here for an authentic Tuscan holiday complete with all manner of amenities including a swimming pool and cooking classes. La Fornella is an ideal respite from Florence's urbanity, and is great location from which to explore the rest of Tuscany.

Run by an ex-pat American and her Italian husband, this charming couple will assist you in creating wonderful itineraries and offer professional concierge services to help you make reservations for local restaurants, tennis courts and golf courses. Tastefully decorated with local antiques, the three apartments sleep 2, 4, or 6 persons, and can be rented on a weekly basis for between E750 and E800 a week.

Contact information: Giacomo Bartoloni Saint Omer and Cassandra Schaffer; *www.lafornella.com; Tel/Fax 055/830-1219; Email: info@lafornella.com.*

Oltrarno

Oltrarno, literally "the other side of the Arno," is home to many of Florence's artisans. It is still looked upon distinct from the city itself even though the walls of Florence encircled this area in 14th century (people remember their history in Europe). Most of the beautiful architecture was destroyed during World War II, not only by the Germans but also by the Allied bombings. Thankfully both sides spared the Ponte Vecchio, The Duomo, and the other great architectural wonders in Florence.

Also spared was the **Palazzo Vecchio** (also known as the **Medici Palace**) and the **Boboli Gardens**. Another place to visit in the Oltrarno is the **Piazza**

Santo Spirito that boasts a 15th century church with the unfinished facade by Brunelleschi.

35. ANNALENA, *Via Romana 34, Tel. 055/222-402, Fax 055/222-403. Email: info@hotelannalena.it. Web: www.hotelannalena.it. Credit cards accepted. 20 rooms, 16 doubles, four singles. Single E120; Double E155. Breakfast included.* ***

This place has at times been a convent, a school for young ladies, a gambling casino, a safe haven for Italian Jews during WWII, and now finally it has become the Hotel Annalena. It takes over the entire floor of a beautiful Florentine palazzo and has all the necessary amenities of a good three-star hotel. The lobby area doubles as breakfast room and evening bar space. The rooms are large with high ceilings and seem to be *fresco* (cool) all year round. Located just beyond the Palazzo Pitti and near one of the entrances to the Boboli Gardens, this hotel is a little off the beaten path which makes for a wonderfully authentic stay. The rooms all have antique style furnishings, terra-cotta floors and come with small terraces overlooking a garden.

36. CLASSIC, *Viale Machiavelli 25, Tel. 055/229-3512, Fax 055/229-353. Email: info@classichotel.it. Web: www.classichotel.it. All credit cards accepted. 20 rooms. Single E125-140; Double E140-170. Breakfast included.* ***

Located in a quaint little palazzo from the nineteenth century situated outside the old city walls, here you can get a real taste of Florentine life. Viale Machiavelli is an exclusive address and this hotel shows it. The lush garden in the rear (there's a glassed-in section for winter guests) is your breakfast location as well as your mid-afternoon slumber spot, and there's a small bar just off the garden for evening drinks. Your rooms are palatial, with immense ceilings and clean bathrooms. I would recommend this gem to anyone who likes to tour and then escape the hectic pace of the city. One minor note, they do not have air conditioning, but when I was there on a 90 degree day each room was very cool. These old palazzi were built to keep cool in the summer and remain warm in the winter. This place is a classic and the choice for discerning vacationers.

37. ISTITUTO GOULD, *Via dei Serragli 49, Tel. 055/212-576, Fax 055/280-274. Email: gould.educativo@dada.it. No credit cards accepted. 25 rooms, 20 with private bath. Single E25; Double E35 per person.* (no stars)

This is a fantastic budget hotel in truly ambient surroundings. The rooms, on the second and third floors of this quaint old palazzo, are quite large. In your search throughout the wonderful building you'll find immense common rooms with comfortable chairs and a quaint little terrace overlooking some rooftops in the rear. The hotel separates the more mature travelers from the younger crowd, so the late night adventures of the young'uns don't keep everyone awake. And the best part of your comfortable stay is that the proceeds benefit a home for boys and girls from eight to 18 who cannot live with their own families. One oddity is that there are limited office hours

(9:00am–1:00pm and 3:00pm–7:00pm). Also, if you want a room with a private bath you need to request that. But even if you do not have one, the common bathrooms are large and accommodating.

38. LUNGARNO, *Borgo S Jacopo 14, Tel. 055/264-211, Fax 055/268-437. Email: bookings@lungarnohotels.com. Web: www.lungarnohotels.it. All credit cards accepted. 66 rooms. Single E230; Double E330-370; Suite E510.* ****

An excellent location right on the river, only a few meters from the Ponte Vecchio, and situated down a quaint, Florentine side street with some great restaurants and food shops. The lounge just off the lobby offers a relaxing view of the river and the Ponte Vecchio. An ancient stone tower is part of the hotel, with a great penthouse suite. If you want the atmosphere of the tower, specify this upon making your reservation. Some of the rooms have terraces overlooking the river, which makes for a perfect place to relax after a tough day of sightseeing. You need to specify this too. This is one of the great hotels in Florence.

39. PITTI PALACE, *Via Barbadori 2, Tel. and Fax 055/239-8711. Web: http://pittipalace.hotel-firenze.net/. All credit cards accepted. 73 rooms. Single E200-250; Double E300-450. Breakfast included. Parking E22.* ***

A comfortable three-star only a few paces from the Ponte Vecchio. The rooms are all different sizes, all furnished in a chic modern style, and some have balconies. The bathrooms are functional and complete with all necessary amenities. The two terraces on the sixth floor offer incomparable panoramic views over the Boboli gardens, Palazzo Pitti, the Duomo and the rest of the city across the river. The breakfast buffet is abundant. A well located, nice hotel. A stay here is comfortable, quiet and accommodating.

40. LA SCALETTA, *Via Guicciardini 13, Tel. 055/283-028, Fax 055/289-562. Email: info@lascaletta.com. Web: www.lascaletta.com. Credit cards accepted. 12 rooms, 11 with private bath. Single E60-100; Double E100-140. Breakfast included.* **

No ifs, ands, or buts about it, this is the best two-star in the Oltrarno. You have to reserve your rooms well in advance. Yes, there's no air conditioning, but it's not needed. This ancient building seems to soak up the cold air in the summer and retain the warm in the winter. The rooms are large, clean and comfortable. The location is ideal and amazingly quiet and relaxing. And best of all there are two incomparable terraces overlooking all the best sights of Florence. The furnishings are eclectic and simple; and the layout is scattered throughout the building, with everything connected by staircases. An excellent choice for your stay in Florence.

Selected as one of my *Best Places to Stay* – see Chapter 10.

41. SILLA, *Via dei Renai 5, Tel. 055/234-2888, Fax 055/234-1437. Email: hotelsilla@tin.it. Web: www.hotelsilla.it. Credit cards accepted. 54 rooms. Single E180; Double E250.* ***

Located on the first floor of an old palazzo, you enter from a lightly traveled side street just off the Lungarno. The white marble stairs are covered with a red carpet that makes you feel very presidential as you ascend to the lobby. The double rooms are rather large while the singles are quite tiny, but all have high ceilings and come complete with the amenities of a good three-star. The large terrace among the flowers and trees is where you have your breakfast and can enjoy a nice view of the Arno. Off the beaten path and boasting a professional staff, which makes the stay here quiet and relaxing.

42. TORRE DI BELLOSGUARDO, *Via Roti Michelozzi 2, Tel. 055/229-8145, Fax 055/229-008. Email: info@torrebellosguardo.com. Web: www.torrebellosguardo.com/. 16 room. Single E170; Double E290. All credit cards accepted. Breakfast E20.* ****

This is the place to stay while in Florence. The ancient towered palazzo that is the hotel will make you feel like you have gone back to the Renaissance. Besides this completely unique and accommodating building, this wonderful hotel has the best views over Florence. And the grounds are filled with gardens and olive trees where horses graze; there is a huge open lawn in front flanked by fir trees. They also have a swimming pool which overlooks the magnificent city of Florence below.

The interior common areas are like something out of a movie script, with vaulted stone ceilings and arches, as well as staircases leading off into hidden passages. You're a short distance outside of the old city walls but here you will find pure romance, complete peace, and soothing tranquility. The hotel is so magnificent that you have to reserve well in advance, since they are booked solid year round. If you aren't already in love, you'll find it or rekindle it in this wonderfully majestic hideaway. This is one of the most unique places to stay in all of Italy! This is my favorite place in Florence, so I've created a map just for this hotel to make it easy for you to stay here!

Selected as one of my *Best Places to Stay* – see Chapter 10.

Florence

S.M. Novella

Arno River

Ponte Vecchio

S. Spirito

Palazzo Pitti

Hotel Torre di Bellosguardo

Boboli Gardens

43. **VILLA CARLOTTA**, *Via Michele di Lando 3, Tel. 055/233-6134, Fax 055/233-6147. Web: http://villacarlotta.hotel-firenze.net. All credit cards accepted. 27 rooms. Five more in a gatehouse building. Single E180-250; Double E250-300. Breakfast included. A meal at their fine restaurant costs only E27.* ****

The hotel is like something out of a dream, with its sunlit tea room used for breakfast, its small garden on the side with fish swimming in the fountain, and elegant dining in the magnificent restaurant below. The location is perfect for those who like to get away from it all. Off the beaten path in a quiet and calm section of town. The rooms are all pleasantly furnished with all necessary amenities. A truly great place to stay.

44. **VILLA CORA**, *Viale Machiavelli 18 20, Tel. 055/229-8451, Fax 055/229-086. Email: reservation@villacora.it. Web: www.villacora.it. All credit cards accepted. 47 rooms. Single E210-310; Double E310-560. Suite E500-1,500Breakfast included.* *****

You'll find this extravagant and ornately decorated hotel on a residential street that curves up to the Florentine hills. It is truly magnificent with its chandeliers, statues, bas-relief covered walls, gilded mirrors and staff that will wait on you hand and foot. If you want to stay in the lap of luxury and are willing to pay for it, this is the place for you. There is a pool-side restaurant, Taverna Machiavelli, where you can eat and relax after a hard day's touring. Another important feature is the rooftop terrace garden, offering excellent views of Florence. A great place to stay if you have the money.

Where To Eat

Before I guide you to the culinary delights you'll encounter in Florence, I've prepared an augmented version of Chapter 9, *Food & Wine*, for you to better enjoy the wonders of Tuscan cuisine. Buon appetito!

Tuscan Cuisine

During the Renaissance, Florence and Tuscany experienced a burst of elaborate cuisine, mainly the result of Catherine de Medici importing a brigade of French chefs, but today that type of cuisine has given way to more basic fare. Tuscan cooking has its roots in frugal peasant fare. Today the food is simple but healthy, with the emphasis on fresh ingredients which accentuates the individual tastes of each dish.

Grilled meats are a staple of the Florentine diet, with bistecca alla Fiorentina rivaling anything Texas could dream of producing. You'll also find beans and olive oil prominently used in many dishes, as well as many types of game that populate the hills of Tuscany. And if you like cheese, my favorite is the full flavored pecorino made from sheep's milk.

Tuscany is not really known for its pasta dishes, but Tuscans do make an excellent pasta alla carrettiera, a pasta dish with a sauce of tomato, garlic, pepper, and parsley. If you want a simple, filling, healthy meal, you'll find one in Tuscany. Just don't expect some extravagant saucy dish. For that go to France.

You don't have to eat all the traditional courses listed below. Our constitution just isn't prepared for such mass consumption, so don't feel bad if all you order is a pasta dish or an entrée with a salad or appetizer.

Antipasto - Appetizer
• Crostini – Chicken liver pate spread on hard, crusty bread
• Pinzimonio – Raw vegetables to be dipped in rich olive oil
• Bruschetta – Sliced crusty bread roasted over a fire covered with olive oil and rubbed with garlic; sometimes comes with crushed tomatoes, or another version has an egg on top (Aqua Cotta)

Primo Piatto - First Course
Zuppa – Soup
• Ribollita – means reboiled. A hearty mushy vegetable soup with beans, cabbage, carrots, and chunks of boiled bread.
• Panzanella – A Tuscan gazpacho (cold soup) made with tomatoes, cucumbers, onions, basil, olive oil, and bread.

Pasta
• Pappardelle alla lepre – Wide homemade pasta with a wild hare sauce
• Pasta alla carrettiera –Pasta with a sauce of tomato, garlic, pepper and parsley
• Tortelli – Spinach and ricotta ravioli with either cream sauce or a meat sauce

Secondo Piatto - Entrée
Carne – Meat
• Bistecca alla Fiorentina – T-bone steak at least two inches thick cooked over coals charred on the outside and pink in the middle. Welcome to Texas!
• Fritto misto –Usually lamb, rabbit or chicken, with peppers, zucchini, artichokes dipped in batter and deep fried
• Arista di Maiale – Pork loin chop cooked with rosemary and garlic
• Trippa alla Fiorentina – Tripe mixed with tomato sauce and served with a variety of cheeses

Pesce – Fish
• Bacca alla Fiorentina – Salted cod cooked with tomatoes and spices (usually garlic and fennel)
• Seppie in Zimino – Cuttlefish simmered with beans

Contorno – Vegetable
- Fagioli all'ucceletto – White beans with garlic and tomatoes and sometimes sage
- Insalata Mista – mixed salad. You have to prepare your own olive oil and vinegar dressing. American's lust for countless types of salad dressings hasn't hit Italy yet.

Formaggio – Cheese
- Pecorino – Cheese made from sheep's milk

Tuscan Wines
Tuscany is known for its full bodied red wines, especially the world famous Chianti. Robust, full-bodied and zesty, the many reds produced by the Chianti vines in Tuscany have attained worldwide acclaim. To be called Chianti a wine must be made according to certain specifications and the vines must be located in certain areas. Within this production zone seven different sub-regions are recognized: Chianti Classico, Chianti Colli Aretini, Chianti Colli Fiorentini, Chianti Colli Senesi, Chianti Colline Pisane, Chianti Montalbano and Chianti Rufina.

Produced between Florence and Siena, Chianti Classico is more full-bodied than the others in its family, and comes from the oldest part of the production zone. If the wine is a Chianti Classico you'll find a black rooster label on the neck of the bottle. An austere wine, ideal when aged and served with meat dishes.

Chiantis can be called *vecchio* (old) if the wine has aged two years and is given the respected and coveted *Riserva* label when aged three years and *Superiore* if aged for five years. With Chianti wines you can expect the best, especially if it is a Classico.

From the Chianti region you should try the following red wines: **Castello di Ama**, **Castello di Volpaia**, and **Vecchie Terre di Montefili**. Outside the region try some **Rosso delle Colline Luchesi** from the hills around Lucca, **Morellino di Scansano** from the hills south of Grossetto, and **Elba Rosso**, made on the island of Elba.

The hills of Tuscany are filled with vineyards large and small supplying grapes to make some of the world's best vintages. When in Tuscany you must sample at least a little of this bounty. Some Tuscans say that their food is bland so that they can enjoy the wine with their meals more. Whatever the reason, you'll love sampling the different varieties.

Centro Storico
1. ANTICO FATTORE, *Via Lambertesca 1-3, Tel. 055/261-225. Closed Sundays. Credit cards accepted. Dinner for two E40.*

This wonderful Tuscan restaurant was virtually destroyed when terrorists

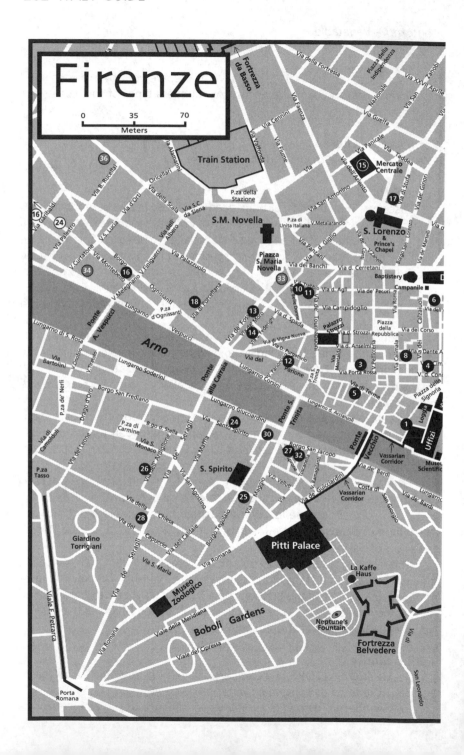

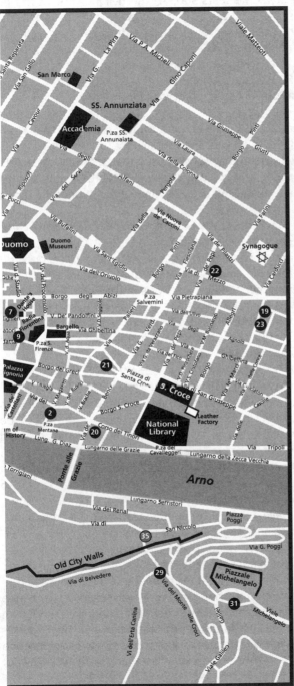

Restaurants ●

Centro Storico
1. Antico Fattore
2. Da Benvenuto
3. La Bussola
4. Da Ganino
5. Oliviero
6. Ottorino
7. Del Pennello
8. Di Verrazzano
9. Vini Vecchi Sapore

Centro
10. Le Belle Donne
11. Buca Lapi
12. Coco Lezzone
13. Garga
14. Latini
15. Nerbone
16. Il Profeta
17. Serrolo Gozzi
18. Tredici Gobbi

Santa Croce
19. Il Cibreo
20. Del Fagioli
21. Leo in Santa Croce
22. La Pentola dell'Oro
23. Il Pizzaiuolo

Oltrarno
24. Angiolino
25. La Casalinga
26. Cavalo Nero
27. Cinghiale Bianco
28. Diladdarno
29. Fuori Porta
30. Del Gallo Nero
31. La Loggia
32. Mama Gina

Nightlife ●

33. Fiddler's Elbow
34. Harry's Bar
35. Il Rifrullo
36. Space Electronic

bombed the Uffizi Gallery some years ago. To the delight of all, it has re-opened. The ambiance and food are as good as ever. Try their tortellini ai funghi porcini (meat or cheese stuffed tortellini with a savory mushroom sauce). It is exquisite. Then for seconds anything on the grill is great, including the lombatina di vitello (veal chop) or the bistecca di maiale (pork steak).

2. DA BENVENUTO, *Via della Mosca 16r, Tel. 055/214-833. Closed Sundays and in August. Credit cards accepted. Dinner for two E35.*

A little off the beaten path, behind the Uffizi gallery, this place is frequented by locals and tourists alike and is authentically Florentine. You'll love the atmosphere here as well as the food. Some dishes available are crostini da fegatini (baked dough stuffed with beans), spaghetti alla carrettiera (with a spicy tomato sauce), and as always meat dishes are plentiful for the main course. Tuscan cooking and character abound here. A wonderful choice while in Florence.

3. LA BUSSOLA, *Via Porta Rossa 58, Tel. 055/293-376. Credit cards accepted. Closed Mondays. Dinner for two E45.*

My favorite place in Florence. You can get superb pizza in this pizzeria/ristorante as well as pasta. They have a marble counter where you sit and watch the pizza master prepare the evening's fare in the wood heated brick oven. Or, if you're into the formal dining scene, try the back with tablecloths, etc. Wherever you sit the food will be excellent. For pasta, try the quattro formaggi (four cheeses) or the tortellini alla panna (cream sauce). You can also get any type of pizza you want here.

4. DA GANINO, *Piazza dei Cimatori 4, Tel. 055/214-125. All credit cards accepted. Closed Sundays. Dinner for two E38.*

The best place to sit in the summer is at the communal wooden benches outside which are hedged in by flower pots. The two rooms inside are made to look rustic with their wooden paneling, yokes hanging from the walls and marble topped tables. Great dishes to try are the petto di pollo alla crema di limone (chicken breast with a lemon cream sauce) or the spaghetti ai funghi porcini (with procini mushrooms). Great food, off the beaten path, while also being in the center of everything.

5. OLIVIERO, *Via delle Terme 51r, Tel. 055/287-643. All credit cards accepted. Closed Sundays and August. Dinner for two E60.*

At Oliviero's you will get a wonderful meal, creatively prepared. Dine here for a culinary adventure; skip it if you want something more traditional. This is where the 'in' crowd sups. The insalata tiepida di polpo (octopus salad) is exquisite as is the tegamino di porcini gratinati al parmigiano e rosmarino (lightly fried grated porcini mushrooms with parmesan and rosemary). I am not too enamored with their pasta dishes, but their fish and meat courses make up for it. A wildly creative cotoletto di vitello farcite con cacio pecorino e pistacchi (veal cutlet cooked with pecorino cheese and pistachio) may not sound delectable, but it is.

The Best Dining in Florence
3. LA BUSSOLA
5. OLIVIERO
10. LE BELLE DONNE
11. BUCA LAPI
12. COCO LEZZONE
15. NERBONE
18. TREDICI GOBBI
19. IL CIBREO
25. LA CASALINGA
31. LA LOGGIA
32. MAMMA GINA

6. OTTORINO, *Via delle Oche 12-16, Tel. 055/218-747 or 055/215-151. Credit cards accepted. Closed Sundays. Dinner for two E47.*

One of the city's oldest restaurants, Ottorino is located on the ground floor of a beautiful medieval tower, brightly lit with long pale wooden communal tables. It serves authentic Tuscan cuisine as well as some dishes that are not very Tuscan. One of my favorites is tagliatelli al coniglio (light pasta in a rabbit sauce). A place to find a great meal in a comfortable atmopshere.

7. DEL PENNELLO, *Via Dante Aligheri 4, Tel. 055/94-848. No credit cards accepted. Closed Sunday for dinner and Mondays. Dinner for two E30.*

The huge antipasto display is the perfect lunch or dinner repast. You can get as much as you want for one low price. But naturally they would rather you not eat them out of house and home. When done grazing, try the spaghetti alla carbonara (with cheese ham, peas, and an egg) or alla bolognese (tasty bologna meat sauce), followed by the petti di pollo alla mozzarella (chicken breasts smothered in mozzarella) or the bistecca di maiale (pork steak). A fine restaurant in an excellent location.

8. DI VERRAZZANO, *Via de' Tavolini 18r, Tel. 055/268-590. Closed Sundays. American Express accepted. Dinner for two E25.*

What a wine bar. This place has excellent though basic food, incredibly refined ambiance, and all at a good price, if you can get in the door. Almost always crowded, especially at lunch. Don't expect a full menu since this is not a restaurant, but you will get tasty panini filled with tasty salami and cheeses, as well as salads, soups and other light fare including coffee and great focaccio. The wines by the glass are local Chianti from the Castello di Verrazzo region (hence the name of the place).

9. VINI VECCHI SAPORI, *Via dei Magazzini 3r, Tel. 055/293-045. Closed Mondays. No credit cards accepted. Dinner for two E20.*

A wonderful wine bar deep in the heart of the centro storico on a side street near the P.za della Signoria. An extensive wine list accompanies the simple, light traditional fare including crostini, salami, cheese, salads and soups. The atmosphere is informal, accommodating and comfortable. This place is open from 10am until the city shuts down. Despite its central location, Vini Vecchi Sapori is only lightly touristed since it is just off of the main tourist path between the Ponte Vecchio and Duomo.

Centro

10. LE BELLE DONNE, *Via delle Belle Donne 16r, Tel. 055/2380-2609. Closed Saturdays, Sundays and in August. No credit cards accepted. Dinner for two E40.*

An eclectically decorated tiny trattoria that is always packed with locals clamoring for the excellent food they prepare. Slightly cramped seating arrangements, but that only adds to the vibrant community-oriented ambiance. Pasta is served in all its forms, soups are plentiful, as are the obligatory meat dishes. And don't forget the desserts. If you are looking for classic Tuscan cooking, with friendly and accommodating wait staff, this is a great place to have a meal. One of my favorites in Florence.

11. BUCA LAPI, *Via del Trebbio 1, Tel. 055/213-768. All credit cards accepted. Closed Sunday for dinner and Mondays. Dinner for two E35.*

One of the very best restaurants Florence has to offer. On a small street, down in the basement of an old building, Buca Lapi treats you to the food of a lifetime (and the spectacle of one too). There is a small open kitchen surrounded on two sides by tables from which you can see all the food being prepared. The decor is bizarre in a fun way, with travel posters covering the walls and ceiling.

The tortelli stuffed with ricotta and spinach in a butter and sage sauce was unparalleled. Or try the spaghetti al sugo di carne e pomodoro (with meat and tomato sauce) for starters, then try either the pollo al cacciatore con spinacio (chicken cooked in tomato-based spicy sauce with spinach) or the cinghiale con patate fritte (wild boar with fried potatoes). A superbly intimate restaurant with wonderful culinary and visual experiences.

12. COCO LEZZONE, *Via dei Parioncino 26, Tel. 055/287-178. No credit cards accepted. Closed Saturdays and Sundays in the Summer and Tuesdays for dinner. In the winter closed Sundays and Tuesdays for dinner. Dinner for two E45.*

Located in what was once a dairy, Coco Lezzone's long communal tables contrast sharply with the white tiled floors. Florentines and tourists alike pack themselves in to enjoy the authentic Tuscan cuisine and atmosphere. The portions are pleasantly large, the meats are amazingly good, especially the arista al forno (roasted pork). Also try the piccione (pigeon) cooked over the grill (don't worry, they're farm raised – they don't go out to the piazza and catch them for dinner.) Where else will you be able to eat pigeon? They also have coniglio arista (roasted rabbit), a must when in Florence since rabbit is a Tuscan specialty.

13. GARGA, *Via del Moro 9, Tel. 055/298-898. Credit cards accepted. Closed Sundays and Mondays. Dinner for two E45.*

If you want to get in on some of the best pasta in Florence, look no further. Try the pennette al gorgonzola e zucchine. For seconds, try the petto di pollo al pomodoro e basilico (chicken breast with tomato and basil) or the scaloppina di vitella al limone (veal with light lemon sauce). The food and the ambiance touch the edge of nouvelle cuisine, so if you're interested in trying something different in a unique atmosphere this place is great.

14. LATINI, *Via Palchetti 6, Tel. 055/210-916. Credit cards accepted. Closed Mondays and Tuesdays for lunch. Dinner for two E40.*

The hams hanging from the ceiling and a huge oxen yoke gives this place a wonderfully local flavor. They specialize in meat dishes (which are wonderful) but you can complement that with one of their insalata mista (mixed salad). The service is brusque in the Tuscan manner and the location down a little street makes the ambiance perfectly authentic. Try the spiedini misti (mixed meat grill) or the pollo arrosto (roasted chicken) and you won't be sorry.

15. NERBONE, *Mercato Centrale, Tel. 055/219-949. No credit cards accepted. Closed Sundays. Meal for two E12.*

When in Florence, you have to come to this truly authentic Florentine eatery. In operation since 1872, this small food stand in the Mercato Centrale serves up great food and the most incredible atmosphere. Known for the best boiled meat sandwiches (pork, beef, or veal) for only E3, which are called panini. The sandwich you get is just the meat, the bread, and some salt, but it is amazingly tasty. You can also order pasta, soup, and salads. To eat your authentic Florentine meal, either stand at the counter or sit at the small area just across the aisle.

16. IL PROFETA, *Via Borgo Ognissanti 93, Tel. 055/212-265. Credit cards accepted. Closed Sundays and Mondays. Dinner for two E38.*

A cheerful unpretentious place with simple, basic food served to you by friendly waiters. The kitchen is visible at the end of the dining room so the sound of pots and pans clattering adds a rustic touch to your meal. They make good pastas, especially the penne carrettiera (garlic, tomatoes and pepper) which is a little like penne all'arrabbiata in Rome, and the house special penne profeta (with cream, ham, and mushrooms) which is really great. Next, sample the finely cooked lombatina di vitella (veal cutlet) or the ever present bistecca alla Fiorentina.

17. SERROLO GOZZI, *Piazza San Lorenzo 8, No telephone. No credit cards accepted. Closed Sundays. Dinner for two E22.*

Come here for a taste of a non-tourist trattoria and a sampling of true Florentine cuisine. This inexpensive, small, rustic trattoria is situated smack dab in the middle of the bustling San Lorenzo market. The seating is at long communal tables that line the walls with benches on one side and chairs on the other. Being just across the street from the food market, Mercato Generale, guarantees you'll have the freshest ingredients. The fare is purely Tuscan. I liked the arista di maiale al forno (pork grilled over the fire) and the vitello arrosto (roasted veal). Super inexpensive, completely authentic, and very satisfying. The service is brusque and informal. A real working man's place.

18. **TREDICI GOBBI** *(13 Hunchbacks), Via del Porcellana 9R. Tel. 055/ 284-015. Credit cards accepted. Dinner for two E35.*

Mainly Florentine cuisine, with a few Hungarian dishes added for flair. A moderately priced restaurant with some expensive meat dishes, such as the excellent bistecca Fiorentina. The pasta is average except for the exquisitely tasty rigatoni with hot sauce. The atmosphere is simple and rustic and the back room with its brick walls is a great spot for dinner. Other fine dishes are the fusilli with rabbit sauce. 'Thumper' never tasted so good. For seconds they also serve wild boar and veal. Don't miss this place while in Florence.

Santa Croce

19. **IL CIBREO**, *Via dei Macci 118r, Tel. 055/234-1100. All credit cards accepted. Closed Sundays, Mondays and August. Dinner for two E65.*

They serve a combination of traditional and nouvelle cuisine here. But, there's no pasta on the menu. Their mushroom soup is excellent as is the typically Roman buffalo-milk mozzarella. All the ingredients are basic and simple, but everything seems to be prepared in a whole new way. If you want to try the Cibreo, the restaurant's namesake, which is a tasty Tuscan chicken stew made from every conceivable part of the bird, you need to order it at least a day in advance while making reservations. A creative, upscale place to dine.

20. **DEL FAGIOLI**, *Corso dei Tintori 47, Tel. 055/244-285. Credit cards accepted. Closed Sundays. Dinner for two E30.*

A straightforward Tuscan trattoria with great food for a good value. The rustic appearance with the wood paneling and antlers hanging on the walls reflects the peasant cuisine served. The menu is not that extensive but you can get a good salsicce alla griglia (grilled sausage) for a dinner and some fagiole and zucchini as an appetizer. Since they are a typical Tuscan restaurant their specialty is grilled meats.

21. **LEO IN SANTA CROCE**, *Via Torta 7r, Tel. 055/210-829, Fax 055/239-6705. All credit cards accepted. Closed Mondays. Dinner for two E42.*

A brightly lit, trying-to-be-upscale restaurant near the church of Santa Croce that serves good food. They prepare dishes from all over Italy so you're not confined to the normal Tuscan peasant fare. You can get the abundant antipasto di casa and sample a variety of local produce and meats. Then you can try a good rendition of the Roman favorite spaghetti all carbonara (ham, cheese, mixed with an egg). Consider also the cordon bleu or the ever tasty filetto di pepe verde (beef with green peppers).

22. LA PENTOLA DELL 'ORA, *Via di Mezzo 24/26r, Tel. 055/241-821. Closed Sundays and August. Only open in the evenings. Credit cards accepted. Dinner for two E45.*

The atmosphere here is rustic as well as refined, the service is courteous, but what draws people to this lovely locale is the menu. Owner and chef Giuseppe Alessi creates amazing dishes from simple ingredients. He has a number of cook books in print, and creates many notable and palate pleasing piatti. Off the beaten path so you won't find many tourists here, unless the secret is already out. An excellent choice while in Florence.

23. IL PIZZAIUOLO, *Via de' Macci 113r, Tel. 055/241171. Closed Sundays and in August. No credit cards accepted. Dinner for two E25.*

If you want a real Florentine experience far away from the thundering herd of tourists, this simple little pizza place is for you. In the area around Santa Croce that is fast becoming known for grand restaurants, this local joint stands out for its traditional authenticity. In some circles the pizza and calzone are considered the best in the city. There's also antipasto and salads but the reason to come here is the pizza. Remember to make reservations since Il Pizzaiuolo is always packed.

Oltrarno

24. ANGIOLINO, *Borgo Santo Spirito 36r. Tel. 055/239-8976. Closed Mondays in summer. All credit cards accepted. Dinner for two E35.*

This is one of the best Tuscan-style trattorie in Florence. The menu changes daily and the tasty offerings are served in a vaulted main room with an exposed kitchen, allowing for tantalizing aromas to surround you throughout your meal. The service if efficient, and the wine list plentiful with a distinct local flavor, a direction in which the menu also leans. You can find crostini (baked dough stuffed with meat and or vegetables), verdure all griglia (grilled vegetables), ravioli, and many other traditional Tuscan dishes. A wonderful place to grab either lunch or dinner while in Florence. Rustic and charming, with an air of elegance.

25. LA CASALINGA, *Via dei Michelozzi 9r, Tel. 055/218-624. Closed Sundays and the first 20 days in August. No credit cards accepted. Dinner for two E25.*

Here in this authentic Oltrarno-style trattoria you'll find a few tourists intermingling with the local artisans and residents. The cooking is classic Tuscan that is simple, tasty and filling. The antipasto is a mixed salad with sliced meats and cheeses thrown in. For seconds you'll find some Tuscan favorites like bolliti misti con salsa verde (mixed boiled meats in a spicy green sauce), lo spezzatino (Tuscan stew), le salsicce con le rape (sausage with turnips), and il baccala alla livornese (cooked cod Livorno style – salty). Sample away and don't forget to wash it all down with some of the great house wine.

Learn to Cook in Florence

Since 1973, Giuliano Bugiali has been teaching Italian cooking to visitors in Florence, and it's all in English. To get information about how to spend an enjoyable culinary experience while soaking up all the glories of this great city, contact **Giuliano Bugiali's Cooking in Florence**, PO Box 1650, Canal Street Station, New York, NY 10013-0870, *Tel. 212/966-5325, Fax 212/226-0601.*

26. CAVALO NERO, *Via dell'Ardiglione 22, Tel. 055/294-744. Closed Sundays, August, Dec 25 and Jan 1. Open only in the evenings. American Express and Via accepted. Dinner for two E65.*

A high end ristorante in a local neighborhood, down a small side street, off the beaten tourist path. A mixture of traditional and creative cuisine where you can get many local favorites as well as cucina nuova concoctions. A pleasantly simple yet refined atmosphere combined with a robust cuisine makes for an excellent meal at the Cavalo Nero. And don't forget the desserts. They are exemplary.

27. DEL CINGHIALE BIANCO, *Borgo San Jacopo 43, Tel. 055/215-706. Credit cards accepted. Closed Tuesdays and Wednesdays. Dinner for two E40.*

Wild game is the specialty here as befits a place named The White Boar, so get ready to enjoy some fine peasant dishes. I like the wrought-iron motif that dominates the place, especially the old cooking pot hanging from the ceiling. A simple place with good food and great atmosphere.

28. DILADDARNO, *Via de' Serragli 108r, Tel. 055/225-001. Closed Mondays, Tuesdays, and from July 16 to August 16. No credit cards accepted. Dinner for two E30.*

This trattoria offers some of the best and most authentic Florentine dishes. Try the trippa alla Fiorentina (boiled tripe), ossobuco (stew made with a veal knuckle in a tomato sauce), ribollita (boiled meats), bistecca (huge grilled steaks of beef), or the rognoncini (stewed kidneys). All can be enjoyed with some tasty house wines. There is a tiny garden inside that can be enjoyed in good weather. Off the beaten track, which is why the prices (and food!) are so good.

29. FUORI PORTA, *Via Monte alle Croci 10r, Tel. 055/234-2483. Closed Sundays and August. No credit cards accepted. Dinner for two E30.*

Just outside one of the old main gates of the city, hence the name "Outside the Gate," this lovely cantina has a rather extensive menu for a wine bar. You can get pastas – such as the tagliatelle con astice e zuchine (with onions and zucchini), crostini, soups and salads and some excellent desserts. The wine list is extensive, filled with both Italian and foreign vintages. Lovely atmosphere, with a quaint terrace, definitely off the beaten path, just outside the old walls of Florence at the foot of the hills of the Piazzalle Michelangelo. A good place to stop in for a filling snack and a relaxing glass of wine.

30. **DEL GALLO NERO**, *Via Santo Spirito 6r, Tel. 055/218-898. Closed Mondays and August. Credit cards accepted. Dinner for two E30.*

Go down the stairs and you'll find yourself in this large vault-like trattoria. The menu is filled with Tuscan antipasti and soups, like the minestra di pane (a tasty bread soup); but my favorites are the series of crostini (stuffed pastry baked in the oven). You can get the crostini stuffed with mozzarella, prosciutto (ham), salami, and all manner of vegetable. They are delicious and filling, especially with a wonderful bottle of Chianti. Make sure you order one with the gallo nero (black rooster) label on the stem. It's the namesake of the restaurant and indicates that the Chianti is of the finest quality.

31. **LA LOGGIA**, *Piazzale Michelangelo 1, Tel. 055/234-2832, Fax 055/234-5288. Credit cards accepted. Closed Wednesdays. Dinner for two E55.*

Come for the view of Florence and stay for the food. Ideally located restaurant and café has a great panoramic view of Florence, and offers excellent local cuisine. This a great place to eat, on the high end of the scale. Try the pollo al diavolo (chicken cooked over an open fire) after the spaghetti al frutti di mare (with seafood). The taglietelle with bacon and broccoli in olive oil is awesome, even at twice the price of ordinary restaurants.

32. **MAMMA GINA**, *Borgo S Jacopo 37, Tel. 055/239-6009, Fax 055/213-908. Web: www.mammagina.it. All credit cards accepted. Closed Sundays. Dinner for two E42.*

Don't be fooled by the small entry, this is a large place with great food. Their tortellini all crema con funghi is simply divine. The best I've ever had. Before that I had some great bruschetta (grilled bread covered with olive oil, garlic and tomatoes). For seconds I had the petti di pollo alla griglia (chicken breasts on the grill). You might also try the penne stracciate alla Fiorentina (a meat and tomato based pasta) and the petti di pollo al cognac con funghi (chicken breast cooked in cognac with mushrooms ... it gives it kind of a cacciatore taste). This is a fantastic place to get great food in a wonderful atmosphere. One of my favorites in Florence.

Seeing the Sights

The sights of Florence are fascinating, incredible – add your own superlatives after you've seen them! Florence is a living breathing museum filled with inspiring open air sights, and some of the best museums in the world. The sights below are numbered and correspond to the *Florence Sights* map on pages 272-273.

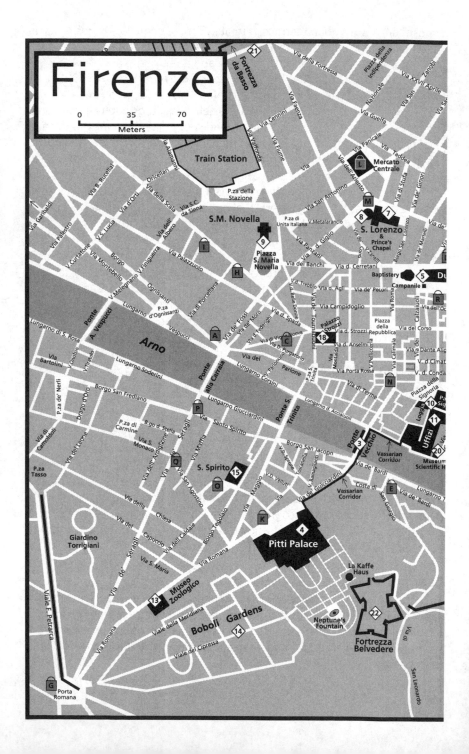

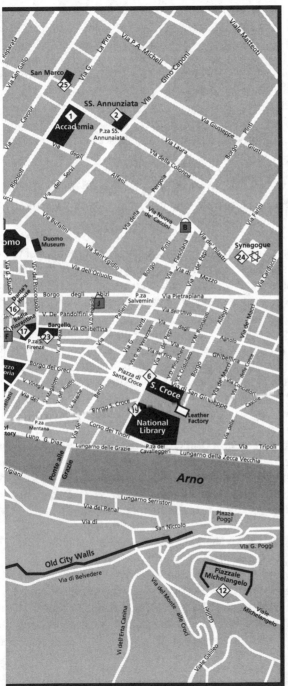

Sights ◇

1. Accademia
2. SS. Annunziata
3. Ponte Vecchio
4. Pitti Palace
5. Duomo, Baptistery, Campanile & Museum
6. Santa Croce
7. San Lorenzo
8. Prince's Chapel
9. Santa Maria Novella
10. Palazzo della Signoria
11. Uffizi Gallery
12. Piazzale Michelangelo
13. Museo Zoologico
14. Boboli Gardens
15. Santo Spirito
16. Dante's House
17. Church of the Badia
18. Palazzo Strozzi
19. National Library
20. Museum of Scientific History
21. Fortressa da Basso
22. Fortressa Belvedere
23. Bargello
24. Tempio Israelico
25. San Marco

Shopping 🛍

A. BM Bookshop
B. Paperback Exchange
C. L'Indice Scrive
D. Il Papiro
E. Il Torchio
F. Bartolucci
G. Gelateria Porta Romana
H. Officina Profumo
I. Tricolore
J. Vestri
K. Firenze Papier Mache
L. Mercato Centrale
M. Mercato di San Lorenzo
N. Mercato Nuovo
O. Mercato di Santo Spirito
P. Vera
Q. Vino e Olio
R. Alessi Paride

1. STATUE OF DAVID AT THE ACCADEMIA
Via Ricasoli 60, *Tel. 055/214-375. Web: www.sbas.firenze.it/accademia.* Open 9:00am–7:00pm Tuesday–Saturday. Sundays 9:00am-1:00pm. Closed Mondays. Admission E6.

The **Accademia** is filled with a wide variety of paintings, sculptures, and plaster molds by artists from the Tuscan school of the 13th and 14th centuries; but the museum's main draw is a must-see for you in Florence. Here you will find a statue that is as close to perfection as can be achieved with a hammer and a chisel, Michelangelo's *David*. This masterpiece was started from a discarded block of marble another sculptor had initially scarred. Michelangelo bought it on his own – no one commissioned this work – since it was less expensive than a new piece of marble, and finished sculpting *David* from its confines at the age of 25 in the year 1504, after four years of labor. It was originally in front of the Palazzo della Signoria, but was replaced with a substitute in 1873 to protect the original from the elements.

Leading up to the *David* are a variety of other works by Michelangelo, most unfinished. These are called *The Prisoners,* since the figures appear to be trapped in stone. These statues were designed to hold the Tomb of Pope Giulio II on their sculpted shoulders, but Michelangelo died before he could bring the figures to life. And now they appear as if they are struggling to be freed from the marble's embrace.

Also included in this wonderful exhibit of Michelangelo's sculptures is the unfinished *Pieta*. Many art critics have spent their entire lives comparing this Pieta with the more famous one in St. Peter's in Rome. This statue looks older, sadder, more realistic, most probably since it was created by Michelangelo at the end of his life. The *Pieta* in Rome appears more vibrant, youthful, optimistic, and alive. Once again, this was probably because he sculpted the *Pieta* in Rome when he was a young man,

Also in the Accademia is the **Sala Dell'Ottocento** (The 19th Century Hall) that is a gallery of plaster model and other works by students and prospective students of the Academy. Despite the medium, plaster, these works are exquisite. The holes you see in the casts are iron markings used as guides so that when carved into marble the figure can be recreated perfectly.

2. PIAZZA & CHURCH OF SS ANNUNZIATA
Tel. 055/239-8034. Open 7:00am–7:00pm.

Just around the corner from the Accademia, this piazza is relatively isolated from the hustle and bustle of Florence's tourist center, so that when you enter it you feel as if you walked back into Renaissance Florence. This is how all the piazzas must have looked and felt back then, no cars, only people milling around sharing the Florentine day.

In the center of the square sits the equestrian *Statue of the Grand Duke Ferdinando I* by **Giambologna** and **Pietro Tacca** (1608). The two bronze fountains with figures of sea monsters are also the work of Tacca (1629).

The church, like the piazza, is also a hidden jewel in Florence. Erected in 1250, reconstructed in the middle of the 15th century by **Michelozzo**, was again re-done in the 17th and 18th centuries, and remains today as it was then. Entering hte Basilica you are instantly struck by the magnificence there in, the carved and gilded ceiling, and the profusion of marble and stucco.

The church is particularly famous for a miracle, which is thought to have taken place here. A certain painter named Bartolomeo was commissioned to paint a fresco in 1252 of the Annunciation. When he was about to paint the face of Mary in the painting he fell asleep, only to find the face painted for him, supposedly by angelic hands, after he awoke. The fresco is located inside the little chapel to the left of the entrance. The fresco became the heart of the Basilica, which was subsequently dedicated to Our Lady Annunciate. So there you have it!

3. PONTE VECCHIO

Literally meaning Old Bridge, the name came about because the bridge has been around since Etruscan times. Not in its present form, of course. The present bridge was rebuilt on the old one in the 14th century by **Neri di Fiorvanti**. Thankfully this beautiful bridge with its shops lining each side of it was spared the Allied and Axis bombardments during World War II. Today the shops on the bridge belong to silversmiths, goldsmiths, and some fine leather stores. In the middle of the bridge are two arched openings that offer wonderful views of the Arno. On the downstream side of the bridge is a bust of **Benvenuto Cellini**, a Renaissance Goldsmith and sculptor, done by Raphaele Romanelli in 1900. At night on the bridge you'll find all sorts of characters hanging out, sipping wine, and strumming guitars.

On the street from the Ponte Vecchio to the Pitti Palace there used to be a series of wonderful old palazzi. Unfortunately the bombers in World War II didn't avoid these buildings as they did the Ponte Vecchio itself. Even so, today the street is filled with lovely reconstructed buildings erected just after the war which makes them older still than most buildings in North America.

4. PITTI PALACE

Piazza dei Pitti. *Tel. 055/287-096.* Building hours: Tuesday-Saturday 9:00am-7:00pm. Most museums only open until 2:00pm. Sundays and Holidays 9:00am-1:00pm. Closed on Mondays.

Built for the rich merchant **Luca Pitti** in 1440, based on a design by Filippo Brunelleschi. Due to the financial ruin of the Pitti family, the construction was interrupted until the palace was bought by **Eleonora da Toledo**, the wife of

Walk With the Medici

Officially inaugurated in 1565, the **Vasarian Corridor** extends over one kilometer from the Palazzo Signoria, through the Uffizi, over the Ponte Vecchio, through the Boboli Gardens, and into the Palazzo Pitti. Along the way it traverses the roof tops, streets and bridges, and cuts through a church and private buildings. It was the private passage used by the Medici to get from their home in the Pitti to the seat of government that they controlled in the Palazzo Signoria. The only way that you can follow in the footsteps of the Medici, and see some wonderful artwork along the way, is by a private tour. The tour lasts two and a half hours, but it is well worth the time and money spent. Of special interest is a collection of self-portraits of famous artists featuring Peter Paul Reubens, John Singer Sargent, Henri Latour, Marc Chagall and many others.

Reservations are required. Book well in advance for the infrequent tours in English on *www.firenze.net* or call *055/265-4321*. Tickets are E26.50 and offer entrance to all the places you pass through. From June 7–July 13, and September 6–December 28 tours offered every Friday and Saturday only.

Cosimo I. It was then enlarged to its present size. And from that time until the end of the 17th century, it was the family home for the Medicis.

Currently it is divided into six different museums; and since the upkeep and security for this building is so expensive, each museum charges their own entrance fee.

The **Museo degli Argenti** (www.sbas.firenze.it/argenti) contains precious objects collected over time by the Medici and Lorraine families. There are works in amber, ivory, silver, crystal, precious woods and enamel work. Located in the former Summer Apartment of the grand dukes of Medici, the collection includes the *Salzburg Treasure* (gold and silver cups, vases and other articles) brought to Florence by the Archduke Ferdinand of Lorraine who was Grand Duke of Tuscany in 1790. The 1st, 3rd, and 5th Mondays and 2nd, and 4th Sundays of the month closed. Admission E6.

The **Museo delle Porcelane** (www.sbas.firenze.it/argenti) is situated in the Boboli Gardens and housed in a quaint little building near the Belvedere Fortress at the top of the hill. This porcelain collection reflects the taste of the Medicis and the many families that resided in the Pitti Palace after the Medici's decline. There are pieces made in Capodimonte, Doccia, Sevres, Vienna, and Meissen and all are delicately exquisite. The 1st, 3rd, and 5th Mondays and

2nd, and 4th Sundays of the month closed. Admission E2 includes entrance to the Boboli Gardens.

The **Galleria Palatina e Apartamenti Reali** *(www.sbas.firenze.it/ palatina)*, also known as the Pitti Gallery, runs the length of the facade of the building and includes paintings, sculptures, frescoes and furnishings of the Medici and Lorraine families. This gallery has some fine works from the 16th and 17th centuries and the most extensive collection of works by Raphael anywhere in the world. Other artists included here are Andrea del Sarto, Fra' Bartolomeo, Titian and Tintoretto, Velasquez, Murillo, Rubens, Van Dyke and Ruisdal.

The royal apartments feature an elaborate display of furnishings, carpets, wonderful silks covering the walls, as well as some fine paintings collected and displayed by the house of Savoy – the most notable of which is a series of portraits of the family of Louis XV of France. Admission E6 includes entrance to the Museo delle Carozze.

The **Museo delle Carrozze** *(www.sbas.firenze.it/palatina)* houses carriages used by the court of the houses of Lorraine and Savoy when they ruled Florence. This was my favorite museum in Florence when I was a child. The carriages are extremely elaborate and detailed, especially the silver decorated carriage owned by King Ferdinand II of the Two Sicilies.

The **Galleria d'Arte Moderna** *(www.sbas.firenze.it/gam)* occupies thirty rooms on the second floor of the palace and offers a thorough look at Italian painting from neo-classicism to modern works covering the years up to 1945. The emphasis is on the art from Tuscany and has some works similar to French impressionists. Organized chronologically and by theme. The 1st, 3rd, and 5th Mondays and 2nd, and 4th Sundays of the month closed. Admission E4 includes entrance to the Galleria del Costume.

The **Galleria del Costume** *(www.sbas.firenze.it/gam)* contains clothing from the 16th century to modern day. All are exhibited in 13 rooms of the Meridiana Wind. It is an excellent way to discern the changes in fashion from the 18th century to the 1920s. Today, because of television, major fashion changes occur almost every year; but back then it could take generations before any noticeable change occurred. Also included are historical theater costumes created by the workshop of Umberto Tirelli.

5. DUOMO & BAPTISTERY, CAMPANILE, & CATHEDRAL MUSEUM

All located at the Piazza del Duomo. *Tel. 055/230-2885.*

Duomo – Church open Monday-Saturday 10:00am–5:00pm, Sunday 1:00pm-5:00pm. Entrance to the dome costs E3.

The Baptistery – Open everyday 2:00pm–5:30pm. E2.

The Campanile – Open 8:30am–6:50pm (9:00am -4:20pm in off season). E3.

Cathedral Museum (Museo dell'Opera del Duomo) – *Web: www.operaduomo.firenze.it.* Closed Sundays. Summer hours - Mon. through Sat. 9:00am-7:30pm. Until 6pm in off-season. Holidays open 9:00am-1:00pm.

Duomo

When you're in Florence the one sight you have to visit is the **Duomo**, Florence's cathedral. It was consecrated in 1436 by Pope Eugenio IV as **Santa Maria del Fiore** (Saint Mary of the Flowers), and that is still its official name, but everybody calls it "The Duomo" because of its imposing dome. It was started in 1296 by Arnolfo di Cambio on the spot where the church of Santa Reparata existed. After di Cambio's death in 1301, the famous Giotto took over the direction of the work, but he dedicated most of his attention to the development of the Bell Tower (Campanile).

When Giotto died in 1337, Andrea Pisano took over until 1349 (death didn't cause his departure, he just moved on to other projects). By 1421 everything else was finished except for the dome, which **Brunelleschi** had won a competition to design and build. It took 14 years just to construct the gigantic dome. Over the years, slight modifications and changes have been made, and in 1887, the current facade of the Duomo was finished by architect **Emilio de Fabris**.

The interior of the Duomo is 150 meters long and 38 meters wide at the nave and 94 meters at the transept. There are enormous gothic arches, supported by gothic pillars, which gives the interior a majestic quality. The dome is 90 meters high and 45.5 meters in diameter and is decorated with frescoes representing the Last Judgment done by Giorgio Vasari and Federico Zuccari at the end of the 16th century. In the niches of the pillars supporting the dome are statues of the Apostles.

The central chapel is home to the **Sarcophagus of San Zanobius** that contains the saint's relics. The bronze reliefs are the work of Lorenzo Ghiberti (1442). When you've finished wandering through the cathedral and admiring the art and stained glass windows, you can go to the top of the Duomo and get some great views of Florence. The way up is a little tiring, but the magnificent photo opportunities – both inside and out – are fabulous. Don't miss these views!

The Baptistery

Definitely considered one of the most important works in the city, the **Baptistery** was built on the remains of an early Roman structure which was transformed into a paleo-Christian monument. The Baptistery, built in the 10th and 11th centuries was dedicated to Saint John the Baptist, the patron saint of Florence. Up until 1128, it was the cathedral of Florence. This small structure just didn't reflect the growing stature of the city of Florence, so they erected the Duomo.

Its octagonal shape is covered with colored marble. On the pavement by the Baptistery you'll find the signs of the Zodiac. Inside is the tomb of Giovanni XXIII by Donatello and Michelozzo in 1427. Next to the altar, you'll see the *Angel Holding The Candlestick* by Agostino di Jacopo in 1320. To the left between the Roman sarcophagi is the wooden statue *Magdalen* by Donatello in 1560.

But the true masterpieces of the Baptistery are the bronze paneled doors by **Ghiberti** and **Andrea Pisano da Pontedera**. The public entrance is the **Southern Door**, created by Andrea Pisano da Pontedera and is of least interest. The east and north doors are far more beautiful and intricate. Michelangelo described the east door as "the door to paradise." On it you'll find stories of the Old Testament, beginning as follows from the top left hand side:

• Creation of Adam; original sin; expulsion of Adam and Eve from Paradise
• Stories of Noah and the universal deluge (coincidentally some of these panels were almost lost in the flooding of 1966)
• Jacob and Esau; Rachel and Jacob; Isaac blesses Jacob
• Moses receives the Ten Commandments on Mount Sinai
• The battle against the Philistines; David and Goliath.

From the top right hand side:
• Adam works the soil; Cain and Abel at work; Cain kills Abel
• Three angels appear to Abraham; Abraham sacrifices Isaac
• Joseph meets his brothers in Egypt; Stories of Joseph
• Joshua crosses the Jordan River; The conquering of Jericho
• Solomon receives the Queen of Sheba in the Temple.

The Campanile
Giotto died while he was attempting to complete the **Campanile**, but after his death **Andrea Pisano** and **Francesco Talenti** both scrupulously followed his designs until its completion. The only part they left out was the spire that was to go on top, which would have made the Campanile 30 meters higher than its current 84. The tower is covered in colored marble and adorned with bas-reliefs by Andrea Pisano and Luca della Robbia and Andrea Orcagna. Sculptures by Donatello, Nanni di Bartolo, and others used to be in the sixteen niches but are now in the Cathedral Museum.

Cathedral Museum (Museo dell'Opera del Duomo)
This is the place where many pieces of artwork that used to be in the Cathedral or the Campanile are now located. Their removal and placement here was mainly done to help preserve them from the environment as well as the onslaught of tourists hordes. Most of the items are statues and bas-relief work. The most famous ones to keep an eye out for are *St. John* by **Donatello**,

Habakkuh by Donatello, *Virgin with Infant Jesus* by **Arnolfo**, and *Choir Gallery* with many scenes by Donatello.

6. SANTA CROCE

Piazza Santa Croce. *Tel. 055/246-6105.* Open 10:00am -12:30pm and 2:30pm - 6:30pm (3-5pm in off season). Closed Wednesdays. E3.

The church of **Santa Croce** sits in the Piazza Santa Croce, surrounded by ancient palazzi renowned for the architecture. The one opposite the church is the **Palazzo Serristori** by Baccio D'Agnolo in the 16th century. Facing the church on the right hand side at #23 is the **Palazzo dell'Antella** built by Giulio Parigi in the 17th century. In this piazza, on any night, when all the shops are closed, you will feel as if you've stepped back into the Renaissance.

In the center of the square is a statue of **Dante Aligheri**, he of *Divine Comedy* fame, sculpted by Enrico Pazzi in 1865. This is a wonderfully ornate yet simple church belonging to the Franciscan Order. Construction was begun in 1295 but its modern facade was created in 1863 by Nicolo Matas. The frescoes on the facade were created in only 20 days by 12 painters working non-stop. It has a slim bell tower whose Gothic style doesn't seem to fit with this modern exterior. The interior, on the other hand, fits perfectly with the simple stonework of the bell tower.

Initially, the walls inside had been covered with exquisite frescoes created by Giotto but these were covered up by order of Cosimo I in the 16th century. What remains is a basic monastic church that conveys piety and beauty in its simplicity. Of the many Italian artistic, religious, and political geniuses that lie buried beneath Santa Croce, the most famous has to be that of **Michelangelo** himself. Other prominent Florentines buried here are **Niccolo Machiavelli**, **Galileo Galilei**, **Dante Aligheri** and **Lorenzo Ghiberti**.

Leather School at Santa Croce

The **leather school** (Scuola del Cuoio) started by the monks more than three decades ago, can be accessed either through the sacristy, or down the road from the entrance to the church, into an entryway at #5 on the street, through a garden, up a set of stairs, and down a hallway. Here you'll find all kinds of fine leather products for sale but the best part is being able to see them being manufactured right in front of you.

The prices are rather high but the selection is good. The main draw is seeing the leather worked. *Tel. 244-533.* Hours are Tuesday-Saturday, 9:00am-12:30pm and 3:00pm-6:00pm. All credit cards accepted.

7. SAN LORENZO

Piazza San Lorenzo. *Tel. 055/216-634.* Open Tuesday-Saturday 9:00am–2:00pm, Sundays and Holidays 9:00am-1:00pm. Closed Mondays.

One of the oldest basilicas in Florence, the architecture of the church is the work of **Filippo Brunelleschi**, done from 1421-1446. However, the church was finished by his pupil **Antonio Manetti** in 1460. The facade was never completed even though Michelangelo himself submitted a variety of designs for its completion.

The interior is made up of three naves with chapels lining the side walls. In the central nave at the far end are two pulpits that are the last two works of **Donatello** who died in 1466 after completing them. You'll find plenty of works by Donatello in this church, including:

• The stucco medallions in the Old Sacristy that represent the *Four Evangelists* that are *Stories of Saint John the Baptist*
• The terra-cotta *Bust of Saint Lawrence* in the Old Sacristy
• The bronze doors with panels representing the *Apostles and Fathers of the Church* in the Old Sacristy.

8. PRINCES' CHAPEL

Piazza Madonna degli Aldobrandini. *Tel. 055/238-8602. Web: www.sbas.firenze.it/cappellemedicee.* Open Tuesday-Saturday 9:00am–2:00pm, Sundays and Holidays 9:00am-1:00pm. Closed 2nd and 4th Sunday, and 1st, 3rd and 5th Monday of every month.

Attached to the church of San Lorenzo, but with the entrance just around the corner to the back of the church, this octagonal building's construction was begun in 1604 on a design by Prince Giovanni dei Medici. It houses the tombs of a variety of Medici princes ... hence the name. Up to 50 of the Medici tombs will be exhumed over the next few years for a controversial DNA testing of the entire family, to finally find out who was related to whom. The reason this is so significant is that some of the Medici's were Popes, and it is speculated that they were not as chaste as they proclaimed to be. The DNA tests will put an end to all the speculation.

It is of interest to many tourists because of the tombs in the New Sacristy which were created by Michelangelo himself. *The Tomb of Lorenzo, Duke of Urbino* (created by Michelangelo) has a statue of the duke seated and absorbed in meditation as well as two reclining figures that represent Dawn and Dusk. On the opposite wall is the *Tomb of Giuliano, Duke of Nemours* (also created by Michelangelo) which shows a seated duke replete in armor, ready for action, as well as two reclining figures that represent night and day. Another Michelangelo work in the New Sacristy is the unfinished *Madonna and Child*.

If you like Michelangelo's brilliant sculptures but want to avoid the crowds that congregate at the museum that houses the David, this is the place to come. And you can get some shopping done in the San Lorenzo market afterwards.

9. SANTA MARIA NOVELLA
Piazza Santa Maria Novella. *Tel. 055/210-113.* Closed Fridays. Open 7:00am–11:30am and 3:30pm–6:00pm Mon–Thurs and Sat, and Sun 3:30pm–5:00pm.

Built in 1278 by two Dominican friars, **Fra Ristoreo** and **Fra Sisto**, the church was created in the Gothic style with green and white marble decorations that are typically Florentine in character. The church was completed in 1470. To the left and right of the facade are tombs of illustrious Florentines all created in the same Gothic style as the church.

The interior of the church is in a "T" shape with the nave and aisles divided by clustered columns that support wide arches. Down the aisles are a variety of altars created by **Vasari** from 1565 to 1571. As a young artist, Michelangelo worked on many of the frescoes as commissioned by his teachers. This is where he got his initial training that helped him create the now famous frescoes in the Sistine Chapel in Rome.

The peaceful and expansive cloisters are a rare treat. Come for a serene visit that harks back to the days of Michelangelo. Hours: weekdays 9:00am - 2:00pm. Holidays 8:00am -1:00pm. Closed Fridays. Entrance E2.

You can spend hours in here admiring these magnificent frescoes created by many Florentine artists including **Domenico Ghirlandaio** (Chapel of High Altar), **Giuliano da San Gallo** (Gondi Chapel), **Giovanni Dosio** (Gaddi Chapel), **Nardo di Cione** (Strozzi Chapel) and more. And if you're tired of sightseeing and need a little break, Florence's best pub, The Fiddler's Elbow, is in the piazza outside the church.

10. PIAZZA, PALAZZO, & LOGGIA DELLA SIGNORIA
Piazza della Signoria
This piazza, with the Palazzo, the Loggia, the fountain, the replica of the statue of David, the cafes and *palazzi* is incomparable in its beauty. Over the centuries great historical and political occurrences, as well as the lives of average Florentines, have all flowed through this piazza.

Today the square is the site of the annual sporting event, **Calcio in Costume** (soccer played in period garb), where the different sections of the city vie for dominance in a game that is a cross between soccer, rugby, martial arts and an all-out war. This annual contest used to be played in the square of Santa Croce but was moved here during modern times. If you are in Florence during June, when the event covers three of the weekends in that month, you definitely have to try and get tickets. The entire piazza is covered with sand, and stadium seats are put up all around the makeshift field, and then the fun begins. The event is a truly memorable experience.

In the small square on the left is **Ammannati's Fountain** with the giant figure of *Neptune*. The statue is commonly called *Biancone* (Whitey) by the locals because of its bland appearance. Giambologna created the equestrian statue representing *Cosimo I dei Medici* on the left of the square.

Palazzo della Signoria – Palazzo Vecchio
Piazza della Signoria. Open Monday–Friday 9:00am–7:00pm, and Sundays 8:00am–1:00pm. *Web: www.palazzovecchio.it.* Closed on Saturdays. Admission E5 for upstairs galleries.

The most imposing structure in the square is the **Palazzo Signoria**. It is 94 meters past the fortified battlements to the top of **Arnolfo's Tower**. In fact I strongly encourage you to go up to top where the art conservationists work. You can walk along the turreted top, and get some terrific views of the Duomo and other aspects of the city.

The entire structure is rather severe, but at the same time elegant. Its construction began in the late 13th century and took hundreds of years to finish. It was once the home of **Cosimo de Medici** and other members of the Medici family before the took over the Pitti Palace.

In front of the building on the platform at the top of the steps, ancient orators used to harangue the crowds, and for this reason this section of the building is called *Arringhiera* (The Haranguing Area). Located here are several important sculptures including the *Marzocco* (a lion symbolizing the Florentine Republic; a stone copy of the original sits in the National Museum); *Judith and Holofernes* created by Donatello in 1460, which is a record of the victory over the Duke of Athens; the copy of Michelangelo's *David* (the original is in the Accademia), and *Hercules and Cacus* created by Baccio Bandinelli.

Above the main door is a frieze with two lions and a monogram of Christ with the inscription *Rex Regum et Dominus Dominantium* (King of Kings and Lord of Lords), which used to record the time that the Florentine republic elected Christ as their King in 1528. The inscription used to read *Iesus Christus Rex Florentinei Populi S P Decreto Electus* (Jesus Christ elected by the people King of Florence) but was changed in 1851.

The interior is mainly filled with artwork glorifying the Medici family who ruled the Florentine Republic for centuries. So if you need a break from religious art and all those paintings of the Madonna and Child, this is the respite you've been looking for. Everything is elaborate and ornate, as befitting the richest family in the world at that time.

You enter through the courtyard which was designed by Michelozzo in 1453. The elaborate stucco decorations on the columns and frescoes on the arches were added in 1565 on the occasion of the wedding between Francesco dei Medici and Joan of Austria. The fountain in the center, *Graceful Winged Cupid* was done by Verrochio in 1476. From here most of the art to see is upstairs, so either take the staircase up or use the elevator.

What follows is a description of the important works to see in each room:

Hall of the Five Hundred – Salone dei Cinquecento
This is the most splendid and artistic hall in Florence. It was designed for public meetings after the Medicis had been thrown from power. When

Cosimo I regained the family's control over Florence, he had the hall enlarged and used it for his private audiences. On the wall opposite the entrance you'll find three large magnificent paintings by Baccio D'Agnolo, Baccio Bandinelli and Giorgio Vassari: *The Conquest of Siena; The Conquest of Porto Ercole; The Battle of Marciano*. On the wall across from this you'll find: *Maximilian Tries to Conquer Livorno; The Battle of Torre San Vincenzo; The Florentines Assault Pisa*. Underneath these painting you'll find sculptures by Vincenzo de Rossi representing *Hercules Labors*.

The ceiling is divided into 39 compartments with paintings by Giorgio Vasari that represent *Stories of Florence and the Medici*. The coup de grace is in the niche of the right wall at the entrance. Here you'll find Michelangelo's unfinished work, *The Genius of Victory*, which was designed for the tomb of Pope Julius II. If you only have a little time, spend it here. This room is magnificent.

Study of Francesco I de Medici

Here you'll find the work of many of Florence's finest artists crammed into as small a space as imaginable. The walls and even the barrel shaped ceiling are covered with paintings, and niches are filled with a variety of bronze statues. Elaborate, ostentatious and overwhelming. It is perpetually roped off, but you are able to view its splendor.

Hall of the Two Hundred – Salone dei Duecento

It is called thus since this is where the Council of two hundred citizens met during the time of the Republic for their important decisions. The walls are adorned with tapestry, the ceiling is ornately decorated, chandeliers hang low, and statues and busts adorn any free spot. The center of the room is occupied by the seating for the Council of 200.

Monumental Quarters – Quartieri Monumentali

These are a series of rooms that get their names from a member of the Medici family. Each are elaborate in their own right, filled with paintings, sculptures, frescoes, and more. From here you'll find many more interesting rooms and paintings as you explore, both on this floor and the one above, but this is the bulk of the beauty in the Palazzo Signoria.

The Loggia della Signoria

In the Piazza, on the right of the Palazzo as you face it, is the expansive and airy **Loggia della Signoria**, a combination of Gothic and Renaissance architecture. It was built by Benci di Cione, Simone Talenti and others during the years 1376–1382. At either end of the steps are two marble lions, one of which is very old, the other made in 1600.

Underneath the arch are some wonderful sculptures: *Persius* by Cellini in 1553 under the left hand arch; *The Rape of the Sabines* by Giambologna in 1583 under the right arch; *Hercules and the Centaur* by Giambologna in 1599 under the right arch also. There is also *Menelaus supporting Patroclus* and a few other less important works. All of them, since they are open to the elements and pollution, have been stained and discolored, but all are excellent studies in human anatomy.

11. UFFIZI GALLERY

Piazzale degli Uffizi. *Tel. 055/238-8651. Web: www.sbas.firenze.it/uffizi or www.uffizi.firenze.it.*Open Tuesday to Saturday 9:00am-2:00pm, Sundays and Holidays 9:00am-1:00pm. Closed Mondays. Admission £6.

The building housing the **Uffizi Gallery** was begun in 1560 by Giorgio Vasari on the orders of the Grand-Duke Cosimo I. It was originally designed to be government offices, but today holds the most important and impressive display of art in Italy, and some would say the world. The gallery mainly contains paintings of Florentine and Tuscan artists of the 13th and 14th centuries, but you'll also find works from Venice, Emilia, and other Italian art centers as well as Flemish, French, and German studies. In conjunction there is a collection of ancient sculptures.

These fabulous works of art were collected first by the Medici family (Francesco de' Medici started it off in 1581) then later by the Lorraine family. The last of the Medici, the final inheritor of that amassed wealth, Anna Maria

Reservation Service for Uffizi & Other Museums

It is strongly recommended that you reserve tickets in advance so that you do not have to stand in the incredibly long lines common at the Uffizi, Accademia and other museums, especially in the summer.

Once you have ordered your tickets you will not have to wait in that incredibly long line outside the Uffizi. Simply walk up to the bookstore to the left side of the entrance, pick up your tickets, and enter at the time designated.

You can also get tickets for the Uffizi and other museums on the web through *www.firenze.net*. The site is self-explanatory and makes life so much easier for people wanting to get into Florence's wonderful museums without having to waste precious hours waiting in line.

Reservations for the Uffizi can be made for a specific day and a specific time of entry, as long as ticket availability last. *Tel. 011/39/055/294-883, Fax 011/39/055/264-406.* Hours: Monday thru Friday 8.30am-6.30pm; Saturday 8.30am-12.30am.

Luisa donated the entire Gallery to the Tuscan state in 1737 so that the rich collection gathered by her ancestors would never leave Florence. Not everything would go as planned, since in the 18th century some pieces were stolen by Napoleon's marauding forces, but most of these were later returned after a ransom was paid. Some items were damaged in the great flood of 1966, and still others were damaged in 1993 when a terrorist car bomb ripped through parts of the Gallery. Even with all these occurrences, the Uffizi is still one of the finest galleries in the world.

As you enter the Uffizi, you will find the statues of Cosimo the Elder and Lorenzo the Magnificent, as well as several busts of the rest of the Medici rulers. It is ironic that they are so prominently displayed since when they ruled most Florentines despised their despotic ways. But now they are immortalized in time because of the philanthropic gesture of their last heir.

Anyway, it would be virtually impossible to list all the paintings and sculptures exhibited, so let me make a list of those that you absolutely must see if you visit the gallery. If you want a more complete listing or an audio guided tour, you can get those as you enter. Also, the museum is in the process of preparing for a move from the upper floor to the two lower floors. If that occurs, the room designations indicated below will no longer be valid.

- *Madonna of the Pomegranate, The Primavera, The Birth of Venus,* and *Annunciation* - Botticelli - Room X (This is the main Botticelli room, but there are Botticelli's strewn from Room X to XIV)
- *Madonna of the Goldfinch* - Raphael - Room XXV
- *Holy Family* - Michelangelo - Room XXV
- *Venus of Urbino* - Titian - Room XXVIII
- *Young Bacchus* - Caravaggio - Room XXXVI
- *Portrait of an Old Man* - Rembrandt - Room XXXVII
- *Portrait of Isabelle Brandt* - Peter Paul Rubens - Room XLI

The most recent purchases are concerned with self-protraits of some of the world's masters including Giotto, Maasaccio, Paulo Uccello, Filippo Lipp, Botticelli, Leonardo, Michelnagelo and others. A rare peek into the past to see what these painters really looked like. Another sight to see at the Uffizi is the view from the Cafetteria Bartolini, located on the second floor at the very end of the second hall way. The food's not that great, but the view is great for photographs.

12. PIAZZALE MICHELANGELO

From this piazza you have a wonderful view over the city of Florence being dissected by the river Arno. Remember to bring your camera since this is the best public view of the city. The best view, public or private is from the Hotel Torre di Bellosguardo, but if you desire that vista you have to spend the night since they don't allow sightseers on their grounds. At the center of the Piazzale

Michelangelo is a monument to **Michelangelo** dominated by a replica of the statue of *David*. Round the pedestal are four statues that adorn the tombs of famous Medicis which Michelangelo created. If you are up here around dinner time and want to grab something to eat, try the restaurant La Loggia on the opposite side of the piazza from the vista, across the road.

If you don't want to walk up the steep hill to the piazza, take bus number 13 from the station.

13. MUSEO ZOOLOGICO LA SPECOLA

Via Romana 17. *Tel. 055/222-451. Web: www.unifi.it/unifi/msn.* Closed Wednesdays. Open 9:00am–noon and until 1:00pm on Sundays.

This is an outing for the entire family. They have vast collection of stuffed animals from all over the world, some extinct, as well as bugs, fish, crustaceans, and more. You won't believe the extent of this collection, and that's just the animals. The best part of the exhibit is the collection of over 500 anatomical figures and body parts that were made in very life-like colored wax between 1175 and 1814. Every part of the body has been preserved separately as well as in whole body displays. They even put human hair on the heads of female reproductions to make them look more realistic.

One exhibit you may not want your kids to see is the part on reproduction, which gets pretty graphic. That room is at the end so you can march ahead and steer your impressionable ones into another room if you choose.

The other stuff is very tame. The last room has miniature wax scenes that are completely realistic depictions of the toll taken by the Black Death (the Plague). One particular tiny image of a rat pulling on a dead man's intestine is quite intense. Look at these pieces as art, not the anatomy tools they were used for, and you'll appreciate them immensely. The museum is used by many art students to study anatomy and you will find them discreetly sketching throughout the entire display.

14. THE BOBOLI GARDENS

Behind the Pitti Palace. *Tel. 055/265-1816.* Closed the last Monday of every month. Open 9:00am-4:30pm (Nov-Feb), 5:30pm (Mar. & Oct.), 6:30pm (April, May & September), 7:30pm (June, July & August). Admission E3.

Hidden behind the Pitti Palace is your respite from the Florentine summer heat and the hordes of tourists. Began in 1549 by Cosimo I and Eleanor of Tudor, the gardens went through many changes, additions, and alterations before they reached their present design. Among its many pathways and well-placed fields, the **Boboli Gardens** are the only true escape from the sun, humidity, and crowds that swarm through Florence in July and August. If you are inclined to walk in a calm, peaceful garden, far from the bustling crowds, or if you wish to enjoy a relaxing picnic, the Boboli is your place.

In the groves and walks of the Boboli you can find many spots to sit and enjoy a picnic lunch, or you can simply enjoy the platoons of statuary lining the walks. Some of the most famous works here include: *Pietro Barbino Riding a Tortoise*, commonly called 'Fat Baby Bacchus Riding a Turtle' (you'll find reproductions of this statue in almost every vendor's stall in Florence); a Roman amphitheater ascending in tiers from the Palazzo Pitti, designed as a miniature Roman circus to hold Medici court spectacles; and *Neptune's Fountain* at the top of the terrace, created in 1565 by Stoldo Lorenzi.

From Neptune's Fountain a path leads to the wonderful **Kaffehaus**. This little cafe offers a superb views of Florence as well as light snacks and drinks. An ideal place to come on a sunny day. After you have refueled, keep going up through the gardens until you reach the **Ex Forte di Belvedere**, which also offers magnificent views of all of Florence. Nearby is **Cypress Alley**, lined with statues of many different origins.

Also in the gardens is the **Museo delle Porcelane** with a delicate porcelain collection from the Medici and Lorraine families.

15. SANTO SPIRITO
Piazza Santo Spirito. *Tel. 055/210-030*. Open 8:00am-Noon and 4:00pm-6:00pm. Closed Wednesday afternoons.

Begun in 1444 by Brunelleschi, and continued after his death in 1446 by Antonio Manetti, Giovanni da Gaiole and Salvi d'Andrea. The last of these built the cupola that was based on Brunelleschi's design. It has a simple, plain, seemingly unfinished facade, in contrast to the interior.

Divided into three naves flanked by splendid capped Corinthian columns, this church looks very similar to San Lorenzo. There is a central cupola with two small naves in the wings of the cross that have small chapels just off of them. Lining the walls are some small chapels capped by semi-circular arches are adorned with elaborate carvings. The main altar, created by Giovanni Caccini (1599-1607), is Baroque in style and intricately displayed. In the chapels off the wings of the cross to the right and left of the main altar are many fine works of art to be enjoyed (two of which are *Madonna con Bambino* by Fillipino Lippi and *San Giovanni and Madonna with Baby Jesus and Four Saints* by Masi di Banco).

Many of these works are difficult to see since light does not find its way into this church very well.

16. DANTE'S HOUSE
Via Santa Margherita 1. *Tel. 055/219-416*. Open 10:00am-6:00pm (until 4:00pm in off season). Closed Tuesdays. Admission E3.

Dante's House and the accompanying museum of his life sits along one of the most medieval streets in Florence, tiny, cramped and evoking the conditions of his time. The house is quaintly picturesque. It was reconstructed a little haphazardly in the 19th century. The ground floor is a precursor with furnishings from Dante's time period. Upstairs is where the museum is (*entrance at Via S. Margherita 1*). It contains various manuscripts from Dante's time including many different versions of the *Divine Comedy*, Dante's most famous work. Not the greatest site in the world, but if you're a Dante fan this is a must see in Florence.

17. CHURCH OF THE BADIA
Via del Proconsolo. Open 9:00am-7:00pm.

Almost directly in front of the Bargello museum, this building was a Benedictine monastery founded in 978. The church is where it is rumored that Dante saw his love Beatrice for the first time. The church and accompanying buildings have gone through many changes. In 1285 the facade was built; in the 1400's extensive renovations were done on the cloisters, and in the sixteenth century the church was given a Baroque look and feel by Matteo Segaloni.

From the courtyard of the building you can admire the campanile of the Palazzo Vecchio, one of the characteristic structures in the skyline of Florence.

The interior of the church contains many notable paintings as well as tombs of respected Florentines, including Ugo di Toscana whose mother founded the monastery and Bernardo Giugni. The organ in the church, built by Onofrio Zeffirini da Cortona in 1558, still works and is used at every mass. Through a door on the right side of the church you enter the amazing *Chapel of the Oranges* (closed during mass) created by Bernardo Rossellino from 1432-38.

18. PALAZZO STROZZI
Piazza degli Strozzi. *Tel. 055/288342.* Hours Mon- Sat. 9:00am-1:00pm. Closed Sundays.

One of the most beautiful Renaissance palazzi in Florence built by and for one of Florence's most powerful families, the Strozzi. Construction was begun August 6th, 1489 because of astrological reasons, was stopped in 1504 for the same reasons, restarted in 1523, and suspended again in 1538 because of the death of Filippo Strozzi il Giovane. In true Italian fashion, work was never totally completed, but constant renovations and reconstructions have occurred.

The proportions of this three-story building are exemplary and is something to be viewed for its Renaissance look and feel. It now houses some cultural institutes not open to the public. However you are allowed to enter the courtyard and look around at the archways and portals.

19. NATIONAL LIBRARY
Piazza Cavaleggeri 1. *Tel. 055/249191.* Open Monday-Friday 10:00am-12.30pm; 3:00pm-6:30pm; Saturdays 10:00am-12.30pm.

The **Biblioteca Nazionale** is one of the most important libraries in Italy, located in the Santa Croce section of Florence in an eclectic building on the Piazza dei Cavaleggeri just off of the Lungarno. It was built between 1911 and 1935. The collection of books was started around 1714 by Angelo Magliabechi and was called at the time Biblioteca Magliabechiana. It was expanded in successive years by incorporating other libraries with the Magliabechi collection; then in 1861 it was renamed the National Library.

Today the library contains over 85 kilometers of shelves, 25,000-plus manuscripts and around 5 million books and 1 million letters. There are many ancient pieces in the library, including *Il Messale* (Catholic Missal) from the 10th century, *Il Codice della Commedia*, the oldest surviving Italian manuscript from before the 10th century, the *Maguntina Bible* from 1462, and *La Commedia* published in Florence in 1481 with comments by Cristoforo Landini and signed by Botticelli. Not your average titles found in libraries elsewhere. If you are a bibliophile make a pilgrimage here.

20. MUSEUM OF SCIENTIFIC HISTORY

Piazza dei Guidici 1, *Tel. 055/239-493* auto info line; *Tel. 055/265-311. Web: www.imss.fi.it.* Hours Monday, Wednesday, Thursday, Friday 9:30am-5:00pm. Tuesday, Saturday 9:30am-1:00pm. Closed Sundays and most holidays.

Located behind the Uffizi is the **Museo di Storia della Scienza**. Situated in the severe Palazzo Castellani which was built in the 14th century, the building was first used as a civil courthouse from 1574 to 1841, and up to 1966 one part of the building was the *Accademia della Crusca*, but the massive flood of that year forced the relocation of that organization.

Since 1930 the Museo di Storia della Scienza has been housed here. The exhibit is mainly a collection of scientific instruments from the 16th and 17th centuries. There are astrolabs, solar clocks, architectural tools and more. Of great interest are the original instruments used by Galileo (rooms IV and V) as well the mummified index finger from his right hand. Also of interest are the map-making materials and ancient geographical tools (room VII). There is also a splendid reconstruction of the map of the world made by Fra Mauro.

On the second floor you will find the precious astronomical clock from the 15th century (room XII) and many instruments created and used in the 17th century, including the amazing mechanical *mano che scrive* (hand that writes) and *l'orologia del moto perpetuo* (clock of perpetual motion). A great museum for those interested in scientific discovery, or for those who need a break from art.

21. FORTREZZA DA BASSO

Viale Filippo Strozzi, 1. *Tel. 055/49721.* The parks inside are open 24 hours a day.

Take the Via Valfonda to the right of the train station to get here, the

Fortress of San Giovanni. Also known as the Fortrezza da Basso ("below") as compared to the Fortrezza Belvedere ("with a good view"). This is an enormous pentagonal fortification built by the decree of Alessandro de' Medici more to eliminate internal strife through a show of force than for defense of the city. Construction was started under the guidance of Sangallo il Giovane in 1534. The outside walls were originally over 12 meters high and the walls nearest the station and the train tracks are the only ones of that height today. On the inside there is an octagonal building of note, the *corpo di guardia* (guard house). The entire structure is used today as an exhibit hall.

22. FORTREZZA BELVEDERE

Via S. Leonardo. *Tel. 055/234-2425.* Open 9:00am-8:00pm. Only the grounds are open to the public.

Also called the Fort of St. George, this fortress was constructed in the 1500s by the decree of the Grand Duke Ferdinand I on a design by Bernardo Buontalenti e Don Giovanni de' Medici. Its battlements were used in the defense of the city for centuries. From the battlements you have an amazing panorama of the city and the valley of the Arno. A great place for photo opportunities.

At the center of the structure is the Palazzina di Belvedere, built between 1560 and 1570, and only open for special exhibits.

23. MUSEO NAZIONALE DEL BARGELLO

Via del Proconsolo, *Tel 055/210-801. Web: www.sbas.firenze.it/bargello.* Open Tuesdays-Saturdays 9:00am 2:00pm and Sundays 9:00am 1:00pm. Holidays 8:30am-1:50pm. Closed Mondays. Admission E4.

Located almost behind the Palazzo Signoria in the quaint Piazza S. Firenze, you will find one of the most important collections of art and artifacts in the world. Located in the building that was the first seat of government in Florence, and was in 1574 the seat of the justice department, police, and customs, this is a rather severe, austere palazzo that was restored from 1858 to 1865. After the great flood of 1966 most of the ground floor had to be redone.

You will find great sculptures from the Renaissance. Featured prominently are those created in Tuscany, which are some of the best ever made. After entering into the small area called Torre Volognana, you are ushered into the *Cortile* (courtyard) area complete with a fountain and six allegorical marble statues by Bartolomeo Ammannati, *Oceano* by Giambologna, *Allegoria di Fiesole* by Tribolo and *Cannone di S. Paolo* by Cosimo Cenni.

Elsewhere in the museum you will find some beautiful works by Michelangelo including *Bacco* (1496-97) *David-Apollo* (1530-32) which is the first large classical sculpture by the artist, and *Bruto* (1530), which means ugly, and is the only bust created by Michelangelo of Lorenzo di Medici. On this floor are also some beautiful bronze statues by a variety of artists.

On the second floor (which you get to by stairs constructed by Neri di Fioravante from 1345-1367) are some interesting bronze animal sculptures including the famous tacchino (turkey) made by Giambologna. The other featured artist in the museum is Donatello whose works are displayed in the Salone del Consiglio Generale, constructed by the same architect who built the stairs. Here you'll find *S. Giorgio* (1416) accompanied by two statues of *David*, one younger in marble (1408-9) and the other more famous one in bronze (circa 1440). Other works by Donatello include the *Bust of Niccolo of Uzzano* made of multi-colored terra-cotta, *Marzocco* (1418-20), a lion that symbolizes the Florentine Republic, *Atys-Amor*, a wonderful bronze, and the dramatic *Crucifixion*.

There are many other works here, too many to mention, but suffice to say that this is a museum that shouldn't be missed while in Florence, especially if you like sculpture. The Accademia and the Uffizi get all the press in Florence, but this is one of the best museums of sculpture anywhere in the world.

24. TEMPIO ISRAELICO

Via Luigi Carlo Ferini, *Tel. 055/234-6654.* Open Sun.-Thurs. 10:00am - 1:00pm & 2:00pm-5:00pm. Fridays 10:00am -1:00pm. Closed Saturdays & Jewish Holidays. E3.

Built from 1874 to 1882, this Byzantine/Moorish synagogue is definitely worth seeing. There is no need to enter unless you are curious, but the building also contains the *Museo Ebraico di Firenze* (Hebrew Museum of Florence), with some ancient ceremonial objects and a sacred torah. The sight to behold is the unique architecture and facade, quite different than most buildings in Florence. Located a little ways away from everything in the Santa Croce section of town.

25. SAN MARCO

Piazza San Marco, *Tel. 055/239-6950. Web: www.sbas.firenze.it/ sanmarco.* Closed the 1st, 3rd and 5th Sunday and 2nd and 4th Saturdays of the each month. E7.

This place is a hidden treasure. Actually this 'place' is the church, the cloisters, the museum next to the church, and the Biblioteca de Michelozzo. The church has some incredible works by Fra Bartolemeo and Michelozzo, as well as Donatello's workshop. The museum has what could be the largest collection of Fra (Beato) Angelico paintings anywhere. The library (biblioteccha) is a spartan presentation of some ancient documents.

You can also visit the rooms on the top floor, where Fra Angelico, the accomplished artist and Dominican friar, lived and worked. Other individuals, such as Savonarola stayed for short and long periods in the little monastic cells.

At the top of the main set of stairs is a beautiful Fra Angelico fresco, and the frescos in each of the cells are by Fra Angelico or his students.

Nightlife & Entertainment

Florence is definitely not known for its nightlife. Most Florentines usually only engage in some form of late night eating and drinking at a restaurant that stays open late. Here are some places to go if you get that itch to be wild; you'll find each listing on the Florence restaurants map, pages 262-263.

33. THE FIDDLER'S ELBOW, *Piazza Santa Maria Novella 7R, Tel. 055/ 215-056. Open 3:00pm-1:15pm everyday.*

If you want to enjoy a true Irish pub outside of Ireland, you've found it. Step into the air-conditioned comfort, sit among the hanging musical instruments, belly up to the dark wooden bar, eye yourself in the mirror, and have a pint. A great place to meet other English speakers, many of whom are living in Florence. It is also a nightspot for young Italians. Whether it's sitting on the patio or inside at one of the many tables you're bound to have some fun.

34. HARRY'S BAR, *Lungarno a Vespucci 22, 50123 Firenze. Tel. 055/ 239-6700. Credit cards accepted. Closed Sundays.*

Based on the famous Harry's Bar in Venice (see the Venice chapter in this book), but with no business connections (Italians obviously have different trademark laws than we do). This is now the place to find the best burgers in Florence. They also mix some strong drinks in the evening, so if you have nothing to do and just want to get out of the hotel room, pop in here.

35. IL RIFRULLO, *Via San Niccolo 55, Tel. 055/213-631. Open from 8:00am to midnight.*

Located in the Oltrarno, this is a charming and relaxing place where you can enjoy a drink in the garden in the summer, in front of the fireplace in the winter, or up at the bar whenever you please. The atmosphere in the front room is all pub, in the back room all taverna, and in the garden, all party. They serve Whitbread Pale Ale, Campbell's Scotch Ale, Stella Artois (Belgian) and Leffe (a Belgian Double Malt on tap), as well as some of the most scrumptious crepes around.

36. SPACE ELECTRONIC, *Via Palazzuolo 37, 50123 Firenze. Tel. 055/ 292-082, Fax 055/293-457.*

The largest and loudest discotheque in the city. They've had music videos playing here before anybody knew what music videos were. I still remember seeing Mick Jagger croon the words to Angie on a big screen here back in my wild days. They continue to be the trendsetters when it comes to club antics. They play all sorts of music, so no one is left out. A fun place with many different levels and dance floors, where you can enjoy the company of your friends, or leave in the company of a newfound one.

Opera

If you are in Florence from December to June, the traditional opera season, and have the proper attire (suits for men, dresses for women) and a taste for something out of the ordinary, try the spectacle of the opera at **Teatro Communale**, Corso Italia 16, *Tel. 055/211-158 or 2729236, Fax 055/277-9410.*

Movies in English

If you want to see an English language film on Mondays or Tuesdays, try **Odeon Original Sound**, Via Sassetti 1, *Tel. 055/214-068. Web: www.cinehall.it.*

For English language films on Wednesdays at 8:30pm, go to the **British Institute**, Lungarno Guicciardini 9, *Tel. 055/2677-8270.*

On Thursdays, you can see films in their original language at **Cinema Fulgor**, Via maso Finiguerra 22r, *Tel. 055/238-1881. Web: cinemafulgor.it.*

Sports & Recreation
Balloon Rides in Tuscany

Contact **The Bombard Society**, 6727 Curran Street, McLean VA 22101-3804. Outside Virginia, toll-free *Tel. 800/862-8537, Fax 703/883-0985. In* Virginia or outside: *Tel. 703/448-9407*; you can call collect. Call for current price and information about the most amazing way to view the most spectacular scenery in the world.

Golf

- **Circolo Golf dell'Ugolino**, Via Chiantigiano 3, 51005 Grassina, *Tel. 055/320-1009, Fax 055/230-1141.* Located 9 km from Florence this is a par 72, 18 hole course that is 5,728 meters long. Open all year round except on Mondays. They have tennis courts, a swimming pool, a pro shop, a nice bar and a good restaurant.
- **Poggio de Medici Golf & Country Club**, Via San Gavino 27, 50038 Scarperia. *Tel. 055/83-0436/7/8, Fax 055/843-0439.* Located 30 km from Florence this is a 9 hole, par 36 course, that is 3,430 meters long, and is open all year round except for Tuesdays. They have a driving range, putting green and a clubhouse with snacks and drinks.

Pools

If you need a break from touring and want to lounge around a pool for the day, below is a list of places that have pools that you can pay to use. Note that some of them are hotels and are conveniently located near the center of town.

- **Costoli**, Viale Paoli, *Tel. 055/678-012,* Open in the summer, 10:00am-6:00pm.

- **Bellariva**, Lungarno Colombo, 6, *Tel. 055/677-521*, Open in the summer.
- **Le Pavoniere**, Viale degli Olmi, *Tel.055/367-506*, Open in the summer.
- **Hotel Villa Medici**, Via Il Prato, 42, *Tel. 055/238-1331*, Open in the summer.
- **Hotel Villa Cora**, Viale Macchiavelli, 18, *Tel. 055/229-8451*, Open in the summer.
- **Hotel Minerva**, Piazza S.Maria Novella, 16, *Tel. 055/284-555*, Open in the summer.
- **Hotel Kraft**, Via Solferino, 2, *Tel. 055/284-273*, Open in the summer.

Tennis
If you have a hankering to serve and volley, here are some tennis clubs in Florence where you can rent a court.
- **Circolo Tennis alle Cascine**, Viale Visarno, 1, *Tel. 055/354-326*
- **Tennis Michelangelo**, Viale Michelangelo, 61, *Tel. 055/681-1880*

Shopping
See the map on pages 272-273 to find manyof the shops in this section.

Antiques
Many of the better known antique stores have been located in the **Via dei Fossi** and **Via Maggio** for years, but there are some interesting little shops in the **Borgo San Jacopo** and the **Via San Spirito**, all located in the **Oltrarno** section of Florence across the river.

When shopping for antiques in Florence, there is one important thing to remember: the Florentines are excellent crafts people and as such have taken to the art of antique fabrication and reproduction. In fact under Italian law, furniture made from old wood is considered an antique, even if it was carved yesterday. These products can be sold as antiques and usually have a price tag to match. But in terms of American understandings, they are not antiques. They only look like it. If you find a 'real' antique by American standards, it is usually designated by a stamp indicating that it is a national treasure and as such cannot be taken out of the country.

Artisans
If you want to see some of this excellent antique fabrication and reproduction work, as well as genuine restoration in progress, you need venture no further than across the river to the Oltrarno section. In these narrow streets you'll find small workshops alive with the sounds of hammers and saws, intermingled with the odors of wood, tanning leather, and glue. When I lived in Florence this was my favorite area to come to. Watching someone creating something out of nothing has always been a relaxing adventure, and besides, not many tourists even venture into these tiny alcoves of Florentine culture.

Some of the best known shops are located in the **Via Santo Spirito**, **Viale Europa**, **Via Vellutini**, **Via Maggio** and the **Via dello Studio**. Strangely enough, on these same streets are your real antique shops. How convenient to have the fabricators and reproducers next door to the 'legitimate' antique dealers. In other words, inspect your goods carefully.

Florentine Craft Tours

Florence is filled with artisan craft shops which create all sorts of time honored traditional crafts, harking back hundreds of years. The best way to find these craft people and their workshops is on free guided tours. Lasting three hours, the tours take place with a minimum of 8 people on Monday and Thursday afternoons (meet at 3pm in Piazza Pitti). Tours are held from March 31 to April 13, May 5 to July 17, and September 15 to December 22. This is a great way to find unique gifts and memories from your visit to Florence.

Reservation Information: *Tel. 055288448, Fax 055288476, Email: centroguide@tiscalinet.it.*

Books & Newspapers in English

A. BM BOOKSHOP, *Borgo Ognissanti 4r, Tel 055/294-575. Open Winter: Mondays 3:30pm-7:30pm, Tuesday-Saturday 9:00am-1:00pm and 3:30pm-7:30pm.*

An extensive collection of English language books.

B. PAPERBACK EXCHANGE, *Via Fiesolana 31r, Tel. 055/247-8154. www.papex.it. Open Mon-Fri 9am-7:30pm, Sat 10am-1pm and 3:30pm-7:30pm.*

The unofficial English-speaking ex-pat meeting place, this store has the largest and best priced selection of new and used English-language paperbacks in Florence.

Cartolerie - Stationary Stores

C. L'INDICE SCRIVE, *Via della Vigna Nuova 82r. Tel. 055/215-165. Credit cards accepted.*

A wide variety of stationary products and unique pens are featured in this store. Most of the items are hand-made, including the diaries, ledgers, guest books, desk sets. etc. A great place to get a gift for someone back home.

D. IL PAPIRO, *Piazza Duomo 24r, Tel. 055/215-262. Email info@ilpapirofirenze.it, Web: www.ilpapirofirenze.it. Credit cards accepted.*

If you like marbleized paper products, this is the store for you. You can get boxes, notebooks, picture frames, pencil holders, basically anything you could imagine. The prices are a little high but that's because of the great location and high quality products. They also have three locations in Rome, all around the Pantheon.

E. IL TORCHIO, *Via de Bardi 17, Tel. 055/234-2862.*

A much less expensive store than **Il Papiro**, with similar stuff, and they make it in front of you while you shop. Located 2 blocks east of the Ponte Vecchio (as you cross the bridge turn left), this place is off the beaten tourist path, but well worth the slight detour.

Ceramics

If you are interested in the famous painted ceramics from Tuscany and Umbria, you don't have to go to the small towns where they are manufactured – there is a great store behind the stalls in the San Lorenzo market called **Florentina**, *Via dell'Ariento 81r, Tel. 055/239-6523.* Owned by a friendly Irish woman and her Italian husband, this store has everything you could want at prices similar to what you would get if you traveled to Deruta in Umbria or Cortona in Tuscany.

Another ceramics store is located near Santa Croce around the corner from the English Bookstore Paperback Exchange. The **Sbigoli Terrecotte**, *Via S. Egidio 4r, Tel/Fax 055/247-9713,* has works from Deruta priced virtually the same as if you were in that town. What this store offers is a workshop where they make, bake and hand paint their own ceramics.

Little Shops

F. BARTOLUCCI, *Via Condotta 12/r, Tel. 055/211-773.*

Near the Piazza Signoria is this great store selling all sorts of wood carved items: cars, motorcycles, clocks, toys, and much more.

G. GELATERIA PORTA ROMANA, *Piazzale di Porta Romana, Tel. 055/ 221-121.*

Located away from the centro storico, just outside the old gates of the city at Porta Romana is this fantastic ice cream store. All their gelato and frozen yogurt is made on site. And it is superb. If you are in the neighborhood, and have a craving for ice cream, you have to stop in.

H. OFFICINA PROFUMO-FARMACEUTICA, *Via della Scala 16/r, Tel. 055/230-2883 or 2649, Fax 055/288-658.*

A beautiful centuries-old establishment with the most refined soaps, shampoos, creams, bath and other personal hygiene products. All products are manufactured with care and artfully displayed.

I. TRICOLORE, *Via della Scala 25/r, Tel. 055/210-166, Web: iltricolore.it.*

The place to get all sorts of Italian law enforcement and military-related products. Badges, hats, flags, shirts, key chains and much more. Unique gifts.

J. VESTRI, *Borgo degli Albizi 11/r, Tel. 055/234-0374, Web: www.ciocolateriavestri.com.*

Fresh chocolate is lovingly made here. A tiny shop that is packed at all times with Florentines coming to get their chocolate fix.

The Paper Mache Store

One store you simply cannot miss is the small studio/gallery of the artist Bijan, **(K) Firenze Papier Mache**, Piazza Pitti 10, *Tel. 055/230-2978, Fax 055/365-768.* He makes beautiful masks covered with intricate sketchings of famous paintings, as well as beautiful anatomical forms, all from paper mache. Even if you don't buy anything, simply browse and savor the beauty of his work. Since the shop is near the Palazzo Pitti, one of your 'must see' destinations while in Florence, there's no reason why you shouldn't take a peak in here.

Markets

L. MERCATO CENTRALE, *immediately north of Piazza San Lorenzo, open Monday–Friday, 7:00am–2:00pm and 4:00pm–8:00pm, Saturday 7:00am-12:15pm and 1:00pm-5:00pm. Sunday 3:00pm-5:00pm.*

This is Florence's main food market for wholesale and retail fish, fresh meat, vegetables, cheeses, oils, breads, and many other delicacies. The meat and fish section is on the ground floor, with a few vegetable stands thrown in, but if you're into healthy food, make your way upstairs to their fruit and vegetable market. When you visit the Mercato Centrale, don't think of leaving without having a sandwich at **Nerbone's** (see review above in *Where to Eat*). A truly authentic Florentine experience.

M. MERCATO DI SAN LORENZO, *near the Duomo, everyday from 8:00am-dark. Closed Sundays in the winter.*

Florence's largest and most frequented street market. It completely dominates the church of San Lorenzo, its piazza, and many adjacent streets. You can find leather jackets, wallets, T-shirts, belts, and much more, most at prices close to half of what you would pay in a store. Remember to bargain, because usually the starting price is rather high. If you've never done this before, the best bet when bargaining is to make a counter offer at half of the initial price. Then let the games begin. Bargaining is much of the fun of buying something in an Italian market.

N. MERCATO NUOVO, *in the Logge del Mercato Nuovo near the Piazza del Signoria, this market is open daily 9:00am–5:00pm.*

Also known as the **Straw Market**, they sell traditional products made from straw but also exquisite leather products, ceramics, linens (like table clothes and napkins), statues, and other hand-made Florentine crafts.

O. MERCATO DI SANTO SPIRITO, *in the piazza in front of Santo Spirito. Open every Sunday from 8:00am-7:00pm.*

A great market filled with antiques, junk, clothes, imported figures from Africa, military surplus, and much more. A local's market, and such, one of the best in Florence if you're looking for a taste of real life in the city.

Food Products

Here's a small list of food stores from which you can get almost all sorts of food products to bring home with you. Three of my favorite items to bring back with me are dried porcini mushrooms, truffles, and Parmigianno Reggiano cheese. Used together they make a great pasta sauce. And the prices are easily one quarter of what you would pay back home.

P. VERA, *Piazza Frescobaldi 3r, Tel. 055/215-465. No credit cards accepted.*

Located in the Oltrarno section of Florence, this store is a food connoisseur's delight. It has the best fresh cheeses, salamis, hams, roasted meats, freshly baked breads, olive oil, soups and salads. If you want fresh fruit you're also in luck – but not here, you have to go to the store across the street.

Q. VINO E OLIO, *Via dei Serragli 29r, Tel. 055298-708. No credit cards accepted.*

You can find any type of wine or olive oil you could dream of in this store. A great place to buy gifts for friends at home. If you don't want to carry them with you on the rest of your trip, the owner will arrange to have them shipped to wherever you choose.

R. ALESSI PARIDE, *Via delle Oche 27-29r, Tel. 055/214-966. Credit cards accepted.*

This store is a wine lovers paradise. They have wines from every region of Italy and there's one room entirely dedicated to Chianti. This store may be a little expensive for picnic supplies, but you can get any manner of wine imaginable here, as well as selected liquors, chocolates, marmalades, and honeys.

Practical Information
Church & Synagogue Ceremonies in English

- **St. James**, American Episcopal Church, Via Rucellai 9, *Tel. 055/294-417.* Located in the Centro section of Florence.
- **St. Marks**, Church of England, Via Maggio 16, *Tel. 055/294-764.* Located in the Oltrarno section of Florence.
- **Synagogue**, Via L.C. Farini 4, *Tel. 055/245-251/2.* Located in the Santa Croce section of Florence.

Consulates
- **British Consulate**, Lungarno Corsini 2,*Tel. 055/284-133*
- **United States Consulate**, Lungarno Amerigo Vespucci 38, *Tel. 055/239-8276*

Emergencies
These are the rapid response numbers for the police, caribineiri and fire departments.
- **Polizia Soccorso Pubbblico** (police), *Tel. 113*
- **Carabinieri Pronto Intervento**, *Tel. 112*
- **Vigili del Fuoco** (fire), *Tel. 115*

Local Festivals & Holidays
- **January 1**, New Year's Day
- **April 25**, Liberation Day
- **Ascension Day**
- **May 1**, Labor Day
- **Month of May**, Iris Festivals
- **Cricket Festival**, Sunday of the Ascension, usually in May, with floats and little (mechanical) crickets sold in cages. Live crickets were once sold, but animal rights activists convinced the city to switch to electronic ones. Political correctness has hit Italy.
- **May and June**, Maggio Musicale Fiorentino
- **Mid-June to August**, Estate Fiesolana. Music, cinema, ballet and theater
- **Three Weekends in June**, Calcio in Costume
- **June 24**, St. John the Baptist's Day celebrated with fireworks
- **August 15**, Ferragosto
- **First Sunday in September**, Lantern Festival
- **November 1**, All Saints Day (Ognissanti)
- **December 8**, Conception of the Virgin Mary (Immacolata)
- **December 25 & 26**, Christmas

Laundry
After you've been on the road for a few days you might need to do some laundry, quickly, easily, and inexpensively. If you're staying at a four-star hotel don't bother reading this because you've already sent your clothes down to be starched and pressed by the in-house staff. For the rest of us, here's some suggestions:
- **Tintoria La Serena**, Via della Scala 30r, *Tel. 055/218-183*. Open seven days a week from 8:00am-10:00pm. The place I always come since you don't need to worry about the exact change or laundry detergent, they do it all. Total of E7.5 for washing and drying one load. Part of a dry cleaners so can get that service done at the same time if need be.

• **Wash & Dry**, now has eight locations, all open seven days a week from 8:00am to 10:00pm. Last wash allowed in at 9:00pm. General number: *Tel. 055/436-1650*. E3 for wash, E3 for dry, E3 for detergent. E6 for large. Located at: Via dei Serragli 87/R and Borgo San Frediano 39/R in the Oltrarno; Via della Scala 52/54R, Via del Sole 29/R, and Via Nazionale 129/R by the train station; Via dei Servi 105/R by the Duomo; and Via Ghibellina 143r and Via dell/Agnolo 21/R in Santa Croce.

Online Access

Internet Land, Via degli Alfani 43r, *Tel./Fax 055/263-8220, www.internetland.it*. Here you can surf the web, scan a document, get one typed and printed, fax a letter home, or e-mail your friends.

Internet Train, *www.internettrain.it*. THE place in Florence to get online. With 14 locations all over the city you are never far from cyberspace. Here are some convenient locations: Galleria Commerciale (the underground walkway leading to the train station), inside the Astor Cafe at Piazza Duomo 20r, Via Porta Rossa 38r near the Piazza della Signoria, Borgo San Jacopo 30r near the Ponte Vecchio.

Postal Services

The **central post office** in Florence, Via Pietrapiana 53-55, is in the Santa Croce section of town; but stamps can be bought at any tobacconist (store indicated by a **T** sign outside), and mailed at any mailbox, which are red and marked with the word Poste or Lettere. You can send duty free gift packages (need to be marked "gift enclosed") home to friends or relatives as long as the cost of the gift(s) in the package does not exceed $50. You will need to box them in official boxes or envelopes which can be bought at cartolerie (stationery stores).

Tourist Information & Maps

• **Information Office**, Via Manzoni 16, *Tel. 055/247-8141*. Located in the Santa Croce area of Florence. Provides city maps, up-to-date information about Florence and the province of Florence, which includes museum hours, events, and bus and train schedules.
• **Hotel Information Office** at the Train Station, Via Stazione 59r. Open 7:00am to 10:00pm. *Tel. 055/282-893/283-500*. They can book hotel rooms for you here; but you have to pay the first night's stay in advance plus a fee of E5 for a deluxe hotel, E4 for a four-star, E3 for a three-star, E2 for a two-star, and E1.5 for a one star.

Tour Operators

• **American Express**, Lungarno Guicciardini 49, *Tel. 055/288-751*. Located in the Oltrarno section of Florence; Via Dante Alighieri 22r, *Tel. 055/50981*.

Located in the Centro Storico section of Florence. They offer a full range of tours.

- **Mercurio Guided Tours**, *Tel. 055/266-141, Fax 055/283-892. Web: www.mercurio-italy.org*. Offer walking tours of Florence for E25, as well as tours of Pisa & Pucca, San Gimignano, Siena & Montalcina.
- **Walking Tours of Florence**, *Tel. 055/580-430. Email: holitaly@dada.it*. One of the best ways to learn all about the Roman, medieval and Renaissance history, and the architecture, people and events of Florence. Every Tuesday, Thursday, and Saturday at 10:00am and Wednesday evening at 6:00pm. Cost is only E20 per person.

Elsewhere in Tuscany

If you have the time, there are a number of great day trips and longer excursions in Tuscany. For many, a trip to Italy is not complete without visiting one of the most famous sights in the world – the **Leaning Tower of Pisa**, – here in Tuscany.

There's also the charming walled city of Lucca with its romantic walkway on the ramparts of the old walls; the winding medieval streets and expansive Campo of **Siena**, with one of the most impressive clock towers in Italy; the ancient town of **Fiesole**, once the Roman Empire's dominant town in Tuscany; the romantic towers and simple beauty of the small hill town of **San Gimignano**; the wonderful churches and market of **Cortona**; and the amazing town of **Montepulciano**.

PISA

Located 56 miles west of Florence, with a population of a little over 100,000 people, Pisa is mainly known for its **leaning tower**. The famous **Campo dei Miracoli** is in the northwestern part of the city. In this square are the **baptistery**, a circular church building used for baptisms; the **Duomo**, built from 1063 to 1160; and the marble **bell tower**, known to the world as the **Leaning Tower of Pisa**. In the cathedral is where the astronomer Galileo first made the observation that later became known as the principle of the motion of a pendulum. But the bell tower is why people come to Pisa. At 179 feet (55 meters) high and 50 feet (15 meters) wide, it was built on unstable ground and as a result began to tip during its construction and is now 15 feet (4.6 meters) out of perpendicular.

A naval base under Roman control, Pisa became a Roman colony after 180 BCE. The town had a Christian bishop by 313 CE. Pisa's finest era was back in the 12th century, when its population was greater than 300,000. Pisa was considered a city of marvels because its merchants and its strong navy had traveled all over the Mediterranean, bringing back not only new products but new ideas and styles in art. The famous **Pisan Romanesque** architecture, with its stripes and blind arcades, had its origins in the Moorish architecture of Andalucia in Spain, whose ideas and styles were brought back by Pisa's world traveling merchants.

During this successful time, the **Duomo** was built and the Baptistery and Campanile were begun. But these weren't the only glory of Pisa. It has been described as being a city of ten thousand towers, most of which do not exist today. The city was badly bombed during WWII, and as a result many of the towers no longer exist. How unfortunate that the one which has survived seems about to fall.

Pisa historically aligned itself with the rulers of Florence, if only for expediency. Their navy was vast and fierce and they were constantly at war somewhere in the Mediterranean, usually against the Muslim world.

Pisa's decline began in 1284, when the mercantile port of Genoa devastated the Pisan navy at the **Battle of Meloria** near Livorno. But the final blow to Pisa's Mediterranean dominance was delivered by nature. The silt from the Arno gradually filled in the Pisan port and the cost of dredging was too great for the city to bear. From that point on Pisa became a pawn that other Italian city-states traded back and forth. Eventually coming under the control of Florence, the Medici dukes gave Pisa a lasting gift, Florence's own university, where Galileo held an honorary title until his death. This institution helped Pisa stay alive and vital, and in touch with the changes going on in the world.

For more information about Pisa, visit their website at *www.pisaonline.it.*

Arrivals & Departures

By car, take the A11 directly to Pisa from Florence. Trains from Florence arrive at the Stazione Centrale, which is a pleasant 10-15 minute walk to the leaning tower and the other tourist sights. Or if you are a little tired, take the No. 1 bus from the station to the sights, or grab a taxi.

Where to Stay

I'm suggesting that you take a day trip up this way from Florence, spend the day, see the sights, explore the old city by the Arno, have lunch and maybe dinner, then catch one of the frequent trains back. But if you happen to tarry a little longer than expected, here's a concise list of hotels in a variety of price ranges that are worthy of your attention.

1. ARISTON, *Via Cardinale Maffi 42, Tel. 050/561-834, Fax 050/561-891. 35 rooms all with bath and radio. Single E50-70; Double E70-90. Breakfast included. All credit cards accepted. ****

Located right by the Leaning Tower and the other main sights in Pisa.

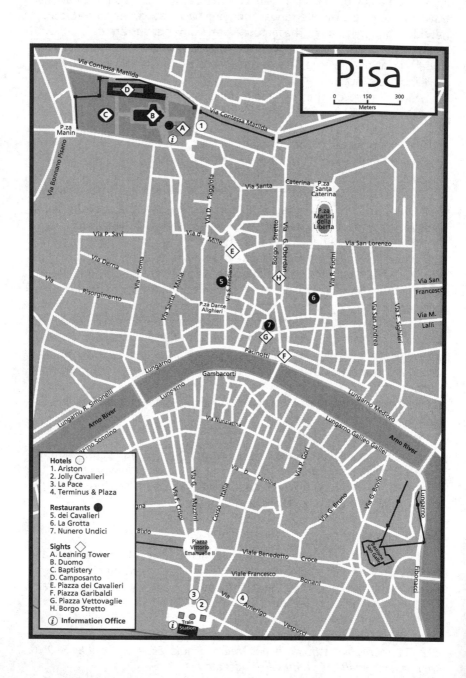

Pisa

0 150 300
Meters

Via Contessa Matilda
Via Contessa Matilda
P.za Manin
Via Bonnano Pisano
Via Santa
Via Santa
Caterina
P.za Santa Caterina
P.za Martiri della Liberta
Via San Lorenzo
Via D. Faggiola
Via P. Savi
Via d. Mille
Borgo Stretto
Via G. Oberdan
Via R. Fucini
Via San Francesco
Via Derna
Via Roma
Via S. Frediano
Via San Andrea
Via E. Sighieri
Via M. Laili
Via
Risorgimento
Via Santa Maria
P.za Dante Alighieri
Lungarno
Pacinotti
Gambacorti
Lungarno
Lungarno R. Simonelli
Arno River
Lungarno Mediceo
Lungarno Galileo Galilei
Arno River
Lungarno Sonnino
Via Nunziatina
Via D. God
Via D. Carmine
Via G. Bovio
Lungarno
Via G. Mazzini
Corso Italia
Via G. Bruno
Via F. Crispi
Bastione San Gallo
Elbonaci
Bixio
Piazza Vittorio Emanuele II
Viale Benedetto
Croce
Via
Amerigo
Bonani
Viale Francesco
Vespucci
Train Station

Hotels ○
1. Ariston
2. Jolly Cavalieri
3. La Pace
4. Terminus & Plaza

Restaurants ●
5. dei Cavalieri
6. La Grotta
7. Nunero Undici

Sights ◇
A. Leaning Tower
B. Duomo
C. Baptistery
D. Camposanto
E. Piazza dei Cavalieri
F. Piazza Garibaldi
G. Piazza Vettovaglie
H. Borgo Stretto

ⓘ **Information Office**

You'll have the tower to keep you company, but this is so far away from the real center of the city located around the river. But even so, this is a good inexpensive option for a short stay in Pisa.

2. JOLLY CAVALIERI, *Piazza della Stazione 2, 56125 Pisa. Tel. 050/ 43290, Fax 050/502-242. Email: pisa@jollyhotels.it, Web: www.jollyhotels.it. Toll free in Italy 167-017703. Toll free in US and NYC 800/221-2626. Toll free in NY State 800/247-1277. 100 rooms. Single E145-170; Double E170-220.* ****

Located near the train station and away from the main sights, this could be an option if you've lingered too long over dinner and don't want to take the train back to Florence or have missed the last one. All the amenities of afour-star including air conditioning, cable TV, piano bar and more. Its location is not so hot in terms of tourist sights, but this is the place to stay in Pisa.

3. LA PACE, *Viale Gramsci 14, Tel. 050/29351. Fax 050/502266. Email: info@HotelLaPace.it, Web: www.hotellapace.it. 70 rooms. Single E70; Double E90. Breakfast included. All credit cards accepted.* ***

Just your basic, run of the mill, three-star hotel located near the train station in Pisa. Located in a commercial gallery that is a little bland. Here you will find peace and quiet but not much else. The rooms are clean and comfortable, but the atmosphere is not too electric. Let's be honest. Pisa is not known as a hot bed for hotels.

4. TERMINUS & PLAZA, *Via Colombo 45, Tel. and Fax 050/500-303. 55 rooms. Single E65; Double E85. Breakfast E6. Credit cards accepted.* ***

A hospitable hotel in an austere building, which is well kept up and finely decorated. The rooms have functionally furnished, nothing special, and the bathrooms are sufficient. The common areas are filled with ambiance and the staff personal and professional. A good option while in Pisa.

Where to Eat

5. DEI CAVALIERI, *Via San Frediano 16, Pisa. Tel. 050/49-008. Closed Saturdays for lunch and Sundays. Credit cards accepted. Dinner for two E32.*

A small place near a public high school, they have good pasta dishes, such as con funghi porcini (with mushrooms), coniglio e asparagi (rabbit and asparagus) or vongole verace (clams in a garlic and oil sauce). For secondo, try either the coniglio al origano (rabbit made with oregano) or the fileto di pesce fresco can patate e pomodoro (fresh fillet of the catch of the day with roasted potatoes and tomatoes).

6. LA GROTTA, *Via San Francesco 103, Tel. 050/578-105. No credit cards accepted. Closed Sundays and in August. Dinner for two E35.*

An old Pisan restaurant built in 1947 that has the look and feel of a cave, hence the name. As such the atmosphere is unique and compliments the rustic Pisan cuisine. Try the risotto ai fiori di zucchini (rice with zucchini flowers), the spaghetti alla vongole (with clam sauce), then for later sample either the coniglio (rabbit) or the vitello (veal). If you're up late, this place stays open until 1 or 2:00am and becomes a wine bar serving drinks and cold plates after 11:00pm. It's one of Pisa's hip hangouts.

7. NUMERO UNDICI, *Via Cavalca 11. Tel. 050/544-294. No credit cards accepted. Closed Saturdays at dinner and Sundays. Dinner for two E23.*

A small, down to earth, local place situated by the University that has a nice outside patio. Located near the old market in Pisa this is the perfect place to sample Pisan home cooking. They make great lasagnas, crepes, and foccace (a crepe-like concoction with meats, cheeses, and vegetables baked inside the crisp doughy exterior), but my favorite was a dish of assorted salamis. Centrally located, good atmosphere and great food.

Graveyard of Ancient Ships

Just a short stroll from the Leaning Tower, archaeologists are unearthing at least ten Roman ships, many complete with cargoes, that sank some 2,000 years ago in a recently rediscovered harbor in Pisa. Merchant vessels, a warship, and a ceremonial boat are all being excavated, along with boxes and boxes of artifacts, from coins and lamps to amphorae that are still full. These artifacts, and the boats themselves, are being readied for removal to the nearby Arsenali Mediciei, a large warehouse structure which is being transformed into a temporary laboratory and museum where the final phases of restoration will occur.

This important find will be open to the public soon, but if you want a sneak preview, visit their website at *www.navipisa.it.* When in Pisa, take some time to visit this historic find.

Seeing the Sights

Much of the main tourist area centers around the **Campo dei Miracoli** (Square of Miracles) and its famous **Leaning Tower**, but Pisa has other attractions that you should explore as well. The sights below are lettered and correspond to the letters on the map of Pisa.

PIAZZA DEL MIRACOLI

It is called the **Square of Miracles** because of the stupendous architectural masterpieces filling the square. These are living testimony to the greatness that the city of Pisa reached at the height of its glory. The square is surrounded by imposing walls begun in 1154, which in turn are surrounded by countless vendors selling a wide variety of trinkets for the tourists.

The following sights are on display in the piazza:

A. THE LEANING TOWER

Tickets E15. You will need to make reservations in advance at **www.duomo.pisa.it** if you want to scale the tower.

The campanile is open once more. You can climb the leaning tower of Pisa again. The 293 steps of the tower can once again be traversed.

The most unique tower in the world because of the fact that it leans, and the degree to which it does. There are other towers in Italy, but none has its beauty and charm, nor are any others on the verge of falling over as is this one.

The lean in the tower was not planned, but it was noticed when the tower reached a height of 11 meters. The builders continued to build even though they realized that the foundation was unstable. The tower was begun in 1174 by Bonanno Pisano and finished in 1350 by Tomaso Pisano, so the family spent many years trying to discover ways to eliminate the list, unsuccessfully. The tower is 55 meters, 22 centimeters high, and its steepest angle is almost 5 meters. This angle has been increasing at almost a millimeter a year.

It was getting so bad that serious measures were undertaken to reduce the list of the tower. Cables were attached around the outside to keep the tower from leaning any further. And a drilling rig removed soil from underneath the side of the foundation opposite the list. Pressure was exerted on the cable to pull the tower into the space vacated by the drilled soil, and the tower's lean has been corrected one-half a degree, or about 16 inches.

During its useful days the tower was employed by **Galileo Galilei** when he conducted experiments with the laws of gravity. Or at least that is the accepted mythology. Today the tower, with its six galleries each surrounded by arches and columns, as well as the bell cell located at the top, is only used for drawing the tourist trade to Pisa.

B. THE DUOMO

Open 8:00am–12:30pm and 3:00pm–6:30pm. In January only open until 4:30pm.

Started in 1063 by Buschetto, it was finally consecrated in 1118 after Rainaldo finished the work. The bronze doors are reproductions, by 16th century Florentine artists, of the originals that were lost in the fire of 1569. The facade is covered with many columns and arches as was the Pisan style at the time.

The interior contains numerous sculptures and mosaics, among which is the famous mosaic *Christ and the Madonna* started by Francesco of Pisa and continued by Cimabue. The celebrated pulpit is the work of Giovanni Pisano, of the same family that built the Campanile. There is also the famous lamp that hangs in the center of the nave that was created by Stolto Lorenzi. It is called the **Lamp of Galileo**, who, as rumor has it, discovered through observation and experimentation the oscillation of pendulum movements. Last but not least is the statuette in ivory by Giovanni Pisano of the *Madonna and Child*.

C. BAPTISTERY

Open 9:00am–1:00pm and 3:00pm–6:30pm. In January only open until 4:30pm.

Begun in 1153 by the architect Diotisalvi, it is circular in form with a conical covering. Later the facade was adapted by Nicola Pisan and his son Giovanni to fit the other works in the square. The interior has five baptismal fonts created by Guido Bigarelli of Como in 1246 and the masterpiece of a pulpit created by Nicola Pisano in 1260.

D. CAMPOSANTO

Open 8:00am–6:30pm. In January open from 9:00am–4:30pm. Admission E3.

A rather serene and unpretentious cemetery, very unlike the foreboding "city of the dead" found in Genoa. This one was started in 1278 by Giovanni di Simone. It was enlarged in the 14th century and stands today like an open air basilica with three aisles. The center soil is rumored to have been brought from the Holy Land. The corridor around the earth is formed by 62 arches in a Gothic style of white and blue marble.

You'll also find some beautiful frescoes along the walls and floors that were partially destroyed during World War II but have since been restored.

E. PIAZZA DEI CAVALIERI

This is the most harmonious piazza in the city after the famous Piazza dei Miracoli with its leaning tower. Literally translated the name means square of the knights, and it is named for the Knights of St. Stephen, an order established by Cosimo I de Medici to defend Florence and her holdings from pirates. The statue above the fountain by Francavilla in 1596 that is opposite the **Palazzo dei Cavalieri** (Knights Palace) is dedicated to this order. On its facade you'll find floral displays, symbols, coats of arms as well as sacred and profane images which are described as graffito style decorations. In niches above the second row of windows you'll find six busts of Tuscan grand dukes, from Cosimo I to Cosimo III de Medici.

The other buildings in this irregularly shaped piazza were built in the 16th and 17th centuries and include the **Church of St. Stephen's**, next to the Palazzo dei Cavalieri on the eastern side. On the western sides is the **Palazzo del Collegio Puteano** built in 1605. The southern side is occupied by the **Palazzo del Consiglio** (Council Chambers) of the order of the Knights of St. Stephen. On the northern side is the **Palazzo dell'Orologio** (Clock Palace). In the same piazza, next to the Palazzo dell'Orologio, the infamous **Muda Tower** (Tower of Hunger) used to sit. This was where Count Ugolino della

Gherardesca was imprisoned with his sons and nephews in 1288 and left to starve to death. This situation was recorded for all to remember in Dante's *Inferno*.

If you're walking from the train station to the Leaning Tower walk through this piazza. It's a nice place to sit and watch Pisan life pass you by.

F. PIAZZA GARIBALDI

This piazza is at the end of the Borgo Stretto with its covered walkways, and is brimming with real Pisan life – not the tourist trap situation like at the Piazza dei Miracoli. From here you are mere meters away from the Piazza Vettovaglie with its outdoor market, and are near the Ponte de Mezzo, from which you can see the beautiful palazzi lining the Arno as it meanders towards the sea. If you are walking from the train station you will most probably pass over this bridge and through this piazza to get to the Piazza dei Miracoli. The area around the Piazza Garibaldi will give you a genuine feel for the real life in Pisa.

G. PIAZZA VETTOVAGLIE

There's a market in this square every morning from 7:00am to 1:30pm. Just off the Via Stretto, here you'll find the hustle and bustle of a small Italian market, with vendors hawking their wares rather vocally. You'll find everything from produce to used clothes in the stalls and around the piazza are little shops that compliment the food being sold outdoors. There are butchers, alimentari, and bakers so that the Pisan housewife can get all she needs here to make her family's daily meals.

The market spills out onto the Via Domenico Cavalca and around the corner. Great sights, sounds, and smells to remember Pisa by. Also, the street just mentioned has a variety of different little restaurants to sample if the market's wares have tempted your appetite.

H. BORGO STRETTO

If you can't get to Bologna to see their famous covered streets, this road has a little taste of it for you. The sidewalks are covered so this street is always filled with people whatever the weather. Just look out for the motor scooters and bicycles that find their way up on the sidewalk at those times. You'll also find street performers and mimes entertaining the bustling crowds. You can either people-watch or shop at the many delightful stores. The market in the Piazza Vettoglie is just off this street.

Practical Information
Car Rental
• **Avis**, Airport, *Tel. 050/42028*
• **Hertz**, Airport, *Tel. 050/49187*

Tourist Information
• **Piazza Duomo**, to the right of the Camposanto, *Tel. 050/560-464.*
• **Piazza Stazione**, just as you exit the doors of the station the office is located directly on the left, *Tel. 050/42-291.* They can give you a map to guide your way through the streets to the sights.

LUCCA

Try not to miss this city. Instead of making this a one-day adventure, I highly recommend staying at least one or two days to savor its beauty and charm. Located 46 miles west of Florence and 14 miles northeast of Pisa, **Lucca** is closer to Pisa than to Florence and it is still one of the least visited cities in Tuscany, but we guidebook writers are starting to change that.

Most motorists coming from the north drive past in their haste to get to Pisa, and most people arriving from Florence fail to take the hour ride further north because Lucca doesn't have an architectural anomaly like the Leaning Tower of Pisa. But what Lucca has, even with a slowly growing tourist trade, is charm, and lots of it.

Lucca's Walls

Lucca main attractions are its walled fortifications surrounding the city. Originally designed to keep marauding Florentines at bay, they are now the site of a flowering greenbelt around the city. This tree-lined garden path on top of the walls and encompassing the ramparts of the old fortifications extends clear around the city and is perfect for a passegiatta (slow stroll). A peaceful and enchanting activity any time of the day. The garden walkway has a thin sliver of asphalt which bicyclists and roller bladers share with strolling pedestrians. But on either side of the walkway is grass, countless trees and shrubs that make this city a wonderfully romantic paradise.

At the battlements, of which there are 10, each coincidentally shaped like a heart, there are plenty of places to cuddle with your loved one, or sit at a wooden table and have a calming afternoon picnic. If you're with a family, the kids can roam free, exploring the nooks and crannies of the walls, while you and your spouse enjoy brief interludes of serenity.

Besides the walls, which with Ferrarra's are the best preserved in Italy, Lucca offers a tight grid road system, a remnant of its Roman occupation, which now gives it the feel of a compact Renaissance town. In this labyrinth of a city is **San Michel in Foro**, which is located on what used to be Lucca's Forum. Every column on this church is different, some are intertwined like corkscrews, some doubled, and some carved with medieval looking monsters.

Often confused with San Michel is Lucca's **Cathedral**. The Duomo rests at the end of the Via Duomo in Piazza San Martino. This structure is perhaps the most outstanding example of the Pisan style of architecture outside of Pisa.

Its porch with three arches, and three levels of colonnades, give it an unusual facade, but typically Pisan.

Explore Lucca!

Besides these sights, Lucca is a city to explore. You can walk its labyrinth of tiny streets and feel a part of the Renaissance. Through your exploration you will find the busy shopping area around Via Fillungo, the 12th century church of **San Frediano**, the Roman **amphitheater** (a must-see so you can compare the different centuries and cultures combined into modern day life), the **Torre Giungi**, which is the tower that overlooks the city. It has one special feature, a garden complete with full-grown trees on the top. Here you can take fine panoramic pictures of the area. Besides these there are plenty of other discoveries waiting for you in Lucca.

Arrivals & Departures

Car is quickest, about one hour away from Florence on the A11 past Prato and Pistoia, two excellent destinations on their own. So if you stop at them, the trip will take somehwat longer. When driving in Italy always remember to *Fare il Pieno* (fill 'er up) whenever you stop for gas, because sometimes gas stations are few and far between.

Trains from Florence take between an hour and an hour and a half depending on how many stops the train has to make. As of press time the trains that depart Florence for Lucca every two to three hours, returning at the same intervals. Make sure you check all this information prior to your departure if you're going for a one-day adventure.

Where to Stay

1. **DIANA**, *Via del Moinetto 11, Tel. 0583/492-202, Fax 0583/47-795. Email: info@albergodiana.com. Web: www.albergodiana.com. Credit cards accepted. 9 rooms, 8 with bath. Single without bath E40-50; Double E60-70.* ******

A nice small hotel in a great location down a cute side street deep in the heart of Medieval Lucca. If you want to stay inside the walls of Lucca at this place, it's best to book in advance, because with its location and relatively inexpensive prices, this hotel is always in great demand. They also have higher end rooms in their "Dependance" section that cost a little more, but a worth it.

2. **LA LUNA**, *Via Fillungo, Corte Compagni 12, Tel. 0583/493-634, Fax 0583/490-021. Email: laluna@onenet.it. Web: www.hotellaluna.com. Credit cards accepted. 30 rooms. Single E70-80; Double E100-110.* *******

This is a professionally run small hotel with beautiful rooms done up in antiques and a comfortable lobby bar area in which to relax. This hotel and the Puccini are the two best places to stay inside the old city walls. The restaurant

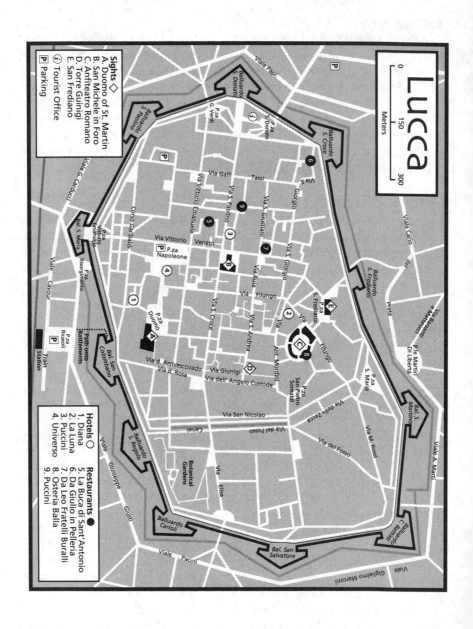

in the tiny square, Pizzeria Italia, though not written up here, is worthy of a visit.

3. PUCCINI, *Via di Poggio 9, Tel. 0583/55421 or 53487, Fax 0583/53487. Email: info@hotelpuccini.com, Web: www.hotelpuccini.com. 14 rooms. Single E60; Double E90. Credit cards accepted. ****

Located right up from the *Piazza San Michelle*, this is a beautifully appointed little three-star hotel that has all necessary amenities. The lobby is small but the accommodations are intimate, comfortable and cozy. The Puccini playing in the lobby is a soothing addition. This is the place to stay in Lucca despite the condescending attitude of the staff.

4. UNIVERSO, *Piazza del Giglio 1 (next to the Piazza Napoleone). Tel. 0583/493-678, Fax 0583/954-854. Credit cards Accepted. 72 rooms. Single E100; Double E150. ****

Established in the 11th century and wonderfully located on the Piazza del Giglio, this is a good option while in Lucca. The rooms are not that large but have all the amenities of a good three-star. It's ideally located near the station and the Duomo but its prices are a little too expensive for my taste. They have a wonderful little bar with seating on the square. A larger, less intimate place than most of the other hotels in Lucca. A close third behind Puccini and La Luna.

Where to Eat

5. LA BUCA DI SANT'ANTONIO, *Via della Cervia 1/3, Tel. 0583/55881. Closed Sunday evenings, Mondays, and in July. All credit cards accepted. Dinner for two E50.*

This is an exceptional restaurant, the most classic and traditional of all places in Lucca. In a splendid location directly behind Piazza San Michele, the atmosphere in here is 19th century opulence. The cooking is festively local with many meat dishes to choose from, as well as tasty grilled vegetables. And the dessert cart is not to be missed. Make reservations here, and dress well when dining. Appearance is important here.

6. DA GIULIO IN PELLERIA, *Via delle Conce 45, Tel. 0583/55948. Closed Sundays and Mondays, and in August. Credit cards accepted. Dinner for two E40.*

A quaint and colorful local trattoria whose menu has not changed for at least 25 years. All sorts of meat and vegetable dishes abound, as well as rustic pies that combine both ingredients. The prices have risen in the past few years because of this places popularity, but they are still reasonable. Come here for fine local cooking in a rustic, authentic atmosphere.

7. DA LEO FRATELLI BURALLI, *Via Tegrimi 1, 55100 Lucca. Tel. 0583/ 492-236. Closed Sundays. No credit cards accepted. Dinner for two E30.*

When in Lucca, don't miss this place. If you're going to have one meal (or two, or three) have it here, but not outside in the thin sliver of seating area on a small side street. You have to come inside and truly the enjoy the vibrancy of this Luccan staple. The energy inside is electric with friends calling to each other across the room, and the food clattering down in front of you as it is served. Try the fettucine all rucola e gamberi (with cheese and shrimp) or the pasta al pomodoro e ragu (with tomato and meat sauce). For seconds sample the pollo arrosto con patate (roasted chicken with potatoes), a cold dish of prosciutto e mozzarella (ham and mozzarella), or some pollo fritto e zucchini (fried chicken and zucchini).

8. OSTERIA BARALLA, *Via Anfiteatro 5, Tel. 0583/44-0240. Closed Sundays and in August. No credit cards accepted. Dinner for two E30.*

After ten years this place has re-opened to rave reviews, and has re-immersed itself into the social life of Lucca. A true local, hosteria that has been painstakingly restored to offer a colorful ambiance. And under the tutelage of chef Alessandro Carmassi, the food is exquisite and traditional. An excellent choice for a meal while in Lucca.

9. PUCCINI, *Corte San Lorenzo 1, 55100 Lucca. Tel. 0583/316-116, Fax 0583/316-031. Web: speweb.monrif.net/prodotti/ristorantepuccini/. Dinner for two E55.*

An expensive but pleasant restaurant that has a somewhat modern ambiance. Try the antipasto di mare (seafood antipasto) or the penne agli scampi (pasta with shrimp). For seconds, I recommend the grigliata mista (mixed grilled meats from Tuscany). A definitely high class eatery that requires proper attire.

Seeing the Sights

Lucca is like a medieval town come to life, with its tiny twisting streets and its converted walls and battlements. It is a great place to explore. Some of the best sights to see include the following:

A. THE DUOMO OF ST. MARTIN

Open 7:00am–7:00pm.

This is perhaps the most outstanding example of Pisan style outside of Pisa. It was begun in the 11th century and completed in the 15th. The facade has three levels of colonnades with three different sized arches. Behind and on the arches are beautiful 12th and 13th century bas-reliefs and sculptures. If you look hard enough you can find a column carved with the tree of life with Adam and Eve crouched at the bottom and Christ at the top, as well as a variety of hunting scenes with real and fantastic animals, dancing dragons, and more, all created by anonymous artists.

The dark interior is a showcase for Lucca's most famous artist, **Matteo Civitali** whose work has not escaped beyond the walls of Lucca. Rumor has it that until his mid-thirties, a ripe old age for some at that time, he was a barber, when he then decided he'd rather be a sculptor. His most famous work is the octagonal *Tempietto* done in 1489. It is a marble tabernacle in the middle of the left aisle. It contains a cedar crucifix, The *Volto Santo* (Holy Image) which is said to have the true portrait of Jesus sculpted on it by Nicodemus, an eyewitness to the crucifixion. Every September 13th the image is removed to join a candlelight procession around town.

Further up the left aisle you can find Fra Bartolomeo's *Virgin and Child Enthroned* as well as the *Tomb of Ilaria del Caretto*, a magnificent work by the Siennese artist Jacopo della Quercia. You will also find the Madonna *Enthroned with Saints* by Domenico Ghirlandaio and a strange *Last Supper* with a nursing mother in the foreground and what looks like cherubs floating above Christ's head.

B. SAN MICHELE IN FORO
Open 7:00am – 7:00pm.

This church is so grand that most people mistake it for Lucca's cathedral. It is located in the old Roman Forum and is a masterpiece of Pisan Gothic architecture. The huge facade rises above the level of the roof, making the church look even larger and grander. You'll notice that every column in the five levels of Pisan-style arcading is different. Some will be twisting, some doubling, some carved with relief monsters and more.

While the entire facade is quite ornate and elaborate, the interior is more austere. It is best known for the place where Puccini started his musical career as a choirboy. As a reminder of this, just down the small road directly in front of the church is a wonderfully intimate place to hang your hat, the Piccolo Hotel Puccini. Besides the memory of Puccini, the interior of San Michelle in Foro contains a glazed terra-cotta *Madonna and Child*, a 13th-century *Crucifixion* hanging over the high altar, and a memorable painting of saints that lived during the plague years.

C. ANFITEATRO ROMANO
A remarkable relic dating from Lucca's ancient Roman past is the **Roman Amphitheater**. Today it is lined with medieval houses, some of which have shops and restaurants on the ground floor. Any marble that was once here was used to build the Cathedral and San Michele. An amazingly well preserved relic from the past despite that desecration.

A great place to lounge at a café, read a book, write some postcards, or watch the Italian children playing their never ending game of calcio. A must see destination while in Lucca.

D. TORRE GUINIGIO
Open 9:00am–7:00pm in the summer and 10:00am–4:00pm in the winter. Admission E3.

A tower rising above a neighborhood that has scarcely changed in 500 years. Here the medieval ancestors of the **Guinigi** family had their stronghold with the tower as their lookout. One of Lucca's landmarks, it is also one of the most elaborate medieval family fortresses.

From the top you have the greatest views over all of Lucca. It's just a short walk up the 230-plus steps to reach the lush garden on the top, complete with trees sprouting from the ramparts. Remember to bring your camera and take some great pictures.

E. SAN FREDIANO
Open 7:00am–7:00pm.
A rather tall church with an even taller campanile (bell tower), both built in the 12th century and completed with colorful mosaics in the 13th century. The interior contains a magnificent baptismal font which is covered with bas-reliefs. The chapels around the central nave are elaborately decorated.

Also inside is the **mummy of St. Zita**, patroness of domestic servants. She was canonized in 1696, long after her birth in 1218. She put in many years of service as a servant for a rich family in Lucca with whom she stayed until her death. She is revered for her selfless acts of charity towards the poor, and now she is pickled in a coffin in Lucca.

Practical Information
Car Rental
• **Avis**, Viale Luporini 1411, *Tel. 0583/51-36-14*
• **Hertz**, Via Catalani 59, *Tel. 0583/58585*

Tourist Information
• **APT**, Vecchia Porta San Donato/Piazzale Verdi. *Tel 0583/419-689*. Hours 9:00am–7:00pm. You can get a map, a list of hotels, or better yet, they can actually help you find the hotel you want and point you in the right direction.

SIENA
Siena is generally described as the feminine counterpart to the masculine Florence, and even its nickname, **City of the Virgin**, belies this feminine quality. Located 42 miles south of Florence, this picturesque walled city is known for its many quality buildings, narrow and hilly streets, immense churches, and ambiant little restaurants. However, the two reasons why I love Siena are that cars are banned from the center of the city, making for a pleasant walking environment (similar to Venice but without the water); and also because of the biannual event called the **Palio**.

Siena is a great place to visit, with plenty to see and do, not the least of which is to be absorbed into the Tuscan pace of life. One slight draw back is that, even though Siena has only around one third the population of Florence, sometimes it seems that there are three times as many. This is because of the layout of the town, where only the streets on the tops of the ridges that the town is built on, are used. This channels most of the population, walking mind you, down the same well trodden streets. The blessing in disguise here, is that just off this beaten path are peaceful alleys and streets, containing unique discoveries to be made.

Another unique feature of Siena is that right inside the old cities walls, also as a result of the layout of the town, with the most of the houses on ridges overlooking valleys, you can find farmland. In the valleys between the ridges of the town, you can see rural life being expressed, complete with roosters crowing and plants being tended and harvested. All of which lends a peaceful and serene quality to all of Siena.

Siena was once a prosperous and artistic city in its own right even before it was absorbed into the Grand Duchy of Tuscany in 1559, which was ruled by Florence. Once it became a part of Florence, Siena was not allowed to pursue its previously prosperous mercantile activities, such as their flourishing wool trade. Because of these actions, and the general despotic rule of Florence, Siena fell into a long period of decline. But today, as other Italian cities have also, Siena has learned how to succeed by marketing its ancient charm. Part of this charm are the well-preserved walls with towers and bulwarks of Siena, which are seven kilometers long and were built from the 13th to the 15th centuries. The old **Fortrezza Medicea** on the outskirts of town is now public gardens. The perfect place to watch the sunset in Siena.

Arrivals & Departures
By Car
Either take the Florence-Siena Superstrada or the slower but more scenic Route 22 that runs through the heart of the Chianti wine region. From Rome take the A1 to the Via di Chiana exit, then head west on route 326 into Siena. You'll have to leave your car at one of the many parking lots on the outskirts of the city center, since no automobiles are allowed into the city.

By Train
From Florence and Rome there are over a dozen trains a day. The trip takes 1 1/2 hours. The train station is located one mile from the center of the city. To get to the centro, just exit the station, cross the piazza and street and catch either bus 15, 2, or 6 and they will all take you into town. Everything from that point on is walking distance. Or take a cab, and it will only be around E5.

Where to Stay
1. DUOMO, *Via Stalloreggi 34-38, 53100 Siena. Tel. 0577/289-088, Fax 0577/43-043. Web: www.hotelduomo.it. Credit cards accepted. 25 rooms. Single E120; Double E150.* ***
Comes with all the amenities of a three-star, including cable TV for those

in need of such entertainment. Located in part of an old palazzo just a little distance away from the Campo, this is a good place to stay within reach of all major sights. The rooms are simply furnished but clean and comfortable.

2. GRAND HOTEL CONTINENTAL, *Via Banchi di Sopra 85, Tel. 0577/ 56011. Fax 0577/560-1555. Web: www.royaldemeure.com. Single E200-280. Double E310-620. Suite E1,200-1,400. Breakfast E27. All credit cards accepted.* *****

Top of the line. The best hotel in Siena. Also the most pricey/ But what elegance, and refinement, and service. A jewel of a hotel on one of the main walking streets in Siena. Here you are in the middle of everything and offered nothing but the best. Stay here if you have the means.

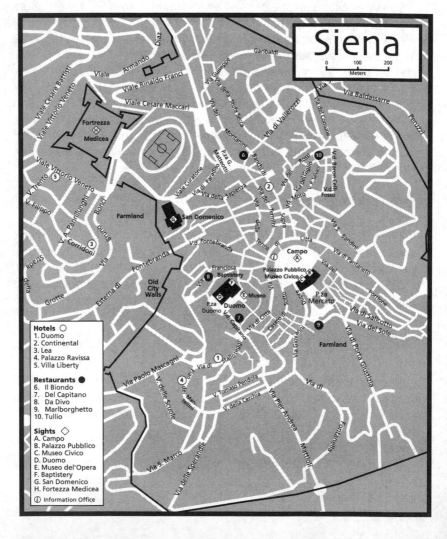

3. **LEA**, *Viale XXIV Maggio 10, 53100 Siena. Tel & Fax 0577/283-207. Email: hotellea@libero.it. Web: www.italiaabc.it/az/lea. 12 rooms. Single E50; Double E70. All credit cards accepted. Breakfast included.* ******

Situated in a small villa from the 1800s, in a tranquil residential area near the center, surrounded by a small garden set with tables and chairs. From the top floors you get a magnificently unique view into the heart of Siena. This hotel offers great prices, spacious rooms, direct dial telephones, simple but comfortable furnishings and well decorated bathrooms. In the morning breakfast is a basic continental fare served in the same room that accommodates the bar and reception area. A great two-star in Siena. A budget travelers paradise.

4. **PALAZZO RAVIZZA**, *Pian dei Mantellini 34, Tel. 0577/280 462, Fax 0577/221-597. Email: bureau@palazzoravizza.it, Web: www.palazzoravizza.it. 30 rooms. E100-140; Double E110-280. Breakfast included. All credit cards accepted.* *******

A quality place to stay in Siena since 1929. The hotel has been owned by the same family for about two hundred years. Situated in a tranquil spot in the centro storico with good views over the city and the surrounding countryside, the furnishings are antique and the atmosphere wonderful. Buffet breakfast is served in their beautiful garden terrace, that has a pleasant view. Evenings can be spent in the large tavern room. Truly a great three-star in Siena and the prices show it.

5. **VILLA LIBERTY**, *Viale Vittorio Veneto 11, 53100 Siena. Tel. 0577/449-666, Fax 0577/44770. Email: info@villaliberty.it. Web: www.villaliberty.it. 12 rooms. Single E130; Double E160. All credit cards accepted. Breakfast included.* *******

Just a little ways outside the walls of Siena near the *fortrezza* this hotel has been renovated in an eclectic Liberty style. Each room is well furnished and comfortable. Everything about this place is accommodating. More of a bed and breakfast than a Holiday Inn. Definitely not a 'cookie-cutter' hotel. A fine choice if you some to Siena. Also, the back garden is a great place to relax in warm weather.

Where to Eat

Siena specialties include **cioccina** (a special variation on pizza) **pici** (thick Tuscan spaghetti served with a variety of sauces), and **pancetta** (sausages and chicken breast added to tomatoes and cooked with red wine).

Siena is also known for its different varieties of salamis that you can buy at any alimentari. **Soppressata**, either sweet or hot, is an excellent salami with black peppercorns added. **Buristo** is heavily spiced salami. **Finocchiona** is made of peppered sausage meat seasoned with fennel seeds. And **Salsiccioli Secchi** are made from lean crusts of pork or boar, spiced with garlic and black or red pepper.

6. **IL BIONDO**, *Vicolo del Rustichetto 10, Tel./Fax 0577/280-739. Closed Wednesdays. Dinner for two E40.*

The ambiance on their terrace is peaceful, and the food is great. Inside it is a plain whitewashed Sienese-style restaurant. They make some good pasta here including spaghetti alla vongole (with clam sauce) and penne alla puttanesca (literally translated it means whore's pasta, made with tomatoes, garlic, black olives, olive oil and meat). For seconds, try the saltimbocca alla Romana (veal shank stewed in tomatoes and spices) or the bistecca alla griglia (beef steak cooked on the grill that would make a Texan proud).

7. **DEL CAPITANO**, *Via del Capitano 6/8. Tel. 0577/288-094. Closed Tuesdays. Most credit cards accepted. Dinner for two E22.*

Small place just down from the Duomo. The atmosphere is typically austere with brick ceiling and whitewashed walls. The food is good and inexpensive. Try the penne all'arrabbiata (with a tomato, garlic, pepper sauce), the spaghetti alla carbonara (with cheese, ham, and egg), or the ravioli all quattro formaggi (thick sauce with four cheeses). For secondo, try the bistecca di maiale (pork steak) or the omelette al formaggio (cheese omelet).

8. DA DIVO, *Via Franciosa 25, Tel. 0577/284-381. Credit crds accepted. Dinner for two E60.*

Two hundred meters form the campo, located behind the Duomo, well off the beaten tourist path, this place has fabulous ambiance and great food. An high end establishment, frequented by locals in search of a superb meal, I cannot recommend this place too highly. Come here and savor a well created and presented Sienese meal.

9. MARLBORGHETTO, *Via di Porta Giustizia 6, Tel. 0577/289-258. Web: www.marlborghetto.it. Closed Tuesdays. Dinner for Two E50.*

Located behind the Campo, just off the Piazza Mercato, in a serene setting with a view of farmland. Yes, you hear correctly, farmland. Complete with clucking chickens, having a meal here is like being in the country, but it is only 100 meters from the center of Siena. As the city is perched mainly on the tops of hills, some of valleys between them have retained their rural nature. Only in America has suburban sprawl decimated both urban and rural areas. So come here to get away from the urban bustle of Siena, sit on their relaxing terrace, and savor their excellent local cuisine.

10. TULLIO, *Vicolo di Provenzano 1, Tel. 0577/280-608. Closed Wednesdays. Credit cards accepted. Dinner for two E50.*

Completely local, boisterously Italian, and serving great local cuisine. Everything from pasta to seafood to huge bistecca fiorentian is served here. Well service is haphazard at best, but who's quibbling. The ambiance is charmingly rustic, and the restaurant is located well off the beaten path, keeping the tourist influx to a minimum. But remember to request to be seated in the non-smoking section if smoking bothers you.

Seeing the Sights
The Palio Race

During the biannual **Palio**, held on July 2 and August 16, is the best time to visit Siena because of the Medieval pageantry, and the worst time to visit because of the crowds. The Palio is a festival awash in colorful banners, historic events, and a wild bareback horse race that runs three times around the **Piazza del Campo**. The race lasts all of 90 seconds but will leave you with memories for a lifetime.

A palio literally is an embroidered banner, the prize offered for winning the race. The first official Palio was run in 1283, though many say the custom dates back farther than that. During the Middle Ages, besides the horse races, there were violent games of primeval rugby (which you can see in Florence twice a year during their **Calcio in Costume** festival) and even bullfights to settle neighborhood bragging rights.

The contestants in the Palio horse race itself are jockeys from the seventeen neighborhood parishes or contrade in Siena. During a Palio ten horses ride in the first race and seven horses ride in the next since the square is not big enough to accommodate all the horses at once. The jockeys willingly risk life and limb for the pride of their small area of the city. At two places in the Piazza del Campo there are right angles at which the horses have to turn, and usually at these points you'll have at least one jockey lose his seat or a horse its footing.

But this is more than a horse race. It is actually a community-wide regression into the Middle Ages, with the coats-of-arms representing each contrade (neighborhood) being displayed prominently by members.

Prior to the Palio race there is a good two hour display of flag throwing by the alferi of each contrada, while the medieval **carroccio** (carriage), drawn by a white oxen, circles the Campo bearing the prized palio each neighborhood wants to claim as its own. The flags and coats-of-arms for each contrade are a colorful collectible whether you come during the Palio or at another time.

To witness this event you have to plan way in advance, since the Palio is jam-packed. You can see the Palio in one of three ways: in the center of the Piazza where people are packed like sardines on a first come first serve basis; in the viewing stands which cost anywhere from E100 to E175; or in one of the offices or apartments that line the piazza. To view from these prime locations, you need to know someone in one of the offices. The Palio is well worth a visit to Siena.

A. THE CAMPO

Eleven streets lead into the square where, in the past, the people of Siena used to assemble at the sound of the **Sunto bell** to learn the latest news. Today it still is the gathering place for all the locals and tourists. You will see at most times of the day the young lounging on the stones and their elders congregating at cafés. The piazza is concave and irregular with a ring of rather austere buildings surrounding it, but even so it is a marvel of architectural harmony. On the curved side of the Campo sits the **Fonte Gaia** (Gay Fountain) made by Jacopo della Quercia. The water from this fountain comes here from 30 km away through a series of pipes and aqueducts from the 13th century.

On the map the Campo looks flat, but it's actually a gradually sloping surface with bricks that seem to float down to the **Palazzo Pubblico**. The campo is a great place to grab a bite to eat at one of the many restaurants, sip a drink at one of the cafés, or to simply rest your tired tourist feet by relaxing on the cobblestone slope.

B. PALAZZO PUBBLICO

At the Campo. Tower open 10:00am–dusk. In the winter open only until 1:30pm. Admission E3.

One of the most attractive and imposing Gothic buildings in all of Tuscany. Most of it was built between 1297 and 1340, with the top story being erected in 1639. This building reflected the wealth and success of Siena, which was almost the same size as London and Paris during the fourteenth century. The little chapel underneath the tower was dedicated by the town to the Virgin Mary when the terrible plague known as the Morte Nera (Black Death) came to an end. In Siena 65,000 people died of the plague in the summer of 1348. That was over half of their population. And about every 7-10 years, the plague would return, decimating the population even further.

The best part of this building is the **Torre del Mangia**. It offers the greatest sights in all of Siena. Unfortunately you have to climb up 400, small steps in a crowded stairway, to top of the bell tower. It is 112 meters high, was built in 1334, and is still in amazing shape. The clock was made in 1360 and

Neighborhood Symbols

On the sides of buildings all over Siena are old metal holders for firebrands, which long ago were used to light the streets at night prior to the advent of electricity. There are also metal rings where citizens could tie up their horses. In each of the separate neighborhoods, or contrade, these functional decorations feature the image of that particular neighborhood. Once there were 59 contrade, but through consolidation only 17 remain: Aquila (eagle), Bruco (caterpillar), Chiocciola (snail), Civetta (owl), Drago (dragon), Giraffa (giraffe), Istrice (porcupine), Leocorno (unicorn), Lupa (she-wolf), Nicchio (shell), Oca (goose), Onda (wave), Pantera (panther), Selva (wood), Tartuca (turtle), Torre (tower), and Valdimontone (ram).

the huge bell was raised to its present position in 1666. Imagine having to haul a bell that weighs 6,764 kilos up a pulley system to the top of the tower? Remember to bring your camera because the views of the countryside and the city are stupendous.

C. MUSEO CIVICO

At the Campo. Open 9:30am–7:30pm Monday–Saturday. Open Sunday 9:30am–1:30pm.

Inside the Palazzo Pubblico is the **Museo Civico**, which is filled with many wonderful paintings, frescoes, mosaics, tapestries, and sculptures. One of which is *Dolore*, Sadness, and features a seated man caught in the throes of that emotion. Upstairs is the famous **Sala del Mappamondo** (Hall of the Map of the World). From its large windows you can look out onto the market square. The other three walls are frescoed with scenes of the religious and civil life of the Siena Republic. In this museum you'll find many examples of the some of the finest Sienese art available.

D. THE DUOMO

Piazza del Duomo. 7:30am–1:30pm and 3:00pm to dusk from December to March. From March to November open 9:00am–7:30pm.

The combination of Gothic and Romanesque architectural elements in the Cathedral of Siena is a result of the large amount of time spent completing it. Despite being incredibly elaborate the facade seems quite harmonious and attractive. The side walls and steeple are striped black and white like the 'Balzana' that is the standard of the town. It was started in 1200 and finished in the 1400s.

Inside the cathedral there is an even more decorative array filling the three naves that are 90 meters long and 51 meters high. The walls are covered with the white and black Balzana stripes. All around the nave you'll see a row of 172 busts of Popes, from Christ to Lucius III, all made in 1400. Beneath them are 36 busts of Roman Emperors. The inlaid floor contains a succession of scenes from the Old Testament, which took from 1372 to 1551 to complete. The earlier ones are done in black and white, and the later scenes have a touch of gray and red in them.

You can't miss the intricate and elaborate pulpit made by **Nicola Pisano** from 1265 to 1268. It is made of dirty white marble and supported by nine darker marble columns resting on four lions. There are 300 human figures and 70 animal figures decorating this delightful work. Besides the pulpit there are countless remarkable paintings, sculptures, reliefs, and stone coffins all throughout the church. The statues on the Piccolo altar have been attributed to **Michelangelo**. In the **Piccolomini Library** you'll find beautiful frescoes of the life of Pope Pius II made by the master Pinturicchio (Admission E2). As you leave the library you'll see the monument to Archbishop Bandini's nephews made in 1570 by Michelangelo.

There were plans to have made this cathedral a small part of a much larger place of worship; but those plans were stunted for a variety of reasons, including the plague and the eventual Florentine conquest of the city. Today, to the right of the Duomo as you face it, near the rear, only a few pillars and walls remain from the plans for that grandiose church.

E. MUSEO DELL'OPERA DEL DUOMO
Piazza del Duomo. 7:30am–1:30pm and 3:00pm to dusk from December to March. From March to November open 9:00am–7:30pm. Admission E3.

In the **museum of the cathedral** is a valuable collection of the treasure of paintings, statues, and fragments the cathedral once displayed. One of the best paintings is Duccio di Buoninsegna's *Maestra* (1308-1311) that was originally on the high altar. You'll find a group of three sculptures, the *Three Graces*, which are Greek works of the 2nd century BCE that were once in the Piccolomini Library. And you can't miss the exquisitely beautiful goldsmith's work, *Rosa d'Oro* (Golden Rose) that was given to the city of Siena by Alessandro VIII in 1658. Another work of interest is the plan of the unfinished facade of the Baptistery by Giacomo di Mino del Pelliciaio.

F. BAPTISTERY OF SAN GIOVANNI
Piazza del Duomo. Open 9:00am–1:00pm and 3:00pm–5:00pm year round. In the summer open until 7:00pm.

Here you can find the **baptismal fonts** by Jacopo della Quercia, the bronze bas-relief of Bishop Pecci by Donatello, and many bronze reliefs of the Old and New Testament. The Baptistery was begun in 1315, but its facade has never been finished.

G. CHURCH OF SAN DOMENICO
Costa San Antonio. Church is open from 9:00am–6:00pm. The Sanctuary is closed 12:30pm–3:30pm Monday–Saturday and all day Sundays.

The Basilica is plain both inside and out, while containing some beautiful works of art. It is a monumental and solitary structure overlooking the surrounding landscape and city. Its simple brick architecture of the 13th century was modified in the 14th and 15th centuries but still remains more like the walls of a convent than a church. Next to the sacristy is the **chapel of St. Caterina** where the saint's head is preserved in a silver reliquary. In the other chapels of the church, and along the walls, you'll find paintings by Sienese artists of the 14th through 16th centuries.

H. FORTREZZA MEDICEA
Via C Maccari.

Not much to see here other than a converted fort into a park where people stroll, joggers exercising, and lovers play. Also the bets place in the city to watch the sunset. Come here for a respite from the urban arena. Bring a book, a picnic lunch, find a place to sit, and relax. There is also a place to eat and shop here, the **Enoteca Italiana**, wine store and enoteche, to the right and left, inside the ramparts, as you enter.

Practical Information
Car Rental
· **Avis**, Via Simone Martini 36, *Tel. 0577/27 03 05*
· **Hertz**, Hotel Lea, Via XXIV Maggio, *Tel. 0577/45085*

Tourist Information
· **Piazza San Domenico**, *Tel 0577/940-809*. Get maps and hotel reservations here if needed. Open 9:00am to 7:00pm.

FIESOLE
Fiesole is five miles east of Florence on a hill overlooking the city. Well before Florence existed, Fiesole dominated this part of the Arno valley. One of the 12 important towns of ancient **Roman Etruria** from 80 BCE on, and later was named the capital city of Roman Etruria. However, in 1125 CE all this dominance came to an end, when Florence sacked and began its control of Fiesole and all of Tuscany. After the takeover, Fiesole was used by many of the Medici family as a refuge from the toil of governing, and the heat of the summer.

Even today Fiesole is a great respite from the heat or the hectic pace of Florence. And it's only a 20 minute bus ride from Florence (the buses leave from the station every 15 minutes). This is a tranquil location for a family vacation that offers access to Florence quickly and easily.

Besides being a refuge, Fiesole's archaeological excavations offers visitors a small glimpse into the ancient past. There are also many fine churches and vistas to enjoy.

Website: *www.comune.fiesole.fi.it.*

Arrivals & Departures
By Bus or Taxi
The easiest and least expensive way to get to Fiesole from Florence is to take the #7 bus from the Piazza della Stazione. The ride takes only 20 minutes. If you take a taxi take just as long and cost you about $25.

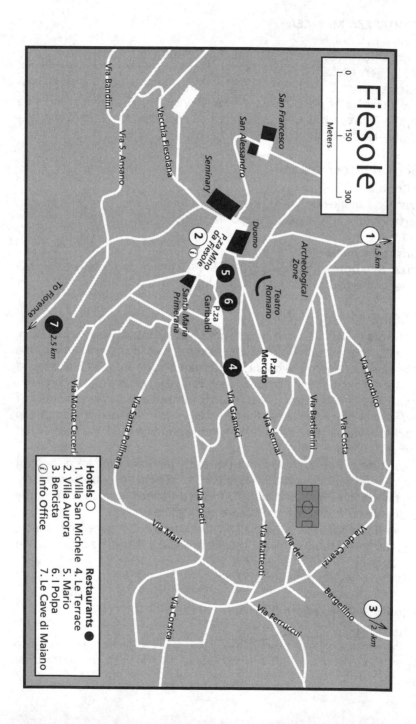

You catch the bus at the side of the train station in Florence under the awnings. Tickets are sold at the Giornalaio inside the station or at the ticket office catty-corner to the bus stop outside. Tickets cost E2.

Where to Stay

1. VILLA SAN MICHELE, *Via Doccia 4, Tel. 055/59-451, Fax 055/598-734, Web: www.villasanmichele.orient-express.com. 36 rooms. Credit cards accepted. Single E600; Double E800-950. Suite E1,100-2,500. Breakfast included.* *****

Located in a converted monastery that has a facade attributed to Michelangelo. If nothing else this hotel will allow you to bring stories of beautiful views, ancient habitations, and opulent surroundings back home. The reception area of the hotel is an old chapel, and in the dining room, the bar is made from an ancient Etruscan sarcophagus. Each room has a four poster bed and everything else is rustically luxurious. The best rooms overlook the gardens that surround the hotel. This is *the* hotel for those of you with plenty of disposable income. Here you can enjoy an outdoor pool during the day, a wonderfully scenic view from the restaurant in the evening, and a boisterous piano bar at night.

2. VILLA AURORA, *Piazza Mino de Fiesole 39, Tel. 055/59-100 or 59-292, Fax 055/59-587. All credit cards accepted. 26 rooms. Single E100-145; Double E145-210 Breakfast costs E9.* ****

Here you've got everything a four-star can offer. If you want to stay in the central square, this is the place. The rooms are large and modern and all have wonderful views. The bathrooms have every modern convenience and some have phones. Attached to a good restaurant, this hotel used to be a theater and osteria for the wealthy patrons who stayed in the villas of Fiesole.

3. BENCISTA, *Via Benedetto da Maiano 4, 50014 Fiesole. Tel. 055/ 59163, Fax is the same. 42 rooms. Single E125; Double E150. Breakfast E7. No credit cards accepted.* ***

You'll need a car to get here as it outside of the town of Fiesole. You'll love the many public areas, all of which are appointed with antique furniture. The rooms (you have to ask for one with a view) are sober but elegant. Opened in 1925, this has been a favorite for travelers ever since. Their restaurant serves up great Tuscan meals made from the freshest ingredients. Breakfast, lunch, and dinner are served in a large room dominated by two large columns. Breakfast in the summer is out on the terrace. A good place to come and relax and recharge your batteries.

Where to Eat

4. LE TERRACE, *Viale Gramsci 19, 50014 Fiesole. Tel. 055/59-272. Closed Tuesdays. Credit cards accepted. Dinner for two E25.*

This is a huge place with both indoor and somewhat cramped outdoor seating, but with stupendous views of a lush green valley below. As you enter you'll pass by the brick wood-burning oven where they make a wide variety of pizzas that will please even the most discerning eater. Besides pizza they make good pastas. Some recommendations: tortellini alla panna e prosciutto (with cream and ham), and tagliatelli della casa (house favorite made with onions, sausage, saffron in a thick cream sauce). If you're interested in meat dishes, try their pollo fritto (chicken fried in olive oil), or the coniglio fritto (rabbit fried in olive oil) and compare whether rabbit really does taste like chicken.

5. MARIO, *Piazza Mino #9, 50014 Fiesole. Credit cards accepted. Dinner for two E37.*

They have two different menus rolled into one. A traditional menu and one they call a cucina creativa (creative cooking) menu. Both are rather sparse, so check them out in the window before you stop here to see if you want anything. They have outside seating on the main square, as well as a few tables inside. Some of the more creative dishes are the ravioline salmone e vongole (little ravioli with a salmon and clam sauce), and the filetto di coniglio alle mele (thin slices of rabbit served with apples).

6. I POLPA, *Piazza Mino #21/22, 50014 Fiesole. Tel. 055/59133. Credit cards accepted. Dinner for two E30.*

Try their country style bruschetta. They brush the coarse toasted garlic bread with succulent olive oil and cover it with fresh tomatoes. Then sample their pennette all fiesolana (with cream sauce and ham). If the meat bug hits you try the scaloppini ai funghi porcini (veal with porcini mushrooms). Reservations on the weekends are recommended.

7. LE CAVE DI MAIANO, *Via delle Cave 16, 50014 Fiesole. Tel. 055/59133. Closed Thursday and Sunday nights. All credit cards accepted. Dinner for two E50.*

One of the most popular restaurants for Florentines escaping their hectic, tourist-jammed city during the summer time. You'll need a car or will have to grab a cab from Fiesole, to get here, since it is about 3-4 kilometers outside of the town of Fiesole proper. You'll be served typical Tuscan food in a truly rustic atmosphere. The restaurant is blessed with a perfect garden environment. They specialize in all types of grilled, roasted, and fried meats.

Seeing the Sights

You can see everything there is to see in Fiesole in less than a day, so you can spend the rest of your time soaking up the great panoramic views, eating wonderful food, and celebrating the tranquillity with some Chianti. But remember, you are only 20 minutes away from the center of Florence by a bus that leaves at least twice an hour. So let me reiterate: if you like the splendor of Florence but can't seem to be able to stomach the noise and congestion, stay here in Fiesole. It will make your tour that much more pleasant and rewarding.

CATHEDRAL OF SAN ROMULUS

Piazza della Cattedrale (also Piazza Mino di Fiesole). Open daily 7:30am–noon and 4:00pm–7:00pm.

Built in the 11th century, the best part of this church is the bell tower whose chimes toll the half hour and the hour. You can hear it all over the countryside informing you of your place in the universe.

THE ARCHAEOLOGICAL ZONE

Open Winter 9:00am–6:00pm, Summer 9:00am–7:00pm. Closed on Tuesdays.

The museum itself houses epics from prehistoric, Etruscan, Roman and medieval times; but the best part of this place is the **Roman Theater**, partially restored, that dates back to the 1st century BCE. It's like a mini-Pompeii or Roman Forum.

ELSEWHERE IN FIESOLE

The steep five minute climb (if you're fit) from the west end of **Piazza Mino** up to the **Church of San Francesco** will give you wonderful views of Florence and the Arno valley, especially from the benches near the **Church of San Alessandro** (open daily 7:30am–noon and 4:00pm–7:00pm.) Remember to bring your camera. The Church of San Francesca itself is relatively nondescript, but the cloisters are worth seeing as is the small museum that has a few Etruscan remains and relics collected by Franciscan missionaries in the Orient many years ago.

Below the church you can see the public gardens and the **Basilica of S Alessandro**, which is on the site of the ancient **Roman temple of Bacchus** Gardens open 7:00am – 7:00pm; Basilica open same hours).

SAN GIMIGNANO

San Gimignano sits majestically on a hill overlooking the **Elsa valley**. Its earthen-colored walls contrast favorably with the surrounding green countryside. The most distinctive feature of this town are its amazing medieval towers. These structures help to create a magical atmosphere of timelessness, despite the hordes of tourists thundering through the tiny streets.

Don't get me wrong, San Gimignano is beautiful. Stunning actually. But if you come here in the summer, the peak of the high season, your experience will be tempered by a pushy polyglot ensemble of camera-toting tourists. But even then, this town is wonderful, as is Venice, Florence and other towns in Italy that also face an annual tourist inundation.

A small Etruscan village during the 3rd and the 2nd century BCE, the town's modern history started around the 10th century when it took its name from the saint himself, Bishop Gimignano. A former Bishop of Modena, he is said to have saved the village from barbarian hordes. After this magical salvation and during the Middle Ages, the town grew in importance because of its strategic location along well-traveled trade routes. This led to the commissioning of wonderful works of art that currently adorn the churches and monasteries in the area.

In 1199 the town became a free municipality, but then the depopulation caused by the Black Death in 1348 forced the town to submit to Florence's control. As the centuries slid by, and trade routes changed, San Gimignano

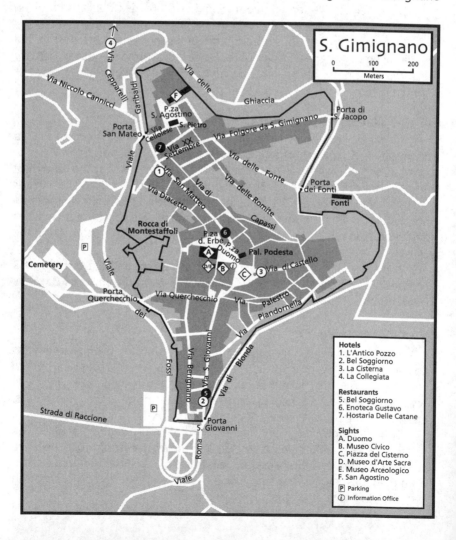

S. Gimignano

Hotels
1. L'Antico Pozzo
2. Bel Soggiorno
3. La Cisterna
4. La Collegiata

Restaurants
5. Bel Soggiorno
6. Enoteca Gustavo
7. Hostaria Delle Catane

Sights
A. Duomo
B. Museo Civico
C. Piazza del Cisterno
D. Museo d'Arte Sacra
E. Museo Arceologico
F. San Agostino

P Parking
ⓘ Information Office

overcame its lack of alternate economic resources by offering its beauty, charm, and cultural heritage as a tourist draw. Despite its modern success, the full time population of the town is still less than it was prior to the Black Death more than 650 years ago!

Arrivals & Departures
By Car
From the north take route 429, from the south the same road is numbered as route 2. Get off at Castel Fiorentino and follow the signs to San Gimignano. Prior to embarking on this trip, please take the time to pick up a road map.

By Train
Take the local train from Florence to Empoli. From here catch a local bus or taxi up to the town.

Where to Stay
1. L' ANTICO POZZO, *Via San Matteo 87, Tel. 0577/942-014, Fax 0577/ 942-117. Email: info@anticopozzo.com, Web: www.anticopozzo.com/. 18 rooms. Single E90; Double E150. All credit cards accepted. Breakfast included.* ***

Located in the center of town in a magnificent 15th century palazzo, this hotel is a wonderful place to stay. Completely restored with all modern amenities, including tasteful furnishings and accommodating restroom facilities, you will be more than comfortable here, while also being in the middle of everything the town has to offer. This place oozes with charm and ambiance. An elegant and refined boutique hotel.

2. BEL SOGGIORNO, *Via S. Giovanni 91, Tel. 0577/940-375, Fax 0577/ 940-375. Email: hbelsog@libero.it. Web: www.hotelbelsoggiorno.it/. 21 rooms. Single or Double E120. All credit cards accepted. Breakfast included.* ***

The hotel consists of two structures from the 1400s that have been completely modernized. Also included with this fine three-star is a wonderful restaurant that is frequented by locals and which serves tasty local dishes (see description following). Rooms have views of either the countryside or the towers and come with tasteful furnishings and functional bath facilities. Not as charming as L'Antico Pozzo, but still a wonderful place to stay.

3. LA CISTERNA, *Piazza della Cisterna 24, Tel. 0577/940-328, Fax 0577/ 942-080. Web: www.sangimignano.com/lacisterna/. 50 rooms. Single E70; Double E120.* ***

Set in the most charming square of this incredibly beautiful town, you will not go wrong staying here. Located in a 14th century palazzo, and containing all necessary modern three-star amenities, La Cisterna is a gem. Furnished in the Florentine style, which consists of simple yet elegant decorations, the hotel also contains a rather good restaurant of its own.

4. LA COLLEGIATA, *Località Strada 27, Tel. 0577/943-201, Fax 0577/ 940-566. Email: info@lacollegiata.it, Web: www.lacollegiata.it/. 20 luxurious rooms. Single E300; Double E450. All credit cards accepted. Breakfast included.* ****

Elegance, charm, serenity, and ambiance is what La Collegiata is all about. Nestled in the hills of Tuscany with wonderful views of San Gimignano, this hotel is a sparkling gem of luxury and comfort. Located in a building from the 16th century, and containing an excellent restaurant, an inviting pool and every imaginable four-star amenity, this is the place to stay in town ... if you have the means. There is an incredible room located in the tower, on the upper floor of which is a large jacuzzi bathtub. From here the entire panorama of the valley can be admired. A truly romantic and sensual setting.

Where to Eat

5. BEL SOGGIORNO, *Via S. Giovanni 91, Tel. 0577/940-375, Fax 0577/ 940-375. Closed Wednesdays and between Jan 6 and March 1. All credit cards accepted. Dinner for two E60.*

Traditional Tuscan cuisine is served up with gusto in this superb eatery, which is attached to the hotel of the same name. By far the best restaurant in town, you will need to make reservations and come dressed appropriately. An elegant and refined ambiance with an extensive menu featuring local vegetables, meats, cheeses, and pasta. You will not go wrong with a meal in this excellent establishment.

6. ENOTECA GUSTAVO, *Via S. Matteo 29, Tel. 0577/940-057. Closed Mondays and in November. All credit cards accepted. Dinner for two E30.*

Despite there being a number of superb restaurants in San Girnignano, all catering to the swarm of Italophiles that make pilgrimages here, I felt it necessary to mention this wonderful little wine bar. Located in the heart of town, this small place is always packed, whether with locals or tourists. It is popular for its great wine list, as well as the fast, inexpensive and delectable food. From 10 in the morning until late at night, here you can find all manner of light and tasty sustenance. A great place to stop for a meal.

7. OSTERIA DELLE CATENE, *Via Mainardi,18, Tel.0577/941-966, Fax 0577/941-966.Closed Wednesdays. All credit cards accepted. Dinner for two E50.*

Arched brick ceilings and white walls are all the adornment this place needs, since the food is superb. Situated in the historic center of San Gimignano, the 'Tavern of the Chains' is famous for its excellent Tuscan cuisine as well as simple and elegant ambiance. All manner of excellent pasta and meat dishes are served here. Make this place one of your stops while in San Gimignano.

Seeing the Sights

A. DUOMO

Piazza del Duomo.

This church is a remarkable monument to Tuscan Romanesque architecture. It is simple, yes; plain, most assuredly; but impressive nonetheless. Though the exterior is nothing to write home about, the interior is resplendent with many fine frescos. Along the walls and in the left aisle, Bartolo di Fredi painted *Scenes from the Old Testament*. In the right aisle are displayed frescoes representing *Scenes from the New Testament*. In the central nave, on both sides of a fresco illustrating the *Martyrdom of St. Sebastiano* by Benozzo Gozzoli, there are two wooden statues by Jacopo della Quercia. On the upper part of the central nave between the two doors are Taddeo di Bartolo's frescoes showing *The Last Judgment*.

But all of this is only prelude for what we find in the right aisle, next to the transept: the famous Chapel of St. Fina built in 1468. With the elegant altar by Benedetto da Maiano and the frescoes by Domenico Ghirlandaio, this entire chapel is a wonderful work of art.

B. MUSEO CIVICO

Piazza del Duomo, *Tel. 0577/940-340*. March 1-Oct. 31: 9:30am-7:20pm; Nov 1-Feb 28: 10:00am-5:50pm. E6.

The Palazzo del Popolo (People's Palace) is home to the **Museo Civico** (Civic Museum) and is situated on the left hand side of the Piazza del Duomo. It is one of the most important monuments in San Gimignano. The museum is rich in paintings from the Florentine and Sienese schools, such as the *Crucifix* by Coppo di Marcovaldo, triptyches by Niccolò Tegliacci and Taddeo di Bartolo, and other works painted by Domenico Michelino, Pinturicchio and Filippino Lippi. On the right hand side of the Palace is the **Torre Grosso** (Great Tower) erected in 1300 from which you can take in commanding views. The hours listed above are for both the museum and the tower.

C. PIAZZA DEL CISTERNO

Just outside of the Piazza del Duomo is the triangular-shaped Piazza del Cisterna, arrayed with brick pavement in a fish scale pattern. Constructed in 1273 and enlarged in 1346, the square is circled by medieval homes and towers, and is a wonderful place to absorb the town's ambiance and charm. As you pass through the passageway from the Piazza del Duomo, you will go by the **Torri Gemelle degli Ardinghello**, constructed in the 1200s.

D. MUSEO D'ARTE SACRA (Museum of Sacred Art)

Piazza Pecori, *Tel. 0577/940-316*. March 1 - March 31 & Nov. 1 - Jan. 20: 9:30am - 5:00pm; April 1 - Oct. 31: 9:30am - 7:30pm. From Jan 21 to Feb 28, the museum is closed. E6.

The museum was opened in 1915 in the sacristy of the Duomo where it remained until 1929 when it was moved to this nearby location. It has recently been reorganized and includes material from local convents, the Duomo, and artifacts donated by private citizens and the Town Council. Some of the most valuable objects include the wooden sculptures from the 14th century. *The Annunciation* is two statues, one representing *The Angel* and the other *The Madonna*, of which only the head and the shoulders still exist. Then there is *The Crucifix*, a figure of Christ which is handless.

There are also splendid psalm books as well as works by Niccolò di Ser Sozzo Tegliacci and Lippo Vanni from the 14th century. In the Silverware room, you will find intricate examples of silversmith's and goldsmith's art, most of which date back to the 17th and 18th centuries. You will also find some exceptional works in silk and satin with gold and silver braids.

E. MUSEO ARCHEOLOGICO

Jan. 1-9: 11.00am - 6pm, Closed Thursdays; Jan 10 - Feb 28: Open only Thurs, Sat, Sun, Mon 11.00am -6:00pm; March 1 - Oct 31: Open every day 11.00am - 6:00pm; Nov 1 Dec 31: 11.00am - 6:00pm, Closed Thursdays. E6.

This archaeological museum has simple but instructive exhibits of Etruscan, Roman and medieval artifacts from the city and the surrounding area. Besides the objects of more common use (plates, bowls, vases, buckles and necklaces), which help to reveal the day-to-day lives of the ancients, I found the funeral urns to be fascinating. They consist of an elongated representative figure of the deceased holding a plate containing a small offering to pay for their passage to the afterlife.

F. CHIESA DI SAN AGOSTINO

Piazza San Agostino.

Located in the northernmost quadrant of the town, near the Porta St. Matteo, the construction of this church began in 1280 and was completed in 1298. Its facade retains the simplicity of its original architectural style. As a way of protecting the door on the main façade, it is infrequently used as an entrance. Use the door on the right hand side of the church. The Cloister was built in the second half of the 15th century.

The interior of the church is in a Romanesque style with Gothic elements and consists of a single great nave with three apses. The roof is supported by a rustic wooden framework. The decorations are in a more elaborate Renaissance style.

The *Chapel of the Blessed Bartolo* contains the saint's mortal remains in a marble monument sculpted by Benedetto da Maiano in 1495. The chapel's walls and vaults were frescoed by Sebastiano Mainardi in 1500. Its terracotta floor is work of Andrea della Robbia. Above the High Altar is *The Coronation of the Madonna and the Saints* painted in 1483 by Piero del Pollaiolo. Other notable works include the frescoes in the Chancel that represent *Episodes from the life of St. Agostino*, and were painted by Benozzo Gozzoli between 1464 and 1465 with the help of two of his pupils, Pier Francesco Fiorentino and Giusto d'Andrea.

Practical Information
• **Information Office**, Piazza del Duomo 1, *Tel. 940-008, Fax 940-903.*
• **Website**, *www.sangimignano.com*

CORTONA
Cortona was a sleepy little town until very recently, when *Under the Tuscan Sun* by Frances Mayes introduced the town's incredible charm and ambiance to the world. Now if you come in the high season, Cortona will be swarming with tourists, which may detract from the whole experience. However, regardless of the tourist influx, the town is a wonderful place to visit.

Cortona is commandingly situated with magnificent views over the **Val di Chiana**, the most extensive valley in the Apennine chain, which stretches to the hills of Siena. The **Sanctuary of Santa Margherita** towers above the town and is in turn overshadowed by the powerful defenses of the **Medici fortress**.

In conjunction, **Lake Trasimeno**, the largest in central Italy, with lovely beaches, is just 9 kilometers away. A short drive from its shores brings you to the Umbrian capital of Perugia. And some of the most important regional towns, such as Florence, Rome and Siena, are within easy reach by either train or car.

Arrivals & Departures
By Car
Take the Autostrada del Sole (State Highway A1). Get off at the Valdichiana exit. Upon exiting the highway take the Siena - Perugia state road and continue towards Perugia. There are 3 exits for Cortona: Cortona via Manzano, Cortona via Lauretana and Cortona via Strada Statale 71. Do yourself a favor and pick up a road map if you're driving.

By Train
Take the train to **Camucia-Cortona** station, which is only 5 kilometer from the town. There's local bus service to Cortona that runs frequently. Buy a ticket for the bus at the newsstand or the train ticket booth.

From Rome you may need to change trains in Chiusi. Remember to ask. From Florence you will most likely have a direct train.

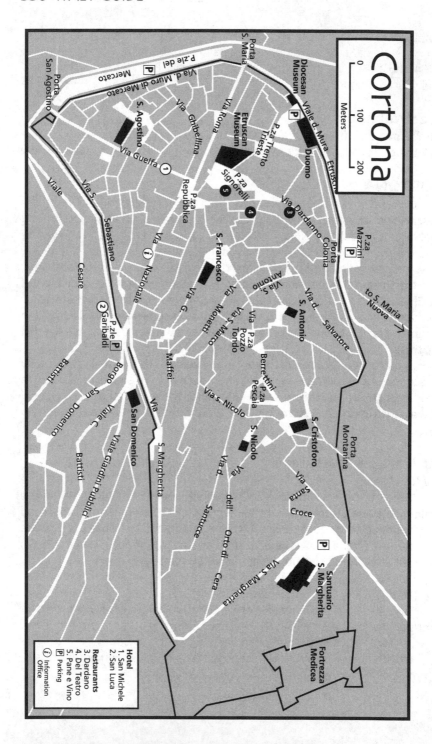

Where to Stay

1. SAN MICHELE, *Via Guelfa 15, Tel.0575/604348, Fax 0575/630147. Email: info@hotelsanmichele.net, Web: www.hotelsanmichele.net. 37 rooms. Single E90, Double E140. All credit cards accepted. Breakfast included.* ****

Great prices for a wonderful four-star deep in the heart of town. This is what you would pay for a two-star in a big city such as Rome, but here, since we are in the country, you get the best for a reasonable price. A great place to stay for the money.

2. SAN LUCA, *Piazza Garibaldi, Tel. 0575/63-460. Email: info@sanlucacortona.com, Web: www.sanlucacortona.com. 60 rooms. Single E60-70, Double E90-100. All credit cards accepted. Breakfast included.* ****

A comfortable newly upgraded four-star with commanding views over the surrounding countryside. They also have a great terrace on the lobby level. The hotel has inviting and comfortable rooms, as well as friendly professional service. A quality hotel with all three-star amenities. My choice for a place to stay in Cortona.

Where to Eat

3. DARDANO, *Via Dardano 24, Tel. 0575/601944. Closed on Mondays. No credit cards accepted. Dinner for two E30.*

The ambiance is all family trattoria, and the waitstaff are wonderfully courteous and friendly. The menu is simple and filled with typical local dishes. For antipasto you can have crostini (baked dough with fillings), bruschetta (Tuscan garlic bread), local prosciutto (ham) and pecorino cheese.

The specialty pasta of the house is ravioli with all sorts of fillings, including cinghiale (wild boar) and anatra (turkey). They also serve up a hearty vegetable soup. For entrees, they offer a wide array of meats on the grill. A wonderful place to eat in Cortona. Authentic and down to earth with great food.

4. DEL TEATRO, *Via Maffei 2, Tel. 0575/630-556. Closedd Wednesdays. All credit cards. Dinner for two E45.*

A refined, elegant, yet down to earth eatery in Cortona. Soft classical music helps make for a serene ambiance. Only a few tables in a series of rooms with terra cotta floors, wood beamed ceilings, and walls decoratively arrayed with quality art. On top of all that, the food is superb. Chef and patron Emiliano Rossi is one of those individuals who cherishes gastronomical tradition, and his culinary creations reflect this appreciation. Upscale yet still inexpensive. A great place to eat in Cortona.

5. PANE E VINO, *Piazza Signorelli 27, Tel. 0575/631-010. Web: www.pane-vino.it. Closed Mondays. All credit cards accepted. Dinner for two E25.*

A gracious local wine bar in the main piazza across from the theater. One draw back is that it is only open at night. Come here for the rustic atmosphere, great wine list, friendly service, and traditional, simple, and organic food.

Seeing the Sights

Though there is not too much in the way of cultural sights in town, this being Italy there is always something to see. The **Etruscan Museum** exhibits the Etruscan chandelier known as the Lamp of Cortona, one of the most celebrated bronzes from that time period. In the **Diocesan Museum** can be found the work of such minor masters as Luca Signorelli and Fra Angelico. The most important medieval churches are those of **S. Francesco** and **S. Domenico**. Renaissance splendor is on display in the **Palazzo Casale** and in the churches of **S. Maria Nuova** and **S. Niccolò**.

If you can, arrange your trip around the **Archidado Games** (circa May 12th to 19th each year), a fierce cross-bow competition between ancient neighborhoods, which compete for the prize of the Golden Dart (Verretta d'Oro). More than 250 townspeople dress in period garb and participate in religious ceremonies commemorating the marriage between Francesco Casali and Antonia Salimberi, which took place in 1397. After which, watch the arrows fly.

Practical Information

• **Websites**, *www.cortona.net* or *www.cortonaweb.net*

MONTEPULCIANO

Montepulciano is a stunningly beautiful little town perched along a narrow limestone ridge high above the verdant plains that surround it. Enclosed by medieval fortifications designed by Antonio da Sangallo the Elder in 1511, the tiny streets are bordered with attractive Renaissance palazzi and churches.

Today Montepulciano is nearly identical to what it was five centuries ago. Its historic center appears to have been frozen in time. The beauty and majesty of the Renaissance and Medieval buildings have remained intact, allowing the town to live up to its moniker as the "Pearl of the 1500s." And it will most likely remain such a jewel since it is not that convenient to get to. It is also a little different from most hill towns in that it does not have a geographic center. While Siena has its Campo, and other towns have a similar piazza that draws the community together, Montepulciano is spread along a ridge. Because of that the life of the time tends to get dissipated along the Corso, and funneled into individual restaurants or cafes. It is my opinion that Montepulciano, because of its layout, no matter how beautiful it is, it will always remain the serene hill town it is today. So come here for a slice of the way Italy used to be.

There are also Etruscan ruins indicating that this town has been inhabited for some time. Despite its lengthy lineage, few Roman ruins remain today. Only after the 6th century AD, when people from Chiusi, which is in an unprotected plain, fled here with the barbarian hordes on their heals, does the historical record contain significant artifacts.

As the town grew in importance, it became a pawn in the power games between Florence, Siena, Perugia and Orvieto, with Siena holding sway because of its size and proximity. However the inhabitants of Montepulciano held no affinity for Siena and in 1202 they swore fidelity to Florence. Heady stuff for a small town. People from Montepulciano have always been known as avant-garde and renegades. This is expressed today in their annual music festival, **Cantiere Internazionale d'Arte** (see the 'Festivals & Events' section below).

Arrivals & Departures
By Car
Located almost equidistant from Orvieto in the south and Siena in the north, Montepulciano is not convenient to get to unless you have a car. To reach Montepulciano take the A1 motorway to the **Val di Chiana** exit and follow the signs.

By Train
Though there is a train station for Montepulciano, the best way to get here is through **Chiusi**. From Chiusi take the blue SITA bus that you catch in front of the station. It runs every half an hour and brings you to the bus station at the base of the walls just outside Montepulciano. The SITA bus costs only E2.50. From there you can either walk or grab an orange local bus, called Pollicino, into town (sign on bus says Centro). Cost is E1.

Your other option is to arrive at **Montepulciano** station and call a cab From the pay phone in the bar across the street from the station, *Tel. 330/732 723, Fax 0578/758-332*; credit cards accepted. The taxi costs E15 each way.

Where to Stay
1. IL BORGHETTO, *Via Borgo Buio 7, Tel. 0578/757-535, Fax 0578/757-354. Email: info@ilborghetto.it, Web: www.ilborghetto.it. 15 rooms, 2 suites. Single E95; Double E105.* ***

A quaint and character-filled little hotel in the heart of Montepulciano. Situated in a 16th century building that has much more ancient foundation dug into the volcanic tufa rock, this is a wonderful place to stay. The rooms are all tastefully furnished and come complete with all three-star amenities. Request one of the rooms with views over the surrounding countryside. The vista is breathtaking.

2. IL MARZOCCO, *Piazza Savonarola 18, Tel. 0578/757-262, Fax 0578/757-530 Email: albergomarzocco@cretedisiena.com, Web: www.cretedisiena.com/albergoilmarzocco. 16 rooms. Single E65; Double E95-125. All credit cards accepted.* ***

Though simply furnished, this hotel has incredible atmosphere. Located inside the old city walls, and situated in a 16th century palazzo, this place has

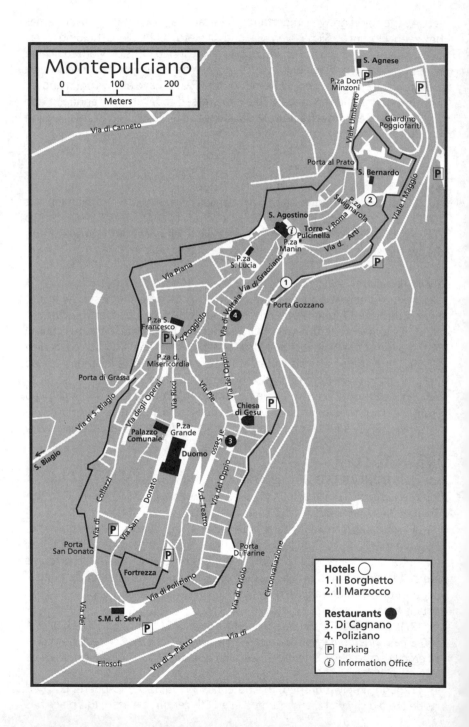

been run by the same family for over 100 years, and has been a hotel since 1860. Il Marzocco is well situated with many terraces that offer stunning panoramic views of the surrounding countryside. An excellent choice for a stay in Montepulciano. Before it was a hotel, it was a post office with space on the ground floor for carriages. That's why their entry is on the first floor. Beware. No elevator.

Where to Eat

3. TRATTORIA DI CAGNANO, *Via del' Oppio ne Corso 30, Tel. 0578/ 758-757. Closed Mondays. All credit cards accepted. Meal for two E40.*

This is where the locals eat in Montepulciano. And for good reason. It is excellent. Enter into a bar/cafe, face an elongated open kitchen and pizza oven, be seated in one of three rooms, and enjoy the rustic charm and superb culinary offerings. They have an extensive list of pizzas, traditional pasta dishes, and a variety of meats to please your palate and fill your stomach. Definitely the place to come in Montepulciano.

4. CAFFÉ POLIZIANO, *Via di Voltaia ne Corso 27, Tel. 0578/758-615. Web: www.ec-net.it/site/caffepoliziano. All credit cards accepted.*

An elegant art nouveau café upstairs and refined restaurant below, this is an upscale option while in Montepulciano. So much so that it seems out of place in this sleepy little town. Whatever the case, come here for a great snack, or an excellent meal. Very reasonably priced for the quality.

Seeing the Sights

The Church of St. Augustine is one of the most beautiful and interesting buildings in Montepulciano. Its facade was designed by Michelozzo Michelozzi (1396-1472) in the first decade of the 15th century. As Brunelleschi's disciple and collaborator in architecture, and Donatello's disciple in sculpture, Michelozzi used simple and elegant Renaissance forms in the lower level. Inside, you can admire works by Barocci, Allori, and Lorenzo di Credi. On the high altar there is a wooden crucifix attributed to Donatello. In front of the church you will see the characteristic 16th century **Pulcinella**, a bell-tower which strikes the hours sonorously.

Another interesting sight is the **Madonna di San Biagio** on the Via di San Biagio. This beautiful church is on the outskirts of Montepulciano and is built of honey and cream-colored stones. It is Sangallo's masterpiece, a Renaissance gem begun in 1518, and which occupied him until his death in 1534.

In the Piazza Grande you will find the **Palazzo Comunale**, onto which, n the 15th century, Michelozzo added a tower and facade to the original structure. On a clear day, the views that can be seen from the tower are superb.

Also in the Piazza Grande is the **Duomo**. It was designed between 1592 and 1630 by Ippolito Scalza. The facade is unfinished and plain, but the interior is elegant and tastefully adorned.

Festivals & Events

Montepulciano's festival season starts in the last week of July and the first week of August when it hosts the **Cantiere Internazionale d'Arte**, an international workshop and festival of art, music, and theater. The festival encourages artists of all ages and levels of experience to participate and collaborate. The ending result is a multicultural, international, dynamic event that is inspirational not only to participate in, but also to behold. *Tel. 0578/ 757089 or 0578/757007, Fax 0578/758307, Email: cantiere@bccmp.com.*

Then there is the **Bruscello** that takes place on August 14th, 15th and 16th when hundreds of players reenact scenes from the town's turbulent history. A truly magical three days. Another colorful spectacle is the **Bravio delle Botti**, on the last Sunday in August. This is a race through the main town streets with 80-kilo casks. These are rolled by *spingitori* (men who push them) representing the 8 quarters of the town. Before the race there is an historical procession featuring more than 200 people all wearing authentic 14th century costumes. Each of the 8 quarters is represented by drummers, flag-wavers, ensigns, ladies, knights, captain, soldiers and a magistrate. A wonderful spectacle akin to Siena's Palio but more rustic in its appeal, and much less crowded.

Agriturismo

AGRITURISMO POGGIO ETRUSCO, *Via del Pelagro 11, Loc. Fontecornino-S. Albino di Montepulciano. Tel/Fax 0578/783-370. In the US 805/963-7289. Web: www.foodartisans.com. Email: Pamela@FoodArtisans.com.*

If you have ever wanted to stay in the countryside of Italy, this is a great place to do so. Owned by an American husband and wife team, this villa, grounds and swimming pool, are a refreshing change from the urbanity of Italy. The wife, Pamela Sheldon Johns, is a cookbook author and culinary expert who also offers courses and workshops on cooking while exploring the backroads of Italian food and culture. The husband, Courtney Johns, is a refugee from Hollywood where he was a successful wardrobe designer, and now operates his own high-end tailor shop and clothing design boutique in Montepulciano (**Il Sarto**, *Tel. 328-053-8590*). If you ever saw the movie *Rocket Man*, which won an Oscar for wardrobe design, you've seen his work.

Practical Information

- **Tourist Office**, Via di Gracciano ne Corso 59/a, *Tel & Fax 0578/757-341. Email prolocomp@bccmp.com.*
- **Website**, *www.ctnet.it/montepulciano*

BOLOGNA EXCURSION

Not located in Tuscany, but an easy day trip from Florence is **Bologna**; a town referred to as "the Fat, Learned, and Turreted." "Fat" because the food is considered the best in Italy; "learned" because it houses the oldest university in Europe; and "turreted" because it once had the most towers of any city in Italy.

Despite all it has to offer, and the fact that it is located just 60 miles north of Florence, Bologna is generally overlooked by tourists. This is cause for rejoicing from dedicated Italophiles everywhere since no Italian city has achieved a better balance between progress and preservation as has Bologna. Much of the city center still looks the same way it did centuries ago. In conjunction, Bologna possesses none of the chaotic congestion of Rome or Florence. Instead it offers a glimpse into the lives of real Italians as they go about their business, and it invites you to enjoy life along with them. Just don't expect the romantic ambiance of Lucca, or the Renaissance splendor of Florence, or the bucolic charm of Venice – except of course for the miles upon miles of covered (arcaded) sidewalks. This is a real, living, breathing Italian city, virtually free of tourists, where you can enjoy the sights and sounds, and food and drink just as they do.

Brief History

Started as an Etruscan settlement of **Felsina**, the town was captured by marauding Gauls, renamed **Bononia**, and kept this name when it became a Roman colony in 139 BCE. As you'll notice by the map, the city center today is still dissected in an orderly fashion along the lines of an ancient Roman camp.

After the Roman Empire dissolved, Ravenna was the stronger of the two cities in the region, but in the 11th century Bologna broke away from its clutches. At which point Bologna became an independent commune of the **Lombard League** during the 12th and 13th centuries. In 1278, Bologna became part of the Papal States but was ruled by a succession of local "first citizens."

Bologna's high point, besides being home to the oldest university in Europe (founded in the 5th century CE as the **Imperial School of Bologna**; which later became a university in the 13th century CE), was probably when **Charles V** was crowned emperor in Bologna in 1530 instead of in Rome. That period marked the end of the Renaissance and the beginning of four and a half centuries of foreign rule. In 1796 the town was incorporated into Napoleon's empire. Then in 1815 it reverted back to Papal rule, and eventually became part of the new Italian state in 1860.

Now Bologna is known for its food and its sights, and as the birthplace of **Guglielmo Marconi**, the inventor who gave us the wireless radio.

Arrivals & Departures

By car, take the A1 directly from Florence to Bologna (or any number of smaller more scenic routes). The trip from Florence lasts 2 hours. By train from Florence, you'll arrive at the station on the outskirts of the old city. The walk to most hotels will take 10 minutes, but a cab is recommended. Train trips from Florence last 1 1/2 hours.

Getting Around Town
By Foot

The center of Bologna is very small, is specifically designed for pedestrian traffic, and in fact in certain areas no private cars are allowed. Walking is really the only mode of transport you'll need.

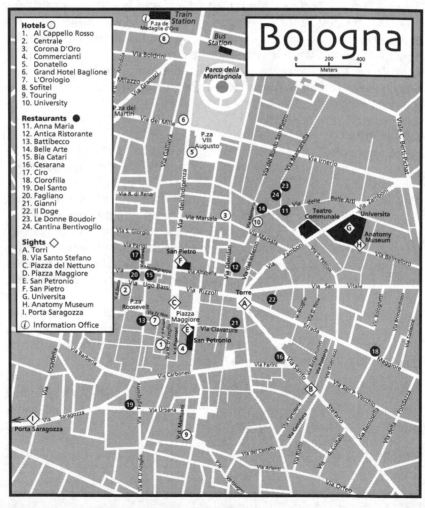

Hotels ○
1. Al Cappello Rosso
2. Centrale
3. Corona D'Oro
4. Commercianti
5. Donatello
6. Grand Hotel Baglione
7. L'Orologio
8. Sofitel
9. Touring
10. University

Restaurants ●
11. Anna Maria
12. Antica Ristorante
13. Battibecco
14. Belle Arte
15. Bia Catari
16. Cesarana
17. Ciro
18. Clorofilla
19. Del Santo
20. Fagliano
21. Gianni
22. Il Doge
23. Le Donne Boudoir
24. Cantina Bentivoglio

Sights ◇
A. Torri
B. Via Santo Stefano
C. Piazza del Nettuno
D. Piazza Maggiore
E. San Petronio
F. San Pietro
G. Universita
H. Anatomy Museum
I. Porta Saragozza
ⓘ Information Office

By Taxi
If you're tired taxi's abound. You can flag one down or call one of these numbers to have one sent to you: *Tel. 051/53-41-41 or 051/37-27-27.* A taxi stand is on the right outside of the station. Most places are a short taxi ride away. The fare to your hotel shouldn't be any more than E5 unless you have loads of luggage.

Where to Stay
1. AL CAPPELLO ROSSO, *Via de Fusari 9. Tel. 051/261-891, Fax 051/ 227-179. Email: info@alcappellorosso.it. Web: www.alcappellorosso.it. 33 rooms all with bath. Single E120-265; Double E160-340. All credit cards accepted. Breakfast E13. *****
A hundred meters from the Piazza Maggiore this is a sublimely refined four star hotel. The rooms are furnished with well-appointed antiques. The bathrooms are nicely accessorized with hairdryers and a complete complimentary toiletry kit. Breakfast is a Bolognese original with local cakes, donuts, rolls and other sweets.

2. CENTRALE, *Via della Zecca 2. Tel. 051/225-114, Fax 051/223-162. 20 rooms 17 with bath. Single without bath E45-60; Single E50-70; Double without bath E55-75; Double E65-85. Credit cards accepted. ***
As the name indicates, this hotel is located in the center of Bologna with shopping and sightseeing all around. On the third floor of a building, you need to catch the lift up to your clean but spartan rooms, some of which have nice views over the rooftops of Bologna. Most rooms face the Via Ugo Bassi and can be noisy. Make sure you request a room that has air conditioning in the summer.

3. CORONA D'ORO, *Via Oberdan 12. Tel. 051/236-456, Fax 051/262-679. Web: http://corona.hotel-bologna.net. 35 rooms all with bath. Double E180 - 290. Credit cards accepted. Breakfast included. *****
The crown prince of the small chain that includes the Orologio and the Commercianti. This hotel has everything you could want in a first class place. The elegant design conserves architectural elements from various periods, which makes the ambiance luxurious. There's an airy lobby with a skylighted atrium, colorful tile floors, frescoes and an abundance of fresh flowers. Most rooms have small balconies, and if you're up high enough you can overlook the rooftops, towers, and domes of Bologna.

4. DEI COMMERCIANTI, *Via De' Pignattari 11. Tel. 051/233-052, Fax 051/224-733. Web: http://commercianti.hotel-bologna.net. 31 rooms all with bath. Double E120-190. Credit cards accepted. ****
Virtually the same location as its sister hotel, L'Orologio, with the same professional manner and service that caters to business travelers. All your needs will be taken care of by the helpful desk staff. Great location for

shopping and sightseeing. All the amenities and professional service you'd expect from a North American hotel except that the rooms are a little smaller. Ideally located in the center of Bologna.

5. DONATELLO, *Via dell'Indipendenza 65. Tel. 051/24-81-74, Fax 051/ 24-81-74. Email: hoteldonatello@digibank.it. Web: www.hoteldonatello.com. 39 rooms all with bath. Single E80; Double E100. Credit cards accepted.* ***

An older hotel whose lobby looks like it's barely hanging onto its former glory. Upstairs the mood is more upbeat with slightly modern appointments. The rooms are spartan with hardly any amenities except for cleanliness and comfort. There are soundproof windows and walls, satellite TV in every room, air conditioning and mini-fridge in each room too. The main draw of this place is location. A good choice for price.

6. GRAND HOTEL BAGLIONI, *Via dell'Indipendenza 8. Tel. 051/225-4454, Fax 051/234-840. Email: ghb.bologna@baglionihotels.com. Web: www.baglionihotels.com. 140 rooms all with bath. Single E150-200; Double E200-350. All credit cards accepted. Breakfast included.* *****

A former 16th century seminary, this is Bologna's most splendid hotel. The color scheme is of salmon, beige, and light blue, giving the whole place a relaxing feel. The hotel has several yards of early Roman roads on display in the basement, so it can also even be considered a small museum. The hotel restaurant, I Carracci, is expensive but exquisite. This is *the* place to stay in Bologna if you have the means. Attentive, personal service with every modern comfort imaginable.

7. L'OROLOGIO, *Via IV Novembre 10. Tel. 051/231-253, Fax 051/260-552. Web: http://orologio.hotel-bologna.net. 29 rooms all with bath. Double E120-190. Credit cards accepted.* ***

A professional hotel that caters mainly to businessmen, but they have all the amenities and service you'd expect from a North American hotel. Part of a group of hotels in the city that also includes the Corona d'Oro and the Commercianti. They all offer shuttle service to the train station at a small charge, free bicycles for your use and all the necessary amenities for their star rating. All three hotels are great places to stay.

8. SOFITEL, *Viale Pietramellara 59. Tel. 051/248-248, Fax 051/249-421. Email: sofitel.bologna@accor-hotels.it. Web: www.accor-hotels.it. 244 rooms all with bath. Single E200; Double E300. All credit cards accepted. Breakfast included.* ****

Another good four star in Bologna, this one situated directly in front of the train station and offering comfort and class. The restaurant serves good Bolognese and international cuisine. Everything about this place is comfortable and accommodating.

9. TOURING, *Via de' Mattuiani 1/2, 20124 Bologna. Tel. 051/584-305, Fax 051/334-763. Email: hoteltouring@hoteltouring.it. Web: www.hoteltouring.it. 40 rooms.. Single E70-120; Double E100-220. Credit cards accepted.* ***

Recently renovated in 2001, this place is much better than it has been in the past. They have a terrace on the roof with a jacuzzi. A good place to relax. This is an elegant hotel with upgraded atmosphere, and the prices are reasonable. I am very impressed with the improvements they have made. Touring is now more than a place to lay your head. Recommended.

10. UNIVERSITY, *Via Mentana 7, 40126 Bologna. Tel. and Fax 051/229-713. Web: www.hotel-university.com. 21 rooms all with bath. Single E160; Double E180. Credit cards accepted. Breakfast included.* ***

This is a clean, modern hotel in the Golden Group Hotel chain that includes the Holiday and Paradise. The entrance hall is not that big and is just off of the breakfast room where you are served a buffet of classic Bolognese breakfast cakes, rolls, fruit, juice, coffee and tea. The rooms and bathrooms are not that large but are comfortable. There are a number of business services available (photocopying, fax, telex, e-mail) that can come in handy.

Where to Eat
Cucina Bolognese

Bologna has arguably the best all-round cuisine in Italy and the citizens of this fair city enjoy it wholeheartedly. The main local dishes are based on pasta, pork, cream, cheese, and ham; and pasta is so revered here that the city government has a giant golden tagliatelli noodle enshrined in its Chamber of Commerce offices.

The cuisine is so good in Bologna because cooks are able to draw on the freshest and best ingredients from the surrounding area. They can get the finest *prosciutto* and *formaggio* from Parma, which is world-renowned for its excellence. They get the freshest fruits and vegetables from the local farms, and the most succulent pork, salami, and other meat products as well. If you came to Bologna and want to remain on a diet ... good luck.

11. ANNA MARIA, *Via Belle Arti 17/a, Tel. 051/266-894. Closed Mondays, six days in January and 15 days in August. All credit cards accepted. Dinner for two E45.*

Anna Maria Monari does everything here, from preparing the sauce to turning the roast to tabulating the check – and she does them all well. You'll find plenty of traditional dishes, including either *tagliatelle, tortellini, tortellone, tagliolini or quadreti in brodo* (different types of pasta in soup); as well as *pasta e fagioli* (pasta and beans) or *trippa coi fagioli* (tripe with beans). They have a great *zuppa di verdure* (vegetable soup), *maiale al forno* (grilled pork) *verdure al forno* (grilled vegetables) or *frittura* (fried). Dining is either inside or outside on their terrace. A wonderful place in Bologna.

12. ANTICA RISTORANTE, *San Lobbe 3d. Credit cards accepted. Closed Sundays. Dinner for two E38.*

Down a twisting alley that is between the Via del Inferno and the Via Oberdan, here you can enjoy a relatively inexpensive meal in quiet and comfortable surroundings. (Bring a map to find it). They serve Bolognese specials like *Tagliatelle Bolognese* (with veal, milk and tomato sauce) and *tortellini al Basilico e pomodoro* (cheese or meat stuffed pasta with a basil and tomato sauce). For secondo they have *castrate* (lamb) and *grigliata mista* (mixed grill with lamb, pork and beef).

13. BATTIBECCO, *Via Battibecco 4/b, Tel. 051/223-298. Closed Sundays and Holidays as well as August. All credit cards accepted. Dinner for two E70.*

Somewhat of an upper crust locale, with many excellent regional and international dishes. You'll find that *Prosciutto di Parma, Parmigiano Reggiano,* and local salamis are featured in almost all the appetizers, soups, and pastas. For seconds try some of their seafood concoctions like *antipasti di gamberetti e calamari* (*antipasta* of small shrimp and squid), or their fresh vegetables either cooked in oven or grilled (*verdure al forno or grigliatta*) or their *scampi reali al whisky* (large shrimp cooked in a whisky sauce). You can also find cold roast beef, which is excellent.

14. BELLE ARTE, *Via Belle Arti 6, Tel. 051/126-76-48. Closed Sundays. No credit cards accepted. Dinner for two E30.*

Set on a side street with outside seating under an awning, and a larger area inside of plain brick with whitewashed walls festooned with pictures, this is a good place to come for a relaxing and tasty meal. Try the *tagliatelle ragu bolognese* or the *tortellini alla panna*. They also have some Roman favorites like *amatriciana* and *arrabbiata*. If you're in search of meat try the *braciola di maiale* (arm of pork) or the *grigliatta misto* (mixed grill with pork, lamb and beef).

15. BIA CATARI, *Via Montegrappa 7/8, Tel. 051/22-48-71. Closed Mondays. Credit cards accepted. Dinner for two E38.*

If you want some seafood, this place specializes in it. They only have inside seating but the space is large, light and comfortable. Try the *antipasto di mare freddo* (cold mixed seafood) or the *cocktail di gamberi* (shrimp cocktail). Skip the pasta altogether and head right to the *fritto misto di mare* (fried mixed seafood) or the *grigliatta mista* (grilled mixed seafood). A great atmosphere with fine service.

16. CESARINA, *Via Santo Stefano 19/b, Tel. 051/232-037. Closed Mondays and Tuesdays at Dinner. All credit cards accepted. Dinner for two E70.*

Enjoy the beauty of Piazza Santo Stefano from the terrace of this restaurant or savor the smells from the kitchen if you sit inside. This place is rather upscale even though they serve many traditional local peasant dishes. Their *fritto misto* (mixed fried vegetables) is simply great and their *tortellini in brodo* (tortellini in soup) is perfect. They also make an excellent *spaghetti alla vongole verace* (with a spicy clam and oil-based sauce), *risotto alla pescatore* (rice with fish), or *scampi alla griglia* (grilled shrimp).

17. CIRO, *Calca Vinazzi de Gessi 5B. Credit cards accepted. Closed Wednesdays. Dinner for two E35.*

Here you can have a peaceful dinner on a private terrace on a small side street away from all the hustle and bustle of Bologna. If you want to watch the pizza chef at work, sit inside around the tile-covered oven. Besides pizza they serve great pastas, especially the *spaghetti alla carbonara* (with cheese, ham, and egg) or the *tortellini al piacere* (tortellini made any way you want them). For seconds try any of their pizzas. Knowing that most people in this city like their cheese, they have an option to double the cheese for an extra E1. This makes the pizza very much like a North American concoction.

18. CLOROFILLA, *Strada Maggiore 64c, Tel. 051/235-343. Closed Sundays. Credit cards accepted. Meal for two E20.*

Specializes in vegetarian meals. They also have wines and beers that were prepared ecologically. You can get fruit salads, regular salads, soybean burgers, *cous cous*, a variety of cheeses, veggie sandwiches, and much more. Even though Italian food itself is fresh and healthy, if you don't even want to see meat on the menu, come here and enjoy an ecologically friendly meal.

19. DEL SANTO, *Via Urbana #7F. Credit cards accepted. Dinner for two E35.*

Real Bolognese cooking in an authentic local *trattoria*. You can sit outside under the arcaded sidewalk and a canopy on a busy road and breathe exhaust fumes, or sit inside in a plainly furnished place. Try any of their *tortellini* or *tortellone* dishes, especially the *alla panna* (with a thick rich cream sauce that you cover with parmesan). For seconds try the *cotoletta alla bolognese* (veal cutlet covered with milk and tomato sauce) or the *scaloppine alla pizzaiolo* (veal covered with melted cheese and tomato sauce).

20. FAGLIANO, *Calca Vinazzi de Gessi. Credit cards accepted. Closed Thursdays. Dinner for two E38.*

Located on a little side street just off the main road, Via Ugo Bassi, they have outside seating under an awning as well as a large inside seating area covered in wood and marble. They make great pastas, especially the local favorites *tortellini alla panna* (with cream sauce) and *tagliatelli alla Bolognese* (with veal, milk and tomato sauce.) They also make a dish that is similar to *penne all'arrabbiata* from Rome, called *penne all'diavolo* (devil's pasta, meaning it's hot and spicy with garlic and hot peppers in a tomato and olive oil base). They also serve pizza for lunch and dinner, as well as some wonderful dishes cooked over the grill. Try the *formaggi alla griglia* (grilled cheeses) or the *grigliatta vegetale* (grilled vegetables).

21. GIANNI, *Via Clavature 18. Tel. 051/22-94-34. Credit cards accepted. Closed Mondays. Dinner for two E38.*

Down a little alley off of the Via Clavature, you can get a taste of real Bologna here. Both in the decor, which is simple brick walls with pictures of the city interspersed, as well as the menu, which changes daily based on the produce available. The staples are the *tortellini* or *tortelloni* pasta dishes (small and large cheese stuffed pasta with a variety of sauces) as well as an antipasto of *prosciutto di Parma* and any form of *maiale* (pork) or *vitello* (veal). A great experience for dining because of its hidden location and great food.

22. IL DOGE, *Via Caldarese 5a. Tel. 051/22-79-80. Closed Mondays. Credit cards accepted. Dinner for two (only pizza) E30.*

A large place on a side street off the Via San Vitale that has a great atmosphere created by wood paneling and stained glass windows and the superb service. As you sit down they bring you a small *bruschetta* (hard garlic bread covered in olive oil and tomatoes). Anything you try here will be good, especially the pizza that they make in the centrally located pizza oven. Each pizza is large, at least 12 inches and they're generous with their toppings – maybe not like in North America, but still a good amount. They also have a good selection of meat and fish dishes.

23. LE DONNE BOUDOIR, *Via Mascarella 5a, Tel. 051/23-54-24. No credit cards accepted. Closed Mondays. Open 7:00pm - 4:00am. Dinner for two E45.*

An eclectic place with posters of old, and some dead, American film stars on the walls. After getting past the café/bar entrance, you enter the cramped surroundings that serves as the dining room. However, if you're over 5'8" tall, you need to sit at one of the booths against the wall so you can stretch your legs. The food is great, especially any of the *tortellini* or *tortelloni* dishes, and the *mozzarelle fritte* (fried balls of mozzarella) and *verdure fritte* (fried vegetables) are delicious. Beware of the waitresses, they are not the most pleasant (to foreigners), but ignore their surliness and enjoy a fabulous meal.

24. CANTINA BENTIVOGLIO, *Via Mascarella 4B. Closed Mondays. Open 8:00pm–2:00am.*

Enter, walk through an entrance corridor, and descend the stairs to a vast renovated wine cellar. On most nights the place will be packed by 9:30pm, not only to hear the tantalizing live music but also to enjoy the *vino*, plates of pasta and *crostini* (sandwiches, like their *pizzaiolo* with mozzarella, tomatoes and oregano) or the *prosciutto* (with mozzarella and ham). If you want a true late night experience, Bologna-Style, try this place.

Seeing the Sights

Bologna is literally made for walking and sightseeing. There are over 20 miles of arcaded sidewalks that turn a brief *passegiatta* a veritable stroll through history. Some of these arcades, or *portici*, date back to the 12th century when the *comune* (the government of Bologna) faced a housing shortage as a result of massive enrollment in the University, so they ordered housing to be built onto existing buildings over the sidewalks. The Bolognese grew attached to these *portici*, not only for their beauty, but also for the protection they offer from the elements.

The best part of Bologna as a walking paradise is that a large part of the historical city center is off-limits to private automobiles, giving you the freedom to move without fear of being run over. Bologna is so well preserved that you can walk down medieval streets and witness countless historically sacred living exhibitions of northern Italian architecture from the 12th through the 18th centuries.

A. TORRI GARISENDA & ASINELLI, PIAZZA DI PORTA RAVEGNANA

Torre degli Asinelli is open daily from 9:00am–6:00pm. In the winter only until 5:00pm. Admission E3.

Known as the **Due Torre** (two towers), these structures were erected in the 12th century as military observation posts. Eventually towers became the fashionable structure to erect as a symbol of your family's wealth (that's why one of Bologna's names is "The Turreted"), as well as a wise military investment for the city. Today only a small handful of them remain, the largest of which is the **Asinelli Tower**, which rises over 320 feet and has a wonderful observation deck from which you can see all of Bologna.

The **Garisenda Tower** right next to it leans a little and appears as if it is trying to affectionately touch the Asinelli Tower. From where the towers are located, five ancient avenues branch off and lead to a gate on the old city walls. The best of these streets to take is the **Via Santo Stefano**.

B. VIA SANTO STEFANO

This is a terrific street to wander along. Stop at the **Piazza del Mercanzi**, which is dominated by the **Merchant's Palace**, an ornate Gothic building that served as the center of Bologna's trade in the 14th century and today houses the chamber of commerce. Inside you will find a gold plated replica of a pasta noodle.

As you proceed down Via Santo Stefano, it's like walking back in time. With each building you pass, the centuries seem to drop away. You'll pass rows of graceful *palazzi* built by the powerful families of Bologna. Numbers 9 through 11 are interesting because of their sculpted terra-cotta facades.

One of the best places along this street is at a small triangular square with a grouping of seven little churches known collectively as **Le Sette Chiese**. You can explore each of their tiny ancient chapels and cloisters of these interconnected buildings and feel as if you are the only one who knows about this humble and hushed place.

C. PIAZZA DEL NETTUNO

In this piazza you're confronted by a startling nude, hugely muscled statue of *Neptune*, trident in hand, attended by four sirens squirting water from their nipples. If you stare at the fountain enough it seems to come to life. Besides the statue you'll find plenty of Bolognese hanging out and communing. A great *piazza* in which to relax, one that merges into the large Piazza Maggiore.

D. PIAZZA MAGGIORE

This *piazza* is one of the most theatrical public spaces in Italy. This vast, raised square is bordered by Gothic and Romanesque facades and the large basilica of **San Petronio**. It is the place to come and socialize for Bolognese. Just off this piazza is a little neighborhood of streets named after the wares they have sold since the Middle Ages where you can find some great stores.

For example, try the **Paolo Atti & Pigli** on Via Caprarie that sells a wide array of fresh breads and pastas. A few doors down is the **Pescheria Brunelli** that sells mountains of fresh fish daily. At the corner of the Via Drapperie and Via Caprarie you'll find a great gourmet store, **Tamburini**, which has anything and everything culinary you could imagine. You'll find hams, salamis, sausages, cheeses, olive oil, bread, pastas, and the best sight is an immense pig, impaled on a large spit being turned ever so slowly over an open fire. The smell is so tantalizing that you can't help but buy something.

E. SAN PETRONIO

Piazza Maggiore, *Tel. 051/220-637*. Open 7:30am–7:00pm.

Located on the south side of the Piazza Maggiore, this Gothic basilica is the largest church in Bologna and is dedicated to the city's patron saint. It was begun in 1390 but it was never completed according to plan. In fact, construction stopped abruptly in 1650 and never continued. The sculpture on the main doorway of the facade is by Jacopo della Quercia. The interior nave is 117 meters long, 48 meters wide and just over 40 meters high, and the decorations are purely Gothic. A majestic church.

F. SAN PIETRO

Via dell'Indipendenza. Open 7:00am–7:00pm.

If you exit Piazza Maggiore and go up Via dell'Indipendenza towards the train station, you'll run into the Cathedral on the right hand side of the street. It was founded in 910 and has a choir created by Tibaldi in 1575, and a Baroque nave created in 1605 which has been added to periodically through time. Even though smaller in scale than San Petronio, I found this church to be filled with much more interesting pieces of artwork.

G. UNIVERSITA
Via Zamboni 33, *Tel. 051/259–021.*

The **University**, founded in 1088, is the oldest such institution in Europe. By the 13th century it had attracted more than 10,000 students from all over Europe. Its alumni include Dante Aligheri, Petrarch, Thomas a Becket, and more recently Federico Fellini. The campus, being in the center of a city, contains both old and new buildings on both sides of the **Via Zamboni**. To see real Italian university life, all you need to do is stroll through the maze of streets that encompass the school. The walls are covered with graffiti and posters and there are many coffeehouses or *trattoria* catering to the students.

H. ANATOMY MUSEUM OF DOMESTIC ANIMALS
Via Belmeloro 8, *Tel. 051/354–243.* Open Monday–Saturday 9:00am–1:00pm and on Wednesday also open 3–5:00pm.

You need to call ahead for an appointment to see these samples of dissected pets. A lesson in anatomy that should not be approached on a full stomach or if you're even a wee bit queasy.

I. PORTA SARAGOZZA & GUARDIA HILL
Through the Porta Saragozza and up the Guardia Hill stands the sanctuary of the **Madonna di San Luca**. As you stroll up the hill, even if it is raining, you will stay completely dry. All thanks to an arcade formed of no fewer than 666 arches. This same walk has been traversed every May since the 15th century as part of a religious procession in which a revered Byzantine image of the Madonna is carried to the sanctuary. Besides this sacred image, from here you can see the vast carpet of red brick of Bologna, reposing quietly below.

Shopping
Since Bologna has over 20 miles of arcaded sidewalks and most of the historic city center is free from automobile traffic, it is definitely made for walking and window shopping. All around the **Piazza Maggiore** and **Nettuno**, in the modern **Galleria** just off the **Via Cavour**, and all along the **Via dell' Indipendenza** and **Marconi** are located the small specialized shops that make shopping in Italy so much fun.

Leather goods for many of Italy's most famous designers are manufactured in and around Bologna, which makes all types of shoes, belts, briefcases, wallets, purses, etc., with or without the famous name label, an extremely good value. You'll find many of these shops on the major streets listed above.

Practical Information
Tourist Information & Maps
• **IAT Office**, Piazza Medaglio d'Oro, Stazione Ferroviara, 40121 Bologna. *Tel. 051/246-541.* Open Monday to Saturday, 9:00am–7:00pm.

Chapter 15

UMBRIA

Umbria – the "Green Heart of Italy" – is a picturesque slice of mother nature's paradise, filled with stunningly beautiful fairy-tale medieval towns. Covered with lush green forest and manicured fields, Umbria is bordered by Tuscany and Lazio, where Florence and Rome are located. The smallest regions of Italy at only 8,500 square kilometers, what Umbria lacks in size it makes up for in art, architecture, natural settings, outdoor sporting activities, delicious cuisine, intricate arts & crafts, welcoming people and a passionate way of life.

Even though it is one of only a few Italian provinces not touching the sea, Umbria's mountains offer plenty of scenic splendor. Besides the natural beauty of the rolling hills and lush valleys, Umbria is filled with stunningly beautiful medieval towns such as the capital, **Perugia**. Spreading majestically over the ridges of a series of hills, Perugia is interlaced with winding cobblestones streets, an aqueduct turned walkway, ancient *palazzi*, Etruscan and Roman arches, and picturesque piazzas. Besides Perugia, the main towns of interest in Umbria include, **Spoleto**, **Todi**, **Gubbio**, **Orvieto**, and **Assisi**; each of which are rewarding destinations in and of themselves. Besides all the natural scenic beauty and scenic medieval towns, one of the main attractions of Umbria is that it is very lightly touristed (except for Assisi which is a major pilgrimage sight). Another is that Umbria is an incredibly inexpensive alternative to the crowding your find in the more well-known areas of Italy.

At most times of the year, when the rest of Italy is swarming with hordes of tourists, you can venture into Umbria and have it almost all to yourself. The locals still outnumber the visitors here.

In Umbria's exotic urban settings you will find some wonderful Etruscan, Roman, Romanesque and Renaissance works of art and architecture. **Perugia** has the imposing and historically significant Etruscan Arch and Roman aqueduct turned walkway. **Orvieto** has its extensive Etruscan Necropolises and an awe-inspiring cathedral. In **Gubbio** there are excellent examples of an ancient Roman temple, mausoleum, and theater just outside of an incredibly beautifully, well preserved and scenic medieval hill town. **Todi** as a whole is an inspiration and a wonderful respite from the hectic pace of modern life.

However, **Spoleto** is the jewel of the region. Second only to Todi in quality of medieval character, this ambient hill town is home to some of the best restaurants in Italy, a direct result of the fact that this town hosts the world-renowned **Spoleto Festival** every summer. But what sets Spoleto apart, not only from towns in Umbria, but from every place I have visited on the planet, is its immediate proximity to pristine, untouched, verdant natural settings. Just

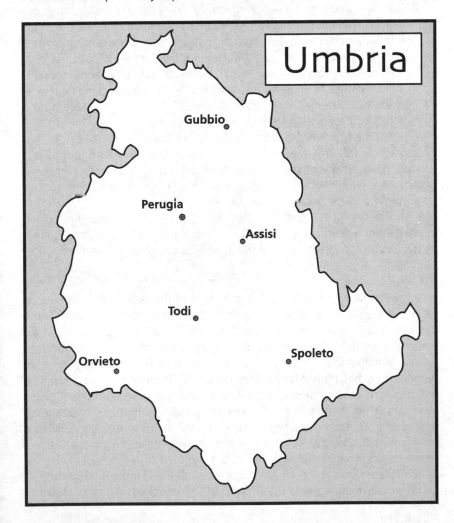

across the Ponte delle Torre — a medieval aqueduct located only a few meters from the centro storico — which spans a deep gorge over to the hillside of Monte Luco, you will find an extensive array of hiking trails through deep forest, with scenic views and the peace and calm that only untouched natural settings can offer. Spoleto is a combination of quaint and colorful medieval setting, complete with cosmopolitan shopping and eating establishments, immediately next door to the purity of nature. A rather unique amalgamation of characteristics.

Umbria – Land of Truffles

Truffles (tartufi) have been described by epicureans as the ultimate indulgence, and if you have ever tasted a dish flavored with them you will realize that this is not only true, but is an incredible understatement. The **tartufo nero** (black truffle) is the more abundant and has a heartier flavor of the two varieties found in Umbria. The **tartufo bianco** (white truffle) is more subtle in flavor and expensive in cost, because it is found in less quantities. Gathered fresh from late September through December, you would be remiss not to savor any dish flavored with these tasty tubers if you venture to Umbria during that time.

Truffles grow wild and are discovered by trained dogs whose keen sense of smell allow them to locate these aromatic morsels despite the fact that the truffles develop over a foot underground. Most truffles are not very large, and weigh very little, but are incredibly expensive, sometimes more than $300 per ounce.

The aroma of *tartufi*, or as the epicureans say, 'perfume', is tantalizingly delicious. Walk into any alimentari or salumeria where they are sold when in season, and the *sapore* (aroma) will overwhelm you.

The Romanesque style is evident in many of the cathedrals in the region, as is the Gothic style, which is particularly exemplified by the cathedral in Orvieto. The Renaissance also flourished and spread throughout the region which has also left us with some stunning architectural wonders. Umbria also boasts some of the Renaissance period's early artists, including the most famous from the Umbrian school, **Pietro Vannucci** (better known as **Perugino**) whose works are exhibited in the National Gallery of Umbria and the Collegio del Cambio in Perugia. An old man when Michelangelo was emerging, Perugino's reputation was negatively impacted by Michelangelo's brilliance.

The medieval towns in Umbria are so well preserved, and are as yet relatively undiscovered, that a visit to the region is truly like walking back in time. Located in every town are prime examples of floating architecture, or *casa pensili* (hanging houses) – archways connecting rooms of buildings located far above the level of the street. So if you want to taste all the flavor of medieval Italy without the congestion of tourists, be a savvy traveler and come to Umbria.

PERUGIA

The capital city of Umbria, the charming old medieval city of **Perugia** is a stunning place to visit. Besides being the seat of some major cultural institutions such as the National Gallery of Umbria in the Prior's Palace, and the home to a number of universities including one specifically for foreigners, Perugia also has the vitality and ambiance of true Italian city.

Perugia retains a quaint medieval charm with stunning old palazzi, winding streets climbing up and down the hills, with archways and buildings traversing the passageways. The main street, Corso Vannucci, and main square, Piazza IV Novembre, are the perfect place for a walk any time day or night, and is where you will find the majority of the population every night strolling along, munching on ice cream, socializing, before and after dinner.

Most of the best shops are located in this area and in the evenings the area is filled with locals taking their evening stroll. A great sense of community thrives in Perugia making the city a fun and lively place to visit. Since it is located near many of the cities of note in the region, Perugia is a perfect place from which to take day trips to the other towns mentioned in this chapter. I cannot recommend this city enough. One of my favorites in all of Italy.

Brief History

Stretching over hilly ridges, Perugia has been the home of human development since prehistoric times. During the 3rd century BCE, Perugia became one of the twelve key cities of the Etruscan federation. After the Etruscans were defeated by Rome, the city was absorbed into the Roman Republic as a colony. Then when the Roman Civil War was won by Octavian, Perugia was razed because of its allegiance to Mark Anthony. Some years later it was rebuilt by Octavian, then Emperor Augustus who gave the city its name (Augustus Perusia).

Once Christianity became the religion of the Empire, Perugia followed suit and started its own diocese in the 5th century CE. Around this time the city was ruled by the Byzantine Empire since the Roman Empire had dissolved and split, until it came under the rule of the papacy in the 8th century. From the 11th century onward Perugia became a 'free' commune (meaning the nobles ruled and the serfs served, but the city wasn't under anyone else's yoke but their own). During the 12th and 13th centuries Perugia fought a series of battles for the control of the region with Chiusi, Cortona, Assisi, Todi and Foligno; and eventually ended up victorious after defeating Assisi in 1202, allowing the city to extend its reach over much of the surrounding area.

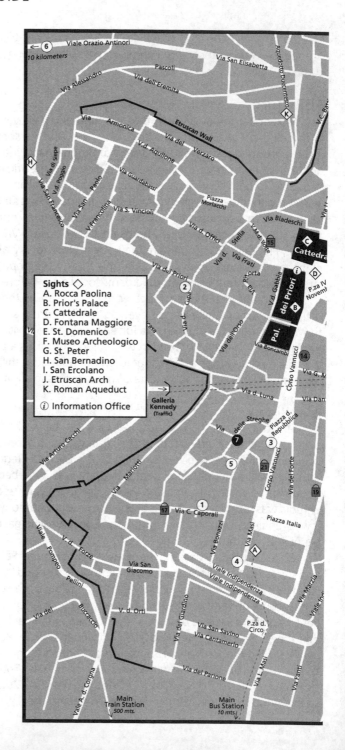

Sights ◇
A. Rocca Paolina
B. Prior's Palace
C. Cattedrale
D. Fontana Maggiore
E. St. Domenico
F. Museo Archeologico
G. St. Peter
H. San Bernadino
I. San Ercolano
J. Etruscan Arch
K. Roman Aqueduct

ⓘ Information Office

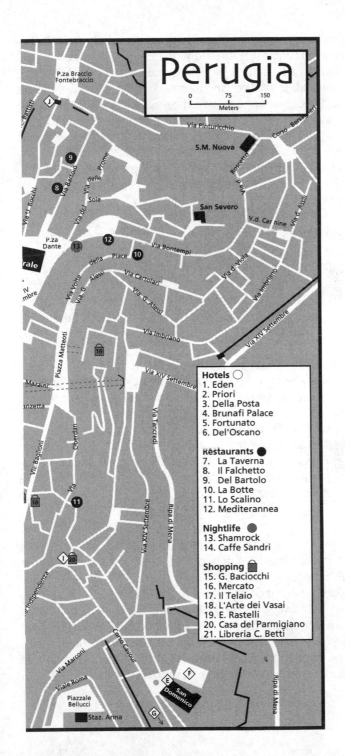

Perugia

0   75   150
Meters

Hotels ○
1. Eden
2. Priori
3. Della Posta
4. Brunafi Palace
5. Fortunato
6. Del'Oscano

Restaurants ●
7. La Taverna
8. Il Falchetto
9. Del Bartolo
10. La Botte
11. Lo Scalino
12. Mediterannea

Nightlife ●
13. Shamrock
14. Caffe Sandri

Shopping 🛍
15. G. Baciocchi
16. Mercato
17. Il Telaio
18. L'Arte dei Vasai
19. E. Rastelli
20. Casa del Parmigiano
21. Libreria C. Betti

Despite dominating the region, internally Perugia was in turmoil. Different factions of nobles fought over the right to govern, never reaching a conclusion, until finally, caught up in their own power struggles, the entire social and economic fabric of the city became frayed. Because of this weakness, in 1540, the city was re-conquered by the forces of Pope Farnese and again came under the rule of the Papal States for three centuries.

Around 1840, a brief flirtation with freedom resulted in Napoleon's forays into the region, at which time the citizens took great pleasure in destroying the Rocca Paolina fortress (an oppressive symbol of papal control of the city) and threw the Swiss Guard out of the city. Twenty years later, on September 14, 1860, the city became part of the kingdom of Italy.

Arrivals & Departures

The reason that Perugia still retains much of its medieval charm is that even though it is in close proximity geographically to Rome and Florence, Italy's two main tourist centers, train schedules are not strategically coordinated between those locations. Whether coming from Florence or Rome, you will have to change trains in **Castiglione del Lago**, and most of the trains which come here are milk runs which tend to stop at every little town along the way.

If you don't rent a car — which I recommend when visiting Umbria — once here, moving around the region can be cumbersome by either bus or train. Renting a car will be more expensive, but it will also allow you to visit remote little hill towns. You can visit Orvieto, Todi and Gubbio from Perugia by train, but a car is best. Gubbio can be easily accessed by bus but a car is also preferred. To visit Assisi both train and bus are good options. To visit Spoleto from Perugia the train is a good option. A bus schedule (orario) for the local line, **Autolinee Regionali**, and a train schedule (Orari Ferroviari) is available at the local tourist office in Piazza IV Novembre.

Orientation

Perugia's centro storico sits on top of the crests of five hills and looks somewhat like the claw of the city's mascot, the Griffin. At the base of the main hill surrounding the train station are more modern urban developments, which though unsightly will not detract from your visit to the quaint, colorful and character-filled old town. The centro storico is bisected by the **Corso Vanucci**, which runs from the cathedral to the **Piazza Italia**, which is where the buses from the main train station let you off. It is also where the escalator arrives — snaking up through the **Papal Fortress** (Rocca Paolina) — from the **Piazza Partigiani**, where the inter-regional bus terminal is located.

Umbria Websites

For up to date information about events and activities in Perugia visit *www.perugia.com*, the official website for the city. This site also has links for *Assisi.com, Gubbio.com, Spoleto.com, Todi.com* among others. Granted they are in Italian, but even so they will help you plan your trip. Another good site, this one with an English option is *www.umbria.org*.

Getting Around Town

Break out your hiking shoes, get a bottle of water and get ready to do some hiking. The only way to explore Perugia is on foot and since it is located on a series of hills, you are going to do some stair- and hill-climbing while here. Aware of this, the Perugini have built escalators in key locations throughout the town making the longer climbs more manageable, while still retaining the charm of this stunning medieval town.

One of the most interesting escalators is the one that comes from the main parking and bus area, **Piazza dei Partigiani**. These *scala mobili* (moving stairs) are underground and surrounded first by modern concrete walls. But these walls soon turn to ancient brick and you find yourself in the remnants of a 16th century underground fortress with vaulted passages, parts of old rooms, pieces of ancient passageways and an odd feeling that you suddenly went back in time. This place is the **Rocca Paolina** (see **A** on map), a fortress built by Pope Paul III in 1540 on the ruins of the Palazzo Baglioni, which was destroyed when the Papal States conquered Perugia. Then when the Papal States were expelled from Perugia, the new fortress the popes built was partially destroyed. Now the *scala mobili* offer a unique introduction to the city, very similar to an amusement park ride. With one defining difference – this is real. Interwoven with these escalators are small roads, even smaller stairways, Etruscan and Roman archways, and a pedestrian aqueduct, making Perugia a perambulating paradise.

Where to Stay

1. EDEN, *Via Cesare Caporali 9. Tel. 075/572-8102, Fax 075/572-0342. 50 rooms. Single E60. Double E80. All credit cards accepted. Breakfast included. ***

A wonderful little two star just off the Piazza Italia where the buses from the train station stop, and the escalator from the bus depot empties. This hotel's main lobby is on the third and fourth floor of an old building. The rooms are spacious, clean and comfortable, come with televisions, and some have spectacular views. Even the rooms overlooking a quiet courtyard are great.

The bathrooms come with blow dryer and courtesy toiletry set. An excellent two star hotel, with wonderful service, in a superb location at excellent prices.

2. PRIORI, *Via del Priori. Tel. 075/572-3378, Fax 075/572-3213, Email: hotelpriori@perugia.com, Web: www.perugia.com/hotelpriori. 50 rooms. No credit cards accepted. Breakfast included. Single E55-70; Double E65-90.* **

Right in the center of town the decor here is 'old Umbrian' with antique furnishings, terra cotta tile floors and flowered drapes. The bathrooms come with blow dryer and courtesy toiletry set and are accommodating though a little cramped. One of the best assets of this place is their large terrace overlooking the rooftops of the city. In the summer the terrace is used for the buffet breakfast which includes juice, fruit, cereal, pastries and coffee and tea. A quaint two star right in the middle of things. Great place to stay at a good price.

3. LOCANDA DELLA POSTA, *Corso Vannucci 97f. Tel. 075/572-8925, Fax 075/572-2413. Web: www.umbriatravel.com/locandadellaposta. 40 rooms. All credit cards accepted. Breakfast included. Single E100-115; Double E140-180; Suite E175-210.* ****

This is the best hotel on the best street in Perugia, Corso Vannucci, the main promenade where all of Perugia comes out at night to promenade, young and old alike joined together in a community ritual of togetherness. The hotel is a 17th century palazzo that once was the old post office. Over the centuries they've had many a luminary stay here, including Frederick II of Prussia, Goethe, and Hans Christian Andersen. In 1990 the entire hotel was completely restored and every modern amenity was added. The hotel retains all of its charm and character, and each room is different from the next adding to the old world ambiance. The bathrooms are large and refined with all modern conveniences.

4. BRUNAFI PALACE, *Piazza Italia 12. Tel. 075/573-2541, Fax 075/572-0210. Toll free in Italy 167/273-226. Toll free fax (USA) 888/661-0219. Email - sina@italyhotel.com, Web: www.summithotels.com. 94 rooms. All credit cards accepted. Breakfast included. Single E245; Double E300.* *****

In the centro storico right next to the Rocca Paolina, this is an extremely elegant and attentive hotel. Recently the Palace Hotel Bellavista has been absorbed in the Brunafi, which resulted in the word 'Palace' being added to the name of the hotel. The ancient palazzo has been completely restored with all modern amenities while retaining its charm, elegance and ambiance. The entrance hall instantly transports you back in time with its tapestries and antique furnishings. The rooms are all differently furnished and are all comfortable and accommodating. A wonderful place to stay in Perugia.

5. FORTUNA, *Via Bonazzi 19. Tel 075/572-2845, Fax 075/573-5040. Web: www.umbriahotels.com/HFortuna. All credit cards accepted. Single E90-105; Double E115-135. ****

Situated in the *centro storico*, just off of the Corso Vanucci, this completely renovated hotel comes with all three star amenities. The second floor houses the breakfast room and evening bar area. The third floor has a nice sitting room with a fire place and there is a big terrace on the fifth floor overlooking the rooftops of Perugia. Wonderful little three star in an ideal location.

6. CASTELLO DELL'OSCANA, *06134 Locanda Cenerente, Perugia. 075/690-125, Fax 075/690-666. Web: www.umbria.org/hotel/oscano. 100 rooms. All credit cards accepted. Breakfast included. Castle: Only 11 rooms in the castle E210-290. Villa Ada: Double E110. La Macina: Weekly rates E300 to 625. Buffet breakfast included and is served in the dining room of the Castle.*

Stunning. Incredibly beautiful. Amazing. Like something out of a fairy tale. Simply unbelievable. A great place to stay. If you have a car, and you have the means, stay here. Near Perugia, but set deep in the surrounding verdant, forested hills, this inspiring medieval castle presents an atmosphere of unparalleled charm and ambiance. There are three locations to choose from: the **Castle** (a medieval structure complete with towers and turrets that is simply but elegantly decorated and equipped with every comfort), the **Villa Ada** (a 19th century residence adjoining the castle that is more modern but no less accommodating), and **La Macina** (a country house down the hill from the other two structures, and comes with complete apartments and has an adjacent pool). A perfect place to spend a honeymoon or simply have the vacation of a lifetime.

Where to Eat

7. LA TAVERNA, *Via delle Streghe 8. Tel. 075/572-4128. Closed Mondays, January 7-21 and all of July. All credit cards accepted. Dinner for two E60.*

Not to be missed. Excellent atmosphere with its vaulted ceilings and arched doorways, simply superb food, and attentive service. Come prepared to have a great meal in authentically medieval surroundings. They make a tasty tagliatelle al ragu di anatra (pasta with duck sauce), linguini con pecorino e olio (pasta with pecorino cheese and oil), and crostini al tartufo nero (baked dough with black truffles). In fact if you come here in truffle season sample anything they make with them. This is an upper echelon restaurant — make sure you dress for the occasion — and most cognoscenti believe it the best in town. I concur.

8. IL FALCHETTO, *Via Bartolo 20, Tel 075/573-1775. Closed Mondays. Open 12:30-2:30pm and 7:30 - 10:00pm. All credit cards accepted. Dinner for two E40.*

Pink tablecloths, vaulted brick ceilings, soothing music, oil lamps on every table, and attentive service all set the scene for a serene meal. In back is where the locals congregate and is a little more boisterous, but both front and rear receive tasty local recipes made with exquisite care and presented with a slight flair. The grilled vegetable antipasto is perfect to start with and the tagliatelle ai porcini (with mushrooms) or al tartufo nero (with black truffles) are both tasty pasta dishes. For seconds they have a number of tasty grilled and oven baked meats and fish.

9. OSTERIA DEL BARTOLO, *Via Bartolo 30. Tel. 075/573-1561. Closed Sundays and January 7-25. All credit cards accepted. Dinner for two E75.*

An elegant small place run by the effervescent and attentive Walter Passeri. They make their bread in-house as are the pastas and desserts. And as befits a restaurant in Perugia they create quality truffle dishes. The menu here changes constantly, but be assured you will receive a superb gastronomical experience. You need to make reservations and you must dress appropriately. Wonderful ambiance, creative cuisine and upscale prices.

10. LA BOTTE, *Via Volte Della Pace 33. Tel. 075/572-2679. Open 12:30-2:30pm and 7:30-10:00pm. Credit cards accepted. Dinner for two E25.*

This is a small, simple, down-to-earth trattoria, off the beaten path, down in the basement of a medieval building off a small side street, that serves a vast array and tasty pasta and meat dishes at incredibly good prices. Locals and travelers alike flock to this little hole in the wall because of the tasty food and accommodating family atmosphere. The entryway looks like a bar or café, but in the back under the while walls and vaulted brick ceilings you'll get some wonderful food, including penne alla vodka (with tomatoes, cream, meat and a touch of vodka), spaghetti alla carbonara (egg, cheese, bacon and peas), or my favorite, penne al panna e funghi (with a creamy mushroom sauce).

11. PIZZERIA LO SCALINO, *Via S. Ercolano 8. Tel. 075/5722-5372. Open 12:00-3:00pm and 7:00-10:00pm. Closed Friday afternoons. Dinner for two E20.*

A tiny local place whose entrance is located on the steps to the church of San Ercolano. A little cramped but comfortable, and frequented by the locals not only for the great pizza, but the warm and accommodating atmosphere. The pizza chefs prepares your pies in a small space in the dining area. Only a few varieties of pizza are available, a few salads, a couple of meat dishes, an excellent bruschetta for appetizer, but what the menu lacks in quantity, the food and local atmosphere makes up for in quality.

11. PIZZERIA MEDITERANNEA, *Piazza Piccinino 11/12, Tel 075/572-1322. Closed Tuesdays. Open 12:30-2:30pm and 7:30pm - midnight. Dinner for two E25.*

All they serve is pizza and it is so good and the atmosphere so electric that people line up to get it. Opening onto a small piazza just past the Duomo sits this festive little pizzeria. A small place with only two rooms, one of which has the pizza oven, this is the favorite hangout for the younger set at night. They only serve pizza, so if you are in the mood for it, give this place a try. If you do not show up early you will definitely have to wait. To get on the list of diners, flag down a waitress and she will give you a number. If you do not want to wait, La Botte is just around the corner.

Seeing the Sights

A. ROCCA PAOLINA

Located in the Piazza Italia, this is fortress built by Sangallo the Younger by the order of Pius III as the Papal States emphatic display of dominance over the city of Perugia. An entire medieval neighborhood, as well as the Baglioni Palazzi were covered over to create this ostentatious display of papal authority which even today makes Perugini leery of the influence of the Pope. In 1860 the fortress was destroyed and what remains underground is now used as a totally unique exhibition space, and a conduit for the escalators from Piazza Partigiani.

B. PRIOR'S PALACE,

Corso Vannucci. *Tel. 075/574-1247.* Closed the first Monday of the month. Open 9am-7pm, holidays 9am-1pm.

Home to the **National Gallery of Umbria** on the third floor, the Prior's Palace is also known as the Town Hall and is an outstanding example of medieval architecture. As such is considered one of the most elegant and famous in all of Italy. Begun in 1293, it was completed in 1443 after the building was consolidated with other homes and pre-existing towers all under one huge roof.

The entrance on Corso Vannucci is through a round portal, almost underneath an imposing tower and guarded by two Griffins – the symbols of the city – sinking their claws into two calves. The entire facade on the Corso is quite imposing and rather fortress-like. Before entering, take some time to check out the ornamental entrance with its friezes, twisted columns, sculptures and ornamental foliage. The Atrium is inside the entrance off of Corso Vannucci and is a covered courtyard with pillars and vaults.

The entrance on the Piazza IV Novembre is just to the left of the tourist information office up a flight of stairs and through a pointed portal. Above the portal are bronze statues of a Griffin and a Lion – the symbol of an old ruling family, the Guelphs. Through the portal is the Sala dei Notari (Lawyer's Room), an impressive hall that has some exquisite frescoes and grandiose arches. The frescoes are some scenes from the Bible and Aesop's fables. Other rooms in the building include the Sala del Consignio Comunale (City Council Hall), which contains a fresco by Pinturicchio, and the Sala Rossa (Red Hall) containing a mural by Dono Doni.

The National Gallery is the third floor and is a must-see in Perugia. It contains masterly examples of the paintings from the Umbrian school, which date from the 13 century CE to the 19th. Perugia's most famous artist, Perugino, is featured in rooms 12-14 with his *Adoration of the Magi* (room 12), *Miracles of San Bernardino* (room 13) and *The Dead Christ* (room 14). Also accessible off of the Corso Vanucci is the **Collegio del Cambio**. To the left of the facade of the Palazzo dei Priori, beyond the archway to the Via dei Priori are three portals, through which you can enter the fresco-laden room containing major works by the cities most famous artist, Perugino.

C. CATHEDRAL OF SAINT LAWRENCE

Piazza IV Novembre.

The steps on the left side of the building facing the Piazza IV Novembre is *the* place to hang out, whether it's sunny or not. You'll have to fight for space with the natives and locals alike, as well as some rather bold pigeons, but this is where you can sit and watch the life of Perugia pass by.

The building itself is an imposing Gothic church constructed between the 14th and 15th centuries CE. It still has an incomplete facade but nonetheless is beautiful. The main entrance is between Piazza Dante and Piazza IV Novembre and has a coarse stone facade with a massive Baroque portal and a large circular window above that. The left side of the building is decorated with ornamental masks by Scalza flanking the plain portal with its ancient wooden doors. Above the portal is the votive Crucifix placed here in 1539. To the right side of the portal is the 15th century pulpit of San Bernardino. To the left of the portal is the *Statue of Pope Julius III*, an intricate bronze by Danti from the 16th century.

The interior is divided by octagonal columns into one nave and two aisles. The Chapel of San Bernardino — to the right as you enter — which is enclosed by beautiful wrought iron railings, contains a stunning fresco by Federico Barocci. In the Chapel of the Holy Ring, enclosed by 15th century wrought iron railings — to the left as you enter — is a silver and gold plated copper tabernacle which contains the onyx wedding ring purported to have been worn by the Virgin Mary. Hmmm? A poor carpenter able to afford an expensive onyx ring? You be the judge of its authenticity.

Also please note the 16th century multi-colored stained glass windows by Arrigo Fiammingo and the 16th century carved choir seats. In the right transept are the tombs of Pope Martino IV, Pope Urbano IV and Pope Innocenzo III as well as the marble sculpture of Pope Leo XIII.

D. FONTANA MAGGIORE

Piazza IV Novembre.

The **Great Fountain** (Fontana Maggiore) is the monumental heart of medieval Perugia, built between 1275 and 1278 with the decorative sculptures created by Nicola and Giovanni Pisano. Topped by a bronze basin, the fountain has an upper stone basin held up by slender columns topped with a variety of capitals.

This basin consists of 24 red marble panels separating some of the Pisano brother's statues which depict scenes from the Bible, historical and mythological figures, and some saints. The lower basin has 50 panels on which are depicted the months of the year, the signs of the Zodiac, scenes from the Old Testament, the founding of Rome and Aesop's fables.

E. BASILICA OF SAINT DOMENICO,
Via Cavour. Open 7:00am-noon & 4:00-7:00pm.

An imposing Gothic church built in the 14th century then rebuilt in the 17th with a huge campanile (bell tower) and separate attached cloisters (not open to the public). On the bare facade is the elegant 16th century portal above a double flight of stairs. The interior is enormous and plain, a simplicity that gives it a peaceful and rather calming effect on the soul. Some elegant pieces include the 18th century organ and the splendid tomb of Pope Benedict XI. The apse is lit by a large, 23 meter high 15th century window. Most of the frescoes that adorn the walls have not survived the test of time. In every chapel there are exquisite paintings depicting a variety of religious themes, as well as a number of crypts containing personages of importance in Perugia.

F. MUSEO ARCHEOLOGICO NAZIONALE DELL'UMBRIA,
Via Cavour. Open 9:00am-5:00pm. Holidays 9:00am-1:00pm. E2.

To get to this museum go through the archway to the left of San Domenico, into the internal courtyard, go down the right portico to the entrance upstairs. The museum wraps around the 1st floor of the courtyard and contains many interesting archaeological relics culled from the many excavations in Umbria. You will find Etruscan, Roman and more recent artifacts. A simple, little museum that is worth a short visit.

G. BASILICA OF SAINT PETER
Borgo XX Giugno. Open 7:00am-noon & 4:00-7:00pm.

Located quite a ways from the centro storico through a rustic working class neighborhood, down the Corso Cavour past St. Domenico, through the Porta San Pietro and along the Borgo XX Giugno. The Basilica of San Pietro was built in the 10th century on the site of an even older cathedral. The church is dominated by a beautiful 15th century campanile. You enter the church through a rather run-down but at the same time elegant porticoed courtyard. Oddly enough there is a bar/café just off of the courtyard where you can grab a refreshment after your long walk over here.

The dark interior contains a single nave with two aisles divided by 18 Roman columns. This church, in contrast to San Domenico, is elaborate in its decoration — very much like San Ercolano — and has a wealth of art work, most of which is rather difficult to see without night vision glasses since the lighting is so poor even on the brightest day. Give your eyes time to adjust and take the time to view magnificent frescoes and paintings adorning virtually every inch of space on the walls. The sacristy contains some works by Caravaggio and Perugino, and the Chapel of the Sacrament has a *Pieta* by Perugino.

Behind the altar, through the intricately carved 17th century choir is a small terrace at the back of the church overlooking an incredibly panoramic view of the surrounding countryside. Take the time to get back here and admire the view, and savor the wood carved choir and doors that lead here.

H. ORATORY OF SAN BERNADINO
Piazza San Francesco. Open 7:00am-noon & 4:00-7:00pm.

The date this building was completed (1461) can be seen on the facade in roman numerals (MCCCCLXI). Masterly crafted by the Florentine Agostino di Antonio di Duccio, the facade is a wonderful series of sculptures of saints in the Perugia-Renaissance style. The 15th century Gothic interior contains the Tomb of Beato Egidio and an ancient 4th century CE Roman-era Christian sarcophagus. In an adjacent building entered through the annex of the Oratory of St. Andrew you get to the Baldeschi Chapel, which houses the Tomb of Bartolo da Sassoferrato, an important 14th century Perugian leader, teacher and lawyer.

I. CHURCH OF SAN ERCOLANO
Via Marzia. Open 7:00am-noon & 4:00-7:00pm.

Dedicated to the patron saint of Perugia, San Ercolano, this church stands on the exact spot where he was martyred when the Goths seized the city in 547 CE. This 13th and 14th century Gothic church is a small octagonal structure with large pointed arches going around it. The interior is accessed through a beautiful double staircase built in 1607. Though more intricate in detail than the original structure, the staircase is the first initiation into the exceptional beauty of this medieval church. At the high altar is a noteworthy Roman-era Christian sarcophagus that contain the remains of San Ercolano. Around the dome are some exquisite frescoes dating to the 16th century which depict a number of scenes from the Bible. Every inch of these walls are covered with frescoes and bas-relief work.

J. THE ETRUSCAN ARCH
Piazza Fortebraccio.

Also known as the **Arch of Augustus**, the original structure was built in the 3rd and 2nd century BCE. Later there were Roman-era additions as well as some during the 16th century. This huge and imposing structure is bordered by some of the old walls of Perugia, clearly indicating the lengths attackers would have to go through to sack the city. Comprised of two powerful Etruscan towers, the right one lowered by an invasion, while the one on the left has an enticing patio on the top and a Roman fountain on the bottom. Above the gate is a sentinel arch, so named because that is where the guards for the city would keep watch. It has since been walled up and now is part of the structure to the left.

K. ROMAN AQUEDUCT
Via di Aquedotto.

What used to be a functioning aqueduct is now a pedestrian street. This may be your only chance to walk along an ancient aqueduct, so take it while you have it. Lining the aqueduct are quaint little homes. Also from this height you get to look down onto other streets and passageways, offering an interesting perspective of this mountain city.

Nightlife & Entertainment
The nightlife and entertainment in Perugia mainly consists of congregating in and around the **Corso Vannucci**, going for a stroll, grabbing an ice cream cone — the preferred social lubricant in Perugia — and meeting with friends at one of the many cafés that line the Corso. This lasts from before dinner through the meal hour and well into the evening, and is especially crowded on Saturday nights when everybody and their grandmother is out for a walk. You will find young and old, well-off and beggars, wild and conservative, families and singles, all connecting despite their differences. Sadly, such community interaction is extremely rare in the U.S. and could help to explain the overall breakdown in American society.

There was a time when the Perugini allowed cars to drive on the Corso Vannucci; but back in the '70s, realizing the detrimental effect cars were having on their community, they put a stop to that practice by closing the street to traffic. Because of this appreciation for maintaining spaces where community can thrive, places such as the Corso Vannucci exist all over Italy. Along this street there are plenty of restaurants, cafés, and pubs in which to stop if refreshment is needed. Two that we recommend are listed below.

13. SHAMROCK, *Piazza Danti 18. Tel. 075/573-6625. Open 7:00pm - 2:00am.*

Great Irish atmosphere. Medieval vaulted ceilings coupled with dark wood furnishings, brass accents, and authentic Irish knickknacks gives this place a true feel of the Blarney. Definitely the best pub atmosphere in Perugia. Located down a dark medieval alleyway in the basement of one of the oldest buildings in the city, just across from the main entrance to the Cathedral. They serve a full complement of ales and have a good bar menu as well as snacks like chips, pretzels and peanuts.

14. CAFFÉ SANDRI, *Corso Vannucci 32. Tel. 075/61012. Open 7:00am - 11:00pm daily.*

The authentically Perugian place to grab a cappuccino or a bite to eat on the Corso Vannucci. Their window displays are tantalizingly spectacular with fruit tarts, cheeses and other delicacies enticing you inside. Sandri is Perugia's landmark café and a local favorite. The frescoed ceilings remain intact and the proprietors come from the same Swiss family, the Schucan's, who founded the café over 130 years ago. When in Perugia, you have to at least stop in for a look.

Shopping

The main pedestrian street **Corso Vannucci** is also the best shopping street in Perugia. Along its route and around its periphery — mainly the parallel streets of **Via Baglioni** and **Via G. Oberdan** — you will find traditional little shops offering a wide variety native arts and crafts as well as local and international fashions.

15. I LEGNI DI GIUSEPPE BACIOCCHI, *Via Maeste delle Volte 8. Tel. 075/57-26-080.*

This artists' shop is located in the basement of a medieval building. Carved wooden figures are his stock in trade and they are simply wonderful. A perfect place to pick up some small gifts for friends, or buy one of his larger magnificent carvings.

16. MERCATO COPERTO, *Open 7:00am-1pm Monday-Saturday.*

Located off of the Piazza Matteoti and through the Palazzo Capitano del Popolo is the covered market of Perugia, which offers dry goods of leather and other crafts in the upstairs section, and fruits, vegetables and other foods on the downstairs.

17. IL TELAIO, *Via Bruschi 2B. Tel. 075/572-6603. Closed Monday mornings. Open 9:30am-1:00pm and 4:00-8:00pm. All credit cards accepted.*

Off the beaten path, this place sells local hand-crafted linens, pillow cases, sheets, tablecloths and everything associated with fabrics and textiles. A wonderful shop to find unique products from Umbria.

18. L'ARTE DEI VASAI, *Via Baglioni 32. Tel. 075/572-3108. Open 9:30am-1:00pm and 3:45-8:00pm. Closed Sundays. All credit cards accepted.*

If you don't want to venture all the way to Deruta to find ceramics, this store has by far the best selection available in Perugia. The perfect place to find hand-crafted, distinctively hand-painted ceramics, bowls, mugs, cups, plates and more.

19. MAGAZZINI DI EGIDIO RASTELLI, *Via Baglioni 17-29. Tel. 075/57-29-050. Open 9:00am-1:00pm and 4:00-7:50pm. Closed Mondays.*

Large cartoleria with all sorts of distinctly unique Italian notebooks, pens, calendars, day planners, sketch pads, and everything else for office, home or school.

20. CASA DEL PARMIGIANO REGGIANO, Via San Ercolano 36. *Tel. 075/573-1233.* All credit cards accepted. Open 7:30am-1:30pm & 4:30-8:00pm.

This is the best place in Perugia to find those exquisitely tasty, pungently aromatic, uniquely Umbrian culinary delight, tartufi. They vacuum seal (sotto vuoto) purchases for you so that they stay fresh.

Bookstores
21. LIBRERIA C BETTI, *Via del Sette 1. Open 10:00am-1:00pm and 4:00pm-8:00pm.*

This tiny bookstore carries a small selection of English language books to the right just as you enter.

Excursions & Day Trips
The other towns listed in this chapter (Orvieto, Todi, Gubbio, Assisi and Spoleto) can all be considered day trips from Perugia, but at the same time, each of these places could be destinations in and of themselves. Deruta, however, is so much closer to Perugia, that it really is the only true day trip.

DERUTA
Located 15 kilometers outside of Perugia, **Deruta** is the generally considered the ceramics capital of Central Italy — something nearby Cortona over the border in Tuscany would dispute heartily. The old town situated on a hill overlooking the valley of the Tiber is beautiful. Unfortunately the new part of the town — which is parallel to and along the Via Tiberina is a slip-shod, unplanned eye sore. So skip the eye sore, and head into the beautiful little hill town filled with the largest selection of **fine ceramic pottery** anywhere.

Don't come expecting any bargains. All you will get here is a large selection. Not really a place to spend much time, except for pottery shopping.

Getting There
By bus is the only way, other than by car, to get to Deruta. Pick up the bus schedule at the information office in Perugia. Buses are infrequent and as a result you need to plan to ensure that you can get there, have time to look around, then be able to catch a bus back.

Practical Information
Festivals
• **Good Friday procession** – La Desolata
• **Mid–July Rock Music festival** – Rockin' Umbria
• **First two weeks of September** – Sagra Musicale Umbria (musical recitals in Perugia's churches)

• **End of October/Beginning November** – Jewel And Antique show
• **2–5 November** – All Souls Fair

Laundry

Le Bolle, Corso G. Garibaldi 43. Open every day 8:00am-10:00pm. Attendant on duty from 2:00-4:00pm & 7:00-10:00pm. Self-service laundromat that is computerized and fully automated. Wash cost: E3 for 8kg (15lbs), E5 for 16kg. Wash takes 25 minutes. Drying cost: E3 for 8kg and E5 for 10kg. Free detergent. If the attendant is not present, call *075/41644* and she will pop down and give you some.

Onda Blu, Via Pinturicchio 102. Open 8:00am-10:00pm every day. Self-service laundromat located near Porta Pesa that is fully automated. Wash cost: E3 for 6.5 kg. Takes 30 minutes. Drying cost: E3 and takes 20 minutes. Detergent costs E3.

Tourist Information

The **tourist information office** is located in the Piazza IV Novembre next to the stairs leading up to the Prior's Palace. Open from 9:00am to 1:00pm and 3:00pm to 6:00pm, *Tel. 075/573-6458 or 572/-3327*. They have useful maps, and all the information you need for buses, trains, walking tours, etc.

SPOLETO

Spoleto is an amazing destination because of the combination of medieval charm, natural setting, excellent restaurants, cosmopolitan shops and art galleries, few tourists, and incredibly friendly and accommodating locals. The ancient medieval town itself, with its winding streets, old buildings is like something out of a fairy tale.

Even though this is one of the better preserved medieval towns in all of Italy, Spoleto is still only lightly touristed. That is except during the world-famous **Spoleto Festival** held in June every year, when tens of thousands of tourists descend here to savor a two week extravaganza of performing arts.

Because of this festival Spoleto has some of the best restaurants in all of Italy, quaint little artisans' shops selling exquisitely created local crafts, and little galleries and studios filled with locally produced painting and sculpture that is of top quality. But that's not all. The main distinguishing feature about Spoleto is that it offers instant access to inspiring natural settings.

Just across the **Ponte delle Torre**, an old medieval aqueduct turned walkway, you are in untouched, pristine nature, laced with hiking trails that snake around the surrounding mountains, and through small local hill towns. In very few places in the world can you go from a quaint medieval town, filled with cosmopolitan amenities, to untouched natural settings after a five minute walk.

Situated on green hillside near the lower border of the Umbra Valley, Spoleto was founded by the original Umbrian people, Later it came under Etruscan influence and eventually was absorbed into the Roman Empire around the 3rd century BCE. Its claim to fame during that period came during the second Punic War, where it played a major role in repelling Hannibal's attacks. After the fall of the Roman Empire, Spoleto was a flourishing Lombard capital, then fell under papal influence and became one of the Pope's summer residences. During the rise of Perugia's power it came under that city's jurisdiction; and with Perugia and Todi in the 14th century it rose up against the excessive and abusive powers of the popes. During Napoleon's sojourn in Italy, Spoleto became one of his local capitals and eventually was absorbed into the newly formed state of Italy on September 17, 1860.

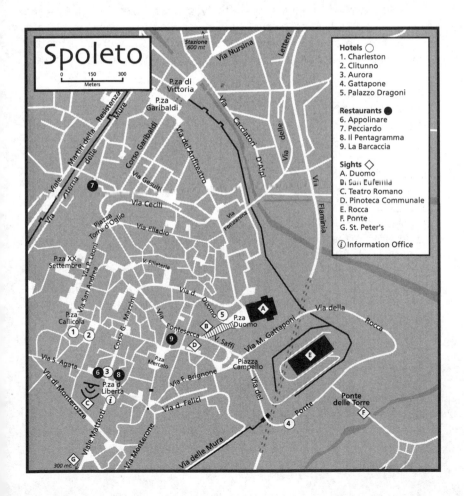

Arrivals & Departures

From Perugia the train leaves every hour and takes an hour to get here. From Rome, the schedule is more erratic but the trip takes only a little over an hour and a half. Check with your local information office for specific schedules.

Orientation

Spoleto is spread up a hillside with the defining structures being the spire of the **cathedral** and the imposing **Rocca** behind it. To the east up the hill is the **Duomo** whose **piazza** is a central focus of the town. The town's tiny roads twist and turn around the undulation of the hillside, so it's best to use a map or have a compass available to keep yourself on the right track.

Getting Around Town

Spoleto is made for walking, with twisting cobblestone streets and winding staircases leading through quaint medieval passageways. Be prepared to hike up and down hills, but the effort will be worth it since the surroundings will instantly transport you back to a simpler place and time.

Where to Stay

1. CHARLESTON, *Piazza Collicola 10. Tel. 0743/223-235, Fax 0743/222-010. Email: info@hotelcharleston.it, Web: www.hotelcharleston.it. 18 rooms. Per person E95-125. All credit cards accepted. Half board included.* ***

In the centro storico, this 17th century palazzo represents a classic blending of the old and new. The common areas are very large and simply furnished and the rooms are comfortably sized with modern 'antique' furnishings. The bathrooms are small but come with hairdryer and complimentary toiletry kit. Buffet breakfast is served in the summer on a small terrace area. Apart from the private garage, guests also have at their disposal a sauna, two bars, and a reading room. The hotel also offers hiking and biking excursions for those that request it at an extra charge. A great place to stay in Spoleto. And if you are wondering about the name of the hotel, Charleston, South Carolina hosts a Spoleto festival every year. The hotel's name comes from that connection.

2. CLITUNNO, *Piazza Sordini. Tel. 0743/223-340. Fax 0743/222-663. Web: www.hotelclitunno.com. 38 rooms. Per person E45-75. All credit cards accepted. Breakfast included.* ***

Located near the Teatro Romano and recently renovated (1994), the Clitunno offers a pleasant mix of the old and new. The best rooms are furnished with the 'faux' antiques with tiled floors and oriental rugs covering them. The others are accommodatingly comfortable with more modern furnishings. The bathrooms are small but well appointed with all manner of amenities, including a phone. A good hotel in a good location.

3. AURORA, *Via Appolinare 3. Tel 0743/220-315, Fax 0743/221-885. Email: info@hotelauroraspoleto.it, Web: www.hotelauroraspoleto.it. 40 rooms. Single E50-70; Double E60-90.* ******

A great two star right next to the Teatro Romana and just down from the Piazza del Mercato, the heart of the centro storico. This hotel is bucking for three star status and as such they are a superb two star, with clean and comfortable rooms and excellent service in an ideal location. The bathrooms are a little small and will need to be upgraded if they want to achieve that extra star, but in terms of price/quality this is a great find.

4. GATTAPONE, *Via del Ponte 6. Tel. 0743/223-447, Fax 0743/223-448. 14 rooms. Standard Single E85-95; Superior Single E112-125; Standard Double E100-145; Superior Double E155-180. Breakfast E12.* ********

Set in a magical location overlooking the green valley and the medieval aqueduct that traverses it. All the bedrooms overlook this picturesque scene and is the reason to stay here. The standard rooms are a little on the small side, but are comfortable and come with baths and showers so you can luxuriate in the tub after a long day of hiking through the mountains. I would suggest springing for the Superior rooms, which are located in the modern extension and offer more space. There are two comfortable bar areas, as well as two terraces below where sheep sometimes wander. This hotel, in its pristine natural setting, is only a short walk to the centro storico. If you are inspired and have the means, without a question, this is *the* place to stay in Spoleto.

5. PALAZZO DRAGONI, *Via del Duomo, 13. Tel. 0743/222-220, Fax 0743/222-225. Web: www.initaly.com/hisres/palazzo/palazzo.htm. 15 rooms, 9 suites. Double E120-270. All credit cards accepted. Breakfast included.* ********

This historic inn just steps from the Duomo, dating from the 14th century, has been lovingly restored and maintained through the years. In fact, the original stone foundations that you can see in the basement date from before 1000 CE, when the residence was two separate structures, with a street running between them! Ask to see it. The common room features vaulted ceilings, as do a number of rooms, with lovely rugs and a medieval feel. The rooms are spacious and charming, and the view from most rooms is incredible, looking out over the rooftops of historic Spoleto. You can see the spire of the Duomo and the walls of the Rocca from the lovely breakfast room on the top floor. Service is friendly and efficient. If you want to feel like you've stepped back into medieval times, this is the place to stay.

Where to Eat

6. APOLLINARE, *Via S. Agata 14. Tel. 0743/223-256. Closed Tuesdays. All credit cards accepted. Dinner for two E60.*

In the heart of Spoleto situated in what was at one time a Franciscan convent, in a short period of time this place has garnered a measure of culinary respect. The ingredients they use are all local but the way they prepare them is in the *cucina nuova* style. They get creative with their dishes so don't expect anything simple and traditional here. Do expect great atmosphere and imaginative food, though at elevated prices. A great place to come if you are into exploring the pleasures of the palate and are not concerned with the effect it has on your wallet.

7. PECCIARDA, *Vicolo San Giovanni 1. Tel. 0743/221-009. Closed Thursdays. No credit cards accepted. Dinner for two E35.*

Exquisite food, attentive service, great local atmosphere in a completely out of the way location, and all at prices that are easy on the pocketbook. This place is fantastic. A real slice of Spoleto. You have to come here if you are in town. Some of the simple but tasty dishes they serve include *gnocchi ripiena* (ricotta cheese dumplings), *stragozzi ai funghi* (local home made pasta with a spicy mushroom sauce) *pollo "alla Pecciarda"* (chicken stuffed with succulent herbs and spices), or a superb *arrosto misto* (mixed grilled meats).

8. IL PENTAGRAMMA, *Via T. Martani 4/6/8. Tel. 0743/223-141. Closed Mondays and January 15-31. All credit cards accepted except American Express. Dinner for two E40.*

With a new owner and a new cook this place is going through a rebirth, not that it was bad to begin with. It's just that now it's fantastic, with great local food and a serene musical atmosphere, at good prices. Try some of their frascarelli con pomodoro e basilica (pasta with tomatoes and basil) or tagliatelle ai funghi porcini (pasta with porcini mushrooms). For seconds the petto di tacchino e purea di fave (turkey breast with pureed fava beans) is rather tasty. They also make some great lamb dishes. To try a little of everything they have an abundant sampler menu for E25 per person, which gives you antipasto, pasta, main course and dessert. This is one of Spoleto's best restaurants.

9. LA BARCACCIA, *Piazza F.lli Bardier 3. Tel. 0743/221-171. Web: www.caribusiness.barcaccia. Closed Tuesdays. Credit cards accepted. Dinner for two E35.*

Located just off of the Piazza del Mercato, the heart of the centro storico, in an isolated piazza of its own, this restaurant offers typical local dishes at good prices. They specialize in cooking with truffles and grilling a wide variety of meats, especially veal. Everything they serve is stupendous and the ambiance is rustic and charming. For primo, try the tortellini al tartufo (meat filled pasta with truffle sauce), the tortellini panna e funghi (meat filled pasta with cream and mushrooms) or the spaghetti alla carbonara (with bacon egg, parmesan and pecorino). A great place to eat while in Spoleto.

Seeing the Sights
A. DUOMO
Rising up from the picturesque main square, the spire on the bell tower

next to the Duomo acts as a beacon. The bell tower was constructed in the 12th century, with stone material removed from ancient Roman ruins. The Romanesque Duomo, built at the same time, has an imposing facade that is preceded by a portico built at the turn of the 16th century. The facade has five Rosetta windows and a mosaic created by Solsterno from 1207 above which are three more Rosetta windows.

The interior (open November-February 8:00am-1:00pm & 3:00-5:30pm; March-October 8:00am-1:00pm & 3:00-6:30pm) is simple with a nave and two aisles. You will find a variety of religious art including some magnificent works by Pinturicchio in the Chapel of Bishop Eroli.

B. SAN EUFEMIA

Located near the Duomo, this is one of the finest examples of simple Umbrian-Romanesque architecture. Constructed in the first half of the 12th century, the facade is basic but inspiring, with a portal window and a sweep of arches on the crown. The interior is white, austere and stark and is divided into three parts – one of which being the women's section above the main floor where women had to sit so as not to distract the men during services. Devoid of much finery, this church is a wonderful example of the piety and beauty of simplicity.

C. TEATRO ROMANO

A well preserved first century CE construction, located just off of the Piazza della Liberta and surrounded on one side by the stables of the 17th century Palazzo Ancaiani. The **church of Santa Agata** occupies what once was the stage area. Also included with the price of entry (E2) is access to the **Museo Archeologico Nazionale** (Via S. Agata, 9:00am-7:00pm; holidays 9:00am-1:00pm) which has a few interesting pieces, including artifacts from a warrior's tomb, jewelry, pottery and other material from the Bronze Age through the Middle Ages.

Outside, the Teatro Romano is a wonderful example of how architecture from different eras has been intertwined into the pastiche of daily life in Spoleto. Another example of that is the **Arco di Druso Minore** and **Arco Romano** nearby. These are two Roman-era arches have been completely incorporated into the surrounding buildings.

D. PINOTECA COMUNALE

Up the Via del Municipio from the Piazza del Mercato — which used to be a Roman Forum — is the Palazzo Comunale with its tall tower, small piazza and large flag out front. Begun in the 13th century and renovated in the 18th, this palazzo is now home to the Pinoteca Comunale (admission E2.5, open 10:00am-1:00pm & 3:00-6:00pm, closed Tuesdays) which contains a small but captivating local museum. My favorite part is the display of old mint pieces that were used to make coins. As you enter, prior to going up to the museum, take a little time to admire the frescoes in the entrance way. Across from the palazzo are some delightful medieval houses set among winding little streets, which should be wandered if you are here.

Included in the price of entry is also access to the remains of an old Roman House, which I found infinitely more interesting than the little museum upstairs. Located to the left of the building, on the Via Visiale, is an excavated Roman home purported to be the home of the mother of Emperor Vespasian. Also included in the price of admission is access to the **Galleria Comunale d'Arte Moderna** (Piazza Sordini 5, 10:00am-1:00pm & 4:00-7:00pm, closed Mondays) with a limited but interesting display of local modern art pieces.

E. ROCCA

This fortress stronghold dominates the view over Spoleto. Finished in the second half of the 14th century, from here you can get wonderful panoramic photos of the town and valley. Once a residence of the popes and other aristocracy, it has since been used as an army base and was a prison until 1982. In 1983 the process of restoring back to its former splendor began. Today you can go on brief guided tours (admission E5, open 3:00-6:00pm Monday-Friday, 10:00am-noon & 3:00-6:00pm Saturday and Sunday). The Rocca is being prepared to house a museum relating to the medieval duchy of Spoleto. The guided tour is well worth the price despite the limited material available.

F. PONTE DELLE TORRE

Past the Rocca is one of the most incredible sights I have ever seen in Italy, a medieval aqueduct spanning a gorge and leading to a pristine, verdant hill covered with hiking trails. This 13th century span connects two hillsides and is 230 meters long and 76 meters high and has towering piers and narrow arcades, which cast incredible shadows over the valley in the late afternoon light. It no longer carries water but serves as a foot bridge over the valley. Because of this sight and where it leads, it makes Spoleto a must-see destination when in Italy.

On the Via della Ponte on the way to the aqueduct, is a little bar, **La Portella**, that has tables set out on an overlooking with views of St Peter's. This is a good spot at which to relax anytime day or night.

G. ST. PETER'S

Located just outside of the old walled city, and visible from the Ponte delle Terme, is this fine church built between the 12th and 13th centuries. The beautiful but simple facade is embellished with numerous ornamental bas-relief decorations. There are three portals in the lower level, the center one surrounded by most of the ornamentation. The interior of the church is divided into three parts and was renovated and updated in 1669. This church, though plain, is one of the most important monuments in the region.

Other churches of interest inside the city walls are San Nicolo, San Filippo, and San Domenico.

Shopping

Spoleto does not have many international boutiques – yet – but what they do have are wonderful little shops selling typical works by local artisans. There are unique stores selling ceramics, fabrics, antiques, handmade note-books as well as shops catering to the needs of the locals like alimentari, salumerie and more. There are also numerous galleries and artists' studios filled with a diverse array of paintings and sculptures. The best shopping is along the **Corso G. Garibaldi**, up the **Via Salaria Vecchia**, and all around the **Piazza del Mercato**.

Practical Information

Festivals

Spoleto Festival, Mid-June to mid-July. Email: tickets@spoletofestival.net, Web: www.spoletofestival.net. A world-renowned festival filled with music, dance, cinematography, theater, art exhibits and more, that goes on every day for a month. An arts extravaganza that has no equal.

Other festivals include:
- **February and March** – Carnival of Spoleto
- **Week After Easter** – Week of the High Middle Ages
- **September** – Experimental Season of Lyrical Opera
- **December 14, 15, 16 and January 1** – Nativity and the Living Crib

Tourist Information

To arrange day trips, find out about bus tours, find train or bus information, get maps, or detailed walking tour information, book a hotel or simply get general information about Spoleto, the **tourist office**, Piazza della Liberta 7, Tel. 0743/49890, Fax 0743/46241, is the place to visit.

GUBBIO

Gubbio is an ancient medieval town that majestically spreads out along the wind-swept ridges of **Mount Ingino**, with the **Torrente Camignano** river flowing through the settlement. This incredibly beautiful little town was founded by the ancient Umbrian people and eventually taken over by the Etruscans, as chronicled to in the **Eugubine Tablets** – the Rosetta Stone for ancient central Italian languages, culture and history – which are located here in Gubbio.

These seven bronze tablets give illuminating insight into how the city was run between the 3rd century and 1st century BCE, and are partially written in the Umbrian language — which is a derivation of Etruscan — and simultaneously in a rudimentary form of Latin.

In 295 BCE, Roman rule began and the town remained safe and secure until the end of the empire, like many of the towns in the region. Then it was destroyed during the Gothic wars of the 5th century CE and eventually came under Lombard control in the 8th century CE. By the 11th century the town was a free, independent commune and as such began to grow in power and importance. This situation instantly led to conflicts with Perugia, another strong city-state in the region, which conquered Gubbio handily in the 12th century. Then the city fell under papal control, which was not as benevolent as one might imagine – it was actually quite despotic. The Dukes of Urbino grabbed control for two centuries, then the Papal States reaffirmed their dominance in 1624 until the city was annexed into the new Italian state in the 1860s.

The layout of the town is very Roman with its structured grid pattern and is quite medieval with its ancient buildings, old city walls, and winding streets and steps flowing up and down the mountain. Also added onto this atmosphere are plenty of more 'modern' Renaissance towers and palazzi mingling with Gothic churches, making Gubbio a stunningly beautiful, 'can't miss' town if you are in Umbria.

The main handicrafts in Gubbio are ceramics as well as wrought iron work, carpentry, and copperware. The main flourish in the cuisine comes from the pungently aromatic white truffle that graces the local dishes mainly in autumn and winter. Gubbio loves a party and has a number of fun medieval festivals to enjoy, especially the **Corsa dei Ceri-Candle Tower Race** held on May 15th, replete with costumes and contests. This festival is on par with the best festivals in Italy. In this reenactment of an ancient tradition, separate sections of the city carry enormous wooden towers topped with wax statues of saints (Ubaldo, George, Anthony and Abbot) on their shoulders through the town, then up to the Basilica of San Ubaldo on Mount Ingino. Despite the Christian trappings, the festival is rooted in pagan rituals celebrating the coming of spring and each saint represents ancient pagan gods of fertility.

Another festival of note, this one on the last Sunday in May, is the **Palio della Balestra** – a crossbow competition. In this festival, archers dressed in period garb vie for an accuracy title. Complete with exciting pageantry, this is a fun festival to witness. Also, from July to mid-August, classical plays are performed in the Roman Theater outside of the main city walls.

Arrivals & Departures

Gubbio can only be reached by car or bus. There is no train service. The bus schedule from Perugia is infrequent. Despite that, Gubbio is a great destination in and of itself, and can also be a quick day trip from Perugia. A bus schedule (orario) for the local line, **Autolinee Regionali**, is available at the local tourist office in Piazza IV Novembre in Perugia.

Orientation

Gubbio is 40 kilometers north-northwest of Perugia. It is separated into two different sections, upper and lower. In the lower section life revolves around the circular **Piazza Quaranta Martiri**. The upper town is centered on the **Piazza Grande**. Surrounding this piazza are most of the main sights of the city.

Getting Around Town

The best way to get around Gubbio, like most Umbrian towns, is by walking. Inside the old city walls the tiny medieval streets lend themselves to exploration by foot. But since it is nestled along a hillside, you should be prepared for some arduous climbs while you explore.

Where to Stay

1. GATTAPONE, Via Ansidei 6. Tel. 075/927-2489, Fax 075/927-1269, Email: hotelgattapone@mencarelligroup.com, Web: www.mencarelligroup.com/ing/hotelgattaponeing/gattapone.htm. Closed January. 28 rooms, all with bath. Single E70-90; Double E90-110. All credit cards accepted. Breakfast included. ***

In an ancient building in the center of Gubbio, close to the Piazza Grande and the Palazzo dei Consoli, this old and respected hotel has recently been granted another star rating, and deservedly so. The general impression of the entire hotel is one of cleanliness, and every room is accommodatingly comfortable and come with air-conditioning, heat, mini-bars, telephones and TVs. Breakfast is either served in your room or at a nearby restaurant, Il Taverna del Lupo (see restaurant section below) that is owned by the same family, Mencarelli. A good place to stay in Gubbio.

2. BOSONE PALACE, Via XX Settembre 22. Tel. 075/922-0688, Fax 075/922-0552, Email: hotelbosonepalace@mencarelligroup.com, Web: www.mencarelligroup.com/ing/hotelpalaceing/bosonepalace.htm. 35 rooms. Single E70-85; Double E85-105. All credit cards accepted. Breakfast included. ***

Located in a 16th century building, this hotel is also run by the Mencarelli family. Maintaining an old world charm and ambiance while offering all modern amenities, the entrance is elegant with aristocratic red divans and a scenic stairway leading up to the guest rooms. Spacious and comfortable, the rooms are decorated with antique furniture and parquet floors covered with oriental rugs. Though on the small side, the bathrooms all have showers and

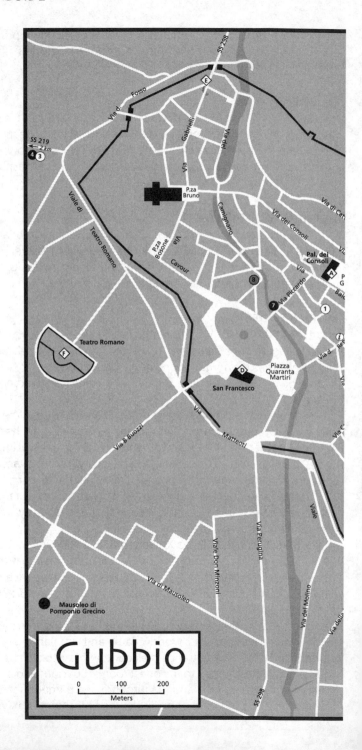

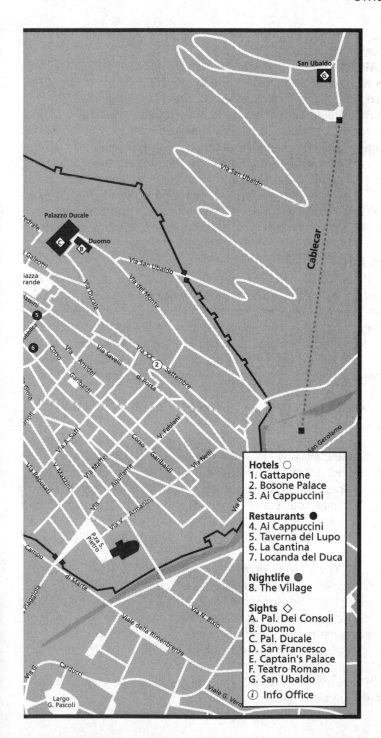

come with a complimentary toiletry kit and hair dryer. An elegant hotel right in the middle of the old city.

3. AI CAPPUCCINI, *Via Tifernate. Tel. 075/9234, Fax 075/661-109. Web: www.venere.com/umbria/gubbio/aicappuccini. 100 rooms. Single E170; Double E210-270. All credit cards accepted. Breakfast included.* ****

Located a kilometer outside the walls of the old city this hotel was once a convent back in the 1600's. While still maintaining the charm of the old structure, the renovations of 1990 have brought this excellent four star hotel into the modern era. Some of the rooms are the old cells the monks used, updated for your comfort of course, and some are located in a new addition to the older structure. Many rooms are around the periphery of a quiet relaxing park area; all are spacious and perfect for relaxing, as is the swimming pool, sun deck and sauna. If you want to stay in the lap of luxury in Gubbio, stay here.

Where to Eat

4. AI CAPPUCCINI, *Via Tifernate. Tel. 075/9234, Fax 075/661-109. Closed Mondays. All credit cards accepted. Dinner for two E75.*

The cuisine is traditional Umbrian which means you'll find truffles, cheese and meats in most dishes. Try their maniche ripiene di ricotta zucchine peperoni e pomodoro (cylinders of pasta stuffed with cheese, zucchini, peppers and tomatoes). For seconds try their succulent petto di anatra tartufato (breast of duck with truffles). A charming atmosphere with seating inside and outside in the park terrace.

5. IL TAVERNA DEL LUPO, *Via G. Ansidei 6. Tel. 075/927-4368. Closed Mondays. All credit cards accepted. Dinner for two E70.*

Run by the Mencarelli group that seems to have a firm grip on the accommodation and culinary options in Gubbio, beyond a doubt this is the best food and most welcoming atmosphere in Gubbio. I recommend trying the menu sampler at E35 per person since you'll get a full meal complete with antipasto, pasta, main course and dessert. The menu consists of traditional Umbrian cuisine: pasta, truffles and meat. The ambiance is charming, romantic, and upscale. Come dressed appropriately and be prepared to pay for the privilege.

6. LA CANTINA, *Via Piccotti 3. Tel. 075/922-0583. Website: www.gubbio.com/lacantina. All credit cards accepted. Dinner for two E35.*

Great atmosphere and wonderful food. This place seems to be crowded all the time and for good reason – it is an excellent restaurant. There are some tiny tables set up just before the entrance in their own little cortille, but the place to be is inside in their expansive and rustic dining hall. Try some tasty tagliatelle al funghi porcini (with mushrooms) or al tartufo (with truffles). For seconds they have meats of all sorts, especially veal, as well as great pizza. A down-to-earth, fun place to eat.

7. LOCANDA DEL DUCA, *Via Picardi 1. Tel. 075/927-7753. All credit cards accepted. Dinner for two E25.*

This is a friendly and irreverent restaurant in a quaint old neighborhood, which serves tasty pastas and meats, but they are really known for their exquisite pizzas. The interior is rustic, set with a wood beamed ceiling; there's a small garden terrace overlooking the small river that flows through Gubbio. A good choice, a little off of the beaten path, and they are open until midnight if you need a late night snack.

Seeing the Sights

A. PALAZZO DEI CONSOLI

Looking out over the town this imposing structure sits at the east end of the Piazza Grande and is the architectural and monumental core of the city. Ringed with some Renaissance *palazzi*, one of which is the **Palazzo Pretorio**, from this piazza you can get some stunning panoramic views.

The Palazzo dei Consoli is really two 14th century buildings, architecturally associated but clearly distinct. Simple and elegant, the palace is graced with a magnificent Gothic portal, in front of which are a set of steps that face out onto the piazza. The facade is divided by vertical pilaster strips, topped with turrets over which looks a small bell tower.

Also known as the Palazzo dei Popolo, the building now houses the **Picture Gallery** which has some paintings from Gubbio dating from the 14th and 16th centuries; and the **Archaeological Museum**, which houses the seven historically significant **Eugubine Tablets**, the Rosetta Stone for Central Italy. These tablets have a corresponding Umbrian language text, which evolved alongside the Etruscan, and a rudimentary form of Latin. There are also some interesting ancient archaeological finds like stone ceramics and coins. Not laid out and catalogued like the Smithsonian, but interesting and educational nonetheless.

B. DUOMO

A simple austere brick cathedral built in the 12th century, located up the hill from the older Roman town. The facade is graced with a plain circular window above a pointed portal. The interior is in a Latin cross plan and has one nave and many pointed arches supporting the ceiling. Simple and plain inside, except for the paintings and frescoes of the 16th century Umbrian artists along the walls, the church also has an incredibly detailed altar space, organ and choir. This cathedral is a wonderful example of austere medieval beauty.

C. PALAZZO DUCALE

Located directly across from the Duomo, this is a prime example of Renaissance architecture. Built in 1470 on the site of an older Lombard palace, this building contains a splendid internal courtyard surrounded by porticos. In the basement there is an archaeological excavation of the alterations made atop the building during the Renaissance. The palace's foundation can be seen as can segments of the original plumbing. Fragments of medieval ceramics found during the excavations are also on display.

The rest of the museum, upstairs, is really just a set of whitewashed walls, scattered antique furnishings, restored pieces from local churches, and an occasional modern art exhibit to fill up the space. Save the E2 cost of entry and buy a drink at The Village instead (see below under *Nightlife*), unless of course you are keenly interested in medieval plumbing.

D. CHURCH OF ST. FRANCIS

Located on the large Piazza Quaranta Martiri, this church was built in the 13th century with a bare facade, a Gothic portal and a small rose window. There is an octagonal campanile at the right side of the church.

The interior has one nave and two aisles. When the sun streams in through the large pointed windows along the sides and the colored windows in the apse, this church simply glows. The attached cloisters evoke images of times past and should be visited if open. Other churches of possible interest to visit in the town, though much simpler in ornamentation, are San Secondo, San Giovanni, and San Pietro.

E. CAPTAIN OF THE PEOPLE'S PALACE

Located on Via dell Capitano del Popolo #6, near the outskirts of this small town, this 13th century building is rather plain, but what's inside is memorable. Home to the **Museum of Torture Instruments**, you can just imagine the displays. They are educational, enlightening and a refreshing reality check concerning the relative safety of modern life.

F. ROMAN THEATER

Located just outside the old city walls, this ancient theater is considered to be one of the largest and best preserved in Italy. Now converted to a verdant park, this old theater is also home to live productions through July and mid-August. Separated into four wedge-shaped sections by flights of stairs with many of the ruins rebuilt and solidified, you really feel as if you've walked back in time.

G. BASILICA OF SAN UBALDO

At the summit of Mount Ingino lies the terminus for the traditional Corsa dei Ceri, the ancient tower up the hill. It can be reached by cable car from the station through the Porta Romana (an immense tower construction evoking a definite medieval feel) or by walking the length of the Corsa dei Ceri through the Porta San Ubaldo. I suggest that route only for the most fit.

Built in the 1514, worthy of note is the engraved marble altar and the glass coffin containing the well-preserved body of St. Ubaldo. The three wooden towers used in the Corso dei Ceri festival are on display here year round. On the hillside above the church are the remains of the 12th century Rocca.

Nightlife & Entertainment
8. THE VILLAGE, *Piazza 40 Martiri #29. Tel. 075/922-2296.*

Art, history, architecture and the surrounding natural setting, coupled with a warm, friendly atmosphere make The Village is the place to come for late night festivities in Gubbio. Located in a renovated old church, I can't think of a better place to come with friends or to meet new ones. They serve Bass and Tenents on tap at E4 a pint and serve some basic Italian-style pub food.

Practical Information
Tourist Information
To arrange day trips, find out about bus tours, find train or bus information, get maps, or detailed walking tour information, book a hotel or simply get general information about Gubbio, the **tourist office** is the place to go, Piazza Oderisi 6, *Tel. 075/922-0693* or *922-0790, Fax 075/927-3409.*

TODI
An ancient and attractive city surrounded by medieval walls, and filled with quaint winding streets, **Todi** rises up among green hills above where the Nala flows into the Tiber. Put this little town on your Umbria itinerary.

Mostly enclosed within the perimeter of the old town walls in a roughly triangular layout, Todi is wonderfully apart from the advance of time, and has yet to succumb to the invading hordes of tourists. There is only one hotel in the centro storico, and a small bed and breakfast which means that the residents of the city still far outnumber the tourists, a situation you will find true all over Umbria, but especially so in Todi.

Todi, like all of Umbria, is not a place to pursue frantic sightseeing forays. Todi has a refreshingly gentle feel to it, and is still untainted by the hustle and bustle of frenetic tour groups trying to suck up the Italian experience as if it were a giant Slurpee. Todi is a town where you can fit right into the flow of real Italian life, wander unobtrusively among the friendly locals, sit with them in the parks as their children play, or smile with them in the piazzas as they pantomime one of the scenes in life's play. This is a place to undertake casual meandering, not only around the hilly cobblestone streets lined with medieval homes – some set into old Roman and Etruscan walls. Todi is also a place to rest and be rejuvenated in a fairy tale setting.

Founded by the Tutere, an ancient Umbrian people, and heavily influenced by the Etruscans who settled along the banks of the Tiber, Todi eventually fell under Rome's control during the 4th century BCE and became known as Tuder. When the Roman Empire collapsed, the city underwent its share of destruction from the Goths and Byzantine Empire.

Beginning in the year 1000 it became an independent commune, during which time it extended its domain as far as Amelia and Terni in the 13th century. But then it became part of other empires again in the 14th century, eventually ending up in the hands of the Papal States. When Napoleon was in control of the Italian peninsula, Todi was an important government seat. After Napoleon it once again came under papal jurisdiction, then was incorporated into the Italian Republic in 1860.

Arrivals & Departures

Todi is difficult to get to because the train and bus schedules are erratic. Also, the train station is a ways out of town (take the bus "C" from Piazza Jacapone) and is on a small regional line, which means the trains move much slower and stop at every town along the way. Check with the information office for schedules.

If you are taking the train into Perugia, be aware that Perugia has three different train stations. Trains from Todi stop first at Porta S. Giovanni station in Perugia, then go onto an even smaller station called **Perugia Santa Ana** (which is where you get off, since it is near the escalators up to the center), but they do not stop at the main train station in Perugia.

Orientation

Located 45 kilometers from Perugia, Todi is a small triangular shaped town sprawled along the crest of a hill. The skyline is dominated by Santa Maria della Consolazione in the lower part of town and the Chiesa di San Fortunato in the upper part. The Piazza del Popolo is definitely the central focus of the town around which are situated most of the major sights.

Getting Around Town

The only way to get around town is by walking. The town is small but even so, getting from the lower part of town to the upper can seem long because of the steep uphill grade. Be prepared to hike while here.

Where to Stay

1. RESIDENZA SAN LORENZO TRE, *Via San Lorenzo 3, Six rooms, four with bath. Tel. & Fax 075/894-4555, Web: www.todi.net/lorenzo. Holiday Jan. 15 – Feb 28. Single without bath E75; Single E80; Double without bath E80; Double E110. Breakfast included. No credit cards accepted.*

Located on the upper floor of a quaint palazzo just off of the Piazza del Popolo, this is a great place to stay in Todi. Though not technically a hotel, I would categorize this bed and breakfast-style residence as a three star, despite the lack of mini-bar and TV in the rooms. What this place lacks in unnecessary modern amenities is more than made up for with its charm, ambiance and incredibly scenic panoramic views. There are two rooms that open onto the most breathtaking vistas you can imagine. Each room is furnished with antique furnishings, which adds to the ambiance, but make sure you specifically request one of the two rooms with a view and your stay here will be stupenda (stupendous).

2. FONTE CESIA, *Via Lorenzo Leony 3, Tel. 075/894-3737, Fax 075/894-4677. Email: fontecesia@fontecesia.it. Web: www.fontecesia.it. 37 rooms. Single E115; Double E140-160. All credit cards accepted. Breakfast included.* ****

Situated in a noble and antique building in the center of Todi, this is an excellent small town four star hotel. Opened in 1994, they have made the decor antique to add a touch of old world character. The rooms are spacious, very comfortable and come with every necessary modern comfort, though the bathrooms are minuscule. Their sundeck is a great place to relax as are the downstairs common areas. A good place to stay in Todi.

Where to Eat
3. UMBRIA, *Via San Bonaventura 13. Tel. 075/894-2390. Closed Tuesdays and at the end of December. All credit cards accepted. Dinner for two E55.*

Where before the food here was average, now it is really good. And before where the service was surly it has come to be professional. I think you'll like the tagliatelle ai funghi (pasta with local mushrooms) or the spaghetti agli 'strioli' (spaghetti with an tasty herb only grown locally). For seconds the salami di cinghiale (wild boar) is a succulently tasty local sausage. An excellent choice while in Todi.

4. LE SCALETTE, *Via delle Scalette 1, Tel. 075/894-4422. Closed Mondays. Open 12:00-2:30pm & 7:00pm-1:00am. Dinner for two E35.*

This is a menu that has something for everyone, whether it's pizza, pasta, meats or vegetarian servings. They have terrace seating with some panoramic views, as well as a quaint medieval interior to add to this place's rustic charm. Here you will find authentic local atmosphere, excellent regional cooking, and attentive service, which will all translate into a wonderful meal. Try their cappollini al tartufo nero (stuffed pasta with truffle cream sauce), or any of their pizza's.

Seeing the Sights
A. SANTA MARIA DELLA CONSOLAZIONE
Located a little ways outside of the city walls, this is a must see location when in Todi. A delightful example of Renaissance architecture, begun in 1508

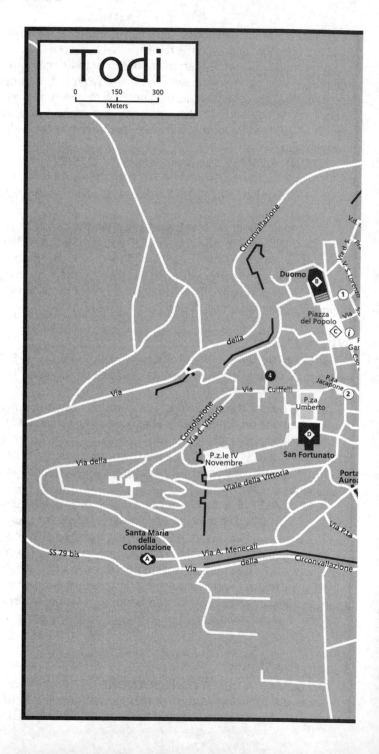

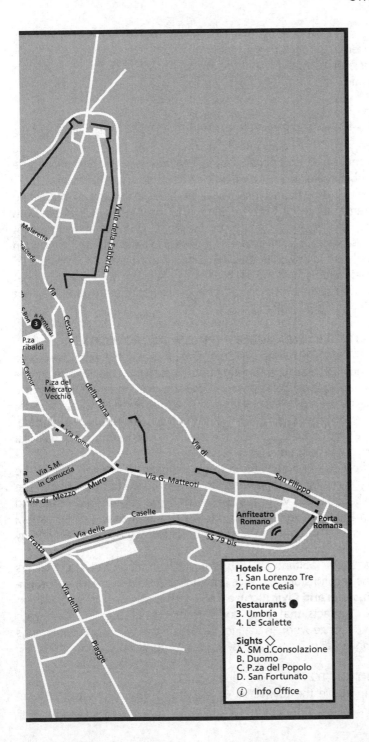

Hotels ○
1. San Lorenzo Tre
2. Fonte Cesia

Restaurants ●
3. Umbria
4. Le Scalette

Sights ◇
A. SM d.Consolazione
B. Duomo
C. P.za del Popolo
D. San Fortunato

ⓘ Info Office

and finished almost a century later, this lovely church, like San Fortunato, stands out from the diminutive skyline of the town. In the shape of a Greek Cross with a large central dome there are four apses each crowned with its own half dome.

B. DUOMO

This church dominates the Piazza Vittorio Emanuele II (also known as the Piazza del Popolo). The rectangular facade with three Rosetta windows and the same number of Gothic portals is simple yet refined. Flanking this facade is the robust bell tower that was once used as a military watchtower.

The interior is divided into three sections. In the left aisle is an interesting bronze of San Martino by Fiorenzo Bacci. The counter facade has a 16th century fresco of the *Last Judgment* by Faenzone. Unfortunately it has not been well preserved but is still powerful. Please also take note of the wooden choir behind the altar, as well as the two paintings portraying *St. Peter* and *St. Paul*, to the left and right of the altar, done by Spagna. For E7.5 you can get a ticket to see the crypt which is a rather non-descript underground area but interesting for medieval history buffs.

C. PIAZZA VITTORIO EMANUELE II (PIAZZA DEL POPOLO)

Besides the aforementioned Duomo, also located in the extensive Piazza Vittorio Emanuele II (more commonly known as the Piazza del Popolo) are the Palazzo dei Priori, Palazzo del Popolo, and Palazzo del Capitano. An extensive piazza that is the heart of this small town, it is located on the site of an ancient Roman Forum and is one the most beautiful medieval squares in all of Europe. Dominated by the Duomo and surrounded by numerous monumental palaces. it transports you back in time.

Across from the Duomo is the turreted **Palazzo dei Priori**, built in the 14th century then joined together with some pre-existing buildings. The trapezoidal shaped tower was originally much higher, but through wars and erosion it remains in its truncated form today. The bronze eagle, the symbol of Todi, that stands out above the second order of windows was made by Giovanni di Gigliaccio in 1339.

The Palazzo del Capitano is a 13th century construction with a set of stairs leading to the second story entrance. The building is the site of the **Roman-Etruscan Museum and Civic Picture Gallery**. There are a number of Roman and Etruscan artifacts that have come from the surrounding area with terracotta and bronze work. In the Picture Gallery you will find fine paintings by many Umbrian and Tuscan artists, as well as gold and ceramic work.

D. SAN FORTUNATO

Rising up above the town this Gothic church (hours: winter 9:30am-12:30pm & 3:00-5:00pm; summer 8:30am-12:30pm & 3:00-7:00pm) was built between the 13th and 15th centuries. The half-completed facade overlooks the top of a scenic but fatiguing series of steps and their accompanying green space. There are three portals, the middle one richly decorated with a variety of colonnades, and is flanked by two statues of *Gabriel* and *Virgin Mary*. The other two are smaller versions of the middle.

The interior can be described as majestic but plain, with its three grandiose naves and the cross vaulting, and stark white walls. The wooden choir behind the altar is as extensive as in the Duomo but it is more accessible and visible here. Unfortunately some the fine frescoes are only in fragments now, as preservation work was not started until this century. But even if the interior art work is a little decayed, the serenity of the space is spiritually invigorating.

E. PARCO DELLA ROCCA

Near San Fortunato is the Parco della Rocca, where you have nice panoramic views, peace and quiet — when there aren't any kids running around — a place to picnic and cuddle, a rose garden to stimulate your nose, all of which make you feel as if you are on top of the world. The peaceful sense of continuity and permanence that Todi evokes is personified by this little park and the residents who frequent it.

Practical Information
Festivals & Fairs
- **March-April** – Antiquarian Exhibition of Italy
- **June-July** – National Antique Fair
- **September 8** – Festa di S. Maria della Consolazione
- **September** – Todi festival
- **October 14** – Festa di San Fortunato (Patron saint of Todi)
- **November 11** – Fair of St. Martin

Tourist Information

To arrange day trips, find out about bus tours, find train or bus information, get maps, or detailed walking tour information, book a hotel or simply get general information about Todi, go to the **tourist office**, Piazza del Popolo 39, *Tel. 075/894-2526*.

ORVIETO

Orvieto is one of Umbria's best cities to visit. Just over the border with Lazio, the province that Rome is in, the stunning city of Orvieto rests picturesquely on the top of a hill bordered by protective cliffs, waiting for you to arrive.

One of the most beautiful towns in all of Italy, Orvieto has a rich array of winding medieval streets and stunning architecture. The town is also famous for the wonderful Orvieto wine that flows from the local vines, as well as the tasty olive oil from the nearby olive groves. Besides its culinary pursuits, the town also is a ceramic center. Local artisans, especially the immensely talented Michelangeli, also create intricate wood carvings as well as delicate lace.

The first inhabitants of Orvieto were Etruscan, after which the city became a protectorate of the Roman Empire. With the empire's decline, Orvieto underwent the inevitable spate of barbarian invasion. It then became a free commune in the 12th century CE and enjoyed a period of artistic and political advancement, until the Papal States suppressed it into their fold in the 14th century. When Napoleon Buonaparte conquered it, he made it an essential center of his dominion until Orvieto was absorbed into the Kingdom of Italy in 1860.

Arrivals & Departures

Orvieto is accessible from Rome by a train which runs every two hours, starting at 6:12am and ending at 8:30pm, and takes an hour and twenty minutes. Returns start at 9:00am and end at 10:30am. Once at the train station you then take the funiculare (cable car) up the hill to the Piazzale Cahen. By the funiculare station is where St. Patrick's Well is located so stop there before you head up into town.

From the station catch the bus 'A' — which should be waiting for you as you exit the funiculare since the bus is timed to its arrival — to the Piazza Duomo and the information office. Or take a taxi. From the Duomo you can get to all sights, hotels, and restaurants.

Orientation

Located on the top of a hill surrounded by cliffs, the **Corso Cavour** divides the city east to west. On the east is the **Piazzale Cahen** and the **Fortrezza** — built in 1364 and now a pleasant public garden with fine views over the surrounding valley — where the funiculare arrives, and at the west is the **Porta Maggior**e.

Getting Around Town

This town is easy to walk since being on the top of a bluff it is mainly flat. Once you take the funiculare up from the station there won't be many more serious hills to traverse.

Where to Stay

1. ITALIA, *Via di Piazza del Popolo. Tel/Fax 0763/42065, Email: hotelita@libero.it, Web: www.bellaumbria.net/grand-Hotel-Italia. 42 rooms. Single E70; Double E100-110. Credit cards accepted. Breakfast included.* ***

This 18th century palazzo in the centro storico of Orvieto offers you a pleasant stay right in the heart of things. The spacious rooms and relaxing

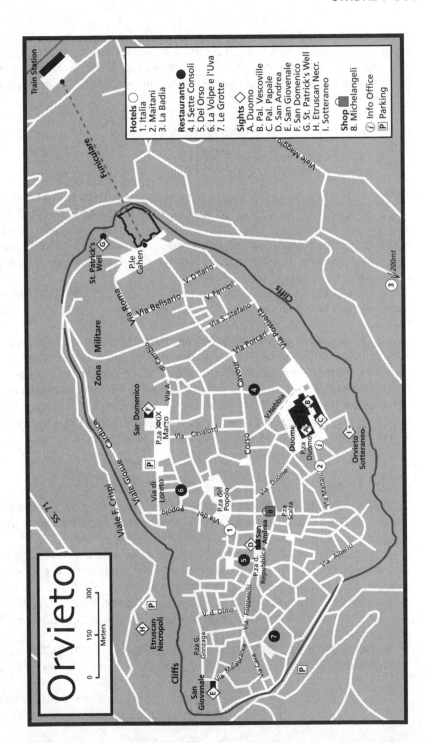

common areas are furnished in a classic but comfortable style, with antiques and a floral theme throughout. The best rooms are those facing the small courtyard (cortile), but all come with every three star amenity. The only real drawback other than that is the minuscule bathrooms Besides that, this is a wonderful place to stay in Orvieto.

2. MAITANI, *Via Lorenzo Maitani. Tel 0763/42011, Fax 0763/660-209. Web: www.argoweb.it/hotel_maitani/maitani.uk.html. Closed January 6-26. 40 rooms. Single E80; Double E130. Suite E150-180. All credit cards accepted. Breakfast E10.* ****

If you want a serene atmosphere you'll find it here in this antique palazzo in the centro storico, only a few steps from the magnificent Duomo of Orvieto. The rooms are all different from one another but are furnished for comfort and style. The bathrooms are all modern, though a wee bit tiny compared to North American standards. There is ample public space downstairs in the lounge/bar area, where you can put your feet up at the end of the day. A wonderful place to stay while in Orvieto, in an ideal setting.

3. LA BADIA, *Tel 0763/301-959 or 305-455, Fax 0763/305-396. Web: www.labadiahotel.it. All credit cards accepted. Single E125; Double E300.* ****

An unbelievably beautiful 12th century abbey at the foot of Orvieto is home to this incredible hotel that has only recently opened for business. Here you will be treated to one of the most unique and memorable experiences in the entire world. The rooms are immense, the accommodations exemplary, the service impeccable, and the atmosphere stupendous. For a fairy tale vacation stay here. Also make sure that you eat at least once at their soon to be world-renowned restaurant offering refined local dishes in an incredibly historic and romantic atmosphere.

Where to Eat

4. I SETTE CONSOLI, *Piazza San Angelo 1/a. Tel. 0763/343-911. Closed Wednesdays and February and March. All credit cards accepted. Dinner for two E40.*

This is one of the best places in town with a comfortable local atmosphere, and a beautiful garden for dining during good weather. If you don't want to make a decision about the food you can order from a series of fixed price menu options that offer you a variety of dishes to sample, and all at good prices. Everything here is fresh and local, especially their salami and cheese, which come in a tasty antipasto platter.

5. TRATTORIA DEL ORSO, *Via della Misericordia. Tel. 0763/341-642. Closed Monday nights, Tuesdays and February. Visa accepted. Dinner for two E40.*

Deep in the heart of Orvieto, nestled down a small side street is this small trattoria passionately operated by Gabrielle (doing the cooking) and Ciro (greeting and seating) where you can find genuine and simple Umbrian cuisine. You should start with the magnificent bruschetta (garlic bread) and proceed to the luscious fettucine alfredo. For seconds there are plenty of meat and vegetable dishes, as well as omelets to choose from. The desserts are home made, so you have to save room for at least one. A great place to sample the local flavor.

6. LA VOLPE E L'UVA, *Via Ripa Corsica 1. Tel. 0763/341-612. Closed Mondays and From July 15 to August 15. American Express and Visa accepted. Dinner for two E35.*

The food, friendly atmosphere and low prices really packs in the customers. Their antipasto salami plate (salumi misti locali) features all sorts of local favorites. The gnochetti con olio pepe e pecorino is a superb mixture of pepper, oil and pecorino cheese over small potato gnocchi. For your entrée you should consider ordering the arrosto di maiale alle erbe (tasty roast pork marinated in herbs) that literally melts in your mouth, or the delicious pollo alla cacciatore (chicken hunter style) or agnello sulla griglia (grilled lamb). For dessert there is good selection of cheese and fruit as well as a rich, creamy chocolate mousse (mousse di cioccolato).

7. LE GROTTE DEL FUNARO, *Via Ripa Serancia 41. Tel. 0763/343-276. Closed Mondays. Dinner for two E40.*

Literally situated in a series of grotte (caves) carved into the tufa layer upon which Orvieto sits, this place offers you a unique dining experience to go along with their delicious food. The whole point of coming here is to eat downstairs in the caves, so avoid the terrace. The have a well rounded menu, but in truffle season that aromatic tuber is featured prominently and any dish seasoned with it should be sampled if you are here from October to December. Try Le Grotte when in Orvieto. You will not be disappointed.

Seeing the Sights
A. DUOMO

Stunning! Elegant! Mesmerizing! No words can really describe this amazing cathedral, located in the Piazza del Duomo, whose facade is covered with bas-reliefs, colorful mosaics, and radiating frescoes. The pointed portals on the facade literally jump out at you, and the rose window — flanked by figures of the Prophets and Apostles — is a treasure to behold. Bring binoculars to admire all the intricate detail, since the facade is an entire museum in and of itself.

Most of its ornamentation was created between the 14th and 16th centuries. The bronze doors are contemporary works by Emilio Greco (1964). A museum featuring more of his art is situated on the ground floor of the Palazzo Papale to the right of the Duomo. Above and beside the doors are the Bronze Symbols of the Evangelists. The exterior side walls are alternating horizontal layers of black basalt and pale limestone in the distinctive Pisan style. This same style is translated into the interior, covering both the walls, and the columns which divide the church into a nave and two aisles. The christening font is the work of several artists and is stunning in its intricacies. The apse is lit by 14th century stained glass windows by Bonino and contains frescoes by Ugolino di Prete Ilario.

In the right transept behind an artistic 16th century wrought iron railing is the beautiful Capella Nuova, which contains Luca Signorelli's superlative Last Judgment. It is purported to be the inspiration for Michelangelo's Last Judgment in the Sistine Chapel. A must see, since it is also considered one of the greatest frescoes in Italian art. The chapel also contains frescoed medallions depicting poets and philosophers ranging from Homer to Dante.

B. PALAZZO VESCOVILLE

Located to the right and at the rear of the Duomo, restored in the 1960s, it now houses the **Archaeological Museum** (open 9:00am – 7:00pm, Holidays 9:00am-1:00pm; admission E2), which has a collection of material excavated from the Etruscan Necropoli that are located nearby the city. A simple, basic introduction to the history of the region.

C. PALAZZO PAPALE

Situated to the right of the Duomo, this was once the residence of a long line of popes when they came to visit the city. This building dates back to the 8th century and is also known as the **Palace of Bonifacio VIII**. On the ground floor you can find the **Museum of Emilio Greco** (open 10:30am-1:00pm and 2:00-6:00pm in winter and 3:00-7:00pm in summer) exhibiting numerous works by this fine sculptor from Catania. On the first floor is the **Cathedral Museum**, which displays miscellaneous works of art, mostly from the Duomo or about the Duomo.

D. SAN ANDREA

On the edge of the Piazza della Repubblica, this plain church is best known for its dodecagonal campanile, a twelve-sided bell-tower. This masterful architectural complement to the church has three orders of windows and a turreted top section. Built between the 6th and 14th centuries on the site of a pre-existing early Christian church, the interior is a single nave with two aisles, a raised transept and cross vaults. The wooden altar by Scalza is worthy of note, as is the pulpit. Situated below the church and accessible by appointment are some ancient ruins dating from the Iron Age up to the medieval period.

E. SAN GIOVENALE

Originally a Romanesque building San Giovenale was reconstructed in the 13th century with Lombard features. The massive square bell tower dwarfs this plain and sturdy looking church. The interior is a simple design with one single nave and two aisles. Note the Romanesque high altar intricately decorated with bas-reliefs as well as the frescoed walls of the Orvieto school from the 13th to the 16th century. This part of town is the ideal location to take relaxing walks, filled with stunning panoramic vistas.

F. SAN DOMENICO

Set back from the Via Arnolfo di Cambio in a less inspiring part of town, this church is famous because St. Thomas Aquinas taught here, and the desk at which he performed his lectures is still inside. You should also take note of the 13th century Tomb of Cardinal de Bray by Arnolfo di Cambio, as well as the Petrucci Chapel built by Michele Sanmicheli, which is below the main church and entered from the a door on the south wall.

G. ST. PATRICK'S WELL

Open daily from 9:00am to 6:00pm, this well, **Orvieto Sotteraneo**, and the **Duomo** are the most famous sights in Orvieto. Built by Antonio Sangallo the Younger for Pope Clement VII, the well served as a reservoir for the nearby fortress if the city was ever put under siege. Hence it is also known as the Fortress Well. Its ingenious cylindrical cavity design was completed in the beginning of the 16th century. Going to a depth of 62 meters, there are two parallel concentric staircases (each with 248 steps ... go on and count them if you want). The water carriers with their donkeys used one spiral staircase for going up and the other for going down. Each staircase has a separate entrance and is ringed by large arched windows. In the public gardens above the well are the overgrown remains of an Etruscan temple.

H. ETRUSCAN NECROPOLISES

Located on either side of the city the foot of the tufa cliffs, the **Necropolis of the Tufa Crucifix** is to the north and the **Necropolis of Cannicella** is to the south. Each date from around the sixth century BCE. Well preserved but ransacked and looted a long time ago, these tombs nonetheless are something to visit while in Orvieto. It's not often that you can come face to face with something that was created almost 2,500 years ago. Inquire at the information office about the ways and means to visit them.

I. ORVIETO SOTTERANEO

If you do nothing else here, make sure that you sign up to go on one of the guided tours of the subterranean passages that snake underneath the entire city. Guided tours are held every day starting at 11am and go until 6pm, and cost E5. Inquire at the information about the times for the tours in English. At last inquiry they were at 12:15 and 5:15pm.Recently excavated and opened for tourists, the tours of these caves under the city take you on a journey through history, including Etruscan wells, a 17th century oil mill, a medieval quarry, ancient pigeon coops and much more, all thoroughly narrated by well-trained guides. These tours are an extraordinary trip back in time and shouldn't be missed.

Shopping

In general there is great shopping in Orvieto, but without the same run-of-the-mill, cookie cutter, international name brand stores you find in most tourist locations. There are many small artisans' shops, unique boutiques, ceramics re-sellers, all of which add to the rich local flavor that Orvieto cultivates. One store in particular you simply must visit is:

8. MICHELANGELI, *Via Gualverio Michelangeli 3B, Tel. 0763/342-660, Fax 0763/342-461. All credit cards accepted.*

An incredible store filled with intricately carved wooden sculptures, toys, figurines, and murals of the most amazing and appealing designs. A ideal store in which to find the perfect gift or keepsake. Michelangeli's work is slowly becoming recognized around the world. It is rustic but refined, and at the very least you should stop in the store, check out the displays, take a look through his portfolios and treat the experience as you would a museum.

Practical Information
Tourist Information

To arrange day trips, find out about bus tours, find train or bus information, get maps, detailed walking tour information, book a hotel, get general information about Orvieto, or book a guided tour for Orvieto Sotteraneo, the **tourist office**, Piazza Duomo 4, *Tel. 0763/301-507 or 301-508, Fax 0763/344-433*, is the place to go.

ASSISI

Dramatically situated on a verdant hill highlighted by olive groves and cypress trees reaching right up to the city walls, the beautiful medieval city of **Assisi** stretches majestically along the slopes of Mount Subasio. Today Assisi stills bears the mark of a robust little medieval town, at least that part which is still encompassed by the old city walls. This stunningly beautiful little Umbrian hill town is a center for art and culture, a major religious pilgrimage site, and a heavily touristed location. As a result, be prepared for crowded streets.

Sadly, some of the town's charm was instantaneously leveled when an earthquake struck in 1997, causing severe damage to the city's structures, especially the Basilica of St. Francis. Many of Giotto's fine frescoes were destroyed in this natural catastrophe. An extensive renovation of the church has just been completed as of going to press. Assisi is a wonderful destination, but you may still find scaffolding and supports in place to secure certain structures of historic significance.

The home of **St. Francis**, Assisi is an original Umbrian settlement, after which it became a part of the Etruscan federation, and later was incorporated into the Roman Empire. In the 3rd century CE it became a Christian town. After the fall of the Roman Empire it was destroyed by the Goths in 545 CE, conquered by the Byzantine Empire and eventually fell into hands of the Lombards.

Incorporated into the Duchy of Spoleto, it became an independent commune in the 11th century and achieved great success in the 13th century. During this period of freedom and economic success, St. Francis was born here in 1182 and **St. Clare** in 1193 (a daughter of a rich family, and a contemporary and disciple of St Francis of Assisi, she founded the order of Poor Clares. She died in Assisi in the convent she founded in 1253).

After the 13th century the city became part of the Papal States, then Perugia, then Milan, and finally fell under the control of the powerful Sforza family. And eventually, as a result of internal strife, Assisi was re-incorporated into the Papal States in the 16th century until it became a part of the new state of Italy in the 19th century.

Arrivals & Departures

Assisi can be somewhat difficult to get to by train or bus, so if you don't rent a car, which is recommended so you can take in all the splendor of Umbria, expect at least a two hour train trip from Rome, or an hour and a half train or bus trip from Perugia. Buses and trains leave every hour and half to two hours from Perugia and are infrequent from Rome. Contact the local tourist office in Perugia for a more detailed schedule.

Orientation

Assisi is directly between Perugia and Foligno, about 13 kilometers from the former. The town is dominated by the **Basilica of San Francesco** on the northwest end. The core of the city surrounds the **Piazza del Comune** with many major sights in an around the square. All streets in the town seem to lead to this piazza, so it is almost impossible to get lost while in Assisi.

Getting Around Town

Assisi, like most Umbrian towns, is made for walking. Many or the smaller streets and the winding staircases are off-limits to cars, but you do have to contend with hills. So bring your walking shoes.

Where to Stay

1. SAN FRANCESCO, *Via San Francesco 48. Tel 075/812-281, Fax the same. 44 rooms. Single E80; Double E150. All credit cards accepted. Breakfast included.* ***

Located near the cathedral, this classic three star hotel is right in the center of things. Some of the rooms have grand views of the cathedral. If you want one you need to request it with your reservation. All rooms have plenty of space and are comfortably furnished with a mixture of antiques and more modern furnishings. This is a good small town three star, a little on the rustic side, with an intimate terrace overlooking the cathedral, a quaint bar area, and a rather well respected restaurant.

2. FONTEBELLA, *Via Fontebella 25. Tel. 075/816-456, Fax 075/812-941. Web: www.venere.com/it/assisi/fontebella. 43 rooms. Single E70-140; Double E95-215. Visa and Mastercard accepted. Breakfast E9. *****

Almost in the center of Assisi with great views over the valley, this is a very nice four star that won the Premium Hotel Award in Italy in 1998. The common areas are spacious and accommodating. The bathrooms are not too big but do come with all modern amenities. The rooms are relatively spacious and comfortable and are designed with a regal yellow and black color scheme. The breakfast buffet, served outside on the terrace in good weather, is quite a spread and is worth the extra money. A fine hotel with all the accoutrements of four star quality. And their restaurant, Il Frantoio, is pretty good too.

3. SUBIASO, *Via Frate Elia 2, 075/812-206, Fax 075/816-691. Toll free in Italy 167/015070. 61 rooms. Single E130; Double E200. All credit cards accepted. Breakfast included. *****

This is the place to stay in Assisi. Almost right at the foot of the Basilica di San Francesco this hotel has some breathtakingly panoramic views over the valley from the balconies of some of the rooms, as well as the sun terrace and garden terrace areas. All rooms are uniquely furnished with attractive antiques and are spacious and comfortable. There are a number of common rooms where you can relax and unwind, and the garden terrace, which houses the restaurant in the summer, is a perfect spot to grab a quiet meal.

4. IL PALAZZO, *Via San Francesco 8. Tel. 075/816-841. Web: www.perugiaonline.com/ilpalazzo/. 40 rooms. All credit cards accepted. Single E55-85; Double E95-125. ***

The Palazzo Bindangoli-Bartocci — in which the hotel resides — was built in the 1500s and still retains its quaint medieval charm. It is perfectly situated between the Basilica of St. Francis and the main square, Piazza del Commune. The foundation of the building is a mixture of stables, storehouses, and inns that were in use in the 12th century. Each room is different in size, shape and antique furnishings but all are decorative and comfortable. In some rooms you have the original oak and beams for ceiling supports. The third floor rooms enjoy a view over the Spoletana valley. Without a doubt this is the best two star in town, and is pressing hard for three star status.

Where to Eat

There are a large number of restaurants since Assisi is such a tourist destination and pilgrimage site. These are my choices for the two best:

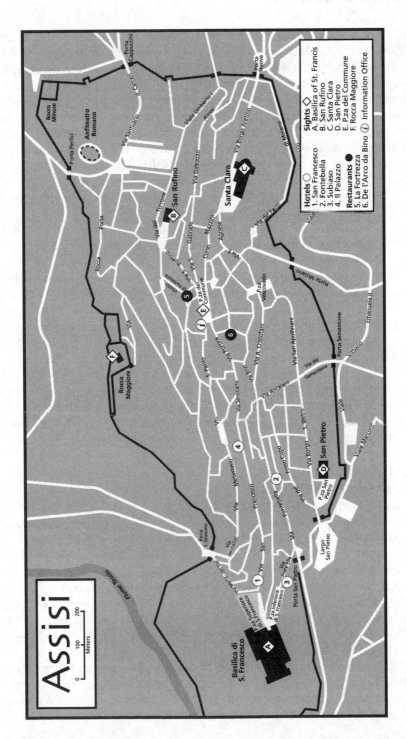

Assisi

0 100 200
Meters

Hotels ◯
1. San Francesco
2. Fontebella
3. Subiaso
4. Il Palazzo

Restaurants ●
5. La Fortrezza
6. De l'Arco da Bino

Sights ◇
A. Basilica of St. Francis
B. San Rufino
C. Santa Clara
D. San Pietro
E. Pza del Commune
F. Rocca Maggiore
ⓘ Information Office

Fiume Tecio

Basilica di S. Francesco

Rocca Minore

Porta Perlici

Anfiteatro Romano

Porta Cappuccini

Porta Nuova

Via dei Carceri o

Via Santuario

Via Eremo delle Carceri

Viale Umberto I

Alesi

Via Porta Perlici

Via del Torrione

San Rufino

Via Galeazzo

Via S. Rufino

Via Borgo Aretino

di Moiano

Santa Clara

Gabriele

Corso Mazzini

Agnese

Via S.

Via del Ponte

Viale

Via Fontebella

Viale
Pietrezza

Pza del Commune

Pza Vescovado

Porta Moiano

S. Paolo

Via A. Cristofani

Via San Apollinare

Via del Sementone

Porta Sementone

Porta Vittorio

Viale

Viale Marconi

Via Ancaloni

Rocca Maggiore

Via

Via Metastasio

Via Seminario

Via Borgo S. Pietro

S. Pietro

San Pietro

Via Ancaloni

Via Francesco

Foro Cupo

Pza San Pietro

Largo San Pietro

Porta Giacomo

Via San Francesco

Via Metastasio

Via Fontebella

Via Frate Elia

Pza Superiore di S. Francesco

Pza Inferiore di S. Francesco

Via Frate Elia

Porta San Pietro

5. LA FORTREZZA, *Piazza del Comune. Tel. 075/812-418. Closed Thursdays and in February. All credit cards accepted. Dinner for two E40.*

In an ideal location right up a small side street from the main piazza, this is a superb local restaurant attached to a two star hotel of the same name. For appetizers, their prosciutto crudo con bruschetta (ham with garlic bread) is superb. For the pasta dish try the succulently rich ravioli alla ricotta e tartufo nero (ravioli with cheese and black truffles) or the tasty pappardelle alla ragu di agnello (pasta with lamb sauce). For the main course its tough to decide between their succulent meat dishes like filetto di vitellone al misto cotto (veal), petto di faraone in crosta (breaded wild chicken breast), the coniglio (rabbit) or piccione (pigeon). A great atmosphere with a wide variety of superb food at more than acceptable prices.

6. TAVERNA DE L'ARCO DA BINO, *Via San Gregorio 8. Tel 075/812-383. Closed Tuesdays, January 8-31, and July 5-15. All credit cards accepted. Dinner for two E55.*

A pleasant, upscale, local place with great atmosphere — vaulted brick ceilings and woodsy wrought iron decor — as well as simply scrumptious food. Try not to miss this place. The specialty of the house is veal and lots of it. And they make it in a variety of different ways, including al tartufo nero (with black truffles), al gorgonzola (with gorgonzola cheese), alla brace (roasted), all'aceto balsamico (with balsamic vinegar), con funghi parmigiano e rucola (with mushrooms and parmesan), as well as a number of other preparations. To start off your meal try their bruschetta al tartufo nero di Assisi (garlic bread spread with black truffles). They also make an excellent fettucine al profumo di bosco (smoked wood-flavored pasta with mushrooms and truffles), which was my favorite, as well as other succulently tasty pastas.

Seeing the Sights
A. BASILICA OF ST FRANCIS

Majestic and picturesque, the basilica and its accompanying cloistered convent have graced this rural landscape for many centuries. The basilica is split into two levels; the lowest is reached from the Piazza Inferiore di San Francesco which is currently being held up — after the earthquake of 1997 — with unsightly but necessary wood and iron brackets and scaffolding. In itself it is an enchanting open space, with a series of quaint 15th century arcades. The lower Church was built between 1228 and 1230 while the Upper Church was built from 1230 to 1253. The church is dominated by the huge square bell tower built in four layers, completed in 1239, with arches gracing the top section.

The **Lower Church** is entered through an intricate double portal surmounted with three rose windows. Inside consists of a single nave divided into five bays with a boule transept and a semi-circular apse. Even in the dim light the star-spangled blue vaults between the arches is stunningly beautiful. The remains of St. Francis are located in a stone urn in the crypt, which is down a staircase located in the middle part of the nave.

The side chapels are all wonderfully decorated with 13th century stained glass windows. On the right you can find the Chapel of St. Stephen, then the Chapel of St. Anthony of Padua and finally the Chapel of St. Mary Magdalene with frescoes by Giotto. In the Chapel of St. Martin on the left you can find some significant frescoes, including *Madonna, Child and Angels* by Cimabue as well as *Life of Christ and St. Francis* by Giotto on the right. The Chapel of St. Nicholas also contains some stunning frescoes by Giotto.

The **Upper Church** is reached — since the earthquake in 1997 it has been off-limits but may have reopened — by steps leading from the lower piazza. The facade faces the town of Assisi and looks over the wide lawn of the Piazza Superiore di San Francesco and has a pure linear Gothic look. The one embellishment is the large rose window staring out at the town. The interior of this level is bright and airy, in contrast to the lower section. It consists of one nave with a transept and a polygonal arch, with stunningly colorful frescoes by Cimabue decorating the walls of the apse as well as the transept.

The inlaid wood choir by the altar is a fantastic piece to admire. It was created between 1491 and 1501 by local artist Domenico Individi. The upper part of the nave is adorned with 13th century stained glass windows. Under the gallery, the walls were covered with some of the most magnificent examples of Giotto's work until the earthquake shook them loose and disintegrated them to powder. Sadly, this whole church is being pieced together, but work may well be complete by the time you visit – and these fantastic frescoes will be available for viewing once again.

B. CATHEDRAL OF SAN RUFFINO

Commonly known as the **Duomo**, the beautiful Romanesque facade is divided into three sections. The uppermost is triangular with a pointed Gothic arch; the middle is divided vertically by pilasters and is decorated with three fine rose windows and myriad carvings; and the lower section has three portals, the left of which is used to enter the church. To the side of the Duomo is the massive bell tower adorned with small arches at the top and an off-set clock on the same level as the top layer of the church.

The interior was renovated in the 16th century and consists of a nave and two aisles. The baptismal font in the right aisle was used to baptize St. Francis, St. Clare, St. Agnes, and St. Gabriel. Assisi definitely is a hotbed of sainthood. The apse contains an outstanding 16th century wood choir. The crypt is a must see. Situated underneath the cathedral, and once part of an earlier church, you can find a Roman sarcophagus which used to contain the remains of San Ruffino. Just down the road from here past Piazza Matteoti is a Roman amphitheater worthy of a short visit.

C. BASILICA OF SANTA CLARA

Classically Gothic, this 13th century church dominates the piazza of the same name. Attached to the left side of the building are three large flying buttresses with a slender bell tower rising up from the apse. The facade is decorated with two closed horizontal bands, is divided into three levels, and has a wonderful rose window and a plain portal flanked by two lions.

The interior is in the form of a Latin cross with a single nave and is as simple and bare as the outside. A good place to come for soul-enriching peacefulness. The crypt, reached by a flight of steps, contains the remains of St. Clare in a glass coffin. In the chapel of St. George is the painted cross which supposedly spoke to St. Francis when it was located in the Church of St. Domain. Located here beyond a lattice window are the remains of St. Clare.

D. CHURCH OF SAN PIETRO

Located just inside the city walls, near the Basilica of St. Francesco, this Romanesque-Gothic 13th century church is built on the site of a previous Catholic place of worship. The facade is rectangular with two orders and beautiful in a simple way. The upper level has three rose windows, and the lower has three portals. The interior contains one nave and two aisles, and has some 14th century frescoes and the ruins of some tombs of the same century. For simple beauty and peaceful serenity this is a fine church to visit.

E. PIAZZA DEL COMMUNE

Located in the heart of the old town, built on the site of an old Roman forum and in the midst of some ancient medieval buildings, is the center of Assisi, the Piazza del Commune. The 14th century **Prior's Palace** houses the town council offices, the **Municipal Picture Gallery** contains Byzantine, Umbrian and Sienese frescoes, the turreted 13th century **Palazzo del Capitano del Popolo** has the 14th century **Municipal Tower** rising out from it.

Next to that is the **Church of Santa Maria Sopra Minerva**, built in the first half of the 16th century over the ancient Temple of Minerva. The facade is all ancient Rome from the Augustan period of the first century BCE, while the rest of the building is medieval.

F. CASTLE OF THE ROCCA MAGGIORE

Pass by the Roman Amphitheater as you go out the Perlici Gate to begin the climb up to this imposing fortress, which once served as protector over the city of Assisi. Built after the Lombard occupation, the fortress with its imposing ramparts and towers completely dominates the town below. A perfect place for kids of all ages to explore a medieval fortress.

Practical Information

Festivals
- **3rd and 4th of October** – Festival of St. Francis, Patron Saint of Italy
- **May Day celebration** – Calendimaggio
- **June 22nd** – Festival of the Vows
- **1st and 2nd of August** – Festival of the Pardon

Tourist Information
To arrange day trips, find out about bus tours, locate train or bus information, get maps, walking tour information, book a hotel, or simply gather general information about Assisi, the **tourist office** at Piazza del Comune 27, *Tel. 075/812-450, Fax 075/813-727* has all that information.

Chapter 16

VENICE

City of Canals & Bridges

Venice is one of the world's most magical cities. No other city in the world is even remotely similar to it. As such it is the most frequented cultural center in Europe, attracting millions of tourists each year. It serves as the capital of the province of Venice (**Venezia**) and the **Veneto region**, which includes the major town of **Verona** and the beautiful and relaxing **Lago di Garda**, both featured in this section.

Venice is a city of canals and bridges which have an indescribable beauty and charm that draws a swarm of visitors each year. Chief among the waterways is the **Grand Canal** which starts at the railway station and **Piazzale Roma** and ends at **Piazza San Marco** (**St. Mark's Square**). Altogether there are more than 200 canals, which are the main thoroughfares of Venice; and crossing the waterways there are about 400 bridges, the most famous of which is the **Rialto** with its many shops.

The historic center of Venice is built on a group of small islands and banks in the middle of **Laguna Veneta**, a crescent-shaped lagoon separated from the **Adriatic Sea** by a barrier of narrow strips of islands and peninsulas. The modern city covers the whole 90 mile (145 km) perimeter of the lagoon and includes ten principal islands in addition to those of the mother city, and two industrial boroughs of **Mestre** and **Marghera** on the mainland.

Some of Venice's islands include: **La Guidecca** with its floating cafés and restaurants; **San Giorgio Maggiore**, with its famous 16th century church of the same name; and **San Michele** with its famous cemetery; **Lido**, a resort built in the 19th century with casinos, hotels, and beaches; **Murano**, noted for its glassworks; colorful **Burano**, famous for its lace; and **Torcello**. Even though Venice is separated from the sea by natural and artificial breakwaters, it only takes a small rainfall for the water level in Venice to rise. As a result, flooding is common from November through March of each year. So if you visit then, remember to bring some galoshes.

Within the Venetian islands, canals, and lagoons, commodities move by barges and tugs, while passenger movement is primarily by *vaporetti* (water buses) or water taxi. The world-famous black *gondolas*, propelled by professional gondoliers, are narrow with high prows and sterns and are used by tourists mainly for short canal passages. Before the modern era gondolas were the main form of transportation for all Venetians who had the means to afford the use of one.

Venice was the late Walt Disney's favorite city. With its scenic canals, ornate bridges, and grandiose palazzi and campi, it easy to see why Venice grabbed his heart. The whole city is so stunningly beautiful that it has an amusement park feel to it. It's almost as if what you're seeing is too magnificent, too stunning to be real. But it is.

But if you're here in high season you will encounter hordes of tourists; and as you shoulder your way through the crowds some of the luster may start to wear off. To escape from the hordes you may choose to escape into one of the stores that seem to take up every doorway, every building front, every available space on every little street. This rampant commercialism makes parts of Walt Disney's favorite city seem like the ugly strip malls that have grown around his theme parks.

Because of the crowds in the high season, Venice is definitely a place to visit in the off-season. Also because of this tourist influx and the commercialism it creates in the San Marco area, it is advised to stay away from this central area, which is around Piazza San Marco.

In the off-season and in the local areas you will share the city almost completely with Venetians. Also in the off-season hotels virtually cut their rates in half allowing you to upgrade your accommodations without any impact on your wallet. Another plus about the off-season is that you will be able to avoid the aroma that can seep its way from the canals during the heat of July and August. All griping aside, even with the tourist hordes and rampant commercialism, Venice is still a vacationer's paradise and it is easy to see Walt's affection for it.

The Early Years

As history books will tell you, Venice was either founded on fear and cowardice, or brilliant necessity and creative ingenuity. With the fall of the Roman Empire, the "barbarian" hordes – Goths and Ostrogoths – swept over Italy in the 5th and 6th centuries CE. Instead of facing this onslaught, the people of the Veneto region found shelter on the scores of offshore islets in the lagoons off the coast, which had previously been inhabited by small settlements of fishermen. Here the future Venetians built their houses on pilings and on islands and learned to move about by poling in shallow boats, which evolved into *gondolas*.

The "barbarians" were good horsemen but bad boatmen, so while they continued to wreak havoc on shore, they left the lagoon to the Venetians. Because of this intimacy with the water, over the centuries Venice grew into a great maritime power. A success based on the astuteness of its merchants and rulers, as well as its centuries-old political, military, and commercial ties with the Byzantium world in Constantinople (now Istanbul) and beyond.

Early Venice was a republic ruled by its **Doges**, who were first elected in 727 CE. The Doges were chosen by the **Council of Ten**, who in turn were elected by the nobles and rich merchants . These aristocrats and business leaders only accounted for about six percent of the population. So Venice wasn't a very representative Republic, but it was a republic none-the-less.

The city-state's chief maritime competitors were Genoa and the Amalfi Coast towns south of Naples, but Venice had the advantage of easier access through low Alpine passes to the heart of Western and Central Europe. This easy access and the ability to put aside moral issues and profit from any venture, helped make Venice a power to be reckoned with in the Mediterranean. In fact, the Venetian Republic was once the most powerful nation in all of Europe, and it lasted for over 1,000 years.

At the height of the republic's power, Venice controlled Corfu, Crete, and the Peloponnesus in what is today Greece. On the mainland it acquired the land westward almost to Milan and eastward down the coast of Yugoslavia.

A variety of problems however, contributed to a sharp decline in the republic's stature from the 16th century on. One of the main problems was the situation on the lagoon. What earlier had assisted them would now bring about their decline. Because of its location on sedentary water, the population of Venice was decimated over three centuries by outbreaks of plague. In one, from 1347 to 1349, three-fifths of its inhabitants died. Noticing this weakness, the **Turks**, who had captured Constantinople in 1453, began to take over Venice's Greek lands and possessions.

Whatever dominion over trade Venice may have had with the Levant ended when the Portuguese opened the Cape Route around Africa. This meant that now the Portuguese had direct access to the spices the Venetians had previously accessed via the land route from Asia through the Levant. This change precipitated a gradual decline in Venice's influence, affluence and power.

In 1797, the city was conquered by **Napoleon**, effectively ending its 1,000 years as a Republic. Later it was ceded to Austria. In 1848 there was an unsuccessful revolt against the Austrians, then in 1866 Venice finally became part of a unified Italy.

Today Venice's glory is all in the past, but we are the welcome beneficiaries of the splendor which remains. The ancient palazzi and attractive vistas of canal and bridge which make the city such a stunning vacation site today. Though its native population continues to decline rapidly, Venice is still one the most romantic and scenic vacation spot in the world. Enjoy your stay.

Arrivals & Departures
By Air

Most international arrivals come into Venice's **Marco Polo airport**. From here you can take a bus, and twenty minutes later be in Venice's Piazzale Roma, where you can take water transport to your hotel. Tickets cost only E3 each way. No reservations. You can buy tickets in the arrivals lounge at the ATVO stand from 8:00am to midnight, *Tel. 041/541-5180 or 520-5530. Email: infomov@atvo.it*. For a bus schedule visit their website: *www.atvo.it*. Buses leave every 20 minutes.

When you catch the bus back to the airport, buy a ticket first at the ATVO ticket office next to the Caribinieri office in Piazza Roma.

You can also catch a boat from the airport directly into the heart of Venice from the airport. It takes about half an hour to forty minutes from the airport to arrive at San Marco. The office at the airport is open daily from 8:00am-midnight, *Tel. 041/541-6555, Email: info@alilaguna.com*. Check out their website for timetables: *www.alilaguna.it*. Price is E10 each way. Though it takes longer than the bus, it certainly is a unique way to enter Venice.

By Bus

When arriving by bus you have to disembark at **Piazzale Roma**, then either walk or catch some form of water transport to your destination. The main local bus service is **ACTV**, *Tel. 041/528-7886*. They have a tourist office in Piazza Roma where you can get maps, tourist information about Venice, and reserve bus seats to a variety of different cities in the region including Mestre, Padua, Mira and Treviso. Once you arrive, you can either walk to your destination or hop on a *vaporetto*. You will also be able to catch water taxis from this location which will be much more expensive.

By Car

If you arrive in Venice by car, be prepared for long waits near **Piazza Roma** before you can deposit your automobile. One of the most welcoming aspects of Venice is that it is automobile free. The only way to get to Venice by car is through the mainland town of **Mestre**, then over the bridge (made by Mussolini) to the parking lots around the Piazza Roma. Once you get rid of your car, you can either walk to your destination or hop on a *vaporetto*.

Sample trip lengths on main roads:
- **Florence**: 4 hours
- **Rome**: 6 hours.

If you want to rent a car, try **Avis**, *Piazza Roma 496/H, Tel. 041/522-5825* or **Hertz**, Piazza Roma, 496/E, *Tel. 041/528-4091*.

By Train

Arriving by train is the most convenient way to get to Venice. The **Stazione di Santa Lucia** is located on the northwestern edge of the city. From here you'll need to either walk to your hotel through the maze of medieval streets, take a *vaporetto* (a water bus) or hire a water taxi. All of these transportation services are located on the canal directly in front of the train station.

Sample trip lengths and costs for direct *(diretto)* trains:
• **Florence**: 3 1/2 hours, E40
• **Rome**: 5 hours, E70

The **tourist information office**, *Tel. 041/719-078*, and **hotel information**, *Tel. 041/715-016*, are located side by side near the front entrance of the station. If you need a hotel reservation get in the right line. If you just want information about upcoming events in Venice, a map, etc., get in the left line.

When standing in line you most likely will be confronted with individuals trying to convince you to stay at their hotels. These are all legitimate agents for hotels that do not get that much business. If you do not want to be pestered simply say *No grazie* (no thank you). But if you take the time to listen to them you will discover that you can sometimes get a three-star hotel at two-star prices.

Orientation

Venice is conveniently separated into six sestieri, or sections, and the houses are numbered consecutively from a point in the center of each section, spiraling out, making finding specific locations an adventure in and of itself. The six *sestieri* are (see map on next page):
• **Cannaregio**, where the Jewish Ghetto is located; not too many tourists here.
• **Santa Croce**, along with San Polo is still considered the 'other side of the canal,' even though the Rialto bridge was built back in 1588 to connect this section of Venice with the more influential San Marco section.
• **San Polo**, site of the famous food market near the foot of the Rialto bridge that is open every morning except Sunday and Monday.
• **San Marco**, which is the cultural and commercial center of Venice and the location that most tourists never leave.
• **Dorsoduro**, where you can have a relaxing meal on the **Zattere**, the series of quays facing the island of **La Guidecca**, and watch the sun go down.
• **Castello**, the location of the **Arsenale**, where many of Venice's ships have been built.

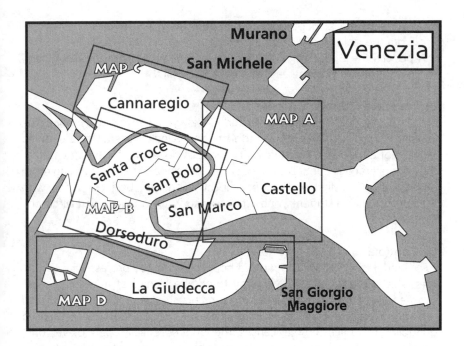

Getting Around Town
By Vaporetti – Water Buses

The least expensive way to travel around Venice and the most efficient is by vaporetti. You can buy these at ticket booths by vaporetti piers, at most tobacconists, and immediately on board from the conductor (the person who opens the gates to the boat). Single tickets cost E5; 24 hour tourist passes cost E10.50; and 72 hour tourist passes cost E22. The main lines are as follows:

- **Accelerato No. 1** – Stops at every landing spot on the **Grand Canal**. Obviously this one takes a little time and is a great way to see the whole canal.
- **Diretto No. 82** – Fastest way to get from the **train station** and **Piazzale Roma** to **Rialto**, **Accademia**, and **San Marco** stops. Often very crowded and as their name suggests, *diretto* indicates a direct trip.
- **Diretto No. 4** – Summer time *vaporetto* that follows the same path as the No. 1.
- **Motoscafo No. 52** – The circle line that travels in both directions around the periphery of Venice and to the smaller islands around Venice, **Isola San Michele** and **Murano** (see *Excursions & Day Trips* section of this chapter for more details). A great ride in and of itself for you to see the peripheral areas of Venice from the water.
- **Vaporetto No. 12** – Goes to **Murano**, **Burano**, and **Torcello**, all smaller islands around Venice (see *Excursions & Day Trips* section of this chapter

for more details); departs from the **Fondamenta Nuove** stop just across from the Isola San Michele.

• **Vaporetti 6** – Goes to the resort of **Lido** and leaves from the **Riva Degli Schiavoni** stop to the east of Piazza San Marco.

By Traghetti – Gondola Ferries

At many points along the Grand Canal, you can cross by using the inexpensive (only E0.40) public gondola ferries called *traghetti* that are rowed by pairs of gondoliers. The times vary for each departure based on whether the gondoliers have enough passengers. In these boats there is standing room only, you'll be traveling with groups of locals, workmen, business people with their briefcases, art students, and other tourists while you are poled across the Grand Canal.

By Gondola

Gondolas are privately operated boats operated by professional gondoliers. This is the most delightful way to admire Venice at a leisurely pace. Granted they are expensive (a half hour ride costs over $50) but they're still fun and romantic if you're so inclined. There are only a little over 400 licensed gondoliers in Venice and the licenses, though theoretically open to everyone, are in practice restricted to the sons (not the daughters) of gondoliers.

If you are going to hire a gondola, take one with a specific destination in mind, such as going to a specific restaurant or specific site instead of just asking the gondolier to pole you around for a while. Even though gondoliers are trained to take you to the prettiest places for your money, by bringing you to a specific destination you and gondolier become part of the Venice of old, because in the not so distant past gondolas were the main form of transportation for all the elite Venetians when they went out to dinner or the opera.

You can also hire a gondola for *serenate* (group rides in which the gondolas feature an accordionist and a singer) at night. These rides can be very expensive, but if it's your honeymoon or a special occasion, who cares?

Remember to bargain with the gondolier for each ride, whether it's a regular trip or a *serenate*. Their prices are not set in stone and it is the accepted custom to bargain.

By Water Taxi

There are plenty of water taxis, but they too are extremely expensive. If you don't want to be part of the maddening crowds, however, this is the quickest way to get from point A to B. If you want to get picked up at a certain place at a certain time, call *041/523-2326 or 522-2303*.

By Foot

Venice is comparable in size to New York City's Central Park, so it's possible for you to walk anywhere you want, as long as you're not in a hurry or worried about getting lost. I've done that plenty of times when I forgot to bring my map with me, but I usually found some out-of-the way shop or café to enjoy on my journeys. And there are signs everywhere pointing visitors in the proper direction.

The true beauty of this city is the absence of cars or buses. The streets are designed for walking, and the pace of life reflects that. This fact alone makes life in Venice seem calmer and more serene than anywhere else. Many Venetians are proud of the fact that throughout their entire lives most of them have never owned an automobile. Not having owned a car myself for more than a decade now, I can understand their pride.

Buy a Map in Venice

In Venice you need a map. This city is one big interconnecting alleyway with little to no address organization or structure. Sometimes street names are repeated in different districts of Venice and many times there are no street signs on the walls. Venice is confusing to get around and the only way I was able to before I figured out the city was to buy a map. I recommend the **F.M.B**. **Piante di Citta** for E5 which you can buy at any giornalaio (newsstand).

Three Day Itinerary In & Around Venice

If you want to stay in a quality hotel, deep in the heart of the Venice where the locals live, away from the hordes of tourists that descend on this city in the summer, stay in Dorsoduro section at either **Messner**, **Alla Salute**, or **Belle Arti**.

DAY ONE
Morning

To get started, find a small café and grab a coffee and light breakfast. Spend some time savoring the sights and sounds of the real Venice. Later compare the different pace here to what you experience in the tourist sections.

After breakfast, go to a newsstand and buy a map of Venice. You are going to need it. Before starting out, map out your route. Then begin walking through the maze of the streets, over the **Accademia** bridge, and make your way to **Piazza San Marco**.

Take your time. Much of the beauty of Venice is simply wandering through its ancient lanes and alleys. By the time you arrive in the square it will probably be around lunch time.

Lunch

For lunch we can go one of two different directions. Option one is to spend a lot of money for little more than the ambiance of sitting at one of the cafés in the Piazza San Marco and admiring the beauty of the surrounding buildings.

If you want a truly authentic Venetian dining experience, go behind the left side of the church of San Marco and follow the road to **Alla Rivetta**, at Ponte S Provolo. At the first bridge look to your right and admire the **Bridge of Sighs** over the canal a little further down. This restaurant is a gondolier hangout when they are not out ferrying tourists around the canals, and the food and ambiance is great.

Afternoon

After lunch, take the time to look through the **Church of San Marco** and the **Palazzo Ducale**. Then admire the **Bell Tower** and the **Clock Tower** in the piazza. This should take all afternoon. On the way back to your hotel for a nap, stop in any church or public building you pass.

Dinner

For dinner try the **Ristorante Al Buso** at Ponte di Rialto. Located right beside the **Rialto** bridge down on the water by the Grand Canal. It only has a few tables set outside for the great canal-side views, A little touristy, but worth it.

On the way back to your hotel stop in the **Campo San Polo** for an after-dinner drink of dessert and savor the life of another truly authentic local piazza.

DAY TWO
Morning

We will start off this by going back to the Rialto bridge area where you had dinner last night. Right on the other side from where your restaurant was last night is the most wonderful daily market (except Sundays) of fruit, vegetable and fish. Here you can grab some fruit to eat for breakfast, stop in a café for some coffee and wander through the stalls where all of Venice's housewives and restaurants buy their food for the day. Don't forget your camera.

Lunch

Make your way across a large portion of Venice either on foot or by vaporetto to **Pizzeria alle Zattere**, *Zattere ai Gesuati 795*. This is a favorite local pizzeria near the Accademia, known not only for its many varieties of pizza but also for the excellent view of Guidecca island from the pizzeria's tables on the Zattere's floating rafts.

Afternoon

After lunch make you way to the famous museum **Accademia**, *Campo della Carita, Dorsoduro*. Here you will find five hundred years of unequaled Venetian art on display. If you want a change of pace try the **Guggenheim Museum** not far away (*Calle Cristoforo, Dorsoduro*). The museum boasts a magnificent 20th century art collection developed by the intriguing American heiress and art aficionado Peggy Guggenheim. There are works by Dali, Chagall, Klee, Moore, Picasso, Pollock and many others. The place to come if modern art is your thing.

Dinner

For dinner we are going back to the *pescheria* fish market area. Huddled in the corner of this vast market, and located near the old post office, is the **Poste Vecie**. To get here, follow a private wooden bridge from the market that leads to this old converted inn with its low ceilings and dark wooden beams. In the summer you can dine in their splendidly relaxing garden that has vines and leaves hanging overhead. Try the *risotto all pesce*, a delicious rice dish for two with assorted sea food.

DAY THREE
Morning

After a simple breakfast either at the hotel or at a café, we are going to take a vaporetto ride on the **Accelerato No. 1** around the entire Grand Canal. This water bus stops at all the landings on the Canal – the perfect way to get a great overview of the city.

Lunch

For lunch, get off the vaporetto at the **Riva di Biasio** landing and make your way to the Campo San Giacomo del'Orio and **La Zucca**. Here you'll find exquisite food in a local restaurant near a beautiful piazza, completely off the beaten path. There is no better way to see how the real Venetians live.

Afternoon & Evening

After lunch we are going on more vaporetto rides. I hope you don't get sea sick. We'll start off by making our way to the vaporetto stop Fondamenta Nuove, where we are going to catch the vaporetto No. 12 and travel to the islands of **Murano**, **Burano** and **Torcello**.

On the island of **Murano**, we are going to go to one of the glass factories and see how the intricate glass pieces are created. The best one to try is **Mazzega SRL**, located at the base of the Ponte Longa, where you can occasionally find young boys flinging themselves into the canal below. After the factory tour wander around and enjoy the peace and tranquility of this tiny island.

On the island of **Burano**, the brightly colored houses here give it the air of an Italian opera set – a perfect background for some excellent photographs. Stop here for a brief walking tour and some gelato at any of the many little cafés. Spend as much time as necessary savoring the incredible back drop of the colorful homes.

On the island of **Torcello**, once a flourishing center of commerce and culture whose greatness dimmed as that of Venice grew, Torcello is now just a solitary village on a lonely island. Today it is remembered for the fact that Hemingway loved its peace and tranquility so much. Let's stop here for dinner at either the **Locanda Cipriani** or the **Osteria Al Ponte del Diavolo**. Both places are rather expensive but well worth it because of the great food and ambiance.

Don't miss the last *vaporetto* back. If you do you'll have to pay an arm and a leg to one of the private water taxis.

Venice Website

For up to date information about events, weather or whatever, in Venice make sure you check out the *www.ciaovenezia.com* website. A must visit site if you are on your way to the most romantic city in the world. Another with great information is *www.turismovenezia.it/eng*.

Evening

To end your stay in Venice, stop back at the **Piazza San Marco**, have a drink or dessert at one of their outside cafés or simply wander around the enjoy the dueling musical ensembles offered by some of the cafes. Being serenaded in a stunning piazza makes for a magical end to three days in Venice.

Where To Stay

In general, where you stay, not just in Venice, but in any city in Italy, will help to determine the type of vacation you will have. This is especially true for Venice since it is such a popular tourist destination. Many of the hotel suggestions here are for places that are off the beaten tourist path, allowing you a respite from the thundering herd of vacationers, giving you a character filled, local living experience while in Venice. See "The Quiet Side of Venice" section a little later in this chapter to better understand which sections of Venice will offer you this local experience.

If you are unable to make suitable reservations prior to arriving in Venice, you should stop by the train station and consult with their friendly, multi-lingual hotel finders service (Santa Lucia Train Station, *Tel. 041/715-016*). In the same office space, but not the same entrance is the general information

Hotels By Map

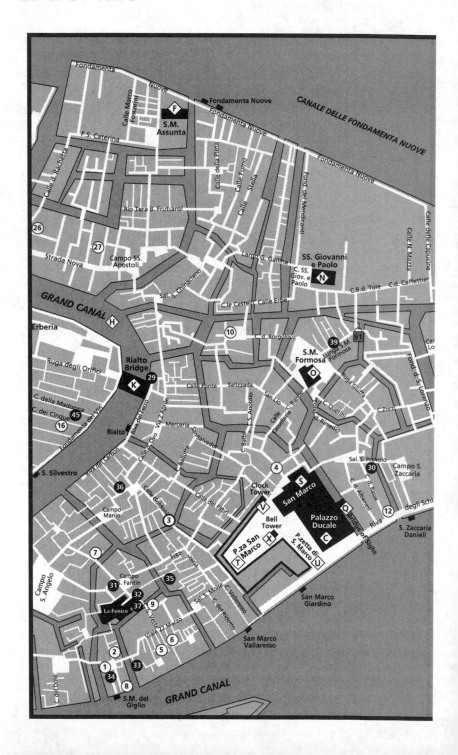

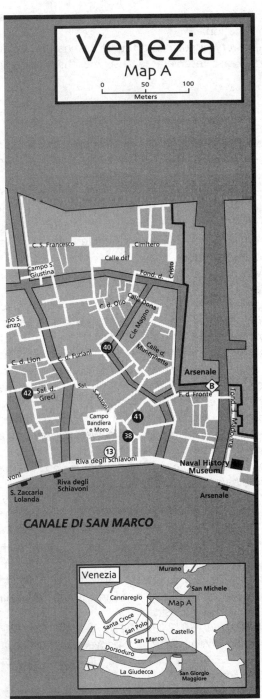

Venezia

Map A

0   50   100

Meters

Hotels ○

1. Ala
2. Bel Sito
3. Bonvecchiati
4. Concordia
5. Do Pozzi
6. Flora
7. Gallini
8. Gritti Palace
9. Kette
10. Santa Marina
12. Danieli
13. Gabrielli Sandwirth
16. Locanda Sturion
26. Abbazzia
27. Bernardi-Semenzato

Eateries ●

29. Al Buso
30. Alla Rivetta
31. Al Teatro
32. Antico Martini
33. Da Raffaele
34. Giglio
35. La Colomba
36. Leon Bianco
37. Vino Vino
38. Al Covo
39. Al Mascaron
40. Archimboldo
41. Corte Sconta
42. Da Remigio
45. Alla Madonna

Sights ◇

B. Arsenale
C. Palazzo Ducale
F. Santa Maria Assunta
H. Grand Canal
K. Rialto Bridge
N. Santi Giovanni e Paolo
O. Santa Maria Formosa
Q. The Bridge of Sighs
S. Basilica di San Marco
T. Piazza San Marco
U. Piazzetta di San Marco
V. Clock Tower
X. Bell Tower

Shops 🛍

61. La Nave de Oro

office for tourists *(Tel. 041/522-6356)*, where you can get maps, directions, and all sorts of necessary information.

To re-emphasize, Venice is very popular as a tourist destination. If you have a specific hotel in mind, please reserve at least six months or more in advance.

San Marco

Directly in the center of Venice, San Marco is the commercial and tourist center of the city. Most people who visit Venice hardly ever leave this section and for good reason. If you only have a little time, even the most seasoned travelers will be able to find everything they desire right here. And at the center of this stage is the Piazza San Marco where people vie with pigeons for space.

The most frequently followed path in this section of Venice is from this piazza along the busy main tourist shopping streets to the Rialto Bridge. You can find everything you'll need right here: history, architecture, restaurants, cafés, shops, sights, fun, and many people.

For each hotel below, I've listed the *vaporetto* stop and map reference.

1. ALA, *Campo Santa Maria dei Giglio 2494, Tel. 041/520-5333, Fax 041/520-3690. E-mail: info@hotelala.it. Web: www.hotelala.it. Credit cards accepted. 85 rooms. Single E100-180; Double E160-290. Breakfast included. Vaporetto Stop – Santa Maria del Giglio. Maps – A & B.* ***

With its own dock on the adjacent canal and an elegant interior decor, the entire establishment is quite exclusive. The rooms are large with all three star amenities; and the bathrooms are as modern as you'll find anywhere. The setting along the canal is what makes this hotel so beautiful and romantic. You'll especially enjoy the beautiful room along the canal where you are served your breakfast. They also have daily Italian and foreign newspapers available for your perusal. A good place to stay while in Venice.

2. BEL SITO, *Campo Santa Maria del Giglio 2517, Tel. 041/522-3365, Fax 041/520-4083. Web: www.hotelbelsito.info. Credit cards accepted. 38 rooms. Single E90-130; Double E120-200. Vaporetto Stop – Santa Maria del Giglio. Maps – A & B.* ***

Handsomely furnished, centrally located, but still slightly off the beaten path so you can get away from the crowds. Professionally managed with impeccable service. The hotel has a quiet micro outdoor café to enjoy at breakfast and to relax at during the day. The rooms are a little on the small side and all but 15 of them overlook the intimate church of Santa Maria del Giglia in the local piazza. A good choice for your visit.

3. BONVECCHIATI, *Calle Goldoni, 30124 Tel. 041/528-5017, Fax 041/528-5230. E-mail: hbonvecc@tin.it. Web: www.hotelbonvecchiati.it. Credit cards accepted. 86 rooms. Single E145-225; Double E130-290. Breakfast included. Vaporetto Stop – San Marco. Map – A.* ****

What a great hotel!! Recently given a fourth star which they most assuredly deserved for years, the Bonvecchiati is a superb place to stay while in Venice. An elegant and refined hotel in a wonderfully central location. "Any hotel can rent you a room," the general manager Domenico Fort likes to say. "While we offer you a true Venetian experience." And he's right! With canal access for direct arrival by water taxi and gondolas, 24-hour concierge service, room service, direct dial telephone, minibar, satellite color TV and laundry service, they treat you like royalty here. On top of all that, their walls are adorned with some fantastic art. The rooms are all furnished in a unique color scheme and are large and comfortable; and the bathrooms are palatial and come adorned with different colored marble. I cannot think of enough great things to say about this place. How about "Stay here when in Venice!"

4. CONCORDIA, *Calle Larga San Marco 367, Tel. 041/520-6866, Fax 041/520-6775. E-mail: VeniceItaly@hotelconcordia.com. Web: www.hotelconcordia.com. Credit cards accepted. 57 rooms. Single E140-250; Double E200-400. Suite E220-450. Breakfast included. Vaporetto Stop – San Marco. Map – A.* ****

The hotel has 20 rooms that overlook the Piazzetta dei Leoni that is part of the Piazza San Marco. Decor is a mixture of modern and elegant antique with a yellow color scheme throughout. The rooms are all wonderfully attractive, especially the ones with a view over the piazzetta. If you to stay in the most exclusive area in Venice and don't mind a little crowd noise in the evenings, you will like this place. A truly refined hotel in the perfect location.

5. DO POZZI, *Via XXII Marzo 2373, Tel. 041/520-7855, Fax 041/522-9413. Email: info@hoteldopozzi.it. Web: www.hoteldopozzi.it. A Credit cards accepted. 35 rooms. Single E80-140; Double E140-220. Breakfast included. Vaporetto Stop – San Marco. Map – A.* ***

Located in the middle of everything but set off on its own small side street, this is a very peaceful and relaxing hotel. They have a garden in the tiny piazza where you can enjoy your breakfast or drinks in the afternoon. You also have air conditioning, phones, mini-bars, room service for breakfast, TVs, and a laundry service, everything a first class hotel can give you – but these aren't first class prices. The reason for that is that some of the rooms are small as are the bathrooms. A good price in a great location.

6. FLORA, *Calle Larga XXII Marzo 2283A, Tel. 041/520-5844, Fax 041/522-8217. E-mail: info@hotelflora.it. Web: hotelflora.it. All credit cards accepted. 44 rooms all bath. Single E110-190; Double E140-240. Breakfast included. Closed November through January. Vaporetto Stop – San Marco. Map – A.* ***

The quaint garden setting where breakfast and afternoon drinks are served in the summer, is dominated by an old well and old pieces of statuary. This area, the breakfast room service, and the general ambiance lend an old fashioned sense of hospitality to the Flora. A great place to stay that is right in the thick of things, where you can still feel you've gotten away from it all.

To get to the rooms, you go up a painted stairway that is something to behold. A good choice for your stay.

7. GALLINI, *Calle della Verona 3673, Tel. 041/520-4515, Fax 520-9103. Email: hgallini@tin.it. Web: www.hotelgallini.it. Credit cards accepted. 50 rooms. Single E80-110; Double E110-160. Breakfast included. Closed November 15 through March 1. Vaporetto Stop – San Marco. Map – A.* **

The hotel has been in the owner's family for over 50 years, and they make sure everything is as perfect as it can be. The place is immaculately clean and your stay here will be in a perfect location for a good price. A comfortable two-star.

My Favorite Venetian Hotels
23. ALLA SALUTE**
24. PENSIONE SEGUSO**
11. SANTO STEFANO***
17. SAN CASSIANO***
3. BONVECCHIATI****
21. CIPRIANI****

☙

---

8. GRITTI PALACE, *Campo Santa Maria del Giglio, Tel. 041/794-611, Fax 041/520-0942. Web: http://gritti.hotelinvenice.com. Credit cards accepted. 96 rooms. Single E287-330; Double E440-650. Suite E900-2,000. Vaporetto Stop – Santa Maria del Giglio. Maps – A & B.* *****

Definitely a top-notch, high-class, deluxe hotel, with lots of local charm. Situated directly on the Grand Canal, this early 16th century palace of the Doge Gritti is one of the world's most celebrated hotels. Here you are treated like royalty, since many of their guests actually are. Enjoy a night here if you're not worried about spending the equivalent of a monthly car or mortgage payment.

9. KETTE, *Piscine San Moise 2053, Tel. 041/520-7766, Fax 041/522-8964. Email: info@hotelkette.com. Web: www.hotelkette.com. All credit cards accepted. 69 rooms, all with bath. Single E120-340; Double E150-360. Suite E210-510. Breakfast included. Vaporetto Stop – Santa Maria del Giglio. Map – A.* ***

If you want luxury for a little less this is the place to stay. The public area is filled with comfortable chairs and international magazines where you can relax outside of the comfort of your room, get a little down time or mingle with the other guests. The rooms are all tastefully decorated, and each has different furnishings. Unfortunately, some rooms face onto close walls from adjacent buildings, but except for this the place is great. Near enough to everything but still far enough away. They are also pet friendly and have babysitting service.

10. **SANTA MARINA**, *Campo Santa Marina 6068, Tel. 041/523-9202, Fax 041/520-0907. E-mail: info@hotelsantamarina.it. Web: www.hotelsantamarina.it. 19 rooms. Single E140-300; Double E190-340. Vaporetto Stop – Rialto. Map – A.* ****

Located in a small square, on three floors of an old *palazzo*, you get a combination of local flavor and tourist amenities in this location. Here you're in the middle of everything tourists want to see, but still far enough away to be a part of the true life of Venice. The staff is amazingly helpful, and your room will be comfortable and quiet. There's a verandah that overlooks the campo with chairs and tables where you can read and relax. Many of the rooms overlook the campo, which is a perfect for people watching. Only open for a few years, the Santa Marina has every modern convenience and is a wonderful place to stay. They are pet friendly and also offer babysitting services.

11. **SANTO STEFANO**, *Campo Santo Stefano 2957, Tel. 041/520-0166, Fax 041/522-4460. Web: www.hotelsantostefanovenezia.com. Credit cards accepted. 11 rooms and with bath. Single E110-220; Double E150-360. Breakfast included. Vaporetto Stop – SM del Giglio. Maps – A & B.* ***

This charming hotel is located on the colorful local Campo Santa Stefano close to the Accademia and Piazza San Marco. Many rooms have a view onto the square. The service is professional and courteous. The rooms are comfortable and well furnished with antiques and glassware from Murano. A high quality place to stay in Venice.

Castello

This part of town offers the perfect chance to escape from the tourist hordes and discover the real Venice. There are plenty of quiet residential neighborhoods here, where old Italian ladies chat with each other from windows overhead while putting out their laundry to dry. If you're looking to shop this isn't the section of Venice for you, but there are some excellent and relatively inexpensive restaurants. Avoid the Riva degli Schiavoni to find the best restaurants.

Castello is home to the **Arsenale** (where many of Venice's boats have been made) and the **Giardini Publici** (Public Gardens), which are a great place to come and relax.

12. **DANIELI**, *Riva degli Schiavoni 4196, Tel. 041/522-6480, Fax 041/ 520-0208. Web: http://danieli.hotelinvenice.com. Credit cards accepted. 235 rooms. Single E235-247; Double E500-1,200. Suites E365-435. Breakfast E33. Vaporetto Stop – San Zaccaria. Map – A.* *****

First opened in 1882 with only 16 rooms, the Danieli has expanded to encompass many surrounding buildings. The magnificent lobby, which is built around a Gothic courtyard, with its intertwining staircases and columns, is truly spectacular. The largest and possibly best hotel in Venice, as well as the most romantic. If you have the means, this is the place to stay.

13. GABRIELLI SANDWIRTH, *Riva degli Schiavoni 4110, Tel. 041/523-1580, Fax 041/520-9455. Email: hotelgabrielli@libero.it. Web: www.hotelgabrielli.it. All credit cards accepted. 100 rooms. Single E160-260; Double E260-450. Closed mid-November to mid-March. Breakfast included. Vaporetto Stop – San Zaccaria. Map – A.* ****

This is a wonderful place to stay. Located in a Gothic palace built in the 13th century with a beautiful rose garden in its center, this hotel is in the middle of everything, but also offers peace and tranquility. You can sun yourself on the roof terrace overlooking the lagoon. One of the best, if not the best views in all of Venice. The best rooms overlook the water and must be specifically requested. All the rooms are tastefully decorated with antiques, chandeliers, and the ever-present roses.

Santa Croce & San Polo

For purposes of clarity we have combined these two geographically connected sections of Venice into one. This area is still considered to be "the other side of the canal," even though the Rialto bridge was built back in 1588 to connect these two sections with the more influential San Marco. Beyond the area around the Rialto, there are plenty of tiny artisan's shops to explore. **Campo San Polo** is the second largest in Venice and is a center for social life in these two neighborhoods. This is a great area just to roam around in and discover the secrets of Venice.

14. AL SOLE, *Santa Croce 136. Tel. 041/523-2144, Fax 041/719-061. Email: info@alsolehotels.com. Web: www.alsolehotels.com. 80 rooms. All Credit cards accepted. Single E60-140; Double E100-270. Breakfast included. Vaporetto Stop – Ferrovia Bar Roma or San Toma. Map – B.* ***

Located near the Piazzale Roma and train station, this is a quaint and comfortable three-star at good prices. Situated in the Palazzo Marcello built in the 14th century, the hotel is filled with antiques. The entrance hall, which is just off the breakfast room where you receive an abundant buffet each morning, is large and luminous. The rooms are all different sizes, so when reserving make sure you request one of the larger ones. They all come with every conceivable amenity for three-stars such as TV, radio, air conditioning, hair dryers, etc.

15. ANTICO CAPON, *Campo Santa Margherita 3004B, Tel. 041/528-5292. Email: hotelanticocapon@hotmail.com. No credit cards accepted. 7 rooms, 6 with bath. Single without bath E40-50; Single E50-70; Double E70-90. Vaporetto Stop – Ca' Rezzonico. Map – B.* *

A super deal in the best local area in Venice. The Campo Santa Margherita and its environs have everything you'll need to feel like a native in this tourist-plagued city. Most mornings there is a small market selling fruit, vegetables, and fresh fish in the piazza. You'll also find places for pizza, pastries, a supermarket, a laundry, and more. The hotel is directly in the middle of all this Venetian life, and three of the rooms face this hustle and bustle while the other four face the uninspiring rear. The rooms are large but the bathrooms are quite small. In fact the shower is located above the toilet. Despite that, this is a great one-star.

16. LOCANDA STURION, *Calle del Sturion. Tel. 041/523-6243, Fax 041/ 522-8378. E-mail: info@locandasturion.com. Website: www.locandasturion.com. 11 rooms. Single E60-160; Double E110-260. All credit cards accepted. Breakfast included. Vaporetto Stop - Rialto. Maps - A&B.* ***

Up a long flight of stairs, therefore not for those weak of heart, this little place is quaint, comfortable and accommodating – not to mention ideally located. The hotel has been in business since the 13th century and is only a few paces from the Rialto bridge and the morning fruit, vegetable and fish market (a must-see while in Venice). Two rooms face out onto the Grand Canal, so if you want the perfect romantic setting for your vacation make sure you request one of these. The rooms and bathrooms are all different sizes but come with every possible three-star amenity. The breakfast room looks out over the Grand Canal and there is also a small library filled with books about Venice.

17. SAN CASSIANO, *Calle della Rosa 2232, Tel. 041/524-1768 Fax 041/ 721-033. Email: info@sancassiano.it. Web: www.sancassiano.it. All credit cards accepted. 35 rooms. Single E65-235; Double E75-335. Breakfast included. Vaporetto Stop - San Stae. Map - B.* ***

By far the best three star in Venice! Located in a 16th century Gothic *palazzo* on the Grand Canal, with a small seating area at their private dock, as well as one in the breakfast room. The rooms are all elegantly furnished, setting a romantic scene for your stay. Try to get one of the rooms on the Grand Canal. The vista is inspiring. A top level hotel, ideally located near San Marco but off the beaten path enough to offer a real Venetian experience. This is an excellent choice while in Venice.

Dorsoduro & Guidecca

If you want to try and get away from it all while in Venice, Dorsoduro is the section in which to do it. There are few stores but many real Venetian sights. You'll find artisans, locals buying fruit from a boat that comes daily from the mainland, as well as high level hotels and museums.

18. AGLI ALBORETI, *Rio Terra Antonia Foscarini, Accademia 884, Tel. 041/523-0058, Fax 041/521-0128. Web: www.aglialboretti.com. All credit cards accepted. 20 rooms. Single E110-130; Double E160-190. Breakfast included. Vaporetto Stop - Accademia. Maps - B&D.* **

I love the little garden off the lobby where you can have breakfast in the mornings or relax in the evenings for dinner or drinks. The rooms are not quite so spacious, but they're comfortable and come with A/C and heat. Located

Hotels ○
1. Ala
2. Bel Sito
7. Gallini
8. Gritti Palace
11. Santo Stefano
14. Al Sole
15. Antico Capon
16. Locanda Sturion
17. San Cassiano
18. Agli Alboretti
19. Belle Arti
20. Calcina
24. Pensione Seguso
25. Villa Maravegie

Eateries ●
28. Al Bacareto
31. Al Teatro
34. Giglio
36. Leon Bianco
43. Ae Oche
44. Al Giardinetto
45. Alla Madonna
46. Antico Capon
47. Cantina do Mori
48. Da Fiore
49. La Zucca
50. Poste Vecie
51. San Toma
52. Al Gondolieri
53. Alle Zattere
54. San Trovaso

Nightlife ●
57. Margaret DuChamp

Shops 🛍
58. Arcobeleno
59. Carta Venezia
60. Livio de Marchi
62. Negozio d'Arte
63. Il Pavone
64. Punto Arte
65. Alberto Valese-Ebru

Sights ◇
A. Accademia
D. Frari
E. Santa Maria del Rosario
H. Grand Canal
K. Rialto Bridge
P. Guggenheim Museum
R. Ponte degli Scalzi

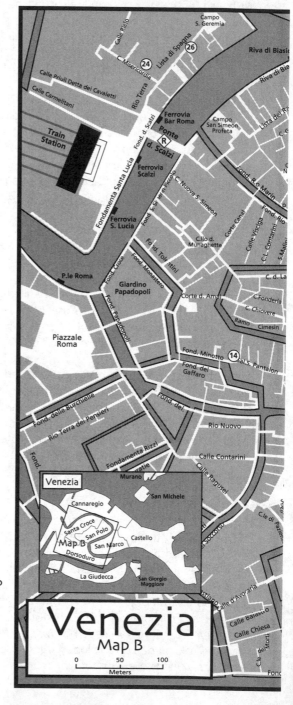

Venezia
Map B

0   50   100
Meters

in the shadows of the Accademia, you are a bridge away from all the major sights, but still have the comfort of a tranquil setting. A comfortable, accommodating and relatively inexpensive two-star hotel. One of the best two stars in Venice and the prices reflect that.

19. BELLE ARTI, *Dorsoduro 912/A, Tel. 041/522-6230, Fax 041/528-0043. Web: www.hotelbellearti.com. Single E95-150; Double E150-210. All credit cards accepted. Breakfast included.* ***

A top notch three star hotel with great rooms, a comfortable and relaxing garden area, superb furnishings, and a character filled ambiance. Despite being located near the Accademia, the hotel is in a quiet part of town, far away from the hordes of tourists. This is an ideal place. Highly recommended.

20. CALCINA, *Fondamenta Zattere dei Gesuati 780, Tel. 041/520-6466, Fax 041/522-7045. Email: info@lacalcina.com. Web: www.lacalcina.com. Credit cards accepted. 30 rooms. Single without bath E65-E80; Single E80-E110; Double E110-190. Vaporetto Stop – Zattere. Maps – B&D.* ***

The hotel has views over the large canal in front, a side canal, and the boring rear. Try to get a great view in the front overlooking La Guidecca island because the sunsets are spectacular. They also have a floating terrace out front from which you can enjoy breakfast or an afternoon cocktail. The rooms are clean and comfortable without any true distinguishing feature, except for the tranquility and calm.

21. CIPRIANI, *Fondamenta San Giovanni 10, La Guidecca, Tel. 041/520-7744, Fax 041/520-3930. Email: info@hotelcipriani.it. Web: www.cipriani.orient-express.com. Credit cards accepted. 98 rooms. Single E375-550; Double E500-800. Vaporetto Stop – Zitelle. Map – D.* ****

This exquisite hotel occupies three beautiful acres at the east end of La Isola del Guidecca. There is a swimming pool, tennis court, saunas, jacuzzis, a private harbor for yachts, a private launch to ferry guests back and forth to San Marco, an American-style bar and two superb restaurants. Sixty rooms overlook the lagoon, while many others look out over the pool. This hotel is probably as close to heaven on earth as you'll find in Venice. They even have a private butler service if needed. The exquisite ambiance makes the Cipriani one of the premier hotels in all of Venice.

22. MESSNER, *Modonna della Salute 216/217, Tel. 041/522-7443, Fax 041/522-7266. Web: www.hotelmessner.it. All credit cards accepted. Single E110. Double E155. Breakfast included.* **

Off the beaten path, in a relatively secluded part of Venice, this two star is clean, quiet and comfortable. A good place to stay for budget travelers. In one of my favorite parts of town, off the beaten path. Highly recommended.

23. ALLA SALUTE, *Fondamenta Ca' Bala, Tel 0415/235-404, Fax 0415/222-271. Email: info@hotelsalute.com. Web: www.hotelsalute.com. 40 rooms. Single without bath E85; Single E120; Double without bath E110; Double E150. All credit cards accepted. Breakfast included.* **

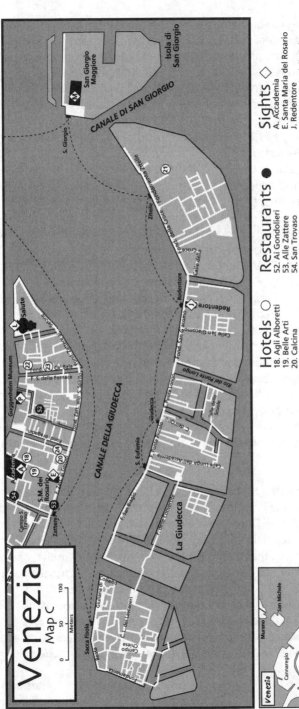

Venezia
Map C

0   50   100
Meters

CANALE DI SAN GIORGIO

Isola di
San Giorgio

San Giorgio
Maggiore

CANALE DELLA GIUDECCA

La Giudecca

S. Giorgio

Salute

Guggenheim Museum

Accademia

S. M. dei Rosario

Redentore

S. Eufemia

Campo S.
Trovaso

Zitelle

Sacca Fisola

Giuliana di Coletto

Campo
Chiesa

Hotels ○
18. Agli Alboretti
19. Belle Arti
20. Calcina
21. Cipriani
22. Messner
23. Alla Salute
24. Pensione Seguso

Restaurants ●
52. Ai Gondolieri
53. Alle Zattere
54. San Trovaso

Sights ◇
A. Accademia
E. Santa Maria del Rosario
J. Redentore
L. Santa Maria della Salute
M. San Giorgio Maggiore
P. Guggenheim Museum

Venezia

Murano
San Michele
Cannaregio
Santa Croce
San Polo
San Marco
Castello
Dorsoduro
La Giudecca
San Giorgio Maggiore
Map D

In a centuries-old building, in a secluded part of town near the Academia, this two star is an ideal place to stay. Filled with pleasant two star comforts, here you will find comfortable rooms as well as accommodating common areas in which to relax. An excellent choice while in Venice on a budget.

24. **SEGUSO**, *Zattere dei Gesuati 779, Tel. 041/528-6858, Fax 041/522-2340. Web: www.pensioneseguso.it. Credit cards accepted. 36 rooms, 18 with bath. Single without bath E90-120; Single E100-154; Double with bath E100-175; Double E110-200. Breakfast included. In high season your room comes with either lunch or dinner. Vaporetto Stop – Zattere. Maps – B&D.* **

Only a two-star but what great atmosphere. The view of the Canal and Guidecca island is especially beautiful when the sun is setting. Recently upgraded, prices are creeping up fast because this place is bucking for three-star status. All the rooms are decorated in a simple fashion and the atmosphere is very much like a bed and breakfast. Slightly expensive for a two-star, but the view is great as is the tranquil setting.

25. **VILLA MARAVEGE**, *Fondamenta Bollani 1058, Tel. 041/521-0188, Fax 041/523-9152. Email: info@pensioneaccademia.it. Web: www.pensioneaccademia.it. All Credit Cards accepted. 27 rooms. Single E90-130; Double E135-280. Breakfast included. Vaporetto Stop – Accademia. Map – B.* ***

This impressive 17th century villa, formerly the Russian consulate, is surrounded by beautiful gardens just off the Grand Canal. There is a patio with chairs and tables and many plants on one side of the villa facing the Grand Canal. The inside is simply beautiful with an upstairs tea room as well as a breakfast room that overlooks a flower garden. All the rooms are large, save number 8, which is a tiny single. Each is furnished in a different manner but are comfortable. Basically this place is marvelous. Because of the location, ambiance and comfort, reservations are sometimes necessary over a year in advance!

Cannaregio

This section in the north of the main island is where the Jewish ghetto is located. This was the first place in Europe where Jews were isolated from the rest of the population The area where they were confined to live was once a cannon foundry, which in Italian is *getto*. Ever since that time, Jewish enclaves have been known by that name. Three of the synagogues in the main square of the tiny island (which comprised the first ghetto) are worth seeing. This area of Venice is alive with local shoppers buying their supplies for the day, with beautiful side streets and canals that are located away from it all.

26. **ABBAZIA**, *Calle Priuli 68, Tel. 041/717-333, Fax 041/717-949. Email: info@abbaziahotel.com. Web: www.abbaziahotel.com. Credit cards accepted. 31 rooms. Single E80-235, Double E90-260. Breakfast included. Vaporetto Stop – Ca' d'Oro. Map – A.* ***

The hotel used to be part of a monastery until about 30 years ago when the monks sold this section of their property. Once inside, you'll be amazed at the beautiful but simple decor. I desperately want one of the wooden abbey benches that line the perimeter of the lobby. A good place to stay in Venice.

27. BERNARDI-SEMENZATO, *Calle del Oca, SS. Apostoli 4363-4366, Tel. 041/522-7257. Fax 041/522-242. Web: www.hotelbernardi.com. Email: info@hotelbernardi.com. Credit cards accepted. 15 rooms. Single E70; Double E100. Breakfast E4 extra. Vaporetto Stop – Ca' d'Oro. Map – A.* **

This place has changed quite a bit in the last few years. It's now a renovated, extremely clean, and wonderful little two-star in a great location. They even have a roof terrace that overlooks Venetian rooftops. Getting up there is kind of rough, but it's still a roof garden. This used to be a budget traveler's paradise but now they're charging a little because they've installed air conditioning and are in the process of putting in TVs in hopes of getting upgraded to a three-star. It used to be a better value but it is still a good place to stay.

Where To Eat

When applicable, each restaurant reviewed below also lists the closest water taxi *(vaporetto)* stop and map reference.

Venetian Cuisine

Venice is not generally known for its cuisine, especially reasonably priced dining, but they do know how to prepare great seafood dishes, which usually comes placed over a bed of rice. Even though pasta is not used as often here as in other regions of Italy, the Venetians make very good *spaghetti alla vongole* (clams) or *alla cozze* (mussels). Another favorite is the *zuppa di pesce* (fish soup), that mixes together every kind of fish that could be found.

Eating most anywhere in Venice you won't get the bang for your buck that you'd get somewhere else in Italy, since many of the restaurants have been created to cater specifically to the tourists. As such they charge rather high prices. With that word of warning, you can also find some wonderful little pizzeria or trattoria that caters to the local population and offers tasty and inexpensive offerings. I'll list some in this section.

Suggested Venetian Cuisine

Traditional Venetian fare is listed below and every course is usually ordered at a full meal. Our constitution just isn't prepared for such mass consumption, however, so don't feel embarrassed if all you order is a pasta dish or an entrée with a salad or appetizer.

Antipasto - Appetizer

• **Insalata di mare** – Seafood salad of shrimp, squid, and clams in a zesty oil, vinegar and herbs sauce.

• **Antipasto misto di mare** – Seafood appetizers taken from a buffet

Primo Piatto - First Course
• **Zuppa di pesce** – Seafood soup with any fish you can imagine cooked into it
• **Spaghetti alla vongole verace** –Spaghetti with an olive oil, garlic and clam sauce
• **Risotto con cozze** – A rice and mussels dish pumped with a variety of spices

Secondo Piatto - Entrée
Pesce (Fish)
• **Grigliata mista di mare** – An assortment of grilled seafood based on whatever the seasonal catch is
• **Bisato anguilla alla veneziana** – Eel cooked with onion, oil, vinegar, garlic and a little bay leaves
• **Fritto misto** – Assorted deep fried seafood

Carne (Meat)
• **Fegato alla veneziana** – Calf's liver sautéed with onions
• **Torresani** – Tiny pigeons served grilled on a spit

Formaggio (Cheese)
• **Asiago** – A dry, sharp cheese from the Veneto mainland

Regional Wines
You'll probably recognize many of the white wines from this region, especially the Friuli wines, such as Pinot Grigio and Pinot Bianco, and the incomparable Soave's which can be found in many stores at home. The reds are not so recognizable except for the Cabernet, and they're not nearly as good as the reds from the Chianti region around Florence. But then again, not many reds can compare to a Chianti.

San Marco
28. AL BACARETO, *Calle Crosera 3447, Tel. 041/5289-336. Credit cards accepted. Closed Saturdays for dinner and Sundays. Meal for two E38. Vaporetto Stop – San Samuele. Map – B.*
This authentic neighborhood *trattoria* serves excellent Venetian dishes. There are a few tables outside from which you can enjoy your meal while reveling in the sights and sounds of the local neighborhood. The seating inside is warm and comfortable, with a dark wooden beamed ceiling. If you're adventurous sample their specialty *fegato alla veneziana* (calf's liver sautéed with onions) or any of their great seafood dishes for seconds. For starters try their *risotto pesce* (rice mixed with seafood) or the *zuppa di pesce* (fish soup).

Restaurants By Map

29. **AL BUSO**, *Ponte di Rialto 5338, Tel. 041/528-9078. Credit cards accepted. Meal for two E32. Vaporetto Stop – Rialto. Map – A.*

Located right beside the Rialto bridge down on the water by the Grand Canal. There are few tables set outside that come with the great canal-side views. It's worth the wait to get one of these tables. The pizza and pasta are both good and inexpensive. Try their *pizza ai frutta di mare* (seafood pizza) or the *spaghetti con pesce* (with seafood). Then for *doppo* (seconds), try the *sogliola alla griglia* (grilled sole), a wonderful finish to any meal.

30. **ALLA RIVETTA**, *Ponte S. Provolo 4625, Tel. 041/528-7302. Credit cards accepted. Closed Mondays. Meal for two E32. Vaporetto Stop – San Zaccaria. Map – A.*

Tucked away at the foot of the Ponte San Provolo behind the Chiesa di San Marco this place is largely overlooked by tourists. A hangout for some of the gondoliers as a drinking hole (they have a bar that faces onto the small canal where the gondoliers park their boats); and for many of the locals because of the food, location, and prices. The atmosphere is all Venetian and the menu is from all over Italy. Enjoy both together. A great place to eat in Venice.

31. **AL TEATRO**, *Campo San Fantin 1916, Tel. 041/522-1052. Credit cards accepted. Closed Mondays and in November. Last orders can be placed at midnight. Dinner for E43. Vaporetto Stop – Santa Maria del Giglio. Maps – A &B.*

Al Teatro stays open late to cater to the exiting theater customers (hence the name). It's actually a ristorante, pizzeria, and bar all rolled into one, with great local ambiance. They have seating outside under canopies in the piazza and plenty of seating inside, but in good weather I believe the atmosphere is best outside. Try the *spaghetti alla vongole* (with a spicy olive oil-based clam sauce or the *risotto di pesce* (seafood rice dish). Then grab some *scampi e calamari fritti* (fried squid and shrimp for seconds).

My Favorite Venetian Restaurants
28. AL BACARETO
30. ALLA RIVETTA
39. AL MASCARON
49. LA ZUCCA
50. POSTE VECIE
60. SAN TROVASO

☞

32. **ANTICO MARTINI**, *Campo San Fantin 1983, Tel. 041/522-4121. All credit cards accepted. Closed Tuesdays and Wednesdays for lunch. Meal for two E105. Vaporetto Stop – Santa Maria Del Giglio. Maps – A.*

Snuggled onto a back street of Venice, this is an excellent and world-renowned restaurant; but it is quite expensive, so save coming here for a special occasion or if you have money to blow. You can be seated in the piazza out front or surrounded by the local decor inside. They make a good *risotto al mare* (seafood rice dish), a tasty *scampi alla provenzale* (shrimp Provencal), and an excellent *branzino alla griglia* (grilled seas bass). Or you can get *tagliata di Angus* (beef steak) or *fegatto alla veneziana* (tasty liver). After your meal ask for the *formaggio* (cheese tray) and sample some of their delicious cheeses. This place is a staple in Venice.

33. **DA RAFFAELE**, *Fondamenta delle Ostreghe 2347, Tel. 041/523-2317. Credit cards accepted. Closed Thursdays and January to mid-February. Meal for two E48. Vaporetto Stop – San Maria del Giglio. Map – A.*

Even though your first impression is of a haven for tourists since the menu is in four languages, the food here is actually very good. Many Venetians frequent this restaurant but they choose to sit inside, where it's endowed with marble and much cooler, leaving the terrace for the tourists, which is also a beautiful place to enjoy a meal. Try the *risotto Raphaele* (made with clams and other seafood), which is for two people. Then later try the assorted fried fish or the grilled sole.

34. **GIGLIO**, *Campo Santa Maria dei Giglio 2477 (next to the Hotel Ala). Tel. 041/523-2368. Meal for two E40. Vaporetto Stop – Santa Maria del Giglio. Maps – A & B.*

There is enclosed piazza seating for any kind of weather, and they have a menu in English for easy ordering. Try the *risotto* with seafood, which is served for two people. Then make sure you try the curried chicken with rice pilaf which is stupendous.

35. **LA COLOMBA**, *Piscina di Frezzeria 1665, Tel. 041/522-1175. All credit cards accepted. Closed Tuesdays. Meal for two E100. Vaporetto Stop – San Marco. Map – A.*

Mainly known for its fish dishes and fine decorations, La Colomba also has a wide variety of grilled, baked, or fried meats and fish. Sitting on a quiet street with some outdoor tables, this is a good place to come and relax until late into the evening (orders still taken up to 11:00pm). You might want to try the succulent *scampi al curry* with rice pilaf. They also make some good pastas, like *spaghetti alla carbonara* (with ham, butter, cheese, and egg) and a great *risotto ai frutti di mare* (with seafood) and a tasty *fresco gazpacho* (cold veggie soup from Spain). Be prepared to spend a little money here; it's very expensive.

36. **LEON BIANCO**, *Salizzada San Luca 4153, Tel. 041/522-1180. No credit cards accepted. Closed Sundays. Open Monday - Saturday 9:00am - 1:00pm and 4:00pm to 9:00pm. Meal for two E18. Vaporetto Stop – Rialto. Maps – A & B.*

A surprising inexpensive little wine bar in Venice's most expensive area, San Marco. There's a wide variety of *tramezzini* sandwiches filled with a variety of meats, cheeses and vegetables to go along with your wine selections. The perfect place to come for a midday snack and a good glass of wine or an ice cold draft beer, as well as for a light dinner.

37. VINO VINO, *Calle Veste 2007A, Tel. 041/522-4121. Credit cards accepted. Closed Tuesdays. Open 10:00am - midnight and 1:00am on Saturdays. Meal for two E20. Vaporetto Stop – Santa Maria del Giglio. Map – A.*

A late night wine bar opened by the owners of the Antico Martini (see number 32 above) to cater mainly to the late night theater crowd and others just leaving their restaurant when it closes at 10:00pm. They serve salads, sandwiches, as well as meat dishes like chicken and lamb all prepared by the kitchen at the Antico Martini and for a much better price (about one quarter as expensive). These two places are bookends for another Martini special, a piano bar that serves late night drinks and entertainment.

Castello

38. AL COVO, *Campiello della Pescaria 3968, Tel. 041/522-3812. No credit cards accepted. Closed Wednesdays and Thursdays and 15 days in August. Meal for two E70. Vaporetto Stop – Riva Degli Schiavoni. Map – A.*

The perfect place to eat is on their patio while sampling the seafood splendor they prepare. One of the owners is American so no need to worry about a language barrier. The service is quite attentive and the food prepared perfectly. Located near San Giovanni in Bragora, this is true Venetian cuisine with wonderful atmosphere. Try the *spaghetti al nero di seppia* (with octopus ink), or the *verdure fritte* (fried vegetables) for seconds. The *zuppa di pesce* (seafood soup) is also good, as is the *ravioli di branzino* (sea bass ravioli). They also make great grilled meats or fish.

39. AL MASCARON, *Calle Lunga Santa Maria Formosa 5225, Tel. 041/522-5995. No credit cards accepted. Closed Sundays and mid-December to mid-January and 15 days in August. Meal for two E35. Vaporetto Stop – Rialto. Map – A.*

Just off of the Campo Santa Maria Formosa, this is a local *trattoria* with a truly rustic atmosphere that serves great food. The menu changes daily but most times you can get great boiled or roasted vegetables as an appetizer or a side dish. Their *spaghetti scoglie* (mix of seafood including mussels, shrimp, clams and more) is stupendous. Also tasty is the *penne al pesce spada* (small noodles with a sauce of swordfish). For seconds any of their fish on the grill, like *branzini* (sea bass) or *sogliola* (sole) are excellent. Highly recommended.

40. ARCIMBOLDO, *Calle dei Furlani 3219, Venezia. Tel. 041/86-569. No credit cards accepted. Closed Tuesdays. Meal for two E30. Vaporetto Stop – Riva Degli Schiavoni. Map – A.*

Located on a small canal, off the beaten path you'll love the local flavor and quiet ambiance of the outside seating. There'll be hardly a tourist around, except for yourself. Try their exquisite *scampi al curry* with rice pilaf and any of their grilled meats. A wonderful place to get away from it all. But bring your map – this is a tough one to find.

41. CORTE SCONTA, *Calle del Pestrin 3886, Tel. 041/522-7024. Credit cards accepted. Closed Sundays and Mondays. Meal for two E35. Vaporetto Stop – Arsenale. Map – A.*

Located near the Piazza San Giovanni in Bragora, this restaurant is always full. Despite its plain decor this place is popular because of its food. And being always filled with locals, makes this a boisterous and authentic night out in Venice. Their menu changes with the tide - i.e. whatever the catch is that day - but they always seem to have a well stocked but diverse *fritture mista di mare* (mixed fried seafood). Since this is a very popular, high end local restaurant, reservations are required.

42. DA REMIGIO, *Salizzada dei Greci, Tel. 041/523-0089. Credit cards accepted. Closed Monday dinners and Tuesdays. Meal for two E60. Vaporetto Stop – Riva del Schiavoni. Map – A.*

A true family style Venetian *trattoria*, in a local part of town, that is frequented mainly by Venetians. Highly recommended. The food is truly Venetian and the atmosphere is rustic and down to earth. As in most Venetian restaurants the specialty is fish. Their mixed seafood grill is scrumptious as are their grilled fish. All at excellent prices

Santa Croce/San Polo

43. AE OCHE, *Calle del Tintor 1552A, Tel. 041/524-1161. www.aeochegroup.it. Credit cards accepted. Closed Mondays. Meal for two E23. Vaporetto Stop – San Stae. Map – B.*

Located near the Campo San Giacomo del'Orto in Santa Croce, this is another inexpensive pizzeria frequented by many Venetians who appreciate the countless varieties of pizza. My favorite is the *pizza mangia fuoco* (literally meaning 'eat fire,' a spicy pizza with salami and hot peppers). For other spicy pizzas, go for the *Diavolo* or *Inferno*. Besides pizza, you can get an *omelet a piacere* (made any way you want). Too bad they're not open for breakfast. The walls are adorned with old commercial signs from the US of A.

44. AL GIARDINETTO, *Rio della Frescada 2910. Tel. 041/522-4100. Credit cards accepted. Meal for two E33. Vaporetto Stop – San Toma. Map – B.*

Located on a quaint little canal under a blanket of vines in a little garden (hence the name). You can enjoy a variety of pizzas that will make you ache for more. Try the *prosciutto e funghi* pizza (ham and mushrooms) and ask for extra mozzarella (*doppia mozzarella*) and you will be very satisfied. A wonderful little place with many dishes from which to choose.

45. **ALLA MADONNA**, *Calle dell Madonna 594, Venezia. Tel. 041/522-3824. All credit cards accepted. Closed Wednesdays, January and seven days in August. Dinner for E55. Vaporetto Stop – Rialto. Maps – A &B.*

Located down a tiny alley off the Grand canal near the Rialto bridge, you get a good mix of locals and tourists here for both lunch and dinner. It is a simple but superb *trattoria* where you can pick out your own fish from the refrigerated display of the catch bought at the morning market nearby. If you don't want any fish they have a variety of grilled and roast meats based on availability. Besides the excellent food, the atmosphere is loud and boisterous which tends to make the meal fun and authentically Venetian. They have excellent *risotto ai frutti di mare* (rice with seafood) and a superb *fritto misto di mare* (mixed fried seafood). You can also enjoy *spaghetti alla vongole* (with clam sauce), *risotto ai frutti di mare* (seafood rice dish) or *pasta e fagioli* (pasta and beans).

46. **ANTICO CAPON**, *Piazza Santa Margherita 3004, Tel. 041/528-525. Web: www.anticocaponristorante.com. Credit cards accepted. Meal for two E25. Vaporetto Stop – Ca' Rezzonico. Map – B.*

Located right below the one-star hotel of the same name, this is a perfect place to enjoy the life of a Venetian piazza. Sit under the awnings or in the sun, but enjoy some good pizza or *crostini* (sandwiches). The *crostino con funghi, prosciutto, e mozzarella* (with mushrooms, ham, and mozzarella) is great, as is the *crostino al inferno* (literally translated it means hell's sandwich; it has tomatoes, mozzarella, hot salami, mushrooms, and *pepperoncini* and is quite tasty, if a little spicy).

47. **CANTINA DO MORI**, *Calle 2 Mori, Tel. 041/522-5401. Tel. 041/522-5401. Open 8:30am-10:30pm. Closed Sundays.*

Can you say "local place?" A great little wine bar near the Rialto. Rustic wood paneling, a few tiny tables, and friendly bar tenders serving tasty edibles and flavorful vintages all make this place perfect for a break in your touring.

48. **DA FIORE**, *Calle del Scaleter 2202, Tel. 041/721-308. All credit cards accepted. Closed Sundays and Mondays, and during August and Christmas. Meal for two E80. Vaporetto Stop – San Silvestro or San Toma. Map – B.*

This is an elegant but at the same time simple old Venetian *trattoria* that offers great fresh seafood. You'll find some *cucina nuova* (nouvelle cuisine) influence here since they have a different menu every day and try to make each meal a magical journey. One of their staples is *risotto di scampi e funghi porcini* (rice with shrimp and mushrooms) that serves two people. After you've digested this, try their *frittura mista al'Adriatico* (mixed seafood from the Adriatic). It's not meant for two, but after the rice dish, it should suffice.

49. **LA ZUCCA**, *Calle del Megio 1762, Tel. 041/524-1570. Credit cards accepted. Closed Sundays. Meal for two E25. Vaporetto Stop – San Stae. Map – B.*

Zucca means pumpkin, and you guessed it, their specialty in the fall and winter is pumpkin pasta. It is extremely delicious, especially with a cream sauce. They also have fresh fish, chicken, and salads but not too much red meat. So if you're a dedicated carnivore, this healthy menu will discourage you. Enjoy your meal at a small table outside or one of their inside tables with views of the canal. Some of my favorite dishes were *maiale al curry con riso pilaf* (curried pork with rice pilaf) or the *pollo ai ferri con tzatziki* (grilled chicken with a tasty yogurt sauce). A great place in Venice. Stop here if you get the chance.

50. **POSTE VECIE**, *Pescheria 1608, Tel. 041/721-822. Web: www.postevecie.com. Credit cards accepted. Closed Tuesdays. Meal for two E50. Vaporetto Stop – Rialto. Map – B.*

Huddled in the corner of the vast *pescheria* fish market (hence the address), and located near the old post office (hence the name). To get here you follow a private wooden bridge that leads to this old converted inn with its low ceilings and dark wooden beams. This restaurant is known for its perfectly prepared fish, especially the grilled variety, and its bountiful antipasto table. In the summer you can dine in the splendid garden that has vines and leaves hanging overhead. Try their superb *risotto di pesce* (rice with seafood for two people), then move onto the exquisite *sogliola ai ferri* (grilled sole).

51. **SAN TOMA**, *Campo San Toma, San Polo 2864A, Tel. 041/523-8819. Credit cards accepted. Closed Tuesdays. Meal for two E30. Vaporetto Stop – San Toma. Map – B.*

Pizza is their specialty, so try a great *pizza rustica* (with mozzarella, tomatoes, salami, and egg). Or indulge yourself in a staple of Venetian cuisine, *risotto di pesce* (rice with seafood, and kind of *paella*-like concoction). The outside seating is best on this out of the way little piazza. You can enjoy your meal and *vino* under the stars or inside in their rustic, wood paneled environment.

Dorsoduro

52. **AI GONDOLIERI**, *Dorsoduro 366. Tel. 041/528-6396. Closed Tuesdays. All credit cards accepted. Meal for two E70. Vaporetto Stop – Santa Maria Della Salute. Map – D.*

The menu mainly consists of meats and cheeses, complemented by seasonal vegetables. My favorite is the exotic *filetto di struzzo alle erbe* (ostrich filet). For the adventurous try the *trippa alla parmigiana* (tripe). Other dishes include *filetto d'Angus al tartufo nero* (beef steak with black truffles) or with *Barolo e porcini* (steak in a red wine and mushroom sauce). And for dessert try something from their extensive cake cart like a *strudel di mele* (apple strudel) or *torte alla frutta* (fruit pies). A fine restaurant located near the Peggy Guggenheim Museum.

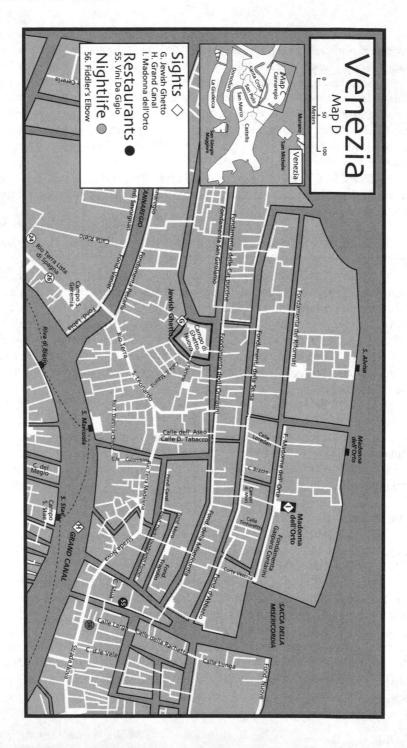

Venezia
Map D

Map C
Cannaregio
Santa Croc
Dorsoduro
San Polo
San Marco
La Giudecca
Castello
San Giorgio Maggiore

Murano
San Michele
Venezia

0   50   100
Meters

Sights ◇
G. Jewish Ghetto
H. Grand Canal
I. Madonna dell'Orto

Restaurants ●
55. Vini Da Gigio

Nightlife ●
56. Fiddler's Elbow

53. **ALLE ZATTERE**, *Zattere ai Gesuati 795,. Tel. 041/520-4224. Credit cards accepted. Closed Tuesdays. Pizza for two E20. Vaporetto Stop – Zattere. Maps – B &D.*

This a favorite local pizzeria near the Campo San Agnese, known for its many varieties of pizza and its excellent view of Guidecca island from the pizzeria's tables on the Zattere's floating rafts. A perfect place to eat when the sun sets. You can get almost any type pizza here, including *margherita* (with sauce and cheese) and *verdure* (with grilled vegetables). There are also seafood salads and seafood pastas from which to choose.

54. **SAN TROVASO**, *Fondamenta Priuli 1016, Tel. 041/520-3703. Credit cards accepted. Closed Mondays. Air conditioned. Meal for two E33. Vaporetto Stop – Accademia or Zattere. Maps – B &D.*

If they seat you in the side room or upstairs with the locals, you feel as if you entered a heated discussion since everyone will be talking at once. Couple this with the clatter of pans and the occasional dropped glass or plate from the kitchen and this place has a great local feel to it. And the food is great, otherwise the locals wouldn't come. Try either the *spaghetti newburg* (with shrimp, tomatoes sauce and cream) or the *spaghetti alla carbonara* (with ham, cream and egg). For *secondo* they have plenty of reasonably priced meats and fish. Take your pick, they're all good.

Cannaregio

55. **VINI DA GIGIO**, *Fondamenta San Felice 3628/a,. Tel. 041/528-5140. Closed Mondays and 15 days in January. All credit cards accepted. Meal for two F60. Vaporetto Stop – Ca' d'Oro. Map – C.*

Located a little off the tourist path, this is a simple local wine bar and *trattoria*. They offer more than 300 different wine choices with your meal of typical Venetian cuisine. Sample their *antipasto di frutti di mare* (antipasto of sea food), then some *tagliatelle nere con sugo di scampi* (dark pasta with shrimp sauce), or *spaghetti alla vongole verace* (with spicy clam sauce), then a *fritto misto di mare and verdure* (mixed fried seafood and vegetables). There is also extensive menu of grilled meats.

Seeing the Sights

Some people say that Venice is really only a living museum and not a real city any longer, but that's what makes it perfect for tourists. Everywhere you look you see something so beautiful, so awe inspiring that Venice at times seems out of this world. I guess that is probably why this was Walt Disney's favorite city.

Medieval in layout and design, this city built on pilings in a marshy lagoon has everything you could imagine for a vacation, except, during high season, reasonable prices. You can find exquisite churches, beautiful synagogues, pristine *palazzi*, spacious *piazze*, magnificent museums, deserted islands only a *vaporetto* ride away, skilled crafts people blowing glass or making masks right in front of you, superb restaurants, relaxing hotels, and so much more.

The sights are spread across the main maps for this chapter: map A (pages 420-421); map B (pages 428-429); map C (page 442) and map D (page 431).

VENICEcard

VENICEcard allows you to use the Aliguna boat service to and from the airport, visit museums, have access to public restrooms, and more, all at cut rate prices. There are one day, three day and seven day passes. Visit their website to find the right one for you: *www.venicecard.com*.

The Quiet Side of Venice

During the summer months Venice is literally crammed with tourists. If you're in need of a little solitude or space, you can find a more serene Venetian experience by going anywhere other than areas around Piazza San Marco, the Rialto Bridge, and the Train station.

Two of the sections of Venice that are less crowded are listed below. Remember that Venice is unbelievably safe, so don't worry about walking, and don't worry about getting lost. You will always find your way. Also, by wandering around you'll inevitably find some charming piazza or café that will seem as if it hasn't been discovered by anyone but you. So strap on your walking shoes and get going.

Castello & St. Elena– There's not much in terms of tourist amenities in these two sections of Venice, but this is where the people live. And that makes it fun to visit. Here you will also be far from the thundering herd of international tourists. Around the **Arsenale** and beyond you'll find real Venetian neighborhoods, with grandmas chatting at each other from window sills above the canals, children playing in the narrow streets, and life peacefully devoid of the rumble of tourist crowds. Also here you'll find some of Venice's rare green, wide open spaces.

Dorsoduro – Here you will wander through some of the best neighborhoods in Venice for a vibrant taste of local color. You'll find artisan's shops, lovely houses, and narrow medieval streets and calming canals. A wonderful respite from tourist Venice.

A. ACCADEMIA

Located in Campo della Carita, Dorsoduro. *Tel. 041/522-2247.* Open Monday–Saturday 9:00am–7:00pm in the summer and 9:00am–4:00pm in winter. Sundays and holidays 9:00am–1:00pm. Vaporetto – Accademia. Maps – B & D.

Five hundred years of unequaled Venetian art are on display at the **Accademia**. The collection began in 1750 when the Republic of St. Mark's decided to endow the city with an academy to feature local painters and sculptors (*Accademica di Pittori e Scultori*). The original academy occupied the current Port Authority building located by the gardens of the royal palace overlooking the harbor of St. Mark's.

During the French occupation of 1807, the collection was moved to the School and Church of the Carita (in Campo della Carita) which was also the former monastery of the Lateran Canons. Since then it has grown and expanded immensely and is a must-see for anyone visiting Venice who is interested in art.

There are far too many excellent paintings and sculptures to list them all, but these are the ones you should not miss:
• *St. George* – Montegna (Room 4)
• *The Madonna degli Alberelli* (Madonna among the little trees) – Giovanni Bellini (Room 5)
• *The Tempest* – Giorgione (Room 5)
• *The Miracle of the Slave* – Jacopo Tintoretto (Room 10)
• *Banquet in the House of Levi* – Veronese (Room 10)
• *The Pieta* – Titian (Room 10). The last work of this amazing artist.
• *Legend of St. Ursula* – Vittore Carpaccio (Room 21)
• *Detail of the Arrival of The Ambassadors* – Vittore Carpaccio (Room 21)
• *Presentation at the Temple* – Titian (Room 24)

B. ARSENALE

Open 9:00am–noon and 3.00pm–7:00pm Monday–Saturday. Vaporetto – Arsenale. Map – A.

The **Arsenale** is an imposing group of buildings, landing stages, workshops, ship yards and more from which the Venetian Navy was built. Begun in 1100, it has been continually enlarged over the years. Surrounded by towers and walls, the Arsenale has an imposing Renaissance entrance created by Giambello in 1460. In the front of the entrance is a terrace with statues that symbolize the victory of the Battle of Lepanto. At the sides are four lions, the symbol of the Venetian city-state.

Nearby is the **Naval History Museum** with its collection of relics and trophies of the Italian Navy as well as that of Venice, which has had a much more auspicious and lengthy existence. There is a wonderfully detailed model of the last *Bucintoro*, the vessel in which the Doge of Venice celebrated the "Wedding of the Sea" between Venice and the sea by throwing a ring into the Adriatic.

This is a great museum, not only because you have to trek through real Venetian neighborhoods to find it, but also as a result of its impressive collection of armaments, models, relics of modern craft used in World Wars I and II. Kids of all ages love this place.

C. DOGES PALACE – PALAZZO DUCALE

Located in St. Mark's Square (Piazzetta San Marco), San Marco. *Tel. 041/ 522-4951*. Open Monday–Sunday 8:30am–7:00pm in the summer and 8:30am–2:00pm in the winter. Vaporetto – San Marco. Map – A.

Another must-see while in Venice. To view it all will take the better part of a day if you perform a thorough inspection. Finished in the 1400s after being started in the 9th century by the Doges Angelo and Giustiniano Partecipazio, this was the seat of the government and the residence of the **Doge**, Venice's supreme head of state. The flamboyant Gothic style was mainly created by a family of skilled Venetian marble craftsmen, the **Bons**. It is still a joy to behold despite the devastation by fire in 1577 of one of the building's wings. Since then it has been rebuilt in its original form. It has a double tier of arcading and

Venice's Suggested Rules of Conduct

Since Venice experiences a massive influx of tourists every year, it is the only Italian city I know of that prints up an official pamphlet advising tourists how to behave while visiting. These rules help travelers from many different cultures remain in harmony with each other and the locals, allowing for daily life of Venice to continue unhindered.

Here are the suggestions Venetians wish tourists to be aware of:

1. When walking on the tiny streets keep to the right, one person behind the other so others coming from the opposite direction may pass.

2. When you stop to admire the view remember to leave space for others to pass; please avoid sitting at any time on the steps of bridges since this will dramatically impede traffic.

3. Always remove backpacks when traveling on the water transport, otherwise you are bound to bump into someone. Remember also to have bought a ticket before boarding.

4. No one, men included, can go bare-chested in Venice; and no one can wear beach attire in the city. This means bikini bottoms for both men and women and bra bathing suit tops or sports bras for women. They also frown on tank tops for both men and women. If you are on Lido near the beach ignore this rule.

5. Remember to dispose of trash in public waste bins and not the streets or canals.

6. It is forbidden to have a picnic lunch in Venice. Seriously. This restriction dramatically cuts down on vagrancy. No worries, there are plenty of great restaurants and cafés. So if you bought lunch supplies save them for later in your room.

If you try to follow these simple rules of living, your stay in Venice will be that much more pleasant for everyone involved.

pink and white patterned walls which gives the building a delicate open air feeling.

Everywhere you roam in this building you will be amazed by the combination of styles and the ornate care in which they were prepared. As you enter you will pass through the **Porta della Carta**, created by the Bon family, with its extravagant Gothic style. Here you'll see the statue of *Doge Frascari* as he is kneeling before the winged lion and the statue of a woman seated at the tallest spire that represents Justice. After passing through you'll enter the courtyard of the Palace, which has a pair of imposing bronze wells in the middle. The one closer to the Poscari Portal is by Alfonso Alberberghetti (from 1559) and the other is by Niccolo del Conti in 1556. Stand here a moment and soak in the typically blended Venetian style of architecture, where they combine Gothic with Renaissance. Also enjoy the countless archways, the exquisite sculptures, and inspiring staircases.

One such staircase is *The Staircase of the Giants*, so named because of the two colossal statues of Mars and Neptune on either side of the landing made by Sansovino and his pupils. Each new Doge of the Republic of Venice was officially crowned on the landing at the top of the stairs.

You will also find some of the most beautiful plaster relief ceilings, marble relief fireplaces, paintings, sculptures, tapestries, medieval weapons rooms and ancient dungeons anywhere in Europe. Keep your eye out for the medieval chastity belt on display in the pistol room. I guarantee it is like nothing you've ever seen before. It really makes you cringe imagining someone having to wear it.

D. FRARI – SANTA MARIA GLORIOSA DE FRARI

Campo dei Frari, San Polo. *Tel. 041/522-2637.* Open Monday–Saturday 9:30am–noon and 2:30pm–6:00pm. Sun open 2:30pm–6:00pm. Vaporetto – San Toma. Map – B.

This Romanesque-Gothic style Franciscan church contains tombs of many famous Venetian persons. The church was begun by Franciscan monks in 1250 from a design by Nicola Pisano and was later made a little more ornate by Scipione Bon, a member of the famous Venetian family of sculptors, in 1338. It was finally finished in 1443.

Today the unadorned facade is not much to look at but is beautiful in its simplicity. It is divided into three sections by pilaster strips surmounted by pinnacles. Over the central portal are statues attributed to Alessandro Vittorio in 1581. There is a Romanesque bell tower that is the second largest in Venice after that of St. Mark's.

The interior is as simple and as equally beautiful as the exterior. It is laid out in a Latin cross with single aisles set off by twelve huge columns. The main draw for this simple church is the **tomb of Titian**, the grand master of painting who died of plague in 1576. There are two works by Titian featured inside,

Assumption of the Virgin done in 1518 hanging over the main altar, and *Pesaro Altarpiece* done in 1526, depicting the Virgin with members of the Pesaro family over the second altar. Another work to note is the statue of *St. John the Baptist* by **Donatello** in the altar of the first chapel.

E. GESUATI – SANTA MARIA DEL ROSARIO

Fondamenta delle Zattere, Dorsoduro. Vaporetto – Accademia or Zattere. Maps – B & D.

This church was erected between 1726 and 1743 for the Dominican friars, and was built over a 14th century monastery. The exterior is simple and tasteful in the basic Classical style. This elliptical shaped church has no aisle, making it seem larger than it really is, and contains superb frescoes on the ceiling of the dome by GB Tiepolo.

The first altar contains the *Virgin in Glory with Three Saints,* a masterpiece done in 1747 by Tiepolo. The second altar has a work by GB Piazzetta, *St. Dominic,* done in 1739. The third altar has the *Crucifixion* created by Tintoretto in 1741.

F. GESUITI – SANTA MARIA ASSUNTA

Campo dei Gesuiti, Cannaregio. Vaporetto – Fondamenta Nuova. Map – A.

Built in the 12th century, this grandiose church was given to the Jesuits (Gesuiti) in 1656. It was remodeled between 1715 and 1730 with a Baroque facade designed by Fattoretto. It contains the statues of the 12 Apostles by Penso, the Groppellio brothers, and Baratta.

This is a single-aisled church laid out in a Latin Cross Style and is decorated with a variety of colored marble inlays. The main attractions to this church are two outstanding paintings: the *Assumption of the Virgin* by **Tintoretto** and the *Martyrdom of St. Lawrence* by **Titian**.

G. JEWISH GHETTO

Near the train station, Cannaregio. Guided tours of the synagogues available every hour on the hour from 10:00am–4:00pm, and Sunday 10:00am–noon. Tours not available Saturday and holidays. Vaporetto – San Marcuola. Map – C.

This was the first Jewish Ghetto in Europe. The word itself, ghetto, originated here in Venice. This area was once a cannon foundry, which in Venetian was called a *getto*. Ever since the Jews were forced into this area in Venice, their enclaves have been known by that name. The location was established by Ducal decree in 1516 and remained an enforced enclave for the Jews in Venice until 1797, ending with Napoleon's victory over the Republic. The Jews were moved here originally from the section of the city known as La Guidecca (see below) so the government could better keep an eye on them.

Here you'll find five synagogues, three of which are open to the public: **Sinagoga Grande Tedesca**, **Sinagoga Spagnole**, and **Levantina**. The small museum, **Museo Ebraica** (Campo del Nuovo Ghetto 2902, *Tel. 71-53-59*, open 10:00am - 4:30pm, closed Saturdays and Jewish holidays. E6 includes a guided tour of three of the synagogues. E3 for the museum only.), contains information about the five centuries of Jewish presence in Venice.

H. GRAND CANAL
Maps – A, B & C.

The **Grand Canal** is shaped like a large upside down "S" bisecting the city. It is almost 2 1/2 miles long, 15 feet deep, and ranges anywhere from 100 to 150 feet across. Usually calm and serene, the canal has become more and more menacing and rough since the introduction of huge ocean liners docking close by.

Lining this wonderful waterway are tremendous old buildings, palaces, and homes dating from every time period and epitomizing every architectural style. You'll also see small canals thrusting off into the darkness, and beautiful gateways and entrances blackened by and beginning to be covered by the water. The best way to see the canal is to take the *vaporetto* around a few times and simply enjoy the view.

I. MADONNA DELL'ORTO
Campo Madonna dell'Orto, Cannaregio. Open 9:00am–5:00pm. Vaporetto – Madonna dell'Orto. Map – C.

This is a simple little church that contains the remains of **Jacopo Robusti**, known as **Tintoretto**, who was buried here in 1594. There are also some exquisite works by the grand master himself, **Titian**. These paintings are in the choir: *Last Judgment*, *Adoration of the Golden Calf*, *Moses Receiving the Tablets of the Law*. The tomb of Tintoretto is marked by a simple stone plaque and is just to the right of the choir.

J. REDENTORE
Campo Redentore. Open 9:00am–5:00pm. Vaporetto – Redentore. Map – D.

Built between 1577 and 1592 by Andrea Palladio and Antonio Da Ponte, as part of a thanksgiving for the end of another of the many plague epidemics that struck Venice. Across Europe more than a third of the population died because of the plagues.

A huge staircase leads up to the facade and the entrance to the church. Inside you'll find the same simple harmony as the outside as well as a magnificent Baroque altar adorned with bronzes by Campagna. In the sacristy you'll find *Virgin and Child* by Alvise Vivarini, *Baptism of Christ* by Veronese, *Virgin and Child with Saints* by Palma the Younger, and a variety of works by Bassaro.

K. RIALTO BRIDGE

Vaporetto – Rialto. Maps – A & B.

One of the best places to view the traffic along the **Grand Canal** and all its charm. This is the oldest of the three bridges spanning the canal and was originally made of wood. It collapsed in 1440 and was rebuilt in wood but still remained rather unstable, so in the 16th century the Doges decided to build a more stable bridge. Michelangelo himself submitted a design for the bridge but a local boy, Antonio Da Ponte, was awarded the contract to design and build it, and it was finished in 1592. The Rialto spans 90 feet and is 24 feet high. There are 24 shops lining the bridge separated by a double arcade from which you can walk out onto the terraces and get those superb views for which it is richly famous.

Every morning, except Sunday, on the San Polo side of the Rialto, the **Erberia** (Vegetable Market) and the **Pesceria** (Fish Market) are held. A sight that should not be missed while in Venice.

L. SALUTE – SANTA MARIA DELLA SALUTE

Campo delle Salute. Open 9:00am–5:00pm. Vaporetto – Salute. Map – D.

One of the sights you'll see from St. Mark's Square across the canal is this truly magnificent church. Adorned with many statues sitting atop simple flying buttresses, this octagonal church is crowned with a large dome, and a smaller one directly above it. It was erected as thanksgiving for the cessation of a plague that struck Venice in 1630. During its construction it had a variety of mishaps like the foundation sinking, and the walls being unable to support the dome.

Inside are six chapels all ornately adorned. On the main altar you'll find a sculpture by Giusto Le Court that represents *The Plague Fleeing The Virgin*. The church is replete with Titian's work, including *The Pentecost* to the left of the third altar, *Death of Abel* on the sacristy ceiling, *Sacrifice of Abraham* in the sacristy, *David and Goliath* on the sacristy ceiling, and an early work *St. Mark and The Other Saints* over the altar in the sacristy.

M. SAN GIORGIO MAGGIORE

Isola San Giorgio Maggiore. Open 9:00am–12:30pm and 2:30pm–6:30pm. Vaporetto – San Giorgio. Map – D.

On an island just off the tip of La Guidecca, this magnificent church by Palladio can be seen and admired from St. Mark's Square, but you should go out and visit because the view of the lagoon and the city from its bell tower are priceless and unforgettable.

The church's white facade makes it stand out wonderfully from the ochre and brown colored monastery buildings surrounding it. It was finished in 1610 by Scamozzi from the plans of the master Palladio whose main work is located in the city of Vicenza. The facade is distinctly his, with its three sections divided by four Corinthian columns. In two niches between the columns are statues of *Sts. George* and *Stephen,* and on either side are busts of *Doges Tribuno Mommo* and *P Zini* all by Giulio Moro. The bell tower we mentioned earlier was erected by Benedetto Buratti from Bologna (a city known at the time for its many towers) in 1791 to replace an older one that collapsed in 1773.

The interior is simple yet majestic. It has a single aisle and is shaped like an inverted Latin cross. Three works to admire are: *Crucifix* by **Michelozzo** in the second altar on the right, and *Last Supper* and *Shower of Mana* by **Tintoretto** at the main altar.

N. SANTI GIOVANNI E PAOLO – SAN ZANIPOLO

Campo Santi Giovanni e Paolo, Castello. Open 9:00am–5:00pm. Vaporetto – Rialto or Fondamenta Nuova. Map – A.

Started by the Dominican monks in 1246, **Santi Giovanni e Paolo** was not finished until 1430, probably due to lack of funds just like their Franciscan counterparts when they were building Santa Maria Gloriosa dei Frari. Like that church, it contains the tombs of many well-known Venetian citizens. The church's style is known as Venetian Gothic with its combination of Gothic and Renaissance styles. Unfortunately, the facade was never finished, but it is still beautiful in its simplicity.

The inside is filled with monuments, sculptures, and paintings depicting a large number of Doges and their families. Don't miss the magnificent 15th century Gothic window by Bartolomeo Vivarini.

O. SANTA MARIA FORMOSA

Campo Santa Maria Formosa, Castello. Open 9:00am–5:00pm. Vaporetto – Rialto or San Zaccaria. Map – A.

This church was initially rebuilt in 1492, and has two 16th century facades and a 17th century belfry. It is in the shape of a Latin cross and has no aisles. The walls are covered with wonderful works by such artists as Vivarini and Palma the Elder. A simple, small church that sits in a part of Venice that most tourists never find. The piazza is filled with the sights and sounds of true modern day Venetian life.

P. GUGGENHEIM MUSEUM

Palazzo Venier dei Leoni, Dorsoduro 701, Calle Cristoforo. *Tel. 041/520-6288.* Open 11:00am-6:00pm every day except Tuesdays and December 25. Admission E6. Students E4. Vaporetto – Accademia. Maps - B & D.

This is a magnificent 20th century art collection developed by the intriguing American heiress and art aficionado Peggy Guggenheim. It is exhibited in Ms. Guggenheim's old home, where she lived until her death in 1979. Here you'll find all the 20th century movements including cubism, surrealism, futurism, expressionism, and abstract art. There are works by Dali,

Chagall, Klee, Moore, Picasso, Pollock and many others. If you love modern art you have to come here.

Q. THE BRIDGE OF SIGHS

Vaporetto – San Marco. Map – A.

From the canal side of Ponte della Paglia you can look directly at this covered bridge connecting the Doges Palace and Prigione Nuovo (New Prison). It was built in the 17th century to transport convicts from the palace to the prison to face their punishment. The name presumably derives from the sighs of prisoners as they crossed the bridge.

When on a tour of the Palazzo Ducale you get the opportunity to walk through the bridge to the prison cells where prisoners were kept.

R. PONTE DEGLI SCALZI

Vaporetto – Ferrovia Bar Roma. Map – B.

Also known as the **station bridge** since it is right near the station, this is the first bridge you'll cross if you're walking from the station to St. Mark's. A simple, single span bridge made of white Istrian stone, it was erected in 1934 to replace a metal bridge built in 1858. The bridge is approximately 130 feet long and 23 feet above water level.

S. BASILICA DI SAN MARCO

Piazza San Marco. *Web: www.basilicasanmarco.it.* Open 9:30am–5:30pm. Vaporetto – San Marco. Map – A.

The church is large, magnificent and seemingly covered in gold leaf. It was built to house the remains of the republic's patron saint, **St. Mark**, as well as to glorify the strength of Venice's sea power. The structure was begun in 829, a year after St. Mark's remains were brought back from Egypt. By 832 the church had all its main structures and by 883 it was fully decorated. Its beauty was slightly marred in 976 from a fire that was set in the Doge's Palace. Then in 1000 the church was demolished because it was not grand enough. The church we know and love today was started in 1063 and was originally a Byzantine plan. It was finished in 1073 and then for centuries it was adorned with superb mosaics, precious marbles, and war spoils brought back by merchants, travelers, and soldiers, so that today the church is a mix of Byzantine, Gothic, Islamic and Renaissance materials.

As such it is garishly and eclectically magnificent inside and out. A description of all the art and architecture in this incredible place would fill another book, so you might want to hire a local tour guide or purchase one of the local guide books inside the church specifically for the Basilica.

T. PIAZZA SAN MARCO

Vaporetto – San Marco. Map – A.

When the Basilica of St. Mark and the Doge's Palace were being erected, the grassy field in front of them was filled in and paved (between 1172-1178). On either side of the pavement, elegant houses were built with arcades running the length of them. Many were taken over by government magistrates, called *Procurati*, which gives these buildings their name today, *Procuratie*. In 1264 the square was re-paved with bricks in a herringbone pattern. Then in 1723 it was paved again with gray trachyte and white marble.

The square is 569 feet long, 266 feet at the side of St. Mark's, and 185 feet long at the side facing St. Mark's. The piazza is alive with orchestra music being played by competing cafés and is a wonderful place to stroll and people watch. You won't find many Venetians here, unless it's the off-season since it gets really crowded with tourists during high season.

U. PIAZZETTA DI SAN MARCO

Vaporetto – San Marco. Map – A.

Directly in front of the Doge's Palace, this little piazza blends into the larger Piazza San Marco and is sometimes lumped together with it. Originally it was a market place for foodstuffs, but in 1536 the Doge mandated that it remain clear for public executions. The two columns at the dock (one with the *Lion of St. Mark* atop and the other with a statue of *St. Theodore*) were brought back from the Orient in 1125 and erected in 1172. Here you'll find some peaceful but expensive outside cafés.

V. CLOCK TOWER

Piazza San Marco. *Tel. 041/523-1879.* Admission E3. Vaporetto – San Marco. Map – A.

Facing St. Mark's, the **Clock Tower** is directly on your left. The clock tower is not the tall brick structure in the middle of the piazza; that's the Bell Tower. The clock tower was built between 1496 and 1499, and the wings were added from 1550-1506. Above the tower is an open terrace upon which stands a bell with two male figures on either side that hammer the bell to indicate the time. These figures have been performing their faithful service for over 500 years and as a result have taken on a dark weather-beaten appearance. Because of this, they are called the Moors.

Beneath the terrace that houses these figures is the symbol of Venice, a golden winged lion. Below the lion is a niche that contains a statue of the Virgin and Child that has been attributed to Alessandro Leopardi sometime in the early 1500s. The clock, just below this, in addition to just telling the time, also indicates the changing of the seasons, the movements of the sun, as well as the phases of the moon.

X. BELL TOWER

Piazza San Marco. *Tel. 522-4064.* Open 9:30am–10pm. Admission E3. Vaporetto – San Marco. Map – A.

Built over old Roman fortifications, the **Bell Tower** has been added to off and on since 888. It has withstood floods and earthquakes, but it finally gave in to less than perfect craftsmanship. On July 14, 1902, it collapsed but was reconstructed and re-opened to the public in 1912. It is the most convenient place to get a bird's-eye view of the city and the lagoon. (The next best place is the bell tower of the church of *San Giorgio Maggiore.*) An elevator can take you to the top where there are five bells that toll on special occasions.

In the distant past a cage used to jut from the wall on the piazza side that sometimes would contain criminals to be exposed to the elements as punishment. This practice was abolished in the 16th century. Another tradition, but one designed for pleasure of the people not punishment of prisoners, was to stretch a rope between the tower and the Doge's Palace and have an acrobat walk the span.

Nightlife & Entertainment

Venice does not really have wild and woolly nightlife. This city shuts down early and any nightlife up to that point is either held in restaurants which are open late, or in the few pubs and bars that exist. Listed below are two of the best.

56. THE FIDDLER'S ELBOW, *3847 Cannaregio (near Ca' d'Oro Vaporetto stop). Tel. 041/523-9930. Open from 5:00pm - 1:30am. Pint E4 half pint E3. Closed Wednesdays but not in the summer. Map - C.*

Come here for a taste of old Ireland. You'll find Harp, Guinness, and Kilkenny on tap, as well as almost any other drink you can imagine. The Irish lads and lassies behind the bar will serve you up proper, so enjoy a pint or two for the homeland (well, their homeland anyway). The premier meeting place for Anglos as well as Italians in Venice. Fiddler's also has pubs in Rome, Florence and Bologna. They are just off the Strada Nuova tucked away in a small *campiello*. A fun place in an ideal location.

57. MARGARET DUCHAMP, *Campo Santa Margherita 3019, 31023 Venezia. Tel. 041/52-86-255. Open 8:00am to 2:00pm. Pint E4 half pint E3. Closed Sundays. Map - B*

Wonderful patio seating and intimate areas inside. Superb atmosphere, excellent bar snacks such as sandwiches, and salads as well as some basic pasta dishes. There is a wide variety of draught beer on tap. They also have fine house wine. The service is so-so but the music lively and entertaining. One of the best places to come to experience authentically relaxed Venetian nightlife.

Opera

If you are in Venice from December to June, the traditional opera season, have brought the proper attire (suits for men, dresses for women), and have a taste for something out of the ordinary, and want to try the spectacle of an opera...you're out of luck. Teatro La Fenice burned down recently and is currently being restored. Since publication, it may have re-opened, so contact them if you want to go.

• **Teatro La Fenice**, Campo S. Fantin 1977, 30124 Venezia. *Tel. 041/786-562 or 786-569, Fax 041/786-580. Web: www.teatrolafenice.it.*

Sports & Recreation

In terms of sporting activities, there really is not much to do in Venice proper except jog along the Grand Canal in the early mornings when the crowds aren't around. For recreation you'll have to go to the island of Lido, where you'll find golf, bicycling, horseback riding, tennis and of course, swimming.

However, I am averse to mentioning Lido, since it really more of a beach resort. The architecture on Lido has little in common with the beauty of Venice, and on Lido they allow cars and buses, so that tranquil feeling you get while in Venice evaporates instantly when you arrive. That being said, if you're in need of some sporting fun, Lido beckons. To get there, take *vaporetto* no. 6 or no. 11.

Bicycling

Having a leisurely bicycle ride on Sundays is a favorite pastime of the people on Lido. To rent a bike, tandem, or tricycle, go to **Giorgio Barbieri**, Via Zara 5, Lido.

Golfing

• **Circolo Golf Venezia**, Via del Forte, 30011 Alberoni. *Tel. 041/731-1333/ 731-015, Fax 041/731-339.* Located 10 km from Venice proper on the island of Lido, this is an 18 hole, par 72, 6,199 meters long course. It's open year round except on Mondays. They have a driving range, pro shop, bar and restaurant.

Swimming

Your choices are the pools at the **Excelsior Hotel** and the **Hotel des Bains** where you can purchase very expensive daily or seasonal tickets; and the public beaches are at **San Nicolo** and **Alberoni** at both the north and the south ends of **Lido**. The rest of the beaches are private and attached to hotels for the use of their guests.

Tennis

There are tennis courts for rent at the **Lido Tennis Club**, Via San Gallo 16, *Tel. 041/760-954*, and from the **Tennis Union**, Via Fausta, *Tel. 041/968-134*. Court time is expensive and packed in the high season.

Shopping

Books & Newspapers in English

Most newsstands in Venice will carry a variety of different international newspapers and magazines. The most current newspaper will most probably be *The International Herald Tribune*. As for books, listed below is a bookstore that has English language titles available:

• **Libreria Internazionale San Giorgio**, Calle Large XXII Marzo 2087, San Marco. *Tel. 041/38-451*. Credit cards accepted.

Glass Products

Venice has been making glass products for more than 1,000 years. The glass blowing furnaces were moved to the island of **Murano** (see *Excursions & Day Trips* below) in 1292 for fire safety reasons. To make sure you're not getting a reproduction or something of inferior quality, always check to see if the letters **VM** are stamped on the bottom of the glasswork. The VM *(Vetro Murano)* is the mark for quality Venetian glass.

All over Venice you'll find cute glass animals and figurines, but on Murano you can see them being made. Two of the five major manufacturers on Murano have shops in Venice (**Salviati** and **Venini**) but the rest sell only from the island of Murano.

Lace Products

The small island of **Burano** (see *Excursions & Day Trips* below) has been producing intricate hand-made lace work for centuries. Mary Tudor of England got her wedding gown made on the island. Since that time the style has been widely copied and some say the French make a better lace now, but an excursion to the island is worth the trip. Burano is also known for its multi-colored homes, which offer a stunning backdrop to any photo.

Masks

Venice is home to one of the world's best carnivals (*Carnevale* in Italian), created so that everyone can sow their wild oats before Lent begins. The merriment generally begins in early February and lasts for several weeks before it culminates on Shrove Tuesday (Mardi Gras). During Carnevale the ancient Venetians used to wear masks all the time, allowing men to court and cavort with impunity and women to be able to walk around unchaperoned, meet their secret lovers or find new ones. Since masks are part of their history, Venetians have become quite adept at creating them.

There are all sorts of traditional masks, many taken from the 16th century *Commedia dell'Arte*. Any of these masks would make for a great wall ornament or Halloween costume. The craftsmen carve wooden molds from which they make plaster casts – basically negative images of the mask – which are then layered with paper mache to shape the masks. Then this covering is either left blank for you to paint or is intricately decorated. There are plenty of stores where you can watch the mask makers at work.

Markets

Erberia (Vegetable Market) and **Pesceria** (Fish Market). The vegetable market is open Monday through Saturday 8:00am to 1:00pm; the fish market is open Tuesday through Saturday 8:00am through 1:00pm

The natives and the restaurants of Venice find their daily produce, cheese, fish, and meats in the large Campo and the adjoining streets near the Chiesa di San Giacomo di Rialto. It is a bustling, crowded, fun adventure just to go there to buy something. You'll have to escape the tourist market set up at the base of the Rialto bridge to find this unique cultural experience. Don't forget your camera.

Paper Products

Venice has been popular for their decorative paper goods for centuries, specifically the marbling effect they produce for the cover of books, desk blotters, pencils, pens, and many other items. When wandering around the back streets of Venice you will surely stumble upon a small shop making and selling their own versions of marbleized paper products. If not there are few listed below for you to find.

Unique Shops

Amazing little shops are all over Venice. However, some of the best and most unique are listed below. If you're looking for inexpensive art, try some of the shops shown here. Or visit two street vendors, Pichio and Renato, located just off St. Mark's square near the **San Marco Giardino** vaporetto stop.

58. ARCOBELENO, *Calle de Botteghe 3457, Tel. 041/523-6818.*

Located down the street from the superb restaurant Al Bacareto, is this unique little art store that sells the pigments to make your own paints. Stored in clear glass jars in the back of the store, even if you are not a painter, the pigment display is a work of art on its own.

59. CARTAVENEZIA, *Santa Croce 2125, Tel. 041/524-1283. Email: cartavenezia@libero.it.*

A truly unique store filled with all sorts of artisan made paper products. Come here for notebooks, diaries, postcards and more. Remember to put on some gloves before picking up any of the products so as not to leave an oily residue.

60. LIVIO DE MARCHI, *Salizade San Samuele 3157a, Tel. 041/528-5694,Website: www.liviodemarchi.com.*

Amazing wooden sculptures of books, teddy bears, and much more. Everything in here would make for a wonderful and unique gift. Get it? "Would." Har har.

61. LE NAVE DE ORO, *Calle Lunga Sante Maria Formosa, Tel. 041/523-7592.*

Wine sold the old fashioned way: from 50-gallon jugs. Bring your own bottle or pick one up here and get it filled up to take away. Not upscale in appearance or presentation but the vintages are superb. A unique Italian cultural experience.

62. NEGOZIO D'ARTE, *Calle Sconda dei Saoneri 2671/B, Tel. 041/275-9367. Web: www.loversoarte.it.*

Come here to find some great prints, amps, etchings and more.

63. IL PAVONE, *Campielo dei Meoni, Tel. 041/522-4298.*

This tiny stationary store has creative rubber stamps, pencils, boxes, notebooks and more, all done up in beautiful designs.

64. PUNTO ARTE, *Calle dei Saoneri 2721, Tel. 041/522-7979. Web: www.etchingvenice.com.*

This is where many of the colorful etchings you see sold in stores all over Venice are created. Come here for the best selection and price.

65. ALBERTO VALESE-EBRU, *Campo San Stefano 3471, Tel. 041/523-8830. www.albertovalese-ebru.com.*

Here you can find unique designs on men's ties, wrapping paper, stationary, books, pens and more. A touch more refined than most of the typical Venetian stationary designs and their prices reflect that.

Excursions & Day Trips

The first three islands mentioned below can all be seen in a four to five hour period. To get to any of them, buy a round-trip ticket for E4 at vaporetto booth #12 at the Fondamenta Nuova. Remember to stamp your ticket before boarding.

If you start in the morning around 9:00am and go first to **Murano**, then **Burano**, and then **Torcello**, you will have worked up a powerful hunger. The same goes if you start the trek at 2:00pm or so, after your lunch in Venice. By the time you get to Torcello, you'll be dying to sample their excellent food in a restaurant with wonderful outdoor seating.

MURANO

Located three quarters of a mile northeast of Venice, Murano is a lagoon town spread among five little islands. The island group is roughly divided in half by a relatively large canal that is spanned by one bridge, the Ponte Longo, from which local kids like to jump off of into the water. It has a relatively quiet and uncrowded feel to it, especially around dinner time, when all the tourists have returned to Venice. Since there are no hotels in the island it has remained relatively tourist free.

Murano today is what Venice must have been like fifty years ago before international tourism really took off. In Venice every ground floor has been turned into a shop, café, or restaurant for tourists. Here people still live in the buildings. But you can find great cafes and restaurants.

Arrivals & Departures

Take *Vaporetto* 52 or 12 from the Fondamenta Nuove. It takes about ten minutes.

Seeing the Sights

This island chain is world-renowned for its **glass blowing** industry, which dates back to 1291 when the furnaces were banned from Venice as a precaution against fire and industrial espionage. At its height in the 16th century, Murano had 37 glass factories and a population of 30,000. Today the population is a little under 8,000.

What used to be the closely guarded secret of glass blowing is today common knowledge, but Murano glass is still in demand all over the world because of the skilled artisans that spend their life preparing the fine works of art. And that's what we've come to Murano to see, a glass blowing exhibition. There are a number of small factories dotting the island group. Check out the **glass factories** on *Fondamenta dei Vetrai*, three of which offer glass blowing exhibitions. If you can't find these, here's one convenient to the vaporetto:
• **Civam**, Viale Garibaldi 24, 30141 Venezia/Murano, *Tel. 041/739-323, Fax 041/739-323.*

Other recommended sights include:
• **Museo dell'Arte Vetraria**, Fondamenta Giustiniano and Fondamenta Manin. *Tel. 041/739-586.* Open Mondays, Tuesdays, Thursdays and Saturdays 10:00am–4:00pm, Sundays 9:00am–12:30pm. Closed Wednesdays. This is the Glass Museum.
• **Santi Maria e Donato**, Campo San Donato. Open 8:00am - noon, 4:00pm - 7:00pm.

BURANO

Located five and a half miles northeast of Venice, Burano occupies four tiny islands that are inhabited mainly by fishermen and lace seamstresses. It was first settled in the 5th and 6th centuries by refugees from Altinum fleeing Attila's Huns. Mainly known for the traditional art of lace making, which the women of the town have been handing down to their daughters for centuries, Burano is also a great place to unwind from the hectic pace of Venice. The brightly colored houses on the island give it the air of an Italian opera set, which also makes it a perfect background for some excellent photographs. There are also plenty of little cafés, *gelaterie*, and *trattoria* to quench a hunger or thirst.

Arrivals & Departures

Take Vaporetto number 12 from Fondamenta Nuove. It takes about 35 minutes. You'll first stop at Burano.

Where to Eat

1. AI PESCATORI, *Via Galuppi 371. Tel. 041/730650. Closed Wednesdays and January. All credit cards accepted. Meal for two E70.*

Come here for great seafood. Located in the center of the island on the main street, this is a nice but expensive local place. Try any of their pasta with fish, like *spaghetti ai frutti di mare* (with the seafood) and any of their grilled or fried fish.

2. AL GATTO NERO, *Via Guidecca 88, Tel. 041/730-120. Closed Mondays. Credit cards accepted. Meal for two E50.*

Off of the main tourist drag is this exquisite, high end trattoria. With seating on a picturesque canal here you can get a genuine Burano experience and some awesome food as well. Make reservations on the weekends, because they can get very crowded.

Seeing the Sights

Take a look at the lace school and satisfy your curiosity about the inner workings of the lace business. The school is **Consorzio dei Merletti**, Palazzo del Podesta in the Piazza B. Galuppi. *Tel. 041/730-034.* Open Monday–Saturday 9:00am–6:00pm, and Sundays 9:00am–4:00pm

One other interesting sight on Burano is the **Church of San Martino**, *Piazza B. Galuppi,* with its leaning tower. Pisa's not the only place with a leaning tower.

Great Little Shop

3. ARTISTICO BOMBON, *Tel. 041/735-551, San Martino*

This adorable little shop serves up the best candies, all made of glass. Despite the fact that the owner has misspelled the French word for candy on the name of his store, everything here is made with exquisite care and tantalizingly tasty detail. The little candies make perfect gifts and are wonderful conversation pieces when placed in bowls at home. Each little wrapped candy is so perfectly crafted that they will tempt even the most discerning guest into believing they're real. Truly whimsical works of art.

TORCELLO

Located six and a half miles northeast of Venice, Torcello was settled between the 5th and 6th centuries by the first wave of refugees from the barbarian hordes. It got its name from the tower (*Torcello* means little tower) from which the bishop of Altinum saw his vision of how to keep his people safe from the barbarians.

Now just a solitary village on a lonely island, it was once a flourishing center of commerce and culture whose greatness dimmed as that of Venice grew. Since the 18th century, Torcello has been nearly deserted, with a population today of only about 100 people. All that remains of its long ago splendor is a group of monuments that face out onto the grassy central piazza.

Most of the land that remains has either been abandoned or has been cultivated, mainly for wine. After you've seen the few sights and walked the few hundred meters of town, the only thing left to do is satisfy your hunger at one of the exquisite outdoor restaurants. Eating, drinking, and making idle conversation is the main activity here. That must be why Hemingway liked it so much.

Arrivals & Departures
 Take *Vaporetto* 12 from Fondamenta Nuove. It takes about 45 minutes. You'll stop at Murano, Mazzorbe, and Burano first. After you get off the boat you'll have a little walk beside a canal to the central square.

Where to Eat
 If you make it to Torcello around meal time, here are two wonderful places at which to eat.
 LOCANDA CIPRIANI, *In town, at the end of the canal. American Express accepted. Tel. 041/730-150 or 73-54-33. Open mid-March–October. Closed Mondays and Tuesdays. Meal for two E60.*
 OSTERIA AL PONTE DEL DIAVOLO, *Via Chiesa 10/11. Tel. 041/730-401 or 041/730-441. In the middle of the canal leading to town. Credit cards accepted. Open for lunch only. Closed on Thursdays and in January. Meal for two E50.*

Seeing the Sights
 • **Cathedral,** Santa Maria Assunta. *Tel. 041/730-084.* Open 10:00am–12:30pm and 2:00pm–6:30pm. Closes two hours earlier in the winter.
 • **Museo dell'Estuario,** Santa Maria Assunta. *Tel. 041/730-761.* Open Tuesday–Sunday 10:30am–12:30pm and 2:00pm–4:00pm. Closed Mondays.

SAN MICHELE
 Located only half a mile north of Venice, here you will find the graves of Ezra Pound, Igor Stravinsky, and Frederick Rolfe. This island cemetery is quite scenic and very peaceful, with its organized paths and beautiful tall trees. Not quite the place to have a picnic, but a place to go that I guarantee you not many tourists visit frequently.
 To get here, take *Vaporetto* 52 from Fondamenta Nuove (5 minutes).

Practical Information for Venice
Consulates
 • **United Kingdom,** Dorsoduro 1051, near the Accademia, *Tel. 041/522-72-07*
 • **United States,** Largo Donegani 1, Milan, *Tel. 01/652-841*
 • **Canada,** Via Vito Pisani 19, Milan, *Tel. 01/669-74-51.* For emergencies: *Tel. 01/66-98-06-00*
 • **Australia,** Via Borgogna 2 , Milan, *Tel. 01/76-01-33-30*

Internet
 • **Internet Point**, Crosera San Pantalon (near the church of San Pantalon),Dorsoduro 3812/a, *Tel. 041/714-666.*

Mail

The main post office is located at Salizada del Fontegho dei Tedeschi 5554, near the Rialto. *Tel. 041/271-7111.* Open Monday–Saturday 8:15am–6:45:00pm. Stamps (*francobolli*) are sold at *tabacchi* all over town. Venice's **postal code** is 30124.

Laundry

• **Bea Vita**, Calle di Chioverette, Open 8am-10pm every day. Located two minutes from the station, you can do a load of wash and dry it in 45 minutes here. Self-service.

Local Festivals & Holidays

• **January 1**, *Primo dell'Anno* (New Year's Day)
• **April 25**, *Festa Del Liberazione* (Liberation Day)
• **February**, usually the first two weeks of February is **Carnevale**, (*www.venice-carnival.com*) a time of riotous celebration where costumes are worn both day and night, and grand balls and celebrations occur frequently.
• **March**, First Sunday after Ascension day; anybody piloting an oar-powered craft can take part in *La Vogalonga*, the "long row." Participants set off at 9:30am from the Bacino di San Marco and follow a marathon-like course around Venice and its islands. Rowers usually return between 11:00am and 3:00pm.
• **May 1**, *Festa del Lavoro* (Labor Day)
• **August 15**, *Ferragosto* (Assumption Day)
• **September**, First Sunday in September is the **Regata Storica**, the historic regatta. The races are preceded by a magnificent procession on the Grand Canal of period boats manned by Venetians in historic costumes. A spectacle to behold. On par with the Palio in Siena.
• **November 1**, *Ognissanti* (All Saints Day)
• **November 21**, *Festa della Madonna della Salute*, which originated as a time of thanks for being spared from the Plague which at one point had decimated more than 60% of Venice's population. Celebrated on two floating bridges built across the Grand Canal from the Giglio to the Dogana.
• **December 8**, *Festa dell Madonna Immacolata* (Immaculate Conception)
• **December 25**, *Natale* (Christmas)
• **December 26**, *Santo Stefano* (Saint Stephen's Day)

Tourist Information & Maps

• **Ente Provinciale per il Turismo** (three different locations): Piazza San Marco 71C, *Tel. 041/522-6356;* Piazzale Roma, *Tel. 041/522-7402;* Santa Lucia Train Station, *Tel. 041/715-016.* They also have an excellent hotel finders service here that comes in real handy if you don't have reservations when you arrive.

Elsewhere Near Venice

VERONA

Located 71 miles west of Venice, Verona has a reputation as being one the most beautiful and romantic of all northern Italian cities. Its presence is dominated by the fast-flowing Adige River that curves dramatically through the city.

Veron'a main claim to fame is that is the home of Romeo and Juliet, made famous by William Shakespeare. However, I wonder if you knew that the play *Romeo and Juliet* was actually first written by an Italian from Vicenza, Luigi da Porto. Shakespeare only adapted this earlier story. Copyright laws weren't in effect back then.

Before those steamy days of romance, Verona had been a flourishing Roman city since the first century BCE. After a brief period of communal government rule in the 12th century, Verona was controlled by the Della Scala family from 1262 to 1387, under whose rule most of Verona's monuments were built. During this time, **Dante Aligheri**, the man who wrote *The Divine Comedy*, visited Verona while exiled from Florence. There is a statue commemorating his stay in the Piazza Dei Signori. Then in 1404 Verona became a part of the Venetian Republic until they were conquered by Napoleon's forces some centuries later.

Verona's website is *www.veronatuttintorno.it*.

Arrivals & Departures
By Train

From Venice you can catch trains approximately every one and a half hours, and the trip itself takes that same length of time. Once on the ground, you'll need to take a taxi into town from the **Porta Nuova Station**.

If you want to take the bus from the train station, take either the #1, 11, or 12 bus from **Mariapiedi A** (the bus stop) directly in front of the station. You have to buy a ticket first, so spend your E0.75 cents for a one-way fare at the *Tabacchi* in the station. The bus will drop you off at the Arena square.

By Car

Take the Autostrada A4 located just after Marghera. You will have to take one of two exits for Verona. Both of which are clearly marked. For a more scenic route take the #11 from Mestre and wind your way through the beautiful scenery in these parts. This will take you directly into the city.

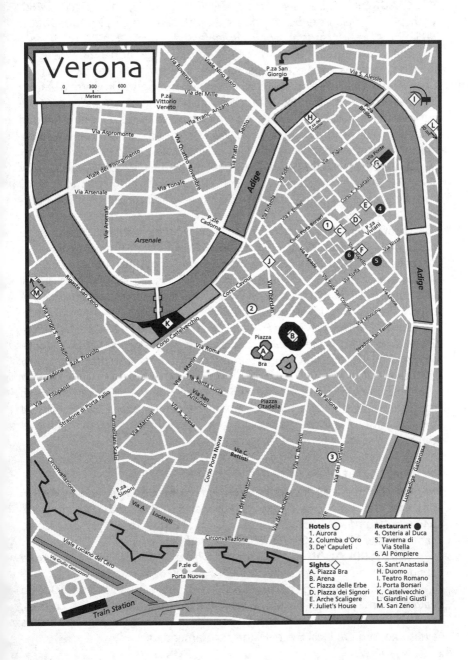

Verona

0 300 600
Meters

Hotels ○
1. Aurora
2. Columba d'Oro
3. De' Capuleti

Restaurant ●
4. Osteria al Duca
5. Taverna di Via Stella
6. Al Pompiere

Sights ◇
A. Piazza Bra
B. Arena
C. Piazza delle Erbe
D. Piazza dei Signori
E. Arche Scaligere
F. Juliet's House

G. Sant'Anastasia
H. Duomo
I. Teatro Romano
J. Porta Borsari
K. Castelvecchio
L. Giardini Giusti
M. San Zeno

Where to Stay

1. AURORA, *Piazza delle Erbe 2, Tel. 045/594-717, Fax 045/801-0860. Web: www.hotelaurora.biz. 19 rooms, all with bath. Single E75-100; Double E85-125. All credit cards accepted. Breakfast included.* **

The best budget hotel in the city. Located in a great piazza, where the bustling market is, this hotel is in an ancient palazzo, with a terrace that has beautiful panoramic views. This is where breakfast is served in warm weather. The best rooms are the ones that face out onto the piazza. All rooms are sufficiently comfortable though not anything special. A great location, a good hotel at an adequate price. You even get TV in your room. Not bad for a two-star.

2. COLUMBA D'ORO, *Via C. Cattaneo 10, Tel. 045/595-300, Fax 045/ 594-974, Email: info@colombahotel.com. Web: www.colombahotel.com. 49 rooms. Single E120-180; Double E175-215. All credit cards accepted. Breakfast E12.* ****

Located only a few steps from the famous arena in Piazza Bra, this hotel has unbeatable location, atmosphere and charm. Originally a monastery, this old palazzo was turned into a hotel at the beginning of the 19th century. The rooms are all elegant and the furnishings refined. The bathrooms are all appointed with marble and come with all necessary four-star amenities. A superb place to stay in Verona.

3. DE' CAPULETI, *Via del Pontiere 26, Tel. 045/800-0154, Fax 045/803-2970. Email: info@hotelcapuleti.it. Web: www.hotelcapuleti.it. 42 rooms. Single E85-105; Double E115-180. All credit cards accepted. Breakfast included.* ***

Only a few paces from the tomb of Juliet, this is a pleasant hotel with comfortable rooms, some of which are on the small side. In a tranquil part of Verona, a little off the beaten path. Comes with all the comforts of a high level three star including an excellent buffet breakfast.

Where to Eat

Besides the places listed below, two which deserve a look include: **Antica Bottega del Vino** (Via Scudo di Francia 3, Tel. *045/800-4535, Web: www.bottegavini.it,* closed Tuesdays); and **Giulietta e Romeo** (Corso Sant'Anastasia 27, Tel. *045/800-9177,* closed Sundays).

4. OSTERIA AL DUCA, *Via Arche Scaligere 2, Tel. 045/594-474. Closed Sundays. Credit cards accepted. Meal for two E26.*

Located in a building from the 1200s, this is a memorable eatery. Oozing with rustic charm, here you will be offered a choice of up to 10 first courses, and the same number or more of entrees for only E13 a person. The food is awesome. A great local place. Highly recommended.

5. LA TAVERNA DI VIA STELLA, *Via Stella 5/c, Tel. 045/800-8008. Closed Mondays. Credit cards accepted. Meal for two E35.*

Near Piazza Erbe and Juliet's House is this rustic eatery serving exquisite local food. It is so rustic here that they have horse on the menu.

6. AL POMPIERE, *Vicolo Regina d'Ungheria 5, Tel. 045/803-0537. Closed Sundays and Mondays for lunch. Credit cards accepted. Meal for two E35.*

Also near Juliet's house, on a small side street is this incredible trattoria. In one corner, surrounded by photos of famous Veronese, is where up to 35 different Italian salamis are sliced. There's also over 100 different types of cheese too! And that's just for antipasto. An excellent choice while in Verona.

Seeing the Sights

Filled with Roman ruins, medieval castles, cobblestone side streets and piazzas, Renaissance palazzi and friendly people, Verona is a perfectly picturesque town to wander through.

A. PIAZZA BRA

The **Forum Boarium** of medieval days of yore is now **Piazza Bra**. The piazza is bounded by the ancient **Roman Arena** to the north, the line of palazzi with their cafés to the west, the 17th century **Gran Guardia** building in the south, and the neo-classic town hall to the east, and in the middle there is a quaint fountain with a park. It is the central meeting place for Veronese.

D. ARENA

Piazza Bra. *Tel. 800–3204.* Tuesdays-Sunday 8:00am-6:30pm in the summer, 8:00am-1:00pm in the winter. Admission E3.

Originally built during the Roman Republican era, the **Arena** must have been completed about 30 CE, judging from mosaics found in an old Roman house in Verona indicating three scenes of gladiators fighting in the arena. These are now in the archaeological museum.

After 325 CE, when the emperor Constantine forbade gladiatorial performances, the arena was used less frequently. That's the official line, but historians tell us that gladiators fought all over the Roman empire as magistrates disregarded Rome's orders, until the emperor Honorius violently put an end to this insubordination in the 5th century. During the Middle Ages the arena was used for capital punishment and trial by combat (sounds a little like gladiators, doesn't it?). By the 16th and 17th centuries, the arena was used for less violent activities like fairs and tournaments, and a variety of performing arts activities. This tradition lives on today.

The arena went through a variety of expansions and today measures 152 by 122 meters. The ancient structure is formed with four concentric rings, with the outermost only retaining four of its original arches. This outer ring used to encircle the entire arena and had 72 arches. Today the second ring is the outer boundary of the arena.

Despite its age, the arena is still used to today for music and theater festivals. Little has had to been done to it to make it functional for modern productions, except add lighting. Even its old drainage system still works perfectly. A testament to the Roman Empire's engineering skills.

C. PIAZZA DELLE ERBE

Open 8:00am–1:30pm.

This used to be the Forum of the old Roman city, whose ruins lie a few meters beneath the current piazza. Today the only Roman feature about the large marble basin taken from the Roman baths, atop which is the *Verona Madonna* statue. Today the square is used during the day as an open air market where you can buy fresh fruits, vegetables, and sundries. Don't miss this place while in Verona.

D. PIAZZA DEI SIGNORI

Locally it is known as **Piazza Dante**, because of the statue erected in 1865. It is bounded on the side nearest Piazza Erbe by the **Domus Nova**, a Baroque building of the 17th century. On the opposite side is the **Loggia del Consiglio**, built at the beginning of Veronese Renaissance. This piazza is the heart of the city.

E. ARCHE SCALIGERE

Just outside of the Piazza del Signori, surrounded by the Scalinger palaces, is the **Chiesa di Santa Maria Antica** and the **cemetery of the Della Scala family** (also knon as Scaligere) which is known to tourists as the **Arche Scaligere**. Here you will find many elaborate shrines, tombs, and sarcophagi. Take some time to wander through and appreciate the beauty of these death monuments.

F. JULIET'S HOUSE

Via Capello 23, *Tel. 803-4303.* Open 8:00am–6:30pm Closed Mondays. Admission E3.

Believe it or not, the Shakespearean story of *Romeo and Juliet* was actually 'borrowed' from a work by a Vicenza author named **Luigi da Porto**, who wrote of the vicissitudes of two unhappy lovers named Romeo Montecchi and Juliet Capuleti. And much of the story was not fiction. We know for sure that these two families did exist. Dante witnessed and wrote about their quarrels when he sojourned here between 1299 and 1304. However, we do not know if Romeo and Juliet were actual people who fell in love, formed a lover's pact, killed themselves, and so on.

No matter – literary expression has triumphed over reality and today we can visit **Juliet's House** in Verona and see the balcony from which she allegedly sealed her tryst with Romeo and eventually their demise. A bronze statue, made by Nereo Costantini, of fair Juliet has been placed in the courtyard in front of the house.

The interior remains as it did in the 14th century, but the exterior of the house is covered in lover's graffiti and handwritten notes forlornly attached to the walls. A testament, I suppose to love's timeless appeal.

G. SANT'ANASTASIA

Corso San Anastasia. Open 9:00am–5:00pm. Admission E2.

Also a Dominican church, **Sant'Anastasia** is quite similar to *SS Giovanni e Paolo* in Venice. The facade is simple and plain, but what is of interest is inside. The first two columns are flanked by hunchback figures *(gobbi)* holding holy water bowls on their backs. These two figures are playfully unique.

The nave is subdivided by columns of red Veronese marble and connected by arches. The walls of the aisles on either side of the columns contain the large circular windows that let light into the church. Everywhere inside you'll find ornate frescoes, bas-relief altars, and sculptures. The **Miniscalchi Altar**, also known as the Altar of the Holy Spirit, is especially exquisite. This work has been attributed to the Venetian master Agnolo.

H. DUOMO

Piazza del Duomo. Open 7:00am–noon and 3:00pm–7:00pm. Admission E2.

The **Duomo** is a composite of varying styles, since the original Romanesque building underwent Gothic modifications in the 15th century. The **bell tower**, with its Romanesque base, should have been finished in the 16th century but was only completed in this century. This church is not nearly as interesting and elaborate as Sant'Anastasia but it does have a beautiful work by Titian, *The Assumption of the Virgin* (at the rear of the church to the left as you face front) dating back to 1535-40. Also on display is the Chiesa di Sant'Elena (to the left of the main altar) and the paleo-Christian remains or an older church found there-in.

Since this church is near the river and the **Ponte Pietra**, it is a perfect launching place to visit the **archeological zone** and the **Roman Theater** (see following).

I. TEATRO ROMANO

Tel. 045/800-0360. Open Tuesday-Sunday 8:00am-6:30pm off-season. Performance days 8:00am-1:30pm. Admission E3.

This ancient theater was excavated between 1834 and 1914. It abuts the slope of Colle di San Pietro and has a relatively modern church, SS Siro e Libera, on its steps as a reminder that in Italy the past, present, and future all fit together seamlessly. The orchestra's diameter is almost 30 meters and the two galleries reach a height of 27 meters. Quite impressive.

The theater's construction has been carbon-dated to the last quarter of the 1st century BCE. If you're interested in archaeology, this is a fun place to roam for a little while. Also, if in Verona June through August you can catch a modern production performed here.

J. PORTA BORSARI

This is the best preserved of the five **Roman gates** in Verona, and is the easiest to find. It was named **Borsari** in medieval times because of the toll tax *(Bursarii)* that were levied here on goods in transit. It is of interest because the entire facade has remained intact. It is assumed that this gate was built during the reign of emperor Claudius (41-54 CE), mainly because of the similarity between it and the Porta Aurea in Ravenna which was made in 43 CE.

The openings on the bottom are 3.5 meters wide and a little more than 4 meters high and are framed by Corinthian columns, which support the rest of the construction. The entire complex rises to a height of 13 meters and is made of white Veronese marble. What is of real interest is that this ancient arch has been completely incorporated into the life of the modern city, as have most Roman ruins in Italy – even going so far as being a part of the modern buildings on either side of it.

K. CASTELVECCHIO

Corso Castelvecchio 2, *Tel. 045/594-734.* Open Tuesday–Sunday 8:00am– 6:30pm. Admission E3.

This structure was the final residence of the Della Scala (Scaligere) family and was built over a period of twenty years from 1354 to 1375. The magnificent three-arched bridge was built for the private use of the residents of the castle. The building itself has served as an army garrison, a military storeroom, and remains today a museum with an exquisite collection of paintings, sculptures, tapestries, ancient jewelry, frescoes and more. Most of the works are religious in nature, so if you haven't had your fill of the Madonna and Child, there's more here.

A relatively unknown Italian artist, G. Francesco Caroto (1480-1555) has many works featured. He studied under Liberale, Mantegna, and was influenced by Leonardo and Raphael and his works show it. One particular painting, though simple in nature, is his *Young Boy With a Drawing.* You can almost feel the boy's joy at creating the stick figure on the paper he holds in his hand.

L. GIARDINI GIUSTI

Via Giardini Giusti 2, *Tel. 045/803-4029*. Open 9:00am to dusk in summer and 9:00am–8:00pm in winter. Admission E5.

The lush garden spaces of the **Palazzo Giusti** are on the same side of the river as the Roman Theater, outside the ancient walls. The gardens are well tended and are punctuated by a variety of different statues, fountains, and a fish pond. The gardens also feature a labyrinth, citrus grove, and an aviary to protect birds in danger of extinction.

Sometimes these gardens are the backdrop for summer productions of the **Theater of Verona**. They are a lovely place to come, relax, and recharge your batteries.

M. BASILICA SAN ZENO

Piazza San Zeno, *Tel. 045/800-6120*. Open Mon-Sat 9:30am-6pm; Sun 1-6pm. Admission E2.

Definitely the most impressive architectural expanse in Verona, though rather bland in terms of its artistic embellishments. Nonetheless, and even despite its distance from the center of town, I would highly recommend a sojourn to this wonderful church and peaceful cloisters.

Simple, austere, and moving, the Romanesque church of San Zeno will fill your heart with wonder and stir your soul to prayer. After recovering from this metaphysical reaction, if you look closely something of a less spiritual nature will grab your eye.

On the right side of the upper section of the apse, you will be appalled to notice graffiti carved into the precious frescoes. And not just recent vandals left their markings. You will also find inscriptions from degenerates dating back to the 14th and 15th centuries.

Sadly, this is not a situation unique to Zeno's. I have seen similar scratchings in the tombs of the Valley of the Kings in Egypt. It seems sad that some members of the human race seem compelled to display their egos by desecrating precious historical relics.

Nightlife & Entertainment
Opera & Theater

If you are in Verona from December to June, the traditional opera season, have the proper attire (suits for men, dresses for women), and would like to see an opera at the opera house, you won't be disappointed. During July and August they offer special productions outside at the **Arena** in Piazza Bra. (Piazza Bra 28. *Tel. 045/590-109 or 800-5151, Fax 045/801-1566 or 801-3287*.) In July and August there is also a drama festival, with an emphasis on Shakespeare's plays, in the **Teatro Romano**, *Tel. 045/800-0360*.

Practical Information

Car Rentals
• **Avis**, Stazione Ponte Nuova, *Tel. 045/800-66-36*
• **Hertz**, Stazione Ponte Nuova, *Tel. 045/800-0882*

Internet
• **Internet Train**, Via Roma 17, *Tel. 045/801-3394*. Open 7 days a week, M-F 11:00am – 10:00pm; Sat and Sun 2:00pm – 8:00pm.

Store Hours
Hours are 9am-1pm and 3:30pm – 8pm, except that they are all generally closed on Monday mornings as well.

Tourist Information
• Piazza Erbe 18, *Tel. 045/800-6997*. Open Mon-Fri 9am-7pm. Sat 9am – 12:30pm.

LAGO DI GARDA
Lago di Garda is a great place to come and relax. Located very near Verona, it is only a short, 20 minute train ride away. While in Verona or Venice, if you want to get away from the crush of urban living, come to Lago di Garda.

At 32 miles long and 10 miles across at its widest point, **Lake Garda** (Lago di Garda) is the largest Northern Italian lake. (You can find the other lakes

described in the Milan section of this book). It is also the mildest in climate, allowing the waters to teem with all sorts of fish and water craft; and the shoreline abounds with all sorts of produce, vegetation, and tourists. As Italy's most visited lake, over the years the hotel and restaurant service has become first-class. You can get from town to town by ferry, hydrofoil *(www.navigazionelaghi.it)* or the Gardesana highway which pass along the shore and through any mountains that get in the way.

Besides scenic natural beauty and your fellow tourists, you'll be able to enjoy some of the most impressive and well-preserved medieval architecture in the region, especially the **Rocca Fortress** at **Riva**, as well as the remains of an ancient Roman villa near **Sirmione**. There are smaller villages along the shore of the lake that warrant exploring as well, including: Gardone Riviera, Limone, Salo, Garda and others.

Since Lago di Garda is divided by three separate Italian provinces, there are a number of official web sites for the lake, or at least parts of the lake. These include:
• *www.gardanet.it*
• *http://gardalake.de*
• *www.gardatrentino.it*

SIRMIONE

On the south side of the lake extending out into the water on a slender peninsula, **Sirmione** is a truly romantic and historic town to spend a few beautiful days. Because it is amazingly beautiful, Sirmione is a tourist magnet, which can detract from its charm. Nonetheless Sirmione is a truly unique town, one not to be missed on a visit to Lake Garda.

An impressive sight just as you enter the town is the **Rocca Scaligera** fortress in the center of town, built in the 12th century to guard the lake. This massive construction with towers and battlements extending out into the water to create a safe harbor is still imposing today (Piazza Carducci. Open 9:00am–12:30pm and 2:00–6:00pm in summer. and 9:00am–1:00pm in winter. Closed Mondays. Admission E3).

Out on the tip of the peninsula is the **Grotte di Catullo**, a grandiose Roman villa complex with rooms, corridors, and underground areas still very well preserved (Via Catullo. Open 9:00am–6:00pm in summer and only until 4:00pm in winter. Closed Monday. Admission E5.) Other features of the town are the well-known **thermal baths** *(www.sirmioneterme.com)* where you can get a massage, sit in a sauna and generally pamper yourself silly; and the enchanting, winding medieval streets. For more information, check out the official Sirmione website at: *www.sirmione.com.*

Arrivals & Departures

If coming by train get off at **Desenzano del Garda** and catch a taxi to your hotel. Cost will be around E20. Once at Sirmione you can travel by ferry to other destinations on the lake.

From Verona, only about 30 km away, by car, take the Autostrada A4 and then the SS 11 at Pescheria del Garda to Sirmione.

From Milan, about 90 km away, by car, take the Autostrada A4 to Desenzano, then take the SS 572 just over six km to the lone road that branches left to Sirmione and its peninsula.

Where to Stay

1. CONTINENTAL, *Via Punta Staffalo 1/9, 25019 Sirmione. Tel. 030/990-5711, Fax 030/916-278. Email: hotelcontinental@yahoo.it. Web: www.continentalsirmione.com. 59 rooms. Single E75-115; Double E125-200. Breakfast included. Half Board per person E80-130; Full board per person E88-14.* ****

The place to stay in Sirmione. All manner of high-end comforts abound, all presented with professionalism and style. Recently renovated, this place has every imaginable comfort. There is even a balcony for every room. But if you want a clear view of the lake, remember to request it. Located on the lakeside, they have a private dock, swimming pool, water sports equipment, and a great buffet breakfast in the mornings. I cannot recommend this hotel highly enough.

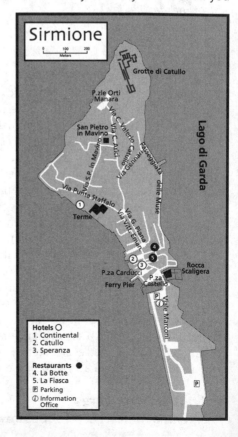

2. CATULLO, *Piazza Flaminia 7. Tel. 030/990-5811, Fax 030/916-444. Email: info@hotelcatullo.it. Web: www.hotelcatullo.it. Closed January 10 and March 15. 57 rooms. Double E110-130. All credit cards accepted. Full board E70-85. Breakfast included.* ***

In the heart of the centro storico, this is a quality choice for Sirmione. For relaxing moments there is an intimate little bar area; or you can sojourn out to the covered terrace with views of the lake. The rooms are spacious and comfortable, and some come with tiny balconies. The bathrooms are well sized and have all necessities.

3. SPERANZA, *Via Casello 6. Tel. 030916-116, Fax 030/916-403. Email: hotelsperanza@tiscali.it. Closed November 25 and February 25. 13 rooms. Single E75; Double E90. Credit cards accepted. Breakfast included.* **

A tiny two star with honest prices, personable owners, and a pleasant atmosphere. Not only is this hotel gracious, clean and comfortable and in the historic old section of Sirmione, but the staff makes you feel as if you are one of the family. Run by two generations of the Sacchella family, the rooms are modern, well-lit and comfortable. The bathrooms are clean, not very big and come with a box shower stall. The best place in Sirmione for budget travelers.

Where to Stay
4. LA BOTTE, *Via Antiche Mura 27, Tel. 030/916-273. Closed Wednesdays. Credit cards accepted. Meal for two E50.*

An extensive menu with pizza to pasta and everything in between. Filled with rustic charm inside, and tables outside in a private piazza seating area under the bell tower. There is something for everyone here.

5. LA FIASCA, *Via S. Maria Maggiore 11, Tel. 030/990-6111. Closed Wednesdays. Meal for two E40.*

Rustic décor with exemplary food. Dishes are served in a refined and elegant style but the food is all local. A great choice while in Sirmione.

Practical Information
• **Tourist Information Office**, Viale Marconi 2. *Tel. 030/916-114*

RIVA DEL GARDA
At the northernmost end of Lake Garda, **Riva del Garda** is a gem of a town with winding medieval streets. Visit the imposing 12th century **Rocca Fortress** with its vast moat. Now a local **museum**, Roman artifacts and other goodies from the past are on display (Piazza Battisti, open 9:00am–1:00pm and 3–5:00pm, only until 4:00pm in the winter; closed Mondays.). Other sights to see include the church of the **Inviolata** and **San Michele**, which is dedicated to the town's citizens who died fighting in WW I. The official website is *www.rivadelgarda.com*.

Arrivals & Departures
By ferry from other parts of the lake, or by car. There is no train service.

Where to Stay
1. EUROPA, *Piazza Catena 9. Tel. 0464/55-433, Fax 0464/521-777. Web: www.rivadelgarda.com/europa. Closed in December. 63 rooms. Single E70-80; Double E110-130. All credit cards accepted. Breakfast included.* ***

A Best Western hotel deep in the heart of the *centro storico*. The restaurant has a terrace overlooking the fort and lake that makes a wonderful setting for a meal. The rooms are spacious as are the bathrooms. The sun terrace on the roof is surrounded by lush potted plants. A good three star in an excellent location.

2. LUISE, *Viale Rovereto 9. Tel. 0464/552-796, Fax 0464/554-250. Web: www.hotelluise.com. Closed from November to Easter. 57 rooms. Double E100-180. All credit cards accepted. Breakfast included. *****

A little ways outside of Riva in a more modern building erected in the '60's that comes with all manner of four star comfort. The rooms are ample and comfortable, with spacious and modern bathrooms.

Where to Eat

3. BELLA NAPOLI, *Via Diaz 29, Tel. 0464/552-139. Credit cards accepted. Meal for two E30.*

Large pizzeria that also serves pasta, meat dishes, salads and more. Deep in the heart of the centro storico, this is great place to eat. Something for everyone with great atmosphere.

4. LA MONTANARA, *Via Montanara 20, Tel. 0464/554-857. Meal for two E30.*

A rustic, local trattoria that serves hearty peasant fare. An ideal place to eat to get a true flavor for the town. It is unlikely that you will find a tourist in here. Highly recommended.

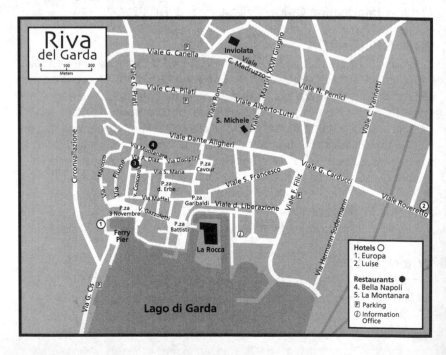

Chapter 17

NAPLES, CAPRI & THE AMALFI COAST

Naples is the gateway to the magical island of **Capri**, the picturesque town of **Sorrento**, as well as the ancient Roman towns of **Pompeii** and **Herculaneum**. Naples is also home to the best archeological museum in Italy, and some say all of Europe.

A little further afield are the beautiful towns of the **Amalfi Coast**. One of these, **Ravello** is a stunning array of buildings perched precariously on the slope overlooking pristine blue waters. If you visit Ravello you will never want to leave. It is simply magical.

From Naples you can also venture deeper into the heart of **Southern Italy** or hop on a ferry down to **Sicily**. On this rustic and beautiful island you can find some of the best preserved Greek archeological ruins anywhere.

NAPLES

To say that **Naples** is a chaotic city is a gross understatement. Cars ignore red lights, scooters drive on sidewalks, and you are forced to thrust yourself into the flow of traffic just to cross a road since hardly anyone obeys traffic laws. There are swarms of people everywhere, filling ominously narrow and dark alleys, and the natives have a hardened surly attitude they have had to adopt to survive in this city.

All of this can at times make Naples less than hospitable. Couple that with the omnipresent threat of getting your pocket picked, it is hard to imagine why people come here. But they do. In droves.

True, Naples is as close to a third world city as you are going to find in the Western world; and as such it is an adventure to visit. It's rough edges, narrow streets and fast pace have kept the flow of international tourism at bay, which makes it an authentic Italian experience. But those same rough edges tend to taint what the city has to offer. A member of the Polizia told me after I reported my wallet stolen, "The streets of Naples are filled with thieves. So be careful." Despite all of this, there is much to see in Naples. Though I would only recommend a visit here to the most experienced Italophile.

Naples is a city to visit if you have already seen Rome, Florence and Venice and want to experience another side of Italy. And even if you do come to visit, it is my recommendation that you stay in Capri or Sorrento and commute into Naples during the day. Nightlife in Naples is drastically curtailed because of the specter of petty street crime. Despite all I have said, please do not avoid Naples. There is much to see and enjoy, as long as you keep your eyes open and your wallet protected.

Among all of this chaos the city flourishes. In many neighborhoods, life is still lived in the gritty labyrinth of the streets, where old and young participate in the cohesive '*piazza* culture' that makes all of Italy so enjoyable. Out in the streets or in the bustling piazzas entertainment is right in front of you, whether it's a family quarrel or two lovers in a corner immersed in their cuddling. As Dickens wrote, "Neapolitans don't just live their lives, they enact them." You'll see this quality all over Naples, especially in **Spaccanapoli** (the historic old town of Naples), and this vibrant zest for life is what makes Naples so irresistible to some.

As Italy's third largest city with 2 million inhabitants, there is much to see in Naples if you can get used to the chaos. The city has an intimacy, tension, and craziness about it that can overwhelm at times. Intermingled among this intense human presence you can find the **Teatro San Carlo**, one of the most beautiful opera houses in the world; the treasures of **Pompeii** grace the **National Museum** (which is a must see if you like archeological treasures); and the archeological excavations of **Napoli Sotteranea** and the **Scavi di San**

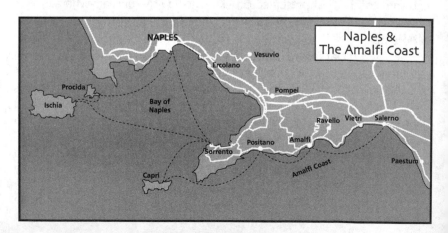

Lorenzo Maggiore should not be missed. Naples has gotten a tough rap over the years because it is a tough city; but if you are looking for a slice of Italian life, pleasantly free from the herd of international tourism, give Napoli a try.

Brief History

Naples was originally a Greek settlement and in the 8th century BCE it was called Parthenope, having been settled by people from Rhodes. Near this site, Ionian settlers founded the 'old town' in 8th century BCE, which they called Parthenope. In the 5th century BCE, the 'new town' of **Neapolis** was founded, and the name, only with slight changes, remains today.

These settlements interacted freely but did not merge until 326 BCE when they became allies of Rome. Though faithful to the alliance, Naples still retained its strong Greek traditions and characteristics until late into the Roman Imperial period. The town itself, and surrounding area, became a favorite of many wealthy Roman merchants and magistrates because of its beautiful scenery, the backdrop of Mount Vesuvius and the artistic flair of the population.

Be Alert, Be Aware in Naples

Though Naples is by far much safer than any American city (whether you want to believe it or not, the U.S. is the most violent country in the Western World) as a large port, Naples attracts people from all over the world, some of whom can be rather unsavory. So be aware, be alert, and make sure you perform all necessary safety precautions. This includes as staying on well traveled, well lit streets, not going down dark alleys, and if it is late at night, taking a cab. Also, in general, if you are robbed, you will only have your pocket picked. You will not be harmed for your possessions as might be in the U.S.

When Rome fell, so did Naples. In 543 CE, the town was overrun by Goths. Ten years later it came under the auspices of the Eastern Roman/Byzantine Empire. When that empire faded in the West, Naples asserted its independence and was free until 1139, when it was conquered by the Normans and incorporated into the Kingdom of Sicily by Roger II. Frederick the I, Roger II's grandson, founded the **University of Naples** that still exists today. In 1179 the capital of the Kingdom of Sicily was moved to Naples.

Spain gained control of the kingdom from 1503 to 1707, and in 1713 the territory passed to the Hapsburgs. Then in 1748 the Bourbons asserted their dominance, and kept control of the city until 1860, when the territory was incorporated into the united Italy we know today.

Arrivals & Departures

The best ways to get to Naples from Rome is first by train, then by car. Bus service to and from Naples is mainly used for getting into remote villages inaccessible by train. The only time you should take a bus to Naples from a major city would be if you're on a tour.

By Car

Located 217 kilometers from Rome, the easiest way to get to Naples by car is by the A2 (Autostrada #2). If you are looking for a more scenic route, the coast road from Ostia Antica will move you past many scenic seaside resorts, including Anzio and Gaeta. But this will take you six hours or more because the roads are small, sometimes only two lanes, and wind endlessly along the coast through little seaside towns. From Rome directly down the A2 should take four hours at most.

By Train

Getting from Rome to Naples by train takes four hours. If you catch a *rapido* you can shave an hour off that time. The train station, Stazione Centrale FS, is located at the eastern end of the city. The **tourist information office** in the station, *Tel. 081/268-779*, can help you locate a hotel if all those in this guide are booked up.

By Ferry

Naples Harbor is always a bustle of activity since Naples is one of Italy's biggest ports. If coming by ferry you will arrive at the **Marine Station** on Molo Angionino. There are ferries to and from the islands of Capri, Ischia, and Procida and the town of Sorrento. From here you can grab a taxi, bus or walk to your final destination.

Getting Around Town

By Bus

Buses can take forever to get you where you want to go, especially at rush hour, but there are times you'll need to take them; for example, when you want to get up to Campodimonte and the National Gallery. The buses congregate at the Piazza Garibaldi outside the train station and each route is posted on the signs at all bus stops for ease of use. You can also get a convenient map from the tourist office that details the main map routes, or you can buy an even better one from a newsstand that lists all the bus routes.

By Foot

You'll obviously need to combine the use of one of the other modes of transport with walking. You'll love the strolls through the *centro storico* and university area, but always be alert. Don't walk at night, especially alone.

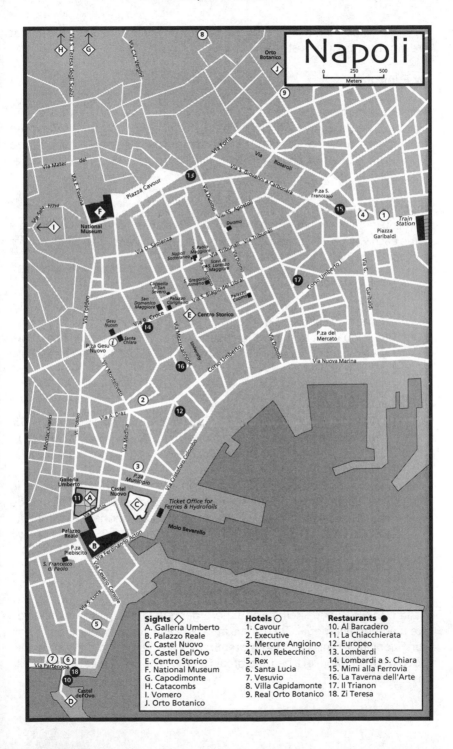

Napoli

0 250 500
Meters

Sights ◇
A. Galleria Umberto
B. Palazzo Reale
C. Castel Nuovo
D. Castel Del'Ovo
E. Centro Storico
F. National Museum
G. Capodimonte
H. Catacombs
I. Vomero
J. Orto Botanico

Hotels ○
1. Cavour
2. Executive
3. Mercure Angioino
4. N.vo Rebecchino
5. Rex
6. Santa Lucia
7. Vesuvio
8. Villa Capidamonte
9. Real Orto Botanico

Restaurants ●
10. Al Barcadero
11. La Chiacchierata
12. Europeo
13. Lombardi
14. Lombardi a S. Chiara
15. Mimi alla Ferrovia
16. La Taverna dell'Arte
17. Il Trianon
18. Zi Teresa

Remember, this is a port city. During the day, don't go down alleys that are empty of people. Just play it smart.

By Funicular

These hillside trams connect the lower city of Naples to the hills of Vomero, where you can see the Castel San Elmo and the Certosa di San Martino. There are three funiculars that can assist in your ascent, the **Centrale** that leaves from Via Toledo, the **Montesanto** that leaves from Piazza Montesanto, and the **Chiai** that leaves from Piazza Amadeo. A one way ticket costs Euro 75 cents.

By Metro

You can take the metro to many places in Naples for only Euro 75 cents a trip each way. It's fast, inexpensive, and safe, but always keep a lookout for pickpockets. They flourish here in Naples.

By Taxi

Naples is a very congested city, and as such it will cost you an arm and a leg whenever you choose to transport yourself by taxi, especially during rush hour. But if you want to spend the equivalent of a meal at a good restaurant just to get from point A to point B, by all means do so. There are strategically placed cab stands all over the city.

Where to Stay

1. **CAVOUR**, *Piazza Garibaldi 32. Tel. 081/283-122, Fax 081/287-488. Email: infor@hotelcavournapoli.it. Web: www.hotelcavournapoli.it. 98 rooms, 40 with bath, 58 with shower. Single E100; Double E170. Lunch or dinner E15. Breakfast included. ****

Elegant and accommodating. Situated in a renovated historic building in the central Piazza Garibaldi. The staff is professional and courteous and do everything to make your stay pleasant. A good three star near the station.

2. **EXECUTIVE**, *Via del Cerriglio 10, Tel./Fax 081/552-0611. Web: http://executive.hotelsinnapoli.com. 19 rooms. Single E90-150. Double E100-245. Credit cards accepted. ****

Located in the *centro storico* in a renovated old convent, this place has a small gym, sauna, and sun deck. The rooms are all comfortable and accommodating. This is a good alternative to the larger hotels in Naples since here you are made to feel special. The rooms are clean and comfortable and have air conditioning, TV, mini-bar and more. Breakfast is served on the sun deck in good weather. More of a bed and breakfast than a hotel. A great choice while in Naples.

3. **MERCURE ANGIOINO**, *Via Depretis 123, Tel. 081/552-9500, Fax 081/ 552-5909. US 1-800/Mercure. Web: www.mercure.com. 85 rooms. Single E100-140; Double E120-200. All credit cards accepted. Breakfast included.* ****

Optimum location in the *centro storico*, near the business district and the Beverello pier where the ferries leave for the islands in the Bay of Naples. Owned by the French chain Mercure, you will receive lavish Gaulish attention. The breakfast room on the first floor is filled to overflowing with the buffet each morning. All the rooms have soundproofed windows so as to block out the noise that makes its way in from the streets below – a necessity in this location. The rooms are all decorated in delicate colors and some are expressly reserved for non-smokers, a rarity in French hotels. The bathrooms are accommodating and have all amenities necessary. The downstairs bar is a great place to relax in the afternoons, or you can order room service from there without a surcharge. A good place to stay.

4. **NUOVO REBECCHINO**, *Corso Garibaldi 356, Tel. 081/553-5327, Fax 081/268-026. 58 rooms. Single E100-140; Double E140-160. All credit cards accepted. Breakfast included.* ***

Convenient location for travelers, right by the station and near the entrance to the Autostrada. Established in 1890, renovated in 1990 it comes with affordable prices. Ask for a room on the fourth floor for the best accommodations. All are furnished in style and elegance, but some don't have sound-proofed windows so request that too. The bathrooms are clean and comfortable and decorated in soft ceramic colors. A good three star in a central location.

5. **REX**, *Via Palepoli 12, Tel. 081/764-9389, Fax 081/764-9227. Web: www.hotel-rex.it. 40 rooms. Single E80-110; Double E110-130. All credit cards accepted. Breakfast included.* ***

In a sweet position, near the lungomare, this hotel occupies part of the Palazzo Coppedé. The Liberty style furnishings in the common rooms hark back to another era, lending a quaint charming air to this place. The rooms are clean and comfortable with colorful bed coverings. All rooms have soundproof windows but only a few have views of the Bay of Naples. A great location at a good price. They have a great map in the entry that shows Naples the way it used to be.

6. **SANTA LUCIA**, *Via Partenope 46, Tel. 081/764-0666, Fax 081/764-8580. Web: www.santalucia.it. 102 rooms, 90 with bath, 12 with shower. Single E150-250; Double E225-290. All credit cards accepted. Breakfast included.* ****

Located within walking distance of the *centro storico* as well as the other major sites, this tranquil romantic hotel is located with a perfect panoramic view of the bay, Mount Vesuvius and Castel dell'Ovo. Like its brethren on the Via Partenope, this is an excellent choice with all the necessary amenities. The only thing it doesn't have is a swimming pool. Opened in 1922, it has been recently renovated and offers complete attention to all details. The hotel restaurant is only open in the evenings, but they will accommodate you for lunch if you make a reservation. The breakfast buffet is overflowing. The rooms are very spacious, come with every imaginable comfort, and are decorated in light blue to continue the seascape you have out the window. The bathrooms come complete with courtesy sets of toiletries. And the service is impeccable.

7. **VESUVIO**, *Via Partenope 45, Tel. 081/764-0044. 081/407-520. Web: www.vesuvio.it. 183 rooms. Single E300-350; Double E350-400. All credit cards accepted. Breakfast included.* ****

Located on the elite hotel row, this beautifully restored old building houses a truly superb hotel. Decorated elegantly with antiques, the charm and character is reflected in their refinement. You will be offered the most attentive service while staying here. The restaurant, Caruso, on the top floor, offers a stunning panoramic view of the Bay of Naples. For over 100 years this seaside hotel has been the address for many illustrious guests. The rooms are extremely comfortable, decorated with wonderful antiques and colorful wall coverings. The bathrooms are immaculate and also come with every imaginable amenity. If you're driving, they have an underground garage since parking on the street is impossible.

8. **VILLA CAPIDAMONTE**, *Via Moiariello 66, Tel. 081/459-000, Fax 081/ 229-344. Web: www.villacapodimonte.it. 60 rooms. Single E165; Double E210. Breakfast included. All credit cards accepted.* ****

Situated above the city near the magnificent tranquility of the park Capidamonte (hence the name), if you want peace and quiet away from the hectic pace of Neapolitan life, stay here. Virtually brand new, the hotel was opened in 1995 and as such it comes with every imaginable creature comfort. You can wind down in the garden, the terrace, the salons, the library or in your comfortable room. Decorated in soft colors to enhance the peaceful tones, most rooms also offer lovely panoramic views. The tennis facilities are a little run down, but still usable. The prices are lower than other four stars because it is so out of the way. As such you would need to take a cab everywhere.

9. **REAL ORTO BOTANICO**, *Via Foria 192, Tel. 081/442-1528, Fax 081/ 442-1346, Email: hoteldelreal@hotmail.com, Web: www.hotelrealortobotanico.it. Single E100-140; Double E170-190.* ***

Located in a completely restored historical building from the 1700s. Situated in a working class neighborhood, right across the street from the Botanical Gardens and just down the street from the world famous National Archeological Museum. The Hotel Real Orto Botanico was opened in June 2001, and comes with every modern three star amenity. The hotel also includes a roof garden area, a state of the art security system, an extensive buffet breakfast served from 7:00am to 10:30am, and an excellent dinner menu. With professional and cordial staff, the Hotel del Real Orto Botanico is a great place to stay in Naples. There is also a great pizzeria right next door.

Where to Eat

10. AL BARCADERO CAFE, *Banchina S. Lucia 2, Tel. 333/222-7023. Open from 10am to 10pm.*

An intimate little cafe in the ritzy part of Naples, near the restaurant Zi Theresa. Set down on the water and away from the frenetic pace of the city, I love this place. Here you can let the hours slip by, while sipping a drink or munching on some simple snacks. Awash with atmosphere, with fishing boats, yachts, Castel Ovo and Mt. Vesuvius all visible.

11. LA CHIACCHIERATA, *Piazzetta M Serao 37, Tel. 081/411 465. Open only for lunch, except Fridays it is also open for dinner. Closed Sundays and August. American Express Cards accepted. Dinner for two E30.*

A small *trattoria* located at the end of the Via Toledo near the Palazzo Reale. They use a lot of vegetables here, especially on their pizza on which they also pile mozzarella and provolone. You can also get some *pasta e fagioli* (pasta and beans), some good *pesce arrosto* (grilled fish), and a superb *capretto al forno* (baked 'kid'). Great food in a great location.

12. EUROPEO, *Via Marchese Campodisola 4/8, Tel. 081/552-1323. Open everyday for lunch. For dinner only Thurs-Sat. Closed Sundays and two weeks in August. American Express and Visa accepted. Dinner for two E40.*

This is a small local *trattoria* that is not so attractive on the ourside but filled with locals and great food inside. Eating here gives you an insight into the cross section of people that make up the community of Naples. They serve a tasty *ostriche e frutti di mare* (oysters and other seafood) appetizer. Then try their *Pizza Margherita* (simple pizza with fresh tomato sauce, oil and mozzarella cheese) or have them put some great sausage on the pizza as well. Or try their superb *spaghetti alle vongole verace* (with spicy clam sauce). For seconds they make a great *frittura di pesce* (fried fish dish).

13. LOMBARDI, *Via Foria 12, Tel. 081/456-220. Closed Mondays. All credit cards accepted. Dinner for two E28.*

Located near the Museo Archeologico Nazionale, this place definitely has the best *Pizza Napoletana* anywhere. Covered in ricotta, mozzarella, vegetables, and almost everything imaginable, this is the tastiest pizza around. They also have a variety of pasta and meat dishes. Also, even with no smoking signs on the walls, nobody adheres to them, so if smoke bothers you ... don't come here.

14. LOMBARDI A SANTA CHIARA, *Via B Croce 59, Tel. 081/522-0780. Closed Sundays and three weeks in August. Credit cards accepted. Dinner for two E33.*

The sister pizzeria to Lombardi's. This place is located in the heart of the *centro storico* right next to the *chiesa di Santa Chiara* and their beautiful cloisters. Here you will find great pizzas of all kinds. For an appetizer try their *mozzarella di bufalo* (buffalo mozzarella) *peperoni, melanzane* (eggplant), and *zucchine* plate. A perfectly situated place to stop for a bite to eat in the middle of a day of wandering around the back streets of Naples. The food is excellent and inexpensive, and the atmosphere is authentically local.

15. MIMI ALLA FERROVIA, *Via A d'Aragona 21, Tel. 081/553-8525. Closed Sundays and a week in August. Credit cards accepted. Dinner for two E60.*

The place to eat near the station. High end service and food. Start with their appetizer of *mozzarella di bufalo, peperoni* or *assagi di paste povere* (a tasty sampling of their pasta dishes). For pasta try their *linguine alla Mimi* (which comes with a great shrimp sauce), then move onto their *frutti di mare e pomodorini* (mixed seafood and small tomatoes). The *calamaretti fritti* (fried calamari) is also good.

16. LA TAVERNA DELL'ARTE, *Rampa S. Giovanni Maggiore 1a, Tel. 081/552-7558. Closed Sundays and August. No credit cards accepted. Dinner for two E40.*

A small local place situated in the heart of the *centro storico* near the University that has superb atmosphere. The service is excellent, either on the terrace or inside. Try the traditional appetizer of *pizze rustiche* (literally country pizza, with a variety of toppings), *salumi artigianali* (literally craftsmen salami – great local salami), *mozzarella fresche* (fresh mozzarella) and *sformato di cipolle* (baked onions). This will definitely fill you up so move directly to a great main course of *maiale in agrodolce* (a sweet and sour pork dish). Definitely my favorite place in Naples.

17. IL TRIANON, *Via P Colletta 46, Tel. 081/553-9426. Web: www.napolibox.it/trianon. Closed Sundays and for lunch, New Years Eve and Christmas. No credit cards accepted. Dinner for two E25.*

Located in the *centro storico*, this is the best pizza in Naples, and that's saying a lot. Besides the many varieties of pizza that come out of their wood burning brick oven, you'll love the high ceilings, slate-yellow walls, tacky print motifs that they call decoration, and the long communal tables. Mainly frequented by University students this place has a fun-filled crowd. Try their filling pizza/lasagna that is loaded with sauce, cheese and meat if a pizza sounds too boring to you, but do not miss this place when in Naples. Great food, local atmosphere.

18. ZI TERESA, *Via Partenope 1, Tel. 081/764-2565. Closed Sunday nights and Saturdays as well as two weeks in August. Credit cards accepted. Dinner for two E65.*

Located across from the Castel dell'Ovo on the water, this is a famous and popular eating spot, and because of that it's rather expensive. It's also surrounded by some of the best hotels in the city, like the Excelsior and the Continental which doesn't help keep prices down. Their terrace is a perfectly romantic spot to have lunch or dinner, but remember to reserve well in advance. Start off with their *antipasto di mare* (seafood antipasto), then move on to their *spaghetti alle vongole* (with clam sauce), then if you're still hungry savor any of their grilled fish. Very high end.

Seeing the Sights

Naples has plenty to offer: world class performing arts, unparalleled museums, centuries-old castles and palaces, and simple pleasures such as strolling along the harbor. But always remember that Naples is a port city so use common sense when walking around, especially at night in the old section.

Napoli Artecard

This excellent money saving card *(www.campaniartecard.it)* offers you free entry to two museums of your choice and entry at 50% to four others, if used in a 60 hour period. The museums on the list are the best: National Museum, Capodimonte, Certosa and Musuem of San Martino, Castel Sant'Elmo, Castel Nuovo, and Palazzo Reale). You also can receive between 15-40% discounts in museum stores, and a 20% discount on parking, theater tickets and ferry tickets. While in Naples, get this card. It only costs E 13 for adults, or E 8 for youths aged 18 to 25.

A. GALLERIA UMBERTO

Between Via San Carlo and Via Toledo. Open 24 hours.

Modeled after the Galleria Emanuelle in Milan, this arcaded shopping area with its glass ceilings is also laid out in a cross pattern. The blending of iron and glass harks back to a bygone era or gentility and refinement. It is hard to believe that modern American shopping malls were based on these beautiful structures. If you like to shop, this should be one of your stops.

B. PALAZZO REALE

Piazza Plebiscito 1. *Tel. 081/794-4021. Web: www.museionline.it.* Open 9:00am–8:00pm. Closed Wednesdays. Admission E4.

The former **Royal Palace** was begun in 1600 by Domenico Fontana and was restored between 1837 and 1841. On the facade are displayed statues of eight former kings who ruled Naples. This extensive palace contains a magnificent marble staircase built in 1651, 17 heavily decorated **apartments**, and the **Biblioteca Nazionale** that contains over 1,500,000 volumes and many ancient manuscripts and relics. You should come to the Royal Palace just to see the National Library, because it is like nothing you can find in North America.

C. CASTEL NUOVO

Piazza Municipio. *Tel. 081/795-2003. Web: www.museionline.it.* Open 9:00am–7:00pm. Closed Sundays. Admission E 5.

Behind the palace is the magnificent, five-towered **Castel Nuovo**, also referred to as **Maschio Angionino**. This was once the residence of kings and viceroys who ruled the Kingdom of Naples, and now houses an interesting little museum. Built between 1279 and 1283, it pre-dated the Palazzo Reale and has been renovated pretty frequently over the years. An imposing structure that adults and children alike love to explore.

D. CASTEL DELL'OVO

Borgo Marinaro. Open 9:00am–noon and 3:00pm–5:30pm.

If your kids like exploring castles, the **Castel dell'Ovo** is located off a causeway from the Via Partenope and sits on a small rocky islet. It was begun in the 12th century and completed in the 16th century and has been used as a lighthouse as well as the first line of defense for the harbor.

Napoli Porte Aperte - 'Open Door Naples'

Be aware that at infrequent times and in true Italian fashion, unannounced, the city opens all of its churches, monuments, and gardens for free. Ask at the tourist office or your concierge whether this rare event will occur during your stay.

E. HISTORIC NAPLES – CENTRO STORICO

Located just north of the harbor, this part of Naples is the best place to walk and get a feel for the real city. It has winding streets dotted with small churches and quaint old buildings. A fun place to explore during the day but be careful at night. Even locals advise that you do not frequent anywhere between the Duomo and the train station at night.

The old main street, called the Spaccanapoli (literally Naples splitter) is a combination of all the streets from the Via Toledo, through the Via Maddaloni, to the Via Croce, and moving onto the Via S. Giagio ai Librai. This wonderful series of streets, as well as the small alleys that are offshoots from it, is lined with shops of traditional artisans such as the **Palazzo dei Strumenti**, Vico San Domenico Maggiore #9, in front of the church of the same name. Up the stairs to the first floor you'll find guitars and other instruments being crafted by hand.

A unique shop is the **L'Ospedale delle Bambole (The Doll Hospital)**, located on Via S Biagio ai Librai. This is the world famous store where you'll find ancient dolls and puppets hanging everywhere or strewn haphazardly about. Walk in and have a look around, the proprietor is very friendly and it's not often you find a store that caters to doll repair. Another can't-miss street in the *centro storico* is the **Via San Gregorio Aremeno**, which is commonly known as the Nativity scene street since they sell figurines for crèches year round.

Church of Santa Anna del Lombardi

Piazza Monteoliveto, Open daily 7:15am–1:00pm.

This church, in the **Piazza Monteoliveto** just off the Piazza della Carita, has a great collection of Renaissance sculpture. The church, a favorite of the Arogonese Court, was built in 1411 and later continued in the Renaissance style. Here you'll find the Pieta, created in 1492 by Guido Mazzoni. Also inside are some amazing frescoes, wonderful terra-cotta statues and a beautiful 16th century choir stall, among other religious art.

Church of Santa Chiara & Gesu Nuovo

Piazza del Gesu Nuovo. Santa Chiara open daily 8:00am–12:30pm and 4:30pm–7:30pm. Gesu Nuovo open daily 7:15am–1:00pm and 4:00pm–7:15:00pm.

Try to see these two churches. The Jesuit **Gesu Nuovo** was erected between 1584 and 1597 and still maintains its triangular grid-like facade. The interior has been sumptuously sheathed with marble facing, stuccoes and frescoes. One of the most appealing is on the counter facade, the *Expuslion of Heliodorus from the Temple* by F. Solimena in 1725 and the *Evangelists* by Lanfranco. An intricately ornate, sumptuous display of stunning art abounds in this church.

The **Santa Chiara** is one of medieval Naples' main monuments. It was built in 1310 and was recreated in the Gothic style after being destroyed by fire during World War II. Inside you'll find medieval tombs and sarcophagi that belong to the house of Anjou. To the left of S. Chiara are also some beautiful cloisters (E4) full of roses and cats. It's a great place to relax among the benches and pillars covered in colorful tiles of scenes of Naples, others of vines, leafs, flowers and grapes. Here you can rest while enjoying the aroma of the roses and escaping from the hectic pace of Naples, at least for a few minutes.

Church of San Domenico Maggiore

Piazza San Domenico Maggiore. Open daily 8:00am–12:30pm and 4:30pm–7:00pm.

From the two churches above, go east down the Benedetto Croce to the next piazza on the left, to the church of **San Domenico Maggiore**. This is another must see destination while in Naples. Built between 1283 and 1324 at the behest of Charles II by incorporating the existing church of Sam Michele Arcangelo a Morfisa. With a Gothic facade added in the 19th century, this is one of the most interesting churches in Naples. When touring this church you will see one of the richest collection of art in all of Naples. It has many early Renaissance pieces as well as over 40 sarcophagi of the Anjou family. Of particular note for American readers is the modern funereal slab for the first Catholic Bishop of New York. He died in Naples after his consecration, while waiting to leave for America.

Capella di San Severo

Via F de Sanctis. Open Mondays and Wednesday–Saturday 10:00am–5:00pm, Sundays 10:00am–1:30pm. Admission E5.

The **Chapel of San Severo** is a short distance east of the church of San Domenico Maggiore, hidden down the small side street of Via F de Sanctis. Built in 1590 as a burial chamber for the Sangro family, it was embellished with the Baroque style in the 18th century. Now a private museum, the chapel is filled with many fine statues including an erotic *Veiled Modesty*. The folds of marble linen covering the naked statue seems translucent. A wonderful small sculpture exhibit. On a more macabre note, you can also find two anatomical machines located downstairs, which are leftovers from the experiments of the Prince Raimondo. He was an inventor and reputed sorcerer, scientist, man of letters, as well as a Masonic Grand Master.

Church and Cloisters of San Gregorio Armeno

Between Via Tribunali and Via S. Baglio S. Librai. Hardly ever open. You need to go there and request entrance.

This vast monastery is one of the oldest and richest in artwork in Naples. Founded by nuns fleeing the heresy of the Byzantine church, the church is splendid, but the cloisters are a rare gem. Most often closed, sometimes you have to ask the nuns if you can enter.

Noteworthy for their remarkable state of preservation, the pillared cloisters open onto a panoramic view of the bay of Naples, have citrus trees all around, as well as a **fountain** in the center depicting the meeting at the well of Christ and the Samaritan woman.

From the cloisters you can enter the wooden choir chamber and peer through the wrought iron grating down onto the church itself. This was where the cloistered nuns celebrated mass.

From here you can pass into the intact rooms of the convent that have been enriched over time by the "dowries" of the girls who became nuns, some of whom came from the most illustrious families in Naples. This array of artwork now constitutes a devotional museum.

Palazzo Cuomo

Via Duomo 288, *Tel. 081/203-175. Web: www.museionline.it.* Open 9:30am–2:00pm and 3:30pm – 7:00pm. Holidays 9:30am-1:30pm. Closed Mondays. Admission E2.6.

The beautiful Renaissance **Palazzo Cuomo**, sometimes spelled Como, was built from 1464 to 1490, and now houses the **Museo Civico "Gaetano Filangieri."** The original collection was partially destroyed in 1943 during the Allies invasion of the Italian peninsula. Opened again in 1948 and made complete with further donations and loans, this is a rather eclectic private collection. Of note are the oriental arms and armor, the fabrics and coin collection, the porcelain, and a number of paintings and sculptures.

Duomo

Via Duomo. Open daily 8:00am–12:30pm and 5:00–7:00pm.

Up the Via Duomo from the Palazzo Cuomo is the **Cathedral**, dedicated to San Gennaro, the patron saint of Naples. Built over the 4th century ruins of a paleo-Christian basilica, this church was erected between 1295 and 1324 in the French Gothic style. After an earthquake destroyed part of it in 1456 it was rebuilt, restored, and altered. It was further updated in the 19th century when part of the facade was replaced, but the church retains its original doors. Of note inside are the Cappella Minutolo (a well preserved Gothic room), the higher church one of the more noteworthy achievements of the Rennaissance in Naples), and the chapel of S. Restituta from the 4th century.

Facing S. Restituta, in the right aisle is a monumental entrance to the **Chapel of San Gennaro**, almost as if it were a facade for a separate church. Incorporated in the Duomo in 1601, on the main altar of the chapel you'll find a silver bust of San Gennaro that contains his skull. In the tabernacle are two vials of dried blood from the saint, which liquifies annually in May and September. An event considered to be a miracle. Believers sigh a breath of relief because the liquification indicates that the saint will continue to protect Naples from Vesuvius' wrath, or whatever might threaten the city. To find the saint's tomb, look under the high altar.

Napoli Sotteranea

Piazza San Gaetano 68. *Tel. 081/296-944. Web: napolisotterranea.org.* Tours Mon-Fri 12, 2, and 4. On Thurs at 9. Sat, Sun and Holidays 10, 12, 2, 4, and 6. Groups need to book in advance. Admission E8.

This is an awesome sight and tour. You get to go on underground tours of **catacombs**, **ancient aqueducts**, **cisterns**, and the remains of **Roman** and **Greek buildings** that lie below modern Naples. During WW II this was used as a refuge from bombings and invading armies. A sight not often seen by visitors. The entrance is to the left of the church of S. Paolo Maggiore. When in Naples, you simply have to do this tour.

Scavi di San Lorenzo Maggiore

P.za San Gaetano. Time Mon-Sat 9am-5pm, Sun 9:30-1:30. Admission E4. Right across the small piazza from Napoli Sotteranea is another excellent archeological excavation deep in the heart of Naples. This is an amazing trip back in time. Self-guided, but with a wonderful map, illustrations and descriptions, this is a sight well worth seeing. There is an excellent miniature model of across from the ticket booth that clearly illustrates what you are about to witness. Located on the street that contains stores that have figurines for crèches.

F. NATIONAL MUSEUM

Piazza Cavour. *Tel. 081/440–166.* Information and reservations: *Tel. 848/800-288. Web: www.cib.na.cnr.it/mann/museo1/mann.html.* Open daily 9:00am–7:00pm. Until 8:00pm on holidays. Closed Tuesdays. Admission E6.5.

On the northwestern outskirts of the *centro storico* just off of Piazza Cavour is the **National Archeological Museum**, which boasts an amazingly rich collection of antiquities. Considered by many to the best archeological museum in Europe, if not the world. The building was originally erected as troop barracks in 1586, then was the home of the University from 1616 to 1790. During this time the University began to house the art treasures of the kings of Naples, the Farnese collections from Rome, and material from Pompeii, Herculaneum, and Cumae. This is definitely a must see destination when in Naples.

One of its best exhibits is the **Gabinetto Segreto**, the secret closet. Filled with erotic statues, mosaics and other pieces of art of a sexual nature, these pieces definitely give you an insight into life back in the Roman era. This titillating exhibit used to be by appointment only, but is now open for all visitors. This exhibit definitely offers a different perspective on history.

G. CAPODIMONTE

Via Milano 1, *Tel. 081/749-9111. Web: www.capodimonte.selfin.it.* Park open daily 7:30am–8:00pm. In off–season open 7:30am–5:00pm. Entrance on Via Capidamonte near the Porta Grande. Buses 24 or C66 will drop you off in front of the entrance.

This 297-acre verdant setting commands wonderful panoramic views of Naples. A peaceful respite from the hectic pace of Naples. Also located at the park is the **Capodimonte Museum** (Open 8:30am-7:30pm. Closed Mondays. Admission E7.5) housed in the Palazzo Reale, and which is filled with arms, armor, porcelain, and paintings, including some great works by **Titian** and **Caravaggio**.

H. CATACOMBS OF SAN GENNARO

Via Capodimonte; entrance near the church of the Madre del Buon Consiglio, Tel. 741-1071. Guided tours only. Fri, Sat and Sun beginning at 9:30am, 10:15, 11, and 11:45. Just across the street from the Capodimonte.

The **Catacombs**, like their Roman counterparts, these contain a maze of passageways and tomb chambers. However the Neopolitan catacombs are slightly better preserved and have some amazing frescoes. Dating from the 2nd century these catacombs come in two levels and are a must see destination when in Naples. Eerie, illuminating, exciting, and fun.

I. VOMERO & THE SURROUNDING HILLS

Certosa di San Martino, museum *Tel. 578-1769.* Open Tuesday–Sunday 9:00am–2:00pm. Admission E4. Castel Sant'Elmo, Open Tuesday–Saturday 9:00am–2:00pm, and Sundays 9:00am–1:00pm.

If you want to get away from the smog and congestion of Naples just hop on one of the *funiculars* and enter a calm antidote in a residential district high above the city. You can also get here by climbing the streets in the Montecalvario section.

The district was built from 1885 onwards, and contains the Villa Floridiana public park in the southern part of Vomero, which has a terrace with a wonderful view overlooking the **Bay of Naples**. Here you'll also find a small museum, **Duca di Martina Museum**, with paintings, porcelain, ivory, china, and pottery here.

Of interest is the **Certosa di San Martino**, an old monastery erected in the 14th century and remodeled during the Renaissance and Baroque periods. You should take the time to the see the cloisters because they give you a glimpse into the monastic life of the times. Their museum contains some interesting nativity scenes (crèches).

Just north of the monastery is the **Castel Sant'Elmo** that was built in 1329 and added to between the 15th and 17th centuries. When the Austrian Empire controlled this region briefly, Peter the Great's son Alexis fled to this castle to escape his father's wrath. Eventually discovered he was returned to Russia. Come here for the view from the ramparts, as well a chance to explore the many passageways that were used for the defense of the harbor.

J. ORTO BOTANICO

Via Foria 223, *Tel. 081/449-759.* Hours 9:00am – 2:00pm.

One of the main botanical gardens in all of Italy, this one was developed from 1807 through 1819. The structure that houses the main part of the gardens is interesting in its own right. If you love plants, and want to see varieties from Asia, Australia and America, stop in. Also a great place to escape the hectic pace of Naples.

Nightlife & Entertainment

RIOT, *Via S Biagio dei Librai 26. No phone. Open from 9:00pm-3:00am.*

To enter come through a wooden door, cross an open courtyard, climb a staircase, and on the right is the secret garden that is the club. It consists of a few rooms in an old building from the 18th century with tall French windows opening out onto a lush terrace of palm trees, pebble paths, and tables at which to sit and enjoy a drink or a smoke.

During the summer they have art exhibits and late night bands, mostly American blues and jazz. The waitresses here are all hip and have a definite attitude. Even so they will serve you drinks and sandwiches outside. It's a bit expensive but the crowd is fun and the atmosphere is like nothing you'll find in the States. I mean how many nightclubs do you know that are in 18th century *palazzi*? It's like something out of an Anne Rice vampire novel. And they are so hip they don't have a phone.

Opera

If you are in Naples from December to June, the traditional opera season, brought with you some proper attire (suits for men, elegant dresses for women), and have a taste for something out of the ordinary, try the **Teatro San Carlo**, Via San Carlo 98f, 80132 Napoli, *Tel. 081/797-2331 or 797-2412, Fax 081/797-2306..*

This is the most distinguished opera in house in Italy after La Scala in Milan. For centuries Naples was considered the apex of European music and the Teatro San Carlo was the premier opera house of that period. Its neoclassic facade dates from its rebuilding in 1816. Most tickets are always sold out, but you can check at the ticket office between 10:00am and 1:00pm and 4:30pm to 6:00pm Sunday through Tuesday during the season.

Sports & Recreation

Golf

• **Circolo Golf Napoli**, Via Campiglione 11, 80072 Arco Felice. *Tel. 081/526-4296.* Located only 5 km from Naples, this is a 9 hole, par 35, course that is 2,601 meters long. It is open year round except Mondays and Tuesdays. They also have a driving range, pull carts, and a bar/restaurant. A good place to come if you're going through golf withdrawal.

Shopping

The main shopping streets with fancy shops are the **Corso Umberto**, **Via Toledo**, and **Via Chiaia**. Along these streets you'll find your international style, upscale, expensive stores. For additional shopping suggestions, see *Seeing the Sights: Historic Naples* above.

English Language Bookstores

• **Feltrinelli**, Via San T. d'Aquino 70. Open Monday through Friday 9:00am to 8:00pm, Saturdays 9:00am to 1:00pm. They have an extensive selection of English language travel guides as well as some paperback novels.

• **Universal Books**, Rione Sirignano. This store has books in many different languages though only a small selection of paperbacks in English.

Antique Fair
Viale Antonio Dohrn, Saturdays and Sundays 8am-2pm. Located in the park of the Villa Communale, just off the bottom left hand corner of our map on page 481.

Excursions & Day Trips
If you have any free time while in Naples, try to visit the two ancient cities of **Pompeii** and **Herculaneum**. They are truly a major wonder of the world: two cities trapped in time by a devastating volcanic eruption. What more could you ask for? You can also take day trips from Naples to the beautiful isle of Capri, as well as the town of Sorrento; even though these places are treated as separate destinations in their own sections.

POMPEII & HERCULANEUM
Thousands of people died and many more lost their homes when Vesuvius erupted in 79 CE, submerging Pompeii and Herculaneum with volcanic emissions. The lava and ash created an almost perfect time capsule, sealing in an important cross-section of an ancient civilization. If you want to take a trip into history, come to one of these magnificent cities buried in time. You will find nothing even remotely similar to this anywhere in the world.

Arrivals & Departures
By car from Rome, take the A2 south, past Naples, connect to the A3 and exit at Pompeii Scavi. Total time elapsed each way, 3 1/2 to 4 hours.

By train from Naples, go one floor below the Central Station to the **Circumvesuviana** station for a local high-speed train to **Ercolano** (Herculaneum) or **Pompeii Scavi**. The trip takes about 30-40 minutes.

Pompeii
Before the city was buried by lava, Pompeii was a major seaport for Rome's linking it to the rest of the Empire. As such it was an established city with a multicultural population of about 25,000 Greeks, Egyptians, Gauls, Iberians and every other nationality in the Roman Empire. By 80 BCE, it was also a favorite resort for wealthy Romans.

Shaken by an earthquake in 62 CE, Pompeii recovered, brushed itself off and went back to business. 17 years later on August 24, 79 CE, Mt. Vesuvius erupted, spewing ash and pumice pebbles which covered the city, preserving it and some of its unfortunate residents. Covered in this manner, for over 1,500 years Pompeii rested undisturbed, then was rediscovered in 1711 when a peasant was digging a well on his property. For two centuries Pompeii served almost entirely as a quarry for works of art, as a plaything for the various dynasties which misruled Naples, and as a romantic stop on the Grand Tour of Europe for elite European society.

Although rudimentary excavations began in 1763, systematic excavations did not get under way until 1911 and have been progressing slowly ever since. Now only about three-fifths of the site has been freed.

Herculaneum has suffered a less severe intrusion from scavengers since on the afternoon of the eruption, rain turned the volcanic ash to mud, which solidified, burying the town thirty to forty feet deep. Electric drills and mechanical shovels are needed to dig here, so progress has been very slow , but the town has been better preserved.

Despite this difference, Pompeii still offers the most fascinating introduction into ancient history. Strolling through this dead city is quite ominous. In places there are human forms and family pets forever preserved, having died in the embrace of the volcanic ash. Along with these macabre scenes, you can easily imagine life going on here since many pieces of every day existence remain. You can see where people planted gardens, shops where they bought food, and walls are still covered with ancient graffiti. These range from erotic drawings advertising the world's oldest profession, to boasts by one of its practitioners to having had over 1,300 men, to drawings of oral sex, to slogans extolling the virtues of one political candidate over another.

In the wealthier homes there are abundant frescoes depicting mythological scenes, as well as frescoes indicating how the owners of the house made a living. The streets have characteristic deep ruts made by wheels of carts – the trucks of antiquity – and are bridged by massive stepping stones, which acted as both a conduit for pedestrians, and also as a traffic calmer.

Some of the best homes to see are the **House of the Faun** and the **House of the Vettii**, both in the residential area north of the **Forum**. Other homes of interest are the **House of the Melander** (located to the east of the Forum), the **Villa of the Mysteries** (located to the west of the main town), and the **House of Pansa** (located to the north of the Forum) that also included rented apartments.

The public **Amphitheater**, in the east of the city, should not be missed because of its scale and level of preservation. A fun activity to try out are finding the locations on the stage where even if a whisper is spoken, even a person standing at the top-most part of the seating area can hear it clearly.

Pompeii is covers 160 acres, and was well supplied with public amenities. Lead water pipes found everywhere show that all but the very humblest of houses were supplied with running water. Most houses either doubled as workshops, or had small workshops in them since the ancient world's slave economy did not foster the development of the factory system. He lives of ancient tradesmen, about which literature tells us almost nothing, become more real for us here than anywhere else in the ancient world. Except possibly, for the abandoned port of Rome, Ostia Antica.

Pompeii has also enriched our knowledge of ancient Romans relations to their gods. Naturally the Imperial cult whereby Emperors were decreed to be gods, was adhered to, though generally only with lip service. Graffiti backs up this blasphemous stance. One such wall scribbling states "Augustus Caesar's mother was only a woman."

In evidence in the remains are symbols of the Greek cult of Dionysis, one of many that flourished in the city. **The Temple of Isis** (to the east of the Forum) testifies to the strong following that the Egyptian goddess had here. The Roman warrior sect of Mithras was well represented, and family cults that worshipped dead ancestors flourished. This is evidenced by the fact that most houses and workshops had private shrines usually housing busts of ancestors. However, the true god of Pompeii was, as with other cities ancient and modern, was money.

Ironically, it was that worship of money that got many people killed. Going back for their hoards of silver and gold spelled death for many of the residents of Pompeii. Under the hail of pumice stone and ashes many were asphyxiated or engulfed. A particularly disturbing cluster of victims, with their children and burdensome possessions is preserved near the **Nocera Gate**.

Most of the remnants of the Pompeian consumer society – the best-preserved artifacts – are not in Pompeii anymore, they are in the National Museum in Naples. So if you can, make a point of visiting there too. After many years of mismanagement, Pompeii is slowly re-emerging to be a true world wonder. An organization called World Monuments Watch has declared Pompeii one of the world's most imperiled cultural sites, but the good news is that they are helping to restore the ancient city to the wonder it once was. Pompeii is unique anywhere in the world, and is a must-see stop when in Italy.

Open April – October 8:30am-7:30pm. Last entry at 6:00pm. November to March 8:30am-5:00pm. Last entry 3:30pm. Admission E10.

Herculaneum (Ercolano)

Closer to Naples, and seventeen miles northeast of Pompeii is the smaller town of Herculaneum. At the time of the eruption Herculaneum had only 5,000 inhabitants, had virtually no commerce, and its industry was solely based on fishing. The volcanic mud that flowed through every building and street in Herculaneum was a different covering from that which buried Pompeii. This steaming hot lava-like substance settled eventually to a depth of 30-40 feet and became rock-hard, sealing and preserving everything it came in contact with. Dinner was left on tables, wine shops abandoned in mid-purchase, sacrifices left at the moment of offering, funerals never finished, prisoners left in stocks, and watchdogs perished on their chains.

Fortunately for the residents, but not for archeologists, the absence of the hail of hot ash that rained down on Pompeii, which smashed the buildings of that city and trapped many residents of that town, meant that many of the inhabitants of Herculaneum were able to get away in time. Despite the absence of preserved human remains, Herculaneum offers complete houses, with their woodwork, household goods, and furniture.

Although Herculaneum was a relatively unimportant town compared with Pompeii, many of the houses that have been excavated were from the wealthy class. It is speculated that perhaps the town was like a retirement village, populated by prosperous Romans seeking to pass their retirement years in the calm of a small seaside town. This idea is bolstered by the fact that the few craft shops that have been discovered were solely for the manufacture of luxury goods.

Archaeologists speculate that the most desirable residential area was in the southwest part of town, which overlooked the ocean in many different housing terraces. Here you will find the **House of the Stags**, famous for its beautiful frescoes, sculpted stags, and a drunken figure of Hercules. Farther north you can find the marvelously preserved **House of the Wooden Partition**. It is one of the most complete examples of a private residence in either Pompeii or Herculaneum. Near this house to the north are the **Baths**, an elaborate complex incorporating a gymnasium and assorted men's and women's baths.

Important to remember as you compare Herculaneum with Pompeii is that this town was only recently excavated since more modern tools were needed for the job. This allowed for more advanced preservation efforts. But both sites are well worth visiting and are highly recommended by the author. Gates to the site open year round 9:00am to 1 hour before sunset. Admission E10.

Practical Information for Naples
Bed & Breakfast Services
• **BBNaples**, *Web: www.bbnaples.it. Email: bbnaples@bbnaples.it*
• **Di Vagando Napoli**, Corso Umberto I #74, *Tel. 081/804-4800, Web: www.divagandonapoli.org/b&b, Email: bbnaples@libero.it.*

Bicycle Rentals
• **Junior Skate Shop**, Riviera di Chiaia 261, *Tel. 081/764-7788. Web: www.junior.it, Email: grindalo.tin.it.*
• **Riciclo**, Via G. Summonte 17, *Tel. 081/552-9988, Email: bidon@bidonville.org.*

Car Rental
• **Avis**, Train Station, Corso Lucci 203, *Tel. 081/878-2459;* or Capodichino Airport, *Tel. 081/761-1365. Web: www.avisautonoleggio.it*

• **Hertz**, Train Station, Piazza Garibaldi 91b, *Tel. 081/599-0924; or Capodichino Airport, Tel. 081/570-8701. Web: www.hertz.it.*

Chartering a Boat

If you are interested in seeing the bay of Naples, the islands, the Amalfi Coast and beyond on your own chartered vessel, the premier company to contract with is **Sail Italia** (Via Roma 10, 80079 Procida, *Tel 081/896-9962, Fax 081/896-9264, Email: info@sailitalia*). Located on the island of Procida, this is a full service boat rental company with dozens of boats available. You can even rent a captain (required if you are not a sailor) and crew. An ideal way to see Italy, from the bow of your own boat, drink in hand, floating beyond the traffic and crowds, one with the waves.

Doll Hospital
• **Ospedale delle Bombole**, Via S. Biagio dei Librai 81, *Tel. 081/203-067, Cell 339/587-2274, Web: www.ospedaledellebombole.it*. Owners: Luigi & Tiziana Grassi.

Embassies/Consulates
• **Canada**, Via Carducci 29, *Tel. 081/401-338*
• **Great Britain**, Via dei Mille 40, *Tel. 081/423-8911*
• **United States**, Piazza della Repubblica, *Tel. 081/583-0111*

English Language Bookstore
• **Universal Books**, Corso Umberto I 22, *Tel. 081/252-0069, Email: unibooks@tin.it*

Hotel Reservation Service
• **Europa Alberghi**, *Tel. 081551-8691, Web: www.sea-hotels.com, Email: info@sea-hotels.com.* Reservation service for three star hotels in Naples.

Internet Centers
• **ClicNet - Internet Point**, Via Toledo 393, 1st Floor, *Tel. 081/552-9370. Web: www.clicnet.it*
• **Internet Bar**, Piazza Bellini 74, *Tel. 081/295-237. Webe: www.internetbarnapoli.it*

Laundromats
• **Bolle Blue**, Corso Novarra 62/64, *Cell 335/664-3057*
• **My Beuatiful Laundrette**, Via Montesanto 2, *Tel. 081/542-2162*

Movies in English
• **Cinema Abadir**, (Tuesdays Only), Via Paesiello 35, *Tel. 081/578-1905 or 578-9447*. Showings at 5, 8 and 10pm.

Postal Services
Post offices are open from 8:00am to 2:00pm on weekdays. The two exceptions to this rule are the **main post office** (**Palazzo delle Poste**) at Piazza Matteoti and the office at the Stazione Centrale, both of which are open Monday through Friday from 8:00am to 7:30pm, and Saturdays from 8:00am to noon.

Scooter Rental
• **Rent Sprint**, Via Santa Lucia 36/1, *Tel. 081/764-1333. Website: wwwrentsprint.com*

Tourist Information
• **Naples Tourist Board**, Piazza del Gesu 7/8, *Tel. 081/551-2701;* or Palazzo Reale - Piazza Plebiscito, *Tel. 081/252-5726. Website: www.inaples.it.*
• **Regional Tourist Board**, Central Station, *Tel. 081/206-666;* Mergellina Station, *Tel. 081/761-2102;* or Piazza dei Martiri 58, *Tel. 081/405-311. Website: www.napoli.it*

The Islands

The islands in the bay of Naples, especially **Capri**, are one of the main reason travelers come down this far on the Italian Peninsula. **Procida** and **Ischia** are less developed than the refined and elegant Capri. However, all offer a refuge from the hectic urban expanse of Naples. Hiking is a main activity on all three islands. My favorite of the three by far is Capri, though all have something to offer.

CAPRI
People flock to Capri for a few very simple reason. It is beautiful, gorgeous, and a vacation delight. Yes it has been taken over by tourism but that is because the scenery is stunning, the restaurants are excellent and the hotels world-class.

With foot paths crossing the island, hiking on Capri is a common activity. It can be done from cafe to cafe and town to town, all along footpaths cut into the verdant hillsides. In other words, very sophisticated hiking. No back woods treks here.

Sun bathing and other water sports are also available. This is an island after all. But the favorite past time on Capri is to just "be." Capri is a place to relax and soak up the incredible atmosphere.

Despite the hordes of tourists that descend in the summer, Capri still maintains a quiet pace, and a strong sense of community among the locals abounds. This community spreads a welcoming aura over all visitors. Capri is one of my favorite destinations. Spend a vacation here and you will definitely not be disappointed.

You arrive at the Marina grande by ferry or hydrofoil. From there, by funiculare or bus is the town of **Capri**. This is the center of the island. Further along, is **Anacapri**, nestled in the mountains, a respite from many of the tourists that descend on Capri. You'll need to take a bus to get here.

From Anacapri you can take a **chairlift** to Monte Solaro for a wonderful view of the whole bay. Highly recommended. A great view over the entire island. Many travelers, hike down to Capri from here.

Capri's most famous sight is the **Blue Grotto**. Try to get here first thing in the morning, before the crowds arrive, or you'll find yourself waiting in a boat at the entrance forever. Other sights include the remains of the debauched Roman Emperor **Tiberius' villa**, dating from 27 AD as well as numerous churches and lush gardens to explore.

In the summer the population of Capri increases dramatically, perhaps more than any other island on the globe. Tourists from all over the world, and temporary residents who summer on the island, flock to the stunning vistas, relaxed pace, and great food.

In winter, life reverts to the dreamy way of life that has been so characteristic of Capri over the centuries. So if you want to see a relatively pristine part of paradise unsoiled by rampant tourism, try to visit in the winter months. However, even with the crowds in the summer, you will be charmed and delighted with Capri's beauty.

Arrivals & Departures

By Ferry (traghetto) or Hydrofoil (aliscafo)

Ferries cost half as much and take twice as long. For both, when buying a ticket you need to know which company you want to use so you can get in the proper line. Signs are available which indicate the destinations each company goes to, and when the next boat is leaving, but it is always best to be prepared. Visit the information office in Naples to get an extensive schedule of the times.

Where to Stay

There are many hotels on Capri. Listed below are some the best. If you desire more options, visit Capri's website: *www.capritourism.com*.

1. CERTOSELLA, *Via Tragara 13, 80071 Capri. Tel. 081/837-0713, Fax 081/837-6113. Closed November and Easter. 12 rooms. Single E160. Double E290-460. All credit cards accepted. Breakfast included.* ***

On the way to the Belvedere Tragara in a central but tranquil location. Operated by the proprietor of the restaurant Canzone del Mare listed below, the food here in their small restaurant, for obvious reasons is superb. The accommodations are pleasant and comfortable with simple furnishings. Some rooms have terraces which are a great place on which to relax in the evenings. The bathrooms are of medium size and come with hair dryers. They have an ample swimming pool for your use too. All the amenities of a three star. A great little hotel.

2. QUISISANA, *Via Camerelle 2, 80073 Capri, Tel. 081/837-0788, Fax 081/837-6080. Email: info@quisi.com. Web: www.quisi.com. 150 rooms, 15 suites. All credit cards accepted. Single E200-250; Double E270-540; Suite E510-770. Closed November 1 to March 31.* *****

One of the more famous hotels in the entire world. An ultra-luxurious hotel with an indoor and outdoor swimming pool, health club, tennis courts, sauna, a great restaurant, as well as excellent views of the whole island. Here you'd be staying in the lap of luxury in one of the more famous hotels in the world. The rooms are large and comfortable and have all the amenities you could expect: mini-bar, TV, air conditioning, room service, hairdryers and even a safe for your valuables. If you have the means, this is *the* place to stay. Their restaurant is highly recommended as well.

3. LA RESIDENZA, *Via F Serena 22, 80073 Capri. Tel. 081/837-0833, Fax 081/837-7564. Email: info@hotellaresidenza.com. Web: www.hotellaresidenza.com. 114 rooms. All credit cards accepted. Single E140-160; Double E260-310; Suites E600-800.* ****

The second largest hotel on the island (the Quisisana is larger), you'll find everything you could want for your stay on Capri: a good restaurant with a great view, a pool with scenic views and relaxing garden setting, a hotel bar, location on the sea, clean and comfortable rooms, transport around the island, and more. But if you want the romantic intimacy of a smaller hotel, this is not the place to stay. It's so large that guests can get lost in the crowd. But if you want anonymity for you and your special friend, this is a good choice.

4. SAN MICHELE, *Via G Orlandi 3, 80071 Capri. Tel. 081/837-1427, Fax 081/837-1420. Web: www.sanmichele-capri.com. 100 rooms. Double E140-180; Breakfast extra. All credit cards accepted.* ***

Oh my, what a view (but you have to request it). Located in Anacapri on the edge of a cliff overlooking the water, almost all the rooms have the most spectacular view you could find anywhere. The excellent restaurant and swimming pool share the same scenery. It doesn't have the intimacy of a smaller hotel, but it has worlds of ambiance, character and charm. The rooms are large and comfortable and bathrooms are immaculate.

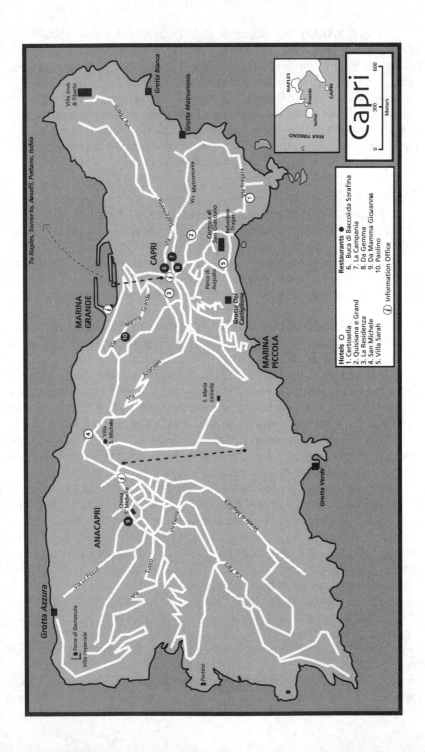

5. VILLA SARAH, *Via Tiberio 3, 80071 Capri. Tel. 081/837-0689, Fax 081/837-7215. Web: www.villasarah.it. Closed from the end of October until Easter. 20 rooms. Single E100-120; Double E140-190. American Express, Mastercard and Visa accepted. Breakfast included.* ***

A villa with a garden located in a tranquil setting away from the bustling crowds along the road that takes you to the Villa Tiberio. The rooms are ample, bright, come with small terraces, are clean and comfortable and are filled with peace and quiet. The bathrooms are also accommodating and come with all necessary amenities. A great place to stay while in Capri.

Where to Eat

6. BUCA DI BACCO DA SERAFINA, *Via Longano 35, Tel. 081/837-0723. Closed Wednesdays and November. All credit cards accepted. Dinner for two E40.*

Small trattoria with an extensive menu. Great atmosphere, off the beaten path, with a small window that has a lovely view. There are many pastas to choose from, as well as meat, fish and pizza. You cannot go wrong eating here.

7. LA CAMPANINA, *Via delle Botteghe 14, Tel. 081/837-0732. Web: www.capannina-capri.com. Closed Wednesdays and November to Easter. All credit cards accepted. Dinner for two E70.*

A fine family run, upscale, but rustic establishment. Near Piazza Umberto where the funiculare stops, here you will get peasant fare for a good price in a great atmosphere. Try their *linguine ai frutti di mare* (with seafood) and their *conniglio "alla tiberiana"* (rabbit stewed with tomatoes and spices).

8. DA GEMMA, *Via Madre Serafina 6, Capri, Tel. 081/837-0461. Web: www.dagemma.com. Closed Mondays and November. All credit cards accepted. Dinner for two E25.*

Many pictures of stars line the walls of the two rooms of great restaurant, one of which is across the small Via Madre Serafina. If there is space in the one with great views, eat there. Even though Gemma is no longer around to run the place, her family continues the tradition of classic Italian food with just enough flair to make them unique and interesting. They are famous for their *spaghetti alle vongole* (with clam sauce) and the *"fritto alla Gemma"* (fried mozzarella and zucchini and other vegetables).

9. DA MAMMA GIOVANNA *(Anacapri) Via Boffe 3/5, Tel. 081/837-2057. Closed Mondays and the ten days after Christmas. All credit cards accepted. Dinner for two E40.*

Located in the heart of Anacapri, this is a small, local *trattoria* that makes great pizzas as well as grilled or oven cooked meats and fish. They have a terrace from which you can watch the night pass as you sip your dry house wine and enjoy the food. A great location in Anacapri. The place to come in this part of the island.

10. **PAOLINO**, *Via Palazzo a Mare 11, Tel. 081/837-6102. Closed Mondays and January 15 to Easter. All credit cards accepted. Dinner for two E60.*

They've got old stoves and other cooking devices supporting the tables, which lends the place a nice down to earth touch that seems to go well with their sky high prices. Try their *ravioli alla caprese* (ravioli with seafood made Capri-style), *spaghetti con pomodoro (with spicy herbed tomatoes)*, or *rucola e gamberi* (pasta with shrimp) for primo. For seconds try any of their seafood on the grill.

Seeing the Sights

To get to the town of Capri after you've made it to the **Marina Grande**, the main harbor on the island, take the funicular (kind of like a trolley rising up the mountain). Once you reach the Piazza Umberto I, you can enjoy the memorable view out onto the Bay of Naples. This is the perfect piazza to have a seat at any one of the cafés and watch the world go by. Granted you'll pay a king's ransom for a coffee but the ambiance and character of the square need to be savored slowly, while seated.

From here you can walk – granted it's a long way – northeast to the **Palace of Tiberius**, the biggest, best preserved Imperial villa on the island. You won't find elaborate mosaic floors or statues in place here, and at first glance the site might seem disappointing, but what makes this place special is the sheer extent of the ruins located in such a superb setting. Built in the first century, the villa was initially 12 stories high but only partial remains of three remain. But the beehive of passageways leading to many small rooms make it evident that this villa functioned as a mini-city, with baths, store rooms and servants' quarters.

The Palace is perched on an imposing hilltop called **Il Salto** (The Leap) from which the Emperor is said to have thrown his enemies (and if you've read any Roman history this is probably true). Open daily 9:00am until 1 hour before sunset. Admission E3.

On the south edge of town is the **Certosa di San Giacomo**, a 14th century Carthusian monastery that was founded in 1371, destroyed in 1553 and rebuilt soon after. It was used as a prison and a hospice in the 1800s and today houses a secondary school and a library. The cloisters and the dark Gothic church are open to the public. The frescoes in the church are interesting to view but those cloisters can be missed, especially the **Museo Deifenbach** with its dark and crusty oil paintings.

From the monastery walk along the Via di Certosa to the **Parco Augusto**. From the terrace here you will find some fine views to the south of the island over the **Marina Piccola** (small harbor) and the **Faraglioni** rock formations. Bring your camera. From here you can follow a road that leads to the Marina Piccola and see the private yachts and fishing boats close up.

My favorite part of the island is the town of **Anacapri**. You get here either by bus or taxi from Capri. Anacapri is more relaxed and down-to-earth as compared to the faster-paced, pretentious nature of Capri. Perched high up on a rocky plateau, its flat-roofed whitewashed buildings are obviously Moorish in style. Here you can find the 18th century **Church of San Michele** (open daily 7:00am–7:00pm) with its sober Baroque design and intricate frescoed floors. Also in Anacapri is the **Villa San Michele**, which is known for its beautiful gardens and vast collection of classical sculpture (open summer 9:00am–6:00pm, winter 10:00am–3:00pm; admission E6). From these gardens are some of the most spectacular views. If you want to go higher, from Anacapri you can walk or take a chair lift up to **Monte Solaro**, which has amazing views over all of Capri. You catch the chair lift from Piazza Vittoria and the trip up here is equally as spectacular as the trip to the Blue Grotto below. Here you will find one of the world's premier picnic spots, so come prepared. But bring a sweater or jacket even on sunny days since the wind tends to cool things down slightly.

Finally, onto the famous **Grotta Azzura** or **Blue Grotto**. You can walk or take a bus down the Via Grotta Azzura from Anacapri. once at the bottom you can hire a boat to take you into the grotto. Or you can come from Marina Grande by motorboat with a number of other people, then transfer to rowboats to enter the grotto. You will have to sit on the floor of the row-boat as the captain (on his back) leads the boat in by pulling hand over hand on a length of fixed chain. The silver-blue light inside is close to indescribable. Suffice to say it is magnificent. The color of the water is caused by refraction of light entering the grotto beneath the surface. Don't foolishly deny yourself the joy of this excursion for fear of being labeled a tourist. The Blue Grotto really is worth seeing no matter how cheesy it appears. Open 24 hours. Boat trips from Marina Grande go from 9:00am–6:00pm. Cost E5.

Walking is by far the best way of getting about the island, but horse-drawn carriages, buses and taxis operate, linking Capri and Anacapri. The island seems bigger than its ten square kilometers suggest, due to an undulating landscape resting upon sheer limestone cliffs. If you are walking during the summer months, remember to rest frequently because the hills are very steep, especially in Capri. Anacapri is easier to walk since it rests on a plateau. Also remember to bring along some water to prevent dehydration even in the cooler, off-season months.

SORRENTO

This is a jewel on the Bay of Naples. A town that caters to tourists, here you can find great restaurants, excellent hotels, world class shops, all in the framework of a small Italian town. This is also an ideal jumping-off point for day trips to the islands in the bay, Pompeii and Herculaneum, the Amalfi Coast and even to venture into Naples. Travelers who chafe at the chaos of Naples stay here and commute in during the day to enjoy the museums and other sights there. This allows them to escape back to Sorrento for a restful evening. In the summer months, this town is hopping.

Sights to see include the churches of **San Francesco**, **San Anonino** and the local **Cattedrale**. The **Museo Correale** is not that extensive, but it can be an educational diversion from lazing about at the beach or by the pool. To get a head start on what there is to do in Sorrento, check out their official website, *www.sorrentoinfo.com*.

Arrivals & Departures

You can get to Sorrento by train from Naples easily in around an hour. There are also ferries and hydrofoil from Capri, as well as Naples.

Where to Stay

1. BELLEVUE SYRENE, *Piazza della Vittoria 5, Tel/081/878-1024, Fax 081/878-3963. Email: info@bellevue.it. Web: www.bellevue.it. Single E190-235; Double E230-300; Suite E320-360. All credit cards accepted. Breakfast included.* ****

In a tranquil location overlooking the sea, they also have a nice flowered garden where you can rest peacefully. There is an elevator that takes you from the garden down to the sea. The rooms either overlook the sea or the garden. Sea views cost a little more. But all rooms are spacious and comfortable and have all necessary four star amenities. A sister hotel to the Sorrento Palace, which is another great hotel in the area, guests of the Bellevue can use the pool and tennis facilities at that location.

2. DEL CORSO, *Corso Italia 134, Tel. 081/807-1016. Fax 081/807-3157. Email: info@hoteldelcorso.com. Web: www.hoteldelcorso.com. 25 rooms. Single E90; Double E125. Breakfast included. All credit cards accepted.* ***

If you're coming to Sorrento on a budget this is the best place to stay. Located on the second floor of an 18th century building on a main road, close by everything, and within walking distance to the train station, this hotel may not be luxurious but it is comfortable and accommodating. They also have a sun deck on the roof and a garden patio where breakfast is served.

3. EXCELSIOR VITTORIA, *Piazza Tasso 34, Tel. 081/807-1044, Fax 081/877-1206. Email: exvitt@exvitt.it. Web: www.exvitt.it. 106 rooms. Single E290; Double E330-470; Suite E600-2,000. All credit cards accepted. Breakfast included.* *****

By far the best hotel in Sorrento. Located in a beautiful villa from the 18th century, this place is an elegant and refined hotel that has hosted many a famous person over the years. The rooms are all spacious and comfortable with beautiful views, antique furnishings, and bathrooms done up in marble. The common areas are stunning and all face the sea. There is a park and pool

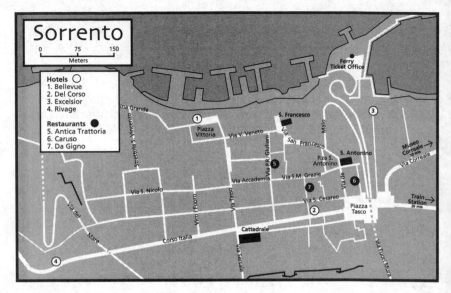

on the hotel grounds where you can relax for hours. And don't forget their famous terrace overlooking the Bay of Naples.

4. RIVAGE, *Via Capo 11, Tel 081/878-1873, Fax 081/807-1253. Email: info@hotelrivage.com. Web: www.hotelrivage.com. 48 rooms. Single E95; Double E100-130. ****

A recently built hotel with every conceivable modern amenity including AC and TV, roof garden, terrace with panoramic views, and sun deck. A little walk from the center of town, just off of a main road, the rooms of the Rivage descends down the cliffs. All of which are spacious and nicely furnished. Your stay here will definitely be comfortable. If you are looking for charm and ambiance, you'll need to look elsewhere. But in terms of the price/quality ratio, the Rivage is a good three star.

Where to Eat

5. ANTICA TRATTORIA, *Via P. Reginaldo Giuliani 33, Tel. 081/807-1082. Web: www.lanticatrattoria.com Closed Mondays (not in summer) and from January to February. All credit cards accepted. Dinner for two E60.*

A refined local place with Sorrentine ceramics strewn around and communal tables in some locations. An ample menu, filled with all sorts of local flavor, especially seafood and pasta. You cannot go wrong by having a meal here. And you'll find you want to come back again and again. Next to the famous gelateria Davide.

6. CARUSO, *Via S. Antonino 12, Tel 081/807-3156. Web: www.ristorantemuseocaruso.com. Closed Mondays and in January. All credit cards accepted. Dinner for two E75.*

Many pictures of past and present luminaries dot the walls attesting to the popularity of this restaurant. Specializing in seafood and other local favorites, and all thrown together with flair. Atmospheric and tranquil, you will have a lovely meal surrounded by others who share your taste for culinary excellence.

7. DA GIGNO, *Via degli Archi 15, Tel. 081/878-1927. Closed Tuesdays. All credit cards accepted. Dinner for two E50.*

Sample some real Neopolitan pizza, great pasta dishes, and all sorts of entrees in a boisterous local atmosphere. A wonderful alternative to many of the touristy and upscale places in town. This is where the locals come. Down a series of side streets, somewhat hard to find, but it's worth the journey.

Practical Information
• **Laundry**, Corso Italia 30, *Tel. 081/878-1185.*
• **Scooter Rental**, Corso Italia 210/a, *Tel. 081/878-1386.*

The Amalfi Coast

The steep slopes and rugged beauty of the **Amalfi Coast** have enchanted visitors for centuries. **Mount Vesuvius** reigns majestically in the distance, dominating the scenery as it once dictated the lives of the area's inhabitants with its eruptions. Dotted with little hillside towns, the serpentine road connecting the towns is usually bumper to bumper traffic. In the off-season the traffic decreases considerably, but then so does the temperature, and bathing in the sea is one of the attractions of this coastline.

The narrow, two-lane road that joins Vietri (near Salerno) to Positano is dug almost entirely out of the rock, and curves maniacally. Built in the 1800s by the King of Naples, Ferdinando di Borbone, this road follows the lay of the mountains on one side and the stunning curves of the sea on the other. However, every turn offers coastal panoramic views of unparalleled proportions – which means that you will be tempted to take your eyes off the road. An error in judgment that is not advised. You'll understand what I mean when you see the tiny size4 of the road and the immense buses that traverse it. Seeing these buses jockey for position generates immense respect for their abilities. So if you want to admire the vistas, have someone else drive.

The entire coastline is filled with high class hotels, excellent restaurants, countless nightlife options, ancient medieval streets and passageways, cultural sights and fun-loving locals. Once you come here, the Amalfi Coast is a place you will want to return to time and time again.

The place to find out about festivals, restaurants, shops, ferry information and more is thre Amalfi Coast website: *www.amalfi.it.* A great resource to help plan your trip.

SALERNO

Just outside of the Amalfi Coast is the port town of **Salerno**, which has an old town with winding medieval streets and steps that merits a look. An amazingly livable town, with an extensive pedestrian street (Corso Vittorio emanuelle II) and a promenade to match along the sea. Near the old town, off of the Piazza Amendola, are the public gardens, on the west side of which is the **Teatro Verdi** where many operas are performed. In the middle of the maze of the old town is the **Duomo** built in 1086, restored in 1768 and then in 1945 after allied bombing took its toll on the facade. Inside a flight of steps leads up to an atrium that has 28 ancient columns and 14 sarcophagi purloined from Paestum. The magnificent bronze doors were cast in Constantinople in 1099.

A little ways north in the Largo Plebiscito is the **Museo Duomo** that contains many relics from Salerno's past. West along Via San Michele is the **Museo Provinciale** with many antiquities, including a huge bronze head of Apollo cast in the 1st century BCE.

Salerno is mainly a jumping-off point to the Amalfi Coast, and visitors use it to rest before embarking on the last leg of their journey to Ravello, Amalfi or Positano. However, when they do stay here, and if they take the time to notice, most people marvel at how much charm Salerno has – much of which is due to the fact that not many tourists frequent this sleepy little town. Which makes Salerno, in my mind, a perfect introduction to real Italian life. Other places have been overwhelmed with tourists. Not so Salerno. Come here for a respite from all that. Then go onto your tourist destinations.

Arrivals & Departures

You can get to Salerno by train from Naples in under an hour, or you can take the Autostrada A3 from Naples.

Vietri

About five kilometers from Salerno (take buses 1, 4 or 9 from the train station) is the ceramic capital of the Amalfi Coast, Vietri. This is a nondescript small town with an abundance of ceramic stores, all of which contain many appealing and intricate designs. Some webnsites to visit to see the ceramics offered include: *www.daedalus.it*, *www.lemaioliche.com*, and *www.santoriellorarte.it*. If you're on the Amalfi Coast, appreciate ceramics, and want a keepsake to bring back with you, come to Vietri.

☙

Where to Stay

1. **DELLE PALME**, *Lungomare Trieste 1, 84100 Salerno. Tel. 089/225-222, Fax 089/237-571. Web: www.jollyhotels.it. 104 rooms. Single E110-125; Double E125-145. Credit cards accepted. Breakfast included. Full board E95-148.* ★★★★

The best hotel in Salerno, is part of the leading chain of Italian hotels. Located at the end of the Lungomare along a busy thoroughfare. The rooms have pastel colored curtains to contrast with the white furniture. The bathrooms are ample with large windows and every modern convenience. All Jolly hotels have professional service, as well as North American-style comforts.

2. **PLAZA**, *Piazza Via Veneto 42, 84100 Salerno. Tel. 089/224-477, Fax 089/237-311. Email: info@plazasalerno.it. Web: www.plazasalerno.it. 42 rooms. Single E70; Double E95. Credit cards accepted. Breakfast included.* ★★★

A great three star ideally located across from the train station and 100 meters from the ferry docks. Also located at the beginning of the walking street area (*zona pedonale*) where you can head out for your evening stroll. This is the best three star in town, and that statement has a lot to do with the presence of a Welsh/Italian manager, Francis/Francesco Policastro, whose fluency in English is a welcome respite. The common areas are pleasant with plants and flowers as adornment. The rooms are simple and comfortable with modern furnishings and come with satellite TV, air conditioning and minibar. The best choice for a stop over in Salerno.

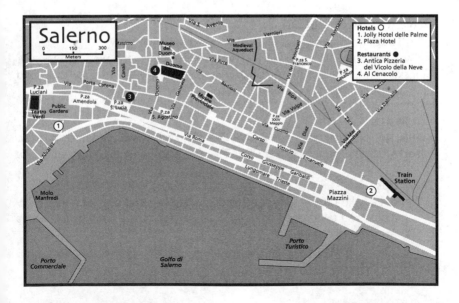

Where to Eat

3. ANTICA PIZZERIA DEL VICOLO DELLA NEVE, *Vicolo della Neve 24, Tel. 089/225-705. Closed Wednesdays, two weeks in August and Christmas. Open only in the evenings. American Express accepted. Dinner for two E35.*

What an amazing place to eat. In one of the areas with the most character and ambiance in the city, this rustic little locale is an ideal trattoria in which to have typical Salernese food at great prices. Everything except for the pizzas and calzones is set up semi-buffet style. The pasta and fagioli (which is awesome), lasagna, and assorted vegetables are on display for your to choose from. Once you tell your waiter what you want, they bake your choices and serve them up promptly. Incredibly popular. If you do not get here early, expect a wait.

4. AL CENACOLO, *Piazza Alfano I 4/6, Tel. 089/238-818. Closed Sunday evenings and Mondays, as well as August 8-22 and December 25 to February 1. Credit cards accepted. Dinner for two E45.*

Basically right in front of the Duomo, this local favorite owned by Pietro Rispoli is a sure thing when it comes to finding fine food and good atmosphere. They have a fixed menu for E23 that comes with antipasto, first, second, and dessert. If you want to order on your own try some of these dishes: *alici marinate* (marinated anchovies), *gamberi in salsa di limone e zucchine* (shrimp in a lemon/zucchini sauce), *ravioli di pesce con vongole e zucchine* (fish stuffed ravioli in a clam/zucchini sauce), or *cannelloni con le melanzane* (cannelloni with eggplant). For seconds they grill a variety of meats and fish. For dessert, their *mousse al cioccolato* (chocolate mousse) is simply sinful. But if you go with the fixed price menu you will be served some great food too.

Practical Information

Bike Tours
• *www.anywherebikeclub.it.* If you are a serious biker, and want to test your skills on the hills of the Amalfi Coast, contact this web site for tours and suggestions.

Car Rental
• **Avis**, Via M. Clemente 18, *Tel/Fax 089/255-092. Web: www.avisautonoleggio.it.*
• **Hertz**, Piazza V. Veneto 38, *Tel. 089/222-106. Web: www.hertzsorrento.com.*

Day Trips
• **Pompei** - Take bus #4 from in front of the train station. Leaves ever 25 minutes and takes one and half hours. An express bus, # 5 or 50, leaves every hour and takes only 50 minutes.

Scooter Rental
• **Tropea**, Piazza V. Veneto 36, *Tel/089/224-673. Fax 089/232-924.*

Driving on the Amalfi Coast

Your heart will be in your throat most of the time when you traverse the small winding road of the Amalfi Coast. The guard rail seems designed for midgets, as does the road itself, but the vehicles in use are regular sized cars and buses.

To drive on the Amalfi Coast, get rid of any competitive attitudes you may have. This is a road designed to foster cooperation, not a winner take all attitude. Here you do not thrust yourself through life, as you might at home. It could spell your demise, as well as that of others. On the Amalfi Coast you need to be patient, and anticipate what others need to do. Giving way is par for the course. Demanding to go first is not. If you can be humble and adapt to others while driving, and you have a strong heart, give it a try. Otherwise, take the bus.

POSITANO

Perched up hillsides in a tangle of houses, alleys, stairways and tourist oriented shops, overlooking a series of pristine beaches, the town of **Positano** has been a part of this beautiful landscape for almost a thousand years. When Emperor Tiberius moved to Capri to escape the intrigue and serious threat of poisoning in Rome, he had his flour brought in from a mill in Positano, one that is still working today. In the 10th century, as a sea power and active trade competitor with Venice, Pisa and Genoa, Positano was one of the most important commercial centers on the Italian peninsula. In the 16th and 17th centuries, filled with the wealth from its trading, was when many of the beautiful Baroque homes scattered on the hills of the town were built.

Because of its timeless beauty, Positano has been the playground of the rich and famous for centuries. Writers, musicians, nobles, aristocrats – all have come here to bathe in the azure waters and relax in the lush green hillsides. Today it is no different. Filled with excellent restaurants, world class hotels, and all manner of water sports, Positano is a perfect holiday destination.

Positano's official web page: *http://positano.starnetwork.it.*

Arrivals & Departures

You can get to Positano by car via the coast road around the tip of the peninsula or the cross peninsula road. You can also come by SITA bus from Salerno by way of Amalfi, where you will have to change buses. You can also catch a ferry from Capri or Salerno during the high season.

Where to Stay

1. **CASA ALBERTINA**, *Via della Tavolozza 3, 84017 Positano. Tel. 089/875-143, Fax 089/811-540. Email: alcaal@starnet.it. Web: www.casalbertina.it. 20 rooms. Single E90-125; Double E125-155. Credit cards accepted. Breakfast included. Full board E60-85.* ***

The hotel is located in quite a tranquil area, but it is also close to the beach, only some 300 steps down to the water. If you don't want to walk back up they have a small shuttle bus to carry you home after your swim. There is a terrace and a solarium for your relaxing pleasure. The rooms are large and well isolated from each other and come in a blue or red color scheme, some of which have nice views over the water. The bathrooms are a little tight but they do have all the modern amenities. Breakfast is a memorable experience filled with meats, cheeses, breads and more, which you can enjoy either in your room or on their little terrace.

The restaurant is superb, with food prepared by Aunt Albertina of the family Cinque that runs the hotel. A true family affair designed to make your stay as relaxing as possible.

2. **POSEIDON**, *Via Pasitea 148, 84071 Positano. Tel. 089/811-111, Fax 089/875-833. Email: poseidon@starnet.it. Web: www.starnet.it/poseidon. 48 rooms. Double E190-280. Credit cards accepted. Breakfast included.* ****

Located in the heart of Positano and run by the Aono family, this a fine four star hotel. Each room has a nice view from their little balconies where you can have your breakfast served. The furnishings are all antique but still comfortable. The restaurant in the summer is located in a quiet garden setting, where the solarium and pool are also located. You also have massage, exercise rooms and baby-sitting service at your disposal.

3. **LE SIRENUSE**, *Via Cristoforo Colombo 30, 84071 Positano. Tel. 089/875-066, Fax 089/811-798. Email: info@sirenuse.it. Web: www.sirenuse.it. 60 rooms. Single E260-690. Double E290-7500. Credit cards accepted. Breakfast included. Full board E180-280.* *****

Definitely the place to stay in Positano – everything about this hotel is beautiful. Nothing overly fancy, nothing too ostentatious, just simply radiant. The rooms are furnished with exquisite taste. The bathrooms are complete with every conceivable comfort. The breakfast buffet is so ample as to dissuade most from lunch. There is a stunningly beautiful pool at your disposal, a sauna, and a small boat to ferry you along the coast. The service here is extremely attentive. The prices have such a wide range because each room comes in a standard, superior and deluxe variety. You need to request which one you want.

Their restaurant, La Sponda, is one of the best, if not the best, in the city. Expensive, yes, but when the excellent Neapolitan cuisine is combined with the great views from the terrace, the price is irrelevant. All the food they make here is great, but I believe the chef concocts the best *spaghetti alle vongole* (with spicy clam sauce) in Positano.

Where to Eat

4. **DA ADOLFO**, *Locanda Laurito, Tel. 089/875-022. Closed November 1 to May 1. Open only for lunch. No credit cards accepted. Meal for two E30.*

To get here you need to catch a boat from the beach at Positano. Located in a truly romantic and isolated setting but not too far from town. A large place, it seats about 100, but the best place to eat is on their extensive balcony overlooking the water. They are usually packed, which is why they only have to be open for lunch and only about half the year. Try some of their flavorful *spaghetti alle vongole* (with clam sauce), *agli zucchine* (with a zucchini sauce), *totani con le patate* (cuttlefish with potatoes), *la parmigiana di melanzane* (eggplant parmesan), or any of their fabulously grilled fish.

5. **LA CAMBUSA**, *Piazza A. Vespucci 4, Tel. 089/875-432. Closed November 11 to December 20. Credit cards accepted. Dinner for two E70.*

Be prepared to be wined and dined in splendor. The perfect place to dine is on the terrace facing the beach. If you don't want to order from the menu they have a daily buffet that features many different plates. They are known for their great seafood, like *insalata di pesce* (seafood salad) or *di gamberetti* (small prawns). For *primo* try their *linguini con scampi* (with shrimp), *con frutti*

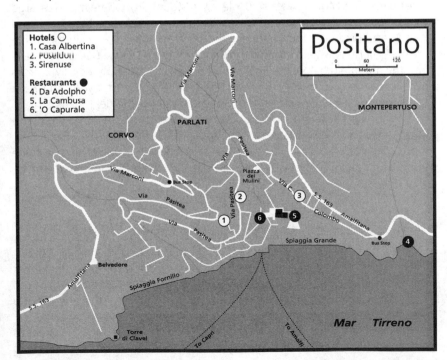

di mare (with seafood), or the *zuppa di pesce* (seafood soup). For seconds you must try any of their grilled fish, served with roasted potatoes. A little expensive, but the food and ambiance are worth the price.

6. 'O CAPURALE, *Via Regina Giovanna 12, Tel. 089/811-188. Closed Tuesdays (not in summer) and January. Credit cards accepted. Dinner for two E35.*

This place has been in the family for over one hundred years and is part of the life of Positano. You can still find some of the older residents of the town playing cards at some of the tables. People come here for the friendly local atmosphere as well as the fine food. Start off with some *linguine all'astice* (with lobster), *agli scampi* (with shrimp), or *bucatini alla 'caporalessa'* (with mozzarella, tomatoes, eggplant, olives, and capers); then move onto *zuppa di pesce* (seafood soup) and *pesce al aqua pazza* (boiled fish).

Seeing the Sights

Positano snakes its way up from the **Harbor** (Marina Grande) where ferries dock coming from Sorrento, Capri and Naples. Along the beach by the harbor are many chic boutiques that you can find in any holiday resort. For more historic sights, try the **Santa Maria Assunta**, a 12th century church that dominates the Positano hillside. The ancient floor is a Byzantine mosaic and on the main altar is a relief of the Madonna and Child in black marble. An hour hike up the hill is **Montepertuso** (Hole in the Mountain), where there is a large cliff pierced by a hole. Legend has it that the devil challenged the Madonna to make a hole in the mountain. He failed in ten attempts, while the Virgin Mother's finger easily created the hole and at the same time pushed the devil into the mountain below the hole. Anyway, enough local mythology ... from here your vantage point is perfect and the little village quaint. If you don't want to walk you can catch a bus at the harbor piazza (Piazza dei Mulini).

A short hike away from Montepertuso is **Nocelle**, another tiny village with great views and a quiet unassuming life. If you are here on New Year's Day, more specifically at dawn of the New Year, you will stumble onto a huge bonfire and banquet that welcomes in, through copious amounts of revelry, all the possibilities that the new year can bring.

AMALFI

What an amazingly beautiful town. Clinging to the rocky coast of the Sorrento peninsula is one of the most picturesque little towns in Italy, **Amalfi**. It is primarily the slow pace, friendly locals and engaging colors of Amalfi that attracts visitors. Set on a backdrop of blue, the pastel colored houses of red and yellow, and the striped fishing boats, fill the canvas of the town. If you want to experience an amazing place, come to Amalfi.

Legend has it that the town was established by Constantine the Great as a respite from the chaos of Rome. By the Middle Ages it had a population of

50,000, but today it is only around 7,000 (when all the tourists leave). During the 16th and 17th centuries it was joined with the other little towns on the Amalfi Coast in competition with the other seafaring states of Venice, Genoa and Pisa.

As a tourist resort, Amalfi offers everything you could need to make your stay pleasant: fine restaurants, wonderful hotels, nightlife, shopping, water sports and sightseeing.

Arrivals & Departures

You can get to Amalfi by car via the coast road or the cross peninsula road. If you go by bus from Naples, catch a SITA bus from Piazza Municipio (*Tel. 081/ 55-22-176*). From Salerno you catch the bus along Via SS Martiri Salernitani (*Tel. 089/22-66-04*). You can also get here by ferry from Sorrento, Capri or Naples.

Where to Stay

1. LA BUSSOLA, *Lungomare dei Cavalieri 16, 84011 Amalfi. Tel. 089/ 871-533, Fax 089/871-369. Email: labussola@amalficoast.it. Web: www.labussolahotel.it. 63 rooms. Single E65-75; Double E100-130. Credit cards accepted. Breakfast included.* ***

La Bussola is strategically placed directly on the walkway along the sea, where they have a private beach. This hotel is located in an old mill and a pasta factory and has been in the hotel business since 1962. The rooms are well decorated and all have balconies. The bathrooms are normal with all necessary modern conveniences. The restaurant is large and has a nice view of the water. On the top floor is a quiet roof garden where you can relax soaking up the wonderful views over the water and the town. A fine three star hotel. A great place to stay in Amalfi.

2. LUNA CONVENTO, *Via Comite 33, 84011 Amalfi. Tel. 089/871-002, Fax 089/871-333. Email: luna@amalficoast.it. Web: www.lunahotel.it. 45 rooms. Single E100-130; Double E125-170. Credit cards accepted. Breakfast included. Full board E90-105.* ****

Located a little ways up from the town. The entry is on the road and the reception on the second floor in a superb inner courtyard. Situated in a convent founded by St. Francis of Assisi in 1222, this place is awash with charm. The library is the old cloisters where you can enjoy a quiet read amongst the white columns and archways. There are two restaurants to choose from, each with its own magnificent view of the water and the hotel's private beach area. There is also an outdoor pool in a garden setting to enjoy. The rooms are large and all furnished differently with pieces made by local artisans, and each has its own little terrace with a view of the water.

There are fifteen internal cells turned into rooms that do not have a view. The bathrooms were modernized in 1994 so they have all modern amenities. The staff is professional and courteous. A wonderful place to stay in Amalfi.

Where to Eat

3. BARRACCA, *Piazza dei Doggi, Tel. 089/871-285. Closed Wednesdays (not from June 15 to September 15) and January 15 to February 15. Credit cards accepted. Dinner for two E45.*

Located in small piazza, here you can find classic seafood cooking prepared with attention and served perfectly. You must try the *spaghetti alle vongole* (with a spicy clam sauce with some tomatoes added for color), *risotto alla pescatore* (fisherman's rice) and for the main course the succulent *gamberini e calamari alla griglia* (grilled shrimp and octopus) or any of the grilled fish they serve. For an after-dinner drink sample one of their home made aromatic liqueurs.

4. LA CARAVELLA, *Via Matteo Camera 12, Tel. 089/871-029. Web: www.ristorantelacaravella.it. Closed Wednesdays (not in the summer) and November. Credit cards accepted. Dinner for two E75.*

Franco Di Pino opened this place back in 1959 and now his wife concocts local specialties in the kitchen. She also makes all the pasta and desserts herself. Fish is the staple of this menu, whether in the pasta, grilled, or fried.

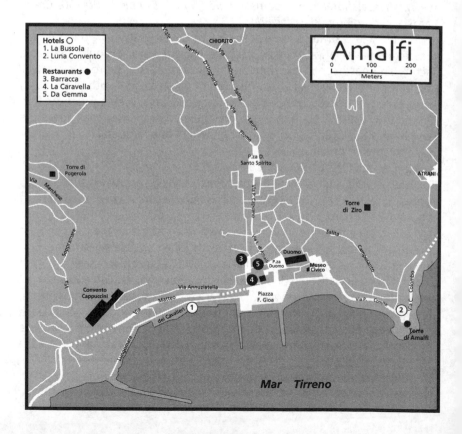

The atmosphere is relaxing and comfortable despite the presence of a main road nearby. A little pricey but worth the expense.

5. DA GEMMA, *Via Fra' Gerardo Sasso 10, Tel. 089/871-345. Closed Wednesdays (not in the summer) and Jan 15 to Feb 15. Credit cards accepted. Dinner for two E55.*

This place represents the best of the local, traditional cuisine in Amalfi. Their *antipasto di mare* (seafood appetizer), *zuppa di pesce* (seafood soup), *linguine all'aragosta* (with lobster sauce), *spaghetti alla cozze* (with mussels), *spaghetti ai frutti di mare* (with mixed seafood) or the *penne alla Genovese* (macaroni-like noodles with a pesto sauce of olive oil, basil and garlic) are all fantastic. And of course their fish, whether boiled, fried or grilled is all fresh and flavorful. Their terrace is a wonderful place to enjoy your meal. For the most part their wine list contains only whites, but that is sensible since they serve mainly fish.

Seeing the Sights

Some of the sights you can see are the **Duomo of Sant'Andrea** built in the Lombard Romanesque style in 1203. Its fine portico with pointed arches was totally rebuilt in 1865. On the west side is a bronze door that was cast in Constinantinople in 1066. In the crypt you will find the remains of the Apostle, Saint Andrew. How they verify these things I will never know. I guess you have to rely on faith?

Near the Duomo is the tiny **Museo Civico** that does its best to offer a history of the town. If you have nothing else to do you may want to try here. High above the town, reachable by a steady hike, is the **Capuccinni Monastery** that offers fine views of the city. Now a hotel, some areas will be off limits to visitors who are not guests of the hotel.

A 15-minute boat ride away is the **Grotta di Amalfi**, an ancient stalactite cave on the coast. The boat ride offers fine vistas, so don't forget your camera. One kilometer away along the coast road is the tiny little village of Atrani, picturesquely sitting along the mouth of a rocky gorge. In the main piazza is the 10th century **church of San Salvatore**, complete with Byzantine bronze doors cast in Constinantinople in 1087.

RAVELLO

Come to Ravello. Drop what you are doing right now. Book a flight, take the train to Salerno, catch the ferry to Amalfi, hop on a local bus, and come up to the amazing little hillside town. What are you waiting for? Come on!

Come here to savor the stillness. Immerse yourself in the richness of life that Ravello offers. Witness the panoramic views that will set your soul free. Come to Ravello but once, and it will remain in your heart forever.

About five kilometers up the hill from Amalfi, **Ravello** is one of the most enchanting spots in the world. Perched on a 350-foot high cliff overlooking the azure sea of the Amalfi Coast, Ravello has preserved its historical monuments through the ages and incorporated them into everyday life. A stunning place to visit or live. As literary luminary Gore Vidal can attest to, since he has made Ravello his home for many decades.

For more information on Ravello, visit their website at *www.ravello.it/ aziendaturismo.*

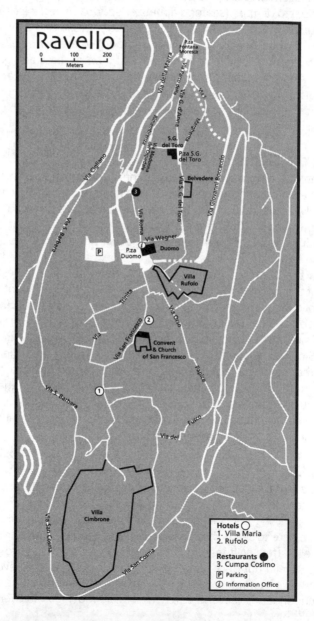

Arrivals & Departures

You can get to Ravello by car via the coast road or the cross peninsula road. If you go by bus from Naples, catch a SITA bus from Piazza Municipio *(Tel. 081/55-22-176)*. From Salerno, catch the bus along Via SS Martiri Salernitani *(Tel. 089/22-66-04)*.

From Amalfi, buses leave from Piazza Flavio Gioia *(Tel. 089/87-10-09)*.

Where to Stay

1. VILLA MARIA, *Via Santa Chiara 2, 84010 Ravello. Tel. 089/857-255, Fax 089/857-071. Email: villamaria@villamaria.it. Web: www.villamaria.it. 18 rooms. Single E150-180; Double E180-220. Credit cards accepted. Breakfast included. Full board E53-97.* ****

This is a recently promoted four star that well deserves the rating. They have a heated pool, a garden terrace area for relaxing, rooms filled with antique furnishings, bathrooms with every modern convenience, beautifulbalconies (Room Number 3's is huge), professional service, and a relaxing atmosphere like a bed and breakfast. An ideal spot for your stay in Ravello. Highly recommended.

2. RUFOLO, *Via S. Francesco 1, Tel. 089/857-133. Fax 089/857935. Web: www.hotelrufolo.it. Double E190-285.* ****

A wonderful four star with every imaginable amenity including incredible views, a large pool, gardens, patios and professional service. This places offers peace and serenity that matches that of the town, and is an ideal choice for an unforgettable stay in Ravello. The views from the restaurant terrace is stunning.

Where to Eat

3. CUMPA COSIMO, *Via Roma 44, Tel. 089/857-156. Closed Mondays (not in Spring and Summer). Credit cards accepted. Dinner for two E40.*

A great little *trattoria*. It comes close to being my favorite in all of Italy. On the walls are photographs of the many personalities who have enjoyed the simple local cooking and the hospitality of the Bottone family. For *primo* try any of their great pastas. For seconds the *agnello, salsicce* and other grilled meats (lamb, sausage, etc., all supplied by the butcher shop run by the same family) are fantastic. You should also try the fresh fish caught daily right in the Bay. For dessert you might want to try some of their *torte* (cakes) and *sorbetti* (Italian ices) made from locally grown oranges.

Seeing the Sights

One of the most important monuments is the **Cathedral**, founded in 1086. Here you can admire the Byzantine mosaic work on the pulpit, the bronze doors, and the civic museum located in the crypt. **Villa Rufolo** is another sight to behold, especially when the views are complimented with the many music festivals they offer. The grand daddy of them all is the **Ravello Music Festival**, which usually begins in July each year. Visit the following two websites to see the musical offerings available and plan your trip accordingly: *www.ravelloarts.org* or *www.ravello.info*.

The **Villa Cimbrone** also contains lush gardens and is known for its breathtaking views, which have been described by many as the best in the world. Other sights to see while in Ravello are: the church of **San Giovanni del Toro** with its mosaic pulpit; the **Villa Episcopio** where King Vittorio Emanuele abdicated the throne; the cloister of the 13th century **convent of St. Francesco** with its amazing library; and the scenic **Piazza Fontana Moresca**.

Southern Italian Living

If you are looking for an authentic Italian adventure, surrounded by rustic countryside and pristine beaches, while residing in a villa filled with all amenities, come to **Capo Vaticano**. Peace and quiet is the norm here, but you also have access, either by car, train, or ferry, to the surrounding area. Down in the toe of Italy's boot, a little over an hour away from Sicily, at Capo Vaticano you can rent one of four villas, while also taking advantage of a beautiful garden of figs, grapes, tomatoes, eggplants, peppers, sweet red onions, salad, beans and many different herbs. Though remote, Capo Vaticano is accessible by plane, with flights occurring daily from London to Lamezia airport.

Call *0963/663-844* or visit *www.capovaticanovillas.com*.

Chapter 18

GENOA, THE ITALIAN RIVIERA, & THE CINQUE TERRE

The seaside splendor of the Ligurean coast is centered around the port city of Genoa. Nearby are some of the most unique places in all of Europe, including the **Cinque Terre**, five wonderful little hill towns perched on cliffs overlooking the water. These relics from the past have been popular for decades with European tourists. Come to the Cinque Terre for a scenic and picturesque experience unparalleled anywhere else in the world. Other options on the Ligurean Coast include the popular resort town/fishing village of **Portofino** in the Golfo di Tigullio as well as towns such as **San Remo** on the **Italian Riviera**. Whatever your desire, you can find it along Italy's Ligurean Coast.

GENOA

Genoa (*Genova*) is a vibrant port city that is known for its excellent restaurants serving the omnipresent pesto sauce, as well as fresh and tasty seafood concoctions. Genoa is still quite walkable. The old town is completely closed off to traffic, and with it's winding Medieval streets it is a relaxing place to walk ... during the day. At night it is somewhat sketchy.

Noted for its medieval, Renaissance, Baroque, and Gothic architecture, Genoa is rich in history. Hundreds of years ago, Venice used to be its main shipping rival, but when that city's trade with the Orient dwindled as result of the Portuguese discovery of a way around Africa in the early 1500s CE, focus shifted westward to the Atlantic, and Genoa's location on the west coast of Italy became a great advantage.

Genoa's prominence as shipping center really got its start during the Crusades (between 800 and 1300 CE). Young knights and their entourages needed convenient locations from which to begin their voyages of salvation, and Genoa was perfectly situated. During that time the city began to develop colonies in Spain and North Africa conquered from the Saracens; and Genovese trading posts and fortresses were established in the eastern Mediterranean and along the Black Sea.

Bombing of the city in World War II damaged both the harbor and industrial plants, but the old city remains today as if transfixed in time, with its winding, narrow streets.

Genoa's Environs

Once you've seen the quaint old world charm of Genoa, it'll be time to really see some sides of Italy not many people experience. Our first stop will be the **Staglieno Cemetery**, which is a veritable city of the dead covering 160 hectares and so large that it even has its own bus system.

You'll find miniature cathedrals, Romanesque chapels, Egyptian temples, *palazzi*, statues, and more. It's not morbid or macabre but a series of monuments erected to celebrate life. You are helping to remember these people by appreciating the stone images left behind to memorialize them. I'm confident all members of the family will enjoy visiting here.

Next, we'll take a train or ferry down to the **Cinque Terre** ("the five lands") that are comfortably removed from both automobile and train access. Each are connected to the other by a small hiking path, which is the main form of transport. These fishing and farming towns, because of their setting, are one of Italy's hidden treasures. What you'll find here is peace, tranquility, great food, wonderful people, beautiful scenery, and memories for a lifetime.

Other highlights in the Genoa area include the postcard-perfect seaside village of **Portofino** and other wonderful seaside towns in the **Golfo di Tigullio** and **Italian Riviera**.

Arrivals & Departures

The best and quickest way to get in and out of Genoa is by train. The city's two main train stations are **Stazione Porta Principe** and **Stazione Brignole**. Porta Principe, not too far from the *centro storico* is the main station.

Getting Around Town
By Bus

The only time you'll really ever need to use the bus is if you want to visit the Staglieno Cemetery. Other than that, all the sights and local flavor are

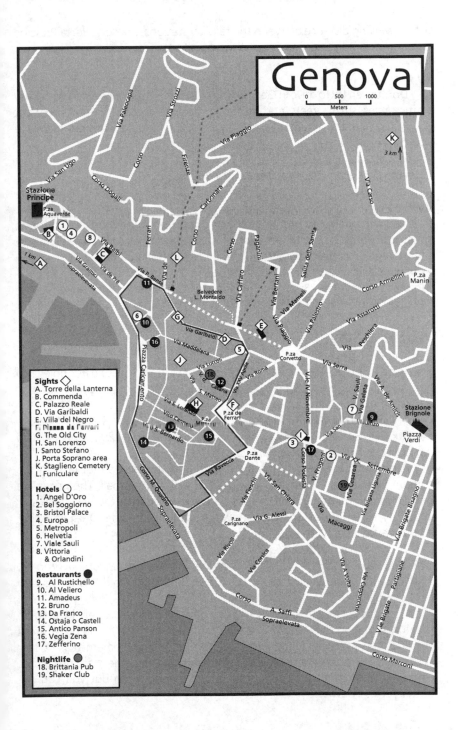

Genova

0 500 1000
Meters

3 km

Sights ◇
A. Torre della Lanterna
B. Commenda
C. Palazzo Reale
D. Via Garibaldi
E. Villa del Negro
F. Piazza de Ferrari
G. The Old City
H. San Lorenzo
I. Santo Stefano
J. Porta Soprano area
K. Staglieno Cemetery
L. Funiculare

Hotels ○
1. Angel D'Oro
2. Bel Soggiorno
3. Bristol Palace
4. Europa
5. Metropoli
6. Helvetia
7. Viale Sauli
8. Vittoria
   & Orlandini

Restaurants ●
9. Al Rustichello
10. Al Veliero
11. Amadeus
12. Bruno
13. Da Franco
14. Ostaja o Castell
15. Antico Panson
16. Vegia Zena
17. Zefferino

Nightlife ●
18. Brittania Pub
19. Shaker Club

within walking distance between the railway stations, Stazione Porta Principe and Stazione Brignole, and around the *centro storico*.

By Car

Don't even try to drive in Genoa. The city is small and congested with busy traffic circles, small streets, and traffic like you've never seen. But if you want to drive out into the mountains or along the coast, here are a few places where you can rent a car:
- **Avis**, Piazza Aquaverde (Stazione Principe). *Tel. 010/25-55-98*
- **Hertz**, Via Casaregia 78/a. *Tel. 010/570-26-25.*

By Taxi

You can hail a cab on the street or grab one of the many **taxi stands** situated around Genoa. To get a radio cab in Genoa, call *010/26-96*. Some of the more prominent taxi stands and their telephone numbers are:
- **Piazza Caricamento**, *Tel. 010/20-46-32*
- **Piazza Aquaverde**, Stazione Principe, *Tel. 010/26-12-46*
- **Piazza Nunziata**, *Tel. 010/29-82-32*

Where to Stay

The best place to find inexpensive hotels is by the main train station, **Stazione Principe**. The area around the other station, Stazione Brignole, also has hotels, though not as many. However, it is in a quieter more residential neighborhood.

1. AGNELLO D'ORO, *Via Monachette 6, 16126 Genoa. Tel. 010/246-20-84. Fax 010/246-23-27. Web: www.hotelagnellodoro.it. 29 rooms all with bath. Single E80-90; Double E90-120.* ***

A pleasant, inexpensive three star hotel down a side street just off the station. The rooms are clean and comfortable if a little small. The prices are good for a three star, but that may be because next door is the best three star in the city, Hotel Europa, and they know they cannot compete. One plus is that if you are traveling with your pet they are accommodating.

2. BEL SOGGIORNO, *Via XX Settembre 19/2, 16124 Genoa. Tel. 010/542-880, Fax 010/581-418. Web: www.belsoggiornohotel.com. 18 rooms, 17 with bath. Single without bath E50-60; Single E70-90; Double without bath E50; Double E70.* **

Their prices are outrageously high for a two star since they are located on the ritzy shopping street Via XX Settembre. They have everything but a street entrance and air conditioning, which will permanently keep them at a two star in Liguria. The rooms are clean and comfortable but the prices are ridiculous. Good accommodations in a wonderful and safe location but you can get better prices elsewhere.

3. **BRISTOL PALACE**, *Via XX Settembre 35, 16121. Tel. 010/59-25-41, Fax 010/56-17-56. E-mail: info@hotelbristolpalace.com. Web: www.hotelbristolpalace.com. 133 rooms all with bath. Single E130-320; Double E150-350; Suite E500-700. Prices dop on the weekends. Buffet breakfast included.* ****

Located on Genoa's premier shopping street, you'll be in the middle of everything here. The rates go down dramatically on the weekends, so this is the best time to come and stay in the lap of luxury of a four star hotel. All the amenities of a good four star including a very respectable restaurant. They are pet friendly and offer baby-sitting service too.

4. **EUROPA**, *Via Monachette 8, 15126 Genoa. Tel. 010/256-955, Fax 010/261-047. Web: www.venere.it/genova/europa. 37 rooms all with bath. Single E85-130; Double E110-200. Breakfast E8.* ***

The best three star in the city. Don't get put off by the small little street it's on just off of the Piazza to the Stazione Principe. Inside it's closer to a four star in luxury. The rooms are quiet and comfortable if a little nondescript in their furnishings. All rooms come with A/C, TV, mini-bar and direct dial phones. They have large common areas and a roof deck that overlooks the entire city. They have parking on-site for E11 extra and an excellent cocktail lounge for evening relaxation. A great place to stay in Genoa. The best three star in town.

5. **METROPOLI**, *Piazza Fontane Marose, Tel. 010/246-8888, Fax 010/ 246-8686. Web: http://bestwestern.worldexecutive.com. 47 rooms. Single E85-130; Double E110-200. American Express and Visa accepted. Breakfast included.* ***

Situated in one of the most beautiful and romantic *palazzi* in the city, you will find peace and tranquility in this hotel. This hotel, part of the Best Western chain, offers comfortable rooms and well-equipped bathrooms. The service is professional and attentive. This is an excellent place to stay in Genoa.

6. **RIO**, *Via Ponte Calvi 5, 16126 Genoa. Tel. 010/29-05-51, Fax 010/29-05-54. 47 rooms, 44 with bath. Single E120; Double E160. Credit cards accepted.* ***

Located deep in the *centro storico* on a relatively wide road, this is a thoroughly modern three star hotel whose prices are so low because of their location. It's safe here during the day, but it is definitely not a place that even I would walk alone in late at night. But what's great about the location is that it is quiet, clean, and comfortable, and you have one of Genoa's best local yet upscale restaurants just across the street. The rooms come with all three star amenities except for A/C.

7. VIALE SAULI, *Viale Sauli 5, Tel. 010/561-397, Fax 010/590-092. Web: www.hotelsauli.it. 56 rooms. Single E70-100; Double E75-150. Credit cards accepted. Breakfast included.* ***

This hotel offers great comfort at good prices. Located in a local area, near the Brignole station, here you will find comfortable communal areas, well appointed rooms, completely soundproofed to the traffic outside. You will find every three star comfort here including AC, TV and more. The service is attentive, and a stay here would definitely be pleasant.

8. VITTORIA & ORLANDINI, *Via Balbi 33, Tel. 010/261-923, Fax 010/ 246-2656. Web: www.vittoriaorlandini.com. 48 rooms. Single E70-100; Double E75-150. Credit cards accepted. Breakfast E3.* ***

Located on the main drag from the main train station, this hotel is a labyrinth inside but well furnished and appointed with objets d'art. They offer a few rooms with access to a peaceful garden. These need to be requested. Also, the north facing rooms have an extra little room for relaxing. All rooms are clean and comfortable as are the bathrooms, and come with every three star amenity. The breakfast room is huge and has a nice view over the old section of town down by the water.

Where to Eat
Genovese Cuisine

Genovese cuisine is dominated by the omnipresent **pesto sauce**, a basil, garlic, pine nuts, and olive oil concoction that they put on everything from lasagna noodles to spaghetti to meat and seafood. Also since they're a port city the "fruits of the sea" (i.e., seafood) are also a big part of any menu you'll find. Essentially the indigenous cuisine reflects the austere tastes and tight budgets of the local fishermen and farmers, so you'll find many creative crépe-type dishes along with pasta and seafood.

Suggested Genovese Cuisine

If you're up for it, try some of these delicious Genovese specialties.

Antipasto - Appetizer

• **Farinata** – a giant crépe made from chickpea flour sprinkled with olive oil and rosemary and then cooked in a wood–burning stove
• **Focaccio** – Crunchy flat bread covered in olive oil
• **Focaccio al formaggio** – the local flat bread with cheese, which is not melted on top but baked inside the pouch of the focaccio
• **Pansotti** – thick chickpea soup

Primo Piatto - First Course
Pasta
• **Pansotti** – Small ravioli stuffed with either mushrooms or spinach, or both, covered with a light walnut sauce
• **Pasta con pesto** – Any type of pasta that is served with the famous light Genovese pesto sauce, which is made from basil, olive oil, and garlic; usually tossed with thin noodles called trenette

• **Gnocchi al pesto** – Semolina dumplings with pesto sauce

Secondo piatto - Entrée
Carne (Meat)
• **Cima all Genovese** – Breast of veal filled with vegetables and hard boiled eggs

Pesce – Fish
• **Fritto misto di mare** – mixed fried seafood
• **Branzino all griglia** – Grilled slab of sea bass
• **Pesce spada con funghi** – Swordfish with mushrooms

Contorno – Vegetable
• **Torta pasqualina** – Vegetables and hard boiled eggs egg rolled in a delicate pastry
• **Insalata mista** – mixed salad. You have to prepare your own olive oil and vinegar dressing. Americans' lust for countless types of salad dressings hasn't hit Italy yet.

9. **AL RUSTICHELLO**, *Via San Vincenzo 59r. Tel. 010/588-556. Credit cards accepted. Dinner for two E35.*
   A small quaint local place that also caters to tourists which is advertised by the sign out front that indicates they speak English and French. I love the brick walls and arched whitewashed ceilings as well as their pasta, pizza, meat and fish. They say they specialize in Genovese cuisine but they have pasta from all over Italy. So if you're a pasta nut like I am, come here for some. They also have a good *cotolette alla Milanese* (lightly breaded veal fried in butter).
   10. **AL VELIERO**, *Via Ponte Calvi 10/12. Tel. 010/291-829. Credit cards accepted. Dinner for two E35.*
   A small, upscale local place that is tucked on a small side street just off the harbor area. The interior is stark white with archways all over the place. It's tiny so get there early or make reservations. They serve great *spaghetti al pesto* (with a garlic, oil, and basil sauce) and *sogliola ai ferri* (sole cooked over an open fire). There are other seafood dishes, of which there are plenty around E15 each, so if you try any of those besides the *sogliola* your price to eat here will go up. But those in the know in Genoa don't care. This is one place to go if you make it to this beautiful city.
   11. **AMADEUS**, *Via PE Bensa 40r (in the Piazza Nunziata). Tel. 010 247-1039. Dinner for two E20.*
   A popular local pizza place especially for the university students, since they serve huge 16 inch pizzas for great prices. The decor is simple and basic, and the only truly interesting feature is the red and white tiled wood-burning oven in the room on the right. Here you can watch all the pizza being prepared. The

food comes super quick since the pizza chef is a maestro, and if you want to linger over a bottle of wine they have no qualms about that. To get pizza American-style ask them to put on extra mozzarella.

12. BRUNO, *Vico della Casana 9. Tel. 010/208-505. Credit cards accepted. Closed Saturdays. Dinner for two E35.*

Located on the first floor of an old *palazzo*, the dining environment with their tall ceilings is terrific. You feel as if you are outside, this place is so big. Try their *penne ai frutti di mare* (with mixed seafood) or their *ravioli al salmone* (with salmon) for primo. Then move onto either a *filetto ai ferri* (grilled filet of steak) of the *pesce spada ai ferri* (grilled swordfish).

13. DA FRANCO, *Archivolto Mongiardino 2. Closed Sundays and Mondays. No telephone number. Credit cards accepted. Dinner for two E33.*

If you like lobster, this is the place for you. Small and local, down a difficult-to-find side street, you have to have a good map to locate this excellent lobster and champagne restaurant. Their menu has other dishes, but this is what they do best, serve up succulent lobster so you can wash it down with sparkling wine. Can you think of a better way to spend the evening?

14. OSTAJA O CASTELL, *Salita Santa Maria di Castello. Tel. 010/298-980. No credit cards accepted. Dinner for two ... hard to say since the menu changes daily.*

This is a small, local, and irreverent place. They make great food and they have fun preparing it and serving it. The menu is a dead giveaway to their attitude. It has snide remarks written on it. For example: "*Antipasto*: we have it/*Primo*: Whatever we have/*Frutta*: costs too much/*Dolce*: right before the check/*Digestivo*: right after the check/*Vino*: It's good" – and so on and so on. The menu changes daily but if you want a fun, intimate atmosphere in a completely local section of town, and you're a little adventurous, come and give it a try.

15. PANSON, *Piazza delle Erbe 5r. Tel. 010/294-903. Credit cards accepted. Dinner for two E40.*

An upscale restaurant in a rustic locale. They've grown huge plants to protect you from the sights in the lively local piazza but the sound still drifts in if you sit on the terrace. Inside seating is better because you can get the true feel of an upscale restaurant in Genoa. Try some of their *risotto di crostacei* (rice with crustaceans) or any of their pasta with *pesto*. They specialize in both seafood and pesto. For seconds the *fritto misto del golfo* (mixed seafood from the gulf) and the *pesce spada* (grilled swordfish) are both excellent.

16. VEGIA ZENA, *Vico del Serragli 15. Tel. 010/299-891. Closed Sundays and Monday nights. Credit cards accepted. Dinner for two E35.*

Great local seafood place with excellent atmosphere, great service, and a truly wild and crazy owner. They serve a superb *grigliatta mista* (mixed grilled fish for two) as well as almost any other seafood pasta or fish you can imagine. Located in the *centro storico*, this is a place to have dinner from about 7:30pm to 9:30pm, since the area gets dark and deserted after ten in the summer. In the winter only come here for lunch.

17. ZEFFERINO, *Via XX Settembre 20. Tel. 010/59-19-90, Fax 010/58-64-64. Credit cards accepted. Closed Wednesdays. Dinner for two E75.*

They call themselves the ambassadors for Italian cuisine, and if you're willing to pay their prices the food will not disappoint. The restaurant is filled with brass nautical and kitchen objects, wine bottles, and pastoral pictures which gives the entire place a rustic ambiance. With their exquisite service and excellent food this is a perfect place for a romantic dinner. Their *pesto* sauce (garlic, oil and basil) on home-made *fazzoletti* is superb. As are all of their seafood dishes, including the *frittura del golfo* (mixed fried seafood from the gulf of Genoa) and the *Gamberi all Carbone* (succulent shrimp cooked over an open fire).

Seeing the Sights

Genoa's best sights, in my humble opinion, lie outside of town, but inside this port city there are some beautiful palaces, churches, squares, and wonderful old streets that have been alive with people and shops for almost two thousand years.

A. TORRE DELLA LANTERNA

Located near the Stazione Principe, down the Via Andrea Doria.

This is a medieval **lighthouse** last restored in 1543 that stands 117 meters high. Before the advent of electricity, a huge fire would be lit on top of the structure to guide ships into the harbor. If you're into lighthouses, you'll like this one.

B. COMMENDA (& CHIESA DI SAN GIOVANNI)

Salita San Giovanni. Open 7:00am–7:00pm.

Situated near the Piazza Aquaverde, in the Chiesa di San Giovanni you will find the small chapel of **San Sepolcro of Jerusalem**. This church is on two levels with definite Gothic influences despite construction having begun in the 12th century. The Commenda, built in the 17th century, is attached. It's décor and tranquil spaces make it a local favorite.

C. PALAZZO REALE

Located at number 10 Via Balbi. *Tel. 010/247-0640.* Open Tuesdays, Thursdays, Saturdays and Sundays 9:00am-1:00pm.

This is a 12th century *palazzo* that was greatly modified in the 17th century. It has beautiful hanging gardens overlooking the harbor. Here you'll also find a rich collection of Ligurean paintings with works by Tintoretto, Van Dyke, Strozzi, and others.

D. VIA GARIBALDI

Genoa's most famous street, laid out in 1558. Many *palazzi* have been converted to banks and offices. **Palazzo Bianchi** (No. 11, open Tuesday–Saturday 9 am–1:00pm and 3:00pm-6:00pm, Sundays 9:00am–noon, admission fee), **Palazzo Rosso** (no. 18, same hours) are of interest. In **Palazzo Tursi** is now Genoa's **Municipio** which has a beautiful courtyard. Paganini's violin is in the Sala delle Giunta, and three letters from Columbus in the Sala del Sindaco.

E. VILLA DEL NEGRO

Piazza Corveto. Open Tuesday–Saturday 9:00am–7:00pm and Sundays 9:00am–12:30pm. Admission E3.

This is an urban oasis that has streams, cascades, grottoes, and walkways all leading to the **Museo d'Arte Orientale (Museum of Oriental Art)**, featuring samurai swords and helmets and much more. The botanical gardens located here were created by Ippolito Durazzo.

Take a Boat Cruise in Genoa

If you want to try something different and enjoy the beauty of Genoa's harbor at night, try a boat cruise that goes until midnight. Affectionately called a booze cruise by some, they also have karaoke and other entertainment. Call **Calata Zingari**, *Tel. 010/256-775* or *010/255-975.*

One of its sections is the remains of the 13th century **Palazzo del Commune** and the 14th century **Torre del Popolo**. Inside you can admire the lovely frescoes and the **Salone dei Gran Consiglio (Grand Council Chamber)**. The *palazzo* has over 3,500 square yards of displays of precious art, archives, libraries, as well as conference rooms and offices.

G. THE OLD CITY

Just around the corner from the Piazza De Ferrari is the pretty **Piazza San Matteo**. Go south from here and you enter the **old city** of Genoa. Your best route is down Via Dante to Piazza Dante and the **Porta Soprano**, the twin-towered gateway from 1155, where Columbus's father was supposedly gatekeeper.

This is a place for exploring (but not at night or alone, especially if you are a woman). Take the Via Ravecca down from Porta Soprana to the 13th century gothic **Church of Sant'Agostino** and its **Museum of Ligurean Sculpture and Architecture** (Tuesday–Saturday 9:00am–1:00pm and 3:00pm-6:00pm, Sundays 9:00am–12:45:00pm, admission E3).

From Sant'Agostino take the Strada di Sant'Agostino to the 12th century **San Donato** (open 9:00am–dusk) with its lovely octagonal campanile (bell tower). Also near here is the **Santa Maria in Castello** (open 9:00am–dusk), which was used by the Crusaders as a hostel. It was rebuilt in the 13th century. Today it has a Romanesque facade. The inside has been adorned with chapels representing the noblest Genovese families. The **Convent** with its three cloisters should also be visited. They also have a small museum with paintings by Brea and some beautiful frescoes from the 15th century.

H. CATHEDRAL OF SAN LORENZO
Via San Lorenzo, Open 9:00am–dusk.

The most elegant and important example of medieval design in and around Genoa. It is beautiful, characterized by its pronounced Roman Gothic style. Over the centuries the cathedral has undergone many reconstructions. In the 13th century the facade was destroyed and replaced by the current black and white striped Gothic styled one we see today. The bell tower was left without a top when constructed in 1427. It eventually got one two centuries later, and it is apparent that it just doesn't quite fit with the rest of the church.

The majestic interior is divided into a nave and two aisles. Remember to visit the **chapel of Saint John the Baptist**. It is one of the greatest works of the Renaissance even though it shows persistent influence of Gothic art in its bas-reliefs. And you have to admire the refined mosaic beauty of the stained glass Rose window. A perfect place to be in early morning as the sun shines through.

I. CHURCH OF SANTO STEFANO
Via XX Settembre. Open 8:00am–7:00pm.

Set in a small *piazza*, the church was used as a Benedictine monastery until the 10th century. The facade is plain and simple and looks like a monastery would. Inside, on the right is a painting of the *Martirio di Santo Stefano* (The Martyring of St. Stephen) by Giulio Romano in 1524. Next to it is the statue of *Mary and Jesus* made in the 17th century. You can gain access to the bell tower from the presbytery on the left. The baptismal font was made in 1676. Notice the relief work of *San Michele Defeating the Devil* done in 1453.

J. BETWEEN VIA SAN LORENZO & VIA GARIBALDI
Built up during the Renaissance, this area's authenticity has survived better than the area around Porta Soprano and the Stazione Principe. Picturesque, old, winding streets containing colorfully local shops, superb traditional restaurants, out of the way pubs, and plenty of interesting people milling about ... at least during daylight hours. Think twice about coming here at night.

There is a quaint, delightful medieval square, **Campetto**; a couple of centuries-old coffee houses in **Piazza Soziglia** (**Kainguti** at #98r and **Romanegro** at #74r); and the sights and sounds of an ancient seafaring city along the twisting cobblestoned paths. For a scenic route that meanders through the center of this section of the *centro storico*, take a series of streets from **Piazza Bianchi** near the water. First in line is the Via Bianchi, which turns into Via degli Orefici to Via Soziglia to Via Luccoli and eventually to the modern **Piazza delle Fontane Marose**. You can take side streets off this main drag of sorts and really grasp the heart of Genoa.

Note: To fully enjoy this section and the entire *centro storico*, I highly recommend purchasing a map of Genoa, one which includes a detailed map of the *centro storico* on the back. The E4 you spend is well worth it.

K. STAGLIENO CEMETERY

Via Piacenza. Open 8:00am–5:00pm, October 24th–November 4th from 7:30am–5:00pm, Christmas Day 8:00am –noon.

To get to this fascinating cemetery, take bus 34 from Piazza Aquaverde or Piazza Corvetto. The trip takes fifteen minutes and will set you back Euro 75 cents for the bus ticket. On the way back, if you took more than an hour walking through the cemetery - and to do it any real justice you will have to spend more than that amount of time - you will have to buy another ticket at the *giornalaio* near the bus stop.

When you get off the bus at the cemetery, go to your left and around the corner, and the entrance gate is right there. You pass by flower stalls on your way in, so if you want to place a flower on someone's grave, by all means indulge yourself. The best way to start your tour of the cemetery, after you've entered the main gates, is to go past the flower stands and enter the small archway to your right. Walk through the small gravestones, some with tiny pictures on them, until you get to a square of cleared area between the gravestone. On your left is a set of stairs leading up to the interesting stuff. Once up, go to your right and then begin the process of weaving through this magnificent collection of art and celebration of life.

This is a veritable city of the dead covering 160 hectares and is so large it has its own bus system There are centuries-old miniature cathedrals, Romanesque chapels, Egyptian crypts, palaces, statues, all laid out in a haphazard fashion that is representative of the *centro storico*. You'll be amazed at the beauty and sadness of the sculptures, some in bronze, others made from marble. Vines and undergrowth twist everywhere, obscuring some of the smaller paths up the hills between the crypts. A perfect place to spend a few hours wandering around. But remember that this is a cemetery, so be respectful when you visit.

When you enter there will be numbered marble crypts on the walls and on the floors (Oscar Wilde is buried in the Protestant section). From here go to the center with its small plots. Take a left and go up the stairs to the monuments and chapels. Remember to try and act as serious as possible, especially when you pass other people, which is infrequent. This is a cemetery, even if it does look like a miniature city or a museum.

Despite this restriction, Staglieno is definitely one of the best sights to see in Genoa, and really one of the most interesting cemeteries in all of Italy.

L. FUNICULARE ZECCHI RIGHI
Largo Zecca. Open 6:00am–10:00pm. Costs the same as a bus ticket.

Take the **Funiculare Zecchi Righi** up to an overlook above the city. Here you can get some great shots of the city itself and other vistas. You can also walk a little way and explore the dilapidated ruins of the **Forts of Begato, Puin, Sperone**. They are up a small winding road that has cars buzzing around it, so if you're with kids make sure they stick to the sides as you walk. The forts are a little distance away from the funicular, but just follow the signs and you'll make it there. The walk is through dense woods that lends a semblance of tranquillity after the hectic pace of Genoa.

Nightlife & Entertainment
18. **BRITANNIA PUB**, *Vico della Casana 76A. Tel. 010/294-878. Credit cards accepted. Pints E3-4.*

In a perfect rendition of an English pub, you can enjoy a few pints of Kilkenny (a great Irish beer), Elephant (a superb beer from Denmark), or Dab (an excellent beer from Holland); as well as satisfy your hunger with sandwiches, hamburgers, hot dogs, salads, or simple Italian appetizers like mozzarella and tomatoes. A place to come for lunch, dinner, or late night for drinks on a romantic interlude.

19. **SHAKER CLUB**, *Via Cesarea 45r. Tel. 010-570-5784. Credit cards accepted. Drinks E4-5.*

You better be dressed well when you come in here, otherwise you'll get the once-over. A piano bar late at night, they also serve drinks and light snacks in the early evenings. There's a bar you can curl up with or small intimate booths in which you can snuggle with your loved one and trade sweet nothings.

Sports & Recreation
Golf
• **Circolo Golf & Tennis Rapallo**, Via Mameli 377, 16035 Rapallo. *Tel. 0185/261-777, Fax 0185/261-779.* Located 25 km from Genoa in the quaint town of Rapallo, this is an 18 hole, par 70, 5,694 meters course that is

open year round. Closed on Tuesdays. They have a good restaurant, pro shop, bar, 6 tennis courts, and driving range.

Practical Information
Consulates
• **United Kingdom**, Via XII Ottobre 2, Genoa *Tel. 010/56-48-33*

Local Festivals & Holidays
• **January–April**, Genoa Opera Company performances in the Teatro Margherita at Via XX Settembre 16a
• **Summer**, Ballet Festival in Nervi's park

Tourist Information & Maps
• **EPT**, Via Roma 11. *Tel. 010/581-407*
• **Information Offices** in both train stations, Stazione Principe and Brignole.

The Italian Riviera

Some describe the entire Ligurean coast as the Italian Riviera, but for sake of precision, in this book we will use that term to mean only those towns west of Genoa up to the French border. This area is separated into two distinct regions: (a) **Riviera delle Palme** (The Palm Riviera), where you will find wonderful beaches, pristine natural surroundings, all manner of water sports, quaint little towns filled with character and ambiance, a variety of superb culinary delights and hospitable locals; and (b) the **Riviera dei Fiori** (The Flower Riviera), closer to the French Riviera and known for its abundant flower and plant life, as well as excellent seaside resorts.

Each consists of a multiplicity of seaside towns set against the vibrant blue of the Mediterranean with intense greens of the Maritime hills as the backdrop. Since the climate is mild year round, the Italian Riviera makes for an excellent vacation spot much of the year. In fact, my favorite time to go is in the off-season when sun worshipers are scarce. Certainly, there aren't any topless bathers either, but tranquility comes at a price.

Many of the seaside towns along the Italian Riviera were popularized at the turn of the century by visiting nobles, aristocrats, and artists. There are plenty of locations from which to choose, complete with water sports, world-class restaurants, scenic nature trails, wonderful museums, stunning architecture, and vibrant community life. the Italian Riviera has it all.

SAVONA

One of the principal cities along the **Riviera delle Palme**, **Savona** boasts Renaissance palaces and villas magnificently decorated, museums filled with works by the Grand Masters, a theater of impeccable tradition, a medieval *centro storico*, as well as a bustling modern street life surrounded by numerous stores for your shopping pleasure.

The **Priamar Palace** has been restored to house the museums and exhibits that record Savona's rich history. It is a pleasure to wander through and soak up the historic pageantry of the region. In the medieval *centro storico* you'll find the **Leon Pancarda** and **Brandale Towers** overlooking this ancient city center as well as the port.

Savona has all the amenities of larger cities, but is also able to maintain somewhat of a quaint and quiet character. If you're looking for a small, sleepy little port, Savona is not for you. But if you want wonderful sights, great nightlife, excellent restaurants and a wild, uniquely Italian vacation, Savona hits the spot.

Arrivals & Departures

Located 33 kilometers from Genoa, you can either come by car on the A10 Autostrada or Route 1 that motors along the sea. Route 1 can get a little crowded in the summer months. When you arrive by train do not be put off by the ultra modern train station. The center of town is more subdued and filled with character.

Where to Stay

1. MARE HOTEL, *Via Nizza 89/r, Tel. 019/264-065 and 805-633, Fax 019/263-277. Web: www.marehotel.it. 65 rooms. Single E80-100; Double E100-150. Credit cards accepted.* ****

This *palazzo* by the sea, about 1.5 kilometers from the center of Savona, offers instant access to the clear blue Mediterranean, as well as intimate privacy on your own beachfront area. The entrance has a modern feel with light gray and bright blue tones everywhere. The restaurant is just as stimulating with giant tanks of fish and lobsters for your viewing and dining pleasure. The rooms are quite ample and furnished in a simple but comfortable style. The bathrooms are large and filled with every modern convenience. A great place to stay.

2. RIVIERA SUISSE, *Via Paleocapa 24, 17100 Savona. Tel. 019/850-853, Fax 019/853-435. Email:g.monti@rivierasuissehotel.it. Web:www.rivierasuissehotel.it. 73 rooms. Single E50-70; Double E75-95. Credit cards accepted.* ***

Centrally located between the train station and the port, this is an old establishment, opened in 1880 but renovated in 1990. The ambiance and simple, pleasant character of this place are its strong points. The bar and restaurant have a grand piano strategically gracing the area. The rooms are all furnished differently. Some are basic with modest bathrooms, but there are fourteen that are more modern and quite a bit more comfortable. Ask for one of these if you stay here.

Where to Eat

3. IN BARBA AL TIRANNO, *Via Cimarosa 4r. Tel. 019/803-029. Closed Mondays (not in summer), two weeks in February and one in October. Credit cards accepted. Dinner for two E70.*

The cuisine here is Ligurean-influenced with a creative flair. You'll find traditional dishes (like *pesto*) alongside wildly imaginative concoctions (like marinated salmon in pear sauce). A fun and tasty dish is the *lasagnette di pesce con zenzero* (fish lasagna with a ginger sauce). They also grill wonderful meats and fish if you want to keep it simple. If you don't want to have to choose, they offer a gourmet menu course for only E28 where you can sample a *primo*, *secondo* and a dessert. For all the creative flair the ambiance is simple, almost like being at home.

4. OSTERIA BACCO, *Via Quadra 17/19r. Tel. 019/833-5350. Closed Sundays, Easter, August and Christmas. Credit cards accepted. Dinner for E45.*

In a festive local atmosphere, Bacco offers up genuine and tasty seafood dishes. All imaginable seafood is prepared here: tuna, swordfish, octopus and more. I really love their fried octopus and potatoes with a sprinkling of rosemary (*fritelle di rosmarino e polpo con patate*). Their *ravioli di pesce* (seafood ravioli) and *spaghetti ai frutti di mare* are also exquisite. Grilled or fried fish is the staple for seconds. The house wine is local, robust and wonderful.

5. VINO E FARINATA, *Via Pia 15/r. No telephone. Closed September. No credit cards. Dinner for two E30.*

In two nondescript rooms with seating for about 120, this place is always packed with locals. The food is great, simple, inexpensive and authentic Ligurean and Savonese dishes. You'll only find regional bottled wine here, as well as a full-bodied local house wine. For real local atmosphere and cooking, this is the place to come. The *pesto* is perfect, the fish grilled delectably, and the service is attentive. You shouldn't miss this place for an authentic evening out.

Practical Information

• **Tourist Information Office**, Via Paleocapa 23/6. *Tel. 019/820-522*

SAN REMO

The historic resort town of **San Remo** is in the heart of the **Riviera dei Fiori** (Riviera of Flowers), close to the French border. Even though there are over 2,000 varieties of flowers in agricultural cultivation in and around San Remo, still the most characteristic plant is the palm. Besides the local flora, San Remo is awash with sumptuous villas in which you will find some of the most amazing art. It is also home to a gloriously romantic medieval section of town (**La Pigna**), with winding cobblestone streets meeting together in small squares and exiting down covered passageways. San Remo contains wonderful hotels built at the turn of the century, is home to exquisite restaurants with some of the most scintillating Ligurean food, boasts an excellent 18-hole golf course, and has all imaginable water sports available. San Remo has it all.

San Remo was popularized in part by the Czarina Maria Alexandrovna who brought the nobles from her country to this small little Ligurean town around the turn of the century. As a sleepy little village in existence for over 1,000 years, San Remo was doing quite fine, thank you very much, but from 1874 to 1906, more than 190 villas and 25 hotels were built to accommodate the influx of nobility from all over the world who were attracted by the Czarina's patronage. Today some of these buildings have been converted to other uses, such as the splendid Bellevue Hotel that is now the **Town Hall**, and the former Riviera Palace Hotel is now the **Tourist Board**.

If you want to be a beach bum, you have everything at your disposal to do so. If, the next day you wish to explore a scenic and silent little medieval town, it is only a couple hundred meters up the hill. Next, if you want to explore stunning villas, filled with opulence you can only imagine, they are just down the road.

Arrivals & Departures

Located 26 kilometers from Imperia and about 20 kilometers from the French border, you can either come by car on the A10 Autostrada or Route 1 that motors along the sea. Route 1 can get a little crowded in the summer months. You can also arrive by train without having to worry about traffic.

Where to Stay

1. BEL SOGGIORNO JUANA, *Corso Matuzia 41, 18038 San Remo. Tel. 0184/667-631, Fax 0184/667-471. 43 rooms. Single E60-80; Double E75-90. Credit cards accepted. Full board E50-70.* ***

Opened in 1910, this hotel has maintained much of its original charm, even if its overall glamour is a bit faded. That is easily made up for by the numerous flowers and plants everywhere in the common areas. Displayed around the hotel you'll also find antique furniture from the turn of the century and well worn Persian carpets. The best common room is where they serve meals with its many columns, lamps, stucco plaster designs and more. Another wonderful sitting area is the beautiful Mediterranean garden verandah with lounge chairs. The rooms have white furnishings with floral bed covers. The bathrooms are a little old but accommodating. Another plus is that here you are only about two meters from the beach.

2. GRAND HOTEL LONDRA, *Corso Matuzia 2, Tel. 0184/668-000, Fax 0184/668-073. 134 rooms. Single E85-100; Double E125-150. Credit cards accepted. Full board E125-150.* ****

Located in a beautiful old *palazzo* constructed in 1850, this is one of the great hotels from the Czarina's era that is still wonderful today. The entrance is impressive with its size and arrangement of period furniture and carpets. The rooms are spacious with red carpets, white furniture, curtains and bed spreads that are an opulent golden yellow. The bathrooms are large and the fixtures modern, but just barely. Other amenities include the ample breakfast buffet, the swimming pool, and the relaxing garden verandah setting. But beware, they are going through some renovations. As a result, when you contact them, find out whether the renovations are completed yet.

3. NAZIONALE, *Corso Matteotti 3, Tel. 0184/577-577, Fax 0184/541-535. Email: nazionale.im@bestwestern.it. 78 rooms. Single E75-100; Double E105-120. Credit cards accepted. Full board E110-160.* ****

The last remaining grand hotel situated near the casino, this wonderful old *palazzo* underwent a perfect reconstruction in 1993 to bring it into the modern world. The doors are now opened by magnetic strip cards and not the quaint keys they used to have, but the renovations couldn't snuff out the ambiance and personal attention that made this hotel one of the best since 1904. The rooms are all well appointed with period pieces and accented with floral curtains and bedcovers. The bathrooms were given the most modern of

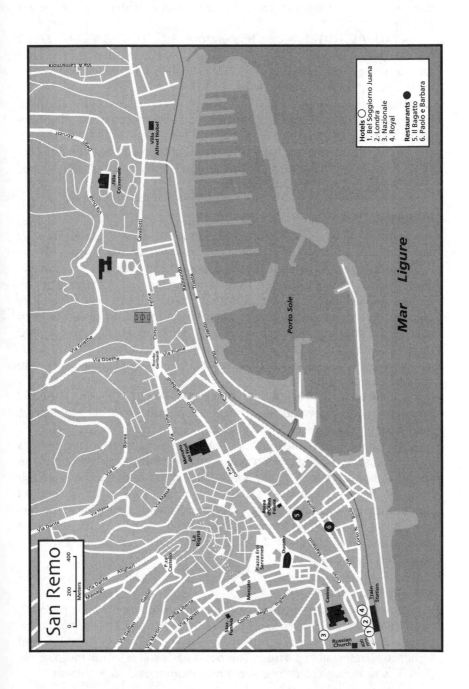

San Remo

Meters
0   200   400

Mar Ligure

Porto Sole

Hotels
1. Bel Soggiorno Juana
2. Londra
3. Nazionale
4. Royal

Restaurants
5. Il Bagatto
6. Paolo e Barbara

makeovers in the reconstruction and now have all amenities. One of the last great hotels left.

4. ROYAL HOTEL, *Corso Imperatrice 80, Tel. 0184/5391. Email: royal@royalhotelsanremo.com. Web: www.royalhotelsanremo.com. 202 rooms. Single E130-280; Double E215-390; Suite E310-670. Credit cards accepted. Full board E70 per person.* *****

Another of the all-time great places to stay. This is a fantastic five star filled with every luxury you could imagine. It is opulent in every detail. There are tennis courts, a swimming pool, sauna, shuttle bus service, beautiful garden verandah, an excellent but expensive restaurant, private beach, child care services and more. This is the place to stay in San Remo if you have the means. Every need you have will be catered to.

Where to Eat

5. IL BAGATTO, *Via Matteotti 145, Tel. 0184/531-925. Closed Sundays and from June 15 to July 15. Credit cards accepted. Dinner for two E70.*

Situated in an old *palazzo*, this place has refined cuisine at a reasonable price. If you don't want to order from the menu, there is a fixed price option for E20 and another for E30 per person. If you go *a la carte* you have to try their *risotto alla marinara* (seafood rice dish). Also all their grilled or oven baked fish dishes are superb. Their wine list is quite extensive with over 400 labels from Italy, the rest of Europe, California and South Africa. Great food, wonderful atmosphere and perfect service. The air conditioning comes in handy in summer too.

6. PAOLO E BARBARA, *Via Roma 47, Tel. 0184/531-653. Closed Wednesdays and in Summer also Thursdays at lunch. Credit cards accepted. Dinner for two E80.*

Only about 30 seats are available here in this elegant restaurant. Barbara is always bustling around making sure everyone is happy, and Paolo is in the kitchen ensuring the food quality is perfect. The staples of the menu are fish from the sea and vegetables from the mountains, all creatively cooked together to develop a culinary symphony in your mouth. Or in layman's terms, scrumptious with an original twist. You can't go wrong here, but you will need to order an entire Italian meal if you're really hungry since the portions are a little small. *Buon Appetito!*

Seeing the Sights

Some of the most refined and elegant **villas** are on the Corso degli Inglesi, which runs from the Casino out of the west side of town. They are not open to the public, but just taking a stroll and soaking up the exquisite gardens and architectural refinement is a treat. This *passegiatta* is akin to, but much better than, a walk through some of the old neighborhoods in New Orleans.

Next, along the eastern part of town on the Corso Felice Cavallotti, are other stunning villas, two of which you can enter and browse through. The first, **Villa Nobel**, was the property of the Swedish scientist who invented TNT, but not wanting to be remembered for such a calamitous invention, devised the concept of and funded the Nobel Prize. In the villa is a permanent collection of Nobel relics and a gallery of Italian Nobel Prize winners. The second, **Villa Ormond**, has incredibly rich and lush gardens accented by spewing fountains and the ever-present palm trees.

Other sights to see are the **Russian Orthodox church** built by Czarina Maria Alexandrovna, the **Borea d'Olmo Palace** that houses the informative **Civic Museum** with its beautifully frescoed vaults in the hallway, and the **San Siro Duomo** and its baptistery. Last but not least, the town does have a magnificent casino, where you can not only gamble but revel in the opulence of yesteryear.

Practical Information
• **Tourist Information Office**, Largo Nuovalini 1. *Tel. 0184/571-571/2/3*

Golfo di Tigullio

North of the celebrated Cinque Terre and just east of Genoa is the bucolic **Golfo di Tigullio**. Frequented for centuries by the *conoscenti* of seaside living, this pristine gulf on the Ligurean Sea is populated with some amazing fishing villages, scenic towns and a relaxed pace of life that brings visitors back over

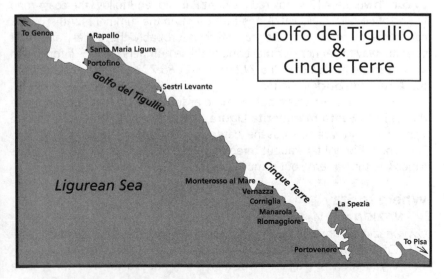

and over again. The most famous town in the area is **Portofino**. A movie set back drop, with tiny cobbled streets, excellent hotels, superb restaurants, and a celebration of life has made this tiny village a place to visit for ages. Other towns to explore in this area, which over time have played host to all manner of celebrities include: **Santa Margherita Ligure**, **Rapallo** and **Sestri Levante**. Try one or sample all; you will not be disappointed.

PORTOFINO

The secluded and protected little fishing village of **Portofino** was discovered many years ago by the super-rich and famous and became one of their favorite playgrounds. Accented by the deep blue of the water and the lush green of the nature preserve hillsides, the colorful buildings of Portofino stand out like a fairy tale set. This beauty has now turned the quiet little town into a haven for the not-so-rich-or-famous, but it still retains its charm and character.

Today, cafés and boutiques line the quaint little streets, and what used to be an exclusive vacation spot is a traffic jam of humanity during the peak summer tourist months. Nonetheless, Portofino will stun you with her beauty despite the summer crowds. And then, after all the ferries and buses have left for the day, the real romance of Portofino begins. If you choose to stay in town, you will have the beauty virtually all to yourself late at night since there are not many hotels in the town itself.

Arrivals & Departures

Located 36 kilometers from Genoa, trains do not come directly to Portofino, which used to give it some of its exclusivity. You can either come by **car** down the A12 Autostrada, exit at Rapallo, and follow the coast road to Portofino, which will entail long traffic jams in the summer months; or you can come by **ferry** from Genoa, which is probably the easiest and least stressful way to get here. Contact one of these numbers for ferry information and reservations: *Tel. 010/265-712* or *0336/688-732*. The ferries leave from the **Aquarium dock** in Genoa.

Another less expensive but far more arduous way to get here is to take the **train** to **Santa Margherita Ligure**, then catch a bus in Piazza Vittorio Veneto, a short walk towards the water from the station, to get to Portofino. The whole trip will take about three hours, however. This will be a little less expensive than a ferry, but is much longer and much more of a hassle.

Where to Stay

NAZIONALE, *Via Roma 8, Tel. 0185/269-575, Fax 0185/269-578. Web: www.nazionaleportofino.com. 13 rooms. Single E125-200; Double E140-350. Credit Cards accepted.* ****

All you get here is a perfect location a few paces away from the seaside *piazza*, a romantic old building, great views, clean and comfortable rooms with TV, mini-bar, and direct dial phone – but not much else. If you come to Portofino, this is a quaint place to stay and enjoy the ambiance of this tiny little village. But you'll need to make reservations about a year in advance, especially for weekend stays.

PICCOLO HOTEL, *Via Duca degli Abruzzi 31, Tel. 0185/269-015, Fax 0185/269621. 22 rooms. Single E100-205; Double E140-350. Credit cards accepted.* ****

Established in 1926 and renovated in 1991, this quaint 'little" (Piccolo) hotel has its own private beach, serene garden, excellent restaurant, day care services, relaxing bar and all the other amenities of a four star hotel. The service is friendly and the rooms are quiet, comfortable and clean. I prefer it to the Nazionale because of the relaxing common areas.

SPLENDIDO, *Viale Baratta 13, Tel. 0185/269-551, Fax 0185/269-614. Web: www.hotelsplendido.com. 86 rooms. Credit cards accepted. Single E490-570; Double E825-1,300; Suite E1,325-4,000. Credit cards accepted.* ****

This place is truly splendid ... and expensive. Definitely the place to stay while visiting Portofino if you have the means. Opened in 1901, Hotel Splendido has a well deserved reputation for excellence. Besides the usual amenities of a four star they have tennis courts, an outdoor swimming pool, a quiet garden, an excellent but expensive restaurant, baby-sitting service, and professional attentiveness. They own a smaller hotel, Splendido Mare, on the Via Roma in town that is less expensive and though not as opulent, does share facilities with the larger hotel, is a great place to stay as well

EDEN, *Vico Dritto 18, Tel. 0185/269-091, Fax 0185/269-047.Web: www.hoteledenportofino.com. 8 rooms. Single E100-120; Double E110-180. Credit cards accepted.* ***

Recently upgraded to a three star, this hotel is in the center of the little fishing village of Portofino. Only eight rooms, so reserve well in advance. They have basically the same amenities as the Nazionale or the Piccolo, even a few more, like TVs in the rooms and a sun deck, but their rooms are not quite as clean or as comfortable. But if you want the beauty and romance of Portofino at more reasonable prices, stay here. They'll eventually be a three or four star if they get their act in gear – leaving budget travelers out in the street in this expensive and elitist town.

Where to Eat

IL PITOSFORO, *Via Molo Umberto I 8. Tel. 0185/269-020. Closed Tuesdays and November. All credit cards accepted. Dinner for two E120.*

Eating here is not going to be inexpensive, so be prepared. You will pay, not only for the food, but also for the magnificent view of the harbor and its *piazza*. Obviously a place designed to fleece the tourists with 130 available seats, but if you're in Portofino come here for a bite. If you only get a pasta dish and a half carafe of wine, that should minimize the damage to your wallet. Try their *linguine all'arragosta* (pasta with lobster sauce), *risotto di mare* (rice covered with seafood), or any of their other tasty, basic, traditional local dishes. Despite all my whining about price it really is a good place to eat.

PUNY, *Piazza Martiri Olivetta 5. Tel. 0185/269-037. Closed Thursdays and January 15 to March 15. No credit cards accepted. Dinner for two E85.*

The most famous restaurant in Portofino, located directly in the main port square with a wonderful terrace overlooking the *piazza* and the port. The green awning shades you from the summer's heat and the baskets of red flowers accent the outside appearance. Inside this has the look of just another local place but it serves superb seafood, pasta, and fresh vegetables. The prices are high because people will pay them, but you can't go wrong here – except if you forget to bring cash. They don't take credit cards.

Seeing the Sights

Leaving the *piazzetta* and its pier lined with fishing nets drying in the sun you can amble up the hill to the **Chiesa** and **Castello di San Giorgio** (both open 9:00am–5:00pm, admission to the Castle is E3). Here you will find the remains of the famous St. George, the dragon slayer. From this vantage point you can walk through lush gardens and have superb scenic views over the town and the water on both sides of the peninsula.

Going in the other direction from town you can hike up to a spot with wonderful views of the area, the **Belvedere**. Portofino is the perfect day trip from Genoa, or a quaint romantic getaway on the coast for a few days.

Practical Information

• **Tourist Information Office**, Via Roma 35. *Tel. 0185/77-10-66*

SANTA MARGHERITA LIGURE

Santa Margherita is one of the more classic, beautiful, elegant and fashionable places in Tigullio, and for that matter in all of Italy. This tiny town has been a glamorous night spot for over 60 years and a fashionable resort since the 19th century. Today it is a representative of true Italian seaside beauty.

Arrivals & Departures

Located 31 kilometers from Genoa, you can either come by **car** down the A12 Autostrada, exit at Rapallo, and follow the coast road to Santa Margherita, which will entail long traffic jams in the summer months; you can come by **ferry** from Genoa, which is probably the easiest and most scenic way to get here; or you can take the **train**. For ferry information and reservations, contact

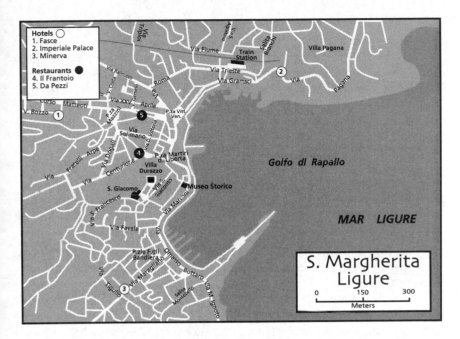

one of these numbers: *Tel. 010/265-712 or 0336/688-732.* The ferries leave from the **Aquarium Dock** in Genoa.

Where to Stay

1. FASCE, *Via L. Bozzo 3. Tel. 0185/286-435, Fax 0185/203 580. Email: hotelfasce@hotelfasce.it. Web: www.hotelfasce.it. 12 rooms, 10 with bath. Credit cards accepted. Single E90; Double E100. Breakfast included. Full board E35-40 per person. ***

Located above the center of town a short walk to the Lungomare, this hotel is a member of the prestigious organization of family hotels, and is operated by Jane, the ever-present British proprietress and her Italian husband. Your rooms are large enough with plenty of space to store your clothes in the white formica units with red trim. There are TVs in the rooms but no air conditioning. You can also get quick four hour laundry service by the hospitable Jane. There is a garden terrace area for relaxing with lounge chairs. If requested, you can get an English-style breakfast with cold cuts and cheese along with the regular continental fare. They also have free bicycles for your use, a roof deck and garden area. A quality inexpensive place to stay in Santa Margherita.

2. IMPERIALE PALACE, *Via Pagana 19. Tel. 0185/288-991, Fax 0185/ 284-223. Email: info@hotelimperiale.com. Web: www.hotelimperiale.com. 102 rooms. Closed from Dec. 1 to March 1. Single E160-225; Double E270-*

430; Single E460-700. Credit cards accepted. Breakfast included. Full board E85-90 per person. *****

Built in 1889, this is the most historic hotel in Santa Margherita which has housed all sorts of royalty and celebrities over the past century. The hotel, with its terraces, balconies and columns, dominates the coastline on this part of the harbor. The entrance hall is a perfect example of elegance with antiques and crystal chandeliers everywhere. In the bar area you will find a piano that is put into use in the evenings, filling the hotel with gentle tunes. The rooms are large and wonderfully appointed with antiques, period pieces and tapestries. The bathrooms are all modern, since the hotel was refurbished in 1992. They come with phones and hairdryers and shower supplies for your convenience. Everything about this hotel is wonderful, including the private beach, swimming pool, tranquil garden and fine restaurant.

3. MINERVA, *Via Maragliano 34/C. Tel. 0185/286-073, Fax 0185/281-697. 28 rooms. Single E100. Double E150. Web: www.venere.it/it/liguria/smargherita/Minerva. Credit cards accepted. Breakfast included. Full board E50-80 per person.* ***

Located in town, this place is only a short walk to the water. They have a peaceful garden area and a terrace with a nice view of the harbor. Their bright entrance hall is filled with Bordeaux-style seats. The rooms have quaint antique furnishings and are quite comfortable with all the amenities of a three star with TV, air conditioning, mini-bar and room service. The bathrooms are clean and modern with phone and hairdryer. This is a good three star.

Where to Eat

4. IL FRANTOIO, *Via del Giunchetto 23/a. Tel. 0185/286-667. Credit cards accepted. Parking available. Closed Tuesdays (except from July 1 to August 31) and November 7-30. Dinner for two E45.*

This is a wonderful restaurant with an ample wine list, fast courteous service and wonderful food, but if you're looking for pizza they don't serve it here. They do make a wonderful *taglierini con scampi* (pasta with shrimp) and *linguini con gamberi* (with prawns) and make exquisite fish dishes. The catch of the day determines that part of the menu. Il Frantoio offers quality meals and fantastic atmosphere.

5. DA PEZZI, *Via Cavour 21. Tel. 0185/285-303. No credit cards accepted. Air conditioned. Closed Saturdays and Dec. 20 to Jan. 20. Dinner for two E25.*

In a simple, basic atmosphere, the Pezzi family caters to a varied and loyal clientele that comes here for the great traditional local dishes prepared to perfection: ravioli, pasta with a delicious pesto sauce, tasty fresh vegetables stuffed or made into pies, *rustiche crostate* (dough stuffed with veggies, fish and/or meat then baked). Everything is served with their good quality house wine and loads of courteous service. A great local place.

Seeing the Sights

The city is guarded by an imposing **castle** built by the Genovese when they controlled this port city. Today it houses the local **Museo Storico**. The central core of the town is referred to as **Pescino**, named for the fishing industry that for centuries was the town's main form of commerce. The harbor is lined with fashionable boutiques, cafés and restaurants, and is filled with a lively atmosphere of commerce. You can still see the fishing boats returning, where their catch is gobbled up by the buyers for the local restaurants, as well some housewives looking for bargains.

Besides wining and dining, you can visit the **Villa Durazzo** and its gardens dating back to 1560. Inside the villa is the **Museo G. Rossi**, dedicated to the famous local journalist and novelist. You should also check out the church of **San Giacomo di Corte**. Located near Villa Durazzo and located on a panoramic hill overlooking the port, it is adorned with precious marbles and frescoes. Besides the beauty of the church, you can get some great photos of the bay and town from this vantage point.

Practical Information

• **Tourist Information Office**, Via XXV Aprile 28. *Tel. 0185/287-486*

RAPALLO

The port of **Rapallo** is the largest community in Tigullio and is a popular resort town in both the summer and winter because of its mild climate. An amphitheater of hills protects Rapallo from cold northern winds, and as a result the climate is temperate year round. Rapallo is bisected by two streams that empty into its large bay, along which you will find a tree-lined promenade and tiny shops, restaurants and cafés.

Arrivals & Departures

Located 30 kilometers from Genoa, you can either come by **car** down the A12 Autostrada, and take the exit at Rapallo; you can come by **ferry** from Genoa, which is probably the easiest and most scenic way to get here; or you can take the **train**. For ferry information and reservations contact one of these numbers: *Tel. 010/265-712* or *0336/688-732*. The ferries leave from the **Aquarium Dock** in Genoa.

Where to Stay

1. EUROPA, *Via Milite Ignoto 2. Tel. 0185/64692. Fax 0185/669-847. Email: info@hoteleuropa-rapallo.com. Web: www.hoteleuropa-rapallo.com. 62 rooms. Credit cards accepted. Single E90-145; Double E140-190. Breakfast included. Full board E50 per person.* ****

Located in a building built in the 1600s, this place is packed with history.

Renovated in 1994 so you have all the necessary amenities for a four star hotel including air conditioning, TV, mini-bar, room service and more. They have a health club, a sauna, relaxing garden area and a good restaurant too. A good four star in the center of everything.

2. RIVIERA, *Piazza IV Novembre 2. Tel. 0185/50248, Fax 0185/65668. Email: info@hotel-riviera.it. Web: www.hotel-riviera.it. American Express and Visa accepted. 20 rooms. Double E120-175. Breakfast included. Full board available. Closed Oct. 30 to Dec. 23.* ***

Ideally situated in the heart of the Lungomare where everyone goes to see and be seen. This is a nice hotel that underwent renovations a few years ago so it is now superb. Some rooms have parquet floors but the best have the wonderful mosaic pavement. These are usually the rooms with balconies that overlook the port. Ask for one of these since the views are tremendous. The bathrooms are clean and modern with hairdryers and shower supplies available. Breakfast is an abundant buffet display of fruits, veggies, rolls and more. The hotel restaurant is also a frequent dining location for the locals since the food is so good and the prices reasonable. *The* place to stay in Rapallo.

3. VILLA MAROSA, *Via Rosselli 10. Tel. 0185/50668/9. No fax. No credit cards accepted. 12 rooms. Single E50-70; Double E70-90. Breakfast included. Full board available.* **

A small two star located along the river, a short stroll from the Lungomare. Quaint and comfortable, this little hotel has clean and comfortable rooms with

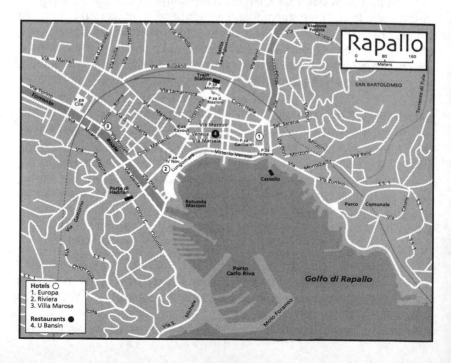

TVs and telephones but not much else. There is a peaceful garden area to relax in the evenings. If you are in Rapallo on a budget, this is good place to stay.

Where to Eat

4. U BANSIN, *Via Venezia 49. Tel. 0185/55913. No credit cards accepted. Parking available. Closed Sundays (but not in the summer) and 15 days in November. Dinner for two E30.*

Rapallo is filled with fine restaurants, but this one takes the cake. Right in the heart of the town, near the *piazza* where the daily market is held, this place serves up fine Ligurean dishes fresh and tasty. In business since 1907, they make all the traditional local dishes like *focaccia al formaggio* (dough stuffed with local cheese and then baked), and at night they grill and fry the catch of the day. Without a doubt this place has the best food and atmosphere in Rapallo (especially on their terrace), as well as quick and courteous service.

Seeing the Sights

On the promenade you will find the open air gazebo-like structure, the **Rotunda Marconi**, from which concerts are performed in the evenings during the summer months. An ancient **Castello**, with its square tower, sloping roof of slate, little windows and draw bridge, overlooks the harbor to the north by the little river San Francesco. Further north around the harbor entrance are the extensive gardens of the **Parco Comunale Casale**. By the river Baote across the harbor are some other gardens, the **Giardini Publici**, smaller but equally as relaxing, from which you can catch a glimpse of the town of Sestri Levante on a clear day.

Other sights to see in Rapallo are the **Sanctuary of Montallegro** (which you can get to by Funicular) and the Gothic ruins of the former convent of **Santa Maria in Christ Valley** up in the hills surrounding the town. Besides sightseeing, Rapallo has everything you could want for an active vacation: horseback riding, golfing, tennis, mini-golf, swimming, bowling, and water sports.

Practical Information

•**Tourist Information Office**, *Via Diaz 9. Tel. 0185/230-346*

SESTRI LEVANTE

Located on the extreme southwest end of the Gulf of Tigullio, the town of **Sestri Levante** is stunningly beautiful. One of its two inlets, the Gulf of Ponente, was renamed the **Baia delle Favole** (Bay of Fables) by Hans Christian Andersen because of its fairy tale beauty. On the other side of the 'island' is the **Baia del Silenzio**, so named for its peace and quiet.

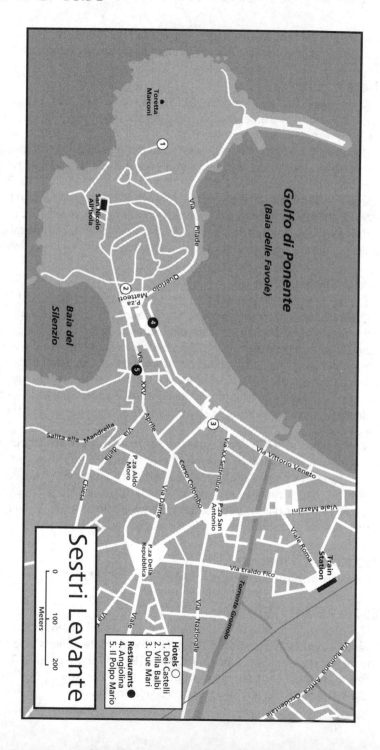

Sestri Levante

Golfo di Ponente
(Baia delle Favole)

Baia del
Silenzio

Toretta
Marconi

San Nicolo
All'Isola

Via Pilade

Via Querciolo

P.za
Matteotti

Via XXV Aprile

Via della Chiesa

Salita alla Mandrella

P.za Aldo Moro

Via Dante

Corso Colombo

Via XX Settembre

Via Vittorio Veneto

P.za San Antonio

Viale Mazzini

Viale Roma

Train Station

Via Eraldo Fico

Via Nazionale

Torrente Gromolo

P.za Della Repubblica

Via Romana Antica Occidentale

Hotels ○
1. Dei Castelli
2. Villa Balbi
3. Due Mari
Restaurants ●
4. Angiolina
5. Il Polpo Mario

0 100 200
Meters

The 'island' really is a peninsula upon which the **Toretta Marconi** (Marconi's Tower) sits watching over the town. The peninsula on which the tower sits at one time was an actual island, but around the 11th century silt had built up from the Gromolo stream between it and the shore. Despite that, it is still known as the 'island' today (things move slower in Italy.) Sestri Levante is a quaint, character-filled little town, perfect for a romantic weekend adventure any time of the year.

Official website: *www.sestri-online.com.*

Arrivals & Departures

Located 51 kilometers from Genoa, you can either come by car down the A12 Autostrada and get off at the Sestri Levante exit; you can come by **ferry** from Genoa, which is probably the easiest and most scenic way to get here; or you can take the **train**. For ferry information and reservations contact one of these numbers: *Tel. 010/265-712 or 0336/688-732.* The ferries leave from the **Aquarium Dock** in Genoa.

Where to Stay

1. **GRAND HOTEL DEI CASTELLI**, *Via Penisola 26. Tel. 0185/487-220, Fax 0185/44767. Email: info@hoteldeicastelli.com. Web: www.hoteldeicastelli.com. 30 rooms. Credit cards accepted. Single E180; Double E220-280. Breakfast included.* ****

Immersed in a park like setting on the peninsula at Sestri Levante, this wonderful hotel is housed in a castle dating back to the 1100s. In the main part of the castle is the central core of the hotel with the salons and common rooms as well as some of the guest rooms. In the tower, separated from the main building but connected by an underground passage, is the restaurant and bar area. All around the hotel are terraces from which you can enjoy stunning views of Sestri and the Gulf of Tigullio. The rooms are all different in size, shape, architectural touches and furnishing, but all are more than amply spacious. The bathrooms are rather large also, some with mosaic tile and all with every modern convenience. Along with the incredibly romantic ambiance, the hotel also has its own private beach, a swimming pool and pristine garden terrace. A wonderful place to stay with all possible four star amenities.

2. **DUE MARI**, *Vico del Caro 18. Tel. 0185/42695, Fax 0185/42698. Web: www.duemarihotel.it. 26 rooms. Credit cards accepted. Double E115-140; Breakfast included. Full board E40-50 per person.* ***

Built in the 1600s, this attractive palazzo was turned into a hotel in 1963 and renovated in 1993 to perfection. Now it is an ideal location for a tranquil stay in the heart of Sestri. The common areas are well lit and filled with antique furnishings. The breakfast room turns into a quaint reading area in the afternoons. The traditional restaurant, which specializes in fish dishes and other healthy fare, is located in the internal garden area. Every room has a view of one of the bays or the internal courtyard. Only the rooms on the third floor have air conditioning, which is a must in August. There are also some relaxing garden areas and a swimming pool to enjoy. A great place to stay.

3. VILLA BALBI, *Viale Rimembranze 1. Tel. 0185/42941, Fax 0185/482-459. Email: villabalbi@villabalbi.it. Web: www.villabalbi.it. 96 rooms. Credit cards accepted. Double E200-250. Breakfast included.* ****

An old historical building constructed by a noble family from Genoa in the 1600s, it was converted into a hotel in 1947 and is a wonderful place to stay. Everything here is pure elegance with wonderful furnishings and architectural displays. The rooms themselves are filled with ambiance and atmosphere and are quite large with furnishings that are quasi-'antique' but comfortable. The bathrooms are large and complete with all necessary modern conveniences. They have a wonderful terrace garden that also houses an outdoor pool that is heated during the cooler months. Also, on their private beach you can place your order from their good restaurant and be served as you sun yourself. A hotel of the highest caliber.

Where to Eat

4. ANGIOLINA, *Viale Rimembranze 49. Tel. 0185/41198. Closed Tuesdays and from November through December. Credit cards accepted. Dinner for two E70.*

A fine restaurant that serves many traditional dishes, like *zuppa di pesce* (fish soup) and *fritto misto e grigliate* (either fried or grilled mixed seafood), but they also get slightly creative with some dishes like the *insalata di polpo e patate* (mixed salad with octopus and potatoes), *triglie al basilico* (mullet with basil sauce) *spaghetti di frutti di mare* (with fruit of the sea, i.e. a variety of sea food) or *seppie ripiene* (stuffed cuttlefish). The portions are extremely generous, the service quick and hospitable, and the atmosphere good, especially in the terrace area, which all makes for a fine meal.

5. IL POLPO MARIO, *Via XXV Aprile 163. Tel. 0185/48-203. Closed Mondays. Credit cards accepted. Dinner for two E80.*

This is a legendary restaurant in Sestri which specializes in seafood. An old traditional *osteria* that has finally been returned to its former glory, the menu is mainly based on the catch of the day straight out of the *Golfo di Tigullio*. The following dishes merit some mention: *Il grande misto di mare all'antica* (all manner of roasted fish with potatoes, tomatoes and other veggies) and *le frittelle con gamberi* (fried fritters and shrimp). Inside it's quaint and comfortable and the terrace seating is splendid too.

Seeing the Sights

Marconi's Tower on the 'island' was where Gugliemo Marconi began his experimentation with short wave radio signals. Without Marconi's efforts from this tower, who knows when radio would have been invented? Also on the peninsula is the rustic little **Church of San Nicolo of the Island**, built around 1511.

A short distance north of the town are the abandoned copper mines in **Libiola**. Active all the way back to Roman times, the mines are now used for archaeological research as well as an eco-museum.

Practical Information
• **Tourist Information Office**, Via XX Settembre 33. *Tel. 0185/497-011*

CINQUE TERRE
If you're searching for something beautiful and off the beaten path, look no further. These five villages are essentially off limits to cars, and to even find them you have to make five separate detours off the main road far away from the coast since the villages are not linked by any road on which an automobile can travel. Because of this remoteness, these villages have preserved their old world charm and have escaped the onslaught of tourism.

The **Cinque Terre** (the five lands) are the five villages of **Monterosso al Mare**, **Vernazza**, **Corniglia**, **Manarola** and **Riomaggiore**. Each is set beautifully in the coastal cliffs and sloping vineyards of Liguria and are connected to each other by a narrow winding country path. Whenever there is a flood, some of the path is usually washed away but still remains traversable on foot – which is the best way to see the Cinque Terre. Settle yourself into a nice hotel in either Monterosso al Mare or Riomaggiore, or a small but nice *pensione* in Vernazza, and walk to the rest. The other two smaller inside villages don't have official hotels or *pensiones* yet. If you get tired and can't walk back, there's always the local train to pick you up and return you to your 'home' village.

The Cinque Terre were situated high up above on the cliffs for protection from marauding pirates. No one knows where these original inhabitants came from since their highland settlements are no longer in existence, but as a result of the high incidence of red hair and light coloring among the residents of Cinque Terre, experts have speculated that they share a Celtic or Nordic background. When the danger of pirates passed, around 1000 CE, the villages resettled themselves closer to the water's edge to take advantage of the bounty from the sea.

Today most of the permanent residents of each village is either a fisherman or a farmer, but some are turning into hoteliers or restaurateurs. The same rugged terrain that protected them long ago from ocean invaders used to also protect them from the modern invasion of mass tourism. But their defenses have started to crumble. In the two border towns, tourism is flourishing and in Vernazza, more and more homes are opening themselves up to become *pensione*. Soon, I fear, the last of Italy's true beauties is going to succumb to the influences of the rest of the world.

Even with more tourists, the sights, scenery, and tranquility here are still extraordinary. Make the trip and you won't be disappointed, especially from October to April, when you'll have the place virtually to yourself and the approximately 6,500 residents of all five villages. There won't be much to do here, except hike from village to village, then casually lunch or dine at a different *trattoria* in a different village each day, and let the cares of the world pass from your mind for a little while.

The map on page 543 shows the location of the Cinque Terre. For more information, go to their official website at *www.cinqueterre.it*.

Arrivals & Departures
By Boat
You can come by boat, which will take you three hours. The train is an hour quicker. But if you're just going for the day, the boat may well be what you're looking for: the trip is designed as a boat cruise, then a three hour stay in Vernazza (the best of the villages), then the return trip.

If you're going to stay a day or two, the trip to Vernazza will cost you E17 round-trip or E9 one way. Contact this number for information and reservations: *Tel. 010/265-712* or *0336/688-732*.

The boat's hours of operation are:
- **July 1–August 26**, Saturdays, leave from the Aquarium dock in Genoa at 9:40am
- **July 2–September 3**, Sundays, leave from the Aquarium dock in Genoa at 8:40am

By Train
Take one of the local trains from Genoa and it will stop in each of the Cinque Terre. A train leaves from Genoa every two hours or so, and the trip takes about two hours.

Where to Stay
If you want first class hotels, stay in either **Monterosso al Mare** or **Riomaggiore**. From these towns you can either hike or take the local train to the other villages. If you don't mind small, intimate, rustic accommodations far off the beaten path, then stay at one of the places listed here.

Usually only the most hardy souls will venture to stay in the inner three villages, giving you even more solitude if that is what you're after. If you're looking for a truly unique Italian holiday adventure, you are going to love the Cinque Terre.

Monterosso al Mare
PORTO ROCA, *Via Corone 1, in Corone, 19016 Monterosso al Mare. Tel. 0187/817-502, Fax 010/817-692. Email: portoroca@portoroca.it. Web:*

www.portoroca.it. 43 rooms. Credit cards accepted. Single E140-260; Double E175-300. ****

Built into a cliff above the village, this beautiful romantic setting is perfect for lovers. You have your own private beach, a quaint little restaurant, and great service. There is a shuttle bus that will run you down to the village since it is quite a hike. If you want to stay in luxury in the Cinque Terre but don't want to be a part of the touristy crowd in Monterosso, stay here.

VILLA ADRIANA, *Via IV Novembre 23, 19016 Monterosso al Mare. Tel. 0187/818-109, Fax is the same. No credit cards accepted. 54 rooms. Single E110; Double E170.* ***

A two star with its own private beach, a good restaurant, with small, comfortable clean rooms. It's located a little on the outskirts of the town, but they have a shuttle bus you can use to get back and forth. The summer months are not so pleasant since they don't have air conditioning, but the rest of the year this is a great place to stay.

Vernazza

Vernazza is the place to stay because of its ambiance, but there are not many lodging options here. Listed below is a quality bed and breakfast. Many locals have opened up their homes and now rent rooms, or offer their homes as bed & breakfasts. To find these places, simply get off the train. You'll be swamped with requests as to whether you need a room.

VILLA L'EREMO SUL MARE, *Tel. 339/268-5617, Email: info@eremosulmare.com. Web: www.eremosulmare.com. Double E90. Breakfast included. No credit cards accepted.*

With only three double bedrooms (two of them air-conditioned), you'll need to book well in advance to ensure a room in this well place bed and breakfast. Be warned that there are only and two bathrooms for guests usage, all shared. But if you can get past that little wrinkle, the two large living rooms with fire place, and a large panoramic terrace make for a great place to stay. Located above the town of Vernazza.

Manarola

CA' D'ANDREAN, *Via Discovolo 25, Manarola 19010. Tel. 0187/920-040, Fax 0187/920-452. Email: cadandrean@libero.it. Web: www.cadandrean.it. 10 rooms. Single E60-70; Double E80-90. Breakfast E5. No credit cards accepted.* ***

Located outside of the village of Riomaggiore near Manarola, you'll be completely isolated here. The only real amenities in the simply furnished rooms are heat and a phone; but they are clean and comfortable if you do not expect too much. There is a small bar area downstairs, just off the tiny entrance way, as well as a beautiful internal garden terrace area complete with lemon trees. A perfect place in which to relax.

MARINA PICCOLA, *Via Discovolo 192, Riomaggiore 19010. Tel. 0187/920-103, Email: info@hotelmarinapiccola.com. Web: www.hotelmarinapiccola.com. All credit cards accepted. 7 rooms. Single E80; Double E110. Breakfast included. Half board E80 per person. Full board E95 per person.* ***

Located outside of the little village, thankfully this place has its own restaurant, of the same name, so you don't have to trek out in the night to find food, as you have to do at the Ca' d'Andrean above. Located on the same street as that hotel too, but a little farther out, this is a pleasant place to stay. The rooms are small but clean and comfortable and most have a view of the sea. The bathrooms also are small but clean. The hotel at *Via Discovolo 202* has three more rooms, all with terraces that overlook the sea. A peaceful place to sit in the evenings.

Where to Eat

Seafood and *pesto* are the specialties of the Cinque Terre, as they are all over Liguria. There are plenty of restaurants in **Monterosso al Mare**, but only a few in the smaller villages (Vernazza, Corniglia, Manarola, Riomaggiore). In addition to the restaurants attached to the hotels listed above, most restaurants here are fairly simple affairs.

Vernazza

TRATTORIA DEL CAPITANO, *Tel. 0187/812-224. Dinner for two E60. No credit cards accepted.*

This is a great place for a meal in Cinque Terre. You'll have a great view of the sea as it crashes on the rocks below. *Pesto* and seafood are the specialties. There's a good *zuppa del mare* (seafood soup) for starters. Follow it with a *pasta con pesto* dish, and finish up with any variety of grilled fish that are pulled from the waters below.

Chapter 19

MILAN & THE LAKE REGION

Milan is Italy's chief industrial, financial, and commercial center. As such it was a target during WW II, and 60 percent of the city, some of the finest architecture in Italy, was destroyed by aerial bombings.

Today Milan is where Italy gets down to business. Image is everything is this frenetic trendy town; but beautiful is not the first word that springs to mind when describing Milan. Known around the world as the capital of high fashion and slick design, Milan is the mecca of elegance and taste. Yet the actual physical presence of Milan is oddly unappealing. The buildings are fundamentally bland and the city seems devoid of vibrant *piazze* and other places for the locals to gather.

As someone who grew up in Rome, each time I visit Milan I search for hints of those items that are purely Italian – a baroque church facade on a small side street, a *palazzo* the warming color of ocher, or a *piazza* with a Bernini fountain teeming with families at play – but am always left disappointed.

Milan has been swallowed up by commercialism. The *piazza* culture found everywhere else in the country has been erased in Milan along with the human face of the city. As a result, many Milanese feel themselves to be, both in physical and spiritual terms, closer to Zurich than to Rome, and more European than Italian.

Even with a lack of overall architectural beauty, the city's Gothic **cathedral** is one of the largest and most attractive churches in the world, rising like a brilliant white crown in the heart of the city. Another great church is that of **Sant' Ambrogio**, built in the 4th century, where St. Ambrose baptized St. Augustine. Nearby stands the former convent of **Santa Maria delle Grazie**, where Leonardo da Vinci's famous but oddly disappointing *The Last Supper* is painted on the refectory wall.

Brera Palace is the home of the **Academy of Fine Arts and Science**. Its galleries contain works by the great Italian masters and other artists. **La Scala**, Milan's opera house, is world-renowned. The city has two famous libraries, three universities, a school of commerce and agriculture, an academy of music, and a celebrated archaeological museum.

There is much to see and do in Milan, but in general, you will find more spectacular and more accommodating Italian cities elsewhere.

Milan Website: *www.provincia.milano.it*.

Insight Into Milan

Milan is a thoroughly modern city steeped in commerce and high fashion. The hectic pace, where meals are rushed, is so unlike any other Italian city that it will seem as if you are in another country. The regular Italian piazza culture that helps create community all over Italy does not exist here. The only way people have a collective experience anymore is by watching the same show or soccer game on the TV. The fast pace, the lack of a sense of community, and the fact that the city is geared around big business all make Milan less Italian and increasingly more European.

Hotels in Milan mainly cater to businessmen who are attending some convention or another. Tourists are basically an afterthought here. And the sights, save for the imposing Gothic Cathedral and Da Vinci's Last Supper, are few and far between, because Milan was virtually razed during World War II and rebuilt soon after. But if you are an opera fan, **La Scala**, the most famous opera house in the world, beckons. And if you want to see the most exquisite selection of foods anywhere in the known world, come here to shop and eat at the many **Peck's** stores. Other than that, Milan can easily be missed.

But if you do come to Milan you ought to see **The Last Supper**, go up on the observation deck of the Cathedral, visit the **Leonardo Da Vinci Museum of Science and Technology**, and go to the **Fiera Sinigallia market** at Porta Ticinese, which is held every Saturday. Otherwise you haven't been to Milan.

Brief History

Because of its location Milan has a long history of raids and invasions. The city started as Mediolanum, a Gallic town, and was taken over by the Romans in 222 BCE. It was burned a number of times – once by the Huns, twice by the Goths, and again by the German, Frederick Barbarossa in 1162.

After a period of civil strife, the house of **Visconti** gained control of this powerful city-state. When the last Visconti duke died in 1447, three years later the rule of the **Sforzas** began, and continued until 1535. Most of the ancient beauty of the city was created by the heads of these two great houses. When the Sforza line died out, Spain seized Milan and held it until 1706. Then the city fell to Austria, which governed it until Napoleon created his short-lived Kingdom of Italy and made Milan its capital. After Napoleon's fall, Milan was restored to Austria. Then finally in 1859 it was included in the new united kingdom of Italy.

Milan's industry, trade, and population swelled in the period between the two world wars. Currently the population hovers around 1.5 million people. The construction boom after World War II included numerous skyscrapers and factories of modern design, and the streets were widened, eliminating what once was a quaint medieval feel to the city, and turning Milan into a city that accommodates the automobile better than it does human beings.

Arrivals & Departures
By Air
When coming to Milan you will either arrive at **Malpensa**, which handles all incoming flights from North America, Australia, and the United Kingdom, or **Linate**, which handles most of the domestic and other European air traffic. Transportation from Milan's airports is not as sophisticated as is it from Rome's Leonardo da Vinci. From Linate there is **bus service** to the Milan Central Train Station leaving every 20 minutes, and **ATM** Municipal Bus Service #73 from Piazza San Babila (corner of Corso Europa) every 15 minutes. Duration for both is 30 minutes. From Malpensa, there is a bus that leaves for the Milan Central Train Station every 30 minutes.

Once at the train station you have access to Milan's extensive Metro system, which takes you virtually everywhere you want to go. If you're in more of a hurry or in need of more comfort, take a taxi from in front of the station.

Directly from the airport into town, the quickest but the most expensive way is to take a taxi. The fare starts at E2 and rises rapidly. Be prepared to pay the cost of a night's hotel room for your ride from the airport.

By Bus
Getting in and out of Milan is best done by train – driving is the worst option and bus is almost as bad. Traffic in and around this region is bumper to bumper. The only saving grace for the bus is that you don't actually have to drive. The only time to use a bus around Milan (if you don't have a car) is if the train doesn't go where you're heading.

All inter-city buses leave from the **Piazza Castello** (at the Cairioli metro stop). Each company has its own office located here.

By Car
Driving in Milan is worse than any other city in Italy, if you can imagine that. It's not the drivers who are so bad, but it's that there are so many cars and the city is so large and spread out.

If you want to rent a car while in Milan you can do so at both airports and at the locations given in the *Renting a Car* section of this chapter.

Sample trip lengths on main roads:

\me: 6 hours

- **Venice**: 4 1/2 hours
- **Florence**: 4 hours.

By Train

The **Stazione Centrale** is Milan's primary railway station and it's like a chaotic mini-mall inside. There are all sorts of shops, eateries, a supermarket, two different levels to get lost in, travel agencies, pickpockets, hustlers, and your trusty **tourist office**, *Tel. 02/669-0532*. This station connects Milan with all other major cities in Italy as well as elsewhere in Europe. The other stations (**Stazione Nord, Porta Genova**, and **Porta Garibaldi**) connect Milan to smaller municipalities like Como and Asti.

A word of advice for first timers to Milan: if you can avoid it stay somewhere else other than around the train station. Located north of the center of Milan, the area around the station is away from all the sights and is not in the best neighborhood. It's safe but the ambiance is not as nice as downtown. You will find the best deals here, but as a first time visitor, it's best to hop on the Metro and stay downtown near the Cathedral.

Sample trip lengths and costs for direct *(diretto)* trains:

- **Rome**: 5 hours, E30
- **Venice**: 3 hours, E20
- **Florence**: 3 hours, E25

Getting Around Town
By Bicycle

They can be rented from **Vittorio Comizzoli**, Via Washington 60, *Tel. 02/498-4694*. I would advise against renting a bike, however, since Milan is such a large city, and is definitely not as picturesque as Rome or Florence, so renting a bike would only put you in harm's way and make your visit less than pleasant.

On Foot

Unlike Florence and Venice, and similar to Rome, Milan is a large city that is not the best walking town. That's why they have a huge Metro system. You can walk the city. It's safe. But to get from point A to point B, why not just take the Metro? It only costs E0.75 cents one way, which is about 80¢. And if the Metro is too much work for you, there's always the ever-present taxis.

By Metro

This is the best way to get around the bustling metropolis of Milano. Find the big red signs with a black "M" which indicate that the **Metropolitana Milanese** is just below. There are three lines: **red** (#1), **green** (#2), and **yellow** (#3).

There are maps everywhere inside and outside the trains, so it is easy to find which train to take. You can also get a map of the Metro system from the

FS information counter at the Stazione Centrale. This is a simple, easy, intuitive metro system to use.

Tickets cost E1 and are sold at local newsstands in the stations, at tobacconist's shops (the ones marked with a blue "T" sign), and at each metro stop.

If you know you're going to be taking the Metro frequently while you're staying in Milan, here are a number of options that can save you money. You can get the following types of tickets at the **Stazione Centrale ATM office**, *Tel. 2/669-70-47*, or the **Duomo office**, *Tel. 0/89-01-97*. The general information number is *02/875-495*.

• **One day ticket** (24 hours after you stamp it) for E2.5.
• **Two day ticket** (48 hours after you first stamp it) for E5.

By Taxi

As in most Italian cities, taxis are everywhere. If you can't locate one on the street, there are plenty of taxi stands all over the city where the taxis line up and wait for fares. Here is a brief list of where some of these taxi stands are located: Piazza del Duomo, Piazza Scala, Piazza Cinque Giornate, Largo San Babila, Largo Treves, Piazzale Baraca and Piazza XIV Maggio.

Here are some radio taxi numbers that may come in handy. But remember that when you call a taxi to come get you, your fare starts when the taxi leaves for your location, not when the taxi picks you up, like it does most everywhere else.

• **La Martesana**, *Tel. 02/52-51*
• **Cooperitiva Esparia**, *Tel. 02/832-12-13*

Renting a Car

I don't recommend renting a car unless you want to take a day trip to a place that cannot be reached by train. Driving in Milan is worse than virtually any city in Italy. But if you desperately feel the need to get behind the wheel of an automobile, here are some rental car agencies you can call.

• **Avis**, Piazza Duomo 6, *Tel. 02/86-343-94/89-01-06-45*; or Stazione Centrale, *Tel. 02/669-02-90/670-16-54*
• **Hertz**, Viale Marelli 314, *Tel. 02/26-22-33-99*

Where to Stay

Milan is not the best city for low-budget tourists. In the center of the city, the best location, you only have a few three star hotels and very few two stars. We've listed the best and least expensive three stars we could find, as well as few excellent two stars.

Another problem with staying in Milan is that it's mainly a business city, which means that most of the hotels are usually booked for some business convention, mainly dealing with fashion or industry. So remember to reserve well in advance.

1. ANTICA LOCANDA SOLFERINO, *Via Castefidardo 2, Tel. 02/656-905. Closed in August. 11 rooms. Email: info@anticalocandasolferino.it. Web: www.anticalocandasolferino.it. Single E120-180; Double E165-180. All credit cards accepted. Breakfast included.* **

In a charming neighborhood with an excellent restaurant literally surrounding the hotel, this place has more character than charm. Meaning, the rooms are somewhat clean, comfortable and well priced, but the proprietress leaves me cold. Also the entrance is located next to the restaurant of the same name which stays open until 1-2am, and the rooms are located above it. This does not make for a good night's rest. Try someplace else unless you are a night owl and like surly service.

2. ARISTON, *Largo Carrobbio 2, Tel. 02/7200-0556, Fax 02/7200-0914. Web: http://aristonhotel.com/ariston. Closed in August. 48 rooms. Single E135-150; Double E195. All credit cards accepted. Breakfast included.* ***

A great environmentally friendly hotel in Milan. The Zurigho is another (see below, #10). Here they do everything in their power to make your stay comfortable and healthy to the environment. Everything from how their furniture was made to the types of cleaning products they use are designed to be as safe as possible on the environment. The mattresses are made from pure unbleached cotton, and are double thickness for orthopedic support and comfort. The lamps use less energy than normal fixtures. There is a no smoking floor, an advanced phenomenon in Italy. And there are free bicycles for you to use during your stay. An excellent hotel that I would recommend even if they weren't committed to helping the environment, but because of that I can think of no better place to stay in Milan. The breakfast consists of tasty organic products.

Milan's Top Hotels
9. VECCHIA MILANO**
2. ARISTON***
5. GRAND HOTEL DUOMO****

3. FELICE CASATI, *Via Casati 18, Tel. 02/2940-4208, Fax 02/2940-4618. Email: felicecasati.mi@bestwestern.it. Web: www.bestwestern.com/prop_98177. Closed in August. 50 rooms. Single E110-135; Double E120-220; All credit cards accepted. Breakfast included.* ***

Between the central station and Porta Venezia near one of Milan's main commercial streets, this Best Western hotel this has clean and accommodating rooms. Another family-run hotel which virtually guarantees a good stay.

Recently renovated, all the furnishings come in calming pastels now. The bathrooms are distinguished by a high level of cleanliness. Breakfast is a little disorganized and is served in a small room which doesn't make for much comfort. If you want it served in your room it comes at a higher price. Metro is within walking distance. A good place to stay in Milan even without A/C.

4. GRAN DUCA DI YORK, *Via Moneta 1a, Tel. 02/87-48-63, Fax 02/869-03-44. Closed in August. 33 rooms. Single E140-190; Double E160-220. All credit cards accepted. Breakfast E6.* ***

Despite not having an official website, which helps travelers get a feel for a hotel prior to arrival, this place is still highly recommended. Located in the heart of the historic center of Milan, only five minutes from the Cathedral and with easy access to a Metro stop, this is good place to stay. They try to give it a castle-like appearance in the common areas; the rooms are plainly furnished but comfortable. In an historic building it has all the necessary amenities of a three star and is in a golden location. They are pet friendly, have a serene garden setting and offer parking services.

5. GRAND HOTEL DUOMO, *Via San Raffaele 1, Tel. 02/8833, Fax 02/8646-2027. Web: www.grandhotelduomo.com. 162 rooms. Single E235-300; Double E330-380; Suite E450-950. Breakfast included. All credit cards accepted.* ****

Situated right in the *centro storico* a stone's throw from the cathedral. If you want location this is the place to stay. The hotel is in an old building, and has great views of the Cathedral from some rooms and the dining room, making a stay here a scenic adventure. This would be my recommendation for anyone who is staying in Milan for the first time, since it is ideally located around all the main shopping and sights. They have a good restaurant where a simple continental breakfast is served but they do offer baby-sitting service and are pet friendly.

6. GRITTI, *Piazza SM Beltrade 4, Tel. 02/80-10-56, Fax 02/89-01-09-99. Email: info@hotelgritti.com. Web: www.hotelgritti.com. 40 rooms. Single E110; Double E150-200. All credit cards accepted. Breakfast included.* ***

A very nice hotel. The entrance hall is decorated with antique furnishings, and the bar is where you can relax and strike up a conversation in the evenings. The rooms are all decorated differently, and are clean and comfortable, and filled with every three star amenity. The bathrooms are a little small, but are new, with red and grey color patterns. Parking is available and the hotel is pet friendly.

7. MANZONI, *Via Santo Spirito 20, Tel. 02/7600-5700, Fax 02/784-212. Email: info@hotelmanzoni.com. Web: www.hotelmanzoni.com. 35 rooms. Single E140; Double E180; Suite E200. All credit cards accepted. Breakfast included.* ***

Located on a quiet street within walking distance of the Duomo and La Scala. This is a completely modern hotel in a high rent district. The rooms are tranquil, clean and comfortable, but there are precious few amenities. If you've come to Milan for shopping, this could be your place of residence since they are ideally located for consumer forays.

8. PALAZZO DELLE STELLINE, *Corso Magenta 61. Tel. 02/481-8431, Fax 02/8520-7540. Email: hotelpalazzostelline@tin.it. Web: www.hotelpalazzostelline.it. Closed in August. 105 rooms. Single E120; Double E180. All credit cards accepted. Breakfast included.* ***

In a unique location outside of the main area of Milan but still with good access by Metro, this is an excellent choice when in Milan. The entrance hall is large and well lit with modern design furnishings that contrast well with the history of the *palazzo*. The rooms are filled with modern, pastel colored furniture. Many have balconies with views over the rooftops of Milan. The bathrooms all come with hydro massage bath as well as shower, have a rich complimentary toiletry kit available and hair dryer for your use.

9. VECCHIA MILANO, *Via Borromei 4, Tel. 02/875-042 and 02/875-971, Fax 02/8645-4292. Email: hotelvecchiamilano@tiscalinet.it. 27 rooms. Single E75; Double E95. Extra person E30. American Express and Visa Accepted. Breakfast Included.* **

This is *the* place to stay in Milan for budget travelers. Though the rooms are clean and comfortable, they are a little spartan. The bathrooms are microscopic and there is no A/C which is a must in some of the summer. It's off the beaten path enough that your stay will be quiet and tranquil in the evenings. A, excellent two star in Milan.

10. ZURIGO, *Corso Italia 11a, 20120 Milano. Tel. 02/7202-2260, Fax 02/ 7200-0013. Email: zurigo@brerahotels.it. Web. http://brerahotels.com/zurigo. Closed December 23 to January 9. 41 rooms. Single E135-150; Double E195. All credit cards accepted. Breakfast included.* ***

Like the Ariston this is an environmentally friendly hotel. The bicycle in the foyer lets you know that bicycles are available for use by the guests free of charge. There is a teeny elevator to bring you up to your rooms which have a jungle feel to them because of the African-style bed covers. The bathrooms are not very big but do have hairdryers and complimentary toiletry kit. A good place to stay with clean and comfortable, if not large, rooms.

Where to Eat
Milanese Cuisine

Milanese cuisine is a melting pot not only of Italy but also of neighboring nations, particularly France. Even so, there still remains a distinct Milanese style of cooking that uses butter, cheese, milk and cream in what is usually categorized as **Northern Italian** cooking. One item that is used frequently in Milanese cuisine is rice, which comes from the multitude of rice paddies on the outskirts of town. One of the staples is *risotto al salto*, leftover rice fried like a pancake.

Suggested Milanese Cuisine
Below are the typical offerings of Milanese cuisine.

Antipasto - Appetizer
• **Antipasto misto** – a variety of different food such as cheese, prosciutto, olives, etc., from a buffet

Primo Piatto - First Course
• **Risotto alla Milanese** – a creamy rice dish made with saffron and marrow and is usually bright yellow in color
• **Risotto** (with a variety of ingredients) – The same creamy sauce as the Milanese risotto but with any number of ingredients such as vegetables, fish, cheese and/or meat
• **Risotto al salto** – Leftover rice fried like a pancake with the consistency of the fried potatoes you usually get for breakfast in the States

Secondo Piatto - Entrée
Pesce – Fish
You can get any type of seafood you want, since many restaurants have fresh fish sent in daily from the coast on ice; as always when you eat fish in a land-locked city, you'll find the prices to be quite astronomical
Carne – Meat
• **Cotoletta alla Milanese** – Breaded thin cutlet of veal sautéed in butter, served crisp on the outside but succulent on the inside
• **Ossobuco** – Usually served with the *risotto alla Milanese*, this is a veal shank cooked with tomatoes and wine then sprinkled with garlic, parsley and a touch of lemon
• **Rostin Negra** – Pork or veal slowly cooked in a pot-roast with a variety of herbs, wine and butter; a truly typical Milanese dish

Formaggio – Cheese
• **Gorgonzola** – a sharp, pungent, pale and delicious local cheese usually mistaken for the French Roquefort, but this is made with cow's milk, not ewe's milk; takes its name from the small town ten miles outside of Milan where it was originally produced

11. AL PORTO, *Piazzale Generale Contore, Tel. 02/8940-7425. No credit cards accepted. Closed Sundays and Mondays for lunch. Dinner for two E60.*
What used to be an old canal toll-house is now a great seafood restaurant filled with maritime decorations of fishing nets, ropes, wheels and more. The menu depends greatly on what fish they are able to purchase, but they'll always have the freshest and most reasonably priced plates in Milan. You can always find an excellent *risotto* or pasta made with fresh seafood. The best

place to enjoy your meal is out on the terrace. I suggest the *scampi alla griglia*, but then I'm partial to shrimp.

12. BAGUTTA, *Via Bagutta 14-16, Tel. 02/7600-2767. American Express, Visa and Mastercard accepted. Closed Sundays. Dinner for two E45.*

One of Milan's famous artsy restaurants, which you will instantly notice since the walls are covered with murals, caricatures, and pictures of famous and some not so famous artists. This is a great place to try food from all over Italy. They have Roman dishes like *penne all'arrabbiata* (spicy tomato based pasta with garlic, oil, parsley, and hot peppers) and the *saltimbocca alla Romana* (veal shank in a zesty tomato-based sauce). They also have *tagliatelli alla Bolognese* (with light veal, tomato and cream sauce) as well as *trenette al pesto Genovese* (pasta with a superb pureed garlic, basil, olive oil, pine nuts sauce). If fish is your desire, try their *fritto misto di mare* (mixed fried seafood)– it's perfect.

13. BEBEL'S, *Via San Marco 38, Tel. 02/657-1658. All credit cards accepted. Closed Wednesdays. and Saturday mornings. Dinner for two E45.*

You can order great pizza from their prominently placed wood-burning brick oven, or you can try the buffet table that has everything you could want for an entire meal. You can also get fresh fish (they sometimes have live lobsters on ice) and grilled meats. They make great Italian staples like *filetto alla griglia* (grilled veal) and *sogliola alla griglia* (grilled sole).

14. DELL'OPERETTA, *Corso di Porta Ticinese 70, Tel. 02/837-5120. American Express, Visa and Mastercard accepted. Closed Sundays. Dinner for two E45.*

This place is a local nightlife favorite with a central bar where patrons can stop for a drink up until 2:00am. There is also *trattoria* dining where you can sample their exquisite *tagliatelline* with a cream of mushroom sauce. The menu changes weekly to keep things lively. Weekend evenings you can sometimes find live jazz or blues bands playing.

15. DEL MONESTERO, *Corso Magenta 29, Tel. 02/869-3069. All credit cards accepted. Air conditioned dining room. Dinner for two E35.*

A small local place that specializes in seafood. Try the *spaghetti ai calamari alla marinara* (with squid and spicy tomato sauce) then the *misto fritto di gamberini e calamari* (mixed fried shrimp and squid). The atmosphere is intimate and friendly and the food is great.

16. IL RISTORANTE (PECK), *Via Victor Hugo 4, Tel. 02/876-774. American Express, Visa and Mastercard accepted. Dinner for two E90.*

This is the place to come and sample everything that the Peck food stores have to offer. Located downstairs from the Bottega del Vino, the setting is relaxing even without windows, the service is excellent and, of course, the food is sublime. The amount of potential choices is far beyond human comprehension, so even if you are a picky eater you are bound to find something to like.

17. IL SOLFERINO, *Via Castelfidardo 2, Tel. 02/659-9886. All credit cards accepted. Closed Saturdays at lunch and Sundays. Dinner for two E60.*

Next door to the Locanda Solferino inn, the atmosphere is cozy, romantic, and fashionable but not fancy. Most of the food is made in a simple way without much garnish or presentation but it is excellent. The *cotoletta alla Milanese* (breaded thin cutlet of veal sautéed in butter, served crisp on the outside but succulent on the inside) is excellent here, as is the *piccantina di vitello ai funghi porcini* (veal with mushrooms) The menu includes fresh pastas and homemade patés. La Briciola and L'Amour are right across the street.

18. LA BRICIOLA, *Corner of Via Solferino and Via Marsala, Tel. 02/655-1012. All credit cards accepted. Closed Sundays and Mondays. Dinner for two E45.*

This place gathers a rather eclectic crowd in the evenings. Not only does it cater to the theater crowd, but the Brera section where the restaurant is located is known as the "artist" section of Milan. Served in an environment of a wood, glass and pink tablecloths, the food here is of local persuasion, with prices to match the upscale clientele but not the peasant fare. You can get the Milanese favorite here, *cotoletta alla Milanese* (lightly breaded veal fried in butter) as well as many other options.

19. LA BRISA, *Via Brisa 15, Tel. 02/872-001. American Express, Visa and Mastercard accepted. Closed Sundays at lunch and Saturdays. Dinner for two E45.*

Just before you enter you can glimpse some Roman ruins that were dug up during a building construction. The restaurant is a plain and simple local place that serves basic but great food, except for the curried rice called *risotto al' Indiana*. At first I thought, how do people from Indiana make rice that is so good, then I realized they meant from India. A quaint little place especially in their terrace garden. You can get great fish and meats and as well as pastas that are all made in-house. If you're in the area, give it a try.

20. LATTERIA UNIONE, *Via dell Unione 6, Tel. 02/874-401. No credit cards accepted. Open for lunch only. Closed Sundays. Lunch for two E30.*

This is actually a *latteria*, or dairy store, which supplies the neighborhood shoppers with cheese, yogurt, butter, milk, eggs, etc., but it also is a fine vegetarian restaurant. It is so popular with the local office workers that it is jam-packed for lunch time. Their menu includes thick minestrone soup, omelets, stuffed tomatoes and peppers, and *risotti* with a variety of vegetable combinations.

Seeing the Sights

Not nearly as scenic as other cities in Italy – chiefly a result of the devastating bombing during World War II – Milan still has some excellent sights to see, including the beautiful Gothic **Duomo**, the world-famous **La**

Scala opera house, the **Galleria**, and Da Vinci's *Last Supper*. But most people don't come here to sightsee, they come to do business.

See the map on page 561 for sights references.

A. DUOMO

Piazza del Duomo. Open 7:00am–7:00pm. October–May 9:00am–4:30pm. Access to the top of the cathedral costs E2. By elevator E3.

If you want Gothic, here you have Gothic at its best. This ornately decorative church was begun in 1386 and is the work of countless architects, artists, and artisans who labored here for centuries, and it is still unfinished today since it is undergoing continuous reconstruction, maintenance, and restoration work. This massive structure is crowned by 135 spires with statues and relief work interspersed everywhere. At night the spires are lit which makes an excellent scene, especially from the dining room at the Hotel Duomo. One of the best ways to get a bird's eye view of the square is to ascend to the outside viewing area above the facade of the cathedral.

The interior, like the exterior, is covered in statues, relief work, and many other decorations. The stained glass windows are of particular interest especially on a bright sunny day. The statue you see in the square is of Vittorio Emanuele II, done in 1896 by Ercole Rosa.

B. VITTORIO EMANUELE GALLERIA

Many buildings and houses were demolished to make this huge arcade which was dedicated to Vittorio Emanuele II. Started on March 7th, 1865, it was finally finished in 1877 – and so was the architect Mengoni. The day before the opening ceremony the architect plunged to his death from the scaffolding.

Created in the form of a cross, the major wing is 195 meters long and the minor wing is 105 meters long. In the center of the cross you'll find a dome that rises 50 meters above the floor. The inside of the gallery is known as the glass sky since it completely covers all people who enter. It's the perfect place to be in a rainstorm.

Inside you'll find shops and restaurants catering to your every need. It is the central meeting place for business people, artists, opera singers, fashion models and tourists alike. It is really the heart and soul of Milan. Devastated in the bombings during World War II, it has been lovingly re-created to its original form.

C. PIAZZA DEI MERCANTI

The **Piazza dei Mercanti** (Merchant's Square) is a small, quaint old square that is not really a part of the modern city of Milan. It is bounded by the **Palazzo della Ragione** (Palace of Reason), built in 1233, and the **Loggia**

of the Osii, built in 1316, on the north and south; and the **Palatine Schools** and the **Panigalaros house** on the east and west.

In the niches of the Loggia of the Osii, you can find the statues of the Milanese saints. But besides the sculptures and ancient architecture, this is a place to come and get away from the pace of modern Milan.

D. TEATRO LA SCALA

Via Dei Filodrammatici 2. *Tel 02/861-781 or 861-772, Fax 02/861-778.* Open Monday–Saturday 9:00am–noon and 2:00–6:00pm. Sundays 9:30am–12:30pm and 2:30pm–6:00pm. Admission E5.

If you are an opera fan you've come to Milan to catch a performance at **La Scala**, the most famous and prestigious of all opera houses in the world. Built between 1776 and 1778 on the old site of the church of Santa Maria alla Scala, it is the work of the architect Giusseppe Piermarini. Developed in the neoclassical style, the facade has a covered portico and gable with a relief work depicting Apollo's Chariot. The building suffered bomb damage during World War II but was rebuilt and renovated as perfectly as could be possible, and re-opened in 1946.

If you can't catch a performance here, just come to visit their museum which offers a variety of operatic costumes, all the way from Ancient Grecian times to the present. There are also many objects that trace the evolution of the theater, as well as 40,000 books that deal with opera and the theater, and records that have over 600 different opera singers recorded.

E. PALAZZO DI BRERA

Via Brera 28, *Tel. 862-634.* Open Tuesday–Saturday 9:00am–2:00pm and Sundays 9:00am–1:00pm. Admission E4.

Built in 1170 by an order of religious men called the Umiliati as a monastery and place of worship. Then in the 13th century the **Church of St. Mary of Brera** was added onto the building and it has been so named ever since. In 1772 the building began its new life as an institute of artistic preservation as commissioned by Mary Teresa of Austria. The first part of the collection was donated by the Abbot Giusseppe Bianconi in return for his appointment as secretary to the new museum. Many of its current works were donations from religious orders by decree of Napoleon himself. In the nineteenth century the collection was enriched by many private donations.

All the works were moved for safekeeping during World War II because of the bombings of the city, then on June 9th, 1950, the collection opened for viewing again. Today you can find works from the 14th century up to present times. Among the most noteworthy are Moccirolo's *Oratorio*, Raphael's well-known *Sposalizio delle Vergine*, Mantegna's *Cristo Morto* and Bramante's *Cristo alla Colonna*.

F. CASTELLO SFORZESCO

Foro Buonaparte. Metro Carioli. Open Tuesday–Sunday 9:30am–5:30pm. What you see today is only a smaller scale of the original citadel. In the beginning it consisted of many forts all enclosed in a great star-shaped fortress with imposing ramparts. Despite its reduction in size it is still Italy's largest castle.

The current fortress was built in 1450 over the ruins of a viscount's fort, which itself had been built over the ruins of the **Porta Giovia Castle**. Under the rule of Lodovico Sforza in 1495, the castle started to take on many artistic accents with works by such masters as Leonardo da Vinci and Bramante. During the Spanish, French, and Austrian control of the area, this beautiful castle was used as a military barracks and was treated so poorly that after a while it could only be considered a ruin. Finally in 1890, when the Austrian troops were forced to leave, the Italians decided to restore it and in 1893 the work began. But in 1943 parts of the building and its museums were damaged in the WWII bombings, but these too were reconstructed.

Today you should visit the castle not only to see its immense towers and walls and stroll through the beautiful park inside, but also to see their extensive art collection, underground archaeological museum and Historic Document Archives. In the **Ancient Arts Museum**, you'll find a wide variety of artistic works, including fabulous gems by Michelangelo and Leonardo da Vinci, Italy's greatest artists. Look for the *Pieta Rondanini*, Michelangelo's last and unfinished work as well as a hall dedicated to ancient arms such as axes, shields, spiked clubs, spears and more. In the **Historic Document Archives**, started in 1902, there are preserved documents, some of which date back to 1385. Any bibliophile will love this collection.

G. ARCO SEMPIONE

Piazza Sempione.

This monument is also called the **arch of peace**. Construction began in 1807 to celebrate Napoleon's victories in war. It consists of three barrel vaults supported by Corinthian columns on pedestals and needs to be seen if you can't make it to Paris and see the Arc de Triomphe. The reclining figures near the top represent the four main rivers in Italy.

H. LEONARDO DA VINCI MUSEUM OF SCIENCE & TECHNOLOGY

Via San Vittore 21, *Tel. 4801-0040*. Metro San Ambrogio. Open Tuesday–Sunday 9:00am–5:00pm. Admission E5 – Adults; E3 kids under 18.

Inaugurated in 1953 for the fifth centenary of Leonardo's birth, this unique museum is a must-see while in Milan. Located on the site of the Olivetano Monastery, this museum now houses a collection of material that gives a complete synthesis of Leonardo da Vinci's work and experiments in many fields. Here you'll find reproductions of his designs and mechanical models of his inventions, some of which you (and the kid inside you) can actually test out. There are also copies of pages from the *Gates Codex* (used to be called the *Codex Hammer* until software billionaire Bill Gates bought it) on display.

If you've had enough of Leonardo's inventions and the Codex you can walk through other wonderful exhibits all related to science and technology. There's one about the history of aviation, one dealing solely with typewriters, one about land transportation, one dedicated to clocks. Besides all of this there is also an excellent reproduction of Leonardo's *Last Supper* painted by Giovanni Mauro Dellarovere at the end of the 16th century. So if you don't want to brave the line and see the real one come here instead.

I. DA VINCI'S "THE LAST SUPPER"

Piazza Santa Maria delle Grazie. *Tel. 498-7588.* Metro Carioli. Open Tuesday–Sunday 8:30am–1:30pm. Admission E3.

To the left of the church of Santa Maria delle Grazie is the refectory of the Dominican convent that houses the most famous of Leonardo's work, *The Last Supper*. Painted between 1495 and 1497, the painting is not standing up to the test of time and man. The humidity in the room doesn't help maintain the fresco and a doorway was built underneath it cutting off one of Christ's legs that was visible under the table. Also restoration work that was done in 1726 and 1770 actually increased the painting's deterioration. Efforts are underway now, using modern techniques, to save the invaluable work, but if I were you I'd see it sooner rather than later since it may not be around for long.

Sports & Recreation
Golf

• **Golf Club Bergamo Ol'Albenza**, Via Congoni 12, 24030 Bergamo. *Tel. 035/640-707, Fax 035/640-028.* Located 50 kilometers from Milan and only 13 kilometers from Bergamo, this is the home course of the famous Italian golfer Constantino Rocca. The main course is an 18 hole, par 72 that is 6190 meters long. The small course is 9 holes, par 36, and 2462 meters long. Open year round except from December 22nd to January 5th and Mondays. They have a restaurant, bar, driving range, and electric carts.

• **Golf Club Carimate**, Via Airldi 2, 22060 Carimate. *Tel. 031/790-226, Fax 031/790-226.* Located 27km from Milan and 15 km from Como this is an 18 hole, par 71 course that is 5,982 meters long. It is open year round except on Mondays. They have a driving range, tennis course, and a fine bar and restaurant.

Shopping

The best and most expensive shopping streets in Milan are the **Via Montenapoleone** and **Via della Spiga**, and all the little alleys surrounding these two parallel streets. Be prepared to spend through the nose here, but at the same time you will get the best service and quality of product available. Taking a stroll down these streets you'll witness the opulence and splendor of Milan's stores and the beauty of these elegant streets.

Fashion & Accessories

Milan is the seat of Italian fashion, and plays a close second to Paris in world fashion. There are plenty of small designer's shops that feature dresses that have either been on the runways during the 'Fashion Week' of spring or fall, or they have deliberately 'copied' these new fashions – or should I say modified them with their own creative direction. Whatever the case, most of these designer outfits will cost you an arm and a leg, but if it's fashion you want, Milan has it.

Home & Office Furnishings

In most everything the Milanese are willing to try any new approach as long as it's aesthetically appealing and has practical application. This is probably best expressed in their home furnishings industry. The city thrives on a culture of modernism and its industry allows this creativity to flow through the production into your home or office.

There are a myriad of showrooms and/or retail stores all over Milan in which you can admire and buy the latest and greatest designs in home and office furniture, lighting fixtures, house wares, and accessories for the office and home. Some of them can be much more fun than going to a museum because it seems as if these pieces are alive.

Bookstores (English-Language)

AMERICAN BOOKSTORE, *Via Camperio 16, Tel. 02/878-920, Fax 02/ 7202-0030. American Express, Mastercard and Visa accepted.*

exclusively an English-language bookstore. The best place to replenish your stock of novels for the rest of your trip.

MONDADORI, *Corso Vittorio Emanuele 34, Tel. 02/705-832. American Express, Mastercard and Visa accepted.*

This store has three floors dedicated mainly to Italian titles, but there is also a fine section of English-language books.

The Peck Stores

Founded by a Czech immigrant Peck, it is now the undisputed gourmet delicatessen chain in the world. There are five Peck stores that serve carry-out gastronomic excellence and one, **Il Ristorante** (#16 in the "Where to Eat" section), that offers creative cuisine consisting of the many ingredients found in their stores. Peck is the place to go for all forms of prepared foods, salamis, cheeses, fruit, vegetables and wine.

Even if you are not going to buy, when in Milan you simply have to come and enjoy the visual feast. They make Dean and Deluca, the famous New York-based specialty food store, pale in comparison. Each store, all located within a stone's throw from one another near the Duomo, carry a variety of different products, designed in this way so you'll have to frequent almost all of them to get the ingredients you need for that special soirée.

21. BOTTEGA DEL MAIALE, *Via Victor Hugo 3, Tel. 02/805-3528.*

Just across the street from Gastronomia Peck, this store offers everything possible created from its namesake, *Il Maiale* (The Pig). You'll find snouts, ears, feet (for *Ossobuco*) as well as salamis, sausages, and cutlets. The hams hanging precariously from the ceiling compete with the salt-cured pork for your attention. Try an *etto* (about 1/4 of a pound) of *salami Milanese* – in my opinion the best salami in Italy.

22. BOTTEGA DEL VINO, *Via Victor Hugo 4, Tel. 02/861-040. American Express, Visa and Mastercard accepted. Dinner for two E30.*

Not just a wine bar and store, this is also a gourmet "fast-food" establishment. At lunch time it is packed with Milanese satisfying their need for excellent cuisine. They have red painted tractor seats set on stools for seating around deli-like counter areas made of beautiful light wood. To wash down all the great food they have in excess of 150 vintages from all over Italy for you to sample by the glass, or you can test the beer on tap.

23. CASA DEL FORMAGGIO, *Via Speronari 3, Tel. 02/800-858.*

This aptly name "House of Cheese" is a cheese lover's fantasy with over 300 varieties from all over Italy. You can get the best mozzarella made with buffalo's milk outside of Rome. They also have cheeses made with olives, spices, and nuts. If you missed out on a visit to Parma or Bologna, try a small cut of their *parmigiano reggiano*. Made from the curds of the cheese making process this dry, brittle cheese simply melts in your mouth.

If you've never seen a skinned rabbit before, look in the window of the *Supermercato* just across the street, they always have a few of them lying there waiting to be bought, heads, tails, eyes and all.

24. GASTRONOMIA PECK, *Via Spadari 9, Tel. 02/871-737.*

This is the main deli that offers everything you could ever imagine wanting. The shelves are packed full of platters of prepared foods, fresh pastas, smoked meats, and vegetables and fruits to go. Why the servers wear polka-dotted bow ties I can't tell you, but everything else in here is a self-explanatory food lover's dream.

25. ROSTICCERIA PECK, *Via Cantu 3, Tel. 02/869-3017. American Express, Visa and Mastercard accepted. Meal for two E25.*

Primarily a takeout place for roasted meats, you can also use their stand-up counter to sample their delicacies. You can get spit roasted chicken as well as pork, beef, and even vegetables all prepared with excellence. They also have perfectly prepared pasta dishes, either hot or cold, that make my mouth water even now. Your meal will be quick, but it will be satisfying.

Markets
Milan definitely has more flea markets and street markets than any other Italian city. Remember, as we've said earlier in the book, always bargain. Don't just accept the first price given. Since you might be pegged as a tourist the price will usually be close to twice as much as offered to Italians. Also, if you're looking for interesting items and you want to avoid the crowds you have to get to each market early.

FIERA SINIGALLIA, *Porta Ticinese. All day Saturdays.*

There are countless peddlers and regular stall holders selling everything from tapes to antiques, as well as books, clothing (new and used) and a variety of curiosities. Definitely the best selection of all the markets. It has grown so big that it merges with the next market on the list below.

MERCATO PAPINIANO, *Viale Papiniano (Porta Ticinese section). Tuesday Mornings and all day Saturdays.*

A good variety of goods, including clothes (new and used), housewares, food, and flowers. The main selection here is food and lots of it. Basically this market and the Sinigallia are one and the same. They stretch from the Porta Ticinese past the Porta Genova and encompass the Piazza San Agostino and beyond. These two combined are quite a sight when you're in Milan on a Saturday. You can spend all day here.

Practical Information
Car Rental
• **Avis**, Linate Airport, *Tel. 02/71-51-23;* Malpensa Airport *02/4009-9375,* plus 10 locations downtown.
• **Hertz**, Linate Airport, *Tel. 02/7020-0297;* Malpensa Airport *02/4009-9010,* plus 5 locations downtown.

Consulates
• **US Consulate**, Via Principe Amadeo 4, *Tel. 02/29-00-18-41*
• **Canadian Consulate**, Via Vittor Pisani 19, *Tel. 02/669-74-51. For emergencies 01/66-98-06-00*
• **United Kingdom Consulate**, Via S. Paolo, *Tel. 02/869-34-42*
• **Australian Consulate**, Via Borgogna 2, *Tel. 02/76-01-33-30*

Local Festivals & Holidays
• **First Sunday in June**, *Festa dei Navigli.* Located along the Navigli (canals) in the Ticinese section this is a folklore celebration with music and a

festival. And even though it is a Sunday most of the stores will be open to accommodate the increased business.
• **December 7**, St. Ambrose day, patron saint of Milan. Features an open-air market surrounding the Basilica of Sant'Ambrogio commonly referred to as "O Bej O Bej."

Postal Services
• **Main Post Office**, Via Cordusio 4, *Tel. 02/869-20-69.* Located near the Duomo, between it and the castle. Open Monday - Friday 8:45am to 7:30am and Saturdays 8:45am to 5:00pm.

Tourist Information & Maps
• **EPT Office**, in Central Station, *Tel. 02/744-065,* or at Linate Airport, *Tel. 02/80-545.* They have maps of the city that are really no help if what you're looking for is down a side street. In conjunction they have information about hotels and can book them for you if you arrive in Milan without a room.

In the next section I explore the best place to get away from Milan, whether for a day trip or longer: the Lake region. Here you will be able to relax amid the natural splendor of either Lago di Maggiore or Lago di Como.

The Lake Region

The northern lake region of Italy has been a preferred spot for vacationers and settlers for centuries. The most important visitor was probably **Julius Caesar**, whose legions left a lasting impression on the landscape with the remains of the forts and cities they built many years ago.

The quaint medieval charm of the lake towns, many of which were founded by the Romans, with their terraced gardens and terra-cotta roofed villas – though stunningly beautiful – pale in comparison to the natural splendor of the breathtaking scenery. This natural beauty has turned what used to be a relatively tourist-free region that could be enjoyed in calm serenity, into a heavily visited area during many times of the year. If you visit in July, August, or early September, the traditional time for Europeans to take their vacations, you will feel as if you're immersed in downtown rush hour instead of the pleasant environs of **Lago Maggiore** or **Lago di Como**. Even during those hectic summer months, the Lake region is splendid vacation spot.

Usually I counsel being car-less in Italy. However, sometimes a car comes in handy in this region. Without the use of an automobile, you may have to restrict yourself to exploring just one lake by ferry. With a car you'll have the

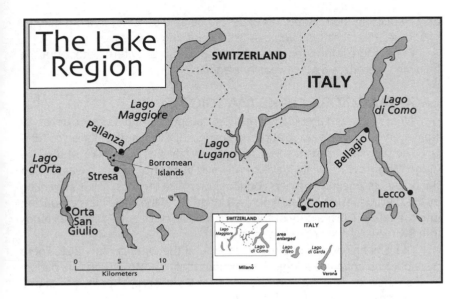

freedom to explore all the lakes at will, and be able to take excursions to wonderful hill towns.

When to Go

Most hotels, restaurants, and shops close during the winter, and ferry service is cut back dramatically, but that time of year is also serenely peaceful. The time to really avoid is July through September, when it seems as if all of Europe has descended on the lakes.

The best time to come is during the Spring months (March to early June) or the Fall months (late September through October). During these periods the ferries operate on a slightly curtailed schedule and some hotels and restaurants are closed, but you will usually have the lakes virtually all to yourself. During these months you may encounter a mist or haze settling over the lakes and periodically obscuring the mountains, but that sometimes can add to the medieval, mystical charm of this wonderful region.

Touring the Lakes

The best way to tour each individual lake is by **ferry**, whether it is a **car ferry** *(traghetto auto)* or a **passenger-only ferry** *(traghetto)*. The ferries take longer than driving a car around the *lungolago* road, but on the water you will be blessed with far superior views of obscure villas and gardens, and best of all you will avoid the maddening traffic that descends during the peak months and even on the weekends in the off-season. The ferries go to all the main towns on each respective lake, so you can enjoy a complete lake experience only by utilizing them. But don't expect to be able to see everything quickly. The ferries take time, and you can't do everything in a day.

To get more information about touring the lakes by ferry, check out the following website: *www.navigazionelaghi.it.*

LAGO MAGGIORE (LAKE MAGGIORE)

What's it like on Lago Maggiore? Magical and relaxing. Come to get away from everything, while also being in the middle of the beauty of Italian culture.

The second largest of the Alpine lakes after Garda is **Lake Maggiore** (**Lago Maggiore** in Italian. It's also known as **Verbano**). The lake was formed during the Ice Age from glaciers coming down from the Alps. This is evidenced by the U-shaped shoreline, its extended length, and the wide inlets advancing into the valley. The majority of the lake is in Italy, but a small section extends into Switzerland in its northern reaches.

The lake has been inhabited since around the ninth century BCE. There have been recent archaeological discoveries that indicate an Iron Age people lived on the lake, who are now referred to as **Golasecca**, after the site of one of their most important burial mounds.

The climate on Lago Maggiore is splendidly mild, which not only assisted human settlement but also a stable agricultural life. These ancient visitors were in all likelihood attracted to the stunning northern scenery, the plentiful game and rich soil, and the beautiful, pristine waters teeming with an abundance of fish. Since the arrival of these early settlers, there have been plenty of visitors to Lago Maggiore, many of them quite famous – Byron, Goethe, and Wagner among them.

It would take volumes to list all of the magnificent towns to visit, with their medieval streets, impressive churches, imposing castles, and more, so I've compiled a list of the best of the best. Once here, use your hotel as a jumping-off point for area sights.

Lago Maggiore Website: *www.lakeweb.it.*

Lakeside Attractions

Visit the **Villa Taranto**, a house built in 1875 and located on the Castagnola between the towns of Intra and Pallanza. (These two towns are so close together it is almost as if they are one and are commonly known as Verbania.) At the villa you'll find over 20,000 species of plants flourishing on over 20 hectares of land. The botanical gardens are quite splendid. Take a relaxing stroll through terraces, lawns, and fountains that make up the grounds. If you're here at the end of April through the beginning of May, you will have stumbled upon the magnificent **Tulip Week**.

If architecture is your pleasure, see the fabulous **Santa Caterina del Sasso**, located between Reno and Cerro on the water. The best way to approach is by boat, where you can get the perfect view of the buildings hewn out of the rock walls of the **Sasso Ballaro**. This monastery was built in the 13th century and added onto over the centuries. Seeing it perched on the cliff walls is mesmerizing.

Another building of architectural interest is the fortified palace on the **Rocca** in Angera. Built by the Visconti family in 1350 on the ruins of an earlier fortress, this place is worth a visit because of the vaulted ceilings and its medieval charm. I also love the tiny village set at the palace's feet that looks as if it hasn't changed in centuries.

Another architectural and historical sight are the remains of the **Vitaliano Castle**, built by Count Ludovico Borromeo between 1519 and 1526 that now rests on one of the three islands that are between Canero and Cannobio. The ferry doesn't stop here (it's really just a speck of an island with a fortified castle on it) but does get close enough for pictures to be taken. Truly magnificent.

Looking for something to bring back home, either for yourself or a friend? Don't miss the **Wednesday Market** at **Luino**, where you can get crafts, food, local clothing, and more. At the same time you can enjoy the sights and sounds of a boisterous local market.

STRESA

For those of you who insist on the best hotels with all the amenities, such as swimming pools, saunas, tennis courts, and more, then you'll want to come to **Stresa**. Called the Pearl of Verbano, Stresa sits below the green slopes of **Mottarone** (which are accessible via a cable car ... a great place for short hikes) and offers a comfortable climate in the summer and mild temperatures in the winter. You also have picturesque beaches, beautiful landscaped gardens, fine restaurants, an abundance of Italian culture and refinement, and much much more. Stresa is an ideal place to stay. And from here you can explore the rest of Lago Maggiore.

Stresa Website: *www.stresa.net.*

Arrivals & Departures

Located 80 miles northwest of Milan, there are a number of daily trains from Milan. If you're driving, take the E 62 to the SS 33, which brings you directly into town.

Where to Stay

1. REGINA PALACE, *Corso Umberto I, Tel. 0323/933-777, Fax 0323/ 933-776. Email: h.regina@stresa.net. Web: www.stresa.net/hotel/regina. 166 rooms. Double E200-250; Suite E350. Breakfast included. All credit cards accepted. *****

A superb hotel situated in an historic and romantic building overlooking the lake. They have a private beach, a pretty garden area for relaxing, outdoor

swimming pool, tennis and squash courts, gymnasium, sun room, sauna, snorkeling equipment, day care, discounts on golf at local courses, and more. The restaurant has perfect views of the lake and the Borromean Islands, and the piano bar offers relaxation in the evening. The rooms here have high ceilings, quaint antique furnishings, and spectacular views of the lake and/or the mountains. Stay here if you have the means.

2. DU PARC, *Via Gignous 1, Tel. 0323/30335, Fax 0323/33596. Email: duparc@internetpiu.com. Web: www.stresa.net/hotel/duparc. Closed October 15 to March 15. 22 rooms. Single E50-100; Double E70-150. Breakfast included. All credit cards accepted. ****

Nestled in a verdant setting, this hotel is set a short distance back from the main street and the shoreline in the upper part of Stresa. Situated in a romantic little villa with panoramic views, this is the perfect choice for those travelers wanting a nice place to stay for not a lot of money. The rooms seem a little small compared with the four and five stars but your stay here will be wonderful. A charming hotel.

3. LA FONTANA, *Via Sempione Nord 1, Tel. 0323/32707, Fax 0323/32708. Email: direzione@lafontanahotel.com. Web: www.lafontanahotel.com. Closed in November. 19 rooms. Single E85. Double E115. Credit cards accepted. Breakfast included.* ***

A tranquil little hotel that has a beautiful internal garden with a fountain. This place started off as a private villa built in the 30's and still has many of the original architectural features. From the third floor you can get good views over the lake. A cute little place with clean comfortable rooms for not a lot of money.

4. SEMPIONE, *Corso Italia 46, 0323/30463. No fax. 17 rooms, 6 with bath, 11 with shower. Single E30-55; Double E50-75. No credit cards accepted.* **

For those travelers on a budget, this is a good two star with clean and comfortable rooms. Not too spacious, but comfortable and accommodating.

Where to Eat

5. L'EMILIANO, *Corso Italia 50, Tel. 0323/31396. Closed Tuesdays, Wednesdays for lunch, and January and February. All credit cards accepted. Dinner for two E80.*

The food here is fabulous. If you want to save some money, order their *menu degustazione* for E28 per person it gives you a first and second course. Their menu is a twist between traditional and *cucina nuova* and mainly consists of fish from the lake. Try their *ravioli di pesce con bisque di crostacei* (ravioli stuffed with fish and served with a crustacean sauce) or their *spaghetti freddi con cozze ed erba cipollina* (cold spaghetti with a sauce of mussels and baby onions). If meat is what you crave, try their *costoletta d'agnello profumate al rosmarino* (lamb cutlets cooked with a touch of rosemary), a succulently exquisite alternative to seafood.

6. PIEMONTESE, *Via Mazzini 25, Tel. 0323/30235. Closed Mondays and holidays. Credit cards accepted. Dinner for two E60.*

Located in the center of Stresa away from the water, the restaurant of the brothers Bellossi specializes in seafood and fish from the lake. In this elegant environment, try some of the *taglierini con vongole verace* (thin spaghetti-like pasta with a spicy oil-based clam sauce) or the tasty *involtini di sogliola e salmone* (rolled filets of sole and salmon). They also offer meat dishes like *costoletta d'agnello al timo con patate arrosto* (lamb cutlet cooked with thyme and served with roast potatoes).

Practical Information

• **Tourist Information Office**, Piazzale Europe 3, *Tel. 0323/31050-30416*

ISOLE BORROMEE (THE BORROMEAN ISLANDS)

Just offshore from Stresa, the three enchanting little **Borromean Islands** will make you feel like you've stepped back in time. The **Isola dei Pescatori** has an ancient and picturesque little fishing village and that's about it, but it is a great place to escape for a while. And to stay if you want utter serenity. The **Isola Bella** has its imposing **Palazzo Borromeo**, complete with a spectacular terraced garden. A tour through the palace brings you in contact with the wealth of the Borromeo family, furnished with Venetian chandeliers and mirrors, puppets, and more. If you visit the island, take the guided tour (*Tel. 30556;* open April–November 9:00am–noon and 1:30pm–5:30pm. Admission E6).

The **Isola Madre** (not on the enclosed map) is world-famous for its **villa** and landscaped **gardens** featuring a wide variety of exotic birds (open April–November 9:00am–noon and 1:30pm–5:30pm; admission E6). Inside the villa you'll find a cute little collection of dolls and puppets dating from the 16th to the 19th centuries. All the islands are just a short ferry ride or small personal boat taxi ride away from Stresa, and are so close that you can visit them all in less than a day.

If you want to stay overnight, here are my recommendations (see map on page 582):

Where to Stay

7. ELVEZIA, *Lungolago Vittorio Emanuele 18, Isola Bella. Tel. 0323/ 30043. Email: info@elveziahotel.com. Web: www.elveziahotel.com. 9 rooms, none with bath. Three bathrooms in the hallway. Single E40-50; Double E65-80. Half board E65. Credit cards accepted.* *

A one star extraordinaire. Though rustic it is a pleasant, and best of all, inexpensive, place to stay on this truly magical island. Be aware that some of the rooms are rather small. Take the half board, since their restaurant is the best place to eat on the island (see below, *Where to Eat*).

8. VERBANO, *Via Ugo Ara 2, Isola dei Pescatori. Tel. 0323/30408, Fax 0323/33129. Email: hotelverbano@tin.it. Web: www.hotelverbano.it. 12 rooms, 8 with bath, 4 with shower. Single E110. Double E150. Breakfast Included. Full board E120. All credit cards accepted.* ***

A truly magical place to stay. Only a short private boat ride away from Stresa, you'll have peace and quiet in the evenings and get the opposite view from the tourists on the mainland, allowing you to savor at the lights of the small town of Stresa reflecting off of the lake. Located in a romantic old building, the hotel has its own private beach – but that's about it. Take them up on the full board meal option, since there are few places to eat on the island … and their restaurant is rather good.

Where to Eat

9. ELVEZIA, *Lungolago Vittorio Emanuele 18, Isola Bella, Tel. 0323/ 30043. Open only in the evenings by reservation only. Closed Mondays and November and March. All credit cards accepted. Dinner for two E45.*
This place has been in the Rossi family for generations. Even though it is large, about 140 seats available, and caters mainly to tourists, they still offer personal attentive service and great food. It's best to find a seat on the verandah porch area overlooking the water. Try their *antipasto di pesce all'isolana* (fish appetizer made island-style), or *le lasagnette alle verdure* (small vegetable lasagna). For seconds any of their fish dishes are superb.

VERBANIA

Verbania is not really a town, its more like a small region, that includes the tiny towns of Pallanza and Intra. The main draw here, as mentioned earlier, is the **Villa Taranto**, a house built in 1875 and located two kilometers north of town, where you'll find over 20,000 species of plants flourishing on over 20 hectares of land. Besides the lovely botanical gardens, there are quaint grounds in which you can take relaxing strolls through terraces, lawns, and fountains (open April–October 8:30am–7:30pm; admission E6.).

Other than that, you can find excellent restaurants, amazing hotels, and peace and tranquility to last you a life time.

Arrivals & Departures

Located on the north shore of Lago Maggiore across from Stresa. You can arrive by ferry from Stresa; by car take the SS 33 to the SS 34 around the lake.

Where to Stay

You'll find that many of the hotels require you to also purchase a full-board meal plan. Inquire about this when making your reservation.

GRAND HOTEL MAJESTIC, *Via Vittorio Veneto 32, Pallanza Tel. 0323/ 504-305, Fax 0323/556-379. Email: info@grandhotelmajestic.it. Web: www.grandhotelmajestic.it. 119 rooms 56 with bath, 63 with shower. Single E155-220; Double E175-240; Suite E500. Breakfast included. *****

Located directly on the lake shore and situated in a romantic old building complete with private beach, indoor swimming pool, private gardens, tennis courts, health club, piano bar, sunbathing terrace, and two restaurants with scenic views over the water. The rooms are expansive, comfortable and come with simple yet elegant furniture, as well as every conceivable amenity. Definitely the place to stay in Verbania.

IL CHIOSTRO, *Via del Ceretti 11, Intra Tel. 0323/53151, Fax 0323/401-231. 49 rooms, only 40 with shower. Single E80; Double E150. Credit cards accepted. Breakfast included.* ***

Located in Verbania's sister town of Intra, this beautiful, quaint, charismatic, romantic hotel is in a 17th century monastery. The second best place to stay while in Verbania in terms of amenities, but the best in terms of character, ambiance and uniqueness. You'll be up the slope of the mountain here, with a stunningly beautiful inner garden courtyard surrounded by arcaded walkways where you can sit and relax. Similar in style to colonial Spanish architecture, you'll find peace and tranquility as well as a good restaurant, room service, lobby bar, tennis courts and more. The rooms have been completely refitted to contain every modern comfort. If only the monks had it so good when they lived here.

CASTAGNOLA, *Via al Collegio 18, Pallanza Tel. 0323/503-414, Fax 0323/556-341. 107 rooms, 3 with bath, 104 with shower. Single E75; Double E100. Visa and Diners Club accepted.* **

What a two star! Located on the mountain overlooking the water and the sister cities of Pallanza and Intra, here you'll find yourself in a tranquil, romantic environment complete with tennis courts, ample park lands for *bocce* or *calcio*, a gymnasium, an excellent restaurant and more. The hotel has huge ceilings, creating the feeling of immense space in your rooms. The bathrooms have been modernized with showers, but are quite small. A great place to stay for the budget traveler and anyone else.

Where to Eat

MILANO, *Corso Zanitello 2, Tel. 0323/556-816. Closed Tuesdays, January 10-February 10 and the first 10 days of August. All credit cards accepted. Dinner for two E50.*

Located on the shoreline, this is the best place to eat in Verbania, especially on their lakeside terrace with the view of the water and the little island of San Giovanni. Situated in an old villa with beautiful gardens and elegant dining rooms, you can't go wrong with the setting or the food. Some of his dishes are a little exotic, like the appetizer *trota alla menta e aceta rossa* (trout with a mint and red vinegar sauce) and the pasta dish *tagliolini agli scampi e zafferano* (pasta with shrimp and saffron) but they all taste fantastic. For seconds their meats are superbly and simply prepared, as are their fish dishes.

LA CAVE, *Viale delle Magnolie 16, Tel. 0323/503-346. Closed Wednesdays and the first two weeks of November. All credit cards accepted. Dinner for two E45.*

On the lake shore, the atmosphere here is comfortable and relaxing. Couple that with fantastic service and superb food, and you have a great place to eat. They present their dishes at your table in a covered cart so you can get an idea of what you're going to get. Try any of their fish and seafood *antipasti*. For *primo*, sample the exquisite *tagliolini all'astice* (pasta with lobster). For seconds you have a wide variety of options from seafood to meat, many of them roasted over an open flame.

Practical Information
• **Tourist Information Office**, Corso Zanitello 8, *Tel. 0323/503-249*

LAGO DI COMO (LAKE COMO)
This lake is a European tourist paradise. Over the centuries **Lake Como** (Lago di Como) has become the destination for royalty – and most recently for the nouveaux riche glitterati – as a result of its intense landscapes and scenery. You can find every imaginable activity around Lake Como including swimming, sailing, canoeing, water skiing, sailing, fishing, golf, hunting, tennis, hiking, rock climbing and much more. If you're not into active vacations and prefer the more sedate pursuits like sightseeing, Como will not disappoint. There are vast parks, exotic gardens, lush villas, picturesque villages, and ancient castles, basilicas, art galleries and museums scattered along the lake.

In this way, it is a tourist paradise since there is so much to do, but as with the rest of the lakes in Northern Italy, they are also great places to relax.

The Lago di Como website is *www.lakecomo.com*.

Como is the perfect jumping-off point from which to explore the lake and its many little towns either by ferry or car. You can also hop on the *funiculare*, located on the north edge of the city, and go up to the **Brunate** section of Como that is dotted with exquisite mansions and gardens. A short way outside of town (5 km) is the village of **Cernobbio**, where you can find the princely **Villa d'Este** with its lush gardens and enormous grounds. The villa is now the area's best five star deluxe hotel, but you can still wander through the grounds even if you're not staying there.

Como produces almost one-fifth of the world's silk supply. Ancient merchants stole the secret of the silk worm from the Chinese many centuries ago, and began production of the seductive cloth along the banks of Lake Como and on the outskirts of the city. As such, you can find many bargains on silk in Como. If shopping is of little interest, you should visit the neo-classic **Villa Olmo** also on the outskirts of town. It is currently the seat of the local government, but the magnificent gardens are open to the public year round (9:00am–noon and 1:30pm–6:00pm).

Arrivals & Departures
Located 70 kilometers north of Milan, you can either take the train from there (four times a day) or drive up the Autostrada A9 straight to the city.

Where to Stay

1. METROPOLE E SUISSE, *Piazza Cavour 19, Tel. 031/269-4444, Fax 031/300-808. Email: info@hotelmetropolesuisse.com. Web: www.hotelmetropolesuisse.com. Closed December 20-January 10. 71 rooms. Single E110-145; Double E135-205. All credit cards accepted. Breakfast included.* ****

One of the oldest hotels in the town. The rooms are spacious each with a different style of furnishings. Some come with antiques from the '30's, others are done in the elaborate Venetian style, and some have more modern assemblies. The bathrooms are accommodating and come with a small complimentary toiletry kit. Each floor has its own sauna for your use. All the amenities of a four star hotel.

2. TERMINUS, *Lungo Lario Trieste 14, Tel. 031/329-111, Fax 031/302-550. Web: www.albergoterminus.com. 38 rooms. Single E110-165; Double E140-210. All credit cards accepted. Breakfast E15.* ***

Renovated to have all modern facilities this charming hotel has also maintained the ambiance of its 19th century roots. The common areas are filled with epochal pieces, tiled and mosaic floors which all helps to give the place character and charm. Each room is different in terms of dimensions and

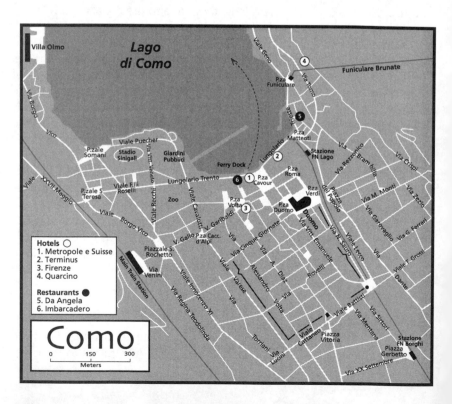

decor. In the small tower there is one room that covers two floors. A splendid place to stay.

3. FIRENZE, *Piazza Volta 16, Tel. 031-300-333, Fax 031/300-101. Email: info@albergofirenze.it. Web: www.albergofirenze.it. 40 rooms. Single E80; Double E130. All credit cards accepted. Breakfast included. ****

In a central location, five minutes from the Duomo, Piazza Cavour or the lake this hotel is in a beautiful building. Going upstairs to the first floor you are confronted with a brightly lit mirrored hall which blends into the bar/breakfast area. The rooms are spacious and accommodating with green doors, parquet floors, cute little lamps on the wall, and beautiful furnishings. Only thirteen rooms so far have A/C so if you come in the summer ask for one of those. The bathrooms with their black and white motif are clean and accommodating. Hair dryers available on request. A good hotel at a good price.

4. QUARCINO, *Salita Quarcino 4, Tel. 031/303-944, Fax 031/304-678. Email: info@hotelquarcino.it. Web: www.hotelquarcino.it. 13 rooms only 3 with bath. Single E60; Double E90. Mastercard and Visa accepted. Breakfast included. ***

Located near the *funiculare* up to Brunate about 10 minutes from the center of Como in a tranquil and lush setting. A favorite of budget travelers. The rooms are spartan but dignified. A quality, low-cost option in Como.

Where to Eat

5. DA ANGELA, *Via Foscolo 16, Tel. 031/304-656. Closed Sundays and August. All credit cards accepted. Dinner for two E75.*

Local food at luxury prices. Located near the Stazione F.N. Lago (not the main train station), this is a popular place in Como. An elegant but rustic atmosphere, try their *coniglio alle olive* (rabbit with olives) or their fantastic *gnocchetti al sugo di salsicce e pomodoro* (little gnocchi in a sauce of tomatoes and sausage).

6. IMBARCADERO, *Via Cavour 20, Tel. 031/277-341. Closed the first ten days in January. Credit cards accepted. Dinner for E60.*

Located a few meters from the water's edge, this relaxed place offers great traditional dishes, simple in preparation but bursting with flavor. In the summer they open up their terrace so you can enjoy a great meal and the sounds, sights, and smells of the lake. An inexpensive and quite satisfying alternative to ordering a la carte is their *menu del giorno*, which offers a different primo and secondo each day for only E25 per person. Fish, soup, pasta, and meat all find their place onto this menu.

Practical Information

• **Tourist Information Office**, Piazza Cavour 17, *Tel. 031/274-064*

BELLAGIO

The location of this village is utterly divine. Surrounded by the lake on three sides, you have fantastic views. And while here you can enjoy strolls through the winding medieval streets or engage in any number of water sports. Down on the eastern shore of the peninsula is the quiet port of **Pescallo** with its many boats. The most famous sights here are the Villa Melzi and the Villa Serbelloni.

The **Villa Melzi**, Lungolario Marconi, open 10:30am-4:00pm, is known for its gardens ornately strewn with monuments and a small little pond of its own covered with lily pads and flowers. The **Villa Serbelloni** is now a five star hotel whose gardens are only open to non-guests from 10:30am to 4:00pm, closed Mondays. Also known for its intricate gardens, the only way to truly appreciate them is by staying there – but the price is rather high.

Bellagio Website: *www.bellagiolakecomo.com.*

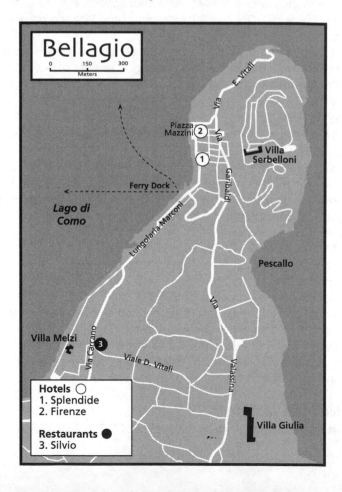

Arrivals & Departures

Located 80 kilometers north of Milan, you can drive here by taking the Autostrada A9 to Como, go through town to the north end near the *funicular*. Here the *lungolago* road turns into the SS 583, which will lead you along the Lake to Bellagio. You can also take the train to Como, and simply take a ferry from there to Bellagio.

Where to Stay

1. SPLENDIDE EXCELSIOR, *Lungolario Marconi 26, Tel. 031/950-225, Fax 031/951-224. Web: www.hsplendide.com. Closed September 20 & March 15. 47 rooms, 13 with bath, 34 with shower. Double E115 130. Credit cards accepted. Breakfast included.* ***

Located along the lakeside road, this hotel is situated in a romantic old *palazzo* built in 1912. The common areas are in the turn of the century style while rooms have been transported from the '70's. Some rooms on the first floor have tiny balconies overlooking the lake. The bathrooms are dated but accommodating. There is a heated indoor swimming pool, a garden area for relaxing, and good restaurant with a scenic view over the lake as well as a piano bar for entertainment at night. They actually feature a small musical ensemble in the evenings. A great place to stay.

2. FIRENZE, *Piazza Mazzini 46, Tel. 031/950-342, Fax 031/951-722. Email: hotflore@tin.it. Web: www.bellagiolakecomo.com/florence. Closed November and March. 34 rooms, all but one single with bath. Single E110-130; Double E160-200. Credit cards accepted. Breakfast included.* ***

In the center of town, this hotel occupies two romantic old buildings, one built in 1720, the other from the past century. The entry hall is like something out of the middle ages, very elegant. The rooms are all different sizes and come with a variety of different furnishings but all are comfortable and spacious. They have a beautiful garden area as well as a really good restaurant and lobby bar that features American jazz in the high season.

Where to Eat

3. SILVIO, *Via Carcano 12, Tel. 031/950-322. Closed January and February. Master card and Visa accepted. Dinner for two E40.*

A family-run place near the Villa Melzi. Mom's in the kitchen, and her son and husband are serving and greeting in the dining room. All you'll find here is whatever they caught on the lake in the morning or during the day. They fry, grill, or bake the fish to perfection and also mix it with *risotto* (rice) or ladle it over pasta. They have a relaxing terrace area that should be enjoyed in the summer. The best place to eat while in Bellagio.

Practical Information

• **Tourist Information Office**, Lungolario A. Marconi, *Tel. 031/950-204*

Chapter 20

ALPINE ITALY

Why go the Rockies, or any other North American winter resort, when you can afford to go to the Alps? The scenery is more majestic in the Alps, the skiing better, and off the slopes the community life in the villages is far more vibrant and enjoyable.

Alpine Italy is a land in and of itself, culturally separate and distinct, but still very much a part of the heart and soul of Italy. Alpine Italy spans a number of different provinces starting in and snaking west to east through Piemonte, Val d'Aosta, Lombardia, Trentino Alto-Adige, Sud Tirol and eventually culminating in Friuli Venezia Giulia. Since Alpine Italy extends from France, passing underneath Switzerland and Austria and ending at Eastern Europe, it encompasses all manner of natural settings, and entails a wide variety of cultural influences. To really do this area justice would entail an entire book. Without that luxury I'll do my best to capture the area's essence in this one small chapter, and few choice destinations.

Alpine Italy's diversity is expressed through its varied cuisine. Italian favorites abound but you can also find more Germanic culinary delights such as *strudel* and *snitzel*; and local beer is as plentiful as the wine, while sausage is as plentiful on the table as pasta.

The scenery is varied as well. You can find cows lolling through the wind swept grasses with bells around their necks just as you would in Switzerland. There are also mountain chalets as you would find in Austria. Spotting an old timer in the traditional attire of *Leiderhausen* is not unheard of either. In all, anywhere you go in Alpine Italy will be a change of pace from a regular Italian vacation. Whether it is for skiing in the winter, hiking in the summer, or just exploring all year round, Alpine Italy is a perfect place to come to get away from it all, and to find scenery, activities and cuisine you would never expect to see while on a trip to Italy.

A prime example of the uniqueness of the area is the "Ice Man," a prehistoric traveler who was frozen in the Alps, and who now resides in a museum in **Bolzano**. This one of a kind glimpse into humanity's past is a rare treasure, and is a must see if you come to Alpine Italy.

Since Alpine Italy is so extensive, we are only going to cover what would be considered some of the major locations. But from these places there are innumerable day trips to scenic little towns, stunning nature preserves, pristine mountain refuges and more. Featured here are the towns of **Aosta** and **Courmayeur** In Val d'Aosta, **Bolzano** and **Merano** in Sud Tirol; and **Bormio** in Lombardia. These are the gems of the region, but there are plenty of other places to explore in Alpine Italy, and so much to do.

AOSTA

If you're interested in Roman ruins with a backdrop of snow-capped mountains, complete with medieval churches, buildings, and towers as a foreground, this unique scene can be yours in **Aosta**. Sitting in the flat lands of the nearby mountains of **Monte Emilius** (3,600 meters) and **Becca di Nona** (3,200 meters) this town was built as a Roman fort and the gateway through the **Great** and **Little St. Bernard** passes.

The Roman fort was erected in 25 BCE and was then called Augustus Praetoria Salassorum, and today an arch dedicated to Augustus remains in the city. The plan of the town still retains the simple structured layout of its Roman origins and the old town is surrounded by the walls erected at that time. These walls form a rectangle 725 meters by 572 meters that contains twenty lookout towers. The city is the capital of the autonomous region known as **Val d'Aosta** and is a prime location for skiing in winter and kayaking, rafting and hiking in the summer. Aosta is a good jumping-off point for any of these activities.

Arrivals & Departures

Aosta is 98 kilometers from Turin, from which three trains leave daily: one in the early am, one at 1:00pm, and one in the late evening. The trip takes about an hour each way. If you don't want to rush, stay the night.

Where to Stay

1. EUROPA, *Piazza Narbone 8, Tel. 0165/236-363, Fax 0165/40-566. Email: hoteleurope@ethotels.com. Web: www.ethotels.com. 71 rooms, all with bath. Per person, per night E50-90. Credit cards accepted. *****

This is an exceptional hotel complete with elegant furnishings, a fitness center, piano bar, two-tiered restaurant that serves local and international food. The rooms are perfect with everything you could want, even a video cassette player for rent.

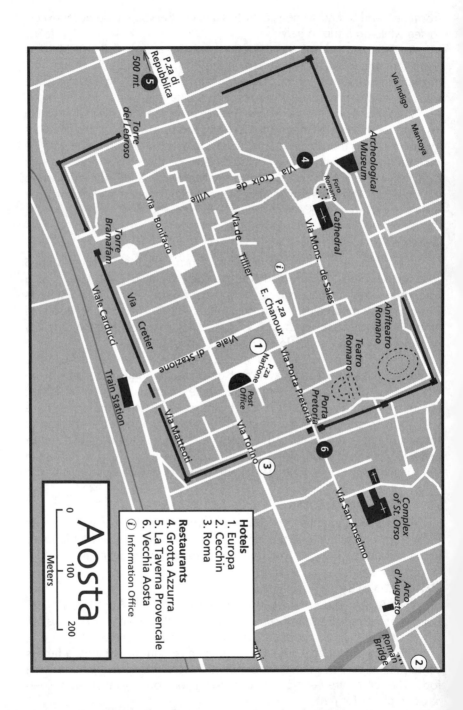

Aosta

0 ___ 100 ___ 200
Meters

Hotels
1. Europa
2. Cecchin
3. Roma
Restaurants
4. Grotta Azzurra
5. La Taverna Provencale
6. Vecchia Aosta
ⓘ Information Office

2. CECCHIN, *Via Ponte Romano 27, Tel. 0165/45262, Fax 0165/31736. Web: www.adava.vao.it/Alberghi/aosta/cecchin.htm. 10 rooms all with bath. Single E70; Double E120. Breakfast E8. Credit cards accepted. Closed in November.* ***

Located right by the ancient Roman bridge, this is a quiet, simple bed and breakfast style hotel with only 10 rooms. Do not be put off by the entrance, which is through a trattoria, this is an informal family run place. The furnishings and accommodations are rustic but comfortable. The bathrooms are basic but have everything you need. There is no air conditioning but it is hardly needed even in the summer.

3. ROMA, *Via Torino 7, Tel. 0165/40821, Fax 0165/32404. Email: hroma@libero.it. Web: www.adava.vao.it/Alberghi/roma/roma.htm. 33 rooms, 3 with bath, 30 with shower. Single E40-55; Double E80-120. Breakfast E6. Credit cards accepted.* ***

Located near the Arch of Augustus, this is a hospitable, clean and comfortable three star housed in a renovated older building. One of the oldest hotels in town, the renovations have given a more modern look and feel to the place. Their restaurant creates some wonderfully appetizing local dishes and their downstairs bar is a place to relax after a tough day. Some of the rooms have just recently got TVs but with the stunning vistas out your window, there's no need to sedate yourself with media *soma*.

Where to Eat

4. LA TAVERNA PROVENCALE, *Via Guido Saba 1, Tel. 0165/236-356. Credit cards accepted. Dinner for two E45.*

A two-tiered brightly lit hotel restaurant attached to the Holiday Inn. They serve the local favorites here all made perfectly. Try the *bouillabaisse* for *primo*, after a fine plate of *grigliata di verdure* (grilled vegetables) for starters. Then you can either move onto a fine fish dish like *pesce persico alle verdure di stagione* (filets of perch cooked with seasonal vegetables) or a great meat dish like *tagliata di manzo ai petali di carciofi* (beef steak with artichoke leaves). Or if you want to save a little money and still get two courses plus dessert, try one of their four fixed price menus from E20-30.

5. GROTTA AZZURRA, *Via Croix de Ville 97, Tel. 0165/262-474. Closed Wednesdays. No credit cards accepted. Dinner for two E40.*

A great little pizzeria, and, as the name suggests – the *grotta azzurra* is the famous grotto under the Isle of Capri in the Bay of Naples – it serves fine fish dishes. Try their *insalata di mare* (seafood salad) and their *spaghetti alla vongole verace* (with a spicy clam sauce), or a fine *zuppa di mare* (seafood soup). And if you can't choose between the fish options, you can always select a pizza made with mounds of cheese.

6. **VECCHIA AOSTA**, *Piazza Porte Pretoriane 2, Tel. 0165/361-186. Closed Tuesday Nights and Wednesdays, two weeks in July and two weeks in October. Credit cards accepted. Dinner for two E45.*

A nice internal ambiance with an ancient Roman feel and look about it. You can be served outside on their terrace also. Here they make some fine local specialties like *ravioli al sugo di arrosto* (roasted ravioli) as well as some great fondues. You can also get a tourist menu for E15 per person, as well as a gastronomic menu for E18. A great place to come and relax and eat simple hearty food.

Seeing the Sights

Take in the Roman ruins and the extant Roman structures, or wander around the medieval and Gothic churches gracing this pleasing town. These are the sights in the town, but outside you will find many too: those of the natural bent. Hiking, skiing, kayaking and other outdoor pursuits can be found in the mountains surrounding Aosta. For more information contact the **tourist office**, Piazza Chanoux 8, *Tel. 0165/23-66-27 or 35655, Fax 0165/34667*, open 9:00am-noon and 3:00pm-8:00pm.

PONTE ROMANO

Located over the **Butheir River** at the eastern part of the city, this is an ancient Roman bridge still in use (after centuries of renovations, of course) even though the course of the Butheir river changed during the Middle Ages and didn't flow underneath the bridge. The humpbacked span is 6 meters wide and 17 meters long and was built in the time of Augustus, at the end of the first century BCE.

ARCO D'AUGUSTO

Piazza Arco d'Augusto.

Not grand or imposing by comparison to those found in Rome, but this **arch** is astounding in that it was built in 25 BCE in homage to Augustus and to commemorate the victory by the Romans over a local tribe called Salassi. This monument, which is perfectly aligned with the Praetorian gate, is 11.5 meters high and represents a combination of Doric and Corinthian styles. The arch used to be adorned with statues, bas-reliefs, and trophies but these were removed during the many "Barbarian" invasions of the Roman Empire. The crucifix that is under the vault was placed there in 1542.

TEATRO ROMANO

Via Bailage. Open Winter 9:30am–noon and 2:00pm–4:30pm. Summer open 9:00am–7:00pm.

This was once a covered **theater** that was used so that shows could be performed in inclement weather. Its construction was begun after the city was erected and sits over private residences that had already been in place. What remains of this theater is the facade (which is 22 meters high), the *cavea* (which was used to help cover the theater), the stage, and the side portico. All are very well preserved.

ANFITEATRO ROMANO
Via dell'Anfiteatro. Contact the Sisters of San Giuseppe in advance to arrange for a visit, *Tel. 0165/262-149.*

Built in the middle of the first century CE, this **amphitheater** used to measure 86 meters by 76 meters and had 60 arches on each of its two floors. It could hold over 2,000 spectators (double the number of inhabitants in the city at the time). It is a little worse for wear, and all that remains today are eight arches that have been incorporated into the **Convent of the Sisters of San Giuseppe**. This could be a more interesting ruin if the city would bother to take the time and money to excavate it properly.

PORTA PRAETORIA
Located between via Sant'Anselmo and Via Porte Pretoriane.

This once was the eastern entrance to the town and dates back to 25 BCE, when the city was founded. It is made of parallel double stone walls and is open at the bottom by three arches. The external wall is 4.5 meters thick and the internal wall is about 3.5 meters. The space between the walls was used as a weapons storeroom. Today over three meters of the gate and wall lie under the ground, due to the periodic flooding of the Dora over the years. The tower next to the gate was built in the 12th century as a residence for the lords of the city. Today the ground floor is used as an exhibit space featuring local artists.

CATTEDRALE
Piazza Cattedrale. Open 7:00am–7:00pm.

Built on the sight of the Roman forum that dates from the fourth century CE, this Romanesque **cathedral** was constructed from 994 to 1026. It was altered many times over the centuries, with addition of the cloister, a neo-classic facade, and cross vaults inside. On a bright sunny day you will really appreciate the spectacle of the sun streaming through the 23 stained glass windows.

COMPLEX OF SAINT ORSO
Via and Piazzetta dell'Orso. *Tel. 0165/262-026.* Winter 9:30am–noon and 2:00pm–5:30pm. Summer 9:00am–7:00pm.

This Romanesque and Gothic complex includes the church of Saints Peter and Orso, the bell tower clock, the crypt, the Museum of Treasure, the cloister of Saint Orso, the buildings of the Priorate, and the ancient cemetery.

Everything about this complex gives us an insight into the religious day to day life from the fifth century to the fifteenth century.

Sports & Recreation
Hiking
The best time to hike in this area is July, August, and the first two weeks of September. Otherwise it can be a little chilly. Contact the tourist office in Aosta listed above, and request a free list of campgrounds, trails, and alpine refuges *(rifugi alpini)* for rent along the many twisting trails of the surrounding peaks. For more detailed information, contact the **Club Alpino Italiano**, *Tel. 0165/40194, Fax 0165/36-32-44*, located above the tourist office in Aosta.

Skiing
High season is November through March, and as such can be very crowded. It is best to make reservations well in advance. Contact the local **tourist office**, Piazza Chanoux 8, *Tel. 0165/23-66-27 or 35655, Fax 0165/34667*, 9:00am-noon and 3:00pm-8:00pm, for a free pamphlet they distribute called *Winter Season, Aosta Valley*. The pamphlet contains up-to-date information about skiing, hotels, events, and more. Courmayeur is the best known ski resort in the area and is Italy's oldest (see below).

Aosta has a *funiculare* to carry skiers up **Mount Emilius**. It is located just behind the train station away from the historic part of town. In the winter, Aosta fills up with skiers from all over the world – not only to sample her slopes but to also bathe in her beauty and charm.

COURMAYEUR
Courmayeur and its sister city five kilometers away, **Entreve**, are located at the base of **Mont Blanc**, the highest peak in the Alps. Entreve is at the entrance to the Mont Blanc Tunnel which offers easy access to France. Both towns serve up some of the best skiing in Italy. The economies of Courmayeur and Entreve are completely geared towards winter sporting activities, and to a lesser but not insignificant degree summer relaxation and hiking, since many hotels stay open year round. In fact there is summer skiing, horse back riding, hang gliding, canoeing and over 280 km of mountain hiking trails in the vicinity.

Courmayeur is Italy's oldest Alpine resort and as such is able to offer skiers of all levels everything they need to have the time of their lives. There are over 140 km of downhill and cross-country skiing runs. Just a few hundred meters from the main square, **Piazzale Monte Bianco**, is the **Funivia Courmayeur**, which transports skiers and sightseers up the first leg of the mountain to reach the choicest slopes this area has to offer. In Entreve there are two more such *funivie* running up Mont Blanc for your skiing pleasure. In the summer the *funivie* carry hikers and nature lovers up into the mountains to explore the area's natural beauty. Courmayeur and Entreve are year round paradises.

Arrivals & Departures

If you're driving from Aosta, take the E 25 straight into Courmayeur. Be aware that during most times of the year there will be a lot of traffic, since this road leads to the **Mont Blanc Tunnel** that cuts through the mountain into France and the ski center of Chamonix.

The only other way to get here is by bus. You'll find the **tourist office** in the bus terminal, *Piazza Monte Bianco, Tel. 0165/842-060.* Here you can get up to date information about skiing, hiking, alpine huts, hotel availability, etc. They also supply superb maps.

Where to Stay

Wherever you stay, you're going to pay through the nose. This is another of those places that was created by the rich and famous many years ago for their pleasure, then left for the not-so-rich-and-famous to enjoy later. But the prices stayed the same.

I strongly recommend making reservations at least six months in advance, summer or winter (in June virtually everything shuts down so shopkeepers, restaurateurs, and hoteliers can take their vacations), especially if you want to stay on a weekend.

PALACE BRON, *Via Plan Gorret 41, Tel. 0165/846-742, Fax 0165/844-015. 27 rooms, 1 junior suite. Minimum 3 day stay. Web: www.palacebron.it. Email: hotelpb@tin.it. Double E200-350. Breakfast included. Credit cards accepted.* ****

Located above the town of Courmayeur, here you can get away from all the hustle and bustle of the ski town and besides the view from the restaurant, lounge, and piano bar is breathtaking. Windows are everywhere to make sure you don't miss the snow-capped beauty. Whitewashed walls, wood paneling and fireplaces dominate the decor downstairs and the rooms come with floral patterned bed spreads, curtains and chairs. Not quite as down to earth and wonderfully all encompassing as the Gran Baita, but here you have a tranquil upscale B&B type setting. You can enjoy the spectacular garden in the summer as well as utilize a shuttle bus to take guests to and from various locations all year round.

PAVILLON, *Strada Regionale 62, 11013 Courmayeur. Tel. 0165/846-120, Fax 0165/8460-122. Email: info@pavillon.it. Web: www.pavillon.it. 50 rooms, 10 of which are junior suites. Single E150-260; Double E200-420. Credit cards accepted.* ****

Near the *funivia* that takes skiers up the mountain, this is one of the largest places in town, and it only has 50 rooms. The exterior with its stone, dark wood, yellow awnings and cascading red flowers is quite impressive. The lobby and the rooms are finished with light wood and earth tones, creating a calming effect. Their restaurant, Le Bistroquet, has magnificent views of the mountains and serves superb food. Other than that they have an indoor swimming pool, sauna, sun deck, weight rooms, and shuttle bus to cart guests back and forth to their destinations. Right in the middle of things. Basically in stumbling distance from many watering holes. A great choice in Courmayeur.

DEL VIALE, *Viale Monte Bianco 74, Tel. 0165/846-712, Fax 0165/844-513. Email: info@hoteldelviale.com. Web: www.hoteldelviale.com. 23 rooms, 12 with bath, 11 with shower. Single E90-150; Double E100-260. Credit cards accepted. ***

Located on the way to Entreve and near the Gran Baita, this is a rustic looking typical little guest house/hotel with great interior decor. The restaurant is a wonderful spot, with its open kitchen separated by only a thick wooden table for the dining area, and with the roaring flame in the fireplace oven. All the ambiance seems to have been used up in the common areas, for the rooms are whitewashed and the furniture is basic Italian modern; though they are comfortable and come with every three star amenity.

CHALET PLAN GORRET, *Via Plan Gorret 45, Tel. 0165/844-832, Fax 0165/844-842. Email: chaletplangorret@libero.it. Web: www.plangorret.it. 6 rooms all with shower. Minimum 3 day stay. Double with half board E140-190. No credit cards accepted. ***

Do you want to stay in a real alpine chalet? This is the place. If you are thinking about staying someplace that is quaint and filled with character and ambiance, you've got the Chalet Plan Gorret. No upscale amenities except for privacy (you're up a hill from the main town near the Palace Bron), along with great views, a small bar area, and good hearty food served with the meal plan. And last but not least, the atmosphere kindles romance. If you like staying in country inns or Bed and Breakfasts, this is the place for you.

Where to Eat

Many of the hotels will require you to purchase a half meal plan depending on the season, which means you get to eat breakfast and one other meal of the day at the hotel. With your other meal here are two restaurants I know you'll love. If these don't please your palate, there are plenty more around.

PIERRE ALEXIS 1877, *Via Marconi 54, Tel. 0165/843-517. Closed Mondays. Visa Accepted. Dinner for two E45.*

An authentic rustic place that serves excellent local salami as an appetizer. The soups and most other offerings have a strong base of cheese in them, and then you get to the fish and meat dishes and the cook goes wild. Maybe it's some sort of French influence, but they have a great *trota in salsa delicata al pepe rosa* (trout in a delicate red pepper sauce) and other interesting dishes. There are also plenty of hearty meat dishes for you Alpine food lovers.

LE RELAIS DU MONT BLANC, *S.S. 26 #18, Tel. 0165/846-777. Closed Tuesdays and Wednesdays for lunch as well as all of June as well as October 15 through November 30. All credit cards accepted. Dinner for two E50.*

A large place, over 100 people can be seated at one time. The restaurant features exquisite fondues. Anything to do with cheese this place does great: *minestra di formaggi* (mixed cheese soup), *maccheroni ai formaggi alpini* (macaroni and alpine cheese). Besides the cheeses, the chef seems to roast the meats to perfection too. You can't go wrong here.

Sports & Recreation
Ski Guides
You can hire **alpine ski guides** to take you on guided skiing through the mountains. You need a group of at least two and no more than eight including the guide. Cost per person (excluding the guide, of course) is E38. You get to ski or hike from Italy to France or vice-versa, then take a bus in the other direction. Loads of fun but exhausting.

BOLZANO
If you like Tuscany, you are going to love Sud Tirol, the region of Italy that contains **Bolzano**. As yet undiscovered by North American tourists, I predict that Sud Tirol will soon become a very popular place indeed, because it has the best of two countries, Austria and Italy, combined into one. Before WWI Sud Tirol was part of Austria, now it is an autonomous region within Italy; and this combination creates a unique blend of cultures, food, and festivities.

The best place to start your exploration of Sud Tirol is Bolzano. With only about 100,000 people, Bolzano has a small town feel but contains all manner of big city amenities. Great shopping, wonderful art galleries, excellent museums, superb restaurants, and world-class hotels make Bolzano an excellent vacation spot. Couple that with its location deep in the heart of the Alps, and Bolzano can be a jumping-off point for all sorts of winter sporting activities, or summer hiking, mountain biking or rafting adventures.

Surrounded by vineyards and apple orchards, and located at the foot of the Alps, this city is the center of commerce and tourism in Sud Tirol. Now with the addition of the one of a kind "**Ötzi**," the "**Ice Man**," an ancient mummified hunter found by two hikers in the Alps in 1991, Bolzano is more popular than ever.

Sud Tirol is a magical place, a natural choice for a unique holiday experience. Protected from cold northerly winds by the Dolomites, the climate is exceptionally warm in comparison to other central European regions. You can even have great hiking adventures as late as November. The pleasant climate and varied landscape offer an ideal backdrop for visitors to enjoy a wealth of activities, including: skiing, mountain biking, hiking, white water rafting, and paragliding. Whether you are looking for winter sports activities, summer alpine hiking, or urbane city living and cultural activities Sud Tirol offers something for everyone.

For more information about Bolzano, visit *www.bolzano.net*, *www.sudtirol.com/bolzano*, or *www.hallo.com*. For information about Sud Tirol, visit *www.suedtirol.info*.

Arrivals & Departures

Bolzano now has a small **airport** which opened in 1999; there are flights from Frankfurt and Rome. (Airport Bolzano Dolomiti, *Tel. 0471/251-681, Email: info@abd-airport.it, Web: www.abd-airport.it.*) By taxi from the airport you are only 25 minutes away from the center of town.

Bolzano can also be reached by train, bus or car. This ease of access makes it a welcoming destination for all travelers. Train from the closest major Italian cities, Venice or Milan, will take about 3-4 hours, depending on the type of train you catch. The Autostrada 22 from the south brings you just outside of town. Travel time by car is slightly less than by train since you have less stops and detours to make.

Getting Around Town

Bolzano is made for walking and biking with miles of trails and bike paths. Public bus service is also extensive. All of which helps make Bolzano a very livable city.

Orientation

Along the confluence of two rivers, the Isarco running along the southern boundary of the town, and the Talvera bisecting the city from the north, Bolzano is set in a natural bowl between stunning mountain peaks. The train station is the starting point for most visitors. To get to the center of town from here simply walk out the station, across the Via Garibaldi, through the piazza in front of the station and up the Viale Stazione.

This will lead to the main piazza of the town, the **Piazza Walther**, where the Duomo is located. Just as you get to the piazza, on the right hand side, at the end of the Viale Stazione is the **information office**. Stop in here for a map. Though Bolzano is laid out on an easy to navigate plan, it cannot hurt to have some guidance as you wander around.

Where to Stay

1. CITTA, *Piazza Walther 21, Tel. 0471/975-221, Fax 0471/976-688. Web: www.hotelalpi.info. Email: info@hotelcitta.info. 102 rooms. Single E85-95; Double E110-150. All credit cards accepted. Breakfast included.* ***

A simply incredible place to stay in Bolzano. Great rooms, excellent location, professional staff, charming ambiance, and a wellness center

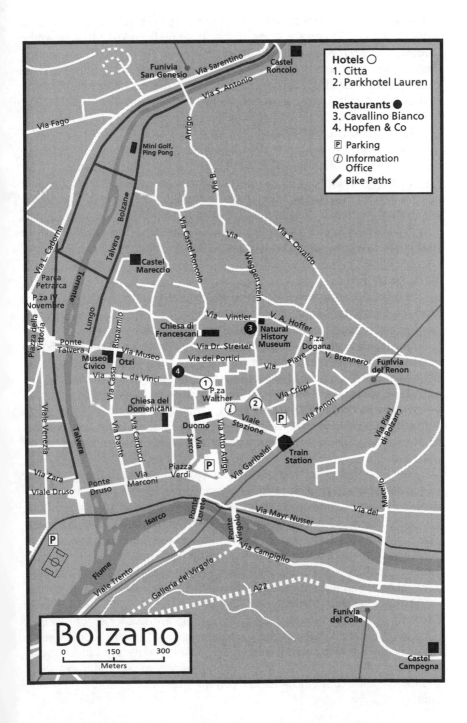

Hotels ○
1. Citta
2. Parkhotel Lauren

Restaurants ●
3. Cavallino Bianco
4. Hopfen & Co

Ⓟ Parking
ⓘ Information Office
Bike Paths

Bolzano

0   150   300
Meters

available for guests makes the Hotel Citta a spa-like retreat as well as a wonderful hotel. Situated in a Liberty style building from 1912 that faces the Duomo, they also have a restaurant/café situated on the main square, Piazza Walther. An ideal place to grab a drink and people watch. But it is the wellness center, complete with dry and wet saunas, Turkish bath, and whirlpool, which makes this hotel truly special. Massage appointments are also available. The Hotel Citta is a wonderful place to stay in Bolzano.

    2. PARKHOTEL LAURIN, *Via Laurin 4, Tel. 0471/311-000; Fax 0471/ 311-148. Email: info@laurin.it. Web: www.laurin.it. 96 rooms. Single E110- 160; Double E160-230. All credit cards accepted. Breakfast included.* ****

    Definitely the best place to stay in Bolzano. Situated in an historic building surrounded by a pleasant garden, a playground for kids, a small pool, and a bar that offers excellent live music, the Parkhotel is a treat. The rooms are all styled differently and come with all 4-star amenities. The bathrooms are resplendent with marble. The ideal place to stay in Bolzano.

Where to Eat

    South Tyrol is not only a fantastic holiday destination, but it also offers many great food products: Speck, wine, apples, dairy products, bread, honey, berries, and grappa are all true delights for your palate.

    I am sure you are wondering ... what the heck is speck? **Speck** is a lightly smoked ham seasoned for a minimum of 22 weeks. It has a milder, more delicate and better-balanced flavor than strongly smoked hams from Northern Europe, which are only seasoned for a short time. Also it has a more distinctive flavor than cured Mediterranean hams, what are called *prosciutto crudo* further south. However you describe it, a trip to Tyrol isn't complete without sampling some Speck. But do not try and take it home. Customs will not let it through.

    One product you can take home is **honey**. Genuine South Tyrolean honey is a wholesome and organic product without any additives. Also, though the growing season is short, you can find a vast array of **fruits** and **vegetables**. Especially flavorful are the strawberries, blackberries, currants and **apples**. You can't miss the apple orchards spreading up the mountain sides all over Sud-Tirol. Every spare piece land seems to be under cultivation. As a result, Sud-Tirol supplies 10% of all of Europe's apples. For more information about Sud-Tirol's agricultural products, access *www.suedtirol.info* or *www.fierabolzano.it*.

    3. CAVALLINO BIANCO, *Via Bottai 6, Tel. 0471/973-267. Closed Saturday nights and Sundays. No credit cards accepted. Dinner for two E40.*

    One of the most characteristic *trattorie* in Bolzano, and the food is superb. As a result it is always packed. Finding a free table is not easy, but it is worth the effort. When here sample anything and everything you can. From soups to sausage, Italian dishes to Austrian, you will love it all. Remember, cash only here.

4. HOPFEN & CO, *Piazza delle Erbe 17, Tel. 0471/303387. Closed Sundays. All credit cards accepted. Dinner for two E40.*
Another traditional place, this one more of the beer garden variety with communal tables serving massive steins of amber ale. Situated on three floors, with an outside area in good weather, here you will find a great meal suffused with tons of character. Also open for breakfast, this is a frequent stop for locals in the mornings. Not fine dining by any stretch of the imagination, but with great salads, sandwiches, pasta etc., I do recommend this place highly.

Seeing the Sights

What's there to do in Bolzano? See Ötzi; rent free biks and ride the trails; shop on Via Portici; take the Funivia to Renon, hop on the 100-year old railway, then hike back; relax at the Caffe Citta in Piazza Walther and enjoy their daily piano music; as well as everything else listed below.

CASTEL MARECCIO

Via Claudia de' Medici, Tel. 0471/976615, Fax 0471/300746. Web: www.comune.bolzano.it. Email: mareccio@comune.bolzano.it. Open 10am-12:30pm and 3pm-5:30pm.
Situated on the outskirts of Bolzano, but still within walking distance, this old castle and set of cloisters is a picturesque example of the architectural beauty of the region. Set in a lush surrounding, this place is like something out of a fairy tale. Though mainly used as an exhibition hall, it is open to guided tours on Tuesdays. It is worth a look, even only from the outside as you stroll along the beautiful and relaxing river walk.

CHIESA DEI DOMENICANI

Mon-Sat 9:30am-5:30pm.
Built in 1272, this is a simple, plain structure on the outside, filled with fragments of the glory of God on the inside. There are incredible, though partial, frescoes by Giotto and students of his style. The damp Alpine air has not helped preserve these artistic jewels. Two of the most famous are the chapels of San Giovanni and of Santa Caterina.

DUOMO

Piazza Walther. Open Mon-Fri. 9:45am-12pm/2pm-5pm. Sat 9:45am-12pm.
The Duomo is a striking focal point for visitors and resident alike. Begun in 1180, but over time pieces were added, others removed, and finally we are left with this glorious adornment to a magical city. The interior is Gothic with three naves and is filled with stunning art created by a variety of artists including Konrad Erlin, Friedrich Pacher, and Karl Hernici. If you are wondering

why the names are not Italian, but seem Germanic, it is because South Tyrol, where Bolzano is located, was until very recently part of Austria, not Italy.

MUSEO ARCHEOLOGICO DI SUD TIROL

Via Museo 43, Tel. 0471/982-098, Fax 0471/980-648, Web: museo@iceman.it, Email: www.iceman.it or www.archaeologiemuseum.it. Open 10am - 5pm Tues- Sun. Thurs 10am-7pm. E8 adults.

This is the place you most likely have come to Bolzano to visit. The one, the only, the home of "**Ötzi**," the "**Ice Man**." The mummy's discovery in 1991 set the world's imagination ablaze. He is incredibly well-preserved for a guy who had been laying about in glacial ice for 5,200 years!

The Ice Man exhibit ties in well with the other exhibits in the museum that document the entirety of the region's history, from the Old Stone Age to more modern times. A great museum to visit, not just for Ötzi, but everything else as well. Remember to rent an audio guide in English for E2 since the displays are only in German and Italian.

MUSEO CIVICO

Via Cassa di Risparmio 14, Tel. 0471/974-625, Fax 0471/980-144. Email: museo.civico@comune.bolzano.it, Web: www.comune.bolzano.it. Closed Mondays. Open Wed 10am-10pm, All other days 10am-6pm. E5.

The **Municipal Museum** (Museo Civico) contains the most extensive collections of art and cultural history of its kind in South Tyrol. There are exquisite artifacts from the Middle Ages to the 20th Century, Romanesque Madonnas and crucifixes, winged Gothic altars as well as entire Gothic rooms, festival masks and local costumes.

MUSEO DI SCIENZA NATURALI

Via Bottai 1 - Bindergasse 1, Tel. 0471/412-960, Fax 0471/412-979, Email: naturmuseum@provinz.bz.it. Web: www.naturmuseum.it or www.museonatura.it. E5.

South Tyrol's **Museum of Natural History** is located in the building that at one time held the administrative offices of Archduke Maximilian. It now offers the visitor an overview of the various typical landscapes of South Tyrol. The principal attraction is its salt-water aquarium.

Sports & Recreation
HIKING AND SKIING

Bolzano is located in a broad valley basin and the mountains are never far away. In just a few minutes any of the cities three cable cars can take you up to the mountain woodlands and meadows on the Renon, Colle and San Genesio mountains. Cost is E3.5 roundtrip.

The Renon cable car is within walking distance form the center. The others you can get to by either a short bicycle ride using the free bikes offered by the town, bus, or taxi. From these spots you can enjoy magnificent views of the surrounding Dolomites., enjoy walks across lush pastureland and fill your lungs with crisp mountain air.

Renon – Bolzano's home mountain beckon with plenty of sun and pretty walks with the unique Sciliar and Alpa di Siusi meadowlands as a backdrop. Take the small, hundred year old railway to other towns and walk back to the cable car. Web: **www.renon.com**.

Colle – A trip to Colle Kohlern mountain by cable car involves riding on the oldest cable way in the world. The original Gondola can be viewed at the upper terminal and is well worth a visit.

San Genesio – The view of the Rosengarten Dolomites from Tschögglberg high plateau is without doubt the finest of all. The sunset enjoyed from Salto mountain are unforgettable, with the Dolomite peaks glowing in the reflected setting sun.

River Walk

Along the Torrente Talvera, on both sides, are walking and bike paths along which you can find sports fields, as well as a location to play mini-golf, ping pong as well as chess on a large board. A great place to walk during the day.

Practical Information

Bicycle Rental

Bolzano offers free bicycle rentals at an outdoor rental stand at the end of the Via Stazione, close to the Piazza Walther. Here you can use an available red bicycle by leaving a E10 deposit and filling out a rental form. Open 8am to 8pm. Both tourists and locals alike use this service.

Car Rental
- **Avis**, Piazza Verdi 18, *Tel. 0471/971467, Fax 0471/980276*
- **Hertz**, Piazza Verdi 42, *Tel. 0471/981411, Fax 0471/303715*. Mon-Fri 8:30am-12:30pm and 2:30pm-6:30pm, Sat 8:30am-12:00pm, Sun closed.
- **Maggiore/Budget**, Via Garibaldi 32, *Tel. 047/ 971531, Fax 0471/971531*

Fruit and Vegetable Market
- **Piazza Erbe**, Fruits and vegetables. Monday to Friday 8am to 7pm. Also open Saturday mornings.

Laundry
- **Lava e Asciuga**, Via Rosmini 81, *Tel. 0471/978414*
- **Lavagett**, Via Sassari 93, *Tel. 0471/923285*

Tourist Information
Piazza Walther 8, *Tel. 0471/307000, Fax 0471/980128, Email:* info@bolzano-bozen.it.

MERANO
Set in a valley among picturesque mountains, **Merano** is located deep in the heart of the Alps, and is a jumping-off point for many outdoor activities in Northern Italy. A small town of around 30,000 people, Merano offers scenic natural beauty and a quaint character-filled medieval townscape.

A tourist town, Merano is filled with travelers during the day, which you can escape by taking any number of different urban walks available. The **Tappeiner Walk** is the best. 4 kilometers of strolling through an outdoor botanical garden with great views over the city.

Another option is to take the bus to the town of **Dorf Tirol**, then from there visit the **Schloss Tirol**, a must see sight if you are in this area, as well as a number of moderate hiking trails through the Alps. Along these trails you will find pleasant little cafes offering refreshments; a truly civilized way to hike in comparison to the rugged, survivalist treks that are the norm in the wilderness of America.

As it is only about 30 minutes from Bolzano by train, Merano can be a day trip from there, if desired.

Arrivals & Departures
Located 24 kilometers from Bolzano, 330 km from Milan, and only 150 km from Innsbruck, Merano can be reached by train, bus and car. The Autostrada 38 skirts the town from the south. Frequent train service is offered from points south, including Bolzano, and points north including Austria.

Though train is incredibly efficient in getting you from one large destination to another, in Merano it is always best to have a car since much of what there is to do and see is outside of town in the beauty of the Alps. Some things to do, such as rafting, will also entail transportation to and from your activity, so not everything will require a car. But there will be activities where a car may be necessary. See Car Rental section below.

Getting Around Town
Merano is a walkable city. Everything of interest is within easy pedestrian access. To get to sights outside of town, public buses are available.

Orientation

Bisected by the River Passirio, the main part of town is on the north shore with the train station on the west and the Duomo to the East. The Corso Liberta which runs from the Piazza Mazzini in the West to the Piazza d. Rena in the East is the city's main street. Along this boulevard is where the tourist office is located.

Where to Stay

1. EUROPA, *Corso Liberta.178, Tel. 0473/232-376 Fax 0473/230-221, Email: info@europa-splendid.com, Web: www.europa-splendid.com. Double E160. All credit cards accepted. Breakfast included.* ***

Located in the center of town, from here you can access the chair lift, are close to the bus stop to go to Dorf Tirol, can stroll the Via Portici with its great shops and restaurants, then you can escape back to the comfort and luxury of this great hotel. A fine choice for staying in the heart of Merano.

2. GRAND HOTEL PALACE, *Via Cavour 2, Tel. 0473/271-000, Fax 0473/271-100. Email: info@palace.it. Web: www.palace.it. 130 rooms. Single E125-170; Double E210-300. All credit cards accepted. Breakfast included.* *****

Far and away the best place to stay in and around Merano. This is a hotel of long and grand tradition in an historic building that is furnished with

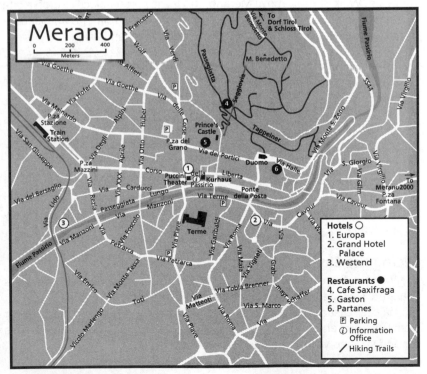

exquisite pieces. The rooms are spacious, comfortable and come complete with every imaginable amenity. You also have a bar with live music, a wonderful hotel restaurant, a covered pool, as well as spa services. If you have the means, this is definitely a **the** place to stay.

3. WESTEND, *Via Speckbacher 9, Tel. 0473/447-654, Fax 0473/222-726. Email: info@westend.it. Web: www.westend.it or www.hotel-westend.it. 22 rooms. Single E50-70; Double E75-100. All credit cards accepted. Breakfast included.* ***

A three star situated in a building from the 1800s, in a lush garden setting right by the river. A well run hotel owned operated by the Strohmer family who also own the Europa. The rooms are of ample size, and wonderfully comfortable and accommodating. The bathrooms are spacious and come with all necessary amenities. The common areas are filled with character and ambiance. There are free bicycles available for guests. A classic place to stay in Merano. Very charming.

Where to Eat

4. CAFÉ SAXIFRAGA, *Tappeiner Walk, Tel. 0473/239-249. Open 10:30am-6pm. Open all year round. Credit cards accepted. Meal for two E25.*

Only two years old, this place is already top notch. Located on the Tappeiner Walk directly above Merano, this is the perfect place to grab a bite to eat or something to drink in the middle of your stroll. The ambiance is incomparable, the view stunning, and the food tasty and filling.

5. GASTON, *Galleria Pobitzer (off Via Portici), Tel 0473/210-245. Closed Mondays. Credit cards accepted. Meal for two E25.*

A café, restaurant and pizzeria all rolled into one magnificent place to eat. Located in a gallery off the main Via Portici, the Gaston will not disappoint. Whether you sample one of the pizzas, a pasta dish, or a local Tirolean favorite, you will leave more than satisfied.

6. PARTANES, *Via Gasse 2, Tel. 0473/210-705. Credit cards accepted. Meal for two E30.*

Run by the Burchia family, this combination restaurant and café serves great food in a modern and relaxed atmosphere. There are two levels for lunch and dinner seating where you can savor Italian and Tirolean favorites. Highly recommended.

Seeing the Sights

What is there to do in Merano? You can take the chairlift to Monte Benedetto for great views over the city; stroll and shop along Via Portici; visit the majectic castle of Schloss Tirol; take the Tappeiner Walk; ride the cable car from Dorf Tirol and hike into the Alps; go up to Merano200 on another cable car and ski; and you can visit the sights listed below.

DORF TIROL

Tourism Office, Via Principale, *Tel. 0473/923-314, Fax 0473/923-012, Web: www.dorf-tirol.it. Email info@dorf-tirol.it*

If you're in Merano, Dorf Tirol should be one of your destinations. From this small little tourist town you can walk to Schloss Tirol and also take a cable car up into the Alps to do some great hiking. The trails up in this part of the Alps are not that strenuous. You are told they are of moderate difficulty but most of them are pretty easy. And along the way ... well there are cafes and restaurants at which you can stop and recharge with some food and drink. A truly civilized way to hike.

To get to Dorf Tirol you need to take a bus from the Merano station or along the Corso Liberta. You can buy a ticket on board for F2. To get to the cable car (Funivia Hochmuth) you'll need to hop on a bus from the center of town. You can use the same ticket you used to get up to Dorf Tirol and just add money on it while on board.

One of the most popular hikes, which only takes about an hour and half, is from Hochmuth, where the cable car drops you off, down to Tiroler Kreuz. From here you can take the bus back to Monte Benedetto and catch the chairlift there down into Merano. Or if you just want the great views from Hochmuth, just take the cable car and grab a bite to eat at the restaurant up there.

Another adventure, this one a little more daring, is to strap yourself into a para-glider with an expert pilot, jump off a cliff and float down from Hochmuth to Dorf Tirol. Cost is E60. Contact Tirolfly at *Tel. 335/767-6891, 225/619-9777,* or *043/923-609, Fax 0473/234-911; Email: tirolfly@yahoo.it.*

KURHAUS

Corso della Liberta.

This truly magnificent building, designed by Vienna architect Friedrich Ohmann in 1914, is, without doubt, the loveliest example of Liberty-style architecture in the entire Alpine region. The great hall holds over 1,000 people and is equipped to host international congresses, conferences, exhibitions and concerts.

MONTE BENEDETTO

Taking the chair life to Monte Benedetto is like going to another world. Up here you can see over the entire valley, sit on one of the benches and relax. Quicker and easier than going to Dorf Tirol's cable car or the one for Merano2000, but does not offer quite as dramatic of views. Chair lift costs E2 one way and E3 round trip.

From here you can also walk about 200 meters (follow the signs) and catch a local bus to Dorf Tirol. You need to buy a ticket in advance. Cost E1.

PRINCES' CASTLE
Via Galilei, *Tel. 0473/230-102.* Tues to Sat 10am to 5pm. Sundays and public holidays 10am to 1pm. Closed on Mondays. E3.

Residence of the Counts of Tyrol starting in 1470 when Merano was the capital of the Austrian province of Tyrol. It is now one of the most complete and well-preserved castles in the Alto Adige province with antique furniture and a rich collection of old arms, weapons and musical instruments.

PUCCINI THEATER
Corso della Liberta.

The civic theatre, dedicated to the famous composer Puccini, was designed in 1900 by Martin Düfler, the most imaginative proponent of German Liberty-style architecture. It is an attractive construction with classical elements and floral decorations.

SCHLOSS TIROL
Tirol Castle, Schlossweg 24, *Tel.0473/220221, Fax 0473/221132. Email: info@schlosstirol.it. Web: www.schlosstirol.it.* June 14 - November 30 Tue-Sun 10am-5pm. E6 adults.

Located just outside of Dorf Tirol, which is only a bus ride away from Merano, the beautiful Tirol Castel (Schloss Tirol) is a must see sight. Built in the first part of the 12th century this castle was the residence of the Counts of Tyrol until 1363, when the last surviving heir gave up her title and handed over all her possessions to the Habsburgs. Completely restored, it now houses a wonderful museum, *South Tyrol Museum of Cultural and Provincial History.* The museum's main focus is the history of the province of Tyrol from its beginnings to modern times. The museum includes the southern palace with its famous Romanesque portals, the frescoes in the double chapel, the wedding chamber of Margarethe Maultasch, and the former dungeon, where the history of the 20th century is depicted on twenty different levels.

THE TAPPEINER WALK
This delightful promenade is one of the main reasons to visit Merano. Located 380 meters above the town along the side of Monte St. Benedetto, this path commands splendid views out over Merano. Here you will find 4 km of exotic vegetation all laid out by local doctor Franz Tappeiner in 1929 who later bequeathed it to the town. A great place to take a relaxing and invigorating stroll. Be sure to stop for sustenance in one of the cozy inns and bars along the path such as the Café Saxifraga.

Sports & Recreation
Bicycling
Free-of-charge bike rental from the Health Spa Center parking lot (*Via*

Piave 9), at the main Railway Station, and on the Via Galileo from the end of May to the end of September. You can get the use of a free bike simply by putting down a refundable deposit. Credit cards accepted.

Ice Skating
The new ice-rink at the **Meranarena** is open for skating from October to March. Located at Via Palade 74, across the river from the main town, near the Maia Race Course, Tel. 0473/236982.

Mountain Biking Tours
Organized by the **Mountaineering School** from April to October. (Tel. 0473/235-223 or 0473/563-845 in winter, or portable phone 0348/260-0813).

Orchestra in The Park
Free daily concerts are available in the Parco Marconi from April to August.

Rafting
Day raft trips are available to rivers and streams in the area. Information available from the **Mountaineering School**, the **Merano Tourist Offices**, or the Rinner family at **Laces Camping Site**, Tel. 0473/623217.

Spa Health Center
In 2005 this will be a place to pamper yourself in a sauna, with a massage, mud bath and more. (Via Piave 9, Tel. 0473/237-724.)

Skiing Year Round
The **Merano 2000** ski area, at over 2,000 meters above sea level, has a total of 40 kms of ski runs and can accommodate up to 7,000 skiers an hour. Located 10 kilometers from Merano, this area is served by a cable-car, five chair lifts and one ski lift. To get to the cable car, take Bus 1A to the Funivia Ivigna. Must get a ticket before getting on board. Cost E1.

Further information is available from the Merano Tourist Offices. The website for Merano 2000 is www.meran2000.net. Unfortunately it is only in German. Another website to visit, which has excellent information about Merano2000 is www.hafling.com.

Practical Information
Car Rental
• **Hertz,** Agenzia Viaggi Burgund, Via Roma 276, Tel. 0473/234-313, Fax 0473/236-419. Mon-Fri 9:30am-12:30pm and 3pm-7pm, Sat 9:30am-12:30, Sun closed.

Tourist Information

Corso Libertà 35, *Tel. 0473/272-000, Web: www.meraninfo.it, Email: info@meraninfo.it.* Open Mon-Frid 9am-12:30pm; 2-6pm, Sat 9:30-12:30pm.

BORMIO

You haven't heard of **Bormio**? Well, that's a big part of its charm. Despite being virtually unknown on this side of the Atlantic, this small village is one of the most important winter and summer sporting centers of the entire Alpine region.

Bormio serves as a base for ski vacations in the winter and hiking adventures into the **Stelvio National Park** in the summer. Stelvio is home to glaciers, trails and alpine refuges, a nature lovers paradise. The town of Bormio itself was famous in ancient times for its nine hot springs, and became a way-station in the 15th and 16th centuries for travelers between the Duchy of Milan or the Republic of Venice into Northern Europe. Today Bormio is a popular ski resort for Italians and other Europeans, but its fame and fun have evaded the radar of North America ... until now.

During the week you will find the town virtually empty, but on the weekends, the skiers of Italy arrive. Whether empty or full, in the old historic center, or around the twisting and turning little roads, you will be awash in charm and character. Even the more modern development on the outskirts cannot negate the beauty that radiates from this adorable little town. Bormio is one of THE places to visit in the entire Alps for all sorts of outdoor leisure activities. If you want to breathe in the crisp Alpine air, luxuriate in thermal baths, ski yourself silly, eat at great restaurants, soak up the charm of a tiny medieval town, or party until dawn, Bormio is the town for you.

Arrivals & Departures

Bormio is located on the edge of the Stelvio National Park. The only way to get here being by road. The closest larger town is Sondrio, 69 kilometers away. The closest Italian airport is Milan.

The road in from Milan is the SS38. Two roads out are either the SS 301 going west or the SS300 going east. Get a map of the region from the **Touring Club Italiano** (Via Marsala 8, 00185, Roma, *Tel. 06/49 98 99)* or the **Italian Government Tourist Offices**, *www.italiantourism.com.*

Another option for getting here if you do not want to be burdened with the expense or hassle of car, and which most people do if they are only going to be heading to Bormio and nowhere else, is to arrange for a bus/van to pick them up at the airport. These can be arranged through your hotel. Most hotels in Bormio work together to have guests picked up at Milan airport and ferried to Bormio. The bus takes about 3 1/2 to 4 hours, and will usually include a stop in Como for a bite to eat. Remember Bormio is really remote, but it is well worth the extra effort getting here.

Orientation

Situated at the meeting point of the SS310 from the west, the SS38 form the south and the SS300 form the east, the small town/ski resort of Bormio is nestled into a valley just on the edge of the Stelvio National Park in the Italian Province of Lombardia.

SS301 turns into Via della Vitttoria and meets SS300 at the Piazza Cavour, the center of town. Radiating from this piazza almost in the form of a trident are the Via Roma to the south, Via de Simoni in the middle and Via Al Forte to the north.

The Via Roma turns into the Via Milano which is where two of the hotels listed are located: Baita Clementi and Palace. South of the Via Roma is the Frodolfo River, across which are the *funiculare* (cable cars) up to the ski areas. The two main roads across the river are the Via Coltura and the Via Funivia where the Genzianella and the Larice Bianco hotels are located.

Where to Stay

If these are booked, which is more than likely since Bormio really is a hot spot, you can find other hotels at the local website, *www.hotels.valtline.it/hotel_bormio.htm*.

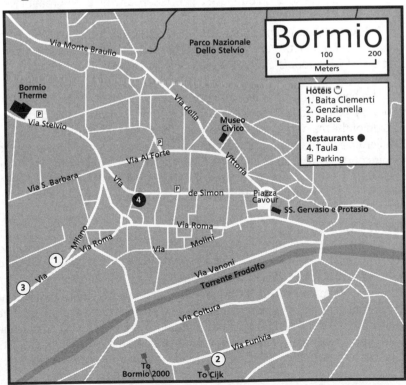

1. BAITA CLEMENTI, *Via Milano 46, Tel. 0342/904-473, Fax 0342/903-649. Email: baita.clementi@novanet.it. Web: www.baitaclementi.com. Closed April 15 - June 20 and Sept. 15 - Dec 12. 41 rooms. Single E70-105. Double E105-170. All credit cards accepted. Breakfast included.* ***

Located just outside the main small town, the style here is rustic but refined with beautiful terra-cotta tile floors. The common areas are accommodating and comfortable. The rooms (12 of which are apartment style and can be rented by groups of people) are elegant with beautiful furnishings. Also available are squash courts, sauna, sun room, massage room, and ping pong. My favorite three star in Bormio.

2. GENZIANELLA, *Via Funivia 6, Tel 0342/904485, Fax 0342-904158. Email: genzia@valtline.it. Web: www.genzianella.com. Closed ion May and November. 40 rooms. Single E45-70; Double E90-140. Visa accepted. Breakfast and lunch included.* ***

Recently upgraded from a two star, this place is in an excellent spot located right near the lifts. Despite this ideal winter sport location, this hotel is a tranquil and comfortable. They offer wonderful accommodations, great prices and attentive service. The common areas are simple though well appointed. The rooms are the same, and most have small balconies to enjoy. The bathrooms are smallish but have all necessary amenities. A great place to stay.

3. PALACE, *Via Milano 54, Tel. 0342/903-131, Fax 0342/903-366. Email: info@palacebormio.it. Web: www.palacebormio.it. Open all year. 80 rooms. Single E90-130; Double E120-180. All credit cards accepted. Breakfast E10.* ****

The best four star in town, and one that is reasonably priced as well. An incredibly comfortable located in a park setting a short walking distance outside of the main small town of Bormio. The common areas are wonderful. Excellent places to relax and meet others. There is also a large covered pool, tennis courts, gym, jacuzzi, massage service as well as a sun room. The rooms come with every imaginable comfort, most with balconies. A truly wonderful place to stay. My favorite in Bormio.

Where to Eat

4. TAULA, *Via Dante 6, Tel 0342/904-771. Closed Wednesdays for lunch and Thursdays. Holidays May 1 - July 1 and November 1 to December 1. All credit cards accepted. Dinner for two E65.*

This is an upscale place. The ambiance is elegant, the service professional and enthusiastic and the food spectacular. All local favorites are served here, some of which you'll need Open Road's *Eating & Drinking in Italy* to decipher what they actually are! Despite their obscure names, they will all tantalize. The desserts are also exquisite. One red mark is that the wine list is limited, featuring mainly local favorites. But overall, this is the best place to eat in Bormio. Located between the Via de Simoni and the Via Roma at the end furthest away from the Piazza Cavour.

Seeing the Sights

In the Piazza Cavour is the **Collegiata dei Ss. Gervasio e Protasio** built in the 11th century and renovated during the Baroque period. Along the Via d. Vittoria, located in the Palazzo de Simoni, is the **Museo Civico**, a series of exhibits commemorating the history of the town. Bormio is not really a town filled with traditional sights. It is a ski town and the focus of the people here is on just that activlty.

Sports & Recreation
Skiing

BORMIO SKI AREA, *Tel. 0342/901-451, Fax 0342/904-305, Email: sib2000@valtline.it, Web: www.sib.bormio.it/piste.htm.*

Bormio is filled with all levels of different slopes, from red to blue to the highest difficulty, black. As a ski resort Bormio can accommodate rank beginners and outright experts. And snowboarding is welcome here as well. All sorts of ski schools abound, all with different prices, but the average is about E30 for a private one on one lesson. A 7-day ski pass cost only between E130 in low season to E150 in high season.

Summer Activities

Hiking, mountain biking and rafting are but some of the activities available in Bormio, and all of the Alps, in the summer months. The ski slopes are open to rampaging mountain bikers, other trails become accessible for hikers, who go out for day trips or spend the nights in mountain refuges (*rifugi*). These are small cabins in the Alps that are well maintained and used by hikers and bikers alike. These places are very different from what we have grown to expect in America, say for example along the Appalachian trail. These mountain refuges are palaces in comparison. Completely enclosed, with simple facilities, they are insulated from the elements. They can get crowded during peak summer months, but they are still a welcome respite from the wind, rain, and cold.

All information associated with these activities is available from the tourist office, or an Italian language website, *www.alpinia.net/.*

Thermal Baths

BORMIO THERME, *Via Stelvio, Tel 0342/901-325, Web: www.bormioterme.it/, Email: info@bormioterme.it. Hours 9am-10pm.*

Prices range from E12 for a thermal bath to E25 for a thermal bath and massage. Also available is aromatherapy, sauna, swimming and all sorts of other spa-like activities, all in a public center located in a modern building in the town of Bormio. Also in this spa is an extensive fitness center you can use for only E12 a day.

Practical Information

- **Tourist Office**, Via Roma, 87, *Tel. 0342/903-594, Email: info@bormio.com, Web: www.bormio.com.*

Chapter 21

TORINO & THE 2006 WINTER OLYMPICS

Situated 78 miles southwest of Milan, with a population just topping one million people, **Turin (Torino)** is the major city in the western Italian Alps. The city lies on the banks of the **Po River** near the foot of the Alps in northwestern Italy. There is enough of interest to justify a one night stay, and maybe a little more.

Because it is the home of automobile makers **Fiat** and **Lancia**, Turin has been called the Detroit of Italy. Besides automobiles, it is also a major industrial center for ball bearings, rubber and tires, clothing, textiles, leather goods, paper, chemicals, and food products. Despite the industrial presence Torino retains the intimacy and pace of a much smaller city.

Torino is really a rare gem of a city and has lately been making itself more accessible, inviting and navigable for tourists. A walk through Torino will take you down and through tree-lined avenues and boulevards, tranquil Baroque *piazze* and arcaded streets. There are over 20 miles of arcaded sidewalks that make a brief *passegiatta* a veritable stroll into history. Some of these arcades, or *portici*, date back to the 12th century.

Every street offers at least one stylish shop or stunning Baroque vista; the museums are excellent; the buildings have maintained their ornate turn-of-the-century facades; the cafes are intimate and plentiful; the food – which includes cheese, wine, pastries and chocolates – is among Italy's best. When you visit you will encounter very few tourists but many friendly natives.

Unless of course, you choose to come during the 2006 Winter Olympics – then Torino will be very crowded. However, the planners for this event are promising many engaging activities to accompany the obligatory events. If you are thinking of visiting Torino, wrapping a visit around the 2006 Olympics might be something to consider.

Short History

Turin has also been a center of learning and religion for many years. The **University of Turin** was founded in 1404, and the **Cathedral of St. John the Baptist** was built from 1491 to 1498. This marvelous church houses the chapel of the **Holy Shroud** and contains a holy relic, the **Shroud of Turin**. Despite the fact that modern carbon dating and other investigative techniques have disproved the robes' authenticity, many of the faithful still believed that this cloth was used to wrap the body of Jesus after his crucifixion.

Torino's name comes from the **Taurini Gauls**, who inhabited this location in pre-Roman times. During the reign of Augustus, the Romans rebuilt and walled the city and gave it the grid pattern that still exists today. In 570 CE, it fell to the Lombards, and under Charlemagne it was assigned to the margraves of Susa. Linked to the House of Savoy in 1046 by a noble marriage, it served as the capital of the Piedmont for several centuries. In 1720 it became the capital of the Kingdom of Sardinia, and in the years 1861 to 1865 it was the capital of a newly united Italy. The city was heavily bombed by Allied air raids during World War II because of its industrial nature, but by 1959 its industries and landmarks had been restored.

Torino Website: *www.turismotorino.org.*

Arrivals & Departures

Your best bet for arrival and departure is the train. Turin is not far from Milan, and travel time by train from Milan or its airport, Malpensa, should be

---

Touring Torino

Torino is made for walking, especially down the arcaded Via Roma. Everywhere you go you'll find exquisitely maintained Baroque and Renaissance architecture. When not promenading, visit the **Royal Armory** (excellent ancient arms and armor), the **Cathedral of St. John the Baptist** (home of the Holy Shroud), the **Palatine Gate** (built by Emperor Augustus), the **Valentino Castle and Park**, Palazzo Madama (which houses the **Museum of Ancient Art**), the **Automobile Museum** (with one of the world's best collection of antique cars, some models dating back to 1893), and you simply cannot miss the **Egyptian Museum** and the **Galleria Sabauda** (collection of Masters art), Torino's two must-see museums. And every Saturday there is a magnificent **flea market** located by the marvelous cast-iron-and-glass food markets.

᠊ᠵ

about no more than an hour and a half. From Rome, the train trip should take about six hours.

Getting Around Town
By Bicycle

You can rent a bicycle at a stand in the beautiful and tranquil **Parco Valentino**. The "shop" is located on the Viale Matteoli and is open from 9:30am–12:30pm and 3:00pm–7:00pm, Tuesday through Sunday. You can rent the bikes for E6 per day or E2 per hour. You need to leave a picture ID and E3 cash as a deposit.

Torino

0 250 500
Meters

Sights ◇	Hotels ○	Restaurants ●
A. Palazzo Madama	1. Amadeus e Teatro	11. Arcadia
B. Palazzo Reale	2. Bologna	12. Dai Saletta
C. St. John the Baptist	3. Conte Biancamone	13. Del Cambio
D. Palatine Gate	4. Genio	14. Il Brande
E. Palazzo dell'Accademia	5. Gran Mogol	15. Neuv Caval 'd Brons
F. Piazza San Carlo	6. Liberty	16. Porto di Savona
G. Valentine Castle & Park	7. Piemontese	17. Spada Reale
	8. Principe e Piemontese	18. Taverna delle Rosa
	9. Turin City Center	
	10. Victoria	

By Bus

This is a large bustling city, but the bus system, as in all Italian cities, is excellent so you can get around easily. At a cost of only E1 per trip, you can go anywhere in the city quickly and efficiently from 6:00am to 12:30am.

Tickets must be bought at a *Tabacchi* prior to boarding the buses, and convenient maps are available at most main bus terminals and at the APT tourist office on Via Roma.

By Taxi

I wouldn't recommend using your car in this big congested city. You can find taxis all over the streets and at conveniently located taxi stands, but if you want to call one from your hotel try one of these three companies:
- **Central Taxi**, *Tel. 011/33-99*
- **Pronto Taxi**, *Tel. 011/57-37*
- **Radio Taxi Torino**, *Tel. 011/57-30*

Where to Stay

Turin's hotels are functional as befits a businesslike town, but several have something approaching charm. One item to note is that the city's hotels are virtually empty on the weekends because Torino has not yet been discovered by tourism. Therefore most of these hotels are more than willing to offer amazing discounts if you stay over the weekend. All you have to do is ask prior to arriving.

1. AMADEUS E TEATRO, *Via Principe Amadeo 41, Tel. 011/817-4951, Fax 011/817-4953. Web: www.turinhotelcompany.it. 26 rooms all with bath. Single E130-190; Double E170-230. Closed in August. Credit cards accepted. Breakfast included.* ***

A small boutique hotel that is well located and at a good price. Recently some rooms and common areas were renovated, bringing this place into the 20th century. The entrance is elegant with blue and white ceramic tile. There is a quaint little *cortile* in the center with a lone palm tree blooming. This is a good three star after its recent renovations. I would recommend it warmly. The rooms have every necessary amenity and are clean, comfortable and spacious.

2. BOLOGNA, *Corso Vittorio Emmanuele II 60, Tel. 011/562-0190, Fax 011/562-0193. 47 rooms, 4 with bath, 33 with shower, 10 with no facilities. Single with bathout E70; Single E90; Double E120. Credit cards accepted.* **

Located in the center city, this is an inexpensive alternative for all travelers. Clean and comfortable with a small but accommodating bar area downstairs. They also have a person at the desk all night long, a rarity in two stars. There are TV in the rooms as well as direct dial phones but no A/C.

3. CONTE BIANCAMANO, *Corso Vittorio Emmanuele II 73, Tel. 011/ 562-3281, Fax 011/562-3789. Web: www.venere.it/it/torino/biancamano/.*

25 rooms, 2 with bath, 23 with shower. Single E130-190; Double E170-230. Breakfast included. All credit cards accepted. ***

If you want quaint old restored buildings at a great price, stay here in this beautiful hotel in a peaceful and tranquil area of Torino near the train station. The public areas are a combination of antique and modern with lovely frescoed and high ceilings with reliefs. The rooms are large, clean and comfortable, if a bit spartan. The staff is always willing to go that extra mile. The only missing ingredient is air conditioning. Stay here when air conditioning is not needed.

4. GENIO, *Corso Vittorio Emmanuele II 47, Tel. 011/650-5771, Fax 011/650-8264. E-mail: genio.to@bestwestern.it. Web: www.bestwestern.it. 120 rooms all with bath. Single E70-110; Double E120 170. Breakfast included. All credit cards accepted.* ^^^

A Best Western hotel right in front of the train station in a quaint old building, with a grand entrance below the porticos between Via Nizza and Via Saluzzo. The entrance hall is large and comfortable with an area to relax directly to the left. Each room, though different in decoration, layout and size, are all clean and comfortable. The Genio is a hotel with a long and storied tradition in Torino, and the staff make a point of attending to your every detail. A great place to stay. They are trying to move up a star and it shows.

5. GRAN MOGOL, *Via Guarini 2 (Piazza Lagrange), Tel. 011/561-2120, Fax 011/562-3160. E-mail: granmogol.to@bestwestern.it. Web: www.bestwestern.it. 45 rooms. Single E70-110; Double E120-170. All credit cards accepted. Breakfast included.* ***

And yet another Best Western, not quite as good as the Genio or Genova e Stazione but on par with the Piemontese. Also situated near the station, this is a comfortable and tranquil hotel. The facade is modern and everything has the look and feel of the recent renovations. All the rooms have similar, standard, basic furnishings a la North America, which means they are kept clean, are comfortable and ample in size and the bathrooms have every necessary amenity. There is air conditioning, satellite TV, room service, etc., that you expect from any three star. The staff here is courteous and work hard to keep your business.

6. LIBERTY, *Via Pietro Micca 15, Tel. 011/562-8801, Fax 011/562-8163. Web: www.venere.com/it/torino/liberty/. 35 rooms all with shower. Single E70-110; Double E110-165. Breakfast included. Lunch or Dinner E25. Credit cards accepted.* ***

Located on the first floor of a Liberty-style older building in the Parisian and Viennese style of the *fin du siècle*, here you have charm, character and superb furnishing taste all rolled into one. In business since the 1800s, this family-operated hotel provides meticulous clothes cleaning services, hot and cold buffet breakfast and a local, home-cooking style restaurant. If you like antiques and comfort stay here. Besides the style they also have air conditioning, TV, radios, and direct dial phones in the rooms, as well as prompt room service. This is the best place to stay in Torino if you're tired of cookie-cutter hotels.

7. **PIEMONTESE**, *Via Berthollet 21, Tel. 011/669-8101, Fax 011/669-0571. E-mail: info@hotelpiemontese.it. Web: www.hotelpiemontese.it. 33 rooms, 2 with bath, 31 with shower. Single E65-105; Double E95-145. Credit cards accepted.* ***

Located in a quiet street near the station and town center, you will find all the amenities of a good three star with excellent attention to detail. They have room service, laundry service, and are pet friendly. The service is North American prompt and courteous, and the rooms try to uphold the same standard but they're not as large as we're used to. They are, however, super clean and comfy. Being a business oriented city, and not a tourist oriented one, prices here, as everywhere in Torino are much lower on the weekends.

8. **PRINCIPI DI PIEMONTE**, *Via P. Gobetti 15, Tel. 011/562-9693, Fax 011/562-0270. Email: torino_principidipiemonte@jollyhotels.it. Web: www.jollyhotels.it. 107 rooms all with bath. Single E180-200; Double E200-250. All credit cards accepted.* ****

How jolly, another Jolly. This is the best of the three in Torino and it is located right in the heart of the city, close to the station, just off of Via Roma, and ideally situated near the few tourist sights and some good cafés and theaters. The eight floors of this rather severe building hide some rather pleasant accommodations. Each floor inside is decorated in a different color, each appealing in its own manner. The top floors offer a great view of the city. The rooms are large and comfortable, and furnished with every amenity. The buffet breakfast is huge and their restaurant I Gentilom offers some superb *cucina piemontese* as well as some international favorites. A truly grand hotel.

9. **TURIN CITY CENTER**, *Via Assietta 3, Tel. 011/516-7111, Fax 011/516-699. 57 rooms, 12 with bath, 45 with shower. Single E180-200; Double E200-250. Breakfast included. All credit cards accepted.* ****

Located on one side of the train station in a beautiful park-like site, this charming old hotel has been completely modernized by the management of the Holiday Inn. They have an excellent restaurant that you should try even if you do not get the full board option. The rooms are perfectly clean and comfortable, and if you don't want to stay in them the hotel has a quaint little bar area. Another relaxing feature is the availability of a refreshing sauna. And to top it off pets are welcome too. Remember, we're in Italy. This is not your typical Holiday Inn. This place has style and character.

10. **VICTORIA**, *Via Nino Costa 4, Tel. 011/561-1909, Fax 011/561-1806. Web: www.hotelvictoria-torino.com. 92 rooms all with bath. Single E120; Double E180. All credit cards accepted. Breakfast included.* ***

A wonderful three star establishment that could easily be one star higher. A little soft around the edges since the decorations are so delicate, but an ideal place to stay for business or pleasure. Located on a tranquil street a few minutes from the train station and right in the center of town. The decor, service and attitude will remind you more of France than of Italy, but it is accommodating nonetheless. In the entry way you will be greeted with bouquets of flowers adorning the classic furniture. Also downstairs are magazines, newspapers and books available for guests. In the rooms you'll find antiques, each furnished different than the next. Air conditioning has not arrived in all the rooms yet, but once it does this place should easily be a four star. The bathrooms are clean and come with all amenities. On a quality/price ratio, this is the place to stay in Torino.

Where to Eat

Besides being known for its industry, the **Piedmont** region and Torino is also be known for their simple cuisine and their tasty wine. The food is a blend of Northern Italian peasant staples mixed in with some elegant French flair. You'll find more butter than olive oil in cooking, a blasphemy in the south, and cheese, mushrooms and truffles are used instead of the abundant tomatoes and peppers down south.

During carnival, they have a special dish called *Tofeja* which is prepared with beans that are soaked for 12 hours, then cooked with minced pork like the skin, ears, and snout (which really doesn't sound appetizing but it is). These are all spiced with parsley and garlic, then rolled up in a light dough mixture (the *Tofeja*), then cooked over night. When not served at carnival it can be found as an hors-d'oeuvre in many restaurants. They also have another appetizer called *capunet* that is boiled cabbage leaves stuffed with minced meat and a variety of spices, as well as a *fresse*, which is a mixture of minced liver, raisins, salt, pepper and cinnamon roasted in the oven with a sauce of red wine, tomato, and brown sugar. A great pasta dish is *agnolotti*, which is a ravioli-like pasta stuffed with boiled cabbage and roasted lamb.

You can also get some tasty cheeses in this region. There is the *toma* which is aged perfectly for three months and used as a snack between dishes but not in cooking. There is also the *tomini*, which is cow and goat milk combined and sold only after 2 or 3 days of production. It's soft, succulent and ever so tasty. My favorite is the *savignon*, which is a combination of buttermilk curds, salt, pepper, and spices that is typical of the village of **Settimo Vittone**. There's nothing like spiced cheese curds.

This region of Italy is also know for its desserts, which are usually tarts filled with fresh fruits like peaches, and sweetened with sugar and cocoa, and sometimes almonds.

The **wines** of the region can be bubbly and sweet, like those from **Asti**. Offered in both a sparkling (*spumante*) and regular version *(Carema* or *Erbaluce)*, they have been produced since the Middle Ages. Both were particularly sweet back then since the only preservation method for wine at the time was the application of sugar. Today the wines are light and dry, with a distinct character that can hold its own against the best the world has to offer.

Restaurant locations can be found on the Torino map, page 621.

11. ARCADIA, *Galleria dell'Industria Subalpina 16, Tel. 011/532-029. Closed Sundays and August. All credit cards accepted. Dinner for two E45.*

Right in the center of Torino this place is swamped for lunch with the business crowd. They serve a local Piemontese-style menu, including a wonderful mixed vegetable dish made local-style (*misto di verdure alla piemontese*) and an assortment of beef dishes like *filetto alla monferrina* (fillet fried in flour). The dessert tray is piled high with local favorites and the waiters are always attentive and alert.

12. DAI SALETTA, *Via Belfiore 37, Tel. 011/668-7867. Closed Sundays and August. Dinner for two E40. Credit cards accepted.*

Run by the Saletta cousins, this place only has seven small tables from which to enjoy their magnificent pasta dishes, most of which are smothered in creamy cheese sauces. You must sample the local *toma* cheese here, the perfect snack between dishes. All of their braised or roasted meats are excellent, but not for the diet conscious. This is another great local place where you can have some perfect Piemontese food and atmosphere. You will need reservations.

13. DEL CAMBIO, *Piazza Carignamo 2, Tel. 011/546-690. Closed Sundays, the first week in January and all of August. Dinner for two E100. All credit cards accepted.*

A super elegant restaurant with over 200 years experience in fine food preparation. Each room is finer than the next and each is a perfect spot for a romantic evening. In this fine environment the service is impeccable and the food exquisite. Their menu changes frequently but you can usually count on getting: *La tartra di verdurine all'antica con fonduta di Castelmagno* (a plate of vegetables chopped for you to dip in a succulent fondue of Castelmagno cheese); *tartufo con fiori zucca* (truffles cooked with pumpkin flowers); or the superb *filetto di vitello con funghi e scalogno* (veal filet with mushrooms and scallions).

14. IL BRANDÉ, *Via Massena 5, Tel. 011/537-279. Closed Sundays and Mondays and August. No credit cards accepted. Dinner for two E45.*

Reservations are definitely necessary to eat at this wonderful little *trattoria* since they only have eight tables. Two cousins by the last name of Mottura run the place and offer a set menu, as well as a series of different dishes with mainly a Normandy (French) influence. Try some of their rabbit dishes or their *gnocchi alle erbe* (small dumplings made of flour covered in herbs and spices) and wash it all down with some excellent *Barolo* wine from Piedmont.

15. **NEUV CAVAL 'D BRONS**, *Piazza San Carlo 157, Tel. 011/562-7483. Closed Sundays. Dinner for two E90. All credit cards accepted.*

What started out as a beer hall in 1947 became known as the Pub Lancia and Steakhouse, and now has given itself a more refined moniker. There are three rooms with a few tables and many decorations. The menu includes everything from seafood to pasta to meat. Try their *gamberini stufato all'Arneis e zafferano* (shrimp stuffed with cheese and saffron) or the *filetto di trota in pan brioche can salsa di sidro* (trout pan-fried in cider). They also have a vegetarian menu, featuring such dishes as a delicious *ravioli di zucchine e porri* (ravioli made with zucchini and leeks) and the *sformata di spinaci con fonduta* (soufflé/fondue of spinach and cheese). If you're in the mood for cheese, go for the *flan di Castelmagno in salsa* (molded cheese soaked in a great sauce).

16. **PORTO DI SAVONA**, *Piazza Vittorio Veneto 2, Tel. 011/817-3500. Closed Mondays, Tuesdays for dinner and all of July. Dinner for two E35. No credit cards accepted.*

The clientele of this place includes actors, authors, businessmen and students. It is a local favorite. The *cucina piemontese* served here is superb, all the way from antipasto to dessert. Try anything on the menu, especially their braised or boiled mixed meats or some of their *gnocchi* with different cheese sauces. An inexpensive and delightfully tasty insight into the heart and soul of Torino.

17. **SPADA REALE**, *Principe Amadeo 53, Tel. 011/832-835. Closed Sundays. Dinner for two E50. All credit cards accepted.*

One of the most frequented restaurants in the city, thanks mainly to the great food and hospitality of the owner Adriano Stefanini. It is open late and caters to actors from the theater, professional athletes, and a wide variety of locals. The cuisine is creative, to say the least, and changes constantly. Mint and curry seem to be the spice staples in many of the dishes. Come here for out of the ordinary cuisine.

18. **TAVERNA DELLE ROSE**, *Via Massena 24, Tel. 011/538-345. Closed Saturdays at Dinner, Sundays, and August. Dinner for two E60. All credit cards accepted.*

A small three room popular local place. The owner and cook Neri Barbieri prepares an excellent antipasto offering, some great pasta dishes like *spaghetti all'aragosta* (with lobster) and *papardelle ai funghi* (large strips of pasta in a mushroom sauce), and superb grilled and roasted meats. A place for a good down home Piemontese meal but at a somewhat high price.

Seeing the Sights

The real sights of Torino are the 11 miles of arcaded sidewalks, stunning Baroque buildings and beautiful and accommodating city layout and design. In terms of museums, the best (see "E" below) houses the Egyptian collection and the Galleria Sabuada. Those seeking spiritual experience will no doubt head to the Cathedral of St. John the Baptist to take in the Holy Shroud.

A. PALAZZO MADAMA

Piazza Castello, Tel. 011/436-1455. Open Tuesdays and Thursdays 2:30pm–7:30pm, Wednesdays, Fridays, and Saturdays 9am–2spm. Admission E4.

Located in the central heart of the old town of Torino, at one end of the Via Roma, is the **Piazza Castello** which contains the massive **Palazzo Madama** that houses the **Museum of Ancient Art**. The core of this building was built in the 13th century on the remains of the Roman east gate to the garrison city. Stark and medieval on one side and a Baroque glass-fronted palace on the other, the Palazzo Madama was enlarged in both the 15th and 16th centuries, with the Baroque west front and the magnificent double staircase. It is a sumptuous reminder of the wealth of the family of Savoy. The museum is on the ground and second floors and has a valuable collection of sculptures, stained glass, paintings and other works.

B. PALAZZO REALE

Piazza Castello, Tel. 011/436-1455. Open Tuesday–Saturday 9am–5pm. Admission E6. Gardens free.

On the north side of the Piazza Castello is the **Palazzo Reale (Royal Palace)**, an austere apricot colored, plain brick building built between 1646 and 1658 for Carlo Emanuele II. It contains 26 sumptuously decorated royal apartments *(Apartamenti Reali)* with gilded walls and an eclectic collection of treasures. Especially noteworthy is the **Apartamento di Madama Felicita**. In the right wing is the **Royal Armory** with a vast collection of arms and armor dating from the 15th to the 17th centuries believed to be the best in Europe. To the east of the palace are the **Royal Gardens**, developed by the creator of the gardens at the Palace of Versailles, Louis le Notre in 1697.

C. CATHEDRAL OF ST. JOHN THE BAPTIST

Piazza San Giovanni, Tel. 011/436-6101. Chapel open Tuesday–Saturday 9am–noon and 3-5:30pm. Church open everyday 7am-noon and 3-5:30pm.

Located west of the Palazzo Reale off Via XX Settembre is the home of the **Holy Shroud of Turin**. This church was built between 1492 and 1498, and the bell tower was added in 1720. The Holy Shroud was purported to have been the linen cloth in which the body of Christ was wrapped after his descent from the cross. Despite the fact that its origin has been carbon dated to the 13th or 14th century, the faithful still believe in its authenticity. The shroud is located in the **Capella della Santa Sindone** (chapel of the Holy Shroud) that is topped with a honeycomb black marble dome. Above the doors is Luigi Ganga's copy of Leonardo da Vinci's *Last Supper*, which is considered the best copy of that fresco ever done.

D. PALATINE GATE
Located northwest of the Cathedral, the arch was built by Emperor Augustus and was the north gate of the old Roman town. It is a simple structure which has two brick towers, but really is a prime example of how history in Italy all blends together into the present.

E. PALAZZO DELL'ACCADEMIA DELLE SCIENZE
Via Accademia delle Scienze 6, *Tel. 011/61-7776.* Open Tuesday–Saturday 9am-2pm and 3pm-7pm. Admission E6.
This palace was initially built as a Jesuit college in 1679 and was converted to the **Academy of Sciences** in 1757. Today it houses the **Museum of Antiquities**, with Greco-Roman and Etruscan material mainly from the Piemontese and Ligurian regions; the **Egyptian Museum (Museo Egizio)**, one of the finest collections of Egyptian antiquities in the world, including a wonderfully evocative statue of Ramses II; and the **Galleria Sabauda**, with its fine collection of canvases by Italian and Flemish masters including Fra Angelico, Mantegna, Bellini and Van Eyck.
Aside from the Shroud, the Egyptian Museum is Torino's chief tourist draw. Any native will tell you that after Cairo, Torino has the finest Egyptian collection in existence.

F. PIAZZA SAN CARLO
This symmetrical square was laid out in 1638. Here you'll find the **Church of Santa Cristina** built in 1637 with a facade by Juvara in 1718; and the **Church of San Carlo** built in 1836. In the center of the piazza stands the equestrian statue of Duke Filiberto Emanuele sculpted in 1838. Running through this beautiful Baroque *piazza* is Turin's main shopping street, **Via Roma**. This street is a perfect place for a *passegiatta* (stroll) as well as window-shopping or people watching.
Located a few blocks from the *piazza* is Torino's most beautiful building, the **Palazzo Carignano**, Via Accademia della Scienza 5. Built in the late 17th century, it is a Baroque marvel of undulating lines and red brick ornament, including motifs of native North American headdresses to commemorate Piemontese participation in a French victory over the tribes of Quebec. Today it houses a wonderful museum about the unification of Italy, **Museo Nazionale del Risorgimento Italiano**, (9:30am-6:30pm Tues-Sat and 9am-12:30pm Sundays, Entrance E5, free on Sundays) since it was the birthplace of Carlo Alberto and Victor Emmanuel, two great Italian patriots. It was also the seat of the Italian Parliament from 1861 to 1864 when the government was here in Torino before it moved to Florence and then Rome. A walk in any direction from this *palazzo* will take you down and through tree-lined avenues and boulevards, tranquil Baroque *piazze* and arcaded streets.

G. VALENTINO CASTLE & PARK

Via Massimo d'Azeglio, *Tel. 011/669-9372.* Open Tuesday–Saturday 9am–6pm and Sundays 10:30am-6pm.

A tranquil respite from the pace of a large city, this park also contains the **Botanical Gardens**, which were established in 1729, and the magnificent **Castello del**, a Disney-like medieval castle created for an exhibition in 1884, which is a great place for kids to visit.

Another great place for kids of all ages is the **Palazzo delle Esposizioni**, which houses the popular and world famous **Museo dell'Automobile** (Tuesday-Sunday 9:30am-12:30pm and 3pm-7pm) featuring car models dating back to 1893. If you're a car buff, and even if you're not, you have to come see this excellent museum.

Nightlife & Entertainment

VINCENZO NEBIOLO, *Via Priocca 10, Tel. 011/436-4558. Closed Sundays and August.*

A quaint little wine bar open from 6:00am to 10:00pm right in the heart of the Mercato di Porta Palazzo. They serve many different wines, most local at E3 per liter, as well as superb *Panini* sandwiches with a variety of cheese and salami fillers.

BRITANNIA PUB, *Via Carlo Alberto 34, Tel. 011/54-33-92. Open from 6:00pm until 2:00am. Pints E4.*

Your traditional English-style pub with Guinness, Harp and Kilkenny on tap. They also serve simple *Panini* and other warm and cold snacks.

DUKE OF WELLINGTON, *Via Caboto 26, Tel. 011/59-99-41. Open from 6:00pm until 2:00am. Pints E4.*

Another English-style pub with a variety of bottled beer and typical English and German offerings on tap. They also serve simple sandwich and *Panini* type food.

Opera

If you are in Torino from December to June, the traditional opera season, have the proper attire (suits for men, dresses for women), and have a taste for something out of the ordinary, try the spectacle of the opera.

• **Teatro Reggio do Torino**, Piazza Castello 215,*Tel 011/88151, Fax 011/ 881-5214.*

Sports & Recreation

Golf

• **Golf Club Associazione Sportiva I Roveri**, Rotta Cerbiatta 24, 10070 Fiano, *Tel. 011/923-5667, Fax 011/923-5669.* Located 20 kilometers from Torino, you can either play the 18 hole, par 72, 6218 meter course or the 9 hole, par 36, 3306 meter course. They are open from March to

November except on Mondays. There's a driving range, gymnasium, putting green, pro shop and restaurant/bar.
- **Circolo Golf Stupinigi**, Corso Unione Sovietica 506 A, 10135 Torino, *Tel. 011/347-2640, Fax 011/397-8038.* Located only 4 kilometers from Torino, this is a 9 hole, par 33, smallish 2170 meter course. They are open year round except August and Mondays. They have a driving range and a restaurant/bar. Good for day trips and short rounds of golf.

Shopping

Torino is a shopper's paradise and the best place for that is the elegant **Via Roma** where you can find all sorts of unique purchases, including shoe stores, tailors, *alimentari*, cafés, restaurants, jewelers, department stores, furriers, and much more. Even if you don't spend any money, Via Roma still is a fun place to window shop and people watch.

Books & Newspapers in English
- **Libreria International Luxembourg**, Via Accademia dell Scienze 3, *Tel. 011/561-38-96.* Mondays 3am to 7:30pm, Tuesday through Friday 8am to 7:30pm. Closed Sundays. There's a good selection of travel books, fiction, and non-fiction works as well as books relating to science and industry.

Practical Information
Car Rental
- **Avis**, Airport, *Tel. 011/470-1528* or Stazione Portanuova, *Tel. 011/669 9800.*
- **Hertz**, Airport *Tel. 011/567-8166* or Via Magellano 12, *Tel. 011/502-080*

Laundry Services
- **Lavanderia Vizzini**, Via San Secondo 30, *Tel. 011/54-58-82.* Open Monday–Friday 8:00am to 12:30pm, and 3:30pm to 6:30pm. Bring in your wash in the morning and pick it up at night. Cost for 4 kilos is E8; 6 kilos is E12.

Postal Services
- **Central Post Office**, Via Alfieri 10 and Via Arsenale 13, *Tel. 011/54-70-97.* Open Monday through Friday 8:30am-5pm, Saturdays 9am-12 noon.

Tourist Information & Maps
Both of these offices will supply you with a workable map of the city and help you find a room if you've arrived without one. In conjunction you can pick up the latest information on what's happening during your stay *(Un Ospite a Torino)* in town and throughout the province.

• **APT Office**, Via Roma 226, *Tel. 011/53-59-01*
• **Information Office**, Porta Nuova Train Station, *Tel. 011/53-13-27. Web: www.turismotorino.org*

Travel Advisory
The local government travel organization strongly suggests that tourists, especially women walking alone, **avoid Via Nizza** next to the train station at night. But as always, in comparison to most American cities, you should be more than safe in Torino.

The 2006 Winter Olympics

From February 10th through the 26th in 2006, Torino and the surrounding area will be brimming with Olympic spirit and vitality. Home to the winter Olympiad, Torino and environs have been busy for many years setting the stage for this grand event. To be held in some of the most picturesque Italian mountains and towns, wrapping a vacation to Italy around the Olympics would be a truly unique experience.

BARDONECCHIA
Probably the most famous town that is part of the 2006 Olympic system is **Bardonnecchia**. Long a part of Italy's skiing history, Bardonnecchia is a great place to vacation winter or summer, and is easily accessible from Torino by train. Filled with many top class hotels and restaurants Bardonecchia is top class all around. Website: *www.comune.bardonecchia.to.it.*

Where to Stay
BUCANEVE, *Viale della Vecchia 2, Tel. 0122/999-332, Fax 0122/999-980, Email: hbucaneve@tin.it. 22 rooms. Single E60; Double E80. Breakfast E8. All credit cards accepted. Closed Sept. 15 – Nov. 30. ***
A small chalet that is particularly accommodating, near both the center of town and the ski lifts. This place is distinguished by warm ambiance and comfortable and typical wood furnishings. The rooms are ample and the bathrooms are all renovated. A top of the line two star. They also have a wonderful restaurant that is highly recommended.
DES GENEYS-SPLENDID, *Via Einaudi 21, Tel. 0122/99-001, Fax 0122/999-295, Email: geneys@libero.it. 57 rooms. Single E80; Double E120. Breakfast E8. All credit cards accepted. Closed Apr. 16-June 20 and Sept 16-Dec 15. ****
A classic hotel nestled in some trees and oozing charm. The rooms are all comfortable and ample. A fine three star.

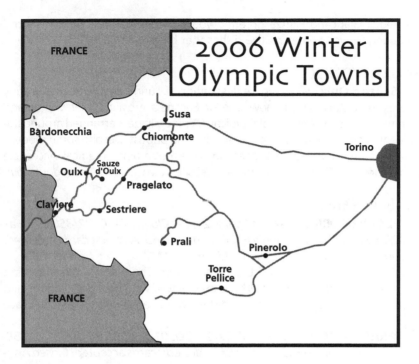

PINEROLO

Pinerolo will host the curling competitions in 2006. It is known as the "Nice of Piedmont" for its mild climate due to the protection afforded by the surrounding hills and mountains. This is a charming little town, not nearly as advanced tourist-wise as Bardonecchia, but that helps to make it alluring. Website: *www.comune.pinerolo.to.it.*

Where to Stay

REGINA, *Piazza Luigi Barbieri 22, Tel. 0121/322-157, Fax 0121/393-133, Email: hotel.regina@piw.it. 15 rooms. Single E65; Double E80. Closed Aug 1-21.* ***

A small hotel with great prices in the heart of the small town of Pinerolo. The structure is nondescript, but the rooms are large and comfortable.

Where to Eat

TAVERNA DEGLI ACAJA, *Corso Torino 106, el. 0121/794-727, Web: www.tavernadegliacaja.it. Closed Mondays, for lunch on Sundays, and August 10-31 and January 1-8. All credit cards accepted. Dinner for two E40.*

An elegant local restaurant that many Italians critics rave about, and I cannot agree more despite my general aversion to *cucina nuovo*. On the corner of a quaint street in the heart of Pinerolo, here you will find the courteous Giancarlo Pilutza greeting you and the talented Fabrizio Finotti preparing for you some creative dishes that burst with flavor.

SAUZE D'OULX

Sauze d'Oulx was a favorite destination of Turin's aristocracy in the early twentieth century, and is now one of Europe's most popular winter and summer vacation spots. The old, typically Alpine village is arranged around the sixteenth century parish church of St. John the Baptist. Despite some modern enhancements to the town, the setting in the mountains is magical. Accessible from Torino by train via the Oulx station. Website: *www.comune.sauzedoulx.to.it.*

Where to Stay

IL CAPRICORNO, *Via Case Sparse 21, Les Clotes, Tel. 0122/850-273, Fax 0122/850-055. 7 rooms. Single E120; Double E165. All credit cards accepted. Closed May 15-June 15 and Sept. 15-Dec. 1. *****

A romantic little chalet nestled in the woods. The rooms come with rustic Alpine furnishings and almost all have excellent views. There is a solarium, and a superb restaurant. The serve local dishes with a semi-creative flair. The place to eat in and around Sauze d'Oulx.

GRAN BAITA, *Via Villagio Alpino 21, Tel. 0122/850-183, Fax 0122/858-439. 32 rooms. Single E55; Double E85. All credit cards accepted. Closed Apr.-June and Sept. 1-Dec. 15. ****

A wonderful little three star in the mountains, near the ski lifts, surrounded by greenery and with luscious views. This place is modern, functional and comfortable. They also have a good restaurant that serves hearty local fare.

SESTRIERE

Sestriere, an ancient village only 60 miles from Torino, This place was adapted in 1934 specifically to be a ski resort. During the Olympics it will host most of the down hill events and has constructed an Olympic village to house some of the athletes. As such, during the Olympics, Sestiere will be a bustling center of activity. Website: *www.comune.sestriere.to.it.*

Where to Stay

GRAND HOTEL PRINCIPI DI PIEMONTE, *Via Sauze 3/b, Tel. 0122/7941, Fax 0122/755-411. 96 rooms. Single E95-170; Double E185-320. All credit cards accepted. Closed Apr. 15-June 31 and Sept. 1-Dec. 15. *****

And elegant hotel in a building from the 1930s, complete with panoramic views, many charming rooms. A little outside of the center of town. Still a great place to stay.

MIRAMONTI, *Via Cesana 3, Tel. 0122/755-333, Fax 0122/755-375, Email: h.miramonti@tiscalinet.it. 30 rooms. Single E 70-125; Double E98-220. Breakfast E7. All credit cards accepted.* ***
In a great spot near the ski slopes, in the mountains, and near a golf course, this place is efficient and comfortable, with rustic furnishings and courteous staff.

Then there is the host to the cross-country skiing, Nordic combined and ski jump events, **Pragelato**. Located in the center of a large basin in the Val Troncea Natural Park, which has 50 kilometers of cross-country ski routes through scenic meadows and pine forests. A very small town, filled with Alpine ambiance and rustic charm. Website: *www.pragelato.it.*

Other tiny Alpine towns that will host Olympic events include: Chiomonte, Claviere, Oulx, Prali, Susa, and Torre Pellice. Many of these smaller towns have websites of their own, which can be accessed from the Bardonecchia website: *www.comune.bardonecchia.to.it.*

This whole area that is playing host to the 2006 Winter Olympics is an Alpine wonderland. Whether you visit Torino and these towns during the Olympics, or come at another time, you will be guaranteed a memorable vacation. Check out the official 2006 Winter Olympiad website for more information: *www.torino2006.org.*

Chapter 22

SICILY

Sicily (Sicilia) is filled with rustic charm. A geological extension of the Apennine Mountains, separated from the toe of the mainland by the **Straits of Messina**, the island is about the size of Vermont. Throughout history, Sicily has always been someone else's prize, making it a great place to visit for amateur archeologists. It was first overrun by the Siculi and Sicans. The Greeks arrived in the 8th century BCE and left behind the ruins of temples and theaters. The Romans made the island their first province. The Arabs contributed a flourishing legacy of crops including oranges, lemons, melons and pistachios which all are part of the vibrant agricultural economy today. The Normans left behind their castles, cathedrals and fair skinned, blue eye genes. And the centuries of Spanish and Austrian control have all laid the foundation for latest ruler, unofficially of course, the Mafia. Today, some claim that the Mafia remains the island's most profitable industry, with an estimated annual income of between $4 and 6 billion.

Don't let that bother you, the whole idea of the Mafia is playfully presented on officially sanctioned tours of local Mafia sights. But the main reason people come here are the extensive historical sites related to the former rulers of the island's. Among the best of the ancient Greek ruins on the island are the Greek theater in **Syracuse**, and the 5th-century BCE **Temple of Concord** in **Agrigento**.

Early Settlements

We know, based on excavations at **Realmonte** near Agrigento, that man's history in Sicily dates back to the early Paleolithic period. There are also early settlements at **Stentinello** and **Lipari** that have been carbon dated to the Neolithic period. During the Copper and Bronze ages, the island's inhabitants traded with many of the other developing Mediterranean settlements. Later Sicily came mainly under the influence of **Greece** and the **Phoenicians**.

Near the end of the Bronze Age, a contingent of people called **Siculi** (which helps explain the island's name) came from the mainland and began to dominate the small settlements of the island, dispersing them and forcing them inland to the mountains for protection. The new people prospered, but were mainly just vassals to the Phoenician and Greek traders. Even though Phoenicia had a greater influence than Greece in Sicily, especially the port cities, they left the main colonization to the Greeks, who started their settlements on the east coast and gradually pushed the Siculi people westward.

By the fifth century BCE, **Syracuse** on the east coast had become the strongest settlement and had Helenized almost all of Sicily. The Siculi looked to the western Phoenician towns of Marsala and Trapani for assistance; they were holding fast against the Greek colonization. As a result a war was fought between the two Sicilian factions, which had to be settled by Roman intervention with the two **Punic Wars** of 264–212 BCE.

With the Roman domination, the interior of the island began to prosper. Splendid villas and fertile fields sprung up throughout Sicily, providing much of Rome's produce.

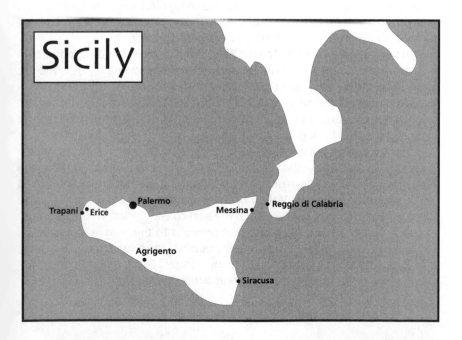

Foreign Invasions

After the fall of Rome, the island was invaded by the Vandals in the 5th century CE, then by the Goths. Eventually the Byzantine Empire took control and almost three centuries of peace lasted until 826. Then the Moors and Saracens took control of Sicily. Their biggest change to the island was to move the capital from Syracuse to **Palermo**, where it remains today.

In 1061, the Norman conquest began (five years before their successful invasion of another island, England) and the island enjoyed its most successful period in history. In 1302, the era of peace and prosperity ended with the Spanish domination. This period saw the rich get richer and the poor get poorer, creating a division between the people and their governors that still exists today. It may be an exaggeration to say that history passed the Sicilians by for the next five hundred years, but not an awful lot of consequence occurred during this long period.

Then on May 11, 1860, **Garibaldi** landed at Marsala and began to dismantle the Kingdom of Sicily and merge it with the Kingdom of Italy. During this time the people were greatly oppressed, which gave rise to the beginnings of what we know today as the **Mafia**. At the beginning of the twentieth century, a massive emigration began, mainly to America and Australia, spreading the Sicilian culture all over the world.

Sicily Today

Besides its rich ancient history, there are many other reasons to visit Sicily: water sports, beaches of rock and sand (including black sand), natural beauty, great food and friendly people (for the most part). For touring, the island can be roughly divided into the north shore and south shore areas.

In the center of the north coast is **Palermo**, the ancient and current capital and the island's largest city with a population of approximately 801,000. Be sure to visit the central market and 12th-century **Monreale Cathedral**, which has impressive biblical mosaics. About 80 km west of Palermo lies the ancient village of **Erice**, atop a mountain, where you can still find the remains of a temple dedicated to Venus.

The **southern coast** has an even milder climate than the North, which means you can enjoy swimming most of the year, although between November and March it can get quite chilly. Among the areas not to be missed are **Agrigento** (to see the **Valley of the Temples**) and **Mt. Etna**, an active volcano just topping 3,200 meters on the east coast. The last time the volcano erupted was in January 1992. The time previous to that was in March 1987, when two people were killed. Although scientists say it can erupt at any time, if you play it safe you shouldn't be in any danger. There is also good winter skiing around Mt. Etna that offers great ocean views.

Arrivals & Departures

By Air

As of press time, there were no direct flights from North America or Australia to either Catania in the east or Palermo in the west. There are some flights on **Ryanair** from London or Dublin to Palermo, as well as on other of the inexpensive European airlines, but that could change. Generally you will have to fly through Milan or Rome first, then transfer to **Alitalia** to get to Sicily.

By Car

The drive down to Sicily through southern Italy is beautifully scenic, especially down the coast, but it takes quite a while. From Rome it will take over 14 hours just to get to Messina. But if you have the time, the scenery is wonderful, and if you don't have the money to fly you can drive, take the train, the ferry, or the hydrofoil.

By Ferry

There are over twenty ferries a day from **Reggio di Calabria** to **Messina** (cost is E5), as well as a hydrofoil service that is faster (E4) but doesn't allow cars. You can also catch ferries from the cities listed below as well as others in Italy:
- **Genoa to Palermo**, 23 hours
- **Naples to Palermo**, 11 hours
- **Naples to Catania to Syracuse**, 15 hours/19 hours
- **Livorno to Palermo**, 19 hours

By Hydrofoil

For a faster alternative to ferries from Naples, try the hydrofoil. It'll cost a little more but the ride will be smoother and it will be over sooner.
- **Naples to Palermo**, 5 hours and 30 minutes

By Train

If you like long train rides you can enjoy the southern Italian scenery and take the train from any place in Italy to Sicily. From Rome it will take over 14 hours just to get to Messina. But if you have the time, the scenery is wonderful, and if you don't have the money to fly this is a nice, scenic option.

The train fare from Rome is E50. The ferry ride from Reggio di Calabria is included in the train fare.

Climate & Weather

Sicilian climate is stable throughout the year but varies based on the topography. To the north, along the coast, you can expect hot summers and mild winters making it perfectly Mediterranean. The temperatures along the southern coast and inland are much higher and you can have more drastic temperature fluctuations. Rain is rare but it does increase with altitude. This makes Sicily, strangely enough, a great place to ski in the winter, since the mountains above 1,600 meters get covered with snow.

In the summer expect to experience the hot and humid *Scirocco* winds that blow in from the Sahara, bringing with it discomfort and clouds of reddish dust.

When to Go

Sicilians will tell you that anytime is a good time to travel to Sicily, and they aren't kidding. As noted earlier, the climate of Sicily does not vary that much during the year, making Sicily a pleasant trip any time of year – although the summers can get unbearably hot at times. The northern coast's climate is more stable than that of the southern coast and inland. If you want to try the beach from November to March, it's not a good idea, since it will be like autumn back in the US.

So the best time to go to Sicily and enjoy good warm weather is September through the first week in November. To enjoy good skiing, go between December and March.

Getting Around Sicily

Sicily is connected by an extensive highway system, a superb train system, and naturally, since Sicily is an island, a complete shipping service involving ferries, hydrofoils, and liners. Your mode of transport will depend on how long you're staying in Sicily and what you want to see.

If you're only visiting coastal towns, it might be fun to take a ferry between them. If you are going to rural, off the beaten path locations, you'll need a car, because even if the train did go to where you're going, the *Locale* would take forever since it stops at every town on its tracks.

By Train

You can get most anywhere in Sicily by train, much the same as on the mainland. There are more extensive rail systems on the east of the island to accommodate the flow of trains from the mainland. Here you should expect delays since the trains may have had trouble getting across on the ferry.

There are some small towns that the trains do not go to, but you should avoid these anyway. You never know when you're going to stumble onto something better left unseen in one of the mountain villages.

By Car

The expressways, called **Autostrada**, are superhighways and toll roads. They connect all major Sicilian cities and have contributed to the tremendous increase in tourist travel. By car is the best way to see Sicily since you don't have to wait for the trains, which are inevitably delayed, something that rarely happens on the mainland.

Driving is the perfect way to see the entire variety of Sicily's towns, villages, seascapes, landscapes, and monuments. The Sicilian drivers may be a little *pazzo* (crazy), but if you drive confidently you'll be fine. A word of caution, again: Sicily is best explored along its coastline and a little inland. Once you start roaming through the mountain towns, unless you know what you're doing, anything could happen.

Basic Information

The **US Consulates** is located at Via GB Vaccarini 1, Palermo. *Tel. 091/ 302-590.*

Food

Most Sicilian food is cooked with fresh ingredients raised or caught a short distance from the restaurant, making their dishes healthy, fresh, and satisfying. There are many restaurants in Sicily of international renown, but you shouldn't limit yourself only to the upper echelon. In most cases you can find as good a meal at a fraction the cost at any *trattoria*. Also, many of the upper echelon restaurants you read about are only in business because they cater to the tourist trade. Their food is good, but the atmosphere is a little hokey.

The traditional Sicilian meal has been influenced by the Middle East, Greece, France, and Spain as a result of the island's past conquests. Other influences include the sea (what better place to find a meal) and the fact that the island's climate is perfect for growing all sorts of herbs and spices, and vegetables and fruits.

Safety & Precautions

Sicilian cities are definitely much safer than any equivalent American city. You can walk most anywhere without fear of harm, but that doesn't mean you shouldn't play it safe. Listed below are some simple rules to follow to ensure that nothing bad occurs:
- At night, make sure the streets you are walking on have plenty of other people. Like I said, most cities are safe, but at night in certain areas the rules change.
- Always have your knapsack or purse flung over the shoulder that is not directly next to the road. Why? There have been cases of Italians on motorbike snatching purses off old ladies and in some cases dragging them a few blocks.
- Better yet, have your companion walk on the street side, while you walk on the inside of the sidewalk with the knapsack or purse.
- Better still is to buy one of those tummy wallets that goes under your shirt so no one can even be tempted to purse-snatch you. That's really all you

should need, but always follow basic common sense; if you feel threatened, scared, alone, retrace your steps back to a place where there are other people.
• Be especially on guard against street thieves and pickpockets in Palermo and other large towns.

Wine

Sicily's best wines are **Etna** (red and white, wide variety) from the Catania area and **Marsala** (white, dry or sweet) from the Trapani province. You should also try some **Casteldaccio,** a dry white from around Palermo, and if you like sweet wine, an **Eloro** from around Syracuse should suffice. If you're on the Eolie Islands, try their unique red and white **Malvasia**.

PALERMO

Palermo started off as a Phoenician city, which the Greeks referred to as Panormos. The city then came under Roman rule during the two **Punic Wars** in 254 BCE. After that they endured Byzantine rule (353–830 CE), then Saracen domination (830-1072), and finally Norman (1072-1194) influence placed its stamp on the city. These conquerors were succeeded by the Hofenstaufens in 1194, then the House of Anjou ruled from 1266 until a popular uprising in 1282.

After that, Palermo came under Argonese and Spanish rule and eventually passed to the Bourbons in the 18th century. It finally became part of Italy on May 27, 1860, when it was liberated by Garibaldi. Today Palermo is Italian but, some say the real rulers are the Mafia.

Palermo is large, busy, noisy, congested and polluted and is completely controlled by Mafia interests. Today there is the beginning of a popular backlash against *La Cosa Nostra's* influence in the city, evidenced by anti-Mafia posters appearing periodically on the walls. But as a tourist you have little to worry about from the Mafia. In Palermo you need to protect yourself against pickpockets and purse snatchers, especially if you roam away from the *centro storico*, but the Mafia has no interest in tourists other than to encourage them to come and spend money.

Centuries ago the city was divided into four quarters, which all merged at the square known as the **Quattro Canti** (four corners) in the center of town. This square is at the intersection of **Corso Vittorio Emanuele** and **Via Maqueda**. The **Albergheria** is northwest of the *quattro canti*, **Capo** is southwest, **Vucciria** is northeast and **La Kalsa** is southeast. Each of these quarters had distinct dialects, cultures, trading practices and markets for their products. There was limited intermingling since intermarriage would result in being ostracized.

Today, the area around the Quattro Canti is where most of the sights are located. Everything here is an eclectic mix of medieval streets and Norman,

Oriental, and Baroque architecture, broad modern avenues and large buildings, and bombed-out vacant lots from World War II.

As such it is not nearly as charming as Florence or Venice, and it also has less historical architecture and museums than Rome; but Palermo is still an interesting city to explore. There's a heavy Middle Eastern influence, almost a *souk*-like atmosphere at some markets that differentiates Palermo from other Italian cities. Stay to see Palermo's sights, marvel in its sounds and smells, and then hop on a train and go explore some other less hectic part of Sicily.

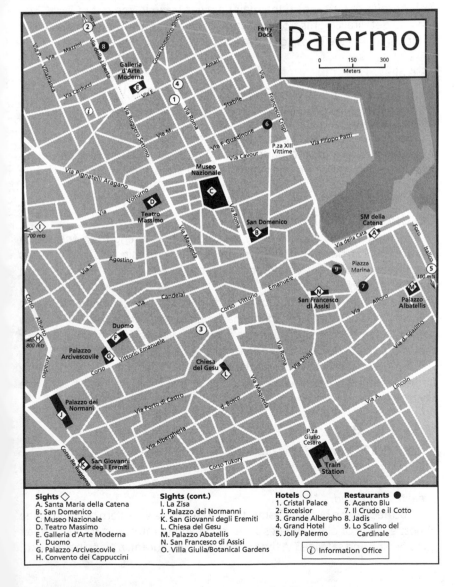

Sights ◇	Sights (cont.)	Hotels ○	Restaurants ●
A. Santa Maria della Catena	I. La Zisa	1. Cristal Palace	6. Acanto Blu
B. San Domenico	J. Palazzo dei Normanni	2. Excelsior	7. Il Crudo e il Cotto
C. Museo Nazionale	K. San Giovanni degli Eremiti	3. Grande Albergho	8. Jadis
D. Teatro Massimo	L. Chiesa del Gesu	4. Grand Hotel	9. Lo Scalino del
E. Galleria d'Arte Moderna	M. Palazzo Abatellis	5. Jolly Palermo	Cardinale
F. Duomo	N. San Francesco di Assisi		
G. Palazzo Arcivescovile	O. Villa Giulia/Botanical Gardens	ⓘ Information Office	
H. Convento dei Cappuccini			

To know what's happening now in Palermo, check out the official website: *www.comune.palermo.it.*

Arrivals & Departures
By Air
You can fly into Palermo from Rome or Milan. The fare is changing all the time, but at last check it was $300 from Rome. It may be even higher by the time you read this, but look for various excursion fares or even package deals with **Alitalia** or **Lufthansa**, the major airlines flying in and out of Sicily. You can also get direct flights from London or Dublin to Palermo, so this could be an option if you are crossing the Atlantic.

By Train
Palermo is about two hours away from Messina by train.

Other Options
Bus will be your best budget travel option, but you can also get here by ferry or hydrofoil from other parts of Sicily or the mainland. Consult the various schedules from the town you plan to depart from for the most up-to-date information.

Getting Around Town
Palermo is a city you can enjoy walking in, but getting from one end of it to another can be tiring. That's why we recommend using the **public buses** whenever you can. They cost E1 for a ticket that lasts an hour. You buy them at *Tabacchi* (stores marked with a blue **T**) or at AMAT's kiosks. If you know you'll be taking the bus a lot, buy an all-day pass for E3. Remember to stamp a single ticket or a day ticket in the machines as you get on the bus. The day pass only needs to be stamped once and kept with you in case an inspector shows up. If you don't have a ticket you will be immediately fined E25.

If you don't want to deal with the push and pull of public transport, simply flag down a taxi, but be prepared to get caught in traffic and watch your fare sky-rocket.

Where to Stay
1. **CRISTAL PALACE**, *Via Roma 477, Tel. 091/611-2580, Fax 091/611-2589. Web: www.venere.it/it/palermo/cristalpalacehotel. 90 rooms, 39 with bath, 51 with shower. Single E120; Double E135. All credit cards accepted. Breakfast included.* ***
Located on the busy Via Roma, this is a completely modern building made almost entirely of glass. Besides super clean and comfortable rooms with air conditioning and satellite TV, the hotel offers a restaurant, a piano bar, a disco,

an American-style bar and a gymnasium. Each room has a separate level for work. The bathrooms are smallish with hairdryers and a minimal courtesy toiletry set. This is a good place to stay.

2. EXCELSIOR PALACE, *Via Marchese Ugo 3, Tel. 091/625-6176, Fax 091/342-139. Web: www.sicily-hotels.com/siti/excelsiorpalace-pa/index.htm. 128 rooms. Single E125-140; Double E180. All credit cards accepted. Breakfast included.* ****

Centrally located, this hotel's former glory was resurrected in 1987 with a complete renovation of the premises. Near the English gardens for relaxing walks and the Via della Iiberta for shopping at their pricey boutiques. In the entrance and other public rooms the lamps are from the island of Murano, off Venice. The rooms are large, and come with soundproof windows to block out the traffic noise, but for some reason only 18 rooms have mini-bars. The best rooms are on the second floor with their beautiful bordeaux bedspreads and wall coverings. The bathrooms are a little small but have everything you need. If you need more room, the 16 suites offer it for about E50 more. And to top it off the service is professional and attentive. A great place to stay.

3. GRANDE ALBERGHO SOLE, *Via Vittorio Emanuele 291, Tel. 091/581-811, Fax 091/611-0182. Web: www.sicily-hotels.com/siti/sole-pa/index.htm. 154 rooms 138 with bath. Single E135-145; Double E190. All credit cards accepted. Breakfast included.* ***

Located a few paces from the Duomo in a hectic central location. The entrance hall is elegantly adorned with antiques along with a small display of archaeological relics. The rooms are adequately comfortable even though the furnishings are a little dated and have TV, radio and A/C. The bathrooms are spacious and come with a minimal courtesy toiletry set, but no hairdryer. Breakfast is Italian, which means coffee and a roll. Recently upgraded to a three star, but I think the designation is a bit of a stretch. But still a pleasant place to stay.

4. GRANDE HOTEL ET DES PALME, *Via Roma 398, Tel. 091/583-933, Fax 091/331-545. Web: www.sicily-hotels.com/siti/thi/despalmes/home.htm. 187 rooms, 103 with bath, 84 with shower. Single E110-195; Double E190-230. All credit cards accepted. Breakfast included.* ****

Located on the busy Via Roma, the windows here are double-paned so you are insulated from the traffic noise. This is a huge, clean, and comfortable hotel whose rooms are adequately sized. The ones with bathtubs instead of showers seem to be bigger. Each room also has a separate floor/area for work space. The entrance hall is magnificently elegant with antique furnishings and huge Doric columns. There is an in-house restaurant where your meal will be good but expensive. There is also room service and an American-style bar downstairs. The bountiful breakfast buffet is served in a 'yellow' room with a beautiful floral arrangement on the center table. One major plus is the presence of a swimming pool. Recently upgraded to four star status and they deserve it, but the prices have gone through the roof.

5. JOLLY HOTEL DEL FORO ITALICO, *Foro Italico 22, Tel. 091/616-5090, Fax 091/616-1441. E-mail: palermo@jollyhotels.it. Web: www.jollyhotels.it. 237 rooms. Single E120-140; Double E140-175. All credit cards accepted. Breakfast included.* ****

Since it is located a ways from the center, the hotel offers shuttle bus service for its guests. Situated on the Foro Italico, it's a fun place people watch in the evenings. The hotel has a pool, nice restaurant, room service, laundry service, air conditioning and satellite TV in the rooms. The place, like all Jolly hotels, is as modern as they come, but it is mainly a businessman's hotel – meaning the rooms are medium sized. The bathrooms are comfortable and come with a complete courtesy toiletry set and a hairdryer. The buffet breakfast is a rich international spread in a room filled with mirrors and lamps made on the island of Murano near Venice. In summer breakfast is served in the gazebo in the interior garden

Where to Stay

6. ACANTO BLU, *Via F Guardinone 19, Tel. 091/326-258. Closed Sundays and September. No credit cards accepted. Dinner for two E30.*

A small little place that serves basic rustic cuisine. You can either enjoy the air conditioning inside or the terrace outside. Try some of the extensive *antipasto* table, especially the fried vegetables with a spicy hot sauce. Next try what they call *riso dei poeti* (rice of the poets), which contains apple, radish and fish. It is quite delectable. Then save the best for last, *funghi infornati cotti nella mollica condita con olio e peperoncini* (fresh mushrooms baked in a mold of bread served up with fresh olive oil and peperoncini).

7. IL CRUDO E IL COTTO, *Piazza Marina 45a, Tel. 091/616-9261. Closed Tuesdays and variable holidays. No credit cards accepted. Dinner for two E35.*

In the beautiful Piazza Marina you can get a great meal at this tiny family run *trattoria*. You have Laura in the kitchen and Franchino and Giovanni greeting people and working as waiters. Get a seat outside so you can enjoy the view. Try their *riso ai frutti di mare* (rice with mixed seafood) then a succulent *bistecca* (steak) or *pesce spada alla griglia* (grilled swordfish) for seconds. To wash it all down get some of their house wine, which comes from the local mountains.

8. JADIS, *Via Liberta 121, Tel. 091/349-323. Closed Sundays and Mondays and August. Open only at night. No credit cards accepted. Dinner for two E36.*

Located a few blocks north of the Museum of Modern Art, this is a very popular place with the arts crowd as well as with people who appreciate good food. You have a choice of outside seating, which is wonderful on cool evenings. Try their *carpaccio di vitello* or their *carpaccio di pesce spada* (steak of veal or swordfish)

9. LO SCALINO DEL CARDINALE, *Via Bottai 18, Tel. 091/3310124. Closed Mondays, for Lunch, and the last half of September. Credit cards accepted. Dinner for two E38.*

A great local place that is always packed during the week. With its terrace in use in the summer there seems to be plenty of space, but in the winter it's difficult to find a spot to eat. Try some of their *crocchette al latte* (croquets with milk) or *al primo sale fritto* (fried with a local cheese). For seconds, try their *pesce spada al profumo di Cardinale* (swordfish with a creamy sauce with sliced bell peppers).

Seeing the Sights
North of Corso Vittorio Emanuele

As you move from the east of Corso Vittorio Emanuele to the west, you may want to catch rides on the frequent **bus #27** to quicken your pace.

A. SANTA MARIA DELLA CATENA

Via Vittorio Emanuele. Open 8am–11:30am and 3:30pm–7pm.

Built in the early 16th century, this church is named after the chain that used to be dragged across the old harbor, **La Cala**, at night to protect the vessels inside. This used to be the main port of Palermo until it started silting up in the late sixteenth century. The main industrial shipping moved north and this little inlet was left to the fishermen. It's a great place to take a short stroll and take in the sights, smells, and sounds of the Sicilian seafarers.

Not far away, located almost at the eastern part of the city, is the **Porta Felice**, which was built in 1582 to compliment the slightly older **Porta Nuova**, which is all the way to the west. Since these two gates were once the ancient boundaries of old Palermo, this is a good place to start your tour, because from here you can get a good feel for the true extent of ancient Palermo.

Past Porta Felice is the popular promenade, **Foro Italico**, with its own little **amusement park**. On summer nights residents come out here to sit, talk, walk, stare, and share the beautiful evenings with each other.

B. CHIESA DI SAN DOMENICO

Piazza San Domenico. Open 7:30am–noon.

Walk down Via Vittorio Emanuele towards the Porta Nuova and take a right on Via Roma to get to the Piazza San Domenico and the church of the same name. This beautiful 17th century church with an 18th century facade is the burial site of many famous Sicilians. At night the facade and the statue-topped marble column are lit up, creating quite a spectacle. The perfect spot to sip an *aperitivo* at one of the outdoor cafés surrounding the piazza.

Just behind the church is the **Oratorio del Rosario di San Domenico**, which contains some interesting stucco work created by Giacomo Serpotta as well as a magnificent altar piece by Van Dyke (Via dei Bambinai #16, open 7:30am–noon).

C. MUSEO NAZIONALE

Piazza Olivella. *Tel. 662-0220.* Open Monday–Saturday 9am–1:30pm, Tuesdays and Fridays also open 3pm–5:30pm. Sundays and holidays only open 9am–12:30pm. Admission E3.

Go back to the Via Roma and walk north to the **National Museum**. Also known as the Museo Archeologico Regionale, if you've been out discovering Sicily's archaeological sites or intend to do so, you'll love this museum. Located in a former monastery, their collection of pre-historic relics, Etruscan, Greek, Egyptian and Roman pieces is quite extensive and well-presented.

The museum has frescoes from Pompeii, bronze works from Greece, Roman sculptures, and much more. Especially imposing are the 56 lion head water spouts taken from 5th century BCE Himera. This is one of the finest antiquities museums in all of Italy.

D. TEATRO MASSIMO

Piazza Verdi. *Tel 091/605-3111, Fax 091/605-3325 or 605-3324.* Hours 9am–1pm and 4pm–7pm. Admission E3.

The **Teatro Massimo** is down Via Maqueda from the National Museum. Also known as Teatro Vittorio Emanuele, this theater was built from 1875 to 1897 and can seat 3,200 attendees. As such it is the second largest theater in Europe, second only to the opera house in Paris. Currently under renovation, you probably will not be able to get a tour inside, but it doesn't hurt to ask.

E. GALLERIA D'ARTE MODERNA

Gallery open Tuesday–Sunday 9am–1pm and 3–6pm. Admission E5.

I know you didn't come to Sicily to look at modern art, but a trip to the **Modern Art Museum** is a breath of fresh air after looking at relics all day long. Italy's art treasures don't all belong to the past, so visit here and see some beautiful and interesting modern works.

Nearby is the main **tourist office**, past the English gardens in front and past the equestrian statue of Garibaldi in the square. Stop here to get ideas about current happenings and what else to see in Palermo and elsewhere in Sicily.

Walk back down Via Roma to the **Quattro Canti** (The Four Corners) – Via Roma, Via Vittorio Emanuele and Via Maqueda – which converge here at what is the center of the old city.

F. DUOMO

Piazza del Cattedrale. Open 7am–noon and 4pm–7pm.

The **Duomo** is three hundred meters past the Quattro Canti on the Via Vittorio Emanuele. The church was begun by the Normans in 1185, and thereafter underwent many architectural transformations from the 13th century to the 18th, though the Norman towers and triple-apsed eastern side remain today. With its many styles, the intricate exterior is a joy to study. The same can't be said for the interior, which was recreated in a bland neoclassic style.

To the left as you enter you'll find six imposing tombs contains the bodies of past kings of Palermo, including Frederick II and Roger II. In the chapel to the right of the choir is the silver sarcophagus that contains the remains of the city's patron saint, Rosalia. The **treasury**, located to the right of the apse, is infinitely more interesting since it contains some exquisite, jewel-encrusted ancient clothing (E1 to enter). You also find remains of some saints preserved here.

G. PALAZZO ARCIVESCOVILE

Via Papireto Bonnello. Open Tuesday–Sunday 9am–1pm and 3pm–6pm.

Immediately southwest of the cathedral is the one-time **Archbishop's Palace** that contains the **Dioclesan Museum**. The museum features many works of art that were salvaged from other churches during the Allied bombings of World War II. If this is closed check out the **Mercato delle Pulci**, just up Via Bonello (next to the Palace) in **Piazza Peranni**. This is a great junk/ antique market held everyday from 8am to 2pm.

A little further down the Via Vittorio Emanuele is the **Porta Nuova**, which was erected in 1535 to commemorate the Tunisian exploits of Charles V.

H. CONVENTO DEI CAPPUCCINI

Open Monday–Saturday 9am–noon and 3pm–5pm. The visit is free but a donation of about E2 per person is expected.

No, this isn't a shrine to that wonderful frothing espresso product, though it is a bizarre yet fascinating place, in a morbid kind of way. To get here, walk 1.5 km west past the Porta Nuova or catch bus #27 going west from the Via Vittorio Emanuele to the Via Pindemonte. After you get off, it's a short walk to the convent. Just follow the signs.

This is like something out of a horror movie. Bodies stacked everywhere. Almost 800 of them. For many centuries this convent was the burial place not only for church members but also for rich laymen. You'll find bodies preserved with a variety of methods with differing results. Some bodies still have their hair and skin. Others have decomposed completely. The saddest sight here, though, are the remains of the tiny infants and young children. A gruesome place to visit, yes; but an experience you will never forget.

I. LA ZISA

Open Monday –Saturday 9am–2pm. Sundays 9am–1pm. The visit is free. Since you're already out here, you might as well walk a short way north to **La Zisa**, a huge palace begun by William I in 1160 and finished by his son William II. Go down the Via Corradino di Svevia, take a right on Via Eugenio L'Emiro (the first road), take an immediate left onto Via Edersi, then take the second right onto Viale Luigi Castiglia and you'll turn left after about fifty meters into the *piazza* that houses La Zisa. This is a wonderful replica of an Arabian palace (Zisa means *magnificent* in Arabic) and was used as a retreat for the king where he had lush exotic gardens tended and wild animals housed.

South of Corso Vittorio Emanuele
J. PALAZZO DEI NORMANNI

Open Monday–Friday 9am–noon and 3pm–5pm and Saturdays and Sundays 9am–11am. The chapel is closed Sundays.

The **Norman** or **Royal Palace**, just past the Porta Nuova going east on Corso Vittorio Emanuele, is a terrific place. Originally built by the Saracens and remodeled and reinforced by the Normans, this is an imposing fortress-like building that sits on the high ground overlooking the city below. Since the *palazzo* is the current seat of the Sicilian Parliament, you must be escorted by a guide through the rooms. Don't playfully attempt to sneak off; security is pretty tight because of the Mafia problems.

One room you can't miss is the **Cappella Palatina** which contains some of the best **mosaics** outside of Istanbul and Ravenna. The tile art describes scenes from the Old Testament. Another room adorned with mosaics, with a flora and fauna motif, is the **Sala di Ruggero**, King Roger's Hall.

K. SAN GIOVANNI DEGLI EREMITI

Corso Re Ruggero. Open 9am–1pm. On Tuesdays, Wednesdays, and Fridays also open 3–5pm.

Founded by Roger II, and built in 1132, the architecture of **St. John of the Hermits** has quite a bit of Arabic influence. Just down the road from the Norman Palace, this church was built over a mosque and is dominated by five Arab-looking domes. To get to the church you must walk up a path lined with citrus trees, behind which are some 13th century cloisters. A beautiful sight to see.

L. CHIESA DEL OF GESU

Via Porto di Castro. Open 7am–noon and 5pm–6:30pm.

Follow Via Porto di Castro from the Norman Palace to this small church with its green mosaic dome. It has a multicolored marble interior and an almost surreal interpretation of the *Last Judgment*. In the church's small courtyard, you can still see the effect of Allied bombings during World War II.

You can see this same bombing effect near the **Palazzo Abatellis** that is home to the **Galleria Nazionale Siciliana** (see below).

M. PALAZZO ABATELLIS

Via Alloro. Open 9am–1:30pm and also open on Tuesdays, Thursdays and Fridays 4pm–7pm. Sundays and holidays open 9am–12:30pm. Admission E4.

This palace houses the **Galleria Nazionale Siciliana**, one of Sicily's wonderful regional art museums. The gallery gives a comprehensive insight into Sicilian painting and sculpture. Some of the work is quite crude, some is magnificent, but if you've never been exposed to Sicilian art, this is your chance to learn.

N. CHURCH OF SAN FRANCESCO DI ASSISI

Via Paternostro. Open only from 7am–11am every day.

You have to be an early bird to catch this sight: the church is known for its intricate rose window that looks magnificent from the inside when the early morning sun streams through it. The zig-zag design on its exterior is common to many of the churches in the area. Built in the 13th century, there were two side chapels added in the 14th and 15th centuries.

O. VILLA GIULIA PARK & BOTANICAL GARDENS

Via Lincoln. Park open until dark. Botanical Gardens open Monday–Friday 9:00am–noon and Saturdays 9am–11am. Admission E2.

This is Palermo's best and most centrally-located park, which gives you a respite from the pace of this hectic city. Besides wildlife roaming around, there are gardens, a small kiddy train and a pretty **Botanical Gardens**. The gardens feature tropical plants from all over the world. It's an uplifting spot after a few days touring through Palermo.

Nightlife & Entertainment

If you are in Palermo from December to June, the traditional opera season, have the proper attire (suits for men, dresses for women), and have a taste for something out of the ordinary, try the spectacle of the opera.

• **Teatro Massimo**, Piazza Verdi. *Tel 091/605-3111, Fax 091/605-3325* or *605-3324*

Shopping

Food shopping can be done at the markets that are located off Via Roma on the **Via Divisi**, as well as between the **Palazzo dei Normani** and the train station at **Piazza Ballaro**.

For inexpensive clothing, try the **Via Bandiera** near Chiesa San Domenico. For more expensive clothing, try along the main thoroughfares of **Via Roma** and **Via Maqueda**.

Practical Information
Car Rental
- **Avis**, Via Principe di Scordia 12, *Tel. 091/586-940*; Aeroporto di Punta Raisi, *Tel. 091/591-684*
- **Hertz**, Via Messina 7, *Tel. 091/381-688;* Aeroporto di Punta Raisi, *Tel. 091/ 213-112-682*

Local Festivals & Holidays
- **July 11-15,** Festival of Santa Rosalia, also known as *Festa di U Fistinu*, with fireworks and general insanity
- **September 4**, pilgrimage-like walk to Monte Pelligrino in honor of Santa Rosalia

Postal Services
The **central post office** in Palermo is at Via Roma 322. Open Monday through Friday 8:30am–5pm, Saturdays 9am–noon.

Tourist Information & Maps
- **Main Information Office**, Piazza Castelnuovo 34, *Tel. 091/583-847*, across from the Modern Art Museum.
- **Information Office**, in the train station, open Monday–Friday, 8am–8pm. If the office at the station is out of information and/or maps, take bus #101 to the *piazza* and the main office. They both supply detailed maps and information about Palermo and other places of interest. There is also a tourist office in the Stazione Maritima and at the airport.

TRAPANI
Located on a sickle-shaped peninsula on the northwest coast of Sicily, **Trapani** is the island's largest fishing port. The city, called *Drapanon* (which means sickle) by locals, used to be the main port for the ancient Greek city of **Eryx** (Erice – see next section). Trapani flourished as a trading center, mainly with customers in Africa and the Middle East. The town has an ancient elegant *centro storico* out on the end of the sickle of a peninsula.

Today the city's lifeblood still depends on the trading of salt, wine, and fish. It's a modern city, developed after most everything else was destroyed during Allied bombing in World War II. Trapani is a friendly city and should definitely be one of your destinations while in Sicily.

Arrivals & Departures
Located 94 km from Palermo as the crow flies, the journey by car is about 110 km; by train you will end up putting in closer to 130 km since the tracks wind along the coast until Castellammare del Golfo then turn inland to follow

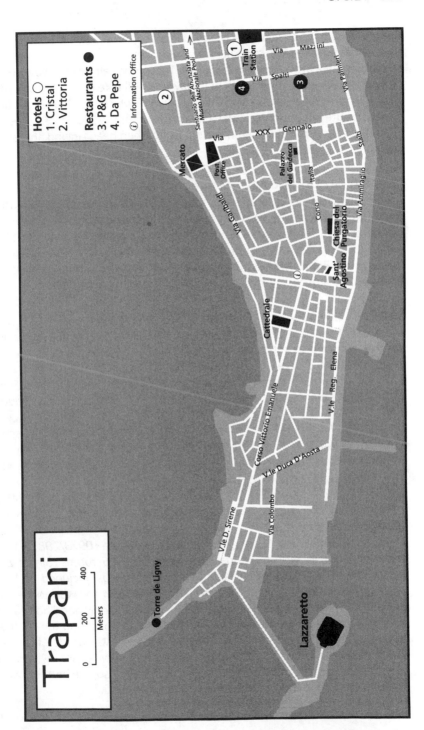

Trapani

Hotels ○
1. Cristal
2. Vittoria

Restaurants ●
3. P&G
4. Da Pepe

ⓘ Information Office

0   200   400
Meters

Torre de Ligny

Lazzaretto

V.le D. Sirene

Via Colombo

V.le Duca D'Aosta

Corso Vittorio Emanuele

Cattedrale

V.le Reg. Elena

Sant'Agostino

Chiesa del Purgatorio

Via Ammiraglio

Corso Italia

Palazzo del Giudecca

XXX Gennaio

Via Garibaldi

Mercato

Post Office

Via

Santuario dell'Anunziata and Museo Nazionale Pepli

②

④

③

①

Train Station

Via Spalti

Via Mazzini

Via Palmieri

Spalti

the main roads. The train usually stops at every town along the way, which means that your journey will take about 3 hours.

By car there are a number of options. The journey along highway 186 out of Palermo, which connects with highway 113, will take about 2 hours. After Alcamo you will be able to get on Autostrada A29 which can shorten the time. The best route but the longest would be to take highway 113 to 187. This runs along the coast until Castellammare del Golfo, then heads inland and passes by Erice along the way.

Getting Around Town

The *centro storico* occupies about a square kilometer on the peninsula, so everything in it is within walking distance. The **train station** lets you off just on the edge of the old town, and the docks along **Via Ammiraglio Staiti** (which runs half the southern length of the old town) are where you can catch ferries to the **Egadi Islands**. To get to the city's museum in the new section of town, you'll need to catch bus #1 or #10 from the train station.

Where to Stay

Most of the hotels in Trapani are located in the new city. The two below are the best and closest to the town's old city.

1. CRISTAL, *Piazza Umberto 1, Tel. 0923/20000, Fax 0923/25555. Web: www.sicily-hotels.com/siti/framon-hotels/crystal/index.html. 70 rooms. Single E85-115. Double E120-160. All credit cards accepted. Breakfast included* ****

Located right next to the train station, it is a lovely experience to spend the night here in the heart of Trapani. Strangely peaceful, quiet and calm, this modern hotel offers all necessary amenities and conveniences to make your stay pleasant and relaxing. The common areas are bright and accommodating. The rooms are large and comfortable, and the bathrooms are clean with all necessities, including a telephone. You also have an excellent restaurant and an ambient garden here.

2. VITTORIA, *Via F. Crispi 4, Tel. 0923/873-0444, Fax 0923/29870. Web: www.sicily-hotels.com/siti/vittoria/homepage.html. 65 rooms. Single E80-90; Double E90-100. All credit cards accepted. Breakfast included.* ***

Located about two blocks from the train station. Exit and walk to the right down Via F. Crispi and you'll run right into it. Really the only good hotel in the *centro storico* area, this place is perfectly situated for exploring the old town as well as getting to the station quickly to explore points outside of Trapani. The rooms have air conditioning, room and laundry service, great views over the sea and the park, and are clean and comfortable. Also, the bathrooms are immaculately kept and have necessary modern amenities.

Where to Eat

3. P&G, *Via Spalti 1, Tel. 0923/547-701. Closed Sundays and August. Credit cards accepted. Dinner for two E45.*

The decorations are not something to write home about, but the food here is excellent. Once you start digging into your antipasto, your mouth will come alive with the flavors of the Mediterranean, not just Italian. Try some of their *cuscus con la cernia* (couscous with stone bass) for *primo*, then move onto some *tonno al forno* (oven cooked tuna steak) or *alla brace* (grilled tuna steak). You should have at least one meal here while in Trapani. There are only 50 seats so make reservations or come early.

4. DA PEPE, *Via Spalti 50, Tel. 0923/28246. Closed Mondays. Credit cards accepted. Dinner for two E45.*

Just down the road from P&G, they're known for their house pasta dish made with the local pasta, *busiati*, which is actually just *fusilli*, a spiral-shaped pasta. The sauce is made with cooked garlic, tomatoes, and basil and is fantastic. And of course for seconds try any of their varieties of *pesce spada* (swordfish) or *tonno* (tuna) steaks.

Seeing the Sights

The look and feel of this medieval port city, with its European and Arab influences, makes it seem as if you've stepped back in time. The medieval and Renaissance fabric of the streets blends well with the tapestry of the Baroque buildings. One of the best structures is the **Cathedral** (Corso Vittorio Emanuele, open 8am–noon and 3pm–6pm). With its Baroque portico and immense exterior, and with its colorful dome and stucco walls, the Cathedral can be an imposing sight compared to the other tiny churches in the old city. A number of them have an interesting mix of Muslim and Christian influences.

Near the cathedral and adjacent to the main tourist office is the small church of **Sant'Agostino** (Piazzetta Saturno, open 8am–noon and 3–6pm). This 14th century church is mainly used as a **concert hall** and its main attraction is its stunning rose colored window.

The most fascinating church to see in Trapani, is the **Chiesa del Purgatorio** (Via Cassaretto, open Monday–Saturday 10am–noon and 4:30pm–6:30pm.), not really because of itself but because of what it has inside. The church is home to a large set of life-sized wooden statues called the **Misteri** that have been paraded through town during Good Friday celebrations every year for the past 600 years. Each statue represents a member of one of the trades, such as fishermen, cobblers, etc. It's quite a sight to see.

The **Torre de Ligny** is a great spot to watch the sunset. Located at the most eastern point of the city the tower also houses the surprisingly interesting **Museo di Preistoria** (open Monday–Saturday 9am-1pm and 4:pm-8pm; admission E2.5), which contains Neanderthal bones, skulls and tools, as well as the remains of prehistoric animals. A must see when here in Trapani.

Located in the heart of Trapani's old **Jewish Ghetto** that was established during the medieval oppression of the Jews, is the 16th century **Palazzo della Guidecca** (Via della Guidecca 43, open 9:00am–1:00pm and 4:00pm–7:00pm). It has a plaque-studded facade with some Spanish-style windows, and is an elaborate and intricate architectural piece.

Walk up the Via Mura di Tramontana Ovest on the north side of the peninsula from the tower and you'll come to the bustling **Mercato di Pesce** (Fish Market). Here you can see fishermen selling their catch, and fruit and vegetable vendors clamoring for your attention. But remember to get here in the morning, because it shuts down by 1:30pm.

Really the only reason to venture into the new city is to come see these last two sights. If you don't want to hike 3 km down a large boulevard, catch either bus #1 or #10 from the station. Remember to buy a ticket at a newsstand or *tabacchaio* first (E 0.75).

This 14th century convent and church, **Santuario dell'Anunziata** (Via Conte Pepoli, open 8:30am–noon and 4–6pm; no charge) contains the town's main treasure, the smiling *Madonna and Child*. This statue has supposedly been responsible for a number of miracles, so it is kept secured here and is usually surrounded by many kneeling worshipers.

Fans of numismatics (that's the study of coins to you and me), hang on to your hats! Beside to the convent and church is the **Museo Nazionale Pepoli** (Via Conte Pepoli; open Monday–Saturday 9am–1:30pm, Sundays until 12:30pm; on Tuesdays, Thursdays and Saturdays also open 4pm–6:30pm; admission E3) that contains a wide variety of artifacts, including an extensive Roman, Greek, and Arab coin collection. Don't miss the 18th century guillotine, the local coral carvings, or the quaint folk-art figurines. It's a great museum for kids of all ages, but remember to come during the day since the lighting isn't quite adequate in the evening.

Nightlife & Entertainment

Trapani closes down around 9:00pm, but just after dinner, along the **Via Vittorio Emanuele** the natives emerge for a stroll or a sip of Sambuca at a sidewalk café. If you're interested in sampling a local delicacy try a *biscotto coi fichi*, a very tasty fig newton-like cookie.

Practical Information

Local Festivals & Holidays

- **Good Friday and Easter Sunday**, *Processione del misteri*, Procession of Wooden Statues
- **Last Three weeks of July**, Luglio Musicale Trapanese; musical festival in the Villa Margherita at 9pm each night

Postal Services
The **central post office** in Trapani is in the Piazza Vittorio Veneto *(Tel. 0923/873-038)* at the end of Via Garibaldi. Open Monday through Friday 8am–5pm, Saturdays 9am–noon.

Tourist Information & Maps
- **Main tourist office**, Piazza Saturno, *Tel. 0923/29000.* They have maps, brochures, and all sorts of information about the town and surrounding area.

ERICE
Only a forty-five minute bus ride from Trapani, don't miss **Erice** when in Sicily. It is a walled mountain town that was once the biggest in the area (Trapani was just its port), and is still completely medieval with its winding streets, alleys, and ancient buildings. You may actually want to stay here rather than in Trapani and do the reverse commute into the larger city, then escape back to this town's silent charms at the end of the day.

The views from Erice's terraces are fantastic. You can see all of Trapani as well as the **Egadi Islands** (Isole Egadi) and on a good day the coast of Africa. Besides the views and the charming streets there is little of importance to see in Erice, but these are types of ancient towns you came to Sicily to see. Don't be upset if there's no Michelangelo's *David* to admire – the town is a masterpiece in itself.

Arrivals & Departures
After a 45 minute bus ride from Trapani, the bus will drop you off at the Porta Trapani at the southwest edge of town. From here cross the piazza to the **tourist office** (open regular business hours, closed Sundays; *Tel. 0923/869-388)* and pick up any information you think you might need.

Where to Stay
If you want to stay in Erice during the summer months, make reservations well in advance. Listed below are the three hotels in the town.

1. ELIMO, *Via Vittorio Emanuele, Tel. 0923/869-377. 21 rooms. Single E100; Double E150. No credit cards accepted. Full board E100.* ***

A quaint little hotel that is the second best in the city. It has a fine restaurant and a relaxing bar for an evening's refreshments, and quaint old surroundings. The rooms have heat and A/C as well as a TV if you get bored with ambiance and views. The rooms are also smallish but clean and very comfortable with rather eclectic furnishings.

2. MODERNO, *Via Vittorio Emanuele 63, Tel. 0923/869-300, Fax 0923/ 869-139. 40 rooms, 6 with bath, 34 with shower. Single E90; Double E120. American Express and Visa accepted. Full board E90.* **

The best hotel in the city with clean rooms and relatively modern furnishings. They have laundry and room service as well as a good in-house restaurant that is large, elegant, and serves superb food, especially their *cous cous di pesce* (a Middle Eastern rice dish with fish) or their *vitello al forno* (veal cooked perfectly in the oven). Request a room with a view, since the panorama is spectacular. Each room is laid out and furnished differently from the others. But each is filled with local products, from the carpets to the bed frames. The bathrooms have a small courtesy toiletry set and hairdryers.

3. PENSIONE EDELWEISS, *Cortile Piazza Vincenzo 5, 91016 Erice. Tel. 0923/869-420, Fax 0923/869-252. 13 rooms, 13 with bath. Single E80; Double E95. American Express and Visa accepted. Full board E80.* **

Since there are only three good hotels in Erice, this makes the Edelweiss the third best hotel in town. In a quiet alley off the Piazzetta San Domenico, this is a simple family-run place that is comfortable and clean, even if the

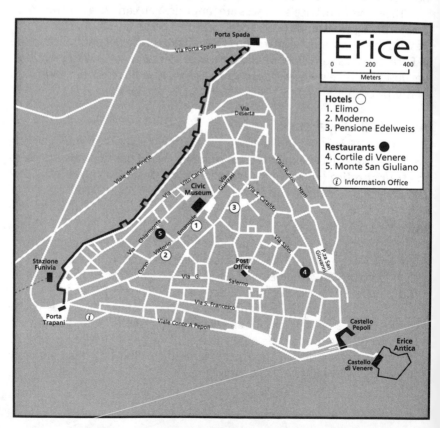

furnishings don't seem to match. If you're a budget traveler this is your only option, even though the accommodations are better than budget.

Where to Eat

You're not going to find an inexpensive meal in Erice unless you grab a sandwich at a sidewalk café, but if you try one of these places, at least you'll be eating well.

4. CORTILE DI VENERE, *Via Sales 31, Tel. 0923/869-362. Closed Wednesdays. All credit cards accepted. Dinner for two E50.*

In the summer you can eat in a splendid courtyard surrounded by buildings from the 17th century. The *gamberi marinati* (marinated grilled shrimp), *spaghetti al pesto ericino* (with a pesto sauce Erice-style) and the *tagliolini al uova di tonno* (thin pasta with a sauce of tuna eggs) are all great. For seconds try some of their *involtini di pesce spada* (rolled swordfish steaks stuffed with spices), *calamari ripieni* (stuffed calamari), or a *costata di Angus alla brace* (an Angus steak grilled over an open flame). Definitely the best food and atmosphere in town.

5. MONTE SAN GIULIANO, *Via San Rocco 7, Tel. 0923/869-595. Closed Mondays. All credit cards accepted. Dinner for two E50.*

If you want to get one of the tables that looks out over the water and the Isole Egadi, you need to get here early or reserve in advance. Their *busiati con pesto ericino* (twisted pasta made with almond paste, garlic, tomatoes, and basil) is exquisite. For seconds, I love their *grigliata di calamari, gamberi e pesce spada* (grilled calamari, shrimp, and swordfish).

Seeing the Sights

As you enter the town you'll be confronted by the **Chiesa Matrice**, whose tower served as a lookout post, then a prison before getting religion (Via Vito Carvini, open 8am–noon and 3pm–6pm). There are five other churches, much smaller in scale, in Erice. When you find them, stick your head inside and take a peek. They are definitely not St. Peter's or the Duomo in Florence, but they do help you step back in time to medieval Erice.

There's a small, really insignificant **museum** (Corso Vittorio Emanuele, open Monday-Saturday 8:30am-1:30pm, Sunday 9am-noon) but the town is a museum in and of itself. After wandering through the streets, avoiding the hordes of tourists in the summertime, walk up past the public gardens and the ancient **Torretta Pepoli**, a restored 15th century tower, and go to the **Castello San Venere** (open Saturday-Thursdays 10am-1pm and 3pm-5pm). Built on the site of an ancient temple to the Greek god Aphrodite and later the Roman god Venus, from here you can get the great views we spoke of earlier. Don't forget your camera.

AGRIGENTO

Even though **Agrigento** is filled with quaint medieval streets and buildings, where butchers and bakers share storefronts with Fendi, nobody comes here just for that experience. Even though the city is not more than 4 km from pristine beaches tourists don't visit for that reason either. The reason people come to Agrigento is for some of the most captivating and well-preserved set of Greek remains and Doric temples outside of Greece – the **Valley of Temples**.

These temples were erected during the 5th century BCE, below the Greek town of Akragas, the forerunner to Agrigento, as testament to the wealth and prosperity of the community. Today Agrigento survives as a result of the tourist trade, and, it is rumored, through Mafia money. But that is the rumor everywhere in Sicilia.

Arrivals & Departures

Since Agrigento is off by itself in the southern part of the island along the coast, with few other towns of tourist interest around, getting here can be quite a haul either by car or by train. To get here by car follow route 115 along the coast, route 640 from Enna (which is on the way from Catania or Messina), or route 189 from Palermo.

Getting Around Town

You can easily walk everywhere in the town itself. The tiny medieval streets are fun to explore. To get the Valley of Temples, you'll need to catch either bus #8, 9 or 10 from the train station. Ask to be let off at the **Museo** (the museum). This a good starting point since it will be able to give you an overview of the entire dig.

Where to Stay

1. BELVEDERE, *Via San Vito 20, Tel. 0922/20051. 35 rooms, 5 with bath, 13 with shower. Single without E55-65; Single E65-75; Double without E75-85; Double E85-95. American Express and Visa accepted.* ******

Located near the train station, I would advise getting a bathroom of your own because there are not many in the halls and they aren't too inviting. Little or no amenities, except a good view from some of the rooms. Try to reserve room #30, which has a large balcony where you can relax in the evenings. A good budget traveler's hotel.

2. DELLE VALLE, *Via dei Templi 94, Tel. 0922/26966, Fax 0922/26412. E-mail: dellavalle@italyhotel.com. 140 rooms. Single E100-140; Double E180-250. Full board E120. All credit cards accepted. Breakfast included.* ********

Located on the road to the temples, you need to take bus #8, 9, or 10 from the station to get here. They have a swimming pool, tranquil and extensive

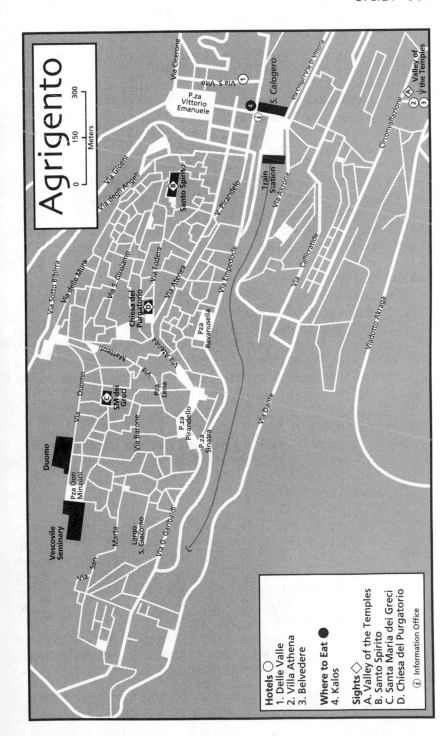

Agrigento

0   150   300
Meters

Hotels ○
1. Delle Valle
2. Villa Athena
3. Belvedere

Where to Eat ●
4. Kalos

Sights ◇
A. Valley of the Temples
B. Santo Spirito
C. Santa Maria dei Greci
D. Chiesa del Purgatorio

ⓘ Information Office

gardens filled with palm and olive trees, four fine restaurants (two of which are in the garden area); and accommodating rooms with all manner of four star amenities. The bathrooms are medium size and come with hairdryer and courtesy toiletry set.

3. VILLA ATHENA, *Via dei Templi 33, Tel. 0922/596-288, Fax 0922/598-770. Web: www.sicily-hotels.com/siti/villathena-ag/index.htm. 40 rooms, 8 with bath, 32 with shower. Single E140; Double E215-270. All credit cards accepted. Breakfast included.* ****

Located in the Valley of the Temples itself, this place has all the amenities you could want, including a pool surrounded by tranquil gardens, a good restaurant, laundry and room service, air conditioning and more. Located in a quaint old romantic building, your rooms are clean as are the bathrooms. The rooms are comfortable and the view from many of the rooms, onto the temples, is exquisite, especially at night, when they are all lit up.

Where to Eat

4. KALOS, *Piazza San Calogero, Tel. 0922/26389. Closed Sunday Nights. Credit cards accepted. Dinner for two E40.*

Located in the small *piazza* near the station and the church of San Calogero, this is a clean, modern looking place, with professional service. Try their *macceroncelli al pistacchio* (macaroni with pistachio sauce, gorgonzola and parmesan cheese). For seconds, get any of their succulent fish or meat cooked on the grill. Great food in a wonderful local environment.

Seeing the Sights

Besides the winding streets and staircases there are only a few sights to see in town. The main show is out at The Valley of the Temples.

A. THE VALLEY OF THE TEMPLES

Open Sunday-Friday 8am-dusk.

After being dropped off by the bus #8, 9, or 10 from town, walk down the hill to the **Museo Nazionale Archeologico di San Nicola** (open Tuesday-Friday 9am-1:30pm and 3pm-5pm, weekends 9:00am-12:30pm) to admire the artifacts removed from the ruins for safekeeping. This museum will help give you a feel for the people that used to worship at these temples. You can find vases, candlestick holders, lion's head water spouts, excellent model reconstructions of the site below, coins, sarcophagi and more.

The **church** that the museum is named after is next door and contains many Roman sarcophagi with intricate relief work. The church isn't open too often. Walking down the road in front will lead you to the Valley of the Temples.

Most of these temples were destroyed by earthquakes and human destruction. Despite the state of the temples, it's still awe-inspiring to walk among structures that once stood erect in the 5th century BCE.

The **Tempio di Giove (Temple of Zeus)** would have been the largest Doric temple ever built had it been completed. It was to be dedicated to the Olympian god Zeus, as you can guess from its name (Jove in English, or *Giove* in Latin, is Zeus). You can still see the remains of one of the standing *telemones*, human figures that were to be the support columns.

The **Tempio della Concordia (Temple of Concord)** is probably the best preserved, most probably because it was converted to a Christian church in the 6th century CE. It has been fenced off to keep scavenging tourists from tearing it apart. But even from a distance it is a joy to behold.

The **Tempio di Giunone (Temple of Juno/Hera)** is not as well preserved but it is still an engaging structure. You may notice some red and black marks in the stone. These could be remnants of fires that were set when the temple was sacked many centuries ago.

Remember to come out and view the temples at night. They are all lit up offering you a stunning and memorable view.

B. SANTO SPIRITO
Piazza Santo Spirito. Accessible 9am–noon and 3pm–6pm.

Built by Cisterian nuns in 1290, this complex contains a church, convent, and charter house. The church contains some fine stucco work. You'll need to ring the bell on the church to gain admittance. Be patient. It's considered rude to keep ringing the bell.

C. CHURCH OF SANTA MARIA DEI GRECI
Via Santa Maria dei Greci. Open 8am–noon and 3pm–5pm.

Built on a 5th century BCE Greek temple, you can still see evidence of the columns in the walls, as well as the base of the columns in the foundation below the church. Make time to search out the entrance in the courtyard. Also inside are some interesting Byzantine frescoes.

D. CHIESA DEL PURGATORIO
Via Fodera. Open 8am–noon and 4pm–7pm.

The main draw for this church are the eight statues inside that represent the eight virtues. Next to the church is the entrance to a network of underground avenues and courtyards, built by the Greeks in the 5th century BCE. This is a must-see adventure while in Agrigento.

Nightlife & Entertainment
The bars and cafés along Via Atenea and in the Piazzale Aldo Moro is where the town congregates for its evening *passegiatta* (stroll). Come out

with the Italians after dinner, sit at a café and sip an *aperitivo,* or stroll among the natives enjoying the relaxing evenings in Agrigento.

Practical Information
Local Festivals & Holidays
• **1st and 2nd Sunday of February**, *Sagra del Mandorlo in Fiore,* Almond Blossom Festival in the Valley of The Temples
• **Late July/Early August**, *Settimana Pirandelliana.* A weeklong festival of plays, opera and ballets all performed in the Piazza Kaos

Tourist Information & Maps
• **Tourist Office**, Piazza Aldo Moro #123, *Tel. 0922/20391,* just to the left as you exit the train station. Here you can get free maps and information about the town and the Valley of the Temples.

SIRACUSA
Most of the old city of **Siracusa** (Syracuse) is situated on an island separated by a narrow channel off the southeastern coast of Sicily. Because of this quaint older town, the scenic **Bay of Porto Grande**, its beautiful natural surroundings, and the monuments and relics of a glorious past, Siracusa is one of the most frequented spots in Sicily.

Founded in 743 BCE by a few colonists from Corinth, **Ortygia** (later to be named Siracusa) grew into a feared and powerful city in the Greek world. In 415 BCE, the city was drawn into the conflict between Athens and Sparta, but when a military expedition from Athens in 413 BCE was completely annihilated the Greeks left the locals alone. To ensure this peace, Siracusa detained over 7,000 Athenians in squalid conditions for over seven years. Over time, Siracusa's power increased and until 212 BCE, Siracusa was arguably the greatest and most powerful city in the world.

Just after that time, the city expanded from its easily defensible island to the mainland. The ruler at the time, Gelon, built the market area and necropolis which is now the famous **Archaeological Park** with its preserved buildings, temples, and theaters that people from all over the world come to see.

After the first Punic War, in which Siracusa was allied with the Romans, the city changed its alliance in the second Punic War to the Carthaginians. Big mistake. The Romans attacked and conquered the city in 212 BCE, and thus began the city's decline. During this two year assault, the city defended itself with an ingenious variety of devices created by the famous scientist and inventor **Archimedes**. After the Romans finally sacked the city, this last great thinker of the Hellenic world was hacked to death in retribution for the many deaths he caused by his ingenious but deadly defensive devices.

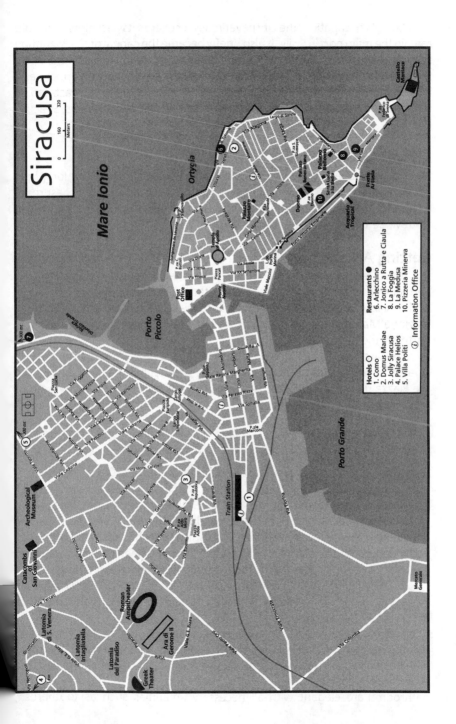

Siracusa

0 160 320
Meters

Mare Ionio

Ortycia

Porto Piccolo

Porto Grande

Castello Menisca

Mare Ionio

Archeological Museum

Catacombs of San Giovanni

Roman Amphitheater

Ara di Gerome II

Greek Theater

Latomia del Paradiso

Latomia Intagliatella

Latomia di S. Venera

Train Station

Mercato Generale

Hotels ○
1. Como
2. Domus Mariae
3. Jolly Siracusa
4. Palace Helios
5. Villa Politi

Restaurants ●
6. Arlecchino
7. Jonico a Rutta e Ciaula
8. La Foggia
9. La Medusa
10. Pizzeria Minerva

ⓘ Information Office

After its occupation, the city never really recovered its past glory, but it did remain the main port in Sicily. It also briefly became the capital of the Byzantine Empire in 663 CE, when the Emperor Constans moved his court here. After that the city, like much of Sicily, was overrun by waves of Arab, Norman, and other conquerors. In conjunction the area has been repeatedly devastated by earthquakes and other natural disasters. Despite all the catastrophes, Siracusa is a great city to visit.

Arrivals & Departures

Nestled down by the southeastern tip of Sicily, Siracusa is a long haul either by car or train. By car the best route to follow is along the coast road, route 115, from Catania. Both by train and by car will take in excess of an hour to traverse the 60 kilometers from Catania.

Getting Around Town

If you're staying in a hotel in or around the center city, Siracusa is a perfect city for walking. From the train station, located almost on the edge of the island, you are within walking distance of the *centro storico* and Stazione Maritima on the island, as well as the Archaeological Park to the north on the mainland.

The Archaeological Park and Museum are about a fifteen minute walk away, so if you're tired you may want to catch either bus # 4, 5 12, or 15 from the Piazza della Poste or from Largo XXV Luglio, which will pass by both of these stops.

Where to Stay

1. **COMO**, *Piazza Stazione 10, Tel. 0931/464-055, Fax 0931/61210. 14 rooms all with shower. Single E75-95; Double E110-120. All credit cards accepted. Breakfast E5.* ***

Recently upgraded to a three star hotel, this wonderful little place is in a good location near the station, has air conditioning, satellite TV, room service and laundry service. Near everything, this small hotel has spotless bathrooms with phones and courtesy toiletry kits. Everything has been recently renovated so it still has a luster about it. Good for budget travelers and above.

2. **DOMUS MARIAE**, *Via Veneto 76, Tel. 0931/24854, Fax 0931/24858. 12 rooms. Single E80; Double without E90; Double E120. No credit cards accepted. Breakfast included.* ***

Located in an old building that has been successfully restored to maintain the original architectural charm while offering all modern comforts, this place has the service and accommodations of a four star at three star prices. The rooms are extremely spacious and finely appointed with antiques. The bathrooms are elegant with all necessary amenities such as toothbrush, toothpaste, hairdryer and more. Situated in the *centro storico* almost directly on the water, this is my favorite place to stay in Siracusa.

3. JOLLY SIRACUSA, *Corso Gelone, Tel. 0931/461-111, Fax 0931/461-126. E-mail: siracusa@jollyhotels.it. Web: www.jollyhotels.it. 100 rooms, 56 with bath, 44 with shower. Single E105-125; Double E140-160. All credit cards accepted. Breakfast included.* ****

Located in the commercial center of Syracuse in a quaint building, the rooms are modern with a separate level to designed as a work space, making them quite large. Every window is soundproof to keep out the traffic noise. The bathrooms are a little small and offer hairdryers as well as a courtesy toiletry set. A clean and comfortable hotel that has a good restaurant (E140 for full board if you're interested), a little American-style bar, room service and laundry service. Located near the train station, you'll find air conditioning and satellite TVs in the accommodating and comfortable rooms.

4. PALACE, *Viale Scala Greca 201, Tel. 0931/491-566, Fax 0931/756-612. 136 rooms, 39 with bath, 97 with shower. Single E100-125; Double E140-160. All credit cards accepted. Breakfast included.* ****

Located outside of town and north of the Greek Theater in the Archaeological Park, this place is somewhat isolated, so getting the E100 full board option at their in-house restaurant would be a good idea. The rooms are old but comfortable and the darker furniture contrasts well with the white floors. The bathrooms come complete with phone and courtesy toiletry kit.

5. VILLA POLITI, *Via M Politi Laudien 2, Tel. 0931/412-121, Fax 0931/36061. Web: www.initaly.com/agri/hotels/politi/politi.htm. 94 rooms, 85 with bath, 9 with shower. 2 Suites. Single E160-190; Double E220-295. All credit cards accepted. Breakfast included.* ****

This is another great place to stay while in Siracusa. The rooms are clean and comfortable, the restaurant offers great local cuisine (E86 full board), and the hotel is located in a quaint historic building. You have air conditioning in the rooms, a disco for dancing at night, a swimming pool surrounded by flowers and vegetation, tennis courts, *bocce* courts, and great views over the sea. It's located a short distance outside of town, but is about equidistant from the town and the Archaeological Park. For a three star, this place offers many four star options and their prices reflect that.

Where to Eat

6. ARLECCHINO, *Via del Tolomei 5, Tel. 0931/66386. Closed Mondays. All credit cards accepted. Dinner for two E50.*

Located in Ortygia, from the entrance you have a great view of the sea. This modern, well-lit place is huge; over 260 people can be seated at the same time. It caters to tourists, but mainly of the Italian variety so the food is good. Try their *antipasto* buffet table for starters that is overflowing with seafood. Then for more seafood with the *spaghetti ai ricci di mare* (with the riches of the sea) or the *tortelloni con scampi allo zafferano* (large cheese stuffed pasta with a shrimp and sauce). For seconds try any of their oven roasted fish as well as their many meat dishes.

7. JONICO A RUTTA E CIAULU, *Riviera Rionisio il Grande 194, Tel. 0931/ 65540. Closed Tuesdays, the end of the year and Easter. All credit cards accepted. Dinner for two E55.*

Located up the coast near the Villa Politi, the best place to eat is on the terrace where you have a fine view of the Ionian Sea. Here you can get some good local dishes at somewhat high prices. Try some of their *spaghetti alla siracusano* (with anchovies and scraped toasted bread sauce), which doesn't sound too appetizing but I like it, or some *spaghetti con tonno fresca* (with fresh tuna sauce). For seconds they serve great tuna and swordfish steaks.

8. LA FOGGIA, *Via Capodieci 29, Tel. 0931/66233. Closed Tuesdays. All credit cards accepted. Dinner for two E40.*

Located in Ortygia, this is a small local place that changes its menu daily based on whatever ingredients chef Nicoletta was able to get at the market. Usually the *antipasto* will be vegetables, like *fritelle di finocchietto* (fried small fennel). Try one of their soups for your *primo* to save yourself for their exquisite fish dishes. Only 25 seats, so make a reservation.

9. LA MEDUSA, *Via San Teresa 21, Tel. 0931/61403. Closed Mondays and August 15 to September 15. American Express accepted. Dinner for two E30.*

Another restaurant in the Ortygia district, this place is run by a Tunisian who has been in Siracusa for over 20 years. You can get some great couscous with either *pesce* or *carne* (a rice-based dish with either fish or meat) for *primo*. The *antipasto* is good too with the *pesce spada marinata* (marinated swordfish), *gamberetti* (small shrimp) and more. For seconds try their *arrosto misto di pesce* (mixed roast fish). Great atmosphere and good food.

10. PIZZERIA MINERVA, *Piazza Duomo 20, Tel. 0931/69404. Closed Mondays and November. No credit cards accepted. Dinner for two E25.*

In the summer this is the perfect pace to end a long walk through Ortygia. The place seats over 130 people, but not all outside in the *piazza* facing the Duomo. Try and get one of these outside seats. You can get any pizza imaginable here, but if you want it American-style you have to order *doppio mozzarella* (double cheese).

Seeing the Sights

The archaeological park and museum is the big draw here, but there are some lovely squares and churches in town that are great for poking around.

ORTYGIA

On the island of **Ortygia**, the ancient nucleus of Siracusa, you can find remains from over 2,500 years of history. A small area, almost half a kilometer across and only one in length, this little parcel of land contains much of the charm and adventure from all of those centuries.

TEMPLE OF APOLLO
Just over the **Ponte Nuovo** from the mainland is the oldest Doric temple in Sicily. Built in the 7th century BCE, little remains of this once glorious temple except for two pillars and parts of some walls. To really get an idea of what it used to look like, go to the Archaeological Museum for a scale model.

PIAZZA ARCHIMEDE
This is Ortygia's **central piazza** and as such is the place to come any time day or night. The square has some bars and cafés with outside seating where you can sit and enjoy the sight of the 12th century fountain with a woodland nymph cavorting under a cover of modern moss. Down a small road from the square is the **Via del Montalto** on which you can find the **Palazzo Montalto** (not open to public), with its fabulous double and triple arched windows. The building's construction was begun in 1397 and is constantly undergoing renovations.

PIAZZA DEL DUOMO
A piazza surrounded by some beautiful 17th and 18th century palazzos and dominated by the impressive Baroque **Duomo**. The square was built over and encompasses an earlier Greek temple, the 5th century BCE Ionic Temple of Athena. You can still see evidence of the previous structure in the walls, where 26 of the original 34 columns remain. Because much of its earlier wealth was stolen and a majority of it was destroyed in the earthquake of 1693, this cathedral contains a wide variety of differing architectural styles, from Greek to Byzantine to Baroque.

The **Palazzo Benevantano** (at #24 on the piazza, not open to the public) is worth a look because of its attractive 18th century facade and serpentine balcony. At the far end of the piazza is the small church of **Santa Lucia alla Badia** built from 1695 to 1703 (open 8:00am-noon and 3:30pm-6:00pm). The church is significant because it contains the remains of the city's patron saint, Santa Lucia.

GALLERIA DI PALAZZO BELLOMO
Via Capodieci 14. Open Tuesday-Sunday 9am-1pm. Admission E3.
Almost behind **Santa Lucia alla Badia** is the **Palazzo Bellomo**, a 15th century palazzo that contains a wonderful gallery of all kinds of artwork, including ancient bibles, medieval carriages, sculptures, tombs, paintings and more. The most famous painting is the Annunciation by Antonello da Messina.
Walk down to the Via Capodieci to arrive at the **Foro Italico**, the main promenade for the citizens of Ortygia. On this tree-lined promenade you'll find

rows of bars and cafés on the land side, and rows of yachts lining the water. It's where the local citizens come to enjoy the evenings before they retire home. At the beginning of this promenade is the fresh water fountain **Fonte Aretusa**. Just past the fountain is the **Aquario Tropical** (open Saturday–Thursdays 9am-1pm, admission E3) that offers 35 different species of tropical fish for your aquarium-viewing pleasure.

CATACOMBS

Via San Giovanni. Open 9am-1pm and 2pm-7pm. Closed Wednesdays. Guide tours of catacombs cost E3.

The **catacombs of San Giovanni** are located under the basilica of the same name, and contain a quantity of faded frescoes. This is an ominous tour through a labyrinth of passageways, most of which were destroyed by looters and their riches stolen, so to see a sarcophagus you need to go to the Archaeological Museum.

ARCHAEOLOGICAL MUSEUM

Viale Teocrito. Open Tuesday–Saturday 9am-1pm and Sunday 9am-12:30pm.

To get to the museum, you can take the 15-minute walk or catch bus #4, 5 12, or 15 from the Piazza della Poste or from Largo XXV Luglio. Since this museum is the most extensive antiquities museum in Sicily, you should spend some time browsing through the collection. The museum contains fossils, skeletons, figurines, sarcophagi and more, but the collection's tour de force is the *Venus Anadiomene*, the coy statue of Venus rising from the sea. If you're into antiquities, this is a great place to spend a few hours.

ARCHAEOLOGICAL PARK

Open Tuesday-Sunday 9am to an hour before sunset. Admission E3.

To get to the park, you can take the 15-minute walk or catch bus #4, 5 12, or 15 from the Piazza della Poste or from Largo XXV Luglio. The structures preserved here were constructed between 475 BCE and the 3rd century CE and many remain somewhat intact. An example of this preservation is the **Greek Theater**, originally made from the side of the hill around 475 BCE. The structure was enlarged in 335 BCE and could seat up to 15,000 people. If you want to see a performance here, come in May and June on the alternate year when classical Greek plays are staged. They are quite stirring mainly because of the ancient backdrop.

Next door to the Greek Theater is the **Latomie del Paradiso**, the **Paradise Quarry**, so named because many of the 7,000 Athenians captured in 413 BCE went to the afterlife from here. In the quarry are two interesting caves: **Grotta dei Cordari**, where rope makers used to work at their craft because the damp cave kept the strands of rope from breaking, and the

Orecchio di Dionisio (Ear of Dionysis), so called because the entrance resembles an ear, and the cave has amazing acoustic qualities. Up from the grotto is the **Roman Amphitheater** which was built in the 3rd century CE. Here they held their vicious gladiatorial games. Just one hundred and forty meters long, it's not quite as impressive as the Colosseum in Rome, but is a treasure in and of itself.

Nightlife & Entertainment
The only real nightlife to speak of is along the Foro Italico promenade. Sip a drink, have a light meal, and watch the citizens of Siracusa walk by.

Practical Information
Car Rental
• **Avis**, Via Savoia 13, *Tel. 0931/61125*

Local Festivals & Holidays
• **May to June**, every even numbered year classical Greek drama is performed at the Greek theater
• **December 13**, *Festa di San Lucia*

Postal Services
The **central post office** in Siracusa is in the Piazza delle Poste, *Tel. 0931/684-16*, located in the *centro storico* island just over the bridge from the mainland. Open Monday through Friday 8:30am-6:30pm, Saturdays 9am-noon.

Tourist Information & Maps
• **Tourist office**, on the island at Via Maestranza 33, *Tel. 0931/652-01*, on the mainland near the catacombs at Via San Sebastiano 45, *Tel. 093/677-10*. There is also one outside of the train station. All three locations can offer you maps of the area and the Archaeological Park, as well as brochures and information about hotels.

INDEX

Things Change!

Phone numbers, prices, addresses, quality of food, etc, all change. If you come across any new information, we'd appreciate hearing from you. No item is too small! Drop us an email note at: Jopenroad@aol.com, or write us at:

Italy Guide
Open Road Publishing, P.O. Box 284
Cold Spring Harbor, NY 11724

Travel Notes

Travel Notes

Travel Notes

Travel Notes

Travel Notes

Travel Notes

Open Road Publishing

U.S.
America's Cheap Sleeps, $14.95
America's Most Charming Towns & Villages, $16.95
Arizona Guide, $16.95
Boston Guide, $13.95
California Wine Country Guide, $12.95
Colorado Guide, $16.95
Hawaii Guide, $18.95
Las Vegas Guide, $15.95
Las Vegas With Kids, $14.95
National Parks With Kids, $14.95
New Mexico Guide, $16.95
San Francisco Guide, $16.95
Southern California Guide, $18.95
Spa Guide, $14.95
Texas Guide, $16.95
Utah Guide, $16.95
Vermont Guide, $16.95
Walt Disney World Guide, $14.95

Middle East/Africa
Egypt Guide, $17.95
Kenya Guide, $18.95

Eating & Drinking on the Open Road
Eating & Drinking in Paris, $9.95
Eating & Drinking in Italy, $9.95
Eating & Drinking in Spain, $9.95
Eating & Drinking in Latin America, $9.95

Latin America & Caribbean
Bahamas Guide, $13.95
Belize Guide, $16.95
Bermuda Guide, $14.95
Caribbean Guide, $21.95
Caribbean With Kids, $14.95
Central America Guide, $21.95
Chile Guide, $18.95
Costa Rica Guide, $17.95
Ecuador & Galapagos Islands Guide, $17.95
Guatemala Guide, $18.95
Honduras Guide, $16.95

Europe
Czech & Slovak Republics Guide, $18.95
Greek Islands Guide, $16.95
Holland Guide, $17.95
Ireland Guide, $17.95
Italy Guide, $19.95
Italy With Kids, $14.95
London Guide, $14.95
Moscow Guide, $16.95
Paris with Kids, $14.95
Prague Guide, $14.95
Rome Guide, $14.95
Scotland Guide, $17.95
Spain Guide, $18.95
Turkey Guide, $19.95

Asia
China Guide, $21.95
Japan Guide, $21.95
Philippines Guide, $18.95
Tahiti & French Polynesia Guide, $19.95
Tokyo Guide, $13.95
Thailand Guide, $18.95

For US orders, include $5.00 for postage and handling for the first book ordered; for each additional book, add $1.00. Orders outside US, inquire first about shipping charges (money order payable in US dollars on US banks only for overseas shipments). Send to:

Open Road Publishing, PO Box 284, Cold Spring Harbor, NY 11724